The Individual in International Law

THE HISTORY AND THEORY OF INTERNATIONAL LAW

General Editors

NEHAL BHUTA
Chair in International Law, University of Edinburgh

ANTHONY PAGDEN
Distinguished Professor, University of California Los Angeles

BENJAMIN STRAUMANN
ERC Professor of History, University of Zurich

In the past few decades the understanding of the relationship between nations has undergone a radical transformation. The role of the traditional nation-State is diminishing, along with many of the traditional vocabularies which were once used to describe what has been called, ever since Jeremy Bentham coined the phrase in 1780, 'international law'. The older boundaries between States are growing ever more fluid, new conceptions and new languages have emerged which are slowly coming to replace the image of a world of sovereign independent nation-States which has dominated the study of international relations since the early nineteenth century. This redefinition of the international arena demands a new understanding of classical and contemporary questions in international and legal theory. It is the editors' conviction that the best way to achieve this is by bridging the traditional divide between international legal theory, intellectual history, and legal and political history. The aim of the series, therefore, is to provide a forum for historical studies, from classical antiquity to the twenty-first century, that are theoretically informed and for philosophical work that is historically conscious, in the hope that a new vision of the rapidly evolving international world, its past, and its possible future, may emerge.

PREVIOUSLY PUBLISHED IN THIS SERIES

A Century of Anarchy?
War, Normativity, and the Birth of Modern International Order
Hendrik Simon

Victims
Perceptions of Harm in Modern European War and Violence
Svenja Goltermann

Sovereignty, International Law, and the Princely States of Colonial South Asia
Priyasha Saksena

Sepúlveda on the Spanish Invasion of the Americas
Defending Empire, Debating Las Casas
Luke Glanville, David Lupher, Maya Feile Tomes

The World Bank's Lawyers
The Life of International Law as Institutional Practice
Dimitri Van Den Meerssche

The Invention of Custom
Natural Law and the Law of Nations, ca. 1550-1750
Francesca Iurlaro

The Individual in International Law

History and Theory

Edited by

TOM SPARKS AND ANNE PETERS

OXFORD
UNIVERSITY PRESS

OXFORD
UNIVERSITY PRESS

Great Clarendon Street, Oxford, OX2 6DP,
United Kingdom

Oxford University Press is a department of the University of Oxford. It furthers the University's objective of excellence in research, scholarship, and education by publishing worldwide. Oxford is a registered trade mark of Oxford University Press in the UK and in certain other countries

Published in the United States of America by Oxford University Press
198 Madison Avenue, New York, NY 10016, United States of America

British Library Cataloguing in Publication Data

Data available

Library of Congress Control Number: 2023948329

ISBN 978–0–19–889891–7

DOI: 10.1093/oso/9780198898917.001.0001

Series Editor's Foreword

Nehal Bhuta

The question of where individuals fit within the framework of international law is a deep-seated inquiry into the fundamental principles and objectives of the international legal order. 'An individual' may refer to a natural person—a single human being—or a legal person, such as an individual State. The essays collected in this volume are concerned with the place of natural persons. The central question is to what degree the international legal system can be understood as prioritising natural persons as both the ultimate aim of its legal norms and one of the origins of normative responsibility.

The subject, in a way, is a venerable one, and reflects a confrontation with the consequences of the statist Eurocentric legal order of early modern Europe. This legal order established the sovereign State as the source of both legal and political governance following the devastating Christian civil wars in Europe. The sovereignty of the State was seen as the most effective way of protecting natural persons from the disastrous effects of civil war and to establish a civil society that could ensure their rights. However, this political and legal theory had difficulty defining constraints on the all-encompassing power of sovereignty, and it appeared to exclude the individual natural person from the international legal order, except when seen through the lens of the State's legal personality. Furthermore, those societies and civilisations deemed unworthy of sovereign statehood, because of their lack of conformity with the Eurocentric standard of civilisation, were unable to enjoy the protections afforded by sovereign status and confronted the international legal order as mere objects of governance through imperial and colonial rulership. In response to the Eurocentric statist image of the international legal order, a particular aspect of interest in international law began to explore how individual natural persons and some collectivities (such as 'peoples') were emerging as subjects of the international legal order. During significant transitional periods in the twentieth century, specifically between 1918 and 1939 and again between 1989 and 2009, there was a growing emphasis on this concern. It was frequently linked to aspirations for a global legal order with cosmopolitan ideals that transcended sovereign statehood itself, and aimed for a global community or *civitas*. However, distinguishing between globalist and imperialist projects was not always straightforward.

The chapters in this wide-ranging volume offer a richer perspective of the topic by combining historical studies with theoretical analyses. The result is a complex picture. We are reminded of the intricate nature of inter-polity legal ordering (albeit largely confined to European historical contexts) that establish the legal personhood and juridical status of natural persons and human groups within multi-polity orders. The current international theoretical landscape is also examined, highlighting the considerable extent to which the place of individual natural persons and human groups, both within and beyond the State, have become the focus of theoretical and doctrinal discussion. The outcome is a profoundly informative account that enables us to rearticulate the nature of the problem, rather than claiming to resolve it in a simplified way.

Acknowledgements

Behind the authors and editors of a volume of this kind stands a community of researchers who have made vital, but often invisible, contributions to the book and the ideas which underpin it. We thank all of those individuals who have helped to develop the concepts and arguments in this volume, and in particular wish to acknowledge those scholars (some of them among the authors of this book's chapters) who commented on the draft chapters to this volume at our authors' workshop in June 2021: Kanad Bagchi, Esra Demir-Gürsel, Dante Fedele, Anneloes Hoff, Francesca Iurlaro, Josh Jowitt, Alexandra Kemmerer, Astrid Kjeldgaard-Pedersen, Edward Kolla, Gustavo Prieto, Daniel R. Quiroga-Villamarín, Miguel Rabado Dorbecker, Mark Somos, Yusra Suedi, Alain Wijffels, and LI Zhenni, and all those who attended and contributed to our discussions.

We are grateful to Robert Cavooris, Lisa Butts, and Alice Noel, together with the rest of the team at Oxford University Press, for their supportive, patient, and friendly collaboration in bringing this volume to print. We thank John Lowrie Morrison OBE for his kind permission to use his beautiful painting, *Mo's Footprints in the Sand—Portuairk Ardnamurchan*, as the cover image for this volume.

Open access publication of the volume has been enabled by the very generous funding by the Max Planck Society, as well as the Hertie School, University of Hamburg, and University of Sydney. We are grateful to the Deutsche Forschungsgemeinschaft and the Fritz Thyssen Stiftung für Wissenschaftsförderung for their financial support of our project workshop.

We are also obliged to our student assistants, notably Julius Barrho, Golzar Falatoon-Zadeh, Sarah Gebel, Moritz Pollack, Philipp Rothkirch, Viola Sauter, Lisa Schultze-Rhonhof, and Marieke Simons, for their editorial assistance, and to several generations of student assistants for their able research assistance. Dr Naomi Shulman provided careful and professional language editing.

Many aspects of this project have been discussed and refined with the generous input of Anne Peters' research group at the Max Planck Institute for Comparative Public Law and International Law in Heidelberg. We thank all those colleagues and friends who took part in seminars at which different parts of the project were discussed. They are too many to name individually, but we are immensely grateful to one and all.

We owe a huge debt of thanks to Anette Kreutzfeld, who has been indispensable in every stage of this process. Anette, your care, attention to detail, meticulous organisation, and good humour have kept this process on track despite the vicissitudes of undertaking a collaborative writing project in circumstances of a pandemic.

Finally, we are indebted to the authors with whom we have had the pleasure to produce this volume. This book was long in the making, in large part because this project (like so many others) has suffered its share of pandemic-related disruptions, and we appreciate their forbearance, their patience, and their continued enthusiasm. Most of all, though, we are grateful for their rich and open engagement with this topic. It has made both for a wonderfully stimulating process and—we think and hope—a fascinating and enriching collection. To all of them: thank you.

Contents

List of Contributors

Editors

Tom Sparks is a senior research fellow at the Max Planck Institute for Comparative Public Law and International Law, Heidelberg, where he works on international environmental law, the humanisation of international law, and legal theory in Professor Anne Peters' research group. He wrote his doctoral thesis at the University of Durham, entitled 'Towards a Human-Centred International Law: Self-Determination and the Structure of the International Legal System'. The thesis won the Global Policy North network of research universities' prize for the best doctoral dissertation of 2018. He is also the author of *Self-Determination in the International Legal System: Whose Claim, to What Right?* (Hart 2023). From 2020 to 2021, Tom was a judicial fellow of the International Court of Justice, where he worked in HE Judge Peter Tomka's chambers.

Anne Peters is Director at the Max Planck Institute for Comparative Public Law and International Law, Heidelberg; a professor at the universities of Heidelberg, Freie Universität Berlin, and Basel; and an L Bates Lea Global Professor of Law at the University of Michigan. She has been a member of the European Commission for Democracy through Law (Venice Commission) in respect of Germany (2011-2015), served as President of the European Society of International Law (2010-2012) and as President of the German Society of International Law (DGIR) (2019-2023). Anne is a member of the Permanent Court of Arbitration and an associate member of the Institut de Droit International. Her current research interests relate to public international law including its history, global animal law, global governance and global constitutionalism, and the status of humans in international law.

Authors

Anne van Aaken is Alexander von Humboldt professor for law and economics, legal theory, public international law, and European law and the Director of the Institute of Law and Economics, University of Hamburg. She was vice-president of the European Society of International Law and chair of the European University Institute Research Council. She is a general editor of the *Journal of International Dispute Settlement* and a member of the editorial boards of the *American Journal of International Law*, the *Journal of International Economic Law, International Theory*, and the *European Journal of International Law* (until 2021). Anne was a guest professor in Europe, Africa, Asia, Latin America, and the United States (Columbia and global law professor at NYU). She has been expert consultant for the IBRD, UNCTAD, GIZ, OECD, and the UN High Level Advisory Board of Effective Multilateralism. Her research focuses on international (economic) law, international governance, behavioural economics/psychology, and international legal theory. She has published widely on these topics.

Başak Çalı is professor of international law and director of the Centre of Fundamental Rights at the Hertie School, Berlin. She is a permanent visiting professor at I-Courts, University of Copenhagen, a fellow of the Human Rights Centre of the University of Essex, UK, and the Chair of European Implementation Network. Her research interests span general public international law and comparative international human rights law, including questions of authority, legitimacy, interpretation, and impact. Başak's authored and edited books relate to the authority of international law, human rights, migration, and procedural questions before international courts and tribunals.

Bhupinder S. Chimni is distinguished professor of international law at O.P. Jindal Global University. Previously he was professor of international law at the School of International Studies, Jawaharlal Nehru University. He has been a visiting professor at Brown, Cairo, IHEID (Geneva), and Tokyo universities and held visiting positions at Harvard, Cambridge, Minnesota, and York universities. He is an associate member of Institut de Droit International, and Member, Academic Council, Institute for Global Law and Policy (IGLP), Harvard Law School. He is former vice-president of the Asian Society of International law and an honorary member of the American Society of International Law. Chimni is a patron of a scholarship for a MA programme at the University of London and holds an honorary doctorate from the University of Gothenburg, Sweden.

Eleanor Cowan is a lecturer in classics and ancient history at the University of Sydney. She is a historian of the Roman Republic and the early (Roman) imperial period. Her research concentrates on communities in conflict, the history of ideas and concepts, the intersection of law and politics, and classical historiography. She holds an LLB in addition to her BA and PhD. Eleanor is the co-founder of the Australasian Roman Law Network. Her current projects include *The Rule of Law in Ancient Rome* and *Domestic Violence in Antiquity*, and her publications cover Roman law in various historical periods.

Rafael Domingo is the Alvaro d'Ors Professor of Law at the University of Navarra. His recent books relate to global law, Roman law, law and religion, and Christianity and the law.

Dante Fedele is research fellow at the French National Centre for Scientific Research (CNRS) and member of the Centre for Judicial History at Lille University. His field of research is legal history with a particular focus on late medieval and early modern diplomacy and international law. He published inter alia on diplomacy from the thirteenth to seventeenth centuries and on the medieval foundations of international law.

Marie-Claire Foblets is director at the Max Planck Institute for Social Anthropology in Halle/Saale, Germany. She is honorary professor at the law faculty of the Catholic University Leuven, the Martin Luther University Halle-Wittenberg, and the University of Leipzig. In 2001, she was elected to the Royal Flemish Academy of Belgium for Science and the Arts (KVAB). In 2004, Marie-Claire received the Francqui Prize, the most prestigious academic award in the humanities in Belgium. She is a full member of the Saxon Academy of Sciences and Humanities, and holds honorary doctorates from the Facultés universitaires

Saint-Louis, Brussels (2016) and the University of Uppsala (2019). Her recent academic work focuses on the accommodation of religious and cultural diversity under State law in Europe.

Angelo Jr Golia is assistant professor of constitutional law and comparative public law at the University of Trento School of Law. His research interests include constitutional theory, legal pluralism, the judicialisation of politics, sociolegal approaches to public law, systems theory, and digital constitutionalism. Recent publications relate to international organisations and digital constitutionalism.

Gleider Hernández is professor of public international Law at the University of Leuven (KU Leuven). Previously, he has worked at the Open Universiteit Nederland and Durham Law School, where he was Deputy Director of the Global Policy Institute. He has held visiting professorships and research fellowships at Harvard Law School (as a Fulbright Scholar), Durham Institute of Advanced Study, Université Paris Nanterre, the University of Amsterdam, McGill University, and the TMC Asser Institute. In summer 2022, Gleider served as English-language Director of Studies at the Hague Academy of International Law. Prior to his academic career, he was associate legal officer at the International Court of Justice clerking for Judges Peter Tomka and Bruno Simma. Elected to the Board of the European Society of International Law in 2018, he was from 2021 to 2023 its Secretary-General and is now President of the Society.

Ruth Houghton is a senior lecturer at Newcastle Law School in the UK. Her research centres on public international law and global constitutionalism, where she focuses on discussions of democracy and constituent power. She utilises feminist methodologies, law and humanities methodologies, and constitutional and political theory. Her work is published in journals such as *Global Constitutionalism* and the *Leiden Journal of International Law* on topics including democracy, utopias, feminist manifestos, and global governance.

Inge Van Hulle is a research professor of legal history at KU Leuven and a Max Planck research group leader at the Max Planck Institute for Legal History and Legal Theory in Frankfurt. She specialises in the history of international law and imperialism during the nineteenth century. Inge is the author of *Britain and International Law in West Africa: The Practice of Empire* (OUP 2020).

Francesca Iurlaro holds a PhD in law from the European University Institute, Florence (2018). She was a global postdoctoral fellow at NYU (2019-2020) and a Alexander von Humboldt postdoctoral fellow at the Max Planck Institute for Comparative Public Law and International Law, Heidelberg (2020-2022). In her book *The Invention of Custom: Natural Law and the Law of Nations* (OUP 2021), she explores how topoi from classical antiquity shaped customary international law. In 2012 she received the Alberico Gentili Prize for her translation of Alberico Gentili's *Lectionis Virgilianae Variae Liber* (1603), a legal commentary on Virgil's *Eclogues*.

Mark Somos is Heisenberg professor at the Max Planck Institute for Comparative Public Law and International Law, Heidelberg. He holds an MPhil in political thought and intellectual history from Cambridge, an AM in government and social policy and a PhD in political science from Harvard, an LLM in international security and law from Sussex University, and a PhD in law from Leiden University. Mark has taught at Sussex, Tufts, Harvard, and Yale; published five scholarly books and over seventy articles; and serves as co-editor-in-chief of *Grotiana*.

Marina Veličković is a Leverhulme early career fellow at the University of Warwick, UK. She is currently researching the role of international law in (re)producing structures of violence in post-conflict settings. She holds a PhD from the University of Cambridge and an LLM in public international law from the London School of Economics.

Alain Wijffels is a retired teacher of comparative law and legal history at the universities of Leiden, Leuven, and Louvain-la-Neuve, and a former research fellow at the French Centre for Scientific Research (CNRS). His current research focuses on Alberico Gentili's annotations as a reader of legal and non-legal works and on the Anglo-Hanseatic relations.

1

Introduction

The History and Theory of the Individual in International Law

Anne Peters and Tom Sparks

1. Centring the Individual: The Humanisation Thesis

In the trial against the Serb politician Duško Tadić, who was ultimately convicted for a range of war crimes committed in the Yugoslav war, the Appeals Chamber of the International Tribunal for the former Yugoslavia (ICTY) issued its famous 1995 decision in which it successfully established its jurisdiction. The Chamber pronounced: 'A State-sovereignty-oriented approach has been gradually supplanted by a human-being-oriented approach. Gradually the maxim of Roman law *hominum causa omne jus constitutum est* (all law is created for the benefit of human beings) has gained a firm foothold in the international community as well.'[1]

This fundamental reorientation of the law of the international community, as evoked by the tribunal—bearing the handwriting of its first President, Antonio Cassese—can be captured as international law's '*humanisation*' (to use the term coined by Theodor Meron)[2] or its '*individualisation*'. That 'gradual' process of change, as identified by the tribunal, refers to one of the key relationships in international law: that between the State and the human individual. Over time, it even amounts to an *exchange* of the human individual for States as the focal point of the international legal order.

But such 'humanisation', as enounced almost thirty years ago, seems to lie in a bygone era. Present-day scholarship is flooded with 'post-humanism',[3] 'transhumanism',[4] and even 'dehumanisation'[5]—paradigms that have been taken up in the legal realm.[6] In parallel, on the political plane we witness a global power

[1] ICTY, *Prosecutor v. Tadić, Decision on the Defence Motion for Interlocutory Appeal on Jurisdiction*, IT-94-1, 2 October 1995, at para. 97.

[2] See below text to note 29.

[3] Stefan Herbrechter et al. (eds.), *Palgrave Handbook of Critical Posthumanism* (Cham: Springer Nature 2022).

[4] Nick Bostrom, 'A History of Transhumanist Thought' *Journal of Evolution and Technology* 14 (2005), 1-25; Janina Loh, *Trans- und Posthumanismus zur Einführung* (Hamburg: Junius 2018).

[5] Maria Kronfeldner (ed.), *The Routledge Handbook of Dehumanization* (Abingdon: Routledge 2021).

[6] Upendra Baxi, *Human Rights in a Posthuman World: Critical Essays* (New Delhi: OUP 2009); Luigi Corrias, 'Dehumanization by Law', in Maria Kronfeldner (ed.), *The Routledge Handbook of*

Anne Peters and Tom Sparks, *Introduction* In: *The Individual in International Law*. Edited by: Tom Sparks and Anne Peters, Oxford University Press. © Anne Peters and Tom Sparks 2024. DOI: 10.1093/oso/9780198898917.003.0001

shift, a rise of States with less individual-centred intellectual and political traditions, democratic retreat in all regions of the world, and the outbreak of a classic inter-State war. Populist leaders and movements, open aggression, and emergency measures are undermining human rights achievements. In addition, the entrenchment of material inequality, the rise of artificial intelligence, and most of all the human-made destruction of the planet urgently demand new paradigms for the international legal order. This political, economic, and ecological constellation has, not least, prompted a return of the State as an actor which seems strong enough to cope with the demands of an uncertain world. States acted vigorously to protect public health in the pandemic, are taking measures collectively to defend Ukraine against Russia's aggression, and are needed to combat ecological disaster. In these and other ways, States are indispensable to protect and shield individuals against powerful new phenomena and formations which threaten human well-being, ranging from big data and big tech, to warlords and organised crime. These contradictions warrant a renewed, deep reflection on the international legal status of the human individual, also in relation to States.

Individuals have played crucial roles in the international legal system. They are its jurists and scholars; the heads of State and plenipotentiaries. When States fight wars, sign treaties, or pollute rivers, it is an individual who pulls the trigger, wields the pen, or opens the valve. Every action that is performed by a State is, at root, the action of one or more individuals acting within structures of authority and attribution.[7] The early theorists of State and law recognised the artificial nature of the personified State,[8] as do the modern rules of attribution,[9] representation,[10] and diplomatic relations.[11] Nevertheless, and for much of the recent history of international law, scholarship has treated the relationship between international law and the individual as one wholly *mediated* by States. Adherents to this worldview denied that human beings could hold any rights or obligations rooted in the international legal order; rather, human interests and needs were the purview of

Dehumanization (Abingdon: Routledge 2021), 201-13; Anna Grear, Emille Boulot, Iván D.Vargas-Roncancio and Joshua Sterlin (eds.), *Posthuman Legalities: New Materialism and Law beyond the Human* (Cheltenham: Edward Elgar 2021); Emily Jones, *Feminist Theory and International Law: Posthuman Perspectives* (Abingdon: Routledge 2023).

[7] Tom Sparks, 'The State', in Jean d'Aspremont and Sahib Singh (eds.), *Concepts for International Law: Contributions to Disciplinary Thought* (Cheltenham: Edward Elgar 2019) 838-49, at 847-49.

[8] See, e.g., Thomas Hobbes, *Leviathan: Or the Matter, Forme and Power of a Common Wealth Ecclesiasticall and Civil* (London: Andrew Crooke 1651), chapter XVI, at 80; Samuel Pufendorf, *Of the Laws of Nature and Nations, in Eight Books* (first published as *De iure naturæ et gentium libri octo,* 1672, this edn Basil Kennett (tr.), London: J Walthoe et al. 1729) at Book I, Chapter I, §VI.

[9] Articles on the Responsibility of States for Internationally Wrongful Acts, annexed to UN General Assembly Resolution 56/83, 12 December 2001, UN Doc. No. A/RES/56/83, Arts. 4-11.

[10] See, e.g., Vienna Convention on the Law of Treaties (VCLT), signed 23 May 1969, in force 27 January 1980, 1155 UNTS 331, Arts. 7-8.

[11] See, e.g., Vienna Convention on Diplomatic Relations, signed 18 April 1961, in force 24 April 1964, 500 UNTS 95, preamble and Art. 1.

domestic legal systems, which collated those and other concerns to form States' interests. Humans were at most protected by standards established by international law—they were 'objects' but not 'subjects' of international law. It was seen as the task of States to implement or translate these international standards into their domestic legal systems.[12] That simplistic picture of the international legal system has likely never been an adequate description of the diverse ways in which international law has involved and addressed humans (and collectives of humans); and, clearly, the Triepelian 'States only'-model does not correctly depict the contemporary international order.

With the explosion of international organisations in the post-World War II era, international law has been forced to come to terms with actors beyond the State. In the same period, the advent of international human rights law with the 1948 Universal Declaration of Human Rights and the founding of the Council of Europe in 1949 recognised inherent legal rights of individuals against States, and in some cases has offered them judicial means of redress.[13] The 1949 Geneva Conventions sought to regulate warfare with the principal intention of protecting persons playing no direct part in hostilities from the worst effects of armed conflict.[14] As early as 1946, the idea of direct duties under international law, even to the extent of attracting a criminal penalty, was forcefully and famously enounced by the Nuremberg judgment:

> It was submitted that International Law is concerned with the actions of sovereign States and provides no punishment for individuals; and further, that where the act in question is an act of State, those who carry it out *are not personally responsible*, but are protected by the doctrine of the sovereignty of the State. In the opinion of the Tribunal, both these submissions *must be rejected. That International Law imposes duties and liabilities upon individuals* as well as upon States *has long been recognized.* [. . .] Crimes against International Law are committed by men, not by abstract entities, and only by *punishing individuals* who commit such crimes can the provisions of International Law be enforced.[15]

[12] See, e.g., Heinrich Triepel, *Völkerrecht und Landesrecht* (Leipzig: Verlag von C L Hirschfeld 1899), 20-21, see also 13-18 and 259-62.

[13] UNGA, Universal Declaration of Human Rights, General Assembly Resolution 217(III); Statute of the Council of Europe, 5 May 1949, ETS No. 001. Under Art. 3 of the Statute, '[e]very member of the Council of Europe must accept the principles of the rule of law and of the enjoyment by all persons within its jurisdiction of human rights and fundamental freedoms'. The Convention for the Protection of Human Rights and Fundamental Freedoms (ECHR), 4 November 1950, ETS No. 005, establishes, in its current version, an individual right of access to the European Court of Human Rights at Art. 34.

[14] René-Jean Wilhelm, 'Le caractère des droits accordés à l'individu dans les Conventions de Genève' *Revue internationale de la Croix-Rouge* (1950) 561-90.

[15] International Military Tribunal, *The Trial of German Major War Criminals*, judgment of 1 October 1946, Part 22 (22 August 1946 to 1 October 1946), 446-47 (emphasis added).

In the 1990s, this bold idea—which for many years after the Nuremberg judgment had remained basically a dead letter—was finally revived and operationalised with the creation of international judicial processes to hold individuals to account for their actions in perpetrating the worst breaches of the law of war, recognised as international crimes: genocide, crimes against humanity, and war crimes. International criminal law, together with international human rights law and international humanitarian law (IHL), forms a triptych of regimes, which numerous authors consider as representing or prompting a deep and structural shift in the nature and telos of the international legal system away from Triepelian State-centrism, and towards 'Humanity's Law' (Ruti Teitel),[16] or an 'International Law for Humankind' (Antônio Augusto Cançado Trindade).[17]

2. Key Concepts

The ostensible reorientation of international law from State sovereignty to human being, as identified by the *Tadić* tribunal is underpinned by the mindset (an 'ism') of *humanism* or *individualism*, a paradigm in which *humanity*, *humankind*, and the *individual human being* are understood as (increasingly important) normative focal points of international law. These normative reference points (section 2.1) and the process and the accompanying mindset (section 2.2) need to be clarified for the purposes of this study.[18]

2.1 The Reference Points: Humanity, Humankind, and the Individual Human Being

Humanity denotes both the collective of all humans on the earth (humankind) and, relatedly, the norm that humans should treat each other with mutual respect ('humanely'), in consideration of their shared quality as humans. The reference to humanity as a collective is one face of the humanisation discourse. It is found in various subfields of international law, such as international environmental and resource law, through the concept of the common heritage of humankind. 'Humanity' also figures prominently in the law of armed conflict. This field is increasingly called international humanitarian law, a label which signals that the overarching purpose of this regime is to secure 'humane' conduct in war. Indeed, a

[16] Ruti Teitel, *Humanity's Law* (Oxford: OUP 2011), 4.

[17] Antônio Augusto Cançado Trindade, 'International Law for Humankind: Towards a New Jus Gentium' *Recueil des Cours* 316 (2005), 9-439.

[18] Our working definitions have been discussed with the authors of this collective volume. Authors were free to deviate from these understandings but were invited to reflect on and explain their use of the relevant terms.

'principle of humanity' undergirds the law of armed conflict and 'is at the heart of international humanitarian law'.[19] The International Court of Justice (ICJ) stated that the 'elementary considerations of humanity' belong to the 'the fundamental general principles of humanitarian law'.[20] A related field is international criminal law, one of the central norms of which is the prohibition of 'crimes against humanity' (Art. 7 International Criminal Court (ICC) Statute). Here, 'humanity' has two reference points and concomitantly two meanings, linked to each other: First, the victimisation of members of the human race and, secondly, crimes which violate human feeling and shock the conscience of humankind.[21]

Another aspect of humanisation (as a transformatory process of international law as a whole) is its focus on the single human being, the individual. The 'individual' or the 'person'—used side by side in treaty law and apparently without distinction[22]—are technical terms of international human rights law to designate the bearer of certain codified rights[23] and the procedural position of those who are entitled to submit individual communications to the treaty bodies.[24] With these terms, the human rights instruments mean 'all *human* beings' (Art. 1 Universal Declaration of Human Rights (UDHR)), or the '*human* person' (as the preambles of the major universal human rights conventions state).[25]

Similarly, the UN Security Council has addressed 'individuals' repeatedly (often besides 'groups', 'undertakings', and 'entities').[26] The most frequent context is targeted sanctions to be imposed by UN member States on individuals designated by

[19] On this principle, see Daniel Thürer, *International Humanitarian Law: Theory, Practice, Context* (Leiden: Martinus Nijhoff Publishers 2011), 66-67, quote at 66.

[20] ICJ, *Military and Paramilitary Activities in and against Nicaragua (Nicaragua v. United States of America)*, Merits, Judgment (1986) ICJ Reports 14, at para. 218; referring to ICJ, *Corfu Channel Case (United Kingdom v. Albania)*, Judgment (1949), ICJ Reports 4, at 22.

[21] The latter meaning is made explicit in the official German translation of the crime: '*Verbrechen gegen die Menschlichkeit*', meaning 'crimes committed in violation of human sentiments'.

[22] See the appearance of both terms in one single provision in, e.g., International Covenant on Civil and Political Rights (ICCPR), 16 December 1966, 999 UNTS 171, Arts. 2(1) and (3). See also International Covenant on Economic, Social and Cultural Rights (ICESCR), 16 December 1966, 993 UNTS 3, preamble and Art. 13; International Convention on the Elimination of All Forms of Racial Discrimination (ICERD), 7 March 1966, 660 UNTS 195, Art. 2; Convention against Torture and Other Cruel, Inhuman or Degrading Treatment or Punishment (CAT), 26 June 1987, 1465 UNTS 85, Art. 22; International Convention for the Protection of all Persons from Enforced Disappearance (ICED), 20 December 2006, 2716 UNTS 3, Art. 19.

[23] See, e.g., ICERD (n. 22), Arts. 1 and 14; ICESCR (n. 22), Art. 6; ICCPR (n. 22), Art. 2(1); CAT (n. 22), Arts 10(1), 13, 22.

[24] See, e.g., Optional Protocol to the International Covenant on Civil and Political Rights, 16 December 1966, 999 UNTS 171, Art. 2; Optional Protocol to the International Covenant on Economic, Social and Cultural Rights, 10 December 2008, A/RES/63/435, Art. 2; International Convention on the Protection of the Rights of All Migrant Workers and Members of their Families (ICRMW), 18 December 1990, 2220 UNTS 3, Art. 77.

[25] See the preambles of ICCPR (n. 22); ICERD (n. 22); CEDAW (n. 24); CAT (n. 22); Convention on the Rights of the Child (CRC), 20 November 1989, 1577 UNTS 3; Convention on the Rights of Persons with Disabilities (CRPD), 13 December 2006, 2515 UNTS 3. The expression 'human person' is here used mostly to designate the carrier of human dignity. In this sense, see also Art. 10 ICCPR.

[26] For examples see UNSC Resolutions S/RES/2574, 11 May 2021 (in the context of the peace process in Colombia) and S/RES/2565, 26 February 2021 (ISIL).

the Council itself or by a sanctions committee.[27] Resultantly, both the 'individual' and the 'human' are well anchored terms of art in contemporary international law.

2.2 The Process: Humanisation and Individualisation

The gradual reorientation of the international legal order as a whole, 'progressively moving from a sovereignty-centred to a[n ...] individual-oriented system'[28]—as Christian Tomuschat put it—has been called, as mentioned, 'individualisation' or 'humanisation'. Theodor Meron initially reserved 'humanisation' to the international law of armed conflict (*ius in bello*). In that context, Meron called 'the direction in which the law of war, or international humanitarian law, has been evolving [... a] humanization of that law, a process driven to a large extent by human rights and the principles of humanity'.[29] This development was seen as a 'tempering of the harshness of humanitarian law by human rights values'.[30] In his general course at the Hague Academy, Meron extended the concept to international law at large. There he defined humanisation as 'the influence of human rights and humanitarian norms [...] spread to many other parts [of international law], though to varying degrees. The humanization of public international law under the impact of human rights has shifted its focus above all from State-centred to individual-centred.'[31]

Twenty years later, the ongoing and deepened transformation of international law in the context of armed conflict has again been scrutinised by Jennifer Welsh, Dapo Akande, and David Rodin, now under the heading of individualisation. These scholars define the individualisation (of war) as 'a process in which individuals (both as agents and as subjects) increase in importance compared with collective entities for the purposes of explaining and normatively assessing the causes, conduct, and consequences of war'.[32] In these debates, the terms individualisation and humanisation are often conflated. While Welsh, Akande, and Rodin use 'individualisation', Gabriela Blum returns to Meron's original label of 'humanisation' to argue

[27] For examples see UNSC Resolutions S/RES/2577, 28 May 2021 (South Sudan); S/RES/2571, 16 April 2021 (Libya); S/RES/2560 (2020) 29 December 2020 (Islamic State). In scholarship, see Leonardo Borlini, *Il Consiglio di Sicurezza e gli individui* (Milan: Guiffrè 2018).

[28] Christian Tomuschat, 'International Law: Ensuring the Survival of Mankind on the Eve of a New Century' *Recueil des Cours* 281 (1999) 9-438, at 237, 161-62.

[29] Theodor Meron, 'The Humanization of Humanitarian Law' *American Journal of International Law* 94 (2000) 239-78, at 239.

[30] *ibid*, 275.

[31] Theodor Meron, 'International Law in the Age of Human Rights' *Recueil des Cours* 301 (2003) 9-489, at 22.

[32] Jennifer Welsh, Dapo Akande, and David Rodin, 'Introduction: Understanding Individualization', in Jennifer Welsh, Dapo Akande, and David Rodin (eds.), *The Individualization of War: Rights, Liability, and Accountability in Contemporary Armed Conflict* (Oxford: OUP 2023), 1-38, at 7-8.

> that the 'humanization of international humanitarian law' marks a shift from collectivism toward cosmopolitan individualism in the regulation of wartime conduct. In other words, wartime regulation has evolved from a predominantly state-oriented set of obligations—which viewed war as an intercollective effort—to a more individual-focused regime.[33]

Antônio Augusto Cançado Trindade, too, has identified a 'historical process of humanization of International Law', as a focus on 'fundamental values', in which the 'realization of superior common goals' has altered the basis of the system as a whole.[34] Alexander Somek describes the 'currently predominant view' as espousing that the international 'community supplants sovereignty with subsidiarity or "humanity" as its major organizing principle. It places the vulnerable individual at the center of the international order.'[35] More recently, Alain Pellet defines humanisation as '*l'irruption de l'individu dans la sphère juridique internationale*'.[36] Importantly, this process 'dépasse la sphère des droits de l'homme *stricto sensu*'.[37] Nevertheless, that process of humanisation remains 'limited', says Pellet.[38] Whichever term is preferred, be it 'humanisation' or 'individualisation' of international law, it has become a familiar trope in the legal discourse.

The process of humanisation/individualisation—as described in this section—comprises both a legal fact (in the law as it now stands) and a gamut of normative attitudes. These attitudes (or mindsets or ideologies) are usually called humanism, anthropocentrism, and individualism. The exact content of these ideologies depends on the social field. In essence, they claim that humankind as a collective or humans as single individuals should be at the centre of reflection and concern.

In international law, humanism/individualism is typically pitted against statism/sovereigntism. For example, Thomas Franck in 1999 put forward the thesis that '[i]n recent decades, the individual has made progress in asserting personal autonomy, while the *sovereign State* has lost some ground: both to *individualism* and to internationalism'.[39] Importantly, the mindset of humanism/individualism in international law which drives and accompanies the process from a State-oriented law set of rights and obligations to a law focused on individual rights

[33] Gabriela Blum, 'The Individualization of War: From War to Policing in the Regulation of Armed Conflicts', in Austin Sarat, Lawrence Douglas, and Martha Merill Umphrey (eds.), *Law and War* (Stanford, CA: Stanford Law Books 2014) 48-83, at 48.

[34] Cançado Trindade, 'Law for Humankind' (n. 17), at 282.

[35] Alexander Somek, *The Cosmopolitan Constitution* (Oxford: OUP 2014), 153. Note that Somek is critical of this view.

[36] He defines humanisation as 'the intrusion of the individual into the international legal sphere': Alain Pellet, 'Le droit international à la lumière de la pratique: L' introuvable théorie de la réalité' *Recueil des Cours* 414 (2021) 25-547, at 370 (our translation).

[37] This process 'goes beyond the sphere of human rights, strictu sensu': *ibid*, 108 (our translation).

[38] *ibid*, 420 (our translation).

[39] Thomas M. Franck, *The Empowered Self: Law and Society in the Age of Individualism* (Oxford: OUP 1999) 224 (emphasis added).

and obligations also implies that individual interests (as opposed to national State interests) *should* be the proper motivation, objective, and ultimate reference point of all workings of international law.

Based on these conceptualisations, and in line with the mentioned usages, we define humanisation (or individualisation) as a process through time by which the international legal order as a whole is reoriented away from States and towards the interests and needs of human individuals—both by themselves and (crucially) in communities—with the help of new legal institutions and mechanisms, imbued by humanism and individualism.

3. The Scope and Depth of Humanisation

Most accounts of the change in the structure and workings of international law have not specified the legal building blocks of that putative humanisation or individualisation process in depth. This omission may be owed to the fact that the international legal order—far from being an unchanging, timeless order having emerged full-formed with the mythical Peace of Westphalia—has changed significantly over the course of its history, including before the Westphalian moment.[40] With this, that legal order's treatment of, respectively, the State (an entity which, itself, has not remained static over time) and the individual has evolved as well. The key elements, factors, drivers, and consequences of 'humanisation' have likewise not remained static over time; these, too, are specific to their own time periods. It is therefore necessary to assess the changing relationship between the State and individual in international law in each time period by reference to the factors which are most appropriate to the legal developments of that time.

In the present day, we discern several developments which are features of the phenomenon of humanisation. The most palpable (and most criticised) reality is the 'rise and rise' of international human rights (section 3.1).[41] The process of humanisation goes far beyond human rights, however. As a direct result of the influence of human rights and through independent processes, individual international entitlements have emerged in many regimes of international law (section 3.2).[42] It

[40] The Westphalian origin of international law has by now been thoroughly debunked. See, e.g., Partel Piirimäe, 'The Westphalian Myth and the Idea of External Sovereignty', in Hent Kalmo and Quentin Skinner (eds.), *Sovereignty in Fragments: The Past, Present and Future of a Contested Concept'* (Cambridge: CUP 2010), 64-80.

[41] Kirsten Sellars, *The Rise and Rise of Human Rights* (Stroud: Sutton Press 2002); Angelika Nußberger (ed.), *Menschenrechte als Alpha und Omega des Rechts? Zur Auseinandersetzung der Fachdiziplinen mit der aktuellen Rechtsprechnung zu den Menschenrechten in Europa* (Tübingen: Mohn Siebeck 2023).

[42] For an attempt to catalogue many of these developing entitlements (as they stood in 2016), see Anne Peters, *Beyond Human Rights: The Legal Status of the Individual in International Law* (Jonathan Huston (tr.), Cambridge: CUP 2016), *passim*. *Beyond Human Rights* is an updated and revised version of Anne Peters, *Jenseits der Menschenrechte: Die Rechtsstellung des Individuums im Völkerrecht* (Tübingen: Mohr Siebeck 2014).

has also been argued that these changes both give rise to and result from an original international legal personality of human beings (section 3.3). Next, the concept of 'responsibility to protect' signals the shift from State sovereignty to humanity as the lead consideration for the structure of international legal order (section 3.4).[43] Finally, further legal phenomena should be seen as a marker of the humanisation of contemporary international law: the participation of individuals in the actual production of international legal norms (treaties, custom, general principles, other); the broadening of the standing of individual claimants before international and domestic forums to vindicate their international rights;[44] and the rise of concepts such as human security and human dignity.[45] We do not dwell on the latter developments in this book.[46]

3.1 The Human Rights Effect

Human rights have become pervasive in the discourse and practice of international law as a whole. Although frequent and rampant violations persist, human rights have become the gold standard of governance. All actors at least pay lip service to human rights.

New international human rights are constantly being spelled out in processes of claims and contestation, ranging from a human right to the internet, through the right of access to energy, to the right to gestational surgery.[47] Notably the human right to a clean, healthy, and sustainable environment meets increasing acceptance.[48] This environmental right is codified in regional human rights instruments,[49] in a rising number of national constitutions and statutes,[50] and has been

[43] For R2P as a marker of 'humanity law', see Ukri Soirilia, *The Law of Humanity Project: A Story of International Law Reform and State-Making* (Oxford: Hart 2021), 105-111.

[44] In current international law, individuals not only have standing before regional human rights courts and investment tribunals, but also enjoy an overarching procedural capacity to act before international or national courts and tribunals to enforce their material rights (Patricia Wiater, *Internationale Individualkläger* (Tübingen: Mohr Siebeck 2020).

[45] Soirilia, *Law of Humanity Project* 2021 (n. 43), 11 and 50.

[46] See Peters, *Beyond Human Rights* 2016 (n. 42), 50-54 and 472-94.

[47] Andreas von Arnauld, Kerstin von der Decken, and Mart Susi (eds.), *The Cambridge Handbook of New Human Rights* (Cambridge: CUP 2020).

[48] Ke Tang and Otto Spijkers, 'The Human Right to a Clean, Healthy and Sustainable Environment' *Chinese Journal of Environmental Law* 6 (2022), 87-108.

[49] African Charter on Human and Peoples' Rights, 27 June 1981, Art. 24; Additional Protocol to the American Convention on Human Rights in the Area of Economic, Social, and Cultural Rights ('Protocol of San Salvador'), 17 November 1988, Art. 11.

[50] See United Nations, Human Rights Council, Report of the Special Rapporteur on the issue of human rights obligations relating to the enjoyment of a safe, clean, healthy and sustainable environment, 30 December 2019, A/HRC/43/53, with a list of countries that possess relevant domestic legislation or constitutional provisions in Annex II: 'Legal recognition of the right to a healthy environment'.

recently endorsed by the UN General Assembly.[51] It will likely become relevant for climate change to which we will revert in the concluding chapter.[52]

The increased salience of human rights also manifests in the extension of those rights' territorial and personal scope: Human rights give rise to extraterritorial obligations, they are invoked against new duty bearers such as business actors and international organisations, and they are claimed for new holders such as animals or nature.

Importantly, what has been called a 'human rights-based approach' has become the standard approach for the analysis and application of virtually all subfields of international law.[53] The human rights-based approach demands first of all that each and every special rule must be interpreted in the light of human rights. Moreover, human rights impact assessments, human rights due diligence, and human rights mainstreaming must be conducted in numerous contexts ranging from the conclusion of an investment agreement to the financing of a World Bank project.[54] In the various legal fields, human rights often operate as a counterforce, e.g. against free trade, foreign investment, resource extraction, or in international finance.[55] In other regimes, human rights function to reinforce legal rules, such as in the fields of development cooperation,[56] in international environmental law,[57] in the international law of armed conflict/IHL,[58] and in the procedural law of international

[51] UNGA, 'The Human Right to a Clean, Healthy and Sustainable Environment', 1 August 2022, A/RES/76/300.

[52] Peters and Sparks, 'Conclusions' (chapter 18), in this volume.

[53] See pivotally Bruno Simma, 'Der Einfluss der Menschenrechte auf das Völkerrecht: Ein Entwurf', in Isabelle Buffard et al. (eds.), *International Law between Universalism and Fragmentation: Festschrift in Honour of Gerhard Hafner* (Leiden: Martinus Nijhoff, 2008), 729-46; Menno T. Kamminga and Martin Scheinin (eds.), *The Impact of Human Rights Law on General International Law* (Oxford: OUP 2009).

[54] Olivier de Schutter et al., *Human Rights Due Diligence, The Role of States* (2012); updated by Mark Taylor, *Human Rights Due Diligence: The Role of States* (2013 Progress Report).

[55] The most intense debate relates to 'business and human rights'. See United Nations, Human Rights Council, Report of the Special Representative of the Secretary-General on the issue of human rights and transnational corporations and other business enterprises (John Ruggie), with Guiding Principles in the Annex, 21 March 2011, A/HRC/17/31, adopted by the UN Human Rights Council, 6 July 2011, A/HRC/RES/17/4 and Open-ended intergovernmental working group (OEIGWG), OEIGWG Chairmanship, third revised draft of 17 August 2021 of a Legally Binding Instrument to Regulate, in International Human Rights Law, the Activities of Transnational Corporations and other Business Enterprises. No new draft has been produced until the time of writing (1 August 2023).

[56] Philip Alston and Mary Robinson (eds.), *Human Rights and Development: Towards Mutual Reinforcement* (Oxford: OUP 2005).

[57] See, e.g., Inter-American Court of Human Rights (IACtHR), *The Environment and Human Rights*, Advisory Opinion OC-23/17, 15 November 2017; Nils Wegner, *Subjektiv-rechtliche Ansätze im Völkerrecht zum Schutz biologischer Vielfalt* (Berlin: Duncker & Humblot, 2018).

[58] Orna Ben-Naftali (ed.), *International Humanitarian Law and International Human Rights Law* (Oxford: OUP 2011); Claus Kreß, 'Die Europäische Menschenrechtskonvention und das völkerrechtliche Gewaltverbot', in Angelika Nußberger (ed.), *Menschenrechte als Alpha und Omega des Rechts? Zur Auseinandersetzung der Fachdiziplinen mit der aktuellen Rechtsprechnung zu den Menschenrechten in Europa* (Tübingen: Mohn Siebeck 2023) 149-68. See also above, section 2.2 on IHL as the first branch of international law the 'humanisation' of which was identified by Theodor Meron.

adjudication.[59] We will revert to the two most recently 'humanising' legal fields—the *ius contra bellum* and climate law—in our concluding chapter.[60]

All mentioned developments are contested and ambiguous. It suffices to recall the claim of a humanisation of IHL mentioned in section 2.2. This idea has drawn on the real practice of co-applying human rights in situations of armed conflict but has not led to a broad recognition of IHL-specific rights and obligations of natural persons. Moreover, several authors still consider IHL as a duty-based regime, imposing obligations on States to cater for human persons who remain 'objects' of protection.[61] Nevertheless, despite contestation and contrary trends, human rights have penetrated all subfields of international law, and have had overall a massive normative impact.

3.2 Beyond Human Rights

International-law-based rights and obligations of individuals have moved beyond human rights and are now widespread and refined.[62] Far from being confined either to particular areas of international law (such as criminal law, humanitarian law, and human rights), or limited to the application of narrow, human-facing doctrines (such as *ius cogens*), contemporary international law is *in toto* a humanised legal system in both broad and deep terms. This is indicated by the sweeping range of norms and regimes which provide for legal rights or obligations of individuals in the contemporary legal system: individuals are treated as independent subjects of law and bearers of special rights in the fields of investment law,[63] consular

[59] Tom Sparks and Mark Somos, 'The Humanisation of Provisional Measures? Plausibility and the Interim Protection of Rights before the ICJ', in Fulvio Palombino, Roberto Virzo, and Giovanni Zarra (eds.), *Provisional Measures before International Courts and Tribunals* (The Hague: TMC Asser Press, 2021) 77-105. An example is the ICJ's provisional measure on the Russian invasion of Ukraine, demanding that Russia suspend its military operations in the territory of Ukraine. Here, the ICJ (over-) stretched its prima facie jurisdiction under the Genocide Convention in response to human suffering in the war (ICJ, *Allegations of Genocide under the Convention on the Prevention and Punishment of the Crime of Genocide* (*Ukraine v. Russian Federation*), Order of 16 March 2022, para. 81).

[60] Peters and Sparks, 'Conclusions' (chapter 18).

[61] Ziv Bohrer, 'Divisions over Distinctions in Wartime International Law', in Anne Peters and Christian Marxsen (series eds.), *Law Applicable to Armed Conflict, Max Planck Trialogues on the Law of Peace and War vol. 2* (Cambridge: CUP 2019) 106-96, at 175 and 182-86. For a contrary view, see Anne Peters, 'The Direct Rights of Individuals in the International Law of Armed Conflict' in Jennifer Welsh, Dapo Akande, and David Rodin (eds.), *The Individualization of War* (Oxford: OUP 2023), 55-88.

[62] For a more extensive argument on these lines, see Peters, *Beyond Human Rights* 2016 (n. 42). The argument on the following pages draws from the work Anne has done here.

[63] Peters, *Beyond Human Rights* 2016 (n. 42), 282. See seminally Zachary Douglas, 'The Hybrid Foundations of Investment Treaty Arbitration' *British Yearbook of International Law* 74 (2004) 151-290; Martins Paparinskis, 'Investment Treaty Arbitration and the (New) Law of State Responsibility' *European Journal of International Law* 24 (2913) 617-47. See from the case law, e.g., International Centre for the Settlement of Disputes (ICSID), *Burlington Resources Inc. v. Republic of Ecuador*, Decision on Reconsideration and Award, 7 February 2017, ICSID Case No. ARB/08/5, para. 177, holding that 'it is generally accepted that the ILC Articles can be transposed to the context of investor-State disputes', and applying the principle of full reparation.

law,[64] diplomatic protection,[65] international labour law,[66] international refugee law,[67] international criminal law,[68] international disaster law,[69] amongst others.

3.3 The International Legal Personality of Humans

Humanisation (or individualisation) also manifests itself in a yet deeper paradigm shift in international law's underlying basis. Rather than being the passive recipient of rights and duties imposed by a State-oriented legal system, the legal personality (personhood or subjecthood)[70] of the individual is increasingly emancipated from States. The concept of person and personality spans various disciplines and has a long and confused history. In law, personhood is a legal artifice,[71] but it is contaminated by non-legal moral meanings.[72] For the purpose of international law, we understand personhood as the capacity of an actor to bear rights or duties in a given (here: the international) legal order.[73]

Humanisation implies that individual human beings are (and should continue to be) recognised as the central,[74] 'primary',[75] and 'original'[76] international legal

[64] Peters, *Beyond Human Rights* 2016 (n. 42), 348. See also Martin Mennecke, 'Towards the Humanization of the Vienna Convention of Consular Rights' *German Yearbook of International Law* 44 (2001) 430-68.

[65] Peters, *Beyond Human Rights* 2016 (n. 42), 388; see also cautiously Flor de María Placo Caballero, *La Cour internationale de Justice et la protection de l'individu* (Paris: LGDJ Schulthess, 2015) *passim*, e.g. 165, 396. For a critical view, see Vasileios Pergantis, 'Towards a "Humanization" of Diplomatic Protection?' *Zeitschrift für ausländisches öffentliches Recht und Völkerrecht* 66 (2006) 351-97.

[66] Peters, *Beyond Human Rights* 2016 (n. 42), 450. See also Hugh Collins, 'Theories of Rights as Justifications for Labour Law' in Guy Davidov and Brian Langille (eds.), *The Idea of Labour Law* (Oxford: OUP 2011) 137-55.

[67] Peters, *Beyond Human Rights* 2016 (n. 42), 450. See also Vincent Chétail, 'Are Refugee Rights Human Rights?', in Ruth Rubio-Marín (ed.), *Human Rights and Immigration* (Oxford: OUP 2014) 14-72.

[68] Peters, *Beyond Human Rights* 2016 (n. 42), 255 on the legal status of victims of crime.

[69] *ibid*, 233. See also International Law Commission (ILC), Protection of Persons in the Event of Disasters, 2016, A/71/10); *Yearbook of the International Law Commission*, 2016, vol. II, part two. On a human rights-based approach to disasters see, e.g., Maria Giovanna Pietropaolo, 'A Human Rights-Based Approach to Humanitarian Assistance' *Journal of International Humanitarian Legal Studies* 7 (2016) 257-93; Karen da Costa and Paulina Pospienszna, 'The Relationship between Human Rights and Disaster Risk Reduction Revisited: Bringing the Legal Perspective into the Discussion' *Journal of International Humanitarian Legal Studies* 6 (2015) 64-86.

[70] We use these terms interchangeably. Both in ordinary and in legal language, the words 'subject' and 'person' tend to be assimilated. Note, e.g., Naffine's interchangeable use of these terms in *Law's Meaning of Life: Philosophy, Religion, Darwin and the Legal Person* (Oxford: Hart 2009). Though see contra Visa A. J. Kurki, *A Theory of Legal Personhood* (Oxford: OUP 2019), 121-24.

[71] Neil MacCormick, 'Persons as Institutional Facts', in Ota Weinberger and Werner Krawietz (eds.), *Reine Rechtslehre im Spiegel ihrer Fortsetzer und Kritiker* (Heidelberg: Springer 1988) 371-79.

[72] Ngaire Naffine, 'Who Are Law's Persons? From Cheshire Cats to Responsible Subjects' *Modern Law Review* 66 (2003) 346-67.

[73] The concept of international legal personality is itself complex and different 'models' are conceivable. See Roland Portmann, *Legal Personality in International Law* (Cambridge: CUP 2010).

[74] Rafael Domingo, *The New Global Law* (Cambridge: CUP 2010), 124-26.

[75] Janne Elisabeth Nijman, *The Concept of International Legal Personality: An Inquiry into the History and Theory of International Law* (The Hague: TMC Asser Press 2004), 473.

[76] Pellet, 'A la lumière de la pratique' 2021 (n. 36), 109.

person (subject), besides and to some extent in opposition to the State. This view is in line with Hersch Lauterpacht's postulate that, 'having regard to the inherent purposes of international law, of which the individual is the ultimate unit, he is in that capacity a subject of international law'.[77]

That vision departs from the classic literature that assumed that the international legal status of individuals was based on treaties concluded between States for the benefit of a third party (*pactum in favorem tertii*).[78] A distinction was made between three types of international treaties: Firstly, treaties granting private third parties (individuals) actionable 'direct' rights against contracting States in international legal proceedings (e.g. the ECHR); secondly, treaties which oblige contracting States to grant rights to third parties (individuals) as part of their domestic law (such as the Agreement on Trade-Related Aspects of Intellectual Property Rights (TRIPS)); and thirdly, treaties that benefit private individuals only 'by rebound'.[79] The mark of all these entitlements or benefits is that they can be nullified by the contracting parties. And to the extent that the rights and duties in question imply that the individual human being is an international legal person (subject), it might be argued (within this State-oriented paradigm) that the States' withdrawal of rights and duties simultaneously means that the States can undo the status as a legal person upon which the rights and duties depend.

Unfortunately, the entire debate is complicated by the muddled understanding of the relationship between legal rights and obligations on the one hand, and legal personality on the other. Some scholars consider the concept of personhood or subjecthood (of individuals or any other actor) irrelevant, empty, or even useless. It is so, they argue, because what matters in practical terms are the individual rights and duties, which can be verified legal-empirically.[80] This pragmatic viewpoint posits that the set of rights and duties constitutes the real and effective legal status of the individual, while the term 'person' is little more than shorthand referring to an unspecified bundle of legal obligations and entitlements.[81] But however

[77] Hersch Lauterpacht, 'The Subjects of the Law of Nations' *Law Quarterly Review* 63 (1947) 428-60, reproduced in Hersch Lauterpacht, *International Law: Being the Collected Papers of Hersch Lauterpacht* (Elihu Lauterpacht ed, Cambridge: CUP 1978), 526. On Lauterpacht see Portmann, *Legal Personality in International Law* 2010 (n. 73), at 127-33.

[78] See Marek St Korowicz, 'The Problem of the International Personality of Individuals' *American Journal of International Law* 50 (1956) 533-62, at 542.

[79] See Rolf Schwartmann, *Private im Wirtschaftsvölkerrecht* (Tübingen: Mohr Siebeck, 2005), 19-22; and further discussion in Peters, *Beyond Human Rights* 2016 (n. 42), chapters 10 and 17.

[80] Kate Parlett, *The Individual in the International Legal System: Continuity and Change in International Law* (Cambridge: CUP 2011), 38; José Alvarez, 'Are Corporations Subjects of International Law?' *Santa Clara Journal of International Law* 9 (2011) 1-36, at 26; Anna Mejknecht, *Towards International Personality: The Position of Minorities and Indigenous People in International Law* (Antwerp: Intersentia 2011), 31.

[81] See already Hans Kelsen, *Reine Rechtslehre* (Leipzig: Franz Deuticke 1934), 177-78. The lesser discussed facet of that argument is that the same objection applies equally to States, the 'personality' or 'sovereignty' of which can similarly be viewed as little more than a bundle of rights and obligations: Sparks, 'The State' 2019 (n. 7); and further Alf Ross, *A Textbook of International Law: General Part* (London: Longmans, Green and Co. 1947), 42-45, esp. at 44.

we conceptualise the legal personhood of the individual—as a mere bundle of rights and obligations or, rather more convincingly, as an empty vessel and a doctrinal pre-condition for being able to hold rights and/or obligations—we need to confront the critique that the international legal personality of the individual seems unstable and revocable: 'Ainsi donc, l'individu destinataire de normes internationales, qu'il s'agisse de droits substantiels ou de moyens de procédure, est toujours dans une situation précaire.'[82] The classical doctrine thus relegates individuals to the status of 'passive', 'secondary', 'delegated', or 'partial' subjects or persons in international law.[83] Their personhood is imperfect, tenuous, situational; and as such can plausibly be denied altogether: 'Individuals [...] derive their legal status only from the will of States (and international organizations) and cannot influence it. [...] Accordingly, one cannot contend that individuals are subjects of international law'.[84]

That classical view is, however, no longer adequate—if adequate it ever were—to the realities of contemporary international law. Far from the international legal personality of individuals being a revocable 'gift' of States, a review of the sources of law enumerated in Article 38(1) of the ICJ Statute demonstrates that not only treaty norms, but also customary international law and general principles of law substantiate individual personality. Put differently, legal foundations for the personhood of individuals can be found in all types of sources of international law. Moreover, the fabric of individual entitlements woven together from these different sources is becoming increasingly dense. This means the recognition of individual legal personality contained therein is increasingly becoming the normal case. In short, there are good reasons to assume that the individual is now the natural person of international law.[85]

3.4 From State Sovereignty to Humanity

The preceding sections have suggested that the 'rise' of the individual in the international legal order is linked to the relative 'decline' of the State in international law. This binarism is a simplification: the international position of the individual is

[82] Christian Dominicé, 'L' émergence de l'individu en droit international public', in Christian Dominicé (ed.), *L'ordre juridique international entre tradition et innovation* (Paris: Presses Universitaires de France 1997), 10-23, at 123: 'In this way, the individual as addressee of international norms, be they substantive norms or procedural ones, is always in a precarious situation' (our translation). In the older literature, see Korowicz, 'Problem of Personality' 1956 (n. 78), 563: 'Today the existence of such international personality of individuals is still entirely dependent on the states which created it, and it is always revocable according to the decisions of these states.'

[83] See only German Constitutional Court (BVerfG) *Kunduz*, 2BvR 477/1, order of 18 November 2020, para. 18 on the 'partial legal personality of the individual'.

[84] Gerhard Hafner, 'The Emancipation of the Individual from the State under International Law' *Recueil des Cours* 358 (2013) 263-441, at 437-41.

[85] Peters, *Beyond Human Rights* 2016 (n. 42), 408-35.

not solely defined by the status of the State. State sovereignty and humanity do not stand in a zero-sum relationship, in the sense that an erosion of State sovereignty would automatically lead to more 'humanity' in the international legal system.[86] Nevertheless, the State has been and still is the most important international actor, the powers and functions of which are the most relevant factors shaping the international legal status of the individual human being. And the more international law caters for individuals 'directly', the relatively less important is what has been called mediation through the States.[87] Therefore, humanisation (or individualisation) as described in the *Tadić* decision and scholarship, is fairly cast as a process of 'from-to', concomitantly implying that the States are becoming less central (both descriptively and normatively) while individuals become more prominent.[88] In addition to a focus on the individual—the 'to' in this process—we therefore also need to look at States.

Following the revolution in political philosophy of the renaissance, with the rejection of the divine right of kings, the State was reconceived as the key vehicle for the emancipation of individuals and for improving the living standards of communities.[89] With States being the key vehicle, in particular around the turn of the twentieth century, human individuals were deemed to be represented—and one might add: ultimately absorbed—by their States on the international legal plane. And because international law could not penetrate the shield of State sovereignty, it had (according to this view) nothing to say about the relationship between States and their own citizens and residents.[90] Individuals could never have international legal rights or obligations: 'For how could International Law, which is a law between States, give rights to individuals concerning their relations to a State?', Lassa Oppenheim asked rhetorically.[91] And he gave the answer: 'International Law *cannot* grant international rights to individuals, for international rights and duties can exist only between States, or between the League of Nations and States.'[92] The international understanding of the State then tipped from imbalance increasingly towards unreality, as the State in that worldview tended ever more to be hypostasised as an end in itself.[93] The underlying mindset might be called *statism*.

[86] Soirilia, *Law of Humanity Project* 2021 (n. 43), at 121 and 163.

[87] For 'mediation', see above, note 12 and accompanying text.

[88] Welsh et al., 'Introduction' 2023 (n. 32), 13.

[89] This was a major feature of the US American Declaration of Independence 1776, and of the French Déclaration des droits de l'homme et du citoyen 1789, as well as the enlightenment legal theorists which helped to provide the intellectual framework for those developments. See, e.g., John Locke, *Two Treatises of Government* (London: Awnsham Churchill, 1690); Jean-Jacques Rousseau, *Du contrat social; ou principles du droit politique* (Amsterdam: Marc Michel Rey, 1762); and for analysis, see Mark Somos, 'Boston in the State of Nature, 1761-1765' *Jus Gentium* 3 (2018) 63-113.

[90] See, e.g., Antoine Hobza, 'Questions de droit international concernant les religions' *Recueil des Cours* 5 (1924), 367-424, at 380. *cf.* also Triepel, *Völkerrecht und Landesrecht* 1899 (n. 12).

[91] Lassa Oppenheim, *International Law—A Treatise*, vol. 1 Peace (3rd edn, Ronald F. Roxborough (ed.), London: Longmans, Green and Co 1920), 457, at § 289.

[92] *ibid*, 459, at § 289 (emphasis in original).

[93] Georg Wilhelm Friedrich Hegel's philosophy strongly influenced legal scholars: 'Der Staat ist nicht um der Bürger Willen da; man könnte fast sagen, er ist der Zweck und sie sind seine Werkzeuge'

Statism was already the subject of prominent criticism in the inter-war period (and thus in the pre-international human rights era), and was pitted against individualism by a number of authors.[94] Jean Spiropoulos formulated the shift of the finality of international law from protecting States to protecting individuals succinctly:

> Depuis que le dogme de la souveraineté absolue a été ébranlé, depuis que l'État a été dépouillé de toute *personification mystique,* enfin que la conviction se fait jour que *l'État n'est pas un fin en soi*, mais simplement un moyen de satisfaction de besoins individuels on commence à se rappeler que tout droit—par conséquent le droit des gens lui-même—n'existe en dernière analyse que pour la *protection des individus*.[95]

Hans Kelsen, too, deplored the hypostatisation of the State: 'L'idée qu'il y aurait entre l'État et les individus, et par suite d'État à État, des rapports qui ne seraient pas des rapports entre individus est une simple illusion, qui ne s'explique que par l'inadmissible hypostase de l'État en un surhomme.'[96] George Scelle conceptualised the State as a mere 'milieu inter-social'—which led him to consider individuals alone as the legal subjects in public international law.[97]

('The State does not exist for the sake of the citizens; it might rather be said that the State is the end and the citizens are its instruments'): Georg Wilhelm Friedrich Hegel, *Vorlesungen über die Philosophie der Geschichte*, vol. I: *Einleitung – Die Vernunft in der Geschichte* (Georg Lasson (ed.), Leipzig: Felix Meiner Verlag 1920), 91; our translation). In legal scholarship, see Adam Heinrich Müller, *Die Elemente der Staatskunst*, vol. 1 (Berlin: J. D. Sander 1809), 68: The State 'is too big, too alive for […] succumbing to one of the aims exclusively: it serves all conceivable objectives, because it serves itself'. ('[…] er ist aber zu groß, zu lebendig, um sich, den Wuenschen der Theoretiker gemaeß, Einem dieser Zwecke aus-schließend und allein hinzugeben: er dient ihnen allen, er dient allen gedenkbaren Zwecken, weil er sich selbst dient'.) Gleider Hernández argues that hypostatisation of the State was the result of a conscious effort to elide the individual, in service of 'an appeal to the rationalist ideals of the period to ensure recognition of international law's character as law': see Hernández, 'Legal Positivism' (chapter 8), in this volume, p. 175.

[94] See Peters, 'Before Human Rights' (chapter 7), in this volume.

[95] Jean Spiropoulos, 'L'individu et le droit international' *Recueil des Cours* 30 (1929) 195-270, at 197: 'As the doctrine of absolute sovereignty has been shaken, as the State has been stripped of all *mystical personification*, as the conviction has grown that the *State is not an end in itself*, but merely a means to meet needs of individuals, it is beginning to be remembered that all law—and therefore the law of nations itself—exists in the last analysis only for the *protection of individuals*' (our translation and emphasis).

[96] Hans Kelsen, 'Les Rapports de Système entre le Droit Interne et le Droit International Public' *Recueil des Cours* 14 (1926), 231-329, at 281: 'The idea that there could be between the State and the individual, and as a result of relations between States, a relationship that is not that of a relationship between individuals is a simple illusion, and one that is explicable only through the inadmissible attribution to the State the character of a super-individual' (our translation).

[97] Georges Scelle, 'Règles générales du droit de la paix' *Recueil des Cours* 46 (1933) 327-703, at 341-43 (quote at 341). See also Georges Scelle, *Précis de droit des gens: principes et systématique*, vol. 1 (Paris: Librairie du Recueil Sirey 1932), 42; *id, Droit international public* (Paris: Les Ed Domat-Montchrestien 1944), 410-11; *id*, 'Some Reflections on Juridical Personality in International Law', in George A. Lipskey (ed.), *Law and Politics in the World Community* (Berkeley, CA: University of

Such diverse approaches allowed their protagonists to break from the conventional narrative of international law as an order comprised of and for States alone.[98] Nevertheless, the conventional narrative was carried over in mainstream scholarship well into the twentieth century. States continued artificially to be conceived as opaque spheres—'billiard balls'[99]—the collisions and interactions of which were the only concern of international law. Under this conception, the internal processes and individuals which compose and act for States were subsumed under and obscured by the metaphysical personality of the State itself.[100] The humanisation thesis is a reminder that such descriptions, never more than caricature, simply cannot capture the complexity of the contemporary international legal system. It acknowledges the sociological fact that States are comprised of individuals, that law is a product of human society, and that absent human beings these social institutions would cease instantly to be.[101]

The reversal of the traditional hierarchy between State sovereignty and humanity has become most tangible in the conceptualisation and application of the 'responsibility to protect' (R2P) as a commitment of the international community.[102] The term was coined, building on scholarship by Francis Deng, by an expert commission established in response to the international community's failure to intervene in the Rwandan genocide of 1995[103] and was subsequently adopted by Heads of States and Governments in the World Summit Outcome Document of 2005.[104] It has been invoked and applied in several UN Security resolutions, notably the authorisation of military intervention in Libya in 2011.[105] R2P is currently operationalised by a UN unit and by the special adviser of the Secretary General on the responsibility to protect.[106] The responsibility to protect holds that each individual State has the responsibility to protect its populations from genocide, war crimes, ethnic cleansing, and crimes against humanity. The international

California Press 1953), 49-58. 'Individuals alone are the legal subjects in public International law' (our translation).

[98] See in detail Peters, 'Before Human Rights' (chapter 7), in this volume.

[99] Arnold Wolfers, *Discord and Collaboration: Essays on International Politics* (Baltimore, MD: Johns Hopkins University Press 1965), 19-24.

[100] *ibid.*

[101] Sparks, 'The State' 2019 (n. 7), at 840-42.

[102] Arguing that State sovereignty is only derivative of the needs or interests of individuals and communities within those States: Anne Peters, 'Humanity as the A and Ω of Sovereignty' *European Journal of International Law* 20 (2009) 513-44.

[103] International Commission on Intervention and State Sovereignty (ICISS), The Responsibility to Protect (2001). Francis M. Deng (ed.), *Sovereignty as Responsibility: Conflict Management in Africa* (Washington DC: Brookings Inst. 1996). See also the journal *Global Responsibility to Protect*, founded in 2009.

[104] World Summit Outcome Document, 16 September 2005, A/RES 60/1, paras 138-39.

[105] UNSC, 17 March 2011, S/RES/1973: 'Reiterating the responsibility of the Libyan authorities to protect the Libyan population and reaffirming that parties to armed conflicts bear the primary responsibility to take all feasible steps to ensure the protection of civilians.'

[106] The position was created in 2008; the current special adviser is George Okoth-Obbo (since 2022).

community must assist the territorial State, and must step in if the State fails to deliver protection. Military intervention, however, is permissible only where authorised by the Security Council. The starting point of this mechanism is the well-being of individual human beings threatened by the worst crimes. The State's position is couched in terms of responsibility, not sovereignty. The key innovation here is the shift of the argumentative burden and the complete reversal of the logic from a *right* to humanitarian intervention to an *obligation* to intervene. This innovative structure marks R2P as emblematic of humanisation. The more recent reluctance to invoke this concept, and especially the failure to bring it to bear on the war in Syria (raging since 2011) therefore dampens the humanisation of international law significantly.

To summarise, the contemporary humanisation (or individualisation) thesis points to the expansion and intensification of direct international individual rights, going beyond human (fundamental) rights proper. It claims that human individuals should be understood as the original or genuine persons of international law and, as a corollary, that States have been displaced as normative reference points of international legal rules. Also relevant are the standing of individuals to enforce their international rights before international courts and tribunals; the intensifying legal practice of granting individual remedies to victims of violations of international law, including monetary compensation; the involvement of individuals in the creation of international law; and the emergence of concepts such as human security and R2P. Overall, the thesis of the humanisation of and inside international law is not merely a descriptive claim, but one with normative force: it argues that individuals *ought to be* the units of concern for international law. Individuals are the core subjects of the system, and international law is being (and should be) reoriented to take account of their interests and needs.[107]

4. The Individual in International Law and Its Critics

The claim that the international legal order has in fact been humanised—has been reoriented to centre the needs and interests of human individuals—and should properly go further in this direction has always met resistance, on doctrinal, analytical, and on normative grounds. Moreover, both technological development and ecological disaster have—in the Anthropocene—prompted new objections against the normative focus of international law on the individual human being. These developments thus confirm and deepen certain of the criticisms. Importantly, the

[107] In order to make this claim, authors need not reject or modify the doctrine of sources as it would be recognised by interlocutors in the positivist/realist tradition. Proponents of the humanisation thesis can retain an account of international law as the legal order which regulates interactions between independent polities, and can provide an internal critique of that account.

philosophical and theoretical scepticism against rights in general, against human rights in particular, and against humanism/anthropocentrism as a mindset is not limited to one specific intellectual camp, but is fed by the entire gamut of ideological positions.[108] In this section, we canvass the most pertinent lines of critique, in order to respond to them in the light of the findings of this book in our concluding chapter.[109]

A first and widespread criticism of humanisation in doctrinal legal scholarship comes from scholars who insist on the centrality of the State for international law in historical, doctrinal, and normative terms. This *'realist' and 'statist' critique* explicitly or implicitly casts the humanisation thesis as failing to take proper account of the power dynamics of the international law-making process. For example, Gerhard Hafner argues that 'reality does not unequivocally support finding a fundamental change' in the telos or structure of the international legal system.[110] Rather, he considers that the 'status of individuals in international law is restricted'.[111] Though Hafner acknowledges the growing number of international law regimes which provide for individual rights or obligations, he diagnoses a continued monopoly on the apparatus of law-making by States, a fact he sees as determinative.[112] On similar grounds, Klaus Ferdinand Gärditz objects to the upgrading of the individual's international legal personality, arguing that individual subjecthood remains 'limited to certain, rather narrow fields of law, which are still based on (and therefore tightly circumscribed by) state consent'.[113] As such, the individual 'remains an object of protection', rather than a meaningful legal subject.[114]

A variation of this statist view accepts the possibility that international law was shallowly humanised (i.e. that international law showed markers of humanisation but without changes to its (ostensible) fundamentally State-centric structure), but only for a time. It casts humanisation as a 'momentary' phenomenon, which has now come to an end.[115] In 2015, William Burke-White argued that there had been

[108] For overviews of the critiques directed against human rights (a core element of humanisation), see Marie-Bénédicte Dembour, 'Critiques', in Daniel Moeckli, Sangeeta Shah, and Sandesh Sivakumaran (eds.), *International Human Rights Law* (Oxford: OUP 2010), 43-64, at 41-59; Justine Lacroix and Jean-Yves Pranchère, *Human Rights on Trial: The Genealogy of the Critique of Human Rights* (Cambridge: CUP 2018); David M. Scott, 'Human Rights', in Jean d'Aspremont and John Haskell, *Tipping Points in International Law: Commitment and Critique* (Cambridge: CUP 2021), 172-95. Against 'the law of humanity project', see comprehensively Soirilia, *Law of Humanity Project* 2021 (n. 43).

[109] See Peters and Sparks, 'Conclusions' (chapter 18), in this volume.

[110] Hafner, 'Emancipation of the Individual' 2013 (n. 84), 276.

[111] *ibid*, 437.

[112] *ibid.*

[113] Klaus Ferdinand Gärditz, 'Bridge of Varvarin' *American Journal of International Law* 108 (2014) 86-94, at 91.

[114] *ibid.* For arguments from a similar standpoint, see also Emma Dunlop, 'Reply to Anne Peters' *European Journal of International Law* 20 (2009) 556-60; Emily Kidd White, 'Reply to Anne Peters' *European Journal of International Law* 20 (2009) 545-49; Tara J. Melish, 'Review of Anne Peters, Beyond Human Rights' *American Journal of International Law* 113 (2019) 654-64.

[115] Soirilia suggests that this 'moment' lasted from 1990 to around 2010: Soirilia, *Law of Humanity Project* (n. 43), 1-3.

a '*reassertion of the centrality of the State* [which] conflicts with the individualization of international law', and predicted:

> For legal rules and regimes that seek to advance this individualization or draw their effectiveness from it [...] the return of the state will likely have pronounced negative consequences. Over time these regimes may be ratcheted back as international law returns closer to its Westphalian origins as a system of sovereignty, among sovereigns.[116]

Indeed, the current roll-back of the international legal system reinvigorates statism as a mindset. More even, this roll-back is further gathering speed with the renewed importance of inter-State collective security mechanisms following Russia's war of aggression against Ukraine.

A second objection finds the humanisation thesis to be unduly value-laden, based on an *outdated natural law paradigm* that cannot explain international law after its secularisation.[117] Rather than seeking to interpret law from the inside and to uncover its internal logic, the critique runs, humanisation scholarship relies on external standards and the demands of an objective morality in order to shape the law. For example, Tara Melish criticises a 'neo-natural' framing of the debate as 'presuppos[ing] a view of law as independent from and superior to politics and power, a view not easily squared with everyday realities'.[118] At the heart of these types of criticism is the suspicion that humanisation is contaminated with an ideological commitment to natural law.

A related issue is the *western origin* of the mindsets of humanism and individualism. At its core, that observation is indisputable: to date, humanisation scholarship has been dominated by a focus on humanitarian law, criminal law, and human rights—the latter two of which in particular are founded upon legal instruments with a specific, western heritage.[119] Beyond this historical consideration, humanisation scholarship, much like the fields it has drawn from, is dominated by the western conception of the individual and individualism.[120] The western

[116] William W. Burke-White, 'Power Shifts in International Law: Structural Realignment and Substantive Pluralism' *Harvard Journal of International Law* 56 (2015) 1-79, at 77.

[117] Secularisation started in the early years of the seventeenth century: Mark Somos, *Secularisation and the Leiden Circle* (Leiden: Brill 2011), 1-47.

[118] Tara J. Melish, 'Review of Anne Peters, Beyond Human Rights' *American Journal of International Law* 113 (2019), 654-64, at 657.

[119] For the argument that human rights, either in the abstract or in the specific context of their development and implementation in international law, are 'western' concepts, see inter alia Raimon Panikkar, 'Is the Notion of Human Rights a Western Concept?' *Diogenes* 30 (1982), 75-102; Bhupinder S. Chimni, 'Third World Approaches to International Law: A Manifesto' *International Community Law Review* 8 (2006) 3-28, at 55-56; Makau Mutua, 'Savages, Victims, and Saviors: The Metaphor of Human Rights' *Harvard International Law Journal* 42 (2011) 201-46, at 205-06.

[120] See Chimni, 'TWAIL' (chapter 11), in this volume; Veličković, 'Marxism' (chapter 13), in this volume; Foblets, 'Anthropological Approaches' (chapter 17), in this volume. See further Bhupinder S. Chimni, *International Law and World Order: A Critique of Contemporary Approaches* (2nd edn, Cambridge: CUP 2017), 148; Adamantia Pollis and Peter Schwab, 'Human Rights: A Western Construct

provenance of many of international law's concepts and institutions is problematic to the extent that it does not fit well with non-western legal cultures, too readily assumes the existence and acceptance of universal legal values, and most of all when it leads to double standards and hypocrisy of the west.[121] Indeed, the humanisation of international law seems lopsided when States of the non-western world are asked (with carrots and sticks, for example with conditionalities) to respect human rights and IHL, while at the same time in some rich States of the north-west refugees are detained, migrant families are separated, drone strikes produce excessive civilian casualties, and when the western lifestyle benefits from unhealthy working conditions and cheap labour in the southern production site countries.

Next, separate but connected paradigms ranging from post-structuralism and critical legal studies through critical post-humanism up to new materialism have all raised objections against the main legal categories of the humanisation debate. These intellectual strands have announced the death of '*man*',[122] and of the '*subject*',[123] have deconstructed the '*human*',[124] and have attacked the concept of *rights*.[125]

These approaches have shifted the image of the individual subject as a wielder of power towards the individual subject as a result of knowledge and power, as a

with Limited Applicability', in Christine M Koggel (ed.), *Moral Issues in Global Perspective: Moral and Political Theory*, vol. 1 (2nd edn, Peterborough, Ontario: Broadview Press 2006), 60-71. For a similar critique emphasising the dominance of male conceptions of individualism, see Houghton, 'Feminist Approaches' (chapter 12), in this volume, and further Catherine MacKinnon, *Are Women Human?* (Cambridge, MA: Harvard University Press 2006), at 43, 180, and *passim*.

121 See notably Stephen Hopgood, *The Endtimes of Human Rights* (Ithaca, NY: Cornell University Press 2013).

122 Michel Foucault, *Les Mots et les Choses* (Paris: Éditions Gallimard 1966), 398: 'En prenant une chronologie relativement courte et un découpage géographique restreint […] on peut être sûr que l'homme y est une invention récente. […] L'homme est une invention dont l'archéologie de notre pensée montre aisément la date récente. Et peut-être la fin prochaine. Si ces dispositions venaient à disparaître comme elles sont apparues […] alors on peut bien parier que l'homme s'effacerait, comme à la limite de la mer un visage de sable.' ('If we take a relatively short chronology and a restricted geographical division [...] we can be sure that man is a recent invention. [...] Man is an invention whose recentness – and maybe whose imminent end – is easily demonstrated by the archeology of our thinking. If these dispositions were to disappear as they have appeared [...] then you can be sure that man would disappear, like a face of sand at the edge of the sea.' (our translation)). For the background to this concept in the post-modern philosophy of Derrida, Deleuze, and others, see James Hartfield, *The 'Death of the Subject' Explained* (Sheffield: Sheffield Hallam University Press 2002).

123 For overviews and critiques of the 'subject', see Jannice Käll, 'Critical Posthumanism, Justice, and Law', in Stefan Herbrechter et al. (eds.), *Palgrave Handbook of Critical Posthumanism* (Cham: Springer Nature 2022), 629-49, at 631 and 634; Jessie Hohmann, 'Diffuse Subjects and Dispersed Power: New Materialist Insights and Cautionary Lessons for International law' *Leiden Journal of International law* 3 (2021), 585-606, at 596.

124 Hohmann recalls that 'according to the new materialism, there is no hard-bordered "human" ': Hohmann, 'Diffuse Subjects' 2021 (n. 123), 593.

125 Influentially Mark Tushnet, 'An Essay on Rights' *Texas Law Review* 62 (1984) 1363-403; Duncan Kennedy, 'The Critique of Rights in Critical Legal Studies', in Wendy Brown and Janet Halley (eds.), *Left Legalism/Left Critique* (Durham, NC: Duke University Press 2002), 178-228 (orig. in Duncan Kennedy, *A Critique of Adjudication (fin de siècle)* (Cambridge, MA: Harvard University Press 1997)).

'constructed' self.[126] They usefully warn against any essentialisation of the subject and against exaggeration of its coherence. Various chapters in this book address these philosophical challenges.[127] Indeed, legal thought needs to digest the philosophical shift towards post-subjectivity, post- (and trans-)humanism, and materialism, and reflect about consequences for legal responsibility and accountability.[128]

Rights are also the subject of another line of critique which, although it accepts the idea of individual rights in general, argues that they need more explicitly to be balanced with individual *duties*. Various strands in virtue ethics, religious laws, and duty-oriented philosophies fear that the insistence on rights as entitlement in any given society (including the international one) fuels egoism, neglects the community, and marginalises *obligations, responsibility, and solidarity*.[129] These observations resonate with critiques of western-style exaggerated individualism.[130]

Others deplore the *'proliferation' of human rights*,[131] 'human rights absolutism',[132] 'rightsism',[133] 'human rights overreach',[134] or an 'inflation'[135] of international human rights. The lamented proliferation is said to weaken the effective protection of a hard core of (in the critics' view) the most fundamental rights. Although clear criteria to distinguish 'real' human rights from 'supposed' ones (to take up Maurice Cranston's (in)famous dichotomy)[136] are rarely forthcoming, the 'proliferation' critiques mostly amount to a denigration of the so-called 'second generation' (economic, social, and cultural) rights, as intruding on the space available for 'true' rights, i.e. the civil and political rights or subsets thereof.[137] A related strand

[126] Catherine Brölmann and Janne Nijman, 'Personality', in Jean d'Aspremont and Sahib Singh (eds.), *Concepts for International Law: Contributions to Disciplinary Thought* (Cheltenham: Edward Elgar 2019), 67-90, at 689.

[127] Chimni, 'TWAIL' (chapter 11), in this volume; Houghton, 'Feminist Approaches' (chapter 12), in this volume.

[128] See in detail Peters and Sparks, 'Conclusions' (chapter 18), in this volume.

[129] Mary Ann Glendon, *Rights Talk: The Impoverishment of the Political Discourse* (New York, NY: The Free Press 1991); John Milbank, 'Against Human Rights: Liberty in the Western Tradition', in Costas Douzinas and Conor Gearty (eds.), *The Meanings of Rights: The Philosophy and Social Theory of Human Rights* (Cambridge: CUP 2014), 39-70; Onora O'Neill, *Justice Across Boundaries: Whose Obligations?* (Cambridge: CUP 2016).

[130] Chimni, 'TWAIL' (chapter 11), in this volume; Foblets 'Anthropological Approaches' (chapter 17), in this volume.

[131] Jacob Mchangama and Guglielmo Verdirame, 'When Defending Liberty, Less Is More: The Danger of Human Rights Proliferation' *Foreign Affairs*, 24 July 2013; Kasey McCall-Smith, 'The Proliferation of Human Rights: Between Devotion and Calculation', in Jan Wouters et al. (eds.), *Can We Still Afford Human Rights?: Critical Reflections on Universality, Proliferation and Costs* (Cheltenham: Edward Edgar 2020), 114-42.

[132] Nathalie R. Davidson, 'Human Rights Realism' *Vanderbilt Journal of Transnational Law* 54 (2021), 31-81, at 35 and *passim*.

[133] *cf.* Jamal Greene, *How Rights Went Wrong: Why our Obsession with Rights is Tearing America Apart* (Boston, MA: Mariner Books 2021), 57 (for the US context only).

[134] For a useful dissection, see Anuscheh Farahat and Ingrid Leijten, 'Human Rights Overreach?' *Netherlands Quarterly of Human Rights* 40 (2022), 83-97.

[135] Dominique Clément, 'Human Rights or Social Justice?: The Problem of Rights Inflation' *International Journal of Human Rights* 22 (2018), 155-69.

[136] Maurice Cranston, 'Human Rights, Real and Supposed', in David D. Raphael (ed.), *Political Theory and the Rights of Man* (London: Macmillan 1967), 43-54.

[137] See, e.g., Eric Posner, *The Twilight of Human Rights Law* (Oxford: OUP 2014).

of critique is motivated by real or feigned concern for democracy. Democracy is presented as being suffocated where 'bloated' human rights ostensibly remove questions from the political realm. The critique here is that setting priorities and making trade-offs for satisfying individuals' and groups' interests should be discussed and decided in political (democratic) processes.[138]

A manifestation of the attempts to cut back human rights is the work of the USA's 'Commission on Unalienable Rights', with the mandate to provide 'advice and recommendations on human rights to the Secretary of State, grounded in [the United States'] founding principles and the 1948 Universal Declaration of Human Rights […] for the promotion of individual liberty, human equality and democracy through U.S. foreign policy'.[139] The report concluded that '[t]here is good reason to worry that the prodigious expansion of human rights has weakened rather than strengthened the claims of human rights and left the most disadvantaged more vulnerable. More rights do not always yield more justice.'[140] With regard to international order, Ingrid Wuerth has deplored the expansion of human rights, claiming that this has made international law 'weaker, less likely to generate compliance, and more likely to produce interstate friction and conflict'. The work of international organisations such as the UN should, in a 'post-human rights era', be focused 'on a stronger, more limited core of international legal norms that protects international peace and security, not human rights'.[141] These arguments feed the narratives of populist and authoritarian politicians. Human rights, and especially the regional human rights courts, have become an easy target for anti-internationalist parties, which portray these institutions as anti-democratic, infringing State sovereignty, leftist, or as a western imposition.[142]

Another critique is '*scholactivism*'.[143] The reproach is that scholars in the field are not 'engaged in a neutral exercise of "diagnosis"'. Instead, they are said to be 'invested in this process of "humanization", if the process is indeed occurring'.[144] In other words, proponents of humanisation are—according to this critique—not conducting valid scholarship (analysing, understanding, and explaining) but rather, when they argue that international law is humanising or individualising,

[138] John Tasioulas, 'Are Human Rights Taking over the Space Once Occupied by Politics?' *New Statesman* (26 August 2019).

[139] Art. 1 of the Commission's Charter of 26 June 2019, approved by Brian J. Bulatao, Under Secretary of State for Management. This commission had been established by the US Secretary of State, Michael Pompeo, a member of the Republican party. Its chair was the Harvard professor Mary Ann Glendon, who had also served as the US ambassador to the Holy See.

[140] Report of the Commission on Unalienable Rights of 26 August 2020, available at https://www.state.gov/report-of-the-commission-on-unalienable-rights/, accessed 27/11/23 at 38.

[141] Ingrid Wuerth, 'International Law in the Post-Human Rights Era' *Texas Law Review* 96 (2017) 279-349 (quotes from the abstract).

[142] *cf.* Soirilia, *Law of Humanity Project* 2021 (n. 43), 140-41, 164.

[143] Tarunabh Khaitan, 'On Scholactivism in Constitutional Studies: Skeptical Thoughts' *International Journal of Constitutional Law* 20 (2022), 547-56.

[144] Emma Dunlop, 'Reply to Anne Peters' *European Journal of International Law* 20 (2009), 556-60, at 556.

pursue a non-scholarly 'project' to evaluate, judge, and change international law in line with their values and beliefs.[145] This putative flaw is exacerbated by the 'absence of any objective yardstick on which to measure the humanisation of international law', which leaves 'the process, or lack of it, [. . .] in the eyes of the beholder'.[146] The engagement with the law of humanisation scholars thus—according to the critics—only feigns scholarly validity, but in reality is no more than activism fuelled by political and moral convictions.

The next observation is that humanisation scholarship has been oblivious to the possibility of abuse of the humanitarian legal vocabulary. Carl Schmitt famously, if cynically, proclaimed that 'he who speaks of humanity cheats'.[147] While scholars diagnosing and applauding the humanisation of international law are not necessarily themselves 'cheating', in this Schmittian sense, it may be that they verge on the naïve in underestimating the potential for others to highjack their noble but indeterminate concepts strategically.[148] Examples of such strategic abuse of humanisation concepts abound, from Venezuela's attempt to refer the USA's sanctions regime to the ICC as a 'crime against humanity',[149] to Russia's disingenuous mobilisation of self-determination and a fictitious genocide against Russian-speakers to claim that its invasion of Ukraine is justified.[150] In light of these—and manifold other—examples, scholars need to remain aware that those who talk 'humanism' or 'universality' may do so only in order to further their special interests.

Finally, we deem most pertinent and profound three final critiques which we attempt to integrate into a renewed conceptualisation of the status of the individual in international law: the reproaches of *neoliberalism*, *veiled colonialism*, and anti-ecological *anthropocentrism*.

The first productive challenge is that humanisation scholarship has (unwittingly) become a bedfellow of *neoliberalism* (broadly speaking).[151] Indeed, the

145 Soirilia, *Law of Humanity Project* 2021 (n. 43), 2 and *passim*.

146 *ibid*, 10.

147 'Wer Menschheit sagt, will betrügen.' Carl Schmitt, *Der Begriff des Politischen* (Berlin: Duncker & Humblot 1932), 55, referring to Proudhon.

148 Soirilia, *Law of Humanity Project* 2021 (n. 43), 11, 13, 80, 124, and 161-63.

149 President of the Republic of the Bolivarian Republic of Venezuela, Referral pursuant to Article 14 of the Rome Statute to the Prosecutor of the International Criminal Court by the Bolivarian Republic of Venezuela with respect to Unilateral Coercive Measures, 12 February 2020, cover letter, available at https://www.icc-cpi.int/sites/default/files/itemsDocuments/200212-venezuela-referral.pdf, accessed 27/11/23.

150 On genocide, see Letter dated 24 February 2022 from the Permanent Representative of the Russian Federation to the United Nations addressed to the Secretary-General (UN Doc. 2022/154): The 'purpose is to protect people who have been subjected to abuse and genocide by the Kiev regime for eight years. And to this end, we will seek the demilitarization and deNazification of Ukraine, as well as the prosecution of those who have committed numerous bloody crimes against civilians, including citizens of the Russian Federation.' See discussion in ICJ, *Allegations of Genocide under the Convention on the Prevention and Punishment of the Crime of Genocide (Ukraine v. Russian Federation)*, Provisional Measures, Order of 16 March 2022, (2022) ICJ Reports 211. On the abusive invocation of self-determination, see Tom Sparks, *Self-Determination in the International Legal System: Whose Claim, to What Right?* (Oxford: Hart 2023), 185-92.

151 Soirila, *Law of Humanity Project* 2021 (n. 43), 141-47. A related reproach is that of the 'managerialism' of humanisation scholarship and the 'human rights audit culture'. Soirilia denounces both

urge to discipline the State can be used to push through the privatisation of public services. The individualism that underpins the humanisation of international law can be employed to overemphasise and overprotect transnational property, trade, and capital rights at the expense of social rights.[152] On these grounds, critical and neo-Marxist thought has recurrently announced the (need for an) 'end' of human rights.[153] Various chapters in the book highlight how international law's reorientation to the individual has been absorbed by global governance machineries that serve global capital more than the human being.[154]

The second forceful and productive critique is that of *neocolonialism*. The work of Third World Approaches to International Law (TWAIL) scholars and of critical black studies have uncovered the colonial roots of many of international law's key doctrines and structures, and argue that modern regimes including international human rights law and governance serve a neocolonial purpose of maintaining the ideological and economic subjugation of the third world (including the 'third world in the first world'[155]).[156] Scholars in this tradition have seen in humanisation a discourse which is, at best, a well-meaning irrelevance, and at worst a purposeful attempt to distract attention from the true problems of the international legal system: inequality, impoverishment, and the ways in which entrenched power structures work against the interests of third world States. It may even be the case, as some TWAIL scholars would argue, that humanisation serves the yet-more insidious purpose of actively limiting the sovereignty of third world States: doctrines such as R2P and human rights provide grounds on which third world States may be sanctioned, controlled, and in extreme cases invaded by their former colonial masters. Critical black studies even reject the concepts of the human, of human rights, and subjecthood, pointing to racialised and 'anti-Black' grounding of these categories. These scholars deplore the 'violence of humanization' and 'the burden of inclusion into a racially hierarchized universal humanity'.[157] They point out that

practices and approaches as falsely depoliticised, technocratic, and expertocratic, and ultimately undemocratic: Soirilia, *Law of Humanity Project* 2021 (n. 43), 133-41, quote at 139). Indeed, the tools of human rights due diligence, human rights mainstreaming, and human rights impact assessments come from the toolbox of new public management and the business sphere.

[152] Jessica Whyte, *The Morals of the Market: Human Rights and the Rise of Neoliberalism* (London: Verso 2019).

[153] Costas Douzinas, *The End of Human Rights: Critical Legal Thought at the Turn of the Century* (Oxford: Hart 2000). See also Hopgood, *Endtimes* 2013 (n. 121); Paul O'Connell, 'On the Human Rights Question' *Human Rights Quarterly* 40 (2018) 962-88.

[154] Veličković, 'Marxist Approach' (chapter 13), in this volume; Chimni, 'TWAIL' (chapter 11), in this volume.

[155] To the best of our knowledge, this term was coined by Trinh T. Minh-ha, 'Wo/Man/Third/World' *Women and Language* (1988) 11, 6-7, 7.

[156] Makau Matua, 'Is the Age of Human Rights Over?', in Sophie A. McClennen and Alexandra Schultheiss Moore (eds.), *The Routledge Companion to Literature and Human Rights* (London: Routledge 2016), 450-58; Colin Samson, *The Colonialism of Human Rights: Ongoing Hypocrisies of Western Liberalism* (Cambridge: Polity Press, 2020).

[157] Zakiyyah Iman Jackson, *Becoming Human: Matter and Meaning in an Antiblack World* (New York, NY: New York University Press 2020), 18.

Black people had been historically enslaved as 'things' and have experienced a life without rights. In their view, the '[r]cognition of personhood and humanity does not annul the animalization of blackness'.[158] Therefore, these scholars could also envisage a society 'after rights'.[159] They refuse to beg for inclusion into a legal order after having historically been denied access to it. In our volume, the third world or post-colonial assessment of the status of the individual in international law is directly addressed by Bhupinder S. Chimni.[160]

Finally, the ongoing *climate and wider environmental catastrophe* poses the third lasting big challenge for humanism and the humanisation of international law. Ecological awareness and environmental law scholars have for decades been exposing the dark side of humanism, in this context mostly denounced as 'anthropocentrism', an undue focus on humans at the expense of proper attention to the ecological sphere. In this debate, the nefarious humanism/anthropocentrism is pitted against the more promising ecocentrism. These debates have generated calls for a post-humanist 'zoocentrism'.[161] This body of scholarship points out that traditional humanism has focused on human interests without embedding humans within the natural world on whom humans depend, and is therefore incomplete to the point of being flawed. We agree, but argue that post-humanism goes too far if it discards the human. We develop our responses to these three great challenges in the concluding chapter.[162]

5. The Need for Historical and Theoretical Investigations

The mentioned contestations of the humanisation thesis and the related attacks on humanism, individualism, legal subjecthood, and legal (human) rights call for a deeper historical and theoretical investigation of the issue, as attempted with this book. The volume is divided into two sections, the first devoted to international law's history. Six chapters examine international law in different time periods, and analyse the interrelationship between the individual and the legal order as it then existed. We acknowledge that the periodisation implied in the sequence of the historical chapters is to some extent arbitrary and surely Eurocentric.[163] However,

[158] *ibid.*

[159] For a powerful account, see Marie Catherine Petersmann, 'In the Break (of Rights and Representation): Sociality beyond the Non/human subject' *International Journal of Human Rights* (2023), 1-25.

[160] See Chimni, 'TWAIL' (chapter 11), in this volume; and further (for an aligned approach) Foblets, 'Anthropological Approaches' (chapter 17), in this volume.

[161] Centrally Rosi Braidotti, *The Posthuman* (Cambridge: Polity Press 2013). See also Susan McHugh, 'Human-Animal Studies: Postzoomanities', in: Stefan Herbrechter et al. (eds.), *Palgrave Handbook of Critical Posthumanism* (Cham: Springer Nature 2022), 823-39.

[162] Peters and Sparks, 'Conclusions' (chapter 18), in this volume.

[163] Oliver Diggelmann, 'The Periodization of the History of International Law', in Bardo Fassbender and Anne Peters (eds.), *The Oxford Handbook of the History of International Law* (Oxford: OUP 2012), 997-1101.

we have chosen this conventional periodisation of the history of international law in order to reassess the story told by the mainstream account on its own terms. These periods were not intended to restrict the authors, however, and were open to adaptation as needed. Beginning with antiquity (Eleanor Cowan, chapter 2), and then progressing through the medieval period (500-1500; Dante Fedele and Alain Wijffels, chapter 3); 1500-1648 (Francesca Iurlaro, chapter 4); 1648-1789 (Mark Somos, chapter 5); 1789-1914 (Inge van Hulle, chapter 6); and 1914-1945 (Anne Peters, chapter 7), these contributions consider what form or forms of international law existed during the periods in question, and how these related to the individual on one side, and on the other to the State. They identify and examine the conceptual framework of the interaction between these entities as it changed over time, by reference to the factors, drivers, or consequences which are of greatest relevance to each time period. In doing so, we seek to avoid both 'history as provenance' and 'history as progress'-narratives, highlighting instead elements of continuity and change both within and between periods.[164] To that end, most chapters focus on select topics that are particularly instructive for the legal role and legal agency of certain types of individuals within the normative context that we would now call international law.

The second part of the volume brings the enquiry up to date and deepens the analysis of the international legal system of the present day by turning to theory. The contributions in this part examine how different theoretical perspectives understand the relationship between individuals and States in contemporary international law and, in particular, to what extent a 'human-centred' international legal system is consistent with each framework's understanding of the international legal order. The chapters examine how the various frameworks can accommodate an understanding of international law that places the individual at its centre. They thus 'test' the theoretical frameworks against the evidence of the positive law. At the same time, they interrogate the assumption that a human-centred vision of the international legal system is necessarily associated with a (neo-)natural law framework (see Gleider Hernández, chapter 8; Rafael Domingo, chapter 9; Tom Sparks, chapter 10). This part broadens the enquiry beyond the opposition of positivism and naturalism by including and considering third world approaches (Bhupinder S. Chimni, chapter 11); feminist approaches (Ruth Houghton, chapter 12); and Marxist approaches (Marina Veličković, chapter 12) to international law. Further chapters discuss global law (Angelo Jr Golia, chapter 14); global constitutionalism (Başak Çalı, chapter 15); international law and economics (Anne van Aaken, chapter 16); and finally anthropological approaches (Marie-Claire Foblets, chapter 17).

[164] These categories are Kennedy's; see David Kennedy, 'The Disciplines of International Law and Policy' *Leiden Journal of International Law* 12 (1999) 9-134, at 88-93.

In the concluding chapter 18, we pull together the findings of the preceding contributions. We respond to the objections levelled against the humanisation as both a practical and scholarly phenomenon in light of the chapters' findings. Based on the controversies, lacunae, and possibilities which the authors in this volume have revealed, we identify especially three challenges that persist: the social, the anti-colonial, and the ecological challenge. These offer impulses for further research on the humanisation of international law that overcomes neoliberalism, decolonises humanisation, and should embed the individual within an environmental, a 'green', humanism.[165] It is hoped that the present volume will stimulate further research into what we deem one of the deepest issues of international legal order.

[165] Peters and Sparks, 'Conclusion' (chapter 18), in this volume, section 4.3.3.

PART 1

THE INDIVIDUAL IN THE HISTORY OF INTERNATIONAL LAW

2
The Individual and International Law in Antiquity

*Eleanor Cowan**

1. Introduction

The history of international law has, until relatively recently, been viewed in terms of the idea that international law regulates the behaviour of sovereign States. This line of thought founds international law in the intellectual and philosophical developments leading up to and following the Peace of Westphalia in 1698 including the writings of earlier thinkers (Hugo Grotius, Alberico Gentili, and others familiar with Roman law concepts and ideas) and the strengthening of legal frameworks and remedies in the aftermath of World War II. Recent trends in international human rights, humanitarian, and international criminal law have begun to recognise a 'diversity of participants' in international law including individuals *as* individuals, but also as groups and non-State actors who have duties and rights (which are enforceable).[1] A chapter on the individual in international law in antiquity must confront three important and challenging questions: can we speak of ancient 'international law'?; what connection (or relevance) might the study of antiquity have for modern thinking about the individual in international law?; and did the ancient world recognise 'the individual' as the subject of international law? In what follows, I aim to facilitate further study in relation to all three questions by surveying some recent works of scholarship and thus seeking to place my own discipline in conversation with others.

* My sincere thanks to the editors of this volume and to the participants in the two-day workshop which accompanied it.

[1] Simone Gorski, 'Individuals in International Law', in Anne Peters (2021-) and Rüdiger Wolfrum (2004-20) (eds.), *Max Planck Encyclopedia of Public International Law* (Oxford: OUP 2013), online edn. See also Rose Parfitt, 'Theorizing Recognition and International Personality', in Anne Orford and Florian Hoffmann (eds.), *The Oxford Handbook of the Theory of International Law* (Oxford: OUP 2016), 583-99.

Eleanor Cowan, *The Individual and International Law in Antiquity* In: *The Individual in International Law.* Edited by: Tom Sparks and Anne Peters, Oxford University Press. © Eleanor Cowan 2024. DOI: 10.1093/oso/9780198898917.003.0002

2. International Law in the Ancient World

There is a growing willingness to view ancient international relations as relevantly concerned with international law.[2] Objections to this view, based on concern about the existence of the sovereign State in antiquity and the capacity of ancient communities to conceive of or adopt norms of international behaviour (as an alternative to perpetual and anarchic states of warfare), continue to be challenged.[3] Study of the ancient world has much to contribute to both the history of international law and our understanding of the intellectual and religious underpinnings of early attempts to formulate ideas and concepts suitable for exploring and explaining relations between ancient communities.[4]

Ancient communities, including those of the ancient Mediterranean and Near East, ancient China, ancient India, and ancient Africa severally testify to a willingness to reflect on and regulate their relationships with, and behaviour in, international settings.[5] International norms and international law modes of thought have been identified in, for example, the Egyptian-Hittite peace treaty of 1270 BCE;

[2] Evidenced, for instance, by entries on 'international law' in standard reference works such as Simon Hornblower, Antony Spawforth, and Esther Eidinow (eds.) *Oxford Classical Dictionary* (Oxford: OUP 2012); see also entries by Jakob Aall Otteson Larsen, Simon Hornblower, and Paul Burton in Sara Elise Phang et al. (eds.), *Conflict in Ancient Greece and Rome: The Definitive Political, Social, and Military Encyclopedia* (Santa Barbara, CA: ABC-CLIO 2016).

[3] Wolfgang Preiser, 'History of International Law, Ancient Times to 1648', in Anne Peters (2021-) and Rüdiger Wolfrum (2004-20) (eds.), *Max Planck Encyclopedia of Public International Law* (Oxford: OUP 2013), online edn and David Bederman, *International Law in Antiquity* (Cambridge: CUP 2001) provide a detailed survey of earlier arguments. See now also Randall Lesaffer, 'Roman Law and the Intellectual History of International Law', in Orford and Hoffman (eds.), *Oxford Handbook* 2016 (n. 1), 38-58; Paul Burton, *Friendship and Empire* (Cambridge: CUP 2011); Paul Burton, 'Roman Imperialism' *Brill's Research Perspectives in Ancient History* 2 (2019), 1-114. On the debate between realist and constructivist readings of ancient international relations, see Neville Morley, *The Roman Empire: Roots of Imperialism* (London: Pluto Press 2010), 32 citing a view he goes on to reject: 'The ancient Mediterranean was undoubtedly anarchic, with no international law, poor and slow communications and no means of enforcing the few rules of conduct between states besides fear of the gods; war was indeed ubiquitous, and it is clear that Rome's militaristic culture was shaped by this environment—as were the cultures of many other states.' See also, Andrew Eckstine, *Mediterranean Anarchy, Interstate War, and the Rise of Rome* (Berkeley, CA: University of California Press 2006) (which deploys realist international relations theory) and Paul Burton, 'Ancient International Law, The Aetolian League, and the Ritual of Surrender, during the Roman Republic: a Constructivist view' *The International History Review* 31 (2009), 237-52.

[4] On the characteristic combination of the rational and the religious in ancient thinking, and hence the fallaciousness of the idea that ancient international law rested solely on religion, see Mikhäil Rostovtseff, 'International Relations in the Ancient World', in Edmund Aloysius Walsh (ed.), *The History and Nature of International Relations* (New York: McMillan 1922), 37-40, at 45; Bederman, *International Law in Antiquity* 2001 (n. 3), 269-70.

[5] See, among many, Preiser 'History' 2013 (n. 3) and entries in Anne Peters (2021-) and Rüdiger Wolfrum (2004-20) (eds.), *Max Planck Encyclopedia of Public International Law* (Oxford: OUP 2013), online edn on regional developments by Shotaro Hamamoto (East Asia); Mohammad Fadel (Islam) and Diane A. Desierto (South and South-East Asia). On ancient Africa, see Taslim Olawale Elias, *Africa and the Development of International law* (2nd edn, Leiden: Brill 1988), 3-6 (on Carthage's relationship with the Mediterranean powers of Greece and Rome). Case studies of ancient international law are provided in Bederman, *International Law in Antiquity* 2001 (n. 3). For sources for the study of international law in antiquity, see Wilhelm Georg Grewe, *Fontes Historiae Iuris Gentium: Sources relating to the history of the law of nations*, vol. 1 (Berlin: Walter de Gruyter 1995).

the extensive systems of international arbitration which existed between ancient Greek States; Roman laws of (war and) peace; patterns of diplomacy between ancient Sumerian city-States; the ancient Chinese doctrines set out in the Tao-Te Ching; and the reflections on diplomacy and warfare in the Indian *Arthasastra* of Kauṭilya.[6] Relationships between ancient communities and between members of these communities and those whom they considered outsiders were arguably concerned with representing mutuality and maintaining a balance of power.[7] They were regulated by laws and customs relating to, for example, the positive treatment of ambassadors, diplomats, and foreigners (including mercantile traders and asylum seekers); the recognition of other religions and gods; treaties and treaty-making (including alliances, peace treaties, tribute, hospitality, surrender, and the treatment of prisoners, and provision for settling disputes); and the declaration and conduct of wars.[8] Important philosophical and religious ideas facilitated, shaped, and underpinned international relations. Among these, the development of philosophies of religious toleration, of natural law, and of just war profoundly affected the behaviour of ancient communities.

The relevance of antiquity in the study of international law has recently been strongly stated.[9] However, the precise relationship (continuity or discontinuity) between ancient and modern international law continues to be debated. This is particularly true in the case of Roman international relations and international law.[10] Roman international customary law consisted of recognisable international

[6] Preiser, 'History' 2013 (n. 3); Bederman, *International Law in Antiquity* 2001 (n. 3), 23 (Sumeria); Olga V. Butkevych 'History of Ancient International Law: Challenges and Prospects' *Journal of the History of International Law* 5 (2003), 189-235 (China). On India, see further Patrick Olivelle, *King, Governance, and Law in Ancient India: Kauṭilya's Arthasastra* (Oxford: OUP 2013), 46-47: 'The maṇḍala or circle theory of kingdoms espoused by Kauṭilya in book 6 also presents the scenario of numerous small states dealing with each other diplomatically and attempting to outwit each other. Foreign policy, therefore, occupies a central position in Kauṭilya's work.'

[7] Michael Rostovtseff, 'International Relations' 1922 (n. 4) and Butkevych 'History' 2003 (n. 6). On balance of power in the ancient Near East, see Alex Ilari Aissaoui, 'Was There a Balance of Power System in the Ancient Near East?' *Diplomacy & Statecraft* 30 (2019), 421-42.

[8] For lists of characteristics of ancient international legal thinking, see Bederman, *International Law in Antiquity* 2001 (n. 3), 267; Butkevych, 'History' 2003 (n. 6); Karl-Heinz Ziegler, *Völkerrechtsgeschichte: Ein Studienbuch* (Munich: Beck 2007).

[9] Butkevych 'History' 2003 (n. 6), 235: 'The analysis of the emergence and becoming of universal principles of law and principles of international law [. . .] bear witness of their much earlier shaping to control international relations of antiquity.' See also Bederman, *International Law in Antiquity* 2001 (n. 3), 16: 'The primary assumption of this study is that there existed at certain times and places in antiquity authentic systems of States which were disposed, through their interactions, to conceive of rules of state behaviour, norms that we might call today the law of nations or international law. This assumption has been debated quite extensively. Indeed, it goes to the heart of my thesis – that ancient peoples were able to envision exogenous limits on State conduct in international relations.'

[10] Early studies are surveyed in Arthur Nussbaum, 'The Significance of Roman law in the history of international law' *Penn Law Review* 100 (1952), 678-87. See now Lesaffer, 'Roman law' 2016 (n. 3), 40-41: 'The question remains whether Roman international law forms a relevant part of modern international law's history. While there is no support for the idea that Roman and modern international law are parts of one evolving system, there is growing consent that certain customs, institutions, and doctrines of the Romans are at the root of their modern variants.' Kaius Tuori, 'The Reception of Ancient Legal Thought in Early Modern International Law', in Bardo Fassbender and Anne Peters (eds.), *The Oxford Handbook of the History of International Law* (Oxford: OUP 2012), 1012-32, at 1014: 'Though

law instruments (treaties) and behaviours (diplomacy, alliances, and the regulation of trade) and was accompanied by the development of a body of ideas, values, and concepts (*fides*, *amicitia*, *maiestas*, *humanitas*, *iustum bellum*, *ius gentium*) with which to evaluate the conduct of international relationships. Perhaps the most influential of these on later thinking were the rituals of the Fetial priests which came to be associated with the idea of just war (*iustum bellum*) and the development, in the Late Republic, of the concept of *ius gentium*, alongside its differentiation from the *ius civile* (the law of individual peoples) and its close relationship to natural law (*ius naturale*). Contemporary debate might be characterised as (a) debate among Roman historians about the lived-experience of Roman international relations and (b) debate among legal theorists and legal historians about the impact of Rome on the later development of international law. As an instance of the former, I note recent critique of the *ius fetiale* and *iustum bellum* which stresses the extent to which Rome claimed to hold itself accountable to (its own) external standard, for instance in the conduct of *iustum bellum*, and to be able to adjudicate matters of (its own) compliance.[11] The Fetial rites themselves fell into abeyance although investment in the idea of just war continued to be important.[12] As an instance of the latter, I note ongoing discussion of the impact and legacy of ancient formulations of *ius gentium*. Cicero, whose writings contain the earliest attested use of *ius gentium*, associated the *ius gentium* with the laws of nature.[13] Later articulations of this idea by Gaius (*Dig.* 1.1.9 Book 1 *Inst.*) and Ulpian (*Dig.* 1.1.1) point to the fact that there

the strong general influence of the Roman legal tradition in the early modern era—be it in general on the European legal traditions, or specifically in the scholarship on international law—is not in doubt, whether or not there was a Roman tradition of international law is debatable.'

[11] Clifford Ando, *Law, Language, and Empire in the Roman Tradition* (Philadelphia, PA: University of Pennsylvania Press 2011) points to the fundamental mismatch between the Roman legal-religious fetial rituals marking just war and Rome's practice which tended to be self-serving (at 31): 'a demand for reparations lay at the heart of Roman declarations of war, and the failure of Rome's opponents to give satisfaction made those wars just. But while Roman sources expend much effort showing that such demands were made, received, and rejected, they never entertain the question of whether the demands were *themselves* just.' For an account of fetial procedure in narrative form, see Liv. 1.24. In addition, claims to have breached *ius fetiale* may also have functioned as a means of explaining defeat after the fact and of holding accountable a general now rendered unpopular. See further Sheila Ager, 'Roman Perspectives on Greek Diplomacy', in Claude Eilers (ed.), *Diplomats and Diplomacy in the Roman World. Mnemosyne* Supplement 304 (Leiden: Brill 2009), 15-43, at 22; Nathan Rosenstein, *Imperatores victi: Military defeat and Aristocratic Competition in the Middle and Late Republic* (Oxford: OUP 1990), 68 for a discussion of the famous case of C. Hostilius Mancinus 137 BCE. The Roman idea of *iustum bellum* was articulated by Cicero, although it may have originated earlier. Precisely what Cicero or other Romans would have considered 'just' about such a war is, however, open to debate. All that may have been meant was that a war was just if it had a cause. For a summary of arguments, see further Ager 'Roman Perspectives', 19-21. See also note 3 above on realist and constructivist readings of Roman international relations.

[12] John Rich, 'The *Fetiales* and Roman International Relations', in James Richardson and Frederico Santangelo (eds.) *Priests and State in the Roman World* (Stuttgart: Franz Steiner Verlag 2011), 187-242.

[13] Cic. *Off.* 3.23 and 3.69 (Cicero, *On Duties*, Book Three, sections 23 and 69); *Har. Resp.* 32 (Cicero, *On the Responses of the Haruspices*) and *Leg.* 2.[8-13]380-87 (Cicero, *On the Laws*, Book Two, sections [8-13] 380-87) discussed by Jed Atkins, *Cicero on Politics and the Limits of Reason: The Republic and Laws* (Cambridge: CUP 2013), 220.

was not a settled definition of *ius gentium* even at the same time as there was widespread recognition of the difference between it and the *ius civile*.[14] Roman international law concepts and thinking had an important afterlife, the precise shape and remit of which continue to be contested.[15]

3. Frameworks for Thinking about the Individual in the Greco-Roman World

An investigation of the individual in international law in the ancient world must perforce recognise the difficulty inherent in conceptualising the ancient individual. Ancient Greco-Roman communities are commonly represented as associations of families rather than associations of individual citizens.[16] After the family, citizenship played a central role in the identity of those (male) members of the community who were entitled to claim it. A recent study of individual liberty in the Greek world has stressed the ways in which individual liberty could be equated to the duties and obligations of citizenship.[17] Christopher Gill has also argued that there is a consistent interest in objective-participant notions of self (*persona*) in Greek and Hellenistic-Roman thought rather than an emergence of individualism.[18] In the case of Roman law, Clifford Ando notes both the contingent ('in motion'/relation) status of Roman legal persons and 'the refusal of Roman legal regulation to imagine individuals as atomized in relation to local and micro networks of

[14] Atkins, *Cicero* 2013 (n. 13), 224-25. See further John R. Kroger, 'The Philosophical Foundations of Roman Law: Aristotle, the Stoics and Roman Theories of Natural Law', in Richard O. Brooks (ed.), *Cicero and Modern Law* (London: Routledge 2009), 229-69.

[15] See note 10, above; and further Paul Remec, *The Position of the Individual in International Law According to Grotius and Vattel* (The Hague: Nijhoff 1960) who argues that (at 61): 'Grotius, therefore, emphatically rejects the Roman notion of natural law common to man and animals' and that it is, in part, Grotius' rejection of 'the distinction made by certain Roman jurists between the law of nature and that of nations' (at 66) which leads to reformulation of his own thought. See also (at 84): 'In essence this was the Roman law conception of "ius gentium" which Grotius rejects.'

[16] The work of Numa Denis Fustel de Coulanges, *The Ancient City* (first published 1864, this edn: Baltimore, MD: Johns Hopkins University Press 1980) has continued to inform modern interpretations of the ancient city. More recently, see Larry Siedentop, *Inventing the Individual* (London: Allen and Unwin 2014), 7: The ancient world was 'a world where action was governed by norms reflecting exclusively the claims of family, its memories, rituals and roles, rather than the claims of individual conscience.' See also, at 28: 'The intermingling of religion and government remained complete. From the sixth to the third century bc changes in the form of polis government – from monarchy to aristocracy, from aristocracy to democracy – did not reduce the authority of the city-state over its members. There was no notion of the rights of individuals against the claims of the city and its gods. There was no formal liberty of thought or action. [...] Ancient liberty consisted of having a share in the government of the city, in public power. It consisted of the privilege and duty to attend the assembly, speak in debates, judge the arguments, take sides and vote, with the further possibility of serving as a magistrate or on a jury, if required. Ancient liberty did not tolerate indifference to the political process. The public thing, *res publica*, was everything.'

[17] Peter Liddel, *Civic Obligations and Individual Liberty in Ancient Athens* (Oxford: OUP 2007).

[18] Christopher Gill, *Personality in Greek Epic, Tragedy, and Philosophy: The Self in Dialogue* (Oxford: OUP 1995) and *id*, *The Structured Self in Hellenistic and Roman Thought* (Oxford: OUP 2006).

affection, social dependency, and obligation. Individualization, individuation, self-fashioning, self-actualizing: in Roman theory, these occur within matrices of social relations and instituted cultural forms.'[19] Beyond citizenship, in Rome, religious, political, and military office-holding as well as one's status as free, freed, or slave also provided an important means of identifying oneself and others. Group identities such as those of the equestrians or freedmen were reinforced performatively (through ceremony and the allocation of space and entitlements) and by distinctions in dress and (for freedpeople) nomenclature.

Powerful cultural traditions of exemplarity nevertheless allowed individuals to be seen. Unlike doctrinal ethics, exempla were particular and contingent.[20] Their use, within a specific argument, rested simultaneously only their uniqueness *and* their typicality.[21] Jorg Rüpke terms this form of individuality 'representative individuality': 'The aim is not individual difference, but perfection in fulfilling a social or religious role, whether as Roman general, Christian martyr, or male Jew, yet fulfilment is a personal feat.'[22] The highly competitive elite political culture of the Republic produced a commemorative culture which concentrated on the achievements of individuals within family groups such as the Scipionic politician-generals. Livy's account of Roman history emphasised the roles of individual men and women as exempla to be imitated or avoided. The emergence of the Principate and the shift to autocratic government (and the corresponding emergence of biographical writing) also stressed the achievements, virtues, and vices of individual emperors.

At the same time, actual action in ancient international relations required and was carried out by and among individuals: generals, diplomats, ambassadors, priests, treaty-makers and breakers, voters. Alongside this mundane observation may be placed a more important one. The Roman *ius gentium* was fundamentally and from the outset concerned with adjudicating disputes between individuals ('a kind of "universal" private law, albeit of Roman making'[23]) and 'Roman jurisprudence bequeathed to the Middle Ages a concept of *jus gentium* that spanned two meanings: that of a universal law, which might well apply to individuals as to

[19] Clifford Ando, 'Self, Society, Individual, and Person in Roman Law', in Maren R. Niehoff and Joshua Levinson (eds.), *Self, Self-fashioning, and Individuality in Late Antiquity. New Perspectives* (Tübingen: Mohr Siebeck 2019), 375-92.

[20] The contrast between exemplarity and doctrinal ethics, and the idea that exempla are particular and contingent, are discussed in Matthew B. Roller, *Models from the Past in Roman Culture* (Cambridge: CUP 2018), 14-15. For the culture of exempla in modernity, see Iurlaro, '1500-1648' (chapter 4), in this volume.

[21] Roller, *Models* 2018 (n. 20), 15-16: 'So while exempla are "unique" in the circumstances of their production (and, as I will argue, in the specific argumentative contexts in which they are invoked), they are "typical" in sharing with other exempla a predicate derived from a shared moral category. Their ontology is double in this way, and they exhibit the one face or the other depending on the circumstances under which they are adduced.'

[22] Jorg Rüpke, *The Individual in the Religions of the Ancient Mediterranean* (Oxford: OUP 2014), 13.

[23] Lesaffer, 'History' 2016 (n. 3), 44.

polities; and that of a law applicable to relations between polities. It also bequeathed a strong association between *jus gentium* and *jus naturale*.'[24] It seems reasonable in the light of this to investigate the individual in Roman international law.

4. The Individual in Ancient International Law: Roman Case Studies

4.1 Individuals as Agents of the *Ius Gentium* (in Private International Law)

4.1.1 The Praetor Peregrinus

By 242 BCE the Romans had created an additional Praetor, the Praetor *inter peregrinos*. The original jurisdiction of this Praetor has proven difficult to understand.[25] He is called *praetor qui inter peregrinos ius dicit* in two Republican statutes and later *praetor qui inter ciues et peregrinos ius dicit*, which has been taken to mean that, by the Principate, this Praetor had capacity to adjudge cases between citizens and peregrines.[26] During the Republic his functions probably included deciding cases between *peregrini* and between peregrines and citizens.[27] Briscoe cites the *ius commercii* of the Latin and Italian communities as the enabling right which brought these cases within the Praetor's jurisdiction, and Daube argues that the Praetor made use of a *formula in factum* and (later) the fiction of *civitas*.[28] Greenidge specifically situates the Praetor's remit in the realm of international law arguing that the Praetor's edict (in some ways analogous to customary law)

[24] *ibid*, 45. See also Remec, *Position of the Individual* (n. 15), 60; citing Hugo Grotius, *De iure belli ac pacis libri tres*, Prolegomena i.1.1.33; i.1.2; ii.4.1.22.: 'It is true that the so-called public aspect is prevalent in these relations among nations in the sense that the actions of sovereign rulers in the interest of the state as a whole have a pre-eminent place. Yet Grotius does not preclude the possibility that individual qua individual could have genuine international relations'. See also, at 63: 'The law of nature thus governs all relations between men as human beings. Hence each individual has a common share in this law not because he belongs to this or that particular community, but because he is a human being' and 69: 'The individual as the indispensable subject of this law has, therefore, a pre-eminent role in the Grotian legal system regulating the "mutual relations among states"'; and 77: 'When Grotius refers to the "free will of man," he clearly means the individual man, not a general will of the civil society.'

[25] The date and evidence for this new praetorship are examined in Cory Brennan, *The Praetorship in the Roman Republic*. (Oxford: OUP 2001), 85-89. Brennan argues (at 89) that the original additional Praetor was stationed in Sicily (*inter peregrinos*), but the argument has been challenged; see John Briscoe, 'Notes in the Functions of the Peregrine Praetor in the Republic' *Latomus* 71 (2012), 996-99. See also David Daube, 'The Peregrine Praetor' *Journal of Roman Studies* 41 (1951), 66-70.

[26] Briscoe, 'Notes' 2012 (n. 25) citing Michael H. Crawford (ed.), *Roman Statutes* (London: University of London Press *BICS Supplement* 1996) p. 1 lines 12 and 89, p. 24 line 8, p. 28 lines 24 and 34 and *TLL* x/1.1314.61.

[27] Briscoe, 'Notes' 2012 (n. 25); contra Brennan, *Praetership* 2001 (n. 25), 85-89. See also Daube, 'Praetor' 1951 (n. 25), 68 who argues that the jurisdiction between citizens and *peregrini* was not part of the original jurisdiction but was introduced by the *Lex Calpurnia* of 149 BCE and the *quaestio repetudarum*.

[28] Briscoe, 'Notes' 2012 (n. 25), 998 and Daube, 'Praetor' 1951 (n. 25), 70.

informed the formation of the *ius gentium* since, in meaningful ways, the Praetor Peregrinus made use of the *ius gentium* as the guiding principle in settling disputes between and non-Romans within the empire.[29] The Praetor Peregrinus, as an individual agent of the private international law, had a considerable independent interpretative role in the development of the law and the application of the law to the circumstances of individuals who presented before his court. These individuals would have recognised themselves as belonging to different legal systems and, via the intervention of the Praetor, had recourse to the *ius gentium* in order to settle disputes.

4.1.2 The Roman General, Sponsio, Deditio, and Imperium

Roman international relations transparently recognised the role(s) that individuals could and did routinely play as the agents of international law. This is especially the case in relation to the role of the Roman magistrate-general (including the consul, praetor, and promagistrates). The Roman general could accept the surrender of a conquered community (*deditio* rites) and he was also able to make a truce (*sponsio*) after an enemy had surrendered on the basis of his (personal) promises and in the absence of a mandate from the Senate or Roman People (although he would anticipate that the Roman People would ratify a treaty afterwards).[30] In addition, Adrian Nicholas Sherwin-White has emphasised the importance of the determination of (international) policy by army commanders on the ground in the course of their campaigns.[31] The character, reputation, status, and wealth of these individuals as well as their personal connections and relationships with the foreigners with whom they were dealing was an important determinate in the success or failure of these international relationships. The use of terms like *amicitia* and *fides*, which simultaneously described inter-personal relationships between individuals and inter-State relationships in the international sphere, highlights the extent to which Roman international relationships were—or could be—viewed as extensions of individual relationships, with the potential for both to co-exist. The career of the late republican general Cn. Pompeius (Pompey the Great) is illustrative of the strong influence which an individual Roman general could have in international affairs. In

[29] Abel Hendy Jones Greenidge, *The Legal Procedure of Cicero's Time* (Oxford: OUP 1901), 30, 92-93, 118 with 47-48 noting also the important role of the *recuperatores* (at 419 'the international court of the *recuperatores*'). On the Praetor's edict, see further Alan Watson, 'The Development of the Praetor's Edict' *Journal of Roman Studies* 60 (1970), 105-19, at 111.

[30] See further Bederman, *International Law in Antiquity* 2001 (n. 3), 200-02, at 200: 'As a matter of necessity, great diplomatic authority was extended to military commanders in the field' and 'But a sponsio was considered really as a personal covenant, entered into by the general on his own authority. If a sponsio was later disavowed by Rome, the only recourse that could be had by the aggrieved nation was against the military leader who sponsored the agreement. This is the rule which gave rise to the Roman practice of noxal surrender (or deditio) of individuals who had made a sponsio which was later repudiated.'

[31] Adrian Nicholas Sherwin-White, *Roman Foreign Policy in the East 168 B.C.-A.D. 1* (Norman, OK: University of Oklahoma Press 1984).

the wake of the series of wars fought between Rome and Mithridates, Pompey was widely recognised as having personally put an end to the problem of pirates in the Mediterranean and to have reorganised the Eastern part of the empire. In helping to secure Pompey's series of extraordinary commands, Cicero had spoken at length of Pompey's particular individual virtues and capabilities.[32] Pompey (along with M. Porcius Cato the Younger) has also been identified as an influential figure in the ethical reformulation of Roman provincial policy.[33] It is unlikely, however, that Pompey's or Cato's views on ethical governance were typical in a system which placed the immediate and future well-being of conquered peoples in the hands of individual Roman generals. At the same time, however individually competent and virtuous Pompey may have been, it is important not to lose sight of the fact that it was the vote of the Roman people which established and enabled his command.

James Richardson has demonstrated that Roman ideas about empire and the language with which these ideas were expressed concentrated on the exercise of power over peoples.[34] He tracks the development of the term *imperium* from the 'power' of an individual or of the Roman people to a particular territory over which that power was exercised.[35] The conceptualisation of relationships between Rome and the other as the exercise of power thrust the individuals wielding that power to the fore, but it was the endorsement of that power by the Roman people (later the Emperor[36]) which informed and underpinned international relations.

4.2 Individuals as the Proper Unit of Concern for Private and Public International Law

4.2.1 *Ius Gentium, Ius Civile*, Legal Fictions, and the Individual: Prisoners of War (POW) and Exiles

A Roman citizen who became a prisoner of war lost their citizenship, or rather had their rights as a citizen suspended. These rights could be reactivated (retrospectively) if the prisoner was able to return to Roman territory by claiming the right of

32 Cic. *Leg. Man.* (*Leg. Imp.*) 3; 5-6; 27-50 (Cicero, *On the Manilian Law/Command of Pompeius*).

33 On a Roman provincial reform agenda. See Kit Morrell, *Pompey, Cato, and the Governance of the Roman Empire* (Oxford: OUP 2017), 269: 'Romans were protecting their allies not only from the threat of enemy arms but from the injustices of Roman rule. That is the sense the phrase bears both in *De Legibus* and in Cicero's letter to Cato of 51, where he proclaims that he has protected the allies by his *aequitas* and *continentia*.'

34 James Richardson, '*Imperium Romanum* between Republic and Empire', in Lukas de Blois et al. (eds.), *The Representation and Perception of Roman Imperial Power: Proceedings of the Third Workshop of the International Network Impact of Empire (Roman Empire, c. 200 B.C. - A.D. 476)*, Rome, *Impact of Empire* series, Vol. 3 (Amsterdam: J. C. Gieben 2002), 137-48.

35 *ibid*, 147: 'Under the republic, *imperium* means power [...] After the middle of Augustus' reign, the word can also mean the extended territory within which that power and control is exercised'.

36 On the Roman Emperor's right to make war and peace and his consultation of the senate, see Richard Talbert, *The Senate of Imperial Rome* (Princeton, NJ: Princeton University Press 1984), 428-30.

postliminium. The status of the citizen's will might nevertheless remain in question since, as a non-citizen (prisoner of war) no valid will could have been made. In order to address this—and as a means of ensuring the property and inheritance were secured—the *Lex Cornelia* (80? BCE) made use of an important legal fiction whereby the POW non-citizen could be considered 'as if' they were a citizen and could thus be covered by the *ius civile*.[37] Clifford Ando has argued that the repeated extension of Roman civil law to non-citizens effectively transformed the Roman Empire since it prepared the way for the declaration of universal citizenship. Prior to 212 CE however, it was these incremental extensions of civil law to aliens which functioned to cover individuals.[38]

The case of exiles, on the other hand, as Ando has demonstrated, the *ius gentium* came into play more directly.[39] Voluntary exile was a common elite response to potential criminal conviction on capital charges under both the Republic and the Principate. During the late Republic exile also became a statutory penalty for particular crimes.[40] Depending on the form of exile, an exiled citizen could lose their citizenship and rights. Interdiction from fire and water, passed after the exile had left by the *concilium plebis*, effectively prohibited the exile from ever returning to Rome or Roman territory. The Roman jurist Marcian (*c.* 220 CE) thus envisaged the exile as existing under the *ius gentium*: *deportatus civitatem amittit, libertatem retinet et iure civili caret, gentium vero utitur*.[41]

4.2.2 War Crimes and Genocide

Romans, like others in the ancient world, accepted the institution of slavery and the act of enslavement of defeated enemies as part of the course of conquest and imperial expansion. The Romans measured a general's entitlement to a triumph according to the body-count of their largest single engagement with the enemy. At the same time, the Romans did hold that some acts, including breaking good faith (*fides*), 'fighting without authorization', and the mistreatment of allies and provincials (including extortion of money, goods, or services), constituted crimes for

[37] Ando, *Law, Language and Empire* 2011 (n. 11), 14.

[38] *ibid*, 17: 'Conceived internally as a set of norms regulating the affairs of citizens, the civil law would seem a tool that could only disjoin, and never unite, citizens and aliens. But in point of fact, despite never shedding that commitment to citizen privilege, Roman law in practice came to embrace an ever-widening portion of the population. This happened at different moments for different reasons—among communities of citizens far from the praetor, among aliens seeking the prestige and power of Roman courts, or among the Romanizing municipalities of Spain. Ultimately, I suggest, the endless construal of aliens as citizens naturalized the truth of that fiction, and a new political and cultural landscape was born from that revolution.'

[39] Clifford Ando, 'Self, Society, Individual, and Person in Roman Law', in Maren R. Niehoff and Joshua Levinson (eds.), *Self, Self-fashioning, and Individuality in Late Antiquity. New Perspectives* (Tübingen: Mohr Siebeck 2019), 375-92.

[40] Gordon P. Kelly, *A History of Exile in the Roman Republic* (Cambridge: CUP 2006).

[41] *Dig.* 48.22.15. The passage is cited and discussed in Ando, *Law, Language and Empire* 2011 (n. 11), 29.

which a general could be held accountable not to an external body but to the senate and people of Rome.[42] Known cases of such prosecutions or calling to account include a small number of Roman generals whose actions constituted unacceptable cruelty.[43] Another instance of an (unsuccessful) attempt to hold a Roman commander directly to account which may have been ethically motivated was seen in Cato the Younger's response to Julius Caesar's acts of genocide *avant la letrre* in Germany. Plutarch describes the event and its aftermath in Rome:

> After Caesar had fallen upon warlike nations and at great hazards conquered them, and when it was believed that he had attacked the Germans even during a truce and slain three hundred thousand of them, there was a general demand at Rome that the people should offer sacrifices of good tidings, but Cato urged them to surrender Caesar to those whom he had wronged, and not to turn upon themselves, or allow to fall upon their city, the pollution of his crime. [. . .] Outside the senate-house, however, Cato could accomplish nothing, since the people wished all along that Caesar should have the chief power; and although Cato had the senate under his influence, it was afraid of the people.[44]

Kit Morrell has demonstrated that Cato argued here for the process of *deditio* (surrender of an offender to the enemy) be used to address what he argued were Caesar's offences.[45] She further argues that this action was consistent with other activities taking place in the years 70-50 BCE whereby Rome's treatment of non-Roman and provincial 'others' became the site of ethical debate about compliance with the law as well as a law reform agenda. Cato's attempt to hold Caesar to account nevertheless failed. This failure was partly a product, as Plutarch recognised, of the operation of divisions within Roman politics. The Roman community were divided about the figure of Caesar and hence about Caesar's culpability. The incident is symptomatic of a systemic problem: that whilst Romans may have acknowledged that their behaviour could be held accountable to standards premised by the *ius gentium* (here specifically the laws of war), these standards were not external and the only measure of Rome's compliance with them was its own.

[42] On Roman war crimes, see Sarah Elise Phang, 'War Crimes', in Phang et al. (eds.), *Conflict in Ancient Greece and Rome* 2016 (n. 2). See now also Tristan Taylor (ed.), *A Cultural History of Genocide*, vol. 1 (London: Bloomsbury 2021).

[43] Phang, 'War Crimes', in Phang et al. (eds.), *Conflict in Ancient Greece and Rome* 2016 (n. 2) details the cases of particular Roman generals.

[44] Plutarch, *Life of Cato the Younger*, in Plutarch, *Lives*, Vol. VIII (Bernadotte Perrin (tr.), Cambridge, MA: Harvard University Press 1919), § 51.

[45] Kit Morrell, 'Cato, Caesar, and the Germani' *Antichthon* 49 (2015), 73-93.

4.2.3. Hostages and Envoys

Romans practised hostage-taking as part of international diplomacy.[46] Roman law also recognised the sanctity of envoys (legates) and stated that corporeal violence against an envoy contradicted the *ius gentium* (Dig. 50.7.18 Pomponius: *si quis legatum hostium pulsasset, contra ius gentium id commissum esse existimatur, quia sancti habentur legati.*). Unlike the Greeks, the Romans did not—prior to expansion into the Greek world—participate in third party dispute resolution or diplomacy.[47] Roman procedure concentrated instead, on the whole, on making clear the justification (and procedural rites) for going to war at the start of a conflict, thus leaving little room for negotiation or compromise once hostilities had been declared. There is some debate about whether or not, even after they encountered Greek diplomatic procedures, the Romans were open to the idea of negotiated solutions to conflict.[48] Rome was not open to arbitration of its disputes and was perhaps even unwilling regularly to engage in mediation although, as Ager argues, Rome was willing to receive 'deprecatory diplomacy' which did not acknowledge any equality between the parties to the dispute but which facilitated an entreaty on behalf of the non-Roman party without infringing the *maiestas* of the Roman people.[49]

Within this context, Romans (like other ancient peoples) acknowledged the special status of diplomats and ambassadors.[50] When Alexandrian ambassadors to Rome were attacked and killed in 57 BCE the Romans were outraged.[51] These ambassadors included well-known individuals who were closely associated with leading families in Rome. In part, the outrage felt in Rome was based on the suspicion that the Egyptian Pharoah, Ptolemy Auletes, had arranged for the attacks on the Alexandrian diplomats to take place in Rome.[52] The prosecution of Caelius for his alleged involvement in the attacks on the Alexandrian diplomats illustrates an (unsuccessful) attempt to hold someone accountable for their part in these acts. Roman diplomatic relations were not carried out by trained specialists and there were no formal or permanent diplomatic stations abroad or in Rome (although family members of friendly kings might live there). Instead, ambassadors were individuals respected within their communities who individually approached magistrates who could arrange for them to be heard by the senate or, later, the emperor. The development of personal and patronage relationships underpinned diplomacy, placing an emphasis on individual actors, although diplomacy itself was governed by conventions which emphasised the primacy of Rome.

[46] Elise Phang, 'Hostages', in Phang et al. (eds.), *Conflict in Ancient Greece and Rome* 2016 (n. 2). On Roman hostage taking, see Joel Allen, *Hostages and Hostage-Taking in the Roman Empire* (Cambridge: CUP 2006).

[47] See further Ager, 'Roman Perspectives' 2009 (n. 11), 17.

[48] *ibid*, 25.

[49] *ibid*, 32-33.

[50] See further Bederman, *International Law in Antiquity* 2001 (n. 3), 114-16.

[51] Cicero, *Pro Caelio* with Timothy Peter Wiseman, *Catullus and his World: A Reappraisal* (Cambridge: CUP 1985), 54-91.

[52] Wiseman, *Catullus* 1985 (n. 51).

The current humanisation thesis argues that individuals rather than States are the proper units of concern for international law.[53] The case studies in this section suggest some possible avenues for exploring further the interplay of general categories of persons and individuals within those categories.

4.3 Rome Acts against Piracy

'A pirate has always been considered an outlaw, a *hostis humani generis*.'[54] Piracy was a perennial problem in the ancient Mediterranean. Rome positioned itself as the dominant power acting against Mediterranean piracy during the second century BCE. Polybius (2.12.6) represented Illyrian pirates as 'the common enemies of all people' and Roman practice and rhetoric continued to proclaim Rome's willingness to act against those deemed to be pirates.[55] Erskine and de Souza have demonstrated that this rhetoric coincided with a more general acceptance of the idea that the Romans could represent themselves as acting with general beneficence.[56] Erskine argues that this reflects a recognition by the Greek States of the eastern Mediterranean that Rome was the dominant power in the area:

> What the Greeks are found doing in the second century B.C. is applying existing political terminology in a new context. This is being done in order to make intelligible an otherwise extraordinary situation in which a long-standing international balance of power simply ceased to exist.[57]

Roman law in the form of the *lex de provinciis praetoriis* (100 BCE) claimed to empower the Romans to act against anyone they identified as pirates and divided the communities of the Mediterranean into those who would act alongside Rome and those who would not.[58] Effectively, this law and the developing rhetoric around piracy enabled the Romans to extend the label 'pirate'. Thus, de Souza observes that:

> [M]any Roman military campaigns of the first half of the first century B.C., which are presented in our sources as being undertaken against pirates, are more likely

[53] See Peters and Sparks, 'Introduction' (chapter 1), in this volume.

[54] Robert Jennings and Arthur Watts, *Oppenheim's International Law: Volume 1 Peace* (9th edn, Oxford: OUP 2008), 746: 'Piracy *jure gentium* is an "international crime", the pirate is considered the enemy of every state, and can be brought to justice "by any nation into whose jurisdiction he may come".'

[55] With Philip de Souza, 'Rome's Contribution to the Development of Piracy' *Memoirs of the American Academy in Rome: Supplementary Volumes Vol. 6, The Maritime World of Ancient Rome* (2008), 71-96, at 77.

[56] See further, Andrew Erskine, 'The Romans as Common Benefactors' *Historia* 43 (1994), 70-87.

[57] *ibid*, 87.

[58] See further de Souza, 'Rome's Contribution' 2008 (n. 55), 78-79.

to have been deliberate attempts to overcome politically and economical autonomous communities that refused to submit to Roman domination.[59]

4.4 Slavery, Human Rights, and *Clementia*

The Romans represented the right to enslave as simultaneously part of the *ius gentium* and against nature (Justinian *Digest* 1.5.4.1).[60] There were numerous and ongoing attempts to regulate the behaviour of Roman masters towards slaves and to ameliorate the lot of enslaved individuals, although movements for the wholescale abolition of slavery as an institution did not emerge. On the whole, as Hunt observes, economic considerations tended to quell or limit opposition to slavery.[61]

Nevertheless, three recent dedicated studies have sought to explore the extent to which ancient thinkers contemplated human rights.[62] In his study, *Human Rights in Ancient Rome*, Richard Bauman notes Livy's repeated reference to *leges humanae* and *ius humanum* in his commentary on Rome's ill treatment of foreigners.[63] Two instances, cited by Bauman, bear repetition. In the first (Liv. 1.28.9-11), Livy recounts the Roman reaction to the punishment of the Alban leader Mettius Fufetius who had failed in his treaty obligations to Rome and was ordered to be torn apart as punishment. Livy notes: 'All eyes were turned away from so dreadful a sight. Such was the first and last punishment among the Romans of a kind that disregards the laws of humanity [*leges humanae*].' At 5.37.4; 36.6 Livy again reflected on human rights when Roman envoys killed a Gallic leader. This was, he claimed, a breach of *ius gentium* since they had violated human rights (*violatores iuris humani*).[64] Notable in much early Roman thinking about *humanitas* is the link between *humanitas*, non-Romans, and ideas of universalism. Bauman traces the emergence and importance of *humanitas* in Rome from the earliest references (mid-second century BCE), including Terence's *homo sum: humani nihil a me alienum puto* (*Heaut.* 77) through to the development of the concept during the late Republic and culminating in the formulation of the Emperor's *clementia*. The transformation of *clementia* from a form of military pardon to mercy shown towards individuals which took place during the constitutional upheavals of the post civil war period should also be considered here

[59] *ibid*, 80.

[60] See further Peter Hunt, *Ancient Greek and Roman Slavery* (Oxford: Wiley-Blackwell 2017), 203-05.

[61] *ibid*, 192: 'the conclusions of philosophers, Christians, and lawmakers were constrained by economic forces, especially the vested interest of the upper classes in the continuation of slavery.'

[62] Richard Bauman, *Human Rights in Ancient Rome* (London: Routledge 1999); Tony Honoré, *Ulpian: Pioneer of Human Rights* (Oxford: OUP 2002). I also include here Giltaij and Tuori's nuanced critical reception of Bauman and Honoré: see Jacob Giltaij and Kaius Tuori, 'Human Rights in Antiquity', in Pamela Slott (ed.), *Revisiting the Origins of Human Rights* (Cambridge: CUP 2015), 39-63. Giltaij and Tuori review earlier scholarship on human rights in antiquity at 47-52.

[63] Bauman, *Human Rights* 1999 (n. 62), 28-30.

[64] I paraphrase Bauman, *Human Rights* 1999 (n. 62), 29 here.

since the emergence of the emperor's pardon transformed the legal landscape.[65] The emperor was represented as—and was perceived to be—accessible to individuals and interested in their specific cases. Saint Paul's appeal to the Emperor as a Roman citizen is perhaps the most famous instance of this phenomenon, but there is widespread evidence of the extent to which individuals expected the emperor to be able to intervene in their particular case. For Honoré, Ulpian's work is recognisably grounded in human-rights thinking:

> Following on the extension of citizenship by the Antonine constitution, he expounds Roman law as a law based on the view that all people are born free and equal and that all possess dignity. These three values, freedom, equality, and dignity, are the essential elements of what we now term human rights.[66]

Both Bauman and Honoré's works have been criticised for varying degrees of historical and conceptual anachronism.[67] The arbitrariness of Roman law, in many ways embodied in the emperor's *clementia*, the pervasive presence of slavery, as well as in the emerging distinction between *honestiores* and *humiliores*, sits uneasily with any real recognition of human rights.[68] At the same time, as Giltaij and Tuori acknowledge, there is space for further consideration and reconceptualisation of human rights in the ancient world:

> [T]here certainly is evidence of some equality-based thinking in the Roman legal sources, even to the point of possibly inspiring modes of legal protection for both slaves and foreigners. In what measure this thinking influenced the Roman legal order in a more general sense is up for debate, with an outcome largely predetermined by the condition of the Roman legal sources.[69]

5. Conclusion

This chapter has sought to address three questions: can we speak of ancient international law?; what connection (or relevance) might the study of antiquity have for modern thinking about the individual in international law?; and did the ancient world recognise 'the individual' as the subject of international law? Contestation and disagreement inform every one of my three central questions. The ancient

[65] Melissa Barden Dowling, *Clemency and Cruelty in the Roman World* (Ann Arbor, MI: Michigan University Press 2003).

[66] Honoré, *Ulpian* (n. 62), 76.

[67] Giltaij and Tuori, 'Human Rights' 2015 (n. 62) and the critical review on Honoré by Ralph W. Mathisen, 'T. Honoré, *Ulpian. Pioneer of Human Rights*' *Journal of Roman Studies* 94 (2004), 279-80.

[68] Giltaij and Tuori, 'Human Rights' 2015 (n. 62), 40.

[69] *ibid*, 62.

world, and especially the reception and interpretation of Roman legal ideas in later periods, offers considerable opportunity to engage with the key questions posed by this book and there is growing willingness to think in terms of 'ancient international law'. Within the Roman Empire, a plurality of local laws and Roman law co-existed and Roman law itself functioned analogously to international law for citizens in different parts of the empire, in relations between citizens and non-citizens as well as in the hunting down of those Rome labelled pirates. Rome's conduct in inter-State relations was primarily concerned with maintaining Roman supremacy, yet some Romans also thought in terms of responsible governance, accountability, *ius gentium*, and perhaps even human rights. The individual is not the primary concern of this thinking, but the operation of recognisable international law instruments and ideas in a world in which the State itself defied simple definition suggests that the ancient world is a good case study of the extent to which legal relationships were social relationships. This chapter has sought to provide a means of putting the ancient world into meaningful conversation with the modern. There is much work still to be done.

3
Individuals and Group Identity in Medieval International Law

*Dante Fedele and Alain Wijffels**

1. Introduction

The issue of the individual in medieval international law raises two preliminary questions. The first is whether or to what extent medieval (legal) anthropological attitudes recognised the individuality of human beings. The second question is how the modern concept of international law may be understood and transposed in the medieval context. This chapter considers the issues in the context of the Latin West, and mainly during the later centuries of the Middle Ages.

The 'invention of the individual'[1] in western culture is neither an innovation of the Renaissance or early modern times, nor of the Middle Ages.[2] Nor is the view contrasting a Germanic (northern European) legal tradition which would have considered mainly social groups and a Romanist (southern, mediterranean) tradition mainly oriented on the individual subject sufficiently supported. Perhaps there is a stronger argument to be made in favour of a contrast, especially from the eleventh century onwards, between a rural culture, which remained overwhelmingly chthonic, and the developing urban culture. Whereas in the former, survival depended overwhelmingly on the acceptance of natural constraints on

* This article is a common work. Sections 1 and 4 were jointly written, section 2 was written by Alain Wijffels, and section 3 by Dante Fedele.

[1] Larry Siedentop, *Inventing the Individual: The Origins of Western Liberalism* (London: Allen Lane/ Penguin 2014/2015), who recognises the development of the notion of individuality in western culture mainly through Christian doctrines' emphasis on the need to secure the soul's salvation, as opposed to the ancient Roman conception of family. In Siedentop's view, the rise of the notion of individualism is also closely associated to that of equality.

[2] See the still relevant debate among medieval historians, one generation ago, on emerging forms of individuality in the context of changing (ecclesiastical) communities: Caroline Walker Bynum, 'Did the Twelfth Century Discover the Individual?' *Journal of Ecclesiastical History* 31 (1980), 1-17; and the critical discussion of the latter by Colin Morris, 'Individualism in Twelfth-Century Religion. Some Further Reflections' *Journal of Ecclesiastical History* 31 (1980), 195-206. Some authors have preferred to phrase the issue in terms of increased awareness of the self, entailing a deeper extent of self-examination: John F. Benton, 'Consciousness of Self and Perceptions of Individuality', in Robert L. Benson and Giles Constable (eds.), *Renaissance and Renewal in the Twelfth Century* (Oxford: Clarendon Press 1982), 263-95. A different, even more complex and controversial issue, is whether one may recognise a medieval humanism, and, if so, what concept of humanity it would have relied on. These latter questions are beyond the scope of the present chapter.

Dante Fedele and Alain Wijffels, *Individuals and Group Identity in Medieval International Law* In: *The Individual in International Law.* Edited by: Tom Sparks and Anne Peters, Oxford University Press. © Dante Fedele and Alain Wijffels 2024.
DOI: 10.1093/oso/9780198898917.003.0003

agriculture and a world vision steeped in the existing hierarchy, the urban community appeared as a man-made world. This was not only expressed through the city's architectural appearance, but fundamentally because the foundational activities of artisans and merchants, industry and trade, necessitated more sophisticated planning which went beyond the natural cycle of the seasons and environmental constraints. The urban culture which assumed that humans had a greater degree of control over their destiny was also reflected in urban social and political institutions. Another contrast can be recognised throughout the Middle Ages in the distribution of learning. However, the learned class, mainly concentrated among the educated clergy, remained a small fraction of the population at large. Even so, centres of learning evolved in the course of the centuries. Whereas until the twelfth century, monastic centres in the countryside had been the main hubs of learning, universities, established in the cities, took over that role and initiated gradually a degree of secularisation of the learned class. All these differentiations reflected disparate anthropologies and affected legal developments. Ordeals, for example, which were first more strongly opposed by both the urban bourgeoisie and the educated clerics, seem to have been supported for much longer by rural populations. Individuality may have found it easier to develop in urban and clerical environments. Moreover, the educated clerical culture was more likely to recognise individuality, because of the Church's essential mission and justification to assist Christians in attaining eternal life. From the early Church days onwards, the emphasis on the salvation of the soul was a strong factor of individualisation, because each person's soul was unique and resisted collectivisation.[3] The individual soul was a factor which, in spiritual terms, was intended, in Christian eschatology, to transcend the apparently most deeply anchored discriminatory social anthropological discriminations.

Nevertheless, tradition and necessity also contributed to various forms of social integration which did not foster the development of individualism. The broad categorisation of the three orders of society, each characterised by their own social and legal normativity, promoted class consciousness. The device of privileges in a wide sense also created particular interest groups which became collectively social and political actors, but depended on the solidarity of its members for their success. Each corporate actor of the medieval multilayered society claimed to represent a common good which trumped particular interests. Medieval legal science largely developed as a science of the art of good governance, aiming at reconciling and ordering the various claims by social and political actors of promoting their commonwealth.

Medieval sources, including legal authorities, tend to privilege a greater degree of individuality as they deal with figures standing higher up in the social and

[3] The point is illustrated by the relevance of penitential manuals for topics of the law of nations: Andrea Padovani, 'Peccati del guerriero nelle *Summae confessorum* medievali e protomoderne', in Dante Fedele, Randall Lesaffer, and Pierre Savy (eds.), *Avant l'État. Droit international et pluralisme politico-juridique en Europe, XIIe-XVIIe siècle* (forthcoming).

political hierarchy.[4] Rulers, at various levels of governance, have a more clear-cut individual profile than those over whom they ruled. Only gradually, especially as access to justice becomes better documented, individual destinies appear in sharper focus in their relationship to the legal systems.

Turning to the notion of international law, it should be remembered that the medieval political constellation was characterised by a plurality of power centres of varying status, in which authority was distributed at different levels. After the 'Gregorian Reform' and the Investiture Controversy, the papacy and the (western) empire claimed universal jurisdiction in their respective domains (the spiritual and the temporal). Territorial entities greatly varied in shape and power, ranging from strong kingdoms to local lords, and including feudal principalities, military orders, cities with varying degree of autonomy, and leagues of cities.[5] Within this political constellation there was no clear link between sovereignty and territory, instead we find a complex interweaving and overlapping of jurisdictions. Each actor in this multilayered system of governance created legal rules (either written or customary law), thus generating a pluralistic legal and political order. International relations were not the sole preserve of 'sovereign' authorities, but were established—both vertically and horizontally—by actors of different stature, including (groups of) individuals. In this context, therefore, 'international law' cannot be understood as it has been by mainstream historiography since the nineteenth century, that is, as inter-State law dominated by the sovereign national State; rather, it should be considered a multi-normative framework that governed inter-polity and cross-jurisdictional relations between a great variety of actors.

The renaissance of legal studies in the twelfth century led to the development of a legal system based on the scholarly interpretation of Roman, feudal and canon law, namely *ius commune*.[6] This supranational system—grounded in the study of a common set of legal texts, the use of a common language, and (for the period considered here) the adoption of a common methodology—provided the basic notions that enabled jurists to deal with each municipal legal system (the *iura*

[4] Exceptionally, a commoner could rise to notoriety and acquire a more individual profile. In the context of the Hundred Years War, the case of Joan of Arc is a striking example of such an exceptional notoriety. A comparison could be made with the representation of portraits in medieval art, which only gradually extended to other persons than rulers and celebrated religious figures towards the end of the Middle Ages. Even doodles can exceptionally illustrate the point: e.g. the small portrait of Joan of Arc sketched in the margin of an entry dated 10 May 1429 in the records of the Parliament of Paris; available via https://commons.wikimedia.org/wiki/File:Contemporaine_afb_jeanne_d_arc.png, accessed 3/12/23.

[5] Jean-Marie Moeglin and Stéphane Péquignot, *Diplomatie et 'relations internationales' au Moyen Âge (IXe-XVe siècle)* (Paris: Presses universitaires de France 2017), 15-96; David Napolitano and Kenneth J. Pennington (eds.), *A Cultural History of Democracy in the Medieval Age* (London: Bloomsbury Academic 2021); Susanne Lepsius, 'The Legal System among Italian City Republics', in Helmut Philipp Aust, Janne E. Nijman, and Miha Marcenko (eds.), *Research Handbook on International Law and Cities* (Cheltenham and Northampton, MA: Edward Elgar 2021), 41-51.

[6] Manlio Bellomo, *The Common Legal Past of Europe 1100-1800* (first published 1988, this edn Lydia G. Cochrane (tr.), Washington, DC: Catholic University of America Press 1995).

propria). Since *ius commune* functioned as an interface that allowed for communication between these systems, its study offers invaluable insights into how jurists managed to rationalise a multilayered legal order.[7] Admittedly, at the time 'international law' as such did not constitute an autonomous branch of legal scholarship: with very few exceptions, no specific section of the Roman, feudal and canon law texts specifically dealt with international law issues.[8] Moreover, in terms of conceptual history, no clear concept of 'international law' was developed in this period. Not even *ius gentium*—which in early modern times was to become *ius inter gentes* and to be translated in national languages as 'the law of nations', '*Völkerrecht*', or '*le droit des gens*'—can be considered an exact equivalent of international law. In fact, although some international law institutions like war, the occupation and fortification of territories, peace treaties and respect for ambassadors were traced back to *ius gentium*,[9] this concept had a much broader scope, which encompassed supranational private law and basic legal principles held to be grounded in human nature. This resulted in a fundamental ambiguity of *ius gentium*, and of its relations to *ius naturale* (natural law), which stimulated considerable debate in late medieval legal scholarship.[10] And yet, despite the lack of a unified concept of international law, *ius commune* jurists could not ignore the numerous issues involved in inter-polity and cross-jurisdictional relations, which they abundantly discussed both in their commentaries on the legal texts studied at university and in the numerous legal opinions (*consilia*) that they delivered on actual disputes.

Indeed, this literature includes substantial comments on the relations between (both universal and territorial) political authorities, conflicts of laws and jurisdiction, diplomacy, treaties, wars, and reprisals. Jurists considered any actor who enjoyed public status to be entitled to undertake such activities – if necessary, with the authorisation of their superior authority. Moreover, actors that did not enjoy public status were occasionally also taken into account. City parties could, under certain conditions, conduct diplomatic activity and conclude treaties. (Groups of) individuals held rights and duties that applied in various situations related to international law. This included the protections accorded to clerics, pilgrims, students, and merchants travelling abroad, the canonistic rules limiting violence in war (*Pax Dei* and *Treuga Dei*) or forbidding the use of certain weapons (arrows and

[7] Alain Wijffels, 'European Private Law: A New Software-Package for an Outdated Operating System?', in Mark Van Hoecke and François Ost (eds.), *The Harmonisation of European Private Law* (Oxford: Hart 2000), 101-16.

[8] Randall Lesaffer, 'Roman Law and the Intellectual History of International Law', in Anne Orford and Florian Hoffman (eds.), *The Oxford Handbook of the Theory of International Law* (Oxford: OUP 2016), 38-58, at 45. For medieval times, the *lex mercatoria* cannot qualify as an expression of international law: Albrecht Cordes, s.v. 'Lex Mercatoria', *Handwörterbuch zur deutschen Rechtsgeschichte*, vol. 3 (2nd edn, Berlin: Erich Schmidt Verlag 2016), col. 890-902.

[9] In particular D. 1.1.5 and Conc. disc. can. c. 9, d. 1.

[10] Dante Fedele, '*Ius gentium*. The Metamorphoses of a Legal Concept (Ancient Rome to Early Modern Europe)', in Edward Cavanagh (ed.), *Empire and Legal Thought. Ideas and Institutions from Antiquity to Modernity* (Leiden: Brill 2020), 213-51.

crossbows) against Christians, the widespread obligation not to engage in piracy, and the infidels' right to *dominium* and jurisdiction over their lands. A vassal's obligation to provide his lord with aid and counsel, including military assistance during a war, was scrutinised, as were citizens' and subjects' obligations to perform public services like those of ambassadors or soldiers. Private individuals were also affected by the distinction increasingly drawn in late medieval scholarship between a community and its members, which was often invoked in the discussion of issues such as a prince's or city's authority to waive the individual rights of their subjects or citizens during peace-making.[11]

The rest of this chapter focuses on two institutions of special interest for an analysis of the relationship between the individual and international law: it first explores the status of prisoners of war and the issues raised by their ransom (*Case Study I*); then it turns to reprisals, which enabled individuals to enforce their individual rights against aliens (*Case Study II*). Both issues appear prominently in legal practice and were discussed by legal scholars. They are of particular relevance for tracing the notion of 'individuality' in medieval (international) law, as they illustrate how the legal focus, both in jurisprudence and in practice, could vary depending on the interests at stake and how to implement them. In that variable legal spectrum, an individual's identity appears to a greater or lesser extent defined by the various social interest groups to which the person belongs.

2. Case Study I: POWs and Ransoms

The widespread practice of ransoming combatants made prisoners in the course of warfare may appear at first sight to offer some indication of individualisation in the context of the laws of war. Nonetheless, more detailed studies show that the individuality of the ransomed prisoner needs to be qualified in the light of their social status and associations.

2.1 Ransoming POWs: The Diversity of Sources and Practices

There was no single body of 'laws of war' governing the ransoming of captured combatants.[12] In the course of the Middle Ages, changes in the composition of

[11] Frederick H. Russell, *The Just War in the Middle Ages* (Cambridge: CUP 1975); James Muldoon, *Popes, Lawyers, and Infidels* (Philadelphia, PA: University of Pennsylvania Press 1979); Peter Haggenmacher, *Grotius et la doctrine de la guerre juste* (Paris: Presses universitaires de France 1983); Dante Fedele, *The Medieval Foundations of International Law. Baldus de Ubaldis (1327-1400), Doctrine and Practice of the Ius Gentium* (Leiden: Brill 2021).

[12] The observation also applies to the medieval laws of war in general: Stephen C. Neff, *War and the Law of Nations, A General History* (Cambridge: CUP 2005), 39-49 and 68-82. The practices of

armies and warfare techniques and strategies also influenced the practice of taking prisoners. Practices differed, depending on various factors such as whether warfare was between Christians of the Latin West, or between Christians and non-Christians, whether the soldiers were fighting as the subjects of their territorial prince, a city-state, as mercenaries, or crusaders. Many of the earlier practices may not have qualified as laws, but expressed different normative usages linked to specific regional, ethnic, social, or occupational cultures. The so-called chivalric code, often referred to as one of the main sources of the medieval law of war(fare), was but one of those normative bodies of rules, and its codification in medieval literature reflects mostly distinctive social-political approaches outside the province of jurisprudence.[13] The customary laws of arms governed a wider range of military forces than the chivalric laws of arms and could extend to both nobles and non-nobles. Military laws, whether issued for specific campaigns or incorporated as more general rules in a broader corpus of statute law (such as the *Siete Partidas*), reflected practices and policies of a particular country without necessarily being connected to a broader *lex* or *consuetudo militaris* in the Latin West. A potentially overarching body of laws was the jurisprudential scholarly literature based on civil and canon law, for which textual fragments of Roman law occasionally offered a more specific support (e.g. the texts compiled under the Digest title D. 49.15, *De captivis, et de postliminio, et redemptis ab hostibus*),[14] The practical literature produced by academic legal scholars (during the later Middle Ages: mainly *consilia*, i.e. legal opinions written on behalf of rulers and office-holders on policy issues, or on behalf of parties involved in litigation) sometimes refers more specifically to contemporary practices, mostly in the context of Italian warfare. However, because of the Italian academic jurists' lasting prestige, and because their reasoning was steeped in *ius commune* scholarship, their opinions would be noted by learned jurists throughout western Europe. *Consilia*, especially those produced in the course of litigation, would refer (explicitly or anonymously) to specific cases and therefore

ransoming non-combatants were often viewed as even more objectionable (in the case of Christian non-combatants ransomed by Christian men-of-arms: Nicholas A.R. Wright, 'Ransoms of Non-Combatants during the Hundred Years War' *Journal of Medieval History* 17 (1991), 323-32). For a general overview of ransoms of POWs in the period, see: Maurice Keen, *The Laws of War in the Late Middle Ages* (Abingdon: Routledge 2016), 156-85.

[13] For example, Anglo-Norman and French chronicles reporting on the Battle of Brémules (1119) differ with regard to the extent of violence. Orderic Vitalis' narrative may be seen as a characteristic, but biased, representation of a chivalrous engagement resulting in very few casualties (though ransoming may have been an incitement to take prisoners rather than slaughtering fellow knights). See the passage quoted in Benjo Maso, '"Zij dorstten niet naar het bloed van hun broeders". De onbloedige strijdwijze in de oorlogvoering in 11de-13de eeuw', in A. J. (Hanno) Brand (ed.), *Oorlog in de middeleeuwen* [Middeleeuwse Studies en Bronnen 8] (Hilversum: Verloren 1989), 89-109, at 91.

[14] Laurent Waelkens, 'La *redemptio ab hostibus* e la *redemptio a domino* nel diritto romano', in Tiziana Faitini and Michele Nicoletti (eds.), *Redimere e riscattare. La* redemptio *tra teologia e politica* [Politica e religione 2017] (Brescia: Morcelliana 2017), 75-90.

often highlight an individual's plea. Civil and canon law scholarship on POWs and ransoms was somewhat contaminated by the debates on the wider issues of just war and on the effects of universal imperial claims, but on the whole, legal scholars were keen to take into account the *Realpolitik* of belligerents and the practical predominance of military customs. Thus, even though authors who departed from the principle derived from ancient Roman legal authorities according to which only wars waged by the empire were proper wars with enemies in a legal sense and produced legal effects, and would therefore argue that autonomous belligerents could in theory enslave captured enemy prisoners, it appears that there was nonetheless a consensus for recognising that enslaving among Christians was not admissible. In contrast, Christians could legitimately enslave non-Christian prisoners captured in warfare.[15]

2.2 Circumstances beyond the Individual POW

Soldiers of all ranks were taken prisoner and ransomed. However, the prisoners' social and, occasionally, political status greatly influenced the handling of their case.[16] In his comparative study of prisoners of war during the Hundred Years War, Rémy Ambühl has emphasised the development of a two-tier system in ransoming practices.[17] In the upper ranks—and one might add: among the upper social classes—no standardisation of ransoming prices (which to some degree may also apply to ransoming practices) was established, in contrast to the standardisation which developed at the lower end of the military ranks. Accordingly, the sources show a greater degree of individualisation of a POW's case as one climbs the ladder

[15] Baldus de Ubaldis' treatment of the issue of POWs provides a good example of civil law scholarship's approach combining general, abstract principles and their application in specific cases. Specific cases, where individuals are inevitably 'fleshed out', appear in Baldus' legal consultations (*consilia*), but on the issue of POWs also in his commentaries: see the recurrent references to the case of count Bulgaruccio di Ugolino da Marsciano, a military commander in the service of Perugia who was taken captive and died before arrangements for his release following an agreement to exchange prisoners had materialised; one of the resulting issues was whether a will he had made while he was still in captivity was valid or not. Such case-sensitive discussions bring the individual's position more in focus. Baldus' opinions and commentaries on prisoners of war are extensively discussed by Fedele, *The Medieval Foundations* 2021 (n. 11), 512-25.

[16] Bert S. Hall, *Weapons and Warfare in Renaissance Europe: Gunpowder, Technology, and Tactics* (Baltimore, MD: The John Hopkins University Press 1997), 39-40, cites the case of Sir John Fastolf in order to argue that, despite new forms of warfare which advantaged to some extent the battle-power of soldiers from lower social classes, the practice of ransoms still maintained the upper classes of warriors in a privileged position (on that case, see Kenneth Bruce McFarlane, 'The Investment of Sir John Fastolf's Profits of War' *Transactions of the Royal Historical Society* 5th series 7 (1957), 91-116).

[17] Rémy Ambühl, *Prisoners of War in the Hundred Years War: Ransom Culture in the later Middle Ages* (Cambridge: CUP 2013); Gerald I. A. D. Draper, 'The Law of Ransom during the Hundred Years War' *The Military Law and Law of War Review* 7 (1968), 263-77.

of military ranks and social status,[18] but such individual differentiation tends to vanish as one considers the lower ranks. A degree of tariffing may nonetheless also have applied to more wealthy POWs who belonged to the landed gentry, as in cases where the ransom price was calculated so as to match the prisoner's annual income (mostly from estates). The practical difficulties of such assessments (in enemy territory) made it difficult to implement such a tariffication and it was not formally codified.

Collective ransoming, as well as agreements about exchanges of groups of prisoners, often took place as the result of negotiations which did not necessarily focus on individual prisoners. In addition to such occasional agreements, a more continual practice of collective deliverance of prisoners through payment was established by religious orders specialising in the redemption of prisoners.

Military discipline was also a concern which could curb individual initiatives and captures. Booty taking in general—not least because of the need to secure the haul, whether chattels or enemy combatants—could seriously disrupt the military efforts while the fighting was still going on. Attempts were therefore made to secure a system of sharing the spoils, which might optimistically also strengthen solidarity between the soldiers of the same company. Such systems, however, could weaken the personal and individual bond created between a master and their prisoner on the battlefield.[19]

Paradoxically, the extreme individualisation in the case of the capture of a prisoner who held an eminent political position would also entail that the interests at stake in handling the captivity and ransoming of such an individual would prevail over the prisoner's capacity to act and take initiatives individually. The ransoming of King John II of France, perhaps one of the most spectacular late medieval examples, became a State matter in the relations between England and France.[20] Somewhat more frequently, the capture of a member of the upper nobility who was also a high-ranking political figure would more easily trigger an intervention of the king and the case would be treated as a political issue which went beyond the individual person of the prisoner.[21]

[18] The ability to pay a ransom could at times be recognised on the battlefield by the soldier's equipment: for a visual illustration, see John Gillingham, 'An Age of Expansion, c. 1020-1204', in Maurice Keen (ed.), *Medieval Warfare, A History* (Oxford: OUP 1999), 59-88, at 67.

[19] On the importance of military company solidarity in the practice of POWs and their release, see Rémy Ambühl, 'The English Reversal of Fortunes in the 1370s and the Experience of Prisoners of War', in Adrian R. Bell and Anne Curry (eds.), *The Soldier Experience in the Fourteenth Century* (Martlesham: Boydell Press 2011), 191-208.

[20] Jules-Marie Richard, 'Instructions données aux commissaires chargés de lever la rançon du roi Jean' *Bibliothèque de l'École des Chartes* 36 (1875), 81-90.

[21] With regard to fourteenth-century warfare from the English perspective, Françoise Bériac-Lainé and Chris Given-Wilson, 'Edward III's Prisoners of War: The Battle of Poitiers and Its Context' *English Historical Review* 116 (2001), 802-14, have emphasised that, from the vantage-point of the English

Ransoming practices would vary, depending on structural factors, some of which could lessen concerns about specific individuals. This may often have been the case in the policies of ransoming or not ransoming between Christians and non-Christians. Long-term armed conflicts (as for example the *Reconquista*, or the Hundred Years War) could contribute to institutionalise some features of ransoming practice. Yvonne Friedman has argued that the differences between the development of war-related captivity and ransom practices in the Latin Kingdom of Jerusalem and on the western side of the mediterranean, during the multi-secular process of the *Reconquista*, were mainly due to the different structural dynamics and the different developments in the balance of power between the chronically warrying sides. In the eastern kingdom, strategic considerations of the Frankish kingdom on the defensive hindered the more elaborate development of ransoming practices and institutions, in contrast to the situation in Spain, where the Christian rulers succeeded in maintaining the expansionist momentum of their fight against the Muslims.[22]

2.3 Factors Fostering the Individual POW's Standing

In general, the lack of any detailed regulations with regard to ransoming and the authorities' general policy of refraining from intervening in the ransoming process gave the two main parties involved, the master and the prisoner, much leeway in negotiating private arrangements between them.

These arrangements started with the way a combatant was captured and gave their faith to their captor. By the acceptance of the capture, a bond was created between master and prisoner. The legal vacuum of the prisoner's status would largely be filled by the contractual freedom of the two parties: negotiations[23] would focus on the ransom price, the modalities of payment, but also on additional issues, such as the conditions in which the prisoner's captivity would be organised and the costs involved (at the prisoner's expense). Not surprisingly, civil law scholarship took advantage of the possibility to address issues insufficiently or uncertainly dealt with by military usages or statutes, and provided principles and solutions on various questions, fleshing out the contractual relationship between master and prisoner,

Crown, political and diplomatic advantage could outweigh the prospects of financial gains derived from ransoms.

[22] Yvonne Friedman, *Encounter Between Enemies: Captivity and Ransom in the Latin Kingdom of Jerusalem* (Leiden: Brill 2002).

[23] Even though ransoms are more part of the *ius in bello* than of the *ius post bellum*, it may be argued that fostering a trading relationship was one way to encourage pacification beyond the battlefield, mirroring the revival of trade in peace-time: Nicolas Offenstadt, *Faire la paix au Moyen Âge. Discours et gestes de paix pendant la guerre de Cent Ans* (Paris: Odile Jacob 2007), 63-74.

but also the claims of third parties. Inevitably, on some issues, the opinion of a particular author could prove difficult to reconcile with prevailing practices. For example, Baldus's qualification of surrender as a form of desertion or treason appears at odds (at least if considered as a blanket rule) with the well-documented usages on the way a combatant acknowledged in battle that they became their captor's prisoner. In any event, by further detailing the conventional relationship between master and prisoner, the civil law contributed to reinforce the individual's role in shaping that relationship.

Although prisoners depended on their own family, social and professional networks for assisting them in raising the funds in order to pay their ransom, many initiatives, and decisions on the assets to make free for financing the operation were their own responsibility. Intermediaries such as messengers or heralds had to be briefed in order to give instructions to the home front. Moreover, during the Late Middle Ages, merchants often acted as brokers at essential stages of the process: money-lending (which in turn required negotiations about the sureties given), money-changing, the handling of licences, and safe-conducts. Even though such arrangements followed certain conventional patterns, the specifics of each agreement necessitated the individual input of the prisoner.

Interventions by the authorities or the prince could sometimes enhance individual circumstances. This was the case when a prisoner would petition the prince for assistance and contribution to the payment of the ransom. Such a petition would include special personal circumstances to back up the prisoner's request. Conversely, when the prince granted a petition, individual qualities or achievements of the petitioner (possibly already mentioned in the original petition) would be included in order to justify the grant.

Access to the courts, in general, may also have contributed to develop the (self-) perception of the individual, not only because of the *locus standi* as such, but also because legal proceedings comprised elaborate fact-finding stages which brought to light individual features of the litigants. For the later centuries of the Middle Ages, court records are an important source of information on ransom practices. Access to justice (whether by the master, their prisoner, or other interested parties) was therefore a factor which reflected individual interests and strategies by various actors in the ransoming process.

2.4 The Economics of the Law of Ransoming: A Double-Edged Sword

It is difficult to assess the impact of ransoming practices on warfare and the laws of war. There is no general agreement on the question whether ransoming practices had the overall effect of attenuating the brutality of warfare and the plight of vanquished or captured enemy soldiers.[24] The spoils of war, including the right of combatants to ransom prisoners they captured in battle, was a strong incentive for many soldiers to join an army or a military expedition,[25] but it could also adversely affect military discipline and strategic considerations.

To some extent, the economics of ransoming—where and when ransoming became a more common practice—appear to have instilled a degree of rationality in dealing with POWs.[26] Some of these rational calculations encouraged group formation and the pooling of interests, such as the *compagnies à butin*. Systems of dividing the spoils were intended to improve discipline and the *esprit de corps*. On the other hand, it may be argued that when, for knights, ransoming replaced the *restauro equorum*, the change caused knights to become more self-sufficient and to resort to self-financing of their warrying careers.[27] In different warzones and in different periods, ransoming led to a more elaborate, sometimes specialised, business of ransoming involving various interest groups and thus contributing to resort to established practices in a wide range of accessory services, each at a cost (custody, messengers, safe-conducts, monetary transactions and the provision of sureties, trade operations as part of the fundraising). All such practices required a degree of personal investment in the actions taken, not least from the POWs themselves.

Capitalist entrepreneurial and mercantile considerations in the management of ransoming POWs were therefore a double-edged sword. On the one hand, especially when the implementation of ransoming depended on interest groups which intervened as third parties, master and prisoner had less leeway in forming and executing the contractual relationship. On the other hand, the flexibility such considerations offered allowed master and prisoner to shape their contractual relationship along more individual lines of initiative and action.

[24] It was at any rate an argument sometimes expressed in medieval times: see, e.g., the (socially biased) plea by Christine de Pisan quoted in Christopher Allmand (ed.), *Society at War, The Experience of England and France during the Hundred Years War* (Woodbridge: The Boydell Press 1998), 83-85. More than ransoming practices, the rulers' or commanders' ordinances on the conduct of armed forces may have been, in the long run, a more important factor in curbing excessive violence in warfare: Neff, *War* 2005 (n. 12), 73-75; Philippe Contamine, *La guerre au Moyen Âge* (Paris: Presses universitaires de France 2017), 458-77. The account by Alexander Gillespie, *A History of the Laws of War*, vol. 2, *The Customs and Laws of War with Regards to Combatants and Captives* (Oxford: Hart 2011), 119-34, is overall pessimistic, emphasising the cases of mass killings, torture, mutilations, and desecration.

[25] Ransoms can be seen as part of the distribution of booties, which were an essential part of the warfare economics. See David Nicolle, *Medieval Warfare Source Book*, vol. 1, *Warfare in Western Christendom* (London: Arms and Armour Press 1995), 246.

[26] For an overall positive assessment of the effects of ransoming and a relatively lenient treatment of POWs in the border regions between England and Scotland, see Andy King, 'According to the Custom Used in French and Scottish Wars, Prisoners and Casualties on the Scottish Marches in the Fourteenth Century' *Journal of Medieval History* 28 (2002), 263-90.

[27] Andrew Ayton, *Knights and Warhorses, Military Service and the English Aristocracy under Edward III* (Woodbridge: The Boydell Press 1999), esp. 84-137.

3. Case Study II: Reprisals

In their oldest form, which can be traced back to the early Middle Ages, reprisals were a self-help measure rooted in custom and intended for the reparation of a wrong suffered at the hands of an alien. Since they were executed either by seizing goods that belonged to members of the wrongdoer's community or by capturing their persons, reprisals have often been understood as a measure rooted in communal solidarity and based on the principle of collective liability. Although this interpretation is not wrong, a closer look at the legal practice and doctrine of reprisals reveals that the legal position of the individuals involved was a matter of concern.

3.1 From *Pignorationes* to Reprisals

Roman law prohibited the seizure of someone's property as compensation for the debts of a third person, considering it contrary not only to 'laws', but also to 'natural fairness, that people be troubled for the debts of others'.[28] A *novella* by Justinian of 537 refers to such seizures as *pignorationes*, and denounces them as an 'abuse' that 'many laws' had already tried to suppress, but which the governors of the provinces were apparently not able to prevent. Anyone who presumed to take property from another in order to indemnify themselves for what was owed to them by a third party was compelled to return to the victim quadruple the amount taken, and was deprived of the right of action against the original debtor.[29]

By Justinian's time, however, the practice had been censured not only by Roman law, but also by the laws of the Barbarian kingdoms established in southern Europe. A letter to the consul of Campania by Theodoric the Great (king of the Ostrogoths from 471 on, and ruler of the Ostrogothic Kingdom of Italy between 493 and 526) condemns creditors who carry out a *pignoratio* against a third party to return twice the amount to the victim.[30] In the subsequent centuries, Barbarian legislations intervened repeatedly against *pignorationes*, but the fact that they attempted to limit—rather than ban—the practice shows that they were unable to wipe it out entirely.[31] The *lex Visigothorum* (mid seventh century) is especially

[28] Cod. 12.60.4 (Honorius and Theodosius II, year 422) and Cod. 11.57.1 (Zeno, years 474-91, whence the quotation is taken), translation: Bruce W. Frier (ed.), *The Codex of Justinian. A New Annotated Translation, with Parallel Latin and Greek Text, Based on a Translation by Justice Fred H. Blume* (Cambridge: CUP 2016), vol. III, 2757.

[29] Auth. 5.5 = Nov. 52.1 (*Ut non fiant pignorationes pro aliis personis*). An excerpt from this novella was later included in the section *Ne uxor pro marito vel maritus pro uxore vel mater pro filio conveniatur* of the *Codex*: Auth. 'Sed omnino' post Cod. 4.12.4.

[30] Cassiodorus, *Variarum libri*, IV.10 in Jacques-Paul Migne (ed.), *Patrologia Latina*, vol. 69 (Paris: J.-P. Migne 1865), col. 618.

[31] References in Alberto Del Vecchio and Eugenio Casanova, *Le rappresaglie nei comuni medievali e specialmente in Firenze. Saggio storico* (Bologna: Zanichelli 1894), 61.

noteworthy, since it explicitly refers to *pignorationes* between people belonging to different jurisdictions. This law limited seizures to cases of denial of justice by a judge of the wrongdoer's community, and stated that any seizure could be carried out either by the judge of the claimant or by the claimant themselves under the former's authorisation. Spelling out in detail the procedure to be followed when one person had a cause of action against another, who resided in the jurisdiction of a different judge, the text says that the judge of the district to which the claimant belonged should send a letter to the wrongdoer's judge, and direct them to hear the cause of the complaint without delay. If the wrongdoer's judge denied justice, the claimant's judge could seize their counterpart's goods for an amount equal to the sum for which the claimant had brought the suit. If the wrongdoer's judge possessed no goods in the neighbourhood, the claimant's judge could seize the goods of anybody living in the former's territory, or deliver the claimant an authorisation to take the goods themselves, up to the said amount.[32]

In the ninth century we find evidence that international treaties, too, regulated the procedures whereby the subject of one party who had suffered a wrong done by the subject of another could obtain redress in the latter's courts: again, *pignoratio* was only allowed in cases of denial of justice. In the so-called *Pactio Sicardi*, concluded in 836 between Sicard, the Prince of Benevento, and the Neapolitans, the parties agreed to request twice, by means of letters carried by the claimant themselves, the compensation of a wrong, before allowing the claimant to seize the goods of the wrongdoer's fellow citizens—initially within the claimant's city, then, if this proved ineffective, also outside it. Specific clauses, moreover, afforded protection to merchants, who could not be subject to either detention or *pignoratio*.[33] This is consistent with the special protection that Germanic and Carolingian legislations provided to merchants and pilgrims.[34] Another treaty, concluded in 840 between Emperor Lothar I (in his role as King of Italy) and the Venetian doge, included—among other provisions on the issue—a clause according to which a *pignoratio* could be made against the judge of one territory who had denied justice to the subject of the other.[35] This document is of particular significance, since it

[32] *Lex Visigothorum* II.2.7 in Karolus Zeumer (ed.), *Leges Visigothorum* [MGH Leges, Leges nationum Germanicarum, t. I] (Hannoverae et Lipsiae: Impensis Bibliopolii Hahniani 1902), 83-84; Hans W. Spiegel, 'Origin and Development of Denial of Justice' *American Journal of International Law* 32 (1938), 63-81, at 65.

[33] *Pactio Sicardi*, cap. 5, 8, and 17, in Fridericus Bluhme (ed.), *Leges Langobardorum* [MGH Leges, t. IV] (Hannoverae: Impensis Bibliopolii Aulici Hahniani 1868), 219 and 221. See Spiegel, 'Origin' 1938 (n. 32), 64.

[34] Claudia Storti, 'Stranieri ed "estranei" nelle legislazioni germaniche', in *Le relazioni internazionali nell'Alto Medioevo* (Spoleto: Fondazione Centro Italiano di Studi sull'Alto Medioevo 2011), 383-436, at 408-10, and Atria A. Larson, 'From Protections for *miserabiles personae* to Legal Privileges for International Travellers: The Historical Development of the Medieval Canon Law regarding Pilgrims' *Glossae* 16 (2019), 166-86.

[35] *Pactum Hlotarii I*, cap. 19 in Alfredus Boretius et Voctor Krause (eds.), *Capitularia regum Francorum* [MGH Leges, Capitularia regum Francorum], t. II (Hannoverae: Impensis Bibliopolii Hahniani 1897), 133. See also *ibid*, cap. 12, 21, and 22, at 132-34.

was the basis of a series of other treaties concluded between Venice and the empire until the reign of Emperor Frederick II.[36] By that time, however, in order to restrict recourse to *pignorationes*, treaties often included a framework intended to allow wrongs to be redressed and legal protection to be ensured for aliens. In fact, in the thirteenth-century mediterranean region 'there were hardly any treaties of friendship which did not contain a restriction of reprisal'.[37]

Similar attempts were also made in legislation, both local and supranational. In his law *Habita* of 1155, Frederick Barbarossa famously forbade the 'perverted custom (*perversa consuetudo*)' of holding students who travelled to or from their place of study accountable for the wrongs of their fellow countrymen. His grandson, Frederick II, completely banned the practice of '*presali*[*e*] *seu represali*[*e*]' in the Kingdom of Sicily. And the Second Council of Lyons (1274)—explicitly referring to the Roman *pignorationes* as an equivalent of '*represali*[*e*]'—forbade their authorisation or execution against clerics and their goods. Although this legislation did not stop the execution of reprisals against aliens in actual practice, the limitations it imposed contributed to their increasing control. The appearance of an official document for their authorisation, in mid thirteenth-century Italy, marked a significant step in the formalisation of the procedures governing their execution, and was quickly followed by the adoption of similar documents across Europe.[38]

3.2 The Scholarly Debate on the Legitimacy of Reprisals

Legal scholars also set out to discuss the legitimacy and requirements of reprisals, generating a doctrinal debate in which Bartolus de Sassoferrato's *Tractatus represaliarum* (1354) is widely recognised as the most significant work.[39] By the end of the fifteenth century, further treatises on the topic were Johannes de Legnano's *De bello, de represaliis et de duello* (1360), Martinus Garatus Laudensis' *De represaliis* (1452-53) and Johannes Jacobus a Canibus' *De represaleis* (1479). This debate clearly shows that, in this period, the meaning of 'reprisals' was much

[36] Roberto Cessi, *Le origini del ducato veneziano* (Naples: Morano 1951), 198-99 (Cessi also provides another edition of the 840 *Pactum* at 237-43), and Gerhard Rösch, *Venedig und das Reich: Handels- und verkehrspolitische Beziehungen in der deutschen Kaiserzeit* (Tübingen: Niemeyer 1982), 7-26.

[37] Spiegel, 'Origin' 1938 (n. 32), 69. For some examples, see Del Vecchio and Casanova, *Le rappresaglie* 1894 (n. 31), 69-71, and Louis Sicking, 'The Pirate and the Admiral: Europeanisation and Globalisation of Maritime Conflict Management' *Journal of the History of International Law* 20 (2018), 429-70, at 440-54.

[38] Philippine C. Van den Brande, '"Remedium repraesaliarum": The Medieval and Early Modern Practice and Theory of Reprisal within the Just War Doctrine' *Grotiana* 41 (2020), 305-29, and Fedele, *The Medieval Foundations* 2021 (n. 11), 564-89. Further references on the late medieval practice of reprisal are found in Frederic L. Cheyette, 'The Sovereign and the Pirates, 1332' *Speculum* 45 (1970), 40-68 and in the literature cited above, note 32 and below, notes 47 and 48.

[39] Extensive analysis of the late medieval and early modern doctrinal debate is found in Ruy de Albuquerque, *As represálias. Estudo de história do direito português (sécs. XV e XVI)* (Lisbon: [n.p.] 1972).

narrower than it is today. They were, in fact, considered the vernacular equivalent of the '*pignorationes*' carried out against a fellow countryman of the original wrongdoer and, as such, they raised issues regarding both the individual rights of the person who resorted to the measure, the individual rights of those against whom it was executed, and the relations between these people's communities. This is why public authorities intervened in the authorisation and execution of reprisals, thus leading modern historiography to consider the latter the 'forerunner of diplomatic protection'.[40]

Since any petitioner who obtained permission from their own polity was entitled to enforce their right against any of their wrongdoer's fellow countrymen who happened to find themselves in the territory controlled by the petitioner's polity, reprisals inevitably affected innocent people. This aspect of reprisals was a source of deep concern for jurists, who shared a widespread distaste for the practice. Bartolus deemed it to be an 'extraordinary' remedy, grounded in *ius divinum* or *ius gentium* rather than *ius civile*, and Albericus de Rosciate (*c.* 1290-1360) stated that it was granted de facto, despite being prohibited de iure.[41] Nevertheless, jurists also felt that—like war, to which they were compared—reprisals were often the only possible way in which someone who had suffered a wrong at the hands of a foreigner, and sought justice in vain before the latter's courts, could get redress: a remedy that, as Baldus de Ubaldis (1327-1400) wrote, had to be authorised 'lest justice perish'.[42] Since they thought that individual people could not be held responsible for a wrong committed by their fellow countrymen, legal scholars insisted that the legitimation of reprisals be contingent upon two requirements: not only the existence of a wrong (and a sufficiently serious one to justify this extraordinary remedy), but also the subsequent denial of justice by the courts of the wrongdoer's community. Bartolus stressed that all legitimate forms of redress had to have been exhausted in the *forum rei* before the petitioner could turn to their own courts and ask for authorisation to carry out reprisals. This requirement was of paramount importance, since it transformed an originally private wrong into a public one, and made the whole community of the wrongdoer responsible before the foreigner private petitioner and their community. In the absence of a superior authority to whom anyone could resort in case of a wrong followed by a denial of justice by a foreign judge, reprisals appeared to be the only available means of

[40] Peter Haggenmacher, 'L'ancêtre de la protection diplomatique: les représailles de l'ancien droit (XIIe-XVIIIe siècles)' *Relations internationales* 143 (2010), 7-12, and Dante Fedele, 'Indemnities in Diplomacy', in Gordon Martel (ed.), *The Encyclopedia of Diplomacy*, vol. II (Hoboken: Wiley-Blackwell 2018), 889-902.

[41] Bartolus de Sassoferrato, *Tractatus represaliarum*, in *id.*, *Consilia, quaestiones, et tractatus* (Venetiis: apud Iuntas 1596), quaestio 1, f. 120ra, nr 5 Albericus de Rosciate, *In Primam Codicis Partem Commentarij* (Venetiis: [Societas aquilae se renovantis] 1586 [reprint Bologna: Forni 1979]), ad Auth. 'Sed omnino' post Cod. 4.12.4, f. 189vb, nr 3.

[42] Baldus de Ubaldis, *In Quartum & Quintum Codicis Libros Commentaria* (Venetiis: [Societas aquilae se renovantis] 1599 [reprint Goldbach: Keip Verlag 2004], ad Auth. 'Sed omnino' post Cod. 4.12.4, f. 23vb, nr 8.

redress. Bartolus explicitly evoked this situation in the proem of his treatise, and linked the recourse to reprisals to the downfall of the Roman Empire and the emergence of cities that recognised no superior.[43]

3.3 The Granting and Execution of Reprisals

Considering reprisals to be a 'hateful remedy (*remedium odiosum*)', which affected innocent people, legal scholars tried to limit both the number of individuals who could ask for it and that of those against whom it could be used. The—often minute—discussion involved issues related to both citizenship and the conflicts of laws and jurisdiction. For instance, Bartolus believed that, as a rule, only citizens who performed public services (*munera*) were entitled to obtain authorisation to carry out reprisals. In his view, if the acquisition of citizenship predated a wrong, a naturalised citizen could even entreat for reprisals to be executed against their city of origin.[44] Baldus on some occasions argued that only native citizens could be subject to reprisal, although on others he agreed with Bartolus that reprisals could also be executed against naturalised citizens. Rebels and outlaws, since they were no longer part of the body politic, could neither ask for nor suffer reprisals. If a treaty had been signed according to which two parties committed to treat each other's citizens as their own, the citizens of one party could not be subject to any reprisal granted by the other. Finally, several groups of individuals—including clerics, ambassadors, merchants attending fairs, students, and pilgrims—were expressly exempted from reprisals.[45]

Having exhausted local remedies in a foreign city, a wronged person had to start proceedings at home in order to obtain proper authorisation for reprisals. Usually, letters or embassies were dispatched to the foreign polity with requests for justice. This stage was sometimes prolonged, especially when the overhasty granting of reprisals risked damaging the commercial interests of the petitioning city. Such interests could eventually also lead to a limited grant, or an outright denial, of the remedy. If diplomacy did not work, and public authorities were determined to resort to reprisal, the ways in which each polity then deliberated on how to proceed depended on their own particular institutional structure. In some cities, like late twelfth- and early thirteenth-century Florence, for instance, legal proceedings were initiated against the wrongdoer's city with a formal summons and the request of legal opinions (*consilia*) from jurists.[46] If granted, reprisals could be carried out either by the public authority or by the petitioner themselves under (some degree

[43] Diego Quaglioni, 'Il proemio del bartoliano "Tractatus represaliarum"' *Pluteus* 2 (1984), 85-92.

[44] Bartolus, *Tractatus represaliarum* 1979 (n. 41), quaestio 5, f. 122ra-122rb, nr 1-3 and 7-11.

[45] Fedele, *The Medieval Foundations* 2021 (n. 11), 576-81.

[46] Lorenzo Tanzini, 'Pratiche e culture del conflitto negli scambi commerciali. I giuristi e la rappresaglia a Firenze alla fine del Duecento' *Nuova rivista storica* 104 (2020), 239-63.

of) public control.[47] Legal scholars usually agreed that a petitioner was entitled to carry out reprisals personally, although they believed that any seized person (and, in the opinion of some, any seized good) had to be handed over to the local magistrate. In accordance with the remedial nature of reprisals, the seized goods were assessed in order that compensation be proportional: the sum recovered could not exceed the amount of the original debt, or the damage caused by the original wrong, plus interest and further expenses. The collective dimension of the liability, however, was greatly reduced by the fact that the (innocent) victim of a reprisal was widely held to be entitled to obtain compensation from the original wrongdoer.[48]

We see therefore that, in the medieval period, the individual's position and rights were matters of concern in both legal practice and doctrine of reprisals. The situation changed in early modern times, when reprisals saw the individual increasingly relegated to a passive role. Over time, the action was monopolised by States, and the remedy—instead of being intended to provide satisfaction for denying justice to a foreigner—became a means by which one State could react against all kinds of (alleged) breaches of international law by another. In this context, reprisals increasingly became a practice tantamount to war.[49]

4. Conclusion

Medieval legal science developed primarily as a science of good, that is, legitimate, governance. Legitimate rulership was required to act, both in domestic matters and in foreign affairs, according to the standards of good governance. Legal scholarship worked out such standards to a large extent by requiring that the ordinary exercise of political power ought to remain within the boundaries of the law. In that sense, good governance required—barring extraordinary circumstances—to follow the rule of law. Although medieval legal scholarship did not follow any systematisation of the law by branches, and therefore ignored a distinct category of (public) 'international law', it dealt with a wide variety of issues of international governance and relations. Several of those issues would qualify today as issues of international law. Legal science did not encompass all the forms of normativity which applied to such issues, not even when such a normativity would have been recognised as a legal normativity.

[47] For examples of the former procedure, see Marie-Claire Chavarot, 'La pratique des lettres de marque d'après les arrêts du Parlement (XIIIe-début XVe siècle)' *Bibliothèque de l'École des Chartes* 149 (1991), 5189, at 63, 84 and 87; for examples of the latter one, see Jurriaan Wink and Louis Sicking, 'Reprisal and diplomacy: conflict resolution within the context of Anglo-Dutch commercial relations c1300-c1415' *Comparative Legal History* 5 (2017), 53-71, at 60-61.

[48] Ruy de Albuquerque, *O Direito de Regresso em Matéria de Represálias (Estudo de História do Direito. Sécs. XV-XVI)* (Coimbra: [n.p.] 1975).

[49] Neff, *War* 2005 (n. 12), 216 and 225-39.

Medieval law and governance dealt with multilayered polities and societies. Group identity of citizens and subjects largely prevailed over their individual identity. However, the standard of the rule of law as a requirement of legitimate rulership entailed the possibility for individuals to seek a remedy at law, before the ruler or their courts, in the event they had suffered an unlawful prejudice. Not surprisingly, individuals claiming justice from the authorities or the courts often provide our main source of information on individuals in disputes involving different polities, whether at war or in peace-time. Even then, however, it is clear that the spectrum of individuation varies, as the individual appears invariably more or less defined by their belonging to a social group. Only at the upper levels of the social and political hierarchy is individualisation more visible, but there again, because of the individual's social position.

A famous controversy among historians relates to the words attributed to Amaury Amalric, abbot of Cîteaux, who lead the armed forces entrusted with the 'Albigensian Crusade' at the siege of Béziers (1209). Some twenty years after the event, Caesarius of Heisterbach reported that while the town was being plundered and the population massacred, Amalric was asked how to differentiate the true believers from the heretics. According to Heisterbach, the abbot is reported to have answered: '*Kill them all for the Lord knows them that are His*'.[50] That order would explain the large numbers of casualties among the population in the aftermath of the taking of the city, even though the numbers mentioned at the time were obviously much exaggerated. Historians disagree whether or not the order was actually given as reported by Heisterbach.[51] Either way, the story is relevant for assessing the lack of focus on the individual. If true, the order would illustrate a 'no quarters' policy which prevailed in many medieval battles, though here extended to a besieged town's civilian population. It would confirm that, when considering military-strategic and political goals, a commander (even when he was a papal legate) could dismiss any concerns based on the individual's soul in this world. If the story does not report Amalric's true words, that may imply a criticism of the undifferentiated slaughter of faithful Christians, and perhaps of an excessive and politically imprudent decision. Either way, and this is all the more noteworthy because the religious beliefs of the city's residents were at stake, neither the men of arms in the theatre of war nor the chronicler would appear to have given overmuch attention to the faith of the individual victims. The fate of the individual soul remained ultimately an issue of the individual's afterlife.

[50] 'Caedite eos. Novit enim Dominus qui sunt eius.' The quotation is understood to refer to *2 Timothy* 2:19.

[51] Jacques Berlioz, '*Tuez-les tous, Dieu reconnaîtra les siens*': *le massacre de Béziers (22 juillet 1209) et la Croisade contre les Albigeois, vus par Césaire de Heisterbach* (Portet-sur-Garonne: Loubatières 1994).

4

From Exemplary Individuals to Private Persons with Rights

International Law, 1500-1647—Vitoria, Gentili, and Grotius

*Francesca Iurlaro**

1. Introduction: Private and Public Individuals in Motion

In early modern doctrines of *ius gentium*, the question of the individual's position was particularly controversial. On the one hand, narratives that focused on the emergence of sovereignty as both a conceptual and historical concept seemed to consider individuals only as sovereigns: sovereigns should be considered individuals and thus are expected to adhere to the principles of natural law. On the other hand, while some scholars defined the concept of sovereignty as a dynamic and ever-changing concept, others portrayed the categories of 'private' and 'public' as mutually dependent rather than mutually exclusive.

From this perspective, early modern *ius gentium* not only used analogies from private law to define what constitutes the public, it also used the concept of the 'public' to define the 'private', as the debates on just war demonstrate. Only a public authority could legitimately declare war: private redress of injustice was permitted only in a state of nature, but when individuals joined the commonwealth, they lost this right once domestic tribunals were established.

Conversely, States had no system of international adjudication except for war. Thus, war, like any process, served as the legitimate method for sovereigns to exercise their right to punish injustices. Who qualified as 'sovereign' and what their prerogatives were defined what the sovereign was allowed to do under the law of nations.[1] In principle, this created an action space for sovereigns functioning as public authorities under the law of nations, a space that, by its very nature, seemed to leave no room at all for individuals.

* I would like to thank all the participants of the 'The Individual in International Law – History and Theory' Authors' Workshop (Heidelberg 17-18 June 2021), especially Professor Alan Wijffels and Dr Dante Fedele for their valuable comments on an early draft of this chapter.

[1] On the question of reprisals and collective punishments, see Fedele and Wijffels, 'Medieval International Law' (chapter 3), in this volume.

Francesca Iurlaro, *From Exemplary Individuals to Private Persons with Rights* In: *The Individual in International Law.* Edited by: Tom Sparks and Anne Peters, Oxford University Press. © Francesca Iurlaro 2024.
DOI: 10.1093/oso/9780198898917.003.0004

Recent literature has shown that this stark division was, in fact, a projection of the contemporary legal mindset. Jurists such as Vitoria, Gentili, and Grotius were very familiar with the reality of their times – a reality in which many individuals exchanged goods, advanced pretences, acted as princes, and suffered injustices. However, it remains an open question whether the individual retained a distinctive legal status within the context of early modern *ius gentium*. The lack of a comprehensive study on the subject (except for Peter Remec's 1960 book, *The Position of the Individual in International Law According to Grotius and Vattel*,[2] which is now somewhat dated) clearly indicates this lacuna in research.

At the same time, it is important not to hastily ascribe rights to individuals that they did not possess under the early modern law of nations. There are, however, two tendencies to be observed in the legal reasoning of authors of the *ius gentium* tradition. As I analyse these tendencies in the current chapter, they represent the 'trends' of arguments often employed by jurists when faced with the reality of individuals engaging in international actions, rather than evidence that individuals' legal status was fully recognised.

The first trend consists of what I refer to as an 'exemplary conception of the legal status of individuals'. In my view, exemplarity of (mis)conduct provides a valuable criterion for understanding the legal prerogatives of individuals. I will explore this hypothesis further by using the idea of literary exemplarity as a proxy for the moral and legal recognition of the role of individuals within *ius gentium*. Individuals are subject to either punishment or protection. Punishing them amounts to an exemplary act for the rest of the community of nations, serving as a warning against replicating behaviours judged to be *hors-la-loi*. Similarly, they are protected in times of war (within what we defined as sovereigns' action space) to prevent an escalation of cruelty and to avoid setting a dangerous precedent for others to follow.

The individual and collective power of examples is based on a specific argument: that individuals and groups can define each other by imitating, projecting, or analogising patterns of behaviour. From this perspective, the literary concept of exemplarity allows us to identify negotiation strategies between individuals and the community and the implications of such strategies for legal discourse.

Contemplating the prerogatives of individuals provides a valuable perspective for examining sovereign powers and the limitations of the distinction between 'public' and 'private' spheres. Against the classic international relations theory of the 'domestic analogy', which conceptualises sovereigns as analogous to individuals,[3] I propose here to reverse the model and to think about individuals as analogous to States. Along these lines, it is possible to identify a second tendency,

[2] Peter Remec, *The Position of the Individual in International Law According to Grotius and Vattel* (The Hague: Martinus Nijhoff 1960).

[3] Hedley Bull, *The Anarchical Society* (New York, NY: Columbia University Press 1977); Chiara Bottici, *Men and States: Rethinking the Domestic Analogy in a Global Age* (Karen Whittle (tr.), London: Palgrave Macmillan 2009).

interwoven with the first, in the legal treatment of individuals under the law of nations: boundaries between individuals and sovereigns are conceived as porous and are defined by expediency. I will address this question by looking at how Francisco de Vitoria, Alberico Gentili, and Hugo Grotius frame these boundaries by employing exemplarity and analogical thinking.

2. Exemplarity and the *Ius Gentium* Tradition

What is exemplarity?[4] In classical literature, the *exemplum* is a 'portable narrative unit',[5] a literary episode deemed to have a paradigmatic moral quality worthy of imitation. It often concerns a hero, a particularly virtuous character, or an episode that is conceived as representative of a specific cultural mentality. The *exemplum* thus serves as a narrative providing a point of reference and grounds for action for members of a society who accept its values as foundational, or it is modified accordingly whenever those values are being renegotiated. Famous *exempla* include the story of Aeneas, portrayed as the hero of Roman piety and virtue in Roman literature and, similarly, parables in the Bible and the lives of saints in the Christian tradition. While memes arguably play a similarly paradigmatic role in contemporary popular culture,[6] in Roman society, *exempla* were ever-evolving literary practices, perpetually shaped by political actors to best represent their specific agendas at any given time.[7] From this perspective, one crucial factor guaranteeing the longevity of the *exempla* tradition is that the Romans learned how to use them to balance the respective claims of individuals within society. In other words, *exempla* offer a semantic strategy of negotiation between individuals and the collectivity.[8] Examples are generally about remarkable individuals, and what distinguishes them is their moral character, their exceptional *genos*, or the social class they represent, but since their symbolic value becomes 'collectively redistributed', it cannot be excessively

[4] Michael Lowrie and Susanne Lüdemann (eds.), *Exemplarity and Singularity: Thinking Through Particulars in Philosophy, Literature, and Law* (London: Routledge 2015) (see, specifically, part II on the Roman practice of exemplarity); Timothy Hampton, *Writing from History: The Rhetoric of Exemplarity in Renaissance Literature* (Ithaca, NY: Cornell University Press 1990); Alessandro Barchiesi, 'Exemplarity: Between Practice and Text', in Jan Papy, Wim Verbaal, and Yanick Maes (eds.), *Latinitas Perennis Volume II: Appropriation and Latin Literature* (Leiden: Brill 2009), 41-62; Matthew Roller, *Models from the Past in Roman Culture* (Cambridge: CUP 2018), 1-31; John D. Lyons, *Exemplum: The Rhetoric of Example in Early Modern France and Italy* (Princeton: Princeton University Press 1989); Dana Hollander, *Exemplarity and Chosenness: Rosenzweig and Derrida on the Nation of Philosophy* (Stanford, CA: Stanford University Press 2008); Irene E. Harvey, *Labyrinths of Exemplarity: At the Limits of Deconstruction* (New York, NY: SUNY Press 2002), 209; see also Jane D. Chaplin, *Livy's Exemplary History* (Oxford: OUP 2000).

[5] Barchiesi, 'Exemplarity' 2009 (n. 4), 41.

[6] Richard Dawkins, *The Selfish Gene* (2nd edn, Oxford: OUP 1989), 368 (on memes as 'units of imitation').

[7] Barchiesi, 'Exemplarity' 2009 (n. 4), 41.

[8] *ibid*, 43 and 45; On examples as flexible units of meanings, see also Maurizio Bettini, *Le orecchie di Hermes* (Torino: Einaudi 2000).

unique. To function as an example, their value has to be relatable, so that it can become collectively appropriated.[9]

Exemplarity plays a fundamental role in early modern literature. After Renaissance humanists prompted a renewed interest in texts of classical antiquity, these writings were given a crucial role in imparting moral and pedagogic function. While that function was exploited in grammar schools and formed the very core of early modern education practices, recent scholarship has shown that the language of natural law and *ius gentium* also relied on these frameworks of meaning.[10] Early modern exemplarity, as both a literary practice and an argumentative legal tool, consists of three fundamental aspects: imitation, hermeneutic application, and negative and positive characterisations.[11]

Imitation is a writing theory that 'contributes to a change in habits of reading'.[12] It implies that the reader can mirror the behaviours described in the text. This capacity, in turn, rests both on the quintessentially human capacity to learn by way of imitation and on the special authoritative appeal of literary models. Only if such authority is perceived as stylistically 'pleasant' can its imitation in writing and reading be deemed a virtue. Therefore, the choice of the most reliable and enlightening authorities implies a careful and ideologically guided selection of canonical authors from the past. This selection process explains why texts from the *ius gentium* refer so frequently to Livy, Virgil, and Cicero, whose writings were considered authoritative both stylistically and substantively. That (almost unchallenged) authority generates the persuasive power of the *exempla* invoked.

Second, literary exemplarity relies on 'hermeneutic application'. The text and its values must be brought to life in the present: in other words, 'the appropriation of past action is understood as the creation of a narrative'.[13] This appropriation implies a close relationship between the *exemplum* and the specific epistemic community it aims to persuade, and provides idealisations that mediate 'between ideals of public virtue and the reader's self-understanding'.[14] In a recent book, James Hankins points to the notion of 'paideuma' to explain the peculiarly elitist value of humanist culture: the concept of *paideuma* 'refers to an intentional form of elite culture that seeks power within a society with the aim of altering the moral attitudes and behaviour of society's members, especially its leadership class'.[15] This

[9] Barchiesi, 'Exemplarity' 2009 (n. 4), 47.

[10] Christopher Warren, *Literature and the Law of Nations* (Oxford: OUP 2015); Benjamin Straumann, *Roman Law in the State of Nature* (Cambridge: CUP 2015).

[11] See also Colin Burrow, *Imitating Authors: Plato to Futurity* (Oxford: OUP 2019); David Scott Wilson-Okamura, *Virgil in the Renaissance* (Oxford: OUP 2010); Timothy Hampton, *Fictions of Embassy* (Ithaca, NY: Cornell University Press 2012).

[12] Hampton, *Writing from History* 1990 (n. 4), 4, quoting from Terence Cave, 'The Mimesis of Reading in the Renaissance', in *Mimesis: From Mirror to Method, Augustine to Descartes* (Dartmouth, NH: New England University Press 1982) 149-65, 155.

[13] Hampton, *Writing from History* 1990 (n. 4), 4.

[14] *ibid*, 19.

[15] James Hankins, *Virtue Politics* (Cambridge, MA: Harvard University Press 2019), 2.

institutionalised elite culture was an attempt to respond to a huge crisis in values, a collapse of the medieval political, cultural, and legal order, by replacing them with the authority of the classical past. From this perspective, European humanism(s) have often been associated with secularisation.[16] However, as has been noted, exemplarity is also a particularly poignant characteristic of theological discourse. In fact, in mediating between sacred texts and the classical past, *exempla* serve to connect pre- and Christian culture.[17]

Third, exemplarity can be characterised either negatively or positively. The power of imitation works both ways: it can inspire imitation as well as moral repulsion.[18] This is particularly relevant for the legal repercussions of exemplarity. It is problematic that a literary *exemplum* from the past is not only enacted as a narrative in the present but also sets an example for future legal conduct. From this perspective, legal scholars have sought to integrate these discussions from literary into legal theory precisely in order to address the question of time: are *exempla* any different from precedents?[19] What is the relationship between *exempla* and the past, and how can the past generate legal meaning both in the present and in the future?

The choice of *exempla*, it has been argued, is never 'innocent':[20] they must resonate emotionally with the audience, meaning that they have to strike a certain chord to achieve the intended rhetorical persuasive impact they are designed to produce. Because *exempla* have to fit into a pre-existing semantic mould to work, they can be used to generate new structures of injustice or carry old ones into the present.[21] At the same time, *exempla* must also be oriented towards the future: 'An example is not a bare particular, but one that points to something beyond it.'[22] It has to produce new knowledge.[23]

The question then arises whether the heuristic value of *exempla* depends on their alleged normative message. Maksymilian Del Mar warns us, against Jerome Bruner's opposing argument in *Making Stories*, that we must resist the temptation

[16] Riccardo Fubini, *Humanism and Secularization from Petrarch to Valla* (Martha King (tr.), Durham, NC: Duke University Press 2003); Ingolf U. Dalferth (ed.), *Reformation und Säkularisierung* (Tübingen: Mohr Siebeck 2017); Rafael Domingo and Giovanni Minnucci, 'Alberico Gentili and the Secularization of the Law of Nations', in Rafael Domingo and John Witte Jr. (eds.), *Christianity and Global Law* (London: Routledge 2020), 98-111.

[17] Barchiesi, 'Exemplarity' 2009 (n. 4), 42; see Robert Maryks, *Saint Cicero and the Jesuits: The Influence of the Liberal Arts on the Adoption of Moral Prohabilism* (London: Routledge 2008).

[18] Festus 72, in *Sextii Pompeii Festi De Verborum Significatu quae Supersunt cum Pauli epitome* (Wallace Lindsay (ed.), Leipzig: Teubner 1913).

[19] Clifford Ando, 'Exemplum, Analogy and Precedent in Roman Law', in Lowrie and Lüdemann (eds.), *Exemplarity and Singularity* 2015 (n. 4), 111-22; Ando argues that precedents always help us think analogically, but not all analogies are necessarily of precedential value (at 114).

[20] Maksymilian Del Mar, 'Exemplarity and Narrativity in the Common Law Tradition' *Law and Literature* 25 (2013), 390-427.

[21] See Randy Gordon's discussion of gender biased domestic violence cases in Randy Gordon, 'Institutionalizing Exemplary Narratives: Stories as Models for and Movers of Law' *Law and Literature* 25 (2013), 337-65.

[22] Del Mar, 'Exemplarity and Narrativity' 2013 (n. 20), 401.

[23] *ibid*, 398.

to assume that 'a narrative always contains, explicitly or implicitly, a lesson to be learned'.[24] Del Mar thus identifies a whole tradition of legal thought (mostly engrained in English common law) that uses *exempla* in a non-moral, non-pedagogic way.[25] By recalling the example of Antigone resisting Creon and vindicating her right to bury her brother according to the unwritten norms of the gods, Del Mar argues that nothing would prevent the reader, hypothetically, from sympathising and siding with Creon. Thus,

> one danger here, then, is that once one identifies narrative with having a moral message (intended or not), one is on the slippery slope to identifying any one narrative with one particular message—and this turns, eventually, into the table-thumping insistence of one interpretation versus another. Ironically, what participants in such disagreements often do not see is that the narrative creates the very possibility of disagreement, that is, of undergoing different emotional experiences of the narrative.[26]

To give literary exemplarity a moral function implies, to a certain extent, the fictional argument that the virtues and vices enshrined in the classical past are also valid in the present.[27] Conversely, if the *exemplum* represents a bad practice, it must be 'crystallised' as an example of 'what not to do' in a recurring situation. Again, a parallel with meme culture might help us understand this specific point. Think, for example, of the ubiquitous Karen Memes that went viral after Amy Cooper's false report to 911, triggering the Central Park birdwatching incident on 25 May 2020. 'Karen', an umbrella name for white women like Amy Cooper, certainly does not serve as a model for virtuous imitation: the paradigmatic value of her *exemplum* lies in her tone-deafness and crass insensitivity to racial matters. Interestingly, Amy Cooper's behaviour generated a whole debate on whether she could be charged on account of her false report and whether this would set a dangerous precedent, discouraging vulnerable people in need from calling the police.[28] But while States seek to introduce new legislation to punish racially biased police calls, the negative

[24] *ibid*, 396; see Jerome Bruner, *Making Stories: Law, Literature and Life* (Cambridge, MA: Harvard University Press 2002).

[25] Del Mar, 'Exemplarity and Narrativity' 2013 (n. 20), 400.

[26] *ibid*, 398.

[27] 'This analogical or synchronic way of thinking about the past was very common in medieval and early modern Europe. It enabled Europeans, for instance, to appeal to political, philosophical, and moral precedents and precepts that they knew from classical Roman texts without worrying too much about the rather different historical, and pagan, contexts from which these originated and to ignore the historically specific circumstances in which these had taken place.' See Judith Pollmann, *Memory in Early Modern Europe* (Oxford: OUP 2017), 48.

[28] 'The Amy Cooper Law makes sense for Amy Cooper, but could be a recipe for abuse. It invites lawsuits against people who call the police for help': Ilann M. Maazel, 'Police Reforms in New York State' *New York Law Journal*, available at https://www.law.com/newyorklawjournal/2020/10/08/police-reforms-in-new-york, accessed 7/06/23 June 2023. California has adopted a Karen Law.

exemplarity of Cooper's behaviour, captured by Karen memes, has identified a specific category of individuals in the aftermath of George Floyd's murder. Thus, the question arises: what happens once an *exemplum* is so effectively used to negatively hypostatise certain categories of individuals that it eventually seeps into the collective unconscious? As I will show in the next section, this was how Gentili and Grotius characterised pirates. Contemporary echoes of this characterisation, which equate terrorists with pirates, are further evidence of this phenomenon.[29]

In early modern *ius gentium*, *exempla* were not merely imbued with vaguely moralising undertones; they were also used so extensively as representations for moral arguments that they attained a canonical status. However, I agree with Del Mar that *exempla* should be seen as spaces for interpretation, which leads to problematic results if readers suggest a specific moral narrative. In the following sections, I will show how Gentili and Grotius use the tools of textual hermeneutics to generate legal meaning and pass them onto future generations based on their specific ideological convictions. Recognising that their agency in crystallising *exempla* into canonical arguments is far from 'innocent' might help us address the question of how they have actively contributed to creating the canon of 'classics of international law'.[30]

3. Exemplarity and Sovereign Prerogatives through the Lens of the Individual

As shown in section 2, the power of examples rests on a specific political argument, namely, that individuals and groups can define each other by imitating, projecting, or analogising patterns of behaviour. The concept of exemplarity allows us to understand sovereign prerogatives against the background of individual ones, and vice versa, especially as far as the use of force in war is concerned.

Francisco de Vitoria provides a relevant example of this tendency in the history of *ius gentium*. In his *De potestate civili*, Vitoria asks the topical question of whether sovereigns are subject to the law or whether their special status exempts them from being subject to any kind of legal obligation (the doctrine known in European political thought as *princeps legibus solutus*). The laws that the king enacts are also binding on him: he is free to make law as he chooses but cannot choose whether he is bound by them or not.

[29] See the infamous Torture Memos and the rhetoric of the *hostis humani generis*, 'Memorandum for William J. Haynes II, General Counsel of the Department of Defense', US Department of Justice, Office of Legal Counsel, footnote 14.

[30] On canon, see Francesca Iurlaro, 'Between Authority and (In)Authenticity: How Literary Canons Shaped *Jus Gentium*' *Leiden Journal of International Law* 35 (2022), 535-47, as well as other contributions in this special issue of the *Leiden Journal of International Law*.

> From what has been said, we may infer the following corollary: that the law of nations does not have the force merely of pacts or agreements between men, but has the validity of positive enactment (*lex*). The whole world, which is in a sense a commonwealth, has the power to enact laws which are just and convenient to all men; and these make up the law of nations.[31]

Here, Vitoria invokes the law of nations to exemplify that sovereigns are indeed bound by law: not only by their domestic legislation but by the laws of the entire world, which is 'in a sense (quasi) a commonwealth'.

However, elsewhere, Vitoria further qualifies the difference between private persons and the political community. In his *De iure belli*, he clarifies that private persons can defend themselves but do not have the right to seek redress for offences or to reclaim stolen property. An exception to this rule applies in cases of an immediate state of necessity: someone who has been struck in the face can respond to the offence with the sword, not to seek revenge but to avoid infamy and dishonour.[32] The political commonwealth has the authority to defend its citizens and to seek redress for the injuries they suffer. If it did not have this power, Vitoria adds, its enemies would become stronger and bolder in their offences, for they could act without fear of being punished. The natural order of things demands not only that princes have the authority to go to war but that the capacity to judge whether to do so is appropriate and just.

Similarly, Gentili argues that only a public authority can declare war. He supports this claim with a famous negative example of individuals who cannot declare war: pirates. Pirates are understood to be 'enemies of mankind', an extralegal category that jeopardises the very foundation of the international order.[33] In Gentili's words, the laws of war do not apply to them because their own behaviour puts them outside the boundaries of the law: 'If law is nothing but community and pact, what law can there be for these subjects who (as Florus says), escaped the civil commonwealth and by so doing they broke the pact of humankind.'[34] Gentili relies on the typical Stoic cosmopolitan argument that an invisible legal vinculum ties humanity together.[35] The very fact that pirates, by their exemplary misconduct,

[31] Francisco de Vitoria, 'On Civil Power', in Anthony Pagden and Jeremy Lawrance (eds.), *Vitoria: Political Writings* (first published 1528, this edn: Cambridge: CUP 1991), 40.

[32] Francisco de Vitoria, 'On the Law of War', in Anthony Pagden and Jeremy Lawrance (eds.), *Vitoria: Political Writings* (first published 1532, this edn: Cambridge: CUP 1991), 300.

[33] Walter Rech, *Enemies of Mankind: Vattel's Theory of Collective Security* (Leiden: Nijhoff 2013).

[34] Alberico Gentili, *De iure belli libri tres* (Hanau: Wilhelm Antonius 1598), 4.

[35] Diego Panizza, 'I valori fondanti della respublica magna nel *De iure belli*', in *Alberico Gentili: (San Ginesio 1552-Londra 1608): Atti dei convegni nel quarto centenario della morte. San Ginesio, 11-12-13 settembre 2008, Oxford e Londra, 5-6 giugno 2008, Napoli 'L'Orientale', 6 novembre 2007* (Milan: Giuffrè 2010), 491-513; Luca Scuccimarra, '*Societas hominum*: Cosmopolitismo stoico e diritto delle genti', in Luigi Lacché (ed.), *Alberico Gentili e gli orizzonti della modernità: ius gentium ius comunicationis ius belli, Atti del Convegno di Macerata in occasione delle celebrazioni del quarto centenario della morte di Alberico Gentili (1552-1608), Macerata 6-7 dicembre 2007* (Milan: Giuffrè 2009) 31-49.

declare themselves to be outside this tacit vinculum makes them unworthy of all forms of legal protection: it would be too dangerous to include them, as their behaviour would set a precedent for the future – although scholarship has shown that in reality pirates were 'vectors of law' and thus anything but excluded from the legal scenario of the early modern sea.[36]

Despite his refusal to turn contemporary practices into standards of behaviour,[37] I suggest that Gentili was well aware that the reality of early modern trade was far more nuanced than his normative expectations. However, I think his reference to the example of pirates should be taken as what it is: a rhetorical *exemplum*. Clearly, the early modern sea was crowded with pirates who could exercise their powers by sovereign authorisation (letters of marque). But Gentili's use of pirates as a limited example of 'what not to do' shows that just because something happens in practice does not mean it has normative value. Indeed, if anything, the fact that it can be construed as a negative *exemplum* can have long-lasting effects on the legal imaginary.

Having clarified that, it is much more interesting to look at how Gentili addresses the private/public divide in a crucial chapter of *De iure belli* devoted to the offences committed by individuals.

In his *De Iure Belli* (I, XXI), Gentili argues that 'private individuals cannot cause injure to the community, as much as they cannot be beneficial to it'. Private individuals are only accountable for their own actions. Similarly, responsibility for their actions cannot be attributed to the whole community. He then distinguishes between two cases: private individuals who exercise their public functions and individuals who explicitly claim personal responsibility for the crime they have committed. In the first case, the offence must be punished like a public offence by the sovereign who received it. The specifically 'public' nature of this case implies that it falls under the jurisdiction of the laws of war. By contrast, in the second situation, the entire State should not suffer the consequences of an injury committed by one of its citizens. This is a consequence of Gentili's assumption that individuals can neither injure nor benefit the community. Here, Gentili seems to suggest one very important aspect: that the 'public' has an inherently positive exemplary quality.

In criticising the behaviour of Venetians, who did not want to respond as a republic to the offences suffered by the king of France at the hands of Venetian

[36] Lauren Benton, *A Search for Sovereignty: Law and Geography in European Empires, 1400-1900* (Cambridge: CUP 2009); Lauren Benton, 'Legalities of the Sea in Gentili's *Hispanica Advocatio*', in Benedict Kingsbury and Benjamin Straumann (eds.), *The Roman Foundations of the Law of Nations: Alberico Gentili and the Justice of Empire* (Oxford: OUP 2010), 269-83; Lauren Benton and Nathan Perl-Rosenthal (eds.), *A World at Sea: Maritime Practices and Global History* (Philadelphia, PA: University of Pennsylvania Press 2020).

[37] Benedict Kingsbury, 'Confronting Difference: The Puzzling Durability of Gentili's Combination of Pragmatic Pluralism and Normative Judgement' *American Journal of International Law* 92 (1998), 713-23; Francesca Iurlaro, 'The Burden of Reason. *Ratio Probabilis, Consensio Omnium* and the Impact of *Humanitas* on Alberico Gentili's Theory of Customary International Law' *History of Political Thought* 38 (2017), 409-38.

merchants, Gentili evokes an *exemplum* from the historian Polybius where the positive exemplarity of the public is particularly evident. Polybius recounts an anecdote that started the Illyrian wars between the regent queen Teuta and the Romans. The Romans claimed that the Illyrians had looted some Roman ships on the Adriatic Sea, but Teuta refused to take responsibility for her citizens' wrongdoing. In compliance with the laws of war, the Romans dispatched two ambassadors. After granting them audience, Teuta responded by assuring them that she would personally ensure that the Illyrians refrained from injuring the Romans, even though doing so ran counter to her people's customs since her subjects were used to freely navigating the sea.[38] The Romans, in turn, compelled her to change her country's laws so as to 'improve the relations between the sovereign and the subject in Illyria'.[39]

Thus, effectively controlling both subjects within the country and at sea is a fundamental aspect of good governance, which Gentili traces back to the responsibility of States to protect their citizens. Furthermore, the *exemplum* showcases Gentili's faith in the power of Rome's civilising mission and in the inherent justice of their public procedures.[40] The contrast between the 'public' sanctity of the ambassadors and the pirates' status as 'outlaws' is striking. In terms of the narrational conflict, it is one that the pirates cannot win. However, Gentili intentionally omits one part of Polybius' story, thus tricking the reader into imagining that Teuta graciously accepted the Romans' imposition. In fact, Polybius reports that Teuta was so outraged by the Romans' request that: 'in despite of the conventions universally observed among mankind, she despatched some men after the ambassadors, as they were sailing home, to kill the one who had used this plainness. Upon this being reported at Rome, the people were highly incensed at the queen's violation of the law of nations, and at once set about preparations for war, enrolling legions and collecting a fleet'.[41] Teuta cannot fully serve as an *exemplum*, not even in the negative sense: her womanhood together with her somewhat controversial status as a semi-public figure (she is a regent, not a proper queen) prevents it. Not only does she fiercely endorse piracy as a distinctively Illyrian customary institution, but she does not punish her subjects when they commit offences on international waters. This shows a tendency—to which I will return in more detail in section 4—to see women as victims rather than as exemplary individuals endowed with power and agency under the law of nations. Had Teuta been a man, perhaps both Polybius and Gentili would have attempted to further analyse her exemplary reaction rather than dismissing it as emotional and instinctive.

[38] Polybius, *Histories*, II, 8.
[39] *ibid.*
[40] Benjamin Straumann, *Crisis and Constitutionalism* (Oxford: OUP 2016), 260-78.
[41] Polybius, *Histories*, II, 8.

A similar duplicity can be found, even more explicitly, in Grotius, who justifies the recourse to private warfare in his unpublished *De iure praedae commentarius* (1604-05):

> In the natural order, as we have already pointed out, every individual is charged with the execution of his own rights. For we have been compounded of mind and body with precisely this purpose in view, namely, that the body may be the servant of the mind. This very point is borne out by the uses of our bodily members, and particularly by the uses assigned to the hands, since we defend ourselves by thrusting the hands forward, and claim a thing as our own by laying our hands upon it.[42]

But it is also natural, according to Grotius' principle of *sociabilitas*, to help each other out as fellow human beings: 'For that matter, even if other bonds are lacking, the universal fellowship of mankind and the communion established by nature, will still cause us to be affected in our turn by ills inflicted upon others. For human beings should not hold themselves aloof from anything that is of human import.'[43]

Rather than basing his claim on a specific exemplary individual, Grotius resorts to the classic Platonic analogy between the human body and the body politic, but he adds an interesting anatomical twist to it:

> Since we ourselves are corporeal entities, other bodies are naturally able to benefit or injure us. Thus, the first law is put into practice through the repulsion of one body from another, and the second law, through the attachment of one body to another. To this end, the lower animals were given their corporeal members and we, our hands and feet, as instruments for the two functions of repelling and attaching. This function of attachment is a gift from God.[44]

He therefore concludes that, as a corollary to the natural function that every individual may exercise with their hands, 'private wars (for these should be dealt with first) are justly waged by any person whatsoever, including cases in which they are waged in conjunction with allies or through the agency of subjects'.[45] How to wage a just private war? 'First of all, let us consider those wars which are undertaken by private individuals. Here we are at once confronted with a rather grave difficulty. For a private war cannot possibly be preceded by a judicial process, since the power

[42] Hugo Grotius, *Commentary on the Law of Price and Booty* (first published 1868, this edn: Martine Julia van Ittersum (ed.), Indianapolis: Liberty Fund 2006), 92.

[43] Grotius, *IPC* 2006 (n. 42), 93.

[44] This passage about the essential role of hands echoes another of Gentili's passages, where he criticises the practice of cutting off thumbs as a way of retaliating against enemies. Gentili condemns this practice because, without thumbs, humans lose the use of their hands altogether: Gentili, *DIB* 1598 (n. 34), III, 2. In support of his argument, Gentili quotes Vesalius' *De humani corporis fabrica* (1555), I, 27.

[45] Grotius, *IPC* 1868 (n. 42), 23.

of judgement resides in the state and the war would cease to be private as soon as the state interposed its authority.' This is Grotius' main problem in *IPC*: how can a private war be just, both substantially and formally, if private persons are bound to have recourse to regular, domestic legal procedures to address their legal claims? Grotius argues that individuals are justified in resorting to war in several situations: if they are faced with a discontinuous administration of legal justice; if reasons of expediency and necessity make it impossible for them to wait for trial; if the absence of tribunals is permanent, such as on the high seas (where no one has jurisdiction as the sea is free); and finally, if they are the victim of an offence. The right to punish is a natural right.[46]

Grotius realises that this framework may grant individuals too large a margin of discretion to wage war and thus set a precedent for future abuse. To this effect, he acknowledges the right to punish as a distinctively sovereign prerogative: even the private acts of a sovereign are, to a certain extent, public.[47] He recognises that there are private individuals who exercise public functions, but every conflict, if it is to be just, requires a sovereign's solemn declaration of war. Individuals can engage in informal war against other individuals, as exemplified with the suppression of armed resistance.[48] The rationale behind this exception is that prioritising the preservation of the commonwealth is more significant than obsessing over formalities. However, even the suppression of armed resistance must be authorised by the sovereign.

4. Exemplarity and Victims: Children and Women

The reluctance to concede unrestrained power to vindicate (rather than to commit) harm is also apparent in how vulnerable groups are treated during times of war. Let us consider, for instance, Vitoria's treatment of women and children. In his *Relectio de iure belli*, Vitoria asks whether it is lawful to kill innocent people in times of war. At first glance, it might seem that it is, and there are many Biblical occurrences that would confirm this argument. But Vitoria suggests that, first, it is never right to kill innocent people intentionally; second, that as they have not committed a crime, it is not lawful to wage war against them; and third, that in a political State, it is unlawful to punish innocent people for the crimes of offenders.[49] Not even in the war against the Turks, he claims, is it lawful to kill children. Nonetheless,

[46] On Grotius' right to punish, see Gustav van Nifterik, 'Grotius and the Origin of the Sovereign's Right to Punish', in Hans Blom (ed.), *Property, Piracy and Punishment: Hugo Grotius on War and Booty in De iure praedae* (Boston, MA: Brill 2009), 396-415; Brad Hinshelwood, 'Punishment and Sovereignty in *De Indis* and *De iure belli ac pacis*' *Grotiana* 38 (2017), 71-105.

[47] Hugo Grotius, *De iure belli ac pacis* (1625), I.III.6.

[48] *ibid*, I.III.6; I.IV.2.

[49] Vitoria, 'On the Law of War' 1991 (n. 32), 314-16.

in a just war, it is conceivable deliberately, in exceptional circumstances, to use cannons on an enemy's fortress even if there is a risk of causing harm to innocent people. Vitoria proposes that if this was not the case, it would be impossible to wage war against guilty parties, which in turn would jeopardise the just cause of war. However, Vitoria dwells on the concern that this behaviour sets a precedent: in war, one must always avoid causing harm that exceeds those harms the war seeks to remedy. Invoking the famous Parable of the Tares, Vitoria claims that there is no need to punish everyone, including innocent people, just for the sake of striking a few enemies. The famous parable is drawn from Matthew: 'While you are pulling the weeds, you may uproot the wheat with them. Let both grow together until the harvest. At that time, I will tell the harvesters: first collect the weeds and tie them in bundles to be burned; then gather the wheat and bring it into my barn.'[50] This parable was used as a counterpart to the *compelle intrare* argument, that is, the idea that infidels should be forced to convert to Christianity.[51] Moreover, it was a relevant illustration of relations between Christians and non-Christians.[52] In line with this, and consistent with his refusal to accept coerced conversions, Vitoria exploits the topical and exemplary value of the parable to impose a customary obligation to protect innocent people, even if they are 'tares', that is, infidels. Furthermore, he adds that one should not commit evil to prevent future evil: 'It is intolerable that someone gets murdered for a future sin.'[53] But it is possible, in compliance with the law of nations, to turn infidels into prisoners of war.[54]

In their respective works, *De iure belli* (1598) and *De iure belli ac pacis* (1625), Gentili and Grotius discuss whether it is lawful to kill women and children in warfare. They argue that women deserve special treatment due to their perceived 'imbecility': except for unique cases (Amazons, Joan of Arc), the 'weakness' of their sex typically prevents women from taking arms in battle, and therefore it is more practical to regard them, along with children, as groups to be protected rather than as targets to be killed.[55] While developing various lines of argument, Grotius essentially reproduces a wide array of sources that he draws directly from Gentili: Seneca, Statius, Livy, Ovid, and Virgil. For the sake of clarity, I will demonstrate how Gentili and Grotius use each of these authors to voice a specific argument about women's 'imbecility' and how the mere rhetorical juxtaposition of all these *exempla* creates new legal interpretations.

[50] Matthew 13: 29-30.

[51] Vincenzo Lavenia et al. (eds.), *Compel People to Come In: Violence and Catholic Conversion in the non-European World* (Rome: Viella 2018).

[52] Roland Bainton, 'The Parable of the Tares as the Proof Text for Religious Liberty to the End of the Sixteenth Century' *Church History* 1/2 (1932), 67-89, at 81. See also Seth Kimmel, *Parables of Coercion* (Chicago, IL: University of Chicago Press 2015); Adriano Prosperi, 'Il Grano e la zizzania', in Pier Cesare Bori (ed.), *L'intolleranza: uguali e diversi nella storia* (Bologna: Il Mulino 1986) 51-86.

[53] Vitoria, 'On the Law of War' 1991 (n. 32), 315-16.

[54] ibid, 319.

[55] Gentili, *DIB* 1598 (n. 34), II, 21; Grotius, *IBP* 1625 (n. 47), III, 4, 9.1. I discuss the same example in Francesca Iurlaro, *The Invention of Custom* (Oxford: OUP 2022).

First, both Gentili and Grotius use a passage from Seneca's tragedy *Octavia* to argue that women cannot be called enemies. Seneca's play—a text of contested attribution[56]—tells the story of Nero's divorce from his stepsister and wife, Octavia. In the passage quoted by Grotius, Nero is asking the prefect to kill Octavia, but the prefect is reluctant to do so. The prefect's reluctance makes Nero question his loyalty:

> Prefect Why doubt my loyalty?
> Nero You spare my foe.
> Prefect A woman is called foe (*foemina hic nomen capit)?*
> Nero If she's called traitor.[57]

To Nero's accusation that women are 'prone to evil and armed with deadly tricks', the prefect responds that God denied women strength—all the more reason, then, to spare Octavia. Instead, Nero specifically labels his wife as his foe, regardless of the prefect's objections, and decides to kill her anyway.

Second, another reason why women cannot be considered enemies under the laws of war is that they are generally untrained in the use of arms. Both Gentili and Grotius base this claim on Statius' *Sylvae*. In his collection of occasional poems, Statius describes the celebrations for Saturnalia, the Roman New Year celebrations under Domitian. These festivities included mock battles involving women and dwarfs:

> Women untrained to the wooden sword take their stand, daring, how recklessly virile battles! You would think Thermodon's bands (i.e. the Amazons) were furiously fighting by Tanais or barbarous Phasis. Then comes a bold array of dwarves, whose term of growth abruptly ended has bound them once and for all into a knotted lump. They give and suffer wounds and threaten death—with fists how tiny! Father Mars and Bloody Virtus laugh, and cranes, waiting to swoop on scattered booty, marvel at the fiercer pugilists.[58]

[56] On Grotius and tragedy, see Mark Somos, 'Enter Secularisation: Heinsius's *De tragoediae constitutione*' *History of European Ideas* 46 (2010), 19-38, at 19; Francesca Iurlaro, 'Grotius, Dio Chrysostom and the Invention of Customary *Ius Gentium*' *Grotiana* 39 (2018), 15-44. Justus Lipsius already considered it 'an inferior work', probably written by yet another author of not more than puerile abilities':Jan Waszink, 'Introduction', in Justus Lipsius, *Politica: Six Books of Politics* (first published 1589, this edn: Jan Waszink (ed.), Assen: Royal van Gorcum BV 2004), at 147.

[57] Anthony J. Boyle (ed.), *Octavia: Attributed to Seneca* (Oxford: OUP 2008), 68-69.

[58] 'Hos inter fremitus novosque luxus spectandi levis effugit voluptas: stat sexus rudis, insciusque ferri ut pugnas capit improbus viriles! credas ad Tanain ferumque Phasim Thermodontiacas calere turmas. hic audax subit ordo pumilorum, quos natura brevis statim peracta nodosum semel in globum ligavit. edunt vulnera conseruntque dextras et mortem sibi (qua manu!) minantur. ridet Mars pater et cruenta Virtus, casuraeque vagis grues rapinis mirantur pugiles ferociores' Publius Papinius Statius, *Sylvae*, I, VI.53.

This passage ridicules the very idea of women in combat. The poet's intention is to make the reader marvel at the exceptional possibility of women engaging in battle despite their lack of training. It is telling that the only scenario in which women can be envisioned as warriors is in a *ludus*, a game in a Saturnalia celebration that temporarily suspends reality and its norms. Does this mean that women can only engage in 'fake' battle? In its early modern iteration, this question was particularly sensitive, both theologically and legally. According to *Deuteronomy* 22:5, 'a woman must not wear men's clothing, nor a man wear women's clothing'. In his polemics against the Puritans, Gentili claims that while scripture prohibits cross-dressing as such, in certain situations it could be justified, such as for theatrical performances.[59]

Similarly, when war permits women to wear 'men's clothing', this exempts them from the protection granted by their natural position of 'imbecility': if they behave like men, they must suffer the consequences. Thus, the act of bearing arms seems to be the legal threshold that distinguishes an enemy from a civilian. Third, and consequently, Gentili and Grotius quote Livy in support of their argument that one must only fight against those who are armed. In book V of his *Ab Urbe Condita*, Livy tells the story of the Falisci, the Italic people who lived in the city of Falerii (now in northern Lazio). Livy explains that it was customary among the Falisci to appoint the same person as both the legal tutor and the pedagogue for a specific group of young boys. One of these tutors was in the habit of taking the boys out to play. One day the tutor brought the boys to the headquarters of Camillus, the Roman chief, asking him to take them as hostages. Camillus told the tutor that Romans never bear arms against children, who are generally spared even during the capture of a city, but only against those who are armed ('arma habemus non adversus eam aetatem cui etiam captis urbibus parcitur, sed adversus armatos').[60] He then gave the boys rods to hit the tutor with while escorting him back to Falerii, their city. The positive exemplarity of Camillus' conduct here is evident: Rome's civilising mission was so morally superior that the Falisci welcomed it, surrendering to Rome in awe of Camillus' moral stature. The argument here recalls the *exemplum* of Teuta discussed in section 3.

Fourth, and consequently, the reference to the capture of a city hints at one final argument: women must not be killed even when they are taken prisoners. Gentili and Grotius use Ovid's *Metamorphosis* to convey this idea. Ovid tells the story of Scylla, princess of Megara and daughter of King Nisus. According to the legend, Nisus had one lock of purple hair that made him and his city invincible. When Megara was under siege by the Cretan king Minos, Scylla fell in love with him. In

[59] See James W. Binns, 'Alberico Gentili in Defense of Poetry and Acting' *Studies in the Renaissance* 19 (1972), 224-72; James W. Binns, 'Women or Transvestites on the Elizabethan Stage? An Oxford Controversy' *Sixteenth Century Journal* 2 (1974), 95-120.

[60] Titus Livius, *Ab Urbe Condita*, 5.27.7.1.

an attempt to win his affection, Scylla cut her father's hair, hoping that such a treasonous act would endear her to Minos. Instead, Minos was shocked by her lack of filial devotion and left Megara immediately. Scylla swam after him, clinging onto his ship. In the meantime, Zeus had metamorphosed her father into a sea eagle. When Nisus saw Scylla and tried to avenge himself, she was also metamorphosed into a sea bird (ciris). Ciris, a Latin poem, whose authorship is unknown, but often attributed to Virgil, tells the same story. Gentili quotes a passage from Ciris where Scylla asks Minos to kill her 'like a prisoner of war' ('*at belli saltem captivam lege necasses*'). 'But the laws of war prohibit the killing of prisoners', Gentili writes: why, then, would it be permissible to kill female prisoners? Gentili links this exemplum with the one from Livy to assert that the suitable punishment for both the tutor of the Falisci and Scylla would be that inflicted on parricides. In short, the applicable legal regime is *ius civile* rather than *ius gentium*. Gentili explicitly blames the conduct of those who have acted otherwise, such as the king Aristomenes who, in his conflict with the Spartans, held the Spartan women hostage and demanded a ransom.[61] Interestingly, Grotius does not mention this incident: he largely accepts this collection of exempla, with little critical examination, from Gentili. Grotius' uncritical use of these exempla solidifies their moral significance for *ius gentium*, isolating them from their original contexts and broader narratives.

Finally, all these themes are condensed into a single reference to Virgil, which Grotius only adds to his 1646 edition of *De iure belli ac pacis*, while Gentili discusses it more extensively. Women must not be killed—not even as prisoners—because they do not qualify as enemies. But what happens if they, while not themselves taking up arms, are nevertheless responsible for wars and the resulting destruction? Gentili responds by evoking the controversial twenty-two verses of book II of the *Aeneid* in which Aeneas contemplates whether to kill Helen, who he considers responsible for the destruction his homeland.[62] Divine intervention puts an end to Aeneas' violent outburst: his mother, Venus, urges him not to surrender to 'uncontrollable anger',[63] and demands he show his famous *pietas*, rather than pointless fury, and protect the memory of his ancestors. Aeneas eventually comes to his senses and refrains from killing Helen. Servius, one of the oldest Virgilian commentators (from the end of the fourth century CE), had already contested the authority of these verses. He argued that they were expunged by Plotius Tucca and Varius Rufus, the two poets Augustus put in charge of editing Virgil's work after his death. The verses were corrected because of inconsistency in the text: it seemed unworthy of Aeneas, depicted throughout the poem as the hero of *pietas*, to succumb to such rage and contemplate the idea of killing a woman.[64]

61 Pausania, *Graeciae descriptio*, IV, 16, 20.

62 Virgil, *Aeneid* (Frederic Ahl (tr.), Elaine Fantham (ed.), Oxford: OUP 2007), 46.

63 *ibid*, 47.

64 Modern philologists still consider the verses in book II to be inauthentic. Most of them find believe that this passage presents one of the 'gravest' interpretative problems of the *Aeneid* as a whole: Pier

Gentili might have not have been aware of these advancements, which resulted from later philological discoveries and techniques. Nevertheless, as demonstrated, it was evident well before the sixteenth century that this Virgilian episode had an air of inauthenticity. But Gentili, with blind trust in Virgil's poetic narrative, defends Aeneas by turning to Julius Caesar Scaliger, one of the greatest humanists of his time and author of an influential treatise on poetry (*Poetices libri VII*, 1561). Indeed, Scaliger claims that Aeneas did not kill Helen because he was acting on divine advice: 'In the human mind, the reason that wins over passion is nothing but a ray of that original light, without which one could say that everything is darkness, and it would really be so.'[65] Aeneas is attempting to save the honour of his citizens: it is natural that he would contemplate vengeance, but this does not imply that he will act on his plan. In Scaliger's interpretation, Venus' intervention simply symbolises human reason's ability to participate in divine judgement. To conclude, Gentili argues that Aeneas would not have killed Helen even if she were guilty, and he encourages the reader never to question the moral integrity of Aeneas as portrayed by Virgil, and to have full trust in Virgil's depiction.

While Grotius quotes the same passage, he does not seem to share Gentili's interpretative authoritarianism.[66] Instead, he specifically refers to Vitoria's paragraph, analysed at the beginning of this section, that appears in *On the Law of War* regarding the killing of innocent people. Grotius not only seems unfettered by Virgilian authority, appearing to feel at liberty to criticise the poet when necessary, but he also adds his own interpretation to the debate concerning this contentious Virgilian passage. By extending the Virgilian text to support a particular legal claim, Grotius effectively adopts the canon, using textual interpretation as a means to convey his own ideas. This is a perfect example of how *exempla* can generate new meaning when lawyers, in appropriating literary texts, enhance them with their legal knowledge in ways that the original poet or writer could not have done. In a later addition to *De iure belli ac pacis*, Grotius suggests, in commenting on this passage, that Tucca and Varius deleted the verses precisely because they presented a legal absurdity –that women could have the status of enemies.[67] Grotius argues that women, unlike children who cannot yet reason, can be held accountable for crimes: but unless they are proven guilty of a specific crime 'or have usurped the Offices of Men', women should not be killed in combat.

Angelo Perotti, 'Qualche osservazione in margine alla scena di Elena' *Latomus* 73 (2014), 629-43, Kenneth J. Reckford, 'Helen in Aeneid 2 and 6' *Arethusa* 14 (1981), 85-99. I discuss this *exemplum* in more detail in Iurlaro, 'Between Authority and (In)Authenticity' 2022 (n. 30); and *Id*, *The Invention of Custom* 2022 (n. 55).

[65] Iurlaro, *The Invention of Custom* (n. 55), 226.

[66] It might be interesting to see this authoritarianism in relation to Gentili's well-known political absolutism, as he developed it in his later *Regales disputationes* (1603).

[67] Hugo Grotius, *De iure belli ac pacis* (Amsterdam: 1646), 528.

Gentili uses the argument of female weakness, based on the positive exemplarity of Aeneas' behaviour, to establish a general rule for treating women with moderation and respect. Aeneas' exemplary behaviour uneasily coexisted with his violent thoughts, which he could entertain freely because they never materialised into actual violence. Gentili's interpretation of and deference towards Virgil preclude the very possibility of Aeneas' violent thoughts becoming action; from this perspective, Gentili's hermeneutic authoritarianism prevents us from ever taking Aeneas' side when he is enraged. But it also generates the scenario in which, as Del Mar pointed out, the moral value of this *exemplum* 'turns, eventually, into the table-thumping insistence of one interpretation versus another'. By contrast, Grotius seems less concerned with the moral value of the *exempla*. What interests him is the legal accuracy of Virgil's text.

5. Conclusion

Do we still believe in the power of imitation? Exemplarity still plays a fundamental role in contemporary culture, although it assumes different forms. How much of this long tradition of exemplarity still shapes contemporary discourses on the individual in international law?

In this short contribution, I have tried to show how various authors of the *ius gentium* tradition use negative and positive exemplarity to construct ideas of individuals 'doing or suffering things international'. The imaginative power of *exempla* provides individuals with a dynamic tool for negotiating the collective semantic space to which they belong. At the same time, however, it may reproduce structures of injustice in the international legal order. Additionally, as I have argued, exemplarity also allows us to appreciate more fully the scope of sovereign prerogatives through the lens of private individuals. Using the concept of exemplarity to cultivate theoretical flexibility helps us appreciate the nuances of the early modern *ius gentium* tradition while also acknowledging the pervasiveness of certain structures of thinking: it is easier to idealise positive and negative examples of individuals and praise or blame them if necessary than to empathise with fellow human beings in the flesh.

5

From Re- to Demoralisation

The Individual in International Law, 1648-1789

Mark Somos

1. Introduction

A survey of the development of the individual's position in international law between the 1648 Treaties of Westphalia and the breakout of the French Revolution in 1789 is not only a fascinating exercise: it also uncovers the dynamic that persists to this day but was set during this specific period between individuals and humankind as a whole, and between the State and the community of all States. Individual rights emerged, evolved, and waned due to religious debates and technological progress.[1] Rights to the freedom of thought and expression drew on doctrines of epistemic humility, according to which neither commoners nor kings knew God's design, in republics and monarchies alike. The Westphalian *cuius regio eius religio* principle proved a rocky but viable compromise paradoxically because Catholics and Protestants agreed on the paramount role of religion in all aspects of life. The territorialisation of sovereignty thus arose from the need to neutralise religion, which was seen as more important than territory but less amenable to rational agreement.[2] In a parallel development, the evolution of the means and costs of war inevitably led to a profound reassessment of individuals' military and financial obligations towards the State, and a renegotiation of the rights concomitant with redefined obligations.[3]

The variations are numerous and as important as the commonalities, but not impervious to usable generalisations. This chapter will show that while the standing of individuals in international law displayed features of the rising individualism that historians have noted in non-legal realms, a countervailing trend saw religious and political authorities uneasily joining forces to construct notions and instruments

[1] A respectable but I think intellectually untenable position is that human rights arose *ab nihilo* with or after the Universal Declaration of Human Rights. See, e.g., Jack Donnelly, *Universal Human Rights in Theory and Practice* (3rd edn, Ithaca, NY: Cornell University Press 2013), 75-92, 106-12 and 116-26.

[2] Mark Somos, *Secularisation and the Leiden Circle* (Leiden: Brill 2011), 4 and 41.

[3] Gerhard Oestreich, *Neostoicism and the Early Modern State* (Cambridge: CUP 1982); Thomas Ertman, *Birth of the Leviathan: Building States and Regimes in Medieval and Early Modern Europe* (Cambridge: CUP 1997).

Mark Somos, *From Re- to Demoralisation* In: *The Individual in International Law*. Edited by: Tom Sparks and Anne Peters, Oxford University Press. DOI: 10.1093/oso/9780198898917.003.0005

of sovereignty by which the State became irremovably lodged between individual and international law.[4] While the Calvinist low nobility that ran provincial governments in the United Provinces and large parts of Germany and Switzerland recognised individual rights under international legal principles that ranged from soldiers' right to conscientious objection to non-Christian non-citizens' universal right to property and freedom of worship, the meteoric rise of French diplomatic law, language and apparatus that set diplomatic templates for Europe and its empires, as well as the French Revolution itself, served primarily to mediate claims to such rights through the State to the exclusion of all other forms of rights claims, whether by individuals, denominations, or transnational entities.[5] Despite gradual secularisation, the religious divide remains the best explanation of why, as a legal standard, cosmopolitanism and 'the common interest of mankind' were soft-power proxies for universal monarchy in the early French Enlightenment (for instance in Mably and Montesquieu), while ostensibly identical standards were invoked to further resist or at least liberalise the State in Britain (from Lilburne to Chatham).

2. Themes

In the period examined, the state of nature, legal epistemology, and recognition were the three key, interrelated but distinct concepts that framed debates and laws regarding the individual's standing in international law. If the state of nature was a state of war, a sovereign who best approximated total control was needed. If the state of nature was one of sociability and natural rights, it not only set limits to the sovereigns' power but also enabled friendly relations with non-Christian States and peoples who were or aspired to be within the ambit of imperial law. International laws also applied to heretics, pagans, and savages, and to enable peace, faith must be kept with all. This cardinal insight is why Grotius' *De iure belli ac pacis* instantly became a classic and recreated international law as a discipline, with the first endowed chair given to Pufendorf to expound Grotius in Heidelberg. Rival formulations of the state of nature explicitly and implicitly structure today's and tomorrow's debates about individual standing in international law.[6]

[4] An important treatment of the rise of early modern individualism is Elizabeth L. Eisenstein, *The Printing Press as an Agent of Change* (Cambridge: CUP 1979). A similarly magisterial account of how States interposed themselves between individual and law are the essays in Michael Stolleis, *Staat und Staatsräson in der frühen Neuzeit: Studien zur Geschichte des öffentlichen Rechts* (Frankfurt: Suhrkamp 1990). On the limits of legal individualism up to Grotius, see Arthur P. Monahan, *From Personal Duties Towards Personal Rights: Late Medieval and Early Modern Political Thought, 1300-1600* (Montreal: McGill-Queen's University Press 1994) and Brian Tierney, *The Idea of Natural Rights* (Grand Rapids, MI: William B. Eerdmans 1997).

[5] Dan Edelstein, *On the Spirit of Rights* (Chicago, IL: University of Chicago Press 2019).

[6] Mark Somos and Anne Peters (eds.), *The State of Nature: Histories of an Idea* (Leiden: Brill 2021). For early uses of Grotius to expand the standing of individuals in international law, see Andreas Harald Aure, *The Right to Wage War (jus ad bellum): The German Reception of Grotius 50 years after De iure belli ac pacis* (Berlin: Berliner Wissenschafts-Verlag 2015).

Knowledge of the prerequisites of salvation, the protection and advancement of which were seen as the chief function of earthly laws, was the second key concept. If priests were needed for salvation, then pre-modern international law that greatly overlapped with ecclesiastical law—whether Catholic or Protestant—had to harmonise with municipal laws to produce a given State's approach to international law, lest the disharmony destroyed both Church and State especially via international law, where the viability of unitary nation-States was most challenged. There was no more feared centrifugal power in this period than religious disagreement between individuals and their State. Popes and bishops continued to excommunicate rulers throughout this period, yet with increasing irrelevance in Europe, though with fluctuating success in Russia. If priests were not necessary for individuals to find salvation, as the 1687 Declaration of Indulgence implied by endorsing individual rights to freedom of thought and expression, then legal epistemology was democratic insofar as knowing, using, debating, and shaping the law became theoretically and often practically open to all. Self-regulating strict Calvinist communities, which spread across the Earth in the brief period examined here and held that the saved cannot be identified by other humans, built both municipal and international law on this foundation, and often produced novel forms of repression of their own (e.g. positivist, not divine).

Finally, the legal philosophy of Rousseau, Vattel and Kant formalised the principle of recognition inherent in Grotius, Hobbes, Pufendorf, and Wolff.[7] Once individuals recognise others as identical to themselves in essence and nature, 'do unto others as you would have them do to you', the optimistic positive Golden Rule deeply entrenched in European legal history, became expressible without religion and applicable to inter-State relations, as well. The negative version, 'do not do to others what you would not want them to do to you', had to await the diffident despondency of nineteenth-century liberalism to become an international law maxim.

Each of these three concepts framed and was fully engaged in the debates over sovereignty, slavery and abolition, property, and the laws guiding relations with non-Europeans in this period. Each will be woven through the fabric of the following sections.

3. Great Legal Thinkers

3.1 Thomas Hobbes (1588-1679)

Although Hobbes is AWOL from recent historiographies of international law, the primary sources from the period examined here make it crystal clear that he

[7] Tarik Kochi, *The Other's War: Recognition and the Violence of Ethics* (London: Birkbeck Law Press 2009).

radically reframed international legal theory. Hobbes claimed to derive all natural, international, and domestic laws from the physiology and phenomenology of the individual. Like Descartes, Hobbes seriously engaged solipsism (what if only I existed, and the rest was illusion?) before he discarded it as self-contradictory and self-paralysing. It is customary to interpret Hobbes' hard-knuckled realism, and prism of violence and the threat of violence, as a function of his experiences in tumultuous early modern England, as well as an intellectual reaction to the unbearable lightness of Pyrrhonean neoscepticism, emblematised by Montaigne and Charron and made famous by Grotius' iconic attempt to refute Carneades' subversive offering of two equally persuasive arguments: one in favour of objective justice; the other, on might as right and all justice as the victor's. Grotius and Hobbes are said to have successfully recast natural law in an anti-neosceptic mode and to have enabled modern international law in the process.[8]

For Hobbes, this is partly right and largely wrong.[9] In *De cive*, *Elements*, and *Leviathan*, Hobbes began from the assumed shared content of his individual readers' mind. Language, he argued, and widely observed patterns of human conduct, must form the building blocks of any system of law, if it is to be credible and useful. An unknowable or privately known but ineffable God was therefore a problem, and so was reason when it exceeded the purview and abilities of the reasonable common man. Yet the fear of death was universal, as was the insatiable lust for more (of everything). For Hobbes, the prudence of trading unlimited freedom for safety under a powerful Sovereign followed inexorably from these premises.[10] History and stupidity—in other words, emotional attachments and the compounded improbability of sovereigns having supreme wisdom and subjects reliably transcending tribalism—have exposed Dante's and papal apologists' models of universal monarchy as untenable; which left sovereign States to endlessly circle one another in a frightful state of nature.

> But though there had never been any time wherein particular men were in a condition of war one against another, yet in all times kings and persons of sovereign authority, because of their independency, are in continual jealousies, and in the state and posture of gladiators, having their weapons pointing, and their eyes fixed on one another; that is, their forts, garrisons, and guns upon the frontiers of their kingdoms, and continual spies upon their neighbours, which is a posture

[8] Richard Tuck, *Philosophy and Government, 1572-1651* (Cambridge: CUP 1993); Richard Tuck, *The Rights of War and Peace: Political Thought and the International Order from Grotius to Kant* (Oxford: OUP 1999), 131-32; Jonathan Israel, *Radical Enlightenment: Philosophy and the Making of Modernity, 1650–1750* (Oxford: OUP 2001).

[9] Mark Somos, 'Reason and Scepticism', in Richard Whatmore and Brian Young (eds.), *A Companion to Intellectual History* (Chichester: Wiley-Blackwell 2016), 417–37.

[10] See Ioannis Evrigenis, *Images of Anarchy: The Rhetoric and Science in Hobbes's State of Nature* (Cambridge: CUP 2014), on the uncommon predicates underlying Hobbes' own rhetorical strategy with which he led the reader to such conclusions.

> of war. But because they uphold thereby the industry of their subjects, there does not follow from it that misery which accompanies the liberty of particular men.
>
> To this war of every man against every man, this also is consequent; that nothing can be unjust. The notions of right and wrong, justice and injustice, have there no place. Where there is no common power, there is no law; where no law, no injustice. Force and fraud are in war the two cardinal virtues. Justice and injustice are none of the faculties neither of the body nor mind. If they were, they might be in a man that were alone in the world, as well as his senses and passions.[11]

Hobbes recast international law in godless terms and challenged his critics to prove the utility, if not the reality, of justice. Moreover, Hobbes' individual was ripped out from nature. Even in the state of nature, interpersonal recognition seems limited to threat—which in turn implies recognition of shared cognition, desires, fear of death, and mutually assured destruction. Hobbesian international law hinged on individual psychology, not providence or revelation. Reason, speech, religion, 'acquired wit', and a host of other characteristics made humans very different from other animals, according to Hobbes, and in need of international law in ways animals never are. Shunning the conventional starting points of divine will in its scriptural and natural manifestations, Hobbes' radical epistemology placed individuals at the core of his ontology of natural and constitutional law, and individualised, fallible sovereigns at the heart of international law. Modern conceptualisations of human rights and international criminal responsibility are built the same way and fundamentally depart from everything pre-Hobbesian, despite occasional cosmetic similarities with, for instance, scholastic or Jesuit rights language.[12]

3.2 Richard Cumberland (1632-1718)

Cumberland's *De legibus naturae* (1672) had a tremendous (and now underappreciated) impact on the evolution of international law.[13] Aimed against Hobbes, it was cited extensively by Pufendorf when he himself was accused of Hobbism.[14] Pufendorf's adaptations of Cumberland were, in turn, extensively borrowed by Thomasius, Wolff, and other luminaries who cited Cumberland early and often. Cumberland made Hobbism more palatable to those unprepared to accept its atheistic implications. In Cumberland's system, some wrongful acts were punished in

[11] Thomas Hobbes, *Leviathan or The Matter, Forme and Power of a Common Wealth Ecclesiasticall and Civil* (London: Andrew Crooke 1651), ch. xiii.

[12] Harro Höpfl, *Jesuit Political Thought: The Society of Jesus and the State, c. 1540–1640* (Cambridge: CUP 2004); Edelstein, *On the Spirit of Rights* 2019 (n. 5), 76-77.

[13] Linda Kirk, *Richard Cumberland and Natural Law: Secularisation of Thought in Seventeenth-Century England* (Cambridge: James Clarke & Co. 1987).

[14] Jon Parkin, foreword, xvii, in Richard Cumberland, *A Treatise of the Law of Nature* (John Maxwell (ed. & tr.), Indianapolis IN: Liberty Fund 2005).

the afterlife, and theology and scriptural exegesis were at least potentially relevant in reconstructing *ius gentium* in the sense of the universal law that applied to all individuals (if not in the sense of *ius inter gentes*).[15] In the genealogy of international law, the tension between the standing, rights, and responsibilities of one individual towards all, on the one hand, and between the individual's standing as derived from inter-State law, on the other hand, resurfaced several times.[16]

Like Hobbes, Cumberland also attempted to build his theory of international law on the physiology of individuals. The natural science of the human body and mind proved, according to Cumberland, that humans were biologically capable of taming and redirecting the passions that naturally arose in their organs.[17] This ability in turn imposed a duty of self-control for others' sake, as well as a duty of self-control and self-improvement for the individual's own sake, since individuals owed themselves the duty to effectively pursue their own greatest happiness, which was unthinkable if passions were allowed to run amok.[18] Self-love is just only when limited by and oriented towards the common good.[19] Rightly self-governed, individuals never lose sight of 'the greatest possible *Happiness of every particular person*'.[20] Individuals' physiological capacity for, and their self- and other-regarding duties to pursue, self-control and self-improvement prove that the state of nature is not a condition of necessary war. Hobbes' pretence to the contrary destroys cardinal elements of international law, including diplomatic immunity and the ability to enter trade agreements.[21]

Individuals are both sociable and need others for happiness, Cumberland thought, and are also best understood when considered in society.[22] Therefore they naturally and inevitably arrive at the concept of the common good, and can judge their own and others' actions by the common good standard. Moreover, any *ius gentium* must assume that individuals can regulate their passions and fully grasp what is and what is not conducive to the common good.[23] Even the famously contested individual right to self-defence must be defined and adjudicated only in the context of the common good; and in the light of reason.[24] From the

[15] Cumberland, Essay I, iii.27; *Inquiry*, I.i.ii-iii.290-1, in *Treatise* 2005 (n. 14).

[16] Arguably, the nuance in Cumberland's distinction between international law as natural law for all individuals or as positive inter-State law (previously known as, respectively, primary and secondary international law) would have pre-empted or at least clarified Lauterpacht's and Lemkin's disagreement about formulating doctrines of individual responsibility under international criminal law after the Holocaust. Philippe Sands, *East West Street* (London: Weidenfeld & Nicolson 2017), esp. 112-13, 291, and 349.

[17] Cumberland, *Inquiry* 2005 (n. 14), ch. II, e.g. xxvi-xxviii.440-51.

[18] *ibid*, II.viii.382-83, V.ix.516-17, V.xvi.530-31, V.xxviii-xxix.556-59, V.xlv-xlvi.606-11, xlviii.614, VI.ii.652, VIII.ii.685-86, *passim*.

[19] *ibid*, VIII.vii.694.

[20] *ibid*, V.xvi.529. Also see V.xxxv.570-71.

[21] *ibid*, ch. V, e.g. V.lv.634-36.

[22] *ibid*, I.i.iv.293, vi.295, xiii.308, II.ii.366, *passim*.

[23] *ibid*, I.xiv.310; xix.317-18.

[24] *ibid*, I.xxiii.327-28; xxxi.349.

social definition of the individual also follows the presumption of shared rationality and a shared knowledge of natural facts ('practical reason') that, according to Cumberland, include moral facts, grounded as they are in observable nature and human physiology.[25]

Cumberland also takes the individual/State analogy into interesting directions. He accepts that the analogy is valid and adds that since individuals collaborate and depend on individuals who are physically closest to them, States too must develop special relations with contiguous and nearby sovereign States.[26] The same practical reason that inevitably prompts individuals in close proximity to recognise their interdependence and their legal obligation to help one another (in keeping with their duties to both each other and to themselves) also prompts States to recognise their moral duty of mutual assistance, the desirability of peace over war, *pacta sunt servanda*, and other international law principles.[27] Individuals who correctly understand that their self-interest is best served by pursuing the common good come together to form political States upon this understanding. Therefore, according to Cumberland, inter-State relations are shaped by a body of public international law that derives its authority and principles from individuals' intention for original State formation and ongoing State preservation.

This is not to deny that municipal legal systems diverge due to historical and practical reasons; but the welfare needs of global society that shapes international law sets limits to the range in which such divergence can lawfully take place. Within these perimeters, international law will support win-win scenarios of inter-State interaction, including commerce and military alliance, even if the States interacting are constitutionally wildly diverse.[28] Here Cumberland derives international law, including general principles and detailed diplomatic and commercial provisions, fully from the natural laws applicable to individuals. Thus, unlike for Hobbes, Cumberland's individuals cannot delegate their autonomy and rights to a sovereign to such a degree that domestic laws and concerns could trump humanity's clear common concerns and the body of international law meant to protect them.[29]

The role of individual interest and judgement as the original and ultimate source of domestic and international law is the reason why princes, magistrates,

[25] *ibid*, II.v.378, vii.380.

[26] *ibid*, I.xxxiv.357.

[27] *ibid*, II.xv.400-01, V.xliii.600-01.

[28] *ibid*, IX.viii.717-18.

[29] Cumberland's train of thought here rhymes with the extraordinary history of British courts expanding habeas corpus into a global norm: Paul D. Halliday, *Habeas Corpus: From England to Empire* (Cambridge, MA: Belknap Press 2010); Geoffrey Robertson, *Crimes Against Humanity: The Struggle for Global Justice* (4th edn, London: Penguin 2012), 2. Harry Potter, *Law, Liberty and the Constitution: A Brief History of the Common Law* (Woodbridge: The Boydell Press 2015), ch. 16 on John Lilburne and ch. 18 on slavery. On countervailing applications of the laws of war to nullify habeas corpus extended into international law, see John M. Collins, *Martial Law and English Law* (Cambridge: CUP 2016), 199 and 248.

judges, and other public representatives may not deviate from the optimal path towards preserving peace even out of considerations of reason of state or *salus populi* limited to a particular nation. The common good of all humanity, presumably understood by all individuals, sets concrete limits to such magistrates' power to perform their international legal functions.[30] Municipal laws may not contravene the law of nations—which in turn must harmonise with natural law as identified and actualised by individuals.[31]

3.3 Samuel Pufendorf (1632-1694) and followers

Pufendorf, holder of the first chair in international law, published the first version of *De jure naturae et gentium* in 1672, the same year as Cumberland's *De legibus naturae*. A partial comparison of their approach to the standing of individuals in international law is instructive. Pufendorf also began from legal epistemology and ontology, regarded humans as irreducibly social and therefore compelled to establish States, but he defined the resulting States as unitary composite moral persons.[32] This move, absent from Cumberland, proved crucial for Vattel and Kant. Like Cumberland, Pufendorf subscribed to the individual/State analogy and deployed the state of nature as a legal fiction for this purpose;[33] but he set limits to the analogy by admitting that due to limited emotional and epistemic capacity, individuals would never reliably recognise that their individual self-interest and self-love aligned with the common good of all humanity. Instead of striving to juridify and institutionalise harmony between individual and universal interests, States are a realistic instrument for shoehorning humanity into manageable units with which individuals can meaningfully identify; and if a problem under international law demands a greater scope or agent, States with similar cultures, languages, and interests can form so-called State-systems.[34] Individuals are wild and ungovernable, and history proves that the only practical way to bring them together is to form States. States must therefore serve as the primary unit of any international order.[35] At the same time, both the creation and survival of the State depends, ultimately, on trust (and trustworthiness) between individuals.

30 Cumberland, *Inquiry* 2005 (n. 14), VII.xi-xiii.680-83.

31 ibid, VIII.iii.687-88.

32 Samuel Pufendorf, *Two Books of the Elements of Universal Jurisprudence* (Thomas Behme (ed.) and William Abbott Oldfather (ed. & tr.) Indianapolis, IN: Liberty Fund 2009), VII.2.13.

33 Michael Seidler, Introduction, 40-42 in Samuel Pufendorf, *An Introduction to the History of the Principal Kingdoms and States of Europe* (Michael Seidler (ed.) and Jodocus Crull (tr.), Indianapolis, IN: Liberty Fund 2013).

34 Pufendorf, *Elements* 2009 (n. 32), II.5.1, 368; David Grewal, 'From the State of Nature to the State of Economy: Pufendorf on Commerce and Natural Law', in Somos and Peters, *The State of Nature* 2021 (n. 6), 177-215.

35 Pufendorf, *An Introduction to the History of the Principal Kingdoms and States of Europe* (Michael Seidler (ed.) and Jodocus Crull (tr.), Indianapolis, IN: Liberty Fund 2013), I.1.13, I.15.31; Ben Holland, *The Moral Person of the State: Pufendorf, Sovereignty and Composite Polities* (Cambridge: CUP 2017).

Though fidelity has long been a key notion, and Johannes Althusius, Grotius, and others have traced the interlinked operations of trust in families, cities, States, and inter-State relations, Pufendorf's systematisation of trust consolidated the standing of the individual in international law in a way that sceptics of the State's moral character could not. The moral aspects of trust and fidelity that all human entities, from individuals to humanity writ large, shared according to Pufendorf made the individual's rights, duties, and opinions more directly linked to international law than for Grotius, for instance, for whom States' moral character was not of the same order as individuals', and who left room for reason of state and the delegation of rights to morally override individual considerations.[36]

In his 1686 *Teutsche Reden*, Veit Ludwig von Seckendorff (1626-1692) pointed out that while municipal laws and laws derived from Christianity are known and accepted only by some nations, the reasoning through which natural law is identified is common to all. Right reason and observable facts form a firmer foundation for deciding matters of war, peace, and inter-State commerce than do either religion or laws applicable or inferable from municipal or imperial laws. In other words, international law is particularly compatible with logic and science and particularly incompatible with religion and parochialism.[37] Inspired by Pufendorf, Johann Christoph Becmann (1641-1717), a Calvinist scholar in Frankfurt, influentially argued that subjects had a personal international human right to religious toleration.[38] Becmann's contemporary, the Franeker and Leiden law professor Gerard Noodt (1647-1725), came to the same conclusion.[39]

According to Tuck, Pufendorf was also the inspiration for John Locke's (1632-1704) assertion (refuting Pufendorf) of the individual's natural right to punish, and to property.[40] Locke's rejection of absolute monarchy is, in important ways, the corollary of these natural rights. Those who aim to become absolute monarchs are like pirates, enemies of humankind and lawful targets of the individual right to punish.[41]

[36] Peter Schröder, *Trust in Early Modern Political Thought, 1598-1713* (Cambridge: CUP 2017), ch. 3, which also details the reception of Pufendorf's moral analogy by Adam Friedrich Glafey and Samuel Rachel, also from the period examined here. See further Holland, *The Moral Person* 2017 (n. 35), and Mark Somos, 'Virtue', in Randall Lesaffer and Janne Nijman (eds.), *The Cambridge Companion to Hugo Grotius* (Cambridge: CUP 2021), 91-117. On Pufendorf's Hobbesian method for generating trust through legal fiction, see Ioannis Evrigenis and Mark Somos, 'Rhetorical Strategy and Legal Force in Pufendorf's State of Nature', in Peter Schröder (ed.), *Contexts and Concepts of Pufendorf's Political and Legal International Thought* (Oxford: OUP 2024), 59-82.

[37] Cited approvingly by Christian Thomasius, *Institutes of Divine Jurisprudence, with Selections from Foundations of the Law of Nature and Nations* (Thomas Ahnert (ed. & tr.), Indianapolis, IN: Liberty Fund 2011), Introductory Dissertation, 58-59.

[38] Johann Christoph Becmann, *Dissertatio de jure subditorum circa sacra* (Frankfurt: Christopher Zeitler 1689).

[39] Gerard Noodt, *Dissertatio quarta de religione ab imperio jure gentium libera* (Leiden: Frederik Haaring, 1706).

[40] Richard Tuck, *The Rights of War and Peace* (Oxford: OUP 1999), ch. 6.

[41] John Locke, *Two Treatises of Government* (London: Awnsham Churchill 1689), ch. 16, para. 176 and ch. 19, para. 228.

Pufendorf endorsed Hobbes' and Cumberland's attempt to ground international law in the epistemic and moral autonomy of individuals, and sided with Hobbes' rejection of the kind of cosmopolitanism with legal effect that Cumberland preferred. However, Pufendorf's State-system introduced a medium between State- and humanity-driven international law, opening a path to the schemes of alliances and federations that ran through Vattel and Kant to the genesis of the Holy Alliance(s), the League of Nations, and the United Nations. In such schemes, individuals' characteristics, including their language, culture, and religion, enabled organisations that united such individuals to claim international legal superiority over those who did not share such characteristics. Furthermore, Pufendorf's emphasis on trust in relationships between individuals, individuals and States, and between States, further extended the individual/State analogy of his predecessors and helped to endow the State with moral characteristics that would be used, by Hegel and others, to diminish the individual's practical standing in international law.[42]

3.4 Christian Thomasius (1655-1728)

Marx did not invent the argument that established religion is institutionally incentivised to keep the masses in ignorance: it is originally a Protestant argument against Catholics. Christian Thomasius was one of the most influential jurists to argue that the clergy tricked the general public into 'blind ignorance' and subverted social and political order by attacking secular rulers.[43]

Thomasius followed Pufendorf in grounding international law in epistemology. Individuals should find the laws of nature for themselves and they could do so because they were rational, Thomasius believed; but reasoning required words, and words gained their meaning from interaction and agreement with other individuals.[44] That is why there can be no solipsist epistemology of international law, and why the attribution of criminal responsibility to individuals requires showing *mens rea*.[45]

In addition to the fact and logical necessity of social interaction, another constraint on the proliferation of individual rights is self-love. According to Thomasius, individuals have duties towards themselves, including developing and exercising

[42] Contrast Vázquez de Menchaca's stance in his 1564 *Controversarium* on natural liberty of all humans as a bulwark against civilisational or religious claims to collective superiority. Benjamin Straumann, *Roman Law in the State of Nature: The Classical Foundations of Hugo Grotius' Natural Law* (Cambridge: CUP 2015), 133.

[43] Christian Thomasius, Essay 1, 'On the History of Natural Law until Grotius', first published in 1707 as the foreword to the first German translation of Grotius' *De iure belli ac pacis*, in Christian Thomasius, *Essays on Church, State, and Politics* (Ian Hunter, Thomas Ahnert, and Frank Grunert (eds. & trs.), Indianapolis, IN: Liberty Fund 2007), 1-48, at 23.

[44] Thomasius, *Institutes* 2011 (n. 37) I.iv. §§ 51-55; *Foundation of the Law of Nature and Nations*, Introduction, § 29, 578.

[45] Thomasius, *Institutes* 2011 (n. 37), I.i. § 66, 71, 72-73.

self-control not to encroach upon other individuals' rights. A person without self-control is unlikely to do well in society, therefore self-love, rightly understood, checks the passion for self-aggrandisement (*libido dominandi*).[46] Thomasius agrees with Cumberland that recognition of others begins with self-recognition as sociable, not only as vulnerable.

But Thomasius follows Hobbes, not Cumberland in bestowing extensive powers on the prince as an individual, so he could protect the people from overweening clerics.[47] Reclaiming conscience as the individual's inalienable internal forum afforded individuals powers that were difficult to conceptualise without the Reformation. As long as priestly and papal authority and biblical interpretation were essential for salvation, the arc for individuals' standing under international law would bend towards insignificance.[48]

Though the primary theatre of war was sovereign legal authority, adiaphora (*Mitteldinge*) were an important battleground. It was one thing to pit sovereign against pope, and municipal against ecclesiastical law. It was quite another to argue that Scripture rightly read was remarkably minimalist about external right conduct, and stripping out millennia of non-scriptural rituals from civil law would reduce to a minimum the scope of individual conduct that either Church or State could lawfully control.[49] If Moses told you to do it, it is Jewish and does not apply.[50] If Jesus told you to do it, it is largely internal and extra-legal. If the Church told you to do it, they are almost certainly wrong and/or lying.[51] If you are wrong about religion, you may go to Hell, though if it is an honest mistake, God will forgive you. In either case, neither the sovereign nor the Church has higher epistemic authority than the individual.[52] In fact, everything that does not affect social order is outside the prince's scope of authority—and the prince's authority over external conduct involving religion is still greater than the clergy's.[53] Thomasius, citing Pufendorf, crucially asserts that 'Christ's kingdom is not of this world, and has nothing in common with civil or human power'.[54] There can be neither political nor religious reason for law to infringe on individual rights to freedom of religion and conscience. Thomasius rendered the separation between Church and State, and between collective and individual responsibility for salvation, almost impermeable. The only exceptions are atheists who, unmotivated by fear of eternal death, cannot

[46] *ibid*, II.ix § 132, 282.

[47] Thomasius, Essay 2, in Thomasius, *Essays on Church, State, and Politics* 2011 (n. 43), 52, § 8.

[48] *ibid*, 60-61, §4; Evrigenis, *Images* 2014 (n. 10).

[49] Thomasius, Essay 4, 'Is Heresy a Punishable Crime?', in Thomasius, *Essays on Church, State, and Politics* 2011 (n. 43), 172 'those who claim that heresy is a punishable crime do not know what faith is'.

[50] Thomasius, Essay 2 (n. 47), 66, § 6.

[51] 'It would be papist to want to exclude jurists from Holy Scripture.' *ibid*, 62, § 4. See also 64, § 5; 68, § 8.

[52] Thomasius, Essay 4 (n. 49), VII.175, 203.

[53] Thomasius, Essay 6, 'On the Right of a Christian Prince in Religious Matters', in Thomasius, *Essays on Church, State, and Politics* 2011 (n. 43), 257-58.

[54] *ibid*, 264.

be trusted by Christian princes to hold social order dear; and zealots (whether Catholic, Protestant, or non-Christian), who believe their religion can justify opposing their prince.[55]

Grounded in the state of nature, individuals hold separately and collectively a pre- and supra-political right to peace among all individuals.[56] The problem with international law, according to Thomasius, is that 'the security of individuals receives too little attention in it'.[57] In terms of norms and priorities, Thomasius called for a humanisation of international law, but noted that individuals' rights are secondary to the rights of all humanity. Marriage, for instance, is primarily aimed at procreation, which is a species-level good. The other consequence of marriage, namely the suppression of extramarital lust, is a secondary benefit because it only helps the individual.[58] Natural laws concerning procreation, such as bans on incest, polygamy, and adultery, are therefore part of international law, rightly understood.[59]

Combining secularising, state of nature, and psychological arguments, Thomasius was a fierce critic of international law's neglect of individuals' security and a staunch advocate of deriving international law from individual moral and epistemic autonomy. Even if he prioritised the welfare of humanity over individual rights, Thomasius was sceptical enough of political and religious authorities' will and ability to protect that collective welfare to regard international law as a key arena for securing individual liberties.

3.5 Johann Gottlieb Heineccius (1681-1741)

Heineccius studied law at Halle under Thomasius, among others, and taught law at Halle and Frankfurt. His 1738 *Elementa juris naturae et gentium*, translated into English and annotated by George Turnbull in 1763, became a key conduit for Halle's humanisation of international law via the secularising individualisation of religion and the epistemic and juridical autonomy that was accorded to individuals by expanding the role of the state of nature in international legal theory. To an extent, Heineccius moderated the secularising arguments of Thomasius, since Halle's theologians forced Christian Wolff to leave, but recalled Heineccius. Heineccius even amended Grotius' *etiamsi daremus* clause to argue that individuals would have duties to God even if no society existed.[60] Nonetheless, Heineccius' moderation

[55] *ibid*, 273-74.
[56] Thomasius, *Institutes* 2011 (n. 37), III.i § 47, 361-02.
[57] *ibid*, III.i § 53, 363.
[58] *ibid*, III.i § 71, 379.
[59] *ibid*, III.iii.
[60] Johann Gottlieb Heineccius, *Elementa Iuris Naturae et Gentium: Methodical System of Universal Law: Or, the Laws of Nature and Nations* (first published 1738, this edn: Thomas Ahnert and Peter Schröder (eds.), with supplements and a discourse by George Turnbull, Indianapolis, IN: Liberty Fund 2008), I.iii.lxxv.60-61.

in reallocating religious autonomy from Pope and Church to the individual was mostly ornamental.

Like Thomasius (and Cicero), Heineccius thought that natural reason was necessary and sufficient to discover the laws of nature and nations, and the presumption that all individuals could access natural reason was equivalent to promulgating these laws and rendering individuals responsible for their observance.[61] I have not, however, found a passage in Heineccius where he followed the mature Thomasius in elaborating a social model of legal epistemology in which individuals could only develop their understanding of natural and international law through initial recognition and concomitant interactions with other individuals.

The individual's state of nature right to self-defence never wholly disappears in Heineccius.[62] The state of nature is a condition of equality and liberty, and individual rights to equality and liberty cannot be wholly alienated by entering any kind of polity.[63] The authority of all executives, legislatives, and municipal legal systems is not only delimited by but it is also directly proportionate to the individual's need for security, which was their motive for leaving the state of nature for the polity in the first place.[64] Reiterating a disavowed Hobbesian distinction, Heineccius argues that while individuals remain in full possession of their original state of nature rights, they surrender the right to judge the sovereigns' intentions to honour or violate the subjects' rights.[65] It is not a stretch to argue that the state of nature rights discourse of this period is the direct precursor to today's international human rights law.[66] Unlike Pufendorf, Heineccius holds that it is possible to become intellectually, economically, and even culturally self-sufficient in the state of nature.[67] Hobbes is wrong that the state of nature is a state of war, but he is right that the laws applicable to individuals in a state of nature are analogous to international law guiding the relationship between States, which are as radically and naturally equal as individuals were in a state of nature.[68]

In a remarkable twist, Heineccius distinguishes between the rights of sovereigns towards their own subjects and towards foreigners. Much of international law, including war and peace, alliances, treaties, and diplomatic laws, falls under the purview of the sovereign's individual rights towards foreigners.[69] This is a curious half-way house or evolutionary side-track in the development of the legal

[61] *ibid*, I.i.xi.18. From this, Turnbull derived the first law of nature to be the individual's duty to remain reasonable. *ibid*, vii.565.

[62] *ibid*, I.vii.clxxxiii.13637.

[63] *ibid*, II.i.iii-vii.324-27, II.vii.cxxvii.439. Though see II.iv.lxxvii.384-85: some individuals have naturally servile minds and can be lawfully kept in servitude.

[64] *ibid*, II.vii.cxxix.441.

[65] *ibid*, II.vii.cxxx.442.

[66] Mark Somos, *American States of Nature: The Origins of Independence, 1761-1775* (Oxford: OUP 2019).

[67] Heineccius, *Elementa Iuris* 2008 (n. 60), II.vi.c-ci.406-07.

[68] *ibid*, II.i.xx.336, II.ix.clxxxviii-cxc.498-500.

[69] *ibid*, II.vii.cxxxiii-cxxxv.450-52.

standing of the individual in international law. While cautiously expanding human rights, Heineccius also shifts responsibility for international legal acts to the sovereign. Vattel's radical transmutation of *ancien regime* princes' individual rights into princely responsibility for war crimes, and his equally radical expansion of human rights, are a continuation of the same swing.

3.6 Emer de Vattel (1714-1767)

Taught by Burlamaqui in Geneva and self-trained in Grotius and Wolff in Neuchâtel, Vattel became a defining authority for Enlightenment international law. His 1758 *Le Droit des gens: Principes de la loi naturelle, appliqués à la conduite et aux affaires des Nations et des Souverains* began as a translation of and notes on Wolff, and turned into one of the most read and cited textbooks of this period. Vattel drew on the state of nature device and accepted the individual/State analogy,[70] but only to a certain extent. He sought to chart a course between the Roman and German reduction of international law to natural law among States, and what many saw as Grotius' excessive positivism that took State practice and treaties as its starting point to work backwards towards first principles.[71] Importantly, Vattel's God is not sovereign over all States, as for Cumberland. The individual/State analogy is limited by Vattel's view that no such common arbitrator is even possible, just as no amount of conquest or alliance-building could produce a universal monarchy.

Vattel began building his system by examining individuals, but reverted to scholastic and Pufendorfian *debilitas*, inability to survive alone, as the feature of individuals most salient to uncovering international law.[72] States, by contrast, can be reasonably self-sufficient, and a 'state or civil society is a subject very different from an individual'. To survive, individuals not only delegate but surrender some of their state of nature rights when they combine into States.[73] States, however, are perfectly free. Even when they violate foundational norms, other States can retaliate, but cannot rightfully judge or morally condemn them.[74] As if in a state of nature, States are perfectly equal: a 'dwarf is as much a man as a giant; a small republic is no

[70] Emer de Vattel, *The Law of Nations, Or, Principles of the Law of Nature, Applied to the Conduct and Affairs of nations and Sovereigns, with Three Early Essays on the Origin and Nature of Natural Law and on Luxury* (transl. first published 1797, this edn: Béla Kapossy and Richard Whatmore (eds.), Indianapolis, IN: Liberty Fund 2008), Preliminaries, § 11, 73; II.i, § 3, 262; II.xviii, § 324, 448; III.xii, § 188, 589; IV.i, § 2, 652; Edward J. Kolla, 'Written in the Hearts of People? Natural and International Law during the Age of Enlightenment', in Somos and Peters (eds.), *State of Nature* 2021 (n. 6), 246-73.

[71] Vattel, *Law of Nations* 2008 (n. 70), Preface, 12.

[72] *ibid*, Preface, 15; Preliminaries, § 8, 71. For more on *debilitas*, see Mark Somos, 'Political Thought and the Historiography of International Law', in Anne Peters and Randall Lesaffer (eds.), *The Cambridge History of International Law*, Vol. 1 (Cambridge: CUP 2024), 107-35.

[73] Vattel, *Law of Nations* 2008 (n. 70), Preliminaries, § 4, 68-69.

[74] *ibid*, Preliminaries, § 8, 71; II.i, § 7, 265.

less a sovereign state than the most powerful kingdom'.[75] In Vattel, the individual/ State moral analogy becomes the direct source of State recognition.

Vattel continues adapting and redeploying Wolff's characterisation of States as unitary moral entities.[76] Just as Thomasius and Heineccius emphasised that individuals' self-love and duty towards themselves constitute the foundation of obligations among all people, and also authorise and limit the power of States, Vattel built on the self-love and duties of States (as moral entities) towards themselves and each other.[77] Once individuals have duly created the State, it becomes obliged to preserve itself, the same way individuals must. It is meaningful to discuss the State's duty to preserve and improve itself and to pursue its own happiness, and the State can only protect itself by protecting the individuals who constitute it.[78] While States are legally obliged not to interfere with or maliciously hinder other States from self-preservation and self-improvement, actively helping other States is at most a moral, never a legal duty.[79] Justice among mutually recognised States is more vital than justice among individuals, precisely because States are more powerful and have greater capacity to cause harm.[80]

This is a very different line of causality and set of priorities than what we find in Thomasius, let alone Hobbes. By reversing Wolff's process of creating norms and authorisation in international law, which runs from individuals to States, Vattel made it easy for the likes of Hegel and Fichte to first anthropomorphise, then deify the State, and relegate individuals into relative insignificance.[81] Yet it would be unfair to blame Vattel for Hegel. While he used the *debilitas* thesis to turn States into the primary unit of international law's analysis, Vattel also raised the legitimating power of the interests and active participation of individuals to a higher level than Locke, Pufendorf, and others who argued that simply being born into and residing in a State automatically constitute tacit consent to the rule of the incumbent; or that given their *debilitas*, individuals surrender their natural rights in exchange for the State's protection. For Vattel, by contrast, individuals' original intent continues to circumscribe State power—even when another sovereign conquers a given State.[82] So do individuals' state of nature rights, such as the right to live somewhere. When someone is exiled and her or his previous State severs all ties, other States cannot keep that individual stateless by refusing to allow her or him to settle down.[83] In

[75] *ibid*, Preliminaries, § 17, 75. States have state of nature duties towards each other: II.xii, § 178 and 352.

[76] Ere Nokkala, 'The Development of the Law of Nations: Wolff and Vattel', in Peter Schröder (ed.), *Concepts and Contexts in Vattel's Political and Legal Thought* (Cambridge: CUP 2021), 64-83.

[77] Vattel, *Law of Nations* 2008 (n. 70), I.ii, § 10 and 85.

[78] *ibid*, I.ii, §§ 16-21, 87-89; II.i, § 4, 262-63.

[79] *ibid*, II.i, § 18, 272.

[80] *ibid*, II.v, § 63, 296; II.xviii, § 339, 459, on how much more dangerous retaliation is between States than between individuals.

[81] See Van Hulle, 'Nineteenth Century' (chapter 6), in this volume.

[82] Vattel, *Law of Nations* 2008 (n. 70), I.v, § 69, 123.

[83] *ibid*, I.xix, §§ 229-30, 226-27; II.ix, § 125, 323.

case of emergency, individuals reactivate 'a remnant of the primitive freedom' and can, for instance in a storm, demand assistance.[84] When push comes to shove, State interests do not override individual rights; but the reverse remains true, as it was in Aquinas.

The underlying presence of individual authorisation and interests does not of course render States helpless. The individual right to self-defence is, according to Vattel, wholly transferred to the State when individuals leave the state of nature.[85] The right to declare war belongs to the government, not the people.[86] Consequently, it is essential to distinguish between private and public enemies, and to guarantee the rights that belong to the latter, as well as to innocent civilians caught up in armed conflict.[87]

Vattel departs from Thomasius and Wolff not only in presenting individuals as self-insufficient and States as at least potentially self-sufficient, but also by siding with Pufendorf concerning the inability of individuals to reliably identify with the interests of humanity as a whole.

> This love of their country is natural to all men. The good and wise author of nature has taken care to bind them, by a kind of instinct, to the places where they received their first breath, and they love their own nation, as a thing with which they are intimately connected. But it often happens that some causes unhappily weaken or destroy this natural impression. The injustice or the severity of the government too easily effaces it from the hearts of the subjects: can self-love attach an individual to the affairs of a country where every thing is done with a view to a single person?—far from it:—we see, on the contrary, that free nations are passionately interested in the glory and the happiness of their country. Let us call to mind the citizens of Rome in the happy days of the republic, and consider, in modern times, the English and the Swiss.
>
> The love and affection a man feels for the state of which he is a member, is a necessary consequence of the wise and rational love he owes to himself, since his own happiness is connected with that of his country.[88]

Note that while Cumberland took care to construct an international legal system in which States with very diverse cultures and constitutions can cooperate; and while Vattel emphasised the equality of all States, which in principle should allow

[84] *ibid*, I.xxiii, § 287, 253; II.ix, §§ 119-20, 320-21.
[85] *ibid*, I.xiii, § 169, 191.
[86] *ibid*, III.i, § 4, 470.
[87] *ibid*, III.v, § 69, 509; III.viii, § 141, 545; III.viii, § 145, 549; III.viii, § 147, 550; III.viii, § 158, 563: 'Let us never forget that our enemies are men. Though reduced to the disagreeable necessity of prosecuting our right by force of arms, let us not divest ourselves of that charity which connects us with all mankind. Thus shall we courageously defend our country's rights without violating those of human nature'; also III.x, § 174, 575.
[88] *ibid*, I.xi, §§ 119-20, 152.

Vattel to follow Cumberland's lead on this score; Vattel nevertheless presents republics as more compatible with the very institution of a State than any other form of government. In this respect, he is again a precursor to a theme that came to dominate international thought from the late eighteenth century, sometimes known as democratic peace theory, according to which it is in the interest of democracies to nudge or even push non-democratic States towards democracy, because an international order of democracies is inherently stable and peaceful.[89]

Turning the State into the primary unit of analysis and agent of international law does not mean, however, that Vattel gives up on universal society. A good State mediates between the individual and humanity. Instead of narrowing the individual's reason and passions, the State helps the individual to anchor and direct them towards an even greater good. 'Universal society', as created by nature before humans invented States, is best approached via States;[90] individuals' disorderly passions and imperfect reason would make it naively idealistic not to interpose the State between individuals and humanity.[91]

According to Vattel, alliances between princes are personal and entirely improper if formed to protect States. Real alliances for this purpose have nothing to do with the prince, even if he negotiated and signed the treaties of alliance.[92] The contracts of princes are private and akin to all private contracts. Extreme caution must be taken to ensure that a prince's private contracts, including debts (even if the prince chose to spend the money on affairs of State) never affect the State.[93] Extraordinarily for his times, Vattel argued that the sovereign who takes his State into an unjust war is solely and personally responsible for the consequences, and must be punished and make reparations without any contribution from his State; he even added that it is 'generally the prince alone who occasions the war'.[94] By contrast, the power to make peace belongs to the nation, not the king.[95] Vattel devotes considerable effort to ensuring that the sovereign's personal capacity becomes hermetically separated from the State's interests.

Vattel's break was radical but one should not exaggerate its originality. As we saw, Heineccius subsumed much of international law under the Sovereign's private rights towards foreigners; and defined the duties of subjects in terms of the rights of the Sovereign towards them.[96] Heineccius also rejected Grotius' distinction

[89] Vattel denies that the form of government makes a difference, but he is not consistent on this score: *ibid*, II.iii, § 38, 282; II.xii, § 185, 356: republics form better alliances, because their treaties of alliance are clearly not based on the personal achievement and preference of a monarch. Republican alliances are also unaffected by the death of signatories. II.xii, § 192, 361.

[90] *ibid*, II.i, § 10, 267.

[91] *ibid*, II.i, § 16, 268-69.

[92] *ibid*, II.xii, § 186, 355.

[93] *ibid*, II.xiv, § 213, 383; II.xiv, § 216, 384-85.

[94] *ibid*, III.xi, §§ 183-185, 586-8. Citation from III.xiii, § 201, 600. It is in this sense that Potter writes: 'Nuremberg had completed what the trial of Charles I began.' 2015 (n. 29), 283.

[95] *ibid*, IV.ii, § 13, 659.

[96] Heineccius, *Elementa Iuris* 2008 (n. 60), II.x.ccxxii-ccxxiii, 523.

between patrimonial and all other States.[97] It was unsustainable, according to Heineccius, to define a State as the private property of any individual.[98] While royal families can legitimately pursue their dynastic interests, they must distinguish them from the public interest.[99] This was an important conceptual move towards a redefinition of individuals as both at the centre of international human rights law and as radically equal. Vattel posited, perhaps unfairly, that Wolff uncritically accepted patrimonial kingdoms and thus became an enemy of freedom.[100] Heineccius' and Vattel's violent opposition to the legitimacy of all patrimonial States, where kings and queens own the State, marked a fundamental shift for the standing of individuals in international law.[101]

4. Conclusion

The 140 years between the Treaty of Westphalia and the trial of Charles I in 1648, and the opening salvos of the French Revolution and the first ratification of the US Bill of Rights in 1789, saw an intensely creative burst of legal theory and practice regarding the status of the individual in international law. In this chapter, secularisation, epistemology, and the legal fiction of the state of nature helped to reconstruct how individuals gained international legal standing at the State's expense in the applicable theories of Hobbes, Cumberland, and Thomasius; how the sovereign reclaimed powers and rights from the individual in the system of Heineccius; and how the legal standing of the individual and the State rose in tandem in Pufendorf and Vattel as the scope of law expanded and incorporated new formal inventions, such as the moralisation and depersonalisation of the State or the State-system.

Yet despite the richness of this period, there is scant evidence of a narrowing or crystallisation of plausible ways to address the standing of the individual in international law. The scope of debate and practice opened wider: it was not until the late nineteenth century that Hobbes' radical epistemic and natural law autonomy, Cumberland's cosmopolitan limits on domestic legislation, or the legal effects of Pufendorf's state of nature began to lose demonstrative appeal, and it took even longer for the deep moralisation of the State by Thomasius, Vattel, and their nineteenth- and twentieth-century followers to begin to ring increasingly hollow.

[97] Emile Simpson, 'States and Patrimonial Kingdoms: Hugo Grotius's Account of Sovereign Entities in *The Rights of War and Peace*' *Grotiana* 39 (2018), 45-76.

[98] Heineccius, *Elementa Iuris* 2008 (n. 60), II.vii.cxlv-cxlvi, 459-60.

[99] ibid, II.ix.ccix, 514.

[100] Vattel, *Law of Nations* 2008 (n. 70), Preface, 13.

[101] For the political context, including a distinction between patrimonial absolutism and (equally unsustainable) patrimonial constitutionalism, see Ertman, *Birth of Leviathan* 1997 (n. 3); For a precise and nuanced overview, see Edelstein, *On the Spirit of Rights* 2019 (n. 5).

6

The Individual in International Law in the Nineteenth Century, 1789-1914

Inge Van Hulle

1. Introduction

The nineteenth century is the age in which State-centrism reigned supreme in international legal theory. This is reflected in the historiography of international law of the nineteenth century, in that 'the history of international law has been predominantly about the relations between European states, understood more or less analogously to individuals in a domestic political community'.[1] The nineteenth century might have idealised territorial sovereignty and the nation-State, but the rapid transformations of technology in communication and transport meant that the horizon of individuals became more global. As individuals together with their crimes, capital, goods, and humanitarian sentiments travelled abroad, so did the potential for conflicts that might trigger international legal action.

The story of the history of international law and its relationship with the individual can be told in a myriad of different ways: the individual as a theorist of international law, as a participant or lobbyist of international law, as (unwitting) international law-makers. I propose that one way to read the role of the individual in nineteenth-century international law is by investigating precisely those moments when individuals acting alone or collectively challenged the status quo by subverting or, alternatively, by reinforcing State authority in international law. Such a particular focus has the potential to offer a broad perspective that encompasses all of the above distinct roles that individuals can play in international law's nineteenth-century lifespan. The first part of this chapter offers a theorist's view of international law and examines how State centrism seeped into legal doctrine, while—at the same time—the increased cross-border activities of individuals spawned discussions by international lawyers of new sub-themes and fields of inquiry which constituted a reflection in legal theory of a state practice that was concerned with especially the economic behaviour of individuals overseas. The second and third parts of the chapter focus on individuals as practitioners and

[1] Martti Koskenniemi, 'Expanding Histories of International Law' *American Journal of Legal History* 56 (2016), 104-12, at 105.

Inge Van Hulle, *The Individual in International Law in the Nineteenth Century, 1789-1914* In: *The Individual in International Law.* Edited by: Tom Sparks and Anne Peters, Oxford University Press. © Inge Van Hulle 2024.
DOI: 10.1093/oso/9780198898917.003.0006

lobbyists and zoom in, first, on the proliferation of calls to diplomatic protection and extraterritoriality as an illustration of how international legal norms were used to protect the interests of merchants and investors especially outside of the west. It also shows how the rise of humanitarianism, which started from the premise of providing aid to those suffering in distant lands, was co-opted by western governments often for geo-political or economic interests. While both diplomatic protection and State-sponsored humanitarian initiatives illustrate the efforts that Western governments took to bolster State-authority through international law, the final section, which deals with 'vernacular international law', also indicates the relative freedom of action that individuals often unwittingly held in crafting international legal instruments. A broad and contextual perspective on individuals' different roles in nineteenth-century international law destabilises the conceptual distinction between the international and the domestic and the global and the local as the actions of individuals blurred the boundaries between nation-States.

This chapter discusses public international law and the individual's role in it as it was conceived of in the west. One of the major outcomes of western States' attempts to control individuals and reassert their authority through international law was that it paved the way for an exclusionary international law that expedited free trade imperialism and colonialism to varying success. International law in the hands of western States who wished to facilitate, demarcate, and regulate this cross-border movement of people and capital provided opportunities for some, especially to merchants and investors, while it attempted to curtail or misuse the actions of those on the fringes of society, such as those considered as vagrants, liberated slaves, the colonised, all-too-eager humanitarians, unruly imperial personnel, or ordinary citizens taking up arms.

2. The Individual as a Theorist

2.1 State Centrism

If the history of international law is at first glance difficult to conceive of as an age in which the individual played a central role, it is because contemporary legal theorists leaned heavily towards State centrism. The birth of modern nation-States provided inspiration. The American colonists' cry for independence marked a transition to 'a world of states from a world of empires' that started in 1776 and that fathered revolutions first in France, then in the Caribbean, Spanish America, and west and central Europe.[2] Certainly after the revolutionary wave of 1848 monarchical constitutionalism replaced—with exceptions—estate-based absolutist

[2] David Armitage, *The Declaration of Independence. A Global History* (Cambridge, MA: Harvard University Press 2008), 104.

governmental models. The demise of empires in the west meant that the western international legal arena was now made up of States, an evolution that did not go unnoticed to the learned commentators of international law.

By the end of the eighteenth century a majority of intellectuals agreed that the origins of the State lay in the existence of a voluntary contract among people, albeit that disagreement continued on the exact limits and substance of this contract. In other words, the State was an artificial construct likened to a machine made of its constituent parts. While such 'mechanistic' understandings of the State remained, by the nineteenth century emphasis shifted towards thinking of the State as a natural organism, much like a person, rather than as an artificial construct founded on a contractual basis.[3] This in itself was a continuation of earlier understandings of the State as a person possessing intellect, as put forward, for example, by Samuel Pufendorf (1632-94). Such anthropomorphic thinking was continued by Emer de Vattel (1714-67), who introduced a liberal conception of international law which built on an analogy between the State and the individual.[4] Vattel argued that, much like individuals, States could be considered to be free and independent 'persons', however operating not from a position of sociability but rather in order to secure their own self-preservation and perfection.[5] The State came to be seen as the holder of fundamental rights and duties under international law and as a kind of organism with a mind of its own and, indeed, its own will.[6] Some authors such as Johann Caspar Bluntschli (1808-81) also emphasised the shared moral sense among States as they were founded on the same 'human nature'.[7] States, indeed, had a 'moral nature identical with that of individuals'.[8] Such a theoretical premise guaranteed freedom of action and equality among States, but at the same time also opened the door towards the individualisation of the international order.[9]

Perhaps most importantly, this implied that only states were recognised as subjects of international law. Lassa Oppenheim (1858-1919), for example, argued that even if seemingly heads of States, diplomatic envoys, and even citizens have 'certain rights' whilst on foreign territory, they derived those rights not directly from the law of nations or from certain treaties, but rather from their own

[3] Michael Stolleis, *Public Law in Germany, 1800-1914* (New York, NY: Berghahn Books 2001), 92-93.

[4] Emmanuelle Jouannet, *The Liberal-Welfarist Law of Nations: A History of International Law* (Cambridge: CUP 2012).

[5] Emer de Vattel, *The Law of Nations, Or, Principles of the Law of Nature* (first published 1758, this edn: Béla Kapossy and Richard Whatmore (eds.), Indianapolis, IN: Liberty Fund 2008), book I, [18-21].

[6] Janne Nijman, *The Concept of International Legal Personality: An Inquiry into the History and Theory of International Law* (The Hague: T. M. C. Asser Press 2004), 112.

[7] Johann Caspar Bluntschli, *Das moderne Völkerrecht der civilisierten Staaten* (2nd edn, Nördlingen: C. H. Beck'schen 1872), 2.

[8] See, e.g., William Edward Hall, *A Treatise on International Law* (2nd edn, Oxford: Clarendon Press 1884), 17.

[9] Jean d'Aspremont, 'The Doctrine of Fundamental Rights of States and Anthropomorphic Thinking in International Law' *Cambridge Journal of International and Comparative Law* 503 (2015), 501-20, at 507; Anthony Carty, *The Decay of International Law. A Reappraisal of the Limits of Legal Imagination in International Affairs* (Manchester: Manchester University Press 1986).

municipal law which reflected merely an incorporation into the domestic legal order of international law.[10] The increased focus during the course of the nineteenth century on the State as the most important and, even, the only legitimate actor in international law was impacted significantly by the thought of Georg W. F. Hegel (1770-1831). While Hegel did not occupy himself extensively with international law, he put forward that the individual State was the supreme entity through which the Weltgeist unfolded itself.[11] For Hegel, however, this was particularly the modern German, Protestant State. For international law, one of the implications was that it was the will of the individual State and not the community of States that mattered in deciding whether or not compacts on an international level could be held to be binding.[12]

State centrism was also reflected in the stress on positivist interpretations of international law. International law needed to be premised on the same empirical bases as the natural sciences. At the same time, under the influence of Karl von Savigny (1779-1861), all law—and thus also by extension international law—was seen as the expression of the historically grounded consciousness of the nation.[13] Von Savigny's historical school impacted the importance attached to State practice as contributing to customary law.[14] The individual rules which international law encompassed could be gleaned through scientific empiricism, namely through the systematic gathering and analysis of State practice constituting international custom. International law was considered to emanate first and foremost from the collective will of States. However, the 'historicist' turn in international legal doctrine meant that international law was interpreted along historical lines and on a path set towards progress and enlightenment.[15] This created a tension between universal aspirations and particularist interpretations of international law. International law was considered as a product of western Christianity and—increasingly—of western 'civilization'.[16] It was thus questioned to what extent European diplomatic practices and internationally binding compacts could be concluded with those polities falling outside of the remit of the Christian world.[17]

[10] Lassa Oppenheim, *International Law*, vol. I (2nd edn, London: Longmans, Green and Co. 1912), Ch. III, 363-64.

[11] Georg Wilhelm Friedrich Hegel, *Lectures on the Philosophy of World History* (first published 1822-23, this edn: Cambridge: CUP 1975), 29-30.

[12] Ingo Hueck, 'Pragmatism, Positivism and Hegelianism in the Nineteenth Century. August Wilhelm Heffter's Notion of Public International Law', in Masaharu Yanagihara and Michael Stolleis (eds.), *East Asian and European Perspectives on International Law* (Baden-Baden: Nomos 2004), 41-55, at 48.

[13] Friedrich Carl von Savigny, *System des heutigen Römischen Rechts* (Berlin: Veit 1840).

[14] Anne Orford, *International Law and the Politics of History* (Cambridge: CUP 2021), 237.

[15] See, e.g., Georg Friedrich von Martens, *Traité de droit international*, vol. I (Paris: Marescquains 1883), 252-54.

[16] Jennifer Pitts, *Boundaries of International Law: Law and Empire* (Cambridge, MA: Harvard University Press 2018), 148-50.

[17] Luigi Nuzzo, 'History, Science and Christianity. International Law and Savigny's Paradigm', in Luigi Nuzzo and Miloš Vec (eds.), *Constructing International Law: The Birth of a Discipline* (Frankfurt am Main: Klostermann 2012), 25-50.

2.2 New Areas of Interest among Legal Theorists

While the State enjoyed an exalted position for legal theorists, the increased movement of individuals and their crimes, capital, and goods nevertheless generated a range of doctrinal attention to subject areas that had previously remained only marginal. The question of the legitimacy of forcible intervention on the territory of third States on the basis of the protection of nationals abroad was given unprecedented scrutiny.[18] Closely tied in with this question was the issue of whether or not forcible intervention was allowed for the collection of public debt, or more narrowly, for private monetary claims.[19] The brunt of foreign intervention for the purposes of debt collection had been borne by Latin American States. They became a locus for the doctrinal opposition to western intervention, most famously in the actions of Argentine Minister of Foreign Affairs, Luis María Drago (1859-1921), and the writings of the Argentine jurist, Carlos Calvo (1824-1906). Calvo argued that intervention for private reasons was often merely a ruse by great powers acting on ulterior motives.[20] Carlo also opposed the increasingly adhered to 'standard of civilization' often applied to justify extraterritorial jurisdiction in Latin America, the Middle East, and South East Asia and—as a response—formulated the doctrine of 'national treatment'.[21]

The nineteenth century was also the 'Zeitalter der Vergleichung' or the age of comparative law across borders.[22] This evolution was directly related to States' interests in the rational organisation of the State and of citizens' behaviour. International lawyers, such as the founding-father of the *Revue de droit international et de législation comparée*, Gustave Rolin-Jacquemyns (1835-1902), considered the scientific study of comparative legislation as a step towards progress and even universal justice.[23] This meant that legislative action based on international legal comparisons increasingly penetrated the domestic sphere of individuals. Comparative law manifested itself first in the area of private law which undergirded the property rights of the new industrial class, but was also aimed at the humanisation of criminal law and the rationalisation of constitutional law.[24] Anything and everything that was related to the facilitation of individuals'

[18] See, e.g., Hall, *A Treatise* 1884 (n. 8), 17.

[19] Amos S. Hershey, 'The Calvo and Drago Doctrines' *American Journal of International Law* 1 (1907), 26-45.

[20] Carlos Calvo, *Le droit international théorique et pratique* (4th edn, Berlin: Puttkammer et Mühlbrecht 1887), 348.

[21] See Peters, 'Before Human Rights' (chapter 7), in this volume.

[22] Michael Stolleis, *Nationalität und Internationalität: Rechtsvergleichung im öffentlichen Recht des 19. Jahrhunderts* (Berlin: Akademie des Wissenschaft und der Literatur 1998), 5.

[23] Gustave Rolin-Jaequemyns, 'De l'étude de la législation comparée et du droit international' *Revue de droit international et de législation compare* 1 (1869), 1-17; also quoted in Martti Koskenniemi and Ville Kari, 'A More Elevated Patriotism: The Emergence of International and Comparative Law (Nineteenth Century)', in Heikki Pihlajamäki, Markus D. Dubber, and Mark Godfrey (eds.), *The Oxford Handbook of European Legal History* (Oxford: OUP 2018), 974-1000, at 974.

[24] Stolleis, *Nationalität* 1998 (n. 22), at 5.

access to international trade, travel, and communication fell within the remit of cross-border legal comparisons: adoption, telegraph- and phone communication, patents, etc.[25] However, not all movement was encouraged: the increased cross-border movement of criminal offenders meant that extradition became an important field of study in international law.[26]

Individuals lived their daily lives not just within the confines of the State, but also within that of the 'nation'. Nineteenth-century revolutionary and democratic change 'altered the locus of sovereignty in Europe' by placing 'the people' or 'the nation' at the centre of the State, rather than the abstract and metaphorical person of the monarch.[27] The concept of the 'nation' as a natural bond between people based on a common language, territory, history, and customs proved of major influence to authors such as Italian jurist, Pasquale Stanislao Mancini (1817-88).[28] His vision was that of the nationality principle as an inalienable right of peoples, but also as an ordering principle that in its legal guise could stimulate universal peace and that jurists needed to use as the foundation of international law.[29]

3. The Individual as a Participant and Lobbyist

3.1 Diplomatic Protection and Extraterritoriality

An unprecedented evolution in transport, communication, and industry meant that people were able to move their capital, corporations, and goods abroad, which also increased the risk that such individuals would encounter bodily harm or would lose their investment outside of the remit of their home States. For that, they claimed their States' protection based on the principle of nationality. While citizenship concerned political participation within the domestic confines of the State, nationality identified a State's responsibility vis-à-vis the individual on an international plane. Nationality, indeed, was the secular articulation of affiliation that replaced earlier associations with kinship and religion. By the turn of the twentieth

[25] See, e.g., J. C. Colfavru, *Le droit commercial comparé de la France et de l'Angleterre* (Paris: Cosse et Marchal 1863); Josef Kohler, *Handbuch des deutschen Patentrechts in rechtsvergleichender Darstellung* (Mannheim: J. Bensheimer 1900); Friedrich Meilli, *Das Telephonrecht: eine Rechtsvergleichende Abhandlung* (Leipzig: Duncker & Humblot 1885). See also Stolleis, *Nationalität* 1998 (n. 22), at 14.

[26] See, e.g., Pasquale Fiore, *Traité de droit pénal et de l'extradition* (Paris: A. Durand et Pedone-Lauriel 1880); Louis Renault, 'Rapport sur l'extradition à l'Institut de Droit International' *Annuaire de l'Institut de Droit International* 5 (1881-1882), 70-102.

[27] Christopher A. Casey, *Nationals Abroad: Globalization, Individual Rights, and the Making of Modern International Law* (Cambridge: CUP 2020), 3.

[28] Luigi Nuzzo, 'Das Nationalitätsprinzip: der italienische Weg zum Völkerrecht', in Serge Dauchy and Miloš Vec (eds.), *Les conflits entre peuples. De la résolution libre à la résolution imposée* (Baden-Baden: Nomos 2011), 93-122.

[29] Pasquale Stanislao Mancini, *Della nazionalità come fondamento del diritto delle genti. Prelezione al corso di dritto internazionale a marittimo pronunziata nella università di Torino* (Turin: Tipografia Eredi Botta 1851).

century, this also meant that to be a stateless person under international law was 'to wander an inhospitable world in quest of a state's protection'.[30] It was the consulate that became the prime representative of the home State to which scorned nationals could turn in a foreign country and, as a result, the number of consulates during the nineteenth century increased to unprecedented numbers.[31]

As the rate of overseas investments rose, investor protection became one of the principal reasons for foreign intervention on behalf of a State's nationals. Whether or not a State intervened was entirely at its discretion, so unsurprisingly—as Calvo had observed—intervening States were often motivated by geo-political reasons next to mere investor protection. Intervention could take the form of blockades, embargos, occupation, or the creation of (partially) foreign financial oversight in the debtor State.[32]

The creation of extraterritorial regimes through treaties was precisely aimed at opening up foreign markets and at facilitating the easy circulation of western capital, merchants, and investors. What is more: by excluding the host State's jurisdictional reach over foreign—and sometimes the host State's own nationals—western States were able to use extraterritoriality as yet another marker and legal amplifier of their own state authority. While the conclusion of treaties that provided for western extraterritorial rights was widespread across the Middle East, Africa, and Latin America, it has been particularly well-researched with respect to the Ottoman Empire, Qing China, Japan, and Siam.[33] With respect to Qing China, some of the foundational treaties were concluded in the years 1842, 1858, and 1860;[34] for Siam in 1855;[35] and for Japan in 1854 and 1858.[36] The Chinese treaties were later branded by Chinese nationalists as 'unequal treaties', which became a

[30] David Armitage, *The Declaration of Independence: A Global History* (Cambridge, MA: Harvard University Press 2008), 105.

[31] Casey, *Nationals Abroad* 2020 (n. 27), 35.

[32] Lea Heimbeck, 'Legal Avoidance as Peace Instrument. Domination and Pacification through Asymmetric Loan Transactions', in Thomas Hippler and Miloš Vec (eds.), *Paradoxes of Peace in Nineteenth-Century Europe* (Oxford: OUP 2015), 111-27, at 113.

[33] Eliana Augusti, 'From Capitulations to Unequal Treaties: The Matter of an Extraterritorial Jurisdiction in the Ottoman Empire' *Journal of Civil Law Studies* 4 (2011), 285-307; Michael R. Auslin, *Negotiating with Imperialism: The Unequal Treaties and the Culture of Japanese Diplomacy* (Cambridge, MA: Harvard University Press 2006); Johannes Berchtold, *Recht und Gerechtigkeit in der Konsulargerichtsbarkeit: Britische Exterritorialität im Osmanischen Reich, 1825–1914* (Munich: R. Oldenbourg 2009); Pär K. Cassel, *Grounds of Judgment: Extraterritoriality and Imperial Power in Nineteenth- Century China and Japan* (Oxford: OUP 2012); Turan Kayaoğlu, *Legal Imperialism: Sovereignty and Extraterritoriality in Japan, the Ottoman Empire, and China* (Cambridge: CUP 2010).

[34] Treaty of Nanking, 1842, 93 CTS 465; Treaty of Tientsin, 1858, 119 CTS 123; Convention of Peace between Her Majesty and the Emperor of China, 1860, 123 CTS 71.

[35] Bowring Treaty, 1855, 113 CTS 83.

[36] Convention of Kanagawa, 1854, 111 CTS 377; the Ansei treaties: Treaty of Peace, Amity and Commerce between Japan and France, 1858, 120 CTS 7; Treaty of Friendship and Commerce between Japan and the Netherlands, 1858, 119 CTS 313; Treaty of Peace, Friendship and Commerce between Japan and Great Britain, 1858, 119 CTS 401; Treaty of Amity and Commerce of Yedo between Japan and the United States of America, 1858, 119 CTS 253; Treaty of Friendship and Commerce between Japan and Russia, 1858, 119 CTS 337.

byword for all similar treaties concluded with non-western powers.[37] Not all of the early treaties comprised extraterritorial rights, but they nevertheless provided a basis for western jurisdictional intrusion.[38]

Initially, extraterritoriality was not perceived as a controversial issue. For example, in the Ottoman Empire a tradition of granting privileges to foreign merchants through capitulations granted by the Sultan had already existed for centuries.[39] Similarly, Japanese and Chinese society recognised a multiplicity of jurisdiction within their realms.[40] However, extraterritoriality came to be considered as particularly heinous by host States as it was now imposed unilaterally and indefinitely and because the presence of consular courts and the crafting of legislation[41] that guaranteed extraterritorial jurisdiction undermined the State authority of its hosts. It implied that foreign nationals were excluded from the jurisdiction of local courts and were able to use the foreign-controlled consular courts to their own benefit.

Like many of the cases of violent foreign intervention, extraterritorial jurisdiction protected trade, property, and investment interests and, with it, a class of wealthy merchants and investors who benefited from the enthusiasm surrounding the discourse of free trade. The US court for China, for example, purposefully ignored crimes that facilitated western economic opportunities, such as the trafficking of opium and arms.[42] However, at the same time, extraterritoriality was also a tool to control wayward and less-than-desirable individuals. One of the reasons, for example, why British extraterritorial jurisdiction grew on the west coast of Africa—most notably in Sierra Leone and the Gold Coast—during the mid-nineteenth century, was to control and punish the violent forays of British subjects against Africans outside of the official boundaries of the British settlements.[43] Tellingly, it was primarily extraterritorial criminal law jurisdiction that proved particularly attractive. Again, one of the prime reasons was to ensure the peaceful continuation of trade relationships with neighbouring African polities.

[37] Inge Van Hulle, 'Unequal Treaties', in Gordon Martel (ed.), *Encyclopaedia of Diplomacy* (Weinheim: Wiley 2018).

[38] The Treaty of Nanking, for example, did not entail provisions relating to extraterritorial jurisdiction.

[39] Augusti, 'From Capitulations to Unequal Treaties' 2011 (n. 33), 285.

[40] Auslin, *Negotiating with Imperialism* 2006 (n. 33), 28.

[41] Within the context of the British Empire, this was most notably done with the passage of the Foreign Jurisdiction Act.

[42] Emily Whewell, *Law across Imperial Borders. British Consuls and Colonial Connections on China's Western Frontiers, 1880-1943* (Manchester: Manchester University Press 2019).

[43] Inge Van Hulle, *Britain and International Law in West Africa: The Practice of Empire* (Oxford: OUP 2020).

3.2 Humanitarianism

The abundance of rights-talk that focused on the socio-political standing of individuals was a steering force behind international legal change and the rise of humanitarianism during the nineteenth century. It should not come as a surprise that, like 'individualism', 'humanitarianism' was a term coined during this era.[44] While the meaning of humanitarianism shifted over time, in the nineteenth century it relied on a discourse of sentiment, compassion, and morality, but it also embraced to varying degrees rights-talk. What is more, humanitarian organisations' cross-border character and their increasing financial capacity for governance meant that many were successful in influencing public opinion and governmental legal actions. Humanitarians organised themselves in a growing number of professional institutions, boards, standing bodies, and committees that gathered information on far-flung human tragedies and that attempted to come up with remedies, sometimes also of an international legal nature. This is in line with what Michael N. Barnett has identified as the three components of humanitarianism: international assistance to the suffering; a belief that such international action was connected to the transcendent; and, finally, the concerted organisation of activities that were designed to improve the condition of humanity.[45]

3.2.1 Abolition and Rights Talk

Nineteenth-century international law was profoundly influenced by 'rights talk' and by humanitarianism, both intimately connected with the socio-political standing of individuals. The drafting of a catalogue of rights that followed the American Declaration of Independence of 1776 in the Constitution[46] and the French Declaration of the Rights of Man and the Citizen of 1789[47] posited equal rights of citizens as the foundation for legitimate governmental power. While the nineteenth century perhaps did not witness the birth of modern-day human rights, the revolutions that took place at the end of the eighteenth century created the intellectual space for new political constellations that provided citizens with rights that protected them from their own governments. At the same time, the principle of equality espoused by revolutionaries was transposed by humanitarians to those suffering overseas. It was used and rephrased to argue for the freedom of enslaved individuals, the protection of religious minorities, or the safety of prisoners of war and of medical personnel during wartime. However, when humanitarianism led

[44] Koenraad W. Swart, 'Individualism in the Mid-Nineteenth Century (1826-1860)' *Journal of the History of Ideas* 23 (1962), 77-90.

[45] Michael N. Barnett, *Empire of Humanity: A History of Humanitarianism* (Ithaca, NY: Cornell University Press 2011), 10.

[46] Constitution of the United States of America, Washington DC, 17 September 1787.

[47] La Déclaration des droits de l'homme et du citoyen, Assemblée national constituante, 26 August 1789.

to new treaty initiatives and to foreign intervention, States often paid lip service to humanitarian demands, while seeking economic and political gain as well.

Even if the emphasis during the course of the nineteenth century came to be primarily on the rights of nation-States, the attention to equality influenced the agitators who advocated against the slave trade; for religious tolerance; and for the plight of women, children, and industrial labourers.[48] Some have considered the natural rights discourse of the Enlightenment as a forerunner of modern-day human rights, that is, rights that pertain to individuals on the basis of their humanity. Samuel Moyn, however, has pointed out that these were confined to the claim of particular political and civic rights within national boundaries.[49]

One of the most profound expressions of humanitarianism translated into international legal action was the campaign for the abolition of the slave trade. The concrete emanation in international law of the sympathy with the enslaved abroad started with attacks against the enslavement and ransoming of 'white slaves' by pirates under the protection of what the west referred to as the 'Barbary States' (i.e. Algiers, Tripoli, and Tunis). Following several US naval campaigns, Algiers was bombarded in 1816 by a joint British-Dutch initiative and promises were extracted that prohibited the enslavement of prisoners of war.[50]

However, it is really the abolition of the transatlantic slave trade that stands as a symbol of nineteenth-century humanitarianism's impact on international law. In 1807 Britain adopted the Act for the Abolition of the Slave Trade, which prohibited the import of enslaved people to British territorial possessions and proscribed the participation of British subjects in the slave trade.[51] In doing so, Britain made a 180-degree turn away from being the foremost participant in the slave trade by the end of the eighteenth century to becoming its most active opponent. This marked the start of an international diplomatic campaign to convince other western states to abolish the slave trade, in which Britain took the foreground. After a failed attempt to outlaw the slave trade at the Congress of Vienna in 1815 and the Congress of Verona in 1822, Britain negotiated a string of bilateral treaties with maritime slave trading States.[52] These inter-western treaties included the right to visit and search ships during peace time—a controversial measure for States such as France and the US—and provided for the set-up of courts of mixed commission for the adjudication of captured slave vessels. It is estimated that at least 80,000 individuals were set free as a result of the decisions rendered by the courts of

[48] Lynn Hunt, 'Revolutionary Rights', in Pamela Slotte and Mila Halme-Tuomisaari (eds.), *Revisiting the Origins of Human Rights* (Cambridge: CUP 2015), 105-18, at 114.

[49] Samuel Moyn, *The Last Utopia. Human Rights in History* (Cambridge, MA: Harvard University Press, 2012).

[50] Jean Allain, *Slavery in International Law* (Leiden: Brill 2012), 61.

[51] An Act for the Abolition of the Slave Trade, 47 Geo. III Sess. 1 c. 36.

[52] What was achieved in Vienna was merely a declaration of principle: Declaration des 8 Cours, relative à l'Abolition Universelle de la Traite des Nègres, 8 February 1815, British Foreign and State Papers, vol. III, 971-972.

mixed commissions, the court in Sierra Leone being the most active one at 65,000 people.[53] Anti-slavery international law culminated in the Berlin Conference of 1885—which adopted another principled declaration against the slave trade—but especially in the Brussels Conference of 1890, which set up an international regime for the suppression of the slave trade.

However, international abolitionist law was about more than calls to freedom of the enslaved and represented merely one example of a new discursive phase in a long history of 'rights talk'.[54] From its inception, it was closely entwined with the transition from mercantilism to free trade. The slave trade treaties that were concluded with west African polities during the 1840s were predicated on the principle of 'legitimate commerce', that is, the idea that the trade in slaves could be replaced by the trade in alternative commodities, provided by European powers. Furthermore, the treaties with non-western polities were often coerced and far from reciprocal. In substance, they also contained clauses that opened up African markets to European goods and that gave European merchants a number of privileges, such as the right to freedom of religious practice and the right to the extraterritorial application of European laws.[55] In addition, after the official abolition of the slave trade and slavery, various forms of unfreedom continued to exist and neither did abolition mark the end of the tutelage of black colonial subjects.[56]

Abolitionist international law built on the diffuse idea of civilisation.[57] By the end of the nineteenth century, the condemnation of the slave trade had become an integral part of the western 'test' of civilisation that political entities needed to pass in order to become accepted members of the European family of nations. These requirements of civilisation were predicated entirely on western cultural, legal, and political values. The standard of civilisation was also used to justify extraterritoriality and use of force in the non-west.[58] Many abolitionists who relied on the famous image and epithet of an enslaved person on bended knee pleading 'Am I not a Man and a Brother?', also believed that Africa was backwards and uncivilised and would benefit from the bible and the plough. For all the moral condemnations of the slave trade, the image of the African in

[53] JP van Niekerk, 'British, Portuguese, and American judges in Adderley Street: The International Legal Background to and some Judicial Aspects of the Cape Town Mixed Commissions for the Suppression of the Transatlantic Slave Trade in the Nineteenth Century' *Comparative and International Law Journal of Southern Africa* 37 (2004), 1-39.

[54] For a differing view, see Jenny Martinez, *The Slave Trade and the Origins of International Human Rights Law* (Oxford: OUP 2012).

[55] Van Hulle, *Britain and International Law in West Africa* 2020 (n. 43).

[56] David Northrupp, *Indentured Labor in the Age of Imperialism, 1834-1922* (Cambridge: CUP 1995).

[57] Michel Erpelding, *Le droit international antiesclavagiste des 'nations civilisée'* (Paris: Institut Universitaire Varenne 2017), 17.

[58] Brett Bowden, *The Empire of Civilization: The Evolution of an Imperial Idea* (Chicago, IL: University of Chicago Press 2014); Gerrit Gong, *The Standard of 'Civilization' in International Society* (Oxford: Clarendon Press 1984). There is an abundant literature on extraterritoriality especially in regions such as China, Siam, the Ottoman Empire, and Japan. A standard work remains: Kayaoğlu, *Legal Imperialism* 2010 (n. 33).

anti-slavery discourse was often stereotypical and ambiguous.[59] Africans were portrayed as child-like, living in a state of nature, and exploited by slave traders. Personal accounts by previously enslaved persons, such as those of Ottobah Cugoano and Olaudah Equiano, while they were exceptions to the image of the 'voiceless' African, also became paternalistic examples of the potential of Africa's moral and religious conversion.[60]

3.2.2 Humanitarian International Law and Intervention

The same humanitarian ethos is what helped to inspire the movement to codify the laws of war. The birth of modern international humanitarian law is said to have started with the drafting of the Lieber Code, created for the purposes of guiding the conduct of the Union forces during the American Civil War.[61] However, the real foundational moment is often identified as when the Swiss philanthropist Henry Dunant inspired by the horrors of the Battle of Solferino in 1859 founded the Red Cross movement and instigated the start of the 'Geneva tradition of humanitarian law', with the adoption of the Geneva Convention for the Amelioration of the Condition of the Wounded and Sick in Armed forces in the Field. Here also a traditionally Whiggish narrative of humanitarian progress culminating in the Additional Protocols of 1977 should be put into perspective.[62] The inter-State codification of the laws of war was also a tool to curtail a burgeoning civil society that witnessed ordinary citizens' readiness to take up arms in defence of the 'nation'.[63] The growing concern to provide a legally protected status to prisoners of war and to other categories of non-combatants is overshadowed by the completely opposite attitude that western States adopted with respect to so-called 'small wars' and colonial use of force.[64]

At the origins of the birth of new republics and nation-States during the nineteenth century lay a nationalist fire that was not solely confined to State borders, but at times burnt brightly beyond it. Indeed, independence struggles and civil wars on

[59] Patrick Brantlinger, 'Victorians and Africans: The Genealogy of the Myth of the Dark Continent' *Critical Inquiry* 12 (1985), 166-203, at 170.

[60] Ottobah Cugoano, *Thoughts and Sentiments on the Evil and Wicked Traffic of the Slavery and Commerce of the Human Species, Humbly Submitted to the Inhabitants of Great-Britain by Ottobah Cuguano, A Native of Africa* (London: s.n. 1787); Olaudah Equiano, *The Interesting Narrative of the Life of Olaudah Equiano or Gustavus Vassa, the African* (London: s.n. 1794).

[61] Amanda Alexander, 'A Short History of International Humanitarian Law' *European Journal of International Law* 26 (2015), 109-38, at 112.

[62] Raphael Schäfer, 'The 150th Anniversary of the St Petersburg Declaration: Introductory Reflections on a Janus-Faced Document' *Journal of the History of International Law* 20 (2019), 510-14, at 511.

[63] Eyal Benvenisti and Doreen Lustig, 'Taming Democracy: Codifying the Laws of War to Restore the European Order, 1856-1874', *New York University*, available at: https://www.law.nyu.edu/sites/default/files/upload_documents/Taming%20Democracy%20%208-24-17.pdf, accessed 8/7/23.

[64] Frédéric Mégret, 'From "Savages" to "Unlawful Combatants": A Postcolonial Look at International Law's "Other" ', in Anne Orford (ed.), *International Law and Its 'Others'* (Cambridge: CUP 2006), 356-71; Van Hulle, *Britain and International Law in West Africa* 2020 (n. 43), 165-205.

distant shores often inspired nationals belonging to neutral States to take up arms in defence of liberty abroad. The actions of unruly volunteers, even though they were difficult to control by neutral governments, could be interpreted by the involved belligerents as unneutral service. Following the example of the United States at the end of the eighteenth century, Great Britain adopted the Foreign Enlistment Act in 1819 to stem the flood of volunteers who joined the Spanish American insurgent armies.[65] The Act criminalised the enlistment by British subjects in the forces of foreign belligerents whenever Britain had pledged neutrality.[66] Nevertheless, the risk of being accused of unneutral service by not sufficiently curtailing the actions of individuals was brought to stark relief in the Alabama Arbitration in 1871 meant to resolve the conflict between the United States against Britain's conduct during the American Civil War, when it had neglected to prevent the fitting out of warships intended for Confederate service in its ports.[67]

The sympathy for suffering overseas did not just trigger very concrete actions on the part of individuals who joined the call to arms, but also provided avenues for European States to assert their authority and sovereignty abroad in the form of humanitarian interventions.[68] The nineteenth century has been referred to as the 'heyday' of humanitarian intervention, even though the term itself did not find entry into legal scholarship until its later decades.[69] Armed interventions whose discourse hinged on the suffering of the oppressed took place, for example, during the Greek war of independence (1821-32), in Lebanon and Syria (1860), and during the Great Balkan Crisis (1875-78).[70] What is clear though is that intervention was often a ruse for the exertion of geo-political control and was also to a large extent premised on the standard of civilisation which allowed western States to justify force overseas.[71]

[65] UK: Foreign Enlistment Act 1819, 59 Geo III. c. 69.

[66] Nir Arielli, Gabriela Frei, and Inge Van Hulle, 'The Foreign Enlistment Act, International Law and British Politics (1819-2014)' *International History Review* 37 (2016), 1-21.

[67] John Bassett Moore, *History and Digest of the International Arbitrations to which the United States has been a Party*, vol. I (Washington DC: Government Printing Office 1898), 495-682.

[68] There is a rich literature on the history of humanitarian intervention. The following is just a selection: Gary Bass, *Freedom's Battle: The Origins of Humanitarian Intervention* (New York, NY: Knopf 2008); Alexis Heraclides and Ada Dialla, *Humanitarian Intervention in the Long Nineteenth Century: Setting a Precedent* (Manchester: Manchester University Press 2015); Fabian Klose, *The Emergence of Humanitarian Intervention. Ideas and Practices from the Nineteenth Century to the Present* (Cambridge: CUP 2015); Brendan Simms and David J. B. Trim (eds), *Humanitarian Intervention: A History* (Cambridge: CUP 2011).

[69] Alexis Heraclides, 'Humanitarian Intervention in the 19th Century: The Heyday of a Controversial Concept' *Global Society* 26 (2012), 215-26.

[70] For an overview, see Mark-Swatek-Evenstein, *A History of Humanitarian Intervention* (Cambridge: CUP 2021).

[71] Anne Orford, *Reading Humanitarian Intervention* (Cambridge: CUP 2009).

4. The Individual as a Law-Maker

Even though mainstream international legal theory recognised only States as subjects of international law, the day-to-day business of law-making and law-theorising was one of individuals. While the idea that the quotidian craft of law-making is the purview of individuals is a commonplace for all periods of history, the decentring of the State in the history of international law in recent literature has happened most thoroughly over the last two decades with respect to the nineteenth century. It is this latter, more sociologically oriented strand of scholarship that has the potential to subvert most profoundly what Doreen Lustig has called the 'statist bias' of international legal histories, that is, the focus on 'the centrality of interstate relations or sovereignty as the focal point for the history of international law'.[72]

For a long time, international law was seen as the providence of a handful of specialists, either intellectuals or professional diplomats and accredited state representatives. Of all of these categories, by far the largest amount of attention has been paid to the lives and writings of learned lawyers: to the manner in which they conceptualised of international normative behaviour, who they considered as forming part of the international community, and to what extent they formed part of this or that particular school of thought.[73] The nineteenth century indeed saw—next to the coining of the term 'international law' (yet another one!)—the birth of international law as a self-standing academic discipline, with its own professional associations, journals, and proliferation of university chairs.[74] As Miloš Vec has highlighted, nineteenth-century lawyers played a decisive role in the creation of legal principles and doctrines, sometimes attaching their names to them.[75] Through their analysis of particularist State practice they thus aided in the universalisation of international law through declaring legal principles.

The sharp peak in the publication of scholarly articles and treatises occasioned by the 'Verwissenschaftlichung' of international law provides a rich resource base for those studying the intellectual history of international law. However, the attention awarded to legal doctrine of this period was also inspired by a critical strand of scholarship that wished to uncover the manner in which international lawyers—some of whom played advisory roles to western governments—aided in providing

[72] Doreen Lustig, 'Governance Histories of International Law', in Markus D. Dubber and Christopher Tomlins, *The Oxford Handbook of Legal History* (Oxford: OUP 2018), 868.

[73] David Kennedy, 'International Law and the Nineteenth Century: History of an Illusion' *Nordic Journal of International Law* 65 (1996), 385-402; See also the various contributions in: Nuzzo and Vec (eds.), *Constructing International Law* (n. 17), 25-50; Ignacio de la Rasilla del Moral, *In the Shadow of Vitoria. A History of International Law in Spain (1770-1953)* (Leiden: Brill 2018).

[74] Martti Koskenniemi, *The Gentle Civilizer of Nations: The Rise and Fall of International Law, 1870–1960* (Cambridge: CUP 2004).

[75] Miloš Vec, 'Principles in 19th Century International Law Doctrine', in Nuzzo and Vec (eds.), *Constructing International Law* (n. 17), 214.

a legal bases for imperial rule and colonial exploitation.[76] While for a long time, focus lay on the histories of white male scholars, over the past few years research scopes have expanded to include examinations of how lawyers and intellectuals from the Global South subverted or strategically adopted the language of western international law in order to resist foreign domination.[77] Also, a new strand of scholarship looks at the overlooked histories of female contributions to the history of international law.[78]

Intellectual histories of international law that trace the lives and ideas of individual authors have become more and more localised and contextualised.[79] The merit of such an approach is that international legal thought becomes more textured: it is seen as a product embedded in authors' social environment, religious and political convictions, education. Intellectuals are seen 'as both universal and particular at the same time, speaking a shared language but doing that from their own, localizable standpoint'.[80] At the same time, the 'state-centric view haunts the imagination of experts preoccupied with the "international"',[81] also in the past. This means that a focus on elite interpretations of international law by international lawyers risks equating their learning opinions with the reality of how international law operated in practice.

There is an abundance of sources at hand for nineteenth-century vernacular international law, as 'the archive was more important in the nineteenth century than in any previous one'.[82] This is certainly the case for the activities of diplomats and higher-level State officials. For example, they played a significant role in the drafting and securing of the unequal treaties concluded in South East Asia, discussed earlier. Diplomats also added their voices to the clamour of creditors who sought compensation for their losses. In fact, they were not averse to encouraging foreign investment and to use defaulting of loans to ask for greater financial concessions and more intrusive ways to secure payment.[83]

[76] See the pathbreaking works of Antony Anghie, *Imperialism, Sovereignty and the Making of International Law* (Cambridge: CUP, 2005).

[77] Arnulf Becker Lorca, *Mestizo International Law: A Global Intellectual History, 1842-1933* (Cambridge: CUP 2015); Liliana Obregón, 'Creole Consciousness and International Law in Nineteenth-Century Latin America', in Anne Orford (ed.), *International Law and Its Others* (Cambridge: CUP 2006); Juan Pablo Scarfi, *The Hidden History of International Law in the Americas* (Oxford: OUP 2017).

[78] Immi Tallgren, *Portraits of Women in International Law: New Names and Forgotten Faces* (Oxford: OUP 2023).

[79] For a discussion of the influence of contextual histories of international law in recent scholarship, see Ignacio de la Rasilla del Moral, *International Law and History: Modern Interfaces* (Cambridge: CUP 2021).

[80] Giulio Bartolini, 'What is a History of International Law in Italy for? International Law through the Prism of National Perspectives', in Giulio Bartolini (ed.), *A History of International Law in Italy* (Oxford: OUP 2020), 3-16.

[81] Koskenniemi, 'Expanding Histories' 2016 (n. 1), 108.

[82] Jürgen Osterhammel, *The Transformation of the World: A Global History of the Nineteenth Century* (Princeton, NJ: Princeton University Press 2014) 50.

[83] Richard Horowitz, 'International Law and State Transformation in China, Siam and the Ottoman Empire during the Nineteenth Century' *Journal of World History* 15 (2004), 445-86, at 472.

Over the past few years, more attention has been awarded to the legal actions of mid-level and lower-level state personnel, indigenous rulers, enslaved individuals, migrants, convicts, pirates, etc., especially within the context of empire.[84] Such histories help us gain a better understanding of how international law operated in practice and provides nuance to the image of an international law neatly crafted in State cabinets that was then theorised upon by an elite class of international lawyers. It also relativises the supposed internationality and universality of international law: the manner in which a rule or legal instrument was applied and interpreted varied from place to place.

Ordinary people acted as international law-makers in far-flung places outside of the immediate control of the metropole that did not feature highly on the list of imperial priorities of western governments. In such a context, individuals negotiated treaties, established extraterritorial control, asserted their rights in local courts, or resorted to force, all with considerable discretion in the application of, or even without, an official mandate. In their resort to and creation of legal instruments they were inspired by a vernacular version of international law that combined elements of the classic law of nations, domestic European law, and indigenous custom.[85] Such vernacular histories of international law for the nineteenth century have been documented in imperial settings, but are yet to be explored in the metropolitan centres of Europe. It requires that we look beyond the classic sources, beyond treaties, treatises, and statutes to trace people's everyday interactions with institutional international law.[86]

Dominant approaches to the history of international law rarely engage with the law-steering roles of individuals on a micro-level. Even the ones that do still primarily revolve around the actions and lives of white men who operated in institutional spaces, such as the corporation, State organs, or international organisations.[87] Histories that focus on the micro-stories of individuals can nevertheless

[84] See various contributions in Saliha Belmessous (ed.), *Empire by Treaty: Negotiating European Expansion, 1600-1900* (Oxford: OUP 2015); Lauren Benton and Lisa Ford, 'Magistrates in Empire: Convicts, Slaves and the Remaking of the Plural Order in the British Empire', in Lauren Benton and Richard Ross (eds.), *Legal Pluralism and Empires, 1500-1850* (New York, NY: New York University Press 2013); Lauren Benton and Lisa Ford, *Rage for Order: The British Empire and the Origins of International Law* (Cambridge, MA: Harvard University Press 2016); Jonathan Chappell, 'Maritime Raiding, International Law and the Suppression of Piracy on the South China Coast, 1842-69' *International History Review* 40 (2018), 473-92; Lisa Ford, *Settler Sovereignty: Jurisdiction and Indigenous People in America and Australia 1788–1836* (Cambridge, MA: Harvard University Press 2010); David Todd, 'Beneath Sovereignty: Extraterritoriality and Imperial Internationalism in Nineteenth-Century Egypt' *Law and History Review* 36 (2018), 105-37; Van Hulle, *Britain and International Law in West Africa* 2020 (n. 43); Nurfadzilah Yahaya, *Fluid Jurisdictions: Colonial Laws and Arabs in Southeast Asia* (Ithaca, NY: Cornell University Press 2020).

[85] Van Hulle, *Britain and International Law in West Africa* 2020 (n. 43).

[86] Jacob Catz Cogan, 'A History of International Law in the Vernacular' *Journal of the History of International Law* 22 (2020), 205-17; Laura F. Edwards, 'Law as Social History', in Markus D. Dubber and Christopher Tomlins (eds.), *The Oxford Handbook of Legal History* (Oxford: OUP 2018), 119-34, at 120.

[87] Balakrishnan Rajagopal, *International Law from Below: Development, Social Movements and Third World Resistance* (Cambridge: CUP 2003), 2.

have an important emancipatory function, particularly when such stories prioritise the role of subaltern groups that are not easily encountered in the archives; archives that indeed privilege the preservation of institutional histories and that must therefore be read 'along the grain' to uncover dynamics of contestation, sentiment, and hidden controversies.[88]

5. Conclusion

During the nineteenth century, international law's subject was the western, Christian sovereign State which interacted with other similarly conceived of States on an equal footing and with concomitant rights and duties. There seemed to be little theoretical manoeuvring space to provide the individual with more than a merely objectified supporting role for the grand Hegelian narrative of the State. However, the nineteenth century presented new and unprecedented challenges for an international order that at least according to western conceptions was neatly carved out into nation-States. Never before had western States been confronted to such an extent with the—at times—barely controllable force of individual actors challenging their authority or calling them into action across the borders of their own jurisdiction. The nationalist, the freedom fighter, the abolitionist, the humanitarian, the investor, the merchant, etc. all tugged at the sleeves of the State demanding more intervention, democratic rights, liberty and safety for the oppressed, or protection of their property with consequences that reverberated overseas. Traces of States' attempts to curtail or promote the calls of individuals can be detected in instances of forcible intervention through diplomatic protection, extraterritoriality, abolitionist international law, and international humanitarian law. What a history of the individual also shows is that the nineteenth century was as much a century of State centrism and it was one in which individuals took a leading role in crafting international law. From the Swedish ambassador in a Parisian salon to the British naval officer on the coast of west Africa, individuals' law-making initiatives made a lasting imprint on the history of international law. This was not just the case for the practice of international law, but also for its theoretical exponent: if the State became the dominant register in which western international law was thought of and spoken about, this was so because its international lawyers who wrote about it and who taught it at their respective law faculties, had made it so.

[88] Ann Laura Stoler, *Along the Archival Grain: Epistemic Anxieties and Colonial Common* Sense (Princeton, NJ: Princeton University Press 2009).

7

Before Human Rights

The Formation of the International Legal Status of the Individual, 1914-45

Anne Peters

1. Introduction

The catastrophic events of World War I and the Russian revolution dismantled the German, Austrian, and Ottoman empires, and Tsarist Russia. A number of small States came into existence, and boundaries in Europe were redrawn. Ethnic violence up to genocide *avant la lettre* in the Balkans and near East was rampant.[1] Millions of humans were victimised: exploited, expelled, expropriated, denationalised, maimed, and killed. Europe was suddenly full of refugees, of *heimatlose*, and of impoverished labourers *en masse*. The new States and new boundaries left inhabitants with the 'wrong' nationality and sharpened the awareness for the vulnerability of religious and ethnic minorities.

These seismic shifts first plunged international law into a deep 'crisis'.[2] But then began an 'extraordinarily active period of legal innovation' in which international legal concepts were developed and received the shape they still have today.[3] The inherited international law was conceptualised as a law between States only,[4] derived from State consent (voluntarism). Public international law was also seen as being strictly separated from domestic law (dualism). And the main method to understand public international law was legal positivism.[5] From those premises, international law evolved to accommodate those human groups and their members which could for various reasons not be protected by one State alone.

The interbellum innovations on individuals followed the path blazed by prior legal developments:[6] *Piracy* and *slave trade* was already regulated by international

[1] The extreme case were the death marches on which the Ottoman authorities sent the estimated 800,000 to 1.2 million Armenians in 1915 and 1916.

[2] Jan de Louter, 'La crise du droit international' *Revue Générale de Droit International Public* 26 (1919), 76-110.

[3] Martti Koskenniemi, History of International Law, World War I to World War II, in Anne Peters and Rüdiger Wolfrum (eds.), *The Max Planck Encyclopedia of Public International Law* (Oxford: OUP 2011), para. 4.

[4] See section 5, below.

[5] See Hernández, 'Legal Positivim' (chapter 8), in this volume.

[6] See Van Hulle, 'Nineteenth Century' (chapter 6), in this volume.

Anne Peters, *Before Human Rights* In: *The Individual in International Law.* Edited by: Tom Sparks and Anne Peters, Oxford University Press. © Anne Peters 2024. DOI: 10.1093/oso/9780198898917.003.0007

law, and several post-war authors began to consider pirates and slave traders as being subjected to direct international duties, and the victims as being directly protected by international rights.[7] *In the laws of war*, post-World War I commentators conceptualised belligerents, recognised insurgents, and 'neutral persons'[8] as potential duty-bearers.[9] Prisoners of war enjoyed 'rights', as expressly codified.[10] Mixed arbitration had already emerged in the eighteenth century, and minority protection regimes had been established at the Berlin Balkan congress of 1878, and rudiments even before.

The new international legal regimes, procedures, and institutions were much more elaborate than the pre-war ones, and concerned new human groups. However, even the new institutions and the new law were weak tools for addressing the enormous transnational challenges after World War I. Ethnic and cultural tensions and strife continued in the multicultural States, non-European peoples remained under foreign domination, and the world economic crisis was soon to erupt. This was the background against which Jean Spiropoulos wrote—in 1929—that 'the problem of the position of the individual in international legal life is currently one of the most debated problems of our discipline'.[11]

This chapter first describes the new international regimes and their significance for the international legal status of individuals (section 2). It then examines the most discussed incidences of individual access to international courts and tribunals (section 3). Another matter was the enforcement of international treaty-based rights in domestic courts (section 4). The practical innovations inspired a doctrinal debate on the international legal personhood of individuals (section 5). The rationales of the upgrading of the international status of the individual, and the broader paradigms and underlying principles, notably democracy and solidarity, rather

[7] *Wheaton's Elements of International Law*, vol. 1 (6th edn, revised by A. Berriedale Keith, London: Stevens and Sons 1929), 40-41. For the controversial argument that the movement to end the transatlantic slave trade aligns with institutional characteristics of contemporary international human rights law, notably because States (pushed by civil society movements) used international law to protect the rights of individuals who were not their own nationals, see Jenny S. Martinez, *The Slave Trade and the Origins of International Human Rights Law* (Oxford: OUP 2012).

[8] Convention (V) respecting the *Rights and Duties* of Neutral Powers and *Persons* in Case of War on Land. The Hague, 18 October 1907. Swiss Bbl. 1909 I 1, AS 26, 499, 0.515.21 (emphasis added). Commenting in 1929, Keith/Wheaton (n. 7) consider the wording of the title *not* to be 'advertent' (at 41). Indeed, nowhere do the provisions of this convention enshrine 'rights'.

[9] On the limited international legal personality of insurgents, see Santi Romano, *Corso di diritto internazionale* (Padova: Cedam 1933), 73-74. But see Josef Kunz, *Kriegsrecht und Neutralitätsrecht* (Berlin and Heidelberg: Springer 1935), 37: the laws of war do not directly bind individuals.

[10] Hague Regulations Respecting the Laws and Customs of War on Land (Annex to the Hague Convention) of 18 October 1907 stipulates 'rights' of prisoners, parlementaires, and commanders (Art. 3; 12; 32-34). The Geneva Convention Relative to the Treatment of Prisoners of War of 27 July 1929 (entered into force 19 June 1931), 118 LNTS 343) mentions 'rights' of prisoners of war in Arts. 42, 62, and 64.

[11] Jean Spiropoulos, 'L'individu et le droit international' *Recueil des Cours* 30 (1929), 195-270, at 195: '[L]e problème de la position de l'individu dans la vie juridique internationale est à l'heure actuelle un des problèmes les plus discutés de notre discipline.' (Here and in the following, all translations are my own.)

than rights and dignity, are discussed in section 6. The chapter concludes that the 'long' post-World War I era was formative for the humanisation of international law (section 7).

2. New International Legal Institutions and Procedures

After 1918, new branches of international law, new institutions, and new procedures were created whose primary purpose was to cushion inter-State tension and competition. The protection of the individual human being as a member of various vulnerable groups was rather a side effect. But growing strands of legal scholarship analysed the implications of the new mechanisms for the international legal status of individuals, and some scholars strove to push individuals to the centre of international law.

2.1 The League of Nations Covenant and the International Labour Organisation

The League of Nations (LoN) Covenant that entered into force in 1920 did not include any general provision on what would now be called human rights. Japan had proposed a clause prohibiting discrimination on racial grounds, but this 'proposal was not really about the principle of universal racial equality' and mainly had 'nationalistic' motives and was made out of 'national pride'.[12] In any case, the Japanese proposal was rejected, notably due to strong opposition by the US, Australia, and the UK. NGO demands for women's rights suffered the same fate.

Article 22 of the Covenant obliged mandatory powers to 'guarantee freedom of conscience and religion' in the mandate territories, and to 'prohibit abuses such as the slave trade' but it did not ban slavery itself.[13] The League was also entrusted 'with the general supervision over the execution of agreements with regard to the traffic in women and children'.[14] In 1924, the League Assembly adopted a 'Declaration *of the Rights* of the Child' which is listed by the UN as a precursor of the 1998 Convention of the Rights of the Child.[15] However, despite its title, the text of the declaration did not spell out any rights of children, but rather duties towards them. For example, Article II said: 'The child that is hungry must be fed; the child

[12] Naoko Shimazu, *Japan, Race, and Equality: The Racial Equality Proposal of 1919* (London: Routledge 1998), 164, also 181, 183, and 184.

[13] See section 2.4, below, on the mandate system.

[14] Covenant of the League of Nations (LoN), 28 June 1919 (SdN, JO February 1920, 3-12), Art. 23(c).

[15] Office of the United Nations High Commissioner for Human Rights, Legislative History of the Convention on the Rights of the Child, vol. I (New York and Geneva: United Nations 2007), 55, available at: https://www.ohchr.org/sites/default/files/Documents/Publications/LegislativeHistorycrc1en.pdf, accessed 7/7/23.

that is sick must be helped; the child that is backward must be helped; the delinquent child must be reclaimed; and the orphan and the waif must be sheltered and succoured'. Importantly, these imperatives were *not* addressed to States directly. Rather, 'men and women of all nations, recognizing that mankind owes to the child the best that it has to give, declare and accept it as their duty that, beyond and above all considerations of race, nationality or creed', children must be given support.[16] So the child was not seen as a holder of international rights of its own but rather as a target of a transnational, primarily societal humanitarianism.

The International Labour Organisation (ILO) was founded with the Peace Treaty of Versailles. (The 'Constitution of the International Labour Organisation' was Part XIII (Arts. 387-427) of the Treaty of Versailles).[17] Simultaneously, the League members committed themselves to 'endeavour to secure and maintain fair and humane conditions of labour for men, women and children'[18] and 'to establish and maintain the necessary international organisations'.[19] The joint undertaking was motivated by the conviction that unfair labour conditions had fuelled the Bolshevik revolution with destabilising effects for central and eastern Europe that had ultimately contributed to the outbreak of the war. The ILO preamble professed: 'peace can be established only if it is based upon social justice; And whereas conditions of labour exist involving such injustice, hardship, and privation to large numbers of people as to produce unrest so great that the peace and harmony of the world are imperilled'. Thus, the ILO drew a connection between peace between States and peace on the labour market.[20]

Otherwise, the purpose of the ILO was to bring about a level playing field on which the national economies could compete. States with a higher level of workers protection would suffer a competitive disadvantage against States with a low level of protection, and therefore a harmonised labour law was desirable. The ILO preamble clearly expresses the objective to prevent a chilling effect: 'the failure of any nation to adopt humane conditions of labour is an obstacle in the way of other nations which desire to improve the conditions in their own countries'. Finally, the international institution for better labour conditions was a reward for the working masses for their contribution to the war effort.[21] All this only peripherally had to do with the

[16] Declaration of the Rights of the Child, 26 September 1924, Records of the Fifth Assembly (LoN OJ, Special Supplement No. 23, 179-82).

[17] Treaty of Peace with Germany, signed 28 June 1919, in *American Journal of International Law Supplement* 13 (1919), 151-386, as amended 20 April 1948, 15 UNTS 40.

[18] This commitment was extraterritorial ('in all countries to which their commercial and industrial relations extend') but was not understood to comprise mandate territories (see references in Taina Tuori, 'From League of Nations Mandates to Decolonization: A Brief History of Rights', in Pamela Slotte and Miia Halme-Tuomisaari (eds.), *Revisiting the Origins of Human Rights* (Cambridge: CUP 2015), 279.

[19] LoN 1919 (n. 14), Art. 23(a).

[20] Heiko Sauer, 'International Labour Organization (ILO)', in Anne Peters and Rüdiger Wolfrum (eds.), *The Max Planck Encyclopedia of Public International Law* (Oxford: OUP last updated 2014), para. 3.

[21] *ibid*, para. 2.

individual worker's dignity. Labour conventions and recommendations were then elaborated in the new tripartite procedures under the auspices of the ILO. Some of them can be seen (or rather later came to be seen) as manifesting a concern for fundamental rights. For example, the forced labour convention of 1930[22] did not contain any rights language. But its 2014 protocol recasts that convention's purpose by '[r]ecognizing that the prohibition of forced or compulsory labour forms part of the body of fundamental rights, *and that forced or compulsory labour violates the human rights and dignity* of millions of women and men, girls and boys [...]'.[23] Out of sixty-seven labour conventions adopted between 1919 and 1939, twenty-seven contain a language of 'rights' or 'entitlements', such as rights to accident compensation, medical treatment, old-age pension, invalidity pension, and maternity leave. These entitlements were mostly to be 'determined by national laws.' The labour conventions simply reflected the bargains struck between capital and labour on concrete practical issues.[24] Therefore, the choice of terminology does not seem deliberate, did not carry a symbolic significance, and did not create 'direct' international rights.

Rather, the mentioned LoN and ILO provisions and the various instruments building on them prompted or even mandated *national* policies of social regulation and for the protection of vulnerable groups. These policies were motivated by intertwined economic, political, and humanitarian considerations that were more paternalist than emancipatory.

2.2 Loss of State Protection: Refugees and Stateless Persons

As a result of the Russian revolution that ended in 1917 with the Bolshevik victory, millions of Russians fled their country. The phenomenon of refugees (including Armenian, Greek, Bulgarian, Assyrochaldean, and later, in the 1930s, Spanish, Italian, and German refugees) grew constantly.

A sizeable number of the refugees were at the same time formally stateless, because the Bolsheviks used denationalisation (stripping persons of their citizenship) as a penalty. Such a systematic policy, later picked up by other States, notably by Fascist Italy and Germany, was completely new in 1917. This also meant that statelessness as a phenomenon reached a hitherto unprecedented extent. Both groups (refugees) and stateless (most of whom were also in flight) shared the fate that they were unprotected by any State. Both issues were therefore tackled simultaneously by the League, and later by the UN.[25]

[22] Convention Concerning Forced or Compulsory Labour, 28 June 1930, ILO No. 29; 39 UNTS 55.

[23] Preamble of the Protocol of 11 June 2014 (P 029) (emphasis added).

[24] Alfred W. Brian Simpson, *Human Rights and the End of Empire: Britain and the Genesis of the European Convention* (first published 2001, this edn Oxford: OUP 2004), 149.

[25] See the joint treatment in, e.g., Egidio Reale, *Le régime des passeports et la Société des Nations* (Paris: A Rousseau 1930), 152 and by the UN in, 'A Study of Statelessness, New York, August 1949, E/

The *refugee problem* reached such a magnitude that 'practically every state felt its repercussions'.[26] Therefore, 'for the first time a serious attempt was made to deal with it systematically, and along international lines'.[27] A refugee convention was drawn up in 1933 and entered into force in 1935.[28] It mainly accorded the refugees a treatment like nationals or like other foreigners in various respects. For example, domiciled refugees were granted 'the same *rights and privileges* as nationals' with regard to access to courts.[29] Again, no special significance was attached to the treaty language of rights (as opposed to the language of protection).

Against the organising principle of international law that each individual must be member of a nation, the existence of *stateless persons* ('*apatrides*', '*Heimatlose*') was an 'anormal fact',[30] an 'anomaly'.[31] Put more starkly, under international law, these stateless persons 'did not exist'.[32] In the old scheme, human beings could step into the 'limelight' of international law only through their nationality by which they were attached to a State.[33] The membership of the individual in a State and the membership of that State in the international legal community were the two 'links' ('*Bindeglieder*' or '*Durchgangspunkte*') which created a 'mediated' ('*vermittelt*') international legal status of the individual, only 'indirectly' based on international law.[34] This legal position of the individual was in the German doctrine called 'international law nativeness' ('*Völkerrechts-Indigenat*').[35] It meant that individuals could enjoy benefits from international law, however 'not as human beings, but as subjects of States which are members of the family of Nations'.[36] Concomitantly, Lassa Oppenheim wrote:

> That Stateless individuals are objects of the Law of Nations in so far as they fall under the territorial supremacy of the State on whose territory they live, there is

1112). After World War II, work began on a convention to protect both groups, was later split up, and ended in two separate conventions.

[26] Carlile Macartney, *Refugees: The Work of the League* (London: League of Nations Union 1930), 5.
[27] *ibid.*
[28] Convention Relating to the International Status of Refugees, League of Nations, Treaty Series, Vol. CLIX, p. 199, No. 3663, 28 October 1933.
[29] *ibid*, Art. 6 (emphasis added).
[30] Jean Pierre Adrien François, 'Le problème des apatrides' *Recueil des Cours* 53 (1935), 283-376, at 371.
[31] Marc Vichniac, 'Le statut international des apatrides' *Recueil des Cours* 43 (1933), 115-246, at 127; I. G. Lipovano, *L'Apatridie* (Paris: Les Éditions Internationales 1935), 137.
[32] Paul Heilborn, *Die Stellung des Menschen im Völkerrecht* (Breslau: Hirt 1927), 5.
[33] Felix Stoerk, 'Staatsunterthanen und Fremde', in Franz von Holtzendorff (ed.), *Handbuch des Völkerrechts auf Grundlage europäischer Staatspraxis, vol. 2: Die völkerrechtliche Verfassung und Grundordnung der auswärtigen Staatsbeziehungen* (Hamburg: Verlag von J. F. Richter 1887), 583-655, at 589.
[34] Rolf Knubben, 'Die Subjekte des Völkerrechts', in Fritz Stier-Somlo (ed.), *Handbuch des Völkerrechts*, vol. 2 (Stuttgart: W. Kohlhammer 1928), 511.
[35] Franz von Liszt, *Das Völkerrecht: systematisch dargestellt* (11th edn, Berlin: Springer 1918), 99.
[36] Lassa Oppenheim, *International Law—A Treatise*, vol. 1 Peace (3rd edn, Ronald F. Roxborough (ed.), London: Longmans, Green and Co 1920), 461.

> no doubt. But since they do not own a nationality, the link by which they could derive benefits from International Law is missing, and thus they lack protection as far as this law is concerned. […] [H]owever much they are maltreated, International Law cannot aid them.[37]

In that scheme, both conferral of nationality by a State to human beings and its counterpart, the denationalisation, according to criteria and under conditions set by the State, were considered a core expression of sovereignty. These acts were seen firmly inside the *domaine réservé*. For that reason, the attempts in the 1930s to deal with the issue of nationality on the plane of international law were revolutionary.[38] The plan to adopt an international instrument harmonising the conferral of nationality questioned the dominant conceptualisation of international law as a law between sovereign States at its core. Any international legal status for stateless persons would expand the authority of international law.[39]

The main argument made by proponents of an international convention on nationality was that the floods of stateless refugees destabilised States and caused inter-State frictions, were therefore a matter of international concern, and hence necessarily fell in the realm of international law.[40] From that perspective, the withdrawal of nationality as a penalty was a 'flagrant violation of fundamental principles of organisation of the international community'.[41] The protection of stateless persons was a task of the League in order to 'assure every individual and group of individuals a place in the sun of the law'.[42] More radically even, the idea of a generalisation of a protection by international law could be made. If international law was directly applied to *apatrides*, there was no reason to refuse its application 'to individuals as such'.[43] A related issue was the lack of choice for women who upon marriage *ex lege* acquired the nationality of their husbands under most domestic laws. The very first scholarly contributions by women dealt with this blatant discrimination.[44]

However, the codification of international principles on nationality, in order to resolve the conflicts that resulted from the diversity of the national laws on

[37] *ibid*, 484-85 (§ 312).

[38] Mira L. Siegelberg, *Statelessness: A Modern History* (Cambridge, MA: Harvard University Press 2021), 9 and 89. On the States-only conception of international law, see section 5, below (text accompanying note 185).

[39] Siegelberg, Statelessness 2021 (n. 38), 88. See, e.g., Lipovano, *L'Apatridie* 1935 (n. 31), 17-20.

[40] Lipovano, *L'Apatridie* 1935 (n. 31), 139-40.

[41] François, 'Apatrides' 1935 (n. 30), 371.

[42] Vichniac, 'Apatrides' 1933 (n. 31), 238: 'assurer une place à tout individu et à tout groupe d'individus au soleil du droit'.

[43] Nicolas Politis, *Les nouvelles tendances du droit international* (Paris: Hachette 1927), 63.

[44] C. Luella Gettys, 'The Effect of Changes in Sovereignty on Nationality' *American Journal of International Law* 21 (1927), 268-77, at 273 notes that the peace treaties explicitly provide that a husband's option should also cover his wife. She finds that these provisions, although they 'may appear to be an infringement of individual rights', were justified 'to preserve family unity'.

nationality, remained 'an enterprise that must be qualified as chimerical' in the interbellum.[45]

2.3 Dissolution of Empires: Option, Plebiscites, and Vested Rights

The nationality of individuals gained extreme salience due to the dissolution of the German and Austro-Hungarian Empires. That dismantlement led to the creation of new States in central and eastern Europe and involved numerous additional boundary changes.

2.3.1 The Right of Option

The various peace treaties (notably of Versailles, Saint Germain, and Trianon) granted those persons who—after the redrawing of boundaries—found themselves in a new State, the right to opt out of this new nationality within a specified period.[46] Against the background of a rich practice, there was some debate whether a right of option had emerged as a customary rule.[47] Another doctrinal question was whether the option was a 'real individual right'.[48] Even for those authors who conceptualised the option as a right of humans, its legal basis was—in the dualist worldview—not international law directly. Rather, the treaties obliged States to revise their domestic law. The individual right of option then rooted in the various national laws.[49] In the background lurked the fundamental question of the overarching purpose of the option. Opinions were divided. The eminent expert on the question, Josef Kunz, argued that the option served 'individual self-determination'.[50] In contrast, the mainstream view was probably that the new criteria introduced by the peace treaties after World War I, firstly satisfied 'the predominant purpose of uniting on the same territory and under a national government individuals of the same race, language, and civilization' and, secondly sought to avoid both persons with multiple nationalities and *heimatlose*.[51] The ultimate

[45] François, 'Apatrides' 1935 (n. 30), 343. Convention on Certain Questions relating to the Conflict of Nationality Laws, 12 April 1930, 179 LNTS 89, No. 4137, Art. 1, emphasised that '[i]t is for each state to determine under its own laws who are its nationals'. For an attempt at the harmonisation of nationality laws, see the 'Harvard' Draft of Convention on Nationality, *American Journal of International Law* 23 (1929), Supplement, Special Number, 13-132.

[46] For detailed study and references, see Josef Laurenz Kunz, *Die völkerrechtliche Option. Band 1: System der Option. Die Option im deutschen Friedensvertrag* (Breslau: Hirt 1925); *Band 2: Staatsangehörigkeit und Option im deutschen Friedensvertrag von Versailles (Nachtrag) und im österreichischen Friedensvertrag von St. Germain* (Breslau: Hirt 1928).

[47] Against the qualification as a customary rule, see Heilborn, *Stellung des Menschen* 1927 (n. 32), 16-19.

[48] In the affirmative, see Ernst Isay, *Mitteilungen der Deutschen Gesellschaft für Völkerrecht* 7 (1926) (discussion of talk by Ebers), 37.

[49] Kunz, *Völkerrechtliche Option* 1925 (n. 46), 176.

[50] *ibid*, 179.

[51] Gettys, 'Effect of Changes' 1927 (n. 44), 269 (quote) and 277.

objective of the option was, from that perspective, to eradicate all possible sources of inter-State frictions arising from the divergence of nationality laws.[52]

2.3.2 Plebiscites

In several border regions, affected populations were allowed to vote in plebiscites on the allocation of their community or district to either of the neighbouring States. The authority on the topic, political scientist Sarah Wambaugh, analysed five plebiscites: three were based on the Treaty of Versailles with Germany (Schleswig, Allenstein and Marienwerder, and Upper Silesia), and two were based on the peace treaty of Saint Germain with Austria or its aftermath (Klagenfurt bassin and Sopron). Wambaugh also examined three attempted plebiscites, a planned plebiscite in the Saar territory, and seven unilateral consultations.[53] The outcomes of the plebiscites that took place in 1920 and 1921 were mostly but not always fully taken into account in the drawing of the boundaries. Their official ideational foundation was the self-determination of peoples which was propagated by various actors as a twin principle to democracy.[54] The beneficiaries of this political principle were 'peoples' as groups, and indirectly their individual members.

2.3.3 Vested Rights

The third novel set of international rules protecting individuals in the context of the dissolution of empires concerned the so-called 'vested rights'. An entire Title of the German-Polish Upper Silesia Convention of 1922 dealt with their protection.[55] In this framework, Germany and Poland committed to '*recognise and respect the rights of every kind*, and in particular concessions and privileges acquired before the transfer of sovereignty by private individuals […] in their respective parts of the plebiscite area'.[56] Such vested rights were notably property rights over factories, and were of high economic value in the densely industrialised region. The convention allowed individuals to bring proceedings for compensation before an international arbitral tribunal (the Upper Silesia Arbitral Tribunal) on grounds of 'revocation of or interference with vested rights'.[57] The Upper Silesian Arbitral Tribunal dealt with a total of approximately 4,000 such individual complaints,

[52] *ibid*, 278.

[53] Sarah Wambaugh, *Plebiscites since the World War: With a Collection of Official Documents* (Washington DC: Carnegie Endowment for International Peace 1933).

[54] Tom Sparks, *Self-Determination in the International Legal System: Whose Claim, to What Right?* (Oxford: Hart 2023), 20-23.

[55] Part I, Title II of the German-Polish 'Geneva' Convention concerning Upper Silesia, signed in Geneva, 15 May 1922; extracts reproduced in PCIJ Series A No. 15, Annex I, 75-85. The full text is reproduced in Georges Kaeckenbeeck, *The International Experiment of Upper Silesia* (Oxford: OUP 1942), 567-822.

[56] Upper Silesia Convention 1922 (n. 55), Art. 4(1).

[57] *ibid*, Art. 5: 'Concerning the question of whether and to what extent the State must provide compensation for the revocation of or interference with vested rights, the arbitral tribunal shall decide directly on the complaint of the entitled person.'

of which most were ultimately found to be unjustified.[58] In the ground-breaking award in favour of the owners of a tobacco factory, *Steiner and Gross* of 1928, the Upper Silesia Arbitral Tribunal decided that such proceedings were also permissible *against the home State* (in that case Poland).[59] This finding implies that the 'rights' were those of individuals, and not of their States. Georges Kaeckenbeeck, who served as president of that Arbitral Tribunal for the duration of its existence, that is, from 1922 to 1937, assumed that the convention granted individual rights and did not only stipulate obligations between States: 'The Arbitral Tribunal's activity relating to the protection of vested rights assumed a pioneering character for the international protection of *individual rights* after a cession of territory.'[60]

The vested rights seemed to be rooted in domestic law, but were indirectly shielded by international law. The Upper Silesia Agreement 'characteristically assumed the necessity of guaranteeing a number of individual rights in order to ensure peace and the maintenance of economic prosperity in the partitioned area'.[61] So these rights were, like the minority rights, instrumental to broad policy objectives.

2.4 The Mandate System of the League of Nations

Mandate territories were created under Article 22 of the Covenant of the League of Nations and placed the former colonies of defeated powers under supervision of the League. The wording of Article 22 was couched in the language of obligations of the mandatory powers, not of rights of the inhabitants. It expressed the philosophy that 'the *tutelage* of such peoples should be entrusted to advanced nations' (Art. 22(2)). The section on class B-mandates stated that 'the Mandatory must be responsible for the administration of the territory under conditions which will guarantee *freedom of conscience and religion* [...], the prohibition of abuses such as the slave trade'.[62] Such obligations were also incumbent on the powers holding the Class-C mandates over the least developed territories.[63] Moreover, such guarantees could also be enshrined in the texts of the mandates themselves (the instruments that transferred the responsibility over the territory to the mandatory power).[64]

58 Kaeckenbeeck, *Upper Silesia* 1942 (n. 55), 482.

59 Upper Silesian Arbitral Tribunal, *Steiner and Gross v. Poland*, 30 March 1928, Case No. 188; in German and Polish in *Schiedsgericht für Oberschlesien: Amtliche Sammlung* vol. I (1930), 2-36 (esp. 30 and 34). For an extract in English, see *Annual Digest of Public International Law Cases*, vol. 4 (London: Longman 1931), 291-92; comment by Kaeckenbeeck, *Upper Silesia* 1942 (n. 55), 47-54.

60 Kaeckenbeeck, *Upper Silesia* 1942 (n. 55), 523 (emphasis added).

61 *ibid*, 528.

62 LoN 1919 (n. 14), Art. 22(5) (emphasis added).

63 *ibid*; see the reference in Art. 22(6): 'subject to the safeguards above mentioned in the interests of the indigenous population'.

64 See, e.g., Mandate for Palestine (League of Nations, Mandate for Palestine, 12 August 1922, UNOG Library; ref.: C. 529. M. 314. 1922. VI), Art. 15. See Simpson, *Human Rights* (n. 24), 146.

A right to *petition* for inhabitants of the mandate territories was not foreseen in the League Covenant, but was introduced in 1923 by the League Council.[65] The inhabitants could petition through the mandatories, and the petition was then considered by the League's Permanent Mandates Commission. The possibility of hearing the petitioners themselves was aired in 1925 and 1926, but was strongly opposed by all mandatory powers.[66] The main motive was to avoid any appearance of a lawsuit. A hearing 'would seem to transform the Commission into a court of law', and this 'would be inconsistent with the very nature of the mandatory system. […] [T]he hearing of petitioners would weaken the authority which the Mandatory should possess in order to carry out its duties successfully […]'.[67]

The contemporary authority on mandates, Quincy Wright, explained that

> the organs of the League itself have been anxious to avoid an appearance of judicial control of the mandatories. The Council and Commission have both insisted that the procedure on petitions is not to be considered a case between the petitioner and the mandatory but a *means of acquiring information*. […] Nevertheless, the appearance of a litigation cannot be wholly avoided.[68]

Such 'appearance of litigation' was underscored by the publicity of the minutes of the Mandates Commission. These were thus apt to influence public opinion.[69] The evolving and ambiguous features of the mandate petition procedure allowed contemporary scholars to interpret it as conferring direct rights on the inhabitants and as implying that the inhabitants were indeed international legal persons.[70]

Overall, the mandate system had the same principal purpose as the refugee, minorities, labour, and nationality/option regimes: to prevent and resolve inter-State tensions. Benefits for individuals were rather a side-effect. This was clearly articulated by William Rappard, director of the Mandates Section of the League of Nations (1920-25) and member of the Permanent Mandates Commission (1925-45). According to Rappard, the mandate system 'was not set up primarily for the

[65] 'Rules of Procedure in Respect of Petitions concerning inhabitants of mandated territories', adopted by the Council on 31 January 1923, LN Document C.P.M 38(1) Official Journal IV 1923 p. II, reprinted in Hessel Duncan Hall, *Mandates, Dependencies, and Trusteeship* (Washington DC: Carnegie Endowment for International Peace 1948), Annex VIII (at 314).

[66] Simpson, *Human Rights* 2004 (n. 24), 148.

[67] League of Nations, *The Mandate System—Origins, Principles, Application* (Geneva: League of Nations Publications 1945), vol. VI, A 1945 1, at 41. Upon these State observations, the Council saw no occasion to modify the procedure (*ibid*).

[68] Quincy Wright, *Mandates under the League of Nations* (Chicago, IL: The University of Chicago Press 1930), 194 (emphasis added).

[69] Tuori, 'Brief History of Rights' 2015 (n. 18), 272 and 283 with further references.

[70] Schulim Segal, *L'individu en droit international positif* (Paris: Sirey 1932), 117-32 and 173.

protection of human rights, but for the settlement of rivalling political claims' in areas which lay on frontiers between the major powers' spheres of influence.[71]

The approach of the League and the mandatory powers was characterised by 'different degrees of paternalism' and by the 'absence of a fully-fledged modern vocabulary of the rights language'.[72] Nevertheless, the mandate system was an early 'international institution where the demands of humanity and the welfare of people were written into the system and were evident in the international regulation and administration of the institution'.[73]

Moreover, already immediately after World War II, the mandate system acquired a human rights colouring which it had not possessed at the time of its actual functioning, as Taina Tuori has demonstrated.[74] For example, Rappard continued that it 'is because, within the admittedly narrow boundaries of *the international protection of certain human rights in backward countries*, the mandates system at least partially succeeded [...] that its lessons should be not be forgotten'.[75] Hersch Lauterpacht in 1950 qualified the right to petition as a 'natural right'.[76] In the same year, the International Court of Justice (ICJ) found that the mandate system's purpose must have been 'a real protection of those *rights* [...] of the peoples' – the ICJ only spoke of peoples' (and States') rights, not of individual rights.[77] Overall, the humanitarian ideals that impregnated the quasi-colonial mandate scheme allowed both a proto-rights debate and a petitions procedure, features that were later reimagined as rights and remedies for mandate populations.

2.5 The Minority Protection Systems

The post-World War I peace treaties' boundary redrawing enlarged the groups that were residing as a minority in States whose majority differed in ethnic, linguistic, religious, or otherwise cultural terms. At least 32 million persons belonged to such minorities, with Germans being the largest group, dispersed in neighbouring countries.

[71] William Rappard, 'Human Rights in Mandated Territories' *The Annals of the American Academy of Political and Social Science* 243 (1946), 118-23, at 119. See also Simpson, *Human Rights* 2004 (n. 24), 149.

[72] Tuori, 'Brief History of Rights' 2015 (n. 18), 285 and 275. See also Simpson, *Human Rights* 2004 (n. 24), 146.

[73] Tuori, 'Brief History of Rights' 2015 (n. 18), 267-92, at 291. See also Simpson, *Human Rights* 2004 (n. 24), 149.

[74] Tuori, 'Brief History of Rights' 2015 (n. 18), 291-92.

[75] Rappard, 'Human Rights' 1946 (n. 71), 123.

[76] Hersch Lauterpacht, *International Law and Human Rights* (first published 1950, this edn Hamden: Archon Books 1968), 244.

[77] ICJ, *International Status of South-West Africa*, Advisory Opinion (1950) ICJ Reports 128, at 136-37 (emphasis added).

In this constellation, new treaties for the protection of minorities were 'one of the cornerstones' of a post-war peace order.[78] But the settlement was characterised by a 'radical hypocrisy'.[79] Only the small States of central and eastern Europe which were new or had gained territory, and which were seen as backward and illiberal were saddled with obligations. The big and victorious powers (France with its Alsatians, the UK with its Irish, Italy with its South Tyrolians, and so on) basically denied they had any minority issues at all. Germany was, although defeated, merely subjected to a temporary regime, and only with regard to Upper Silesia.

A gamut of bilateral treaties, provisions in the peace treaties, and unilateral declarations to the League of Nations granted members of minority groups substantive rights or privileges: the right of option of nationality;[80] special rules governing child-rearing, schooling, and religion; financial support; and political autonomy. These provisions 'formed schemes or embryonic codes of rights, enumerated, but not elaborately defined'.[81]

In the covering letter presented to Poland with the minorities treaty of 24 June 1919, the President of the Paris Peace Conference, Georges Clemenceau, depicted the minorities protection system as 'an established procedure in the public law of Europe'.[82] Indeed, international commitments for the protection of religious minorities had been imposed on central and eastern Europe States since the seventeenth century. But contemporaries saw a 'fundamental difference' between prior minority protection systems and the new system set up under the guarantee of the League.[83] The completely novel feature of the Versailles minority protection system was the 'guarantee' by the League of Nations that replaced the previous supervision by the Great Powers.[84] It was the international organisational machinery and the procedures of petition and complaint, not the treaty provisions in substance that were unprecedented.[85]

[78] Jacob Robinson et al., *Were the Minorities Treaties a Failure?* (New York, NY: Institute of Jewish Affairs of the American Jewish Congress and the World Jewish Congress 1943), V. See the excellent accounts by Inis Lothar Claude, *National Minorities: an International Problem* (Cambridge: Harvard University Press 1955) and by Simpson, *Human Rights* (n. 24), 107-45, on the League system, see 121-45.

[79] Simpson, *Human Rights* 2004 (n. 24), 124.

[80] See section 2.3.1, above.

[81] Simpson, *Human Rights* 2004 (n. 24), 126.

[82] Clemenceau to Paderewski, writing on behalf of the Supreme Council of the Principal Allied and Associated Powers (covering letter presented to Poland with the minorities treaty), 24 June 1919: reproduced in Oscar J. Janowsky, *Nationalities and National Minorities (with special Reference to East-Central Europe)* (New York, NY: Macmillan 1945), 179-84, at 179.

[83] Helmer Rosting, 'Protection of Minorities by the League of Nations' *American Journal of International Law* 17 (1923), 641-60, at 641.

[84] See, e.g., *Traité concernant la reconnaissance de l'indépendance de la Pologne et la protection des minorités of 28 June 1919*, in Clive Perry (ed.), *Consolidated Treaty Series*, vol. 225 (New York, NY: Oceana 1919), 412-24, at Art. 12.

[85] Report of Work of the League of Nations in Relation to Protection of Minorities Prepared by a Committee Constituted by the Council of the League in its Resolution of 7 March 1929 in Pablo de Azcárate, *League of Nations and National Minorities: an Experiment* (New York, NY: Carnegie Endowment for International Peace 1945), Appendix (163-209), at 200-01.

2.5.1 Procedures within the League of Nations

The petitions and complaints procedures were designed as an exercise of reconciliation among the involved States. The initial League guarantee made no provision for complaint by individuals. This had been discussed, but rejected because it would constitute an infraction to State sovereignty.[86] The original purely inter-State complaint system remained virtually unused. It was superseded by a procedure of individual complaints based on a Council decision of 1920.[87] In the entire history of the scheme (between 1921 and 1939), about 900 petitions were submitted. The final stage, consideration by the Council of the League, was reached in only twelve cases (until 1931). Theoretically, the Council could take action but never did so. The minority regime also gave rise to four advisory opinions by the Permanent Court of International Justice (PCIJ).[88]

In order to legitimise the revolutionary step of individual complaints and to pay lip service to State sovereignty, the complaints were labelled as mere 'sources of information'.[89] Concomitantly, the minority groups (or any of their members) were not party to this procedure. All proceedings took place in camera, and the individual petitioner was not involved and not even kept informed.[90] The Tittoni report which invented the procedure made both points clear at the outset: 'But this act must retain the nature of a petition, or a report pure and simple; it cannot have the legal effect of putting the matter before the Council and calling upon it to intervene.'[91] Proposals to reform the petitions scheme in the direction of a more judicial procedure, for example through publicity, were rejected exactly in order to safeguard the diplomatic character, so as not to endanger the success of the relevant inter-State 'negotiations'.[92]

2.5.2 Upper Silesia

The most important bilateral minority treaty was the Upper Silesia Convention between Germany and Poland of 15 May 1922, which was operational from 1922 to

[86] Simpson, *Human Rights* 2004 (n. 24), 129 with further references.

[87] Report of M. Tittoni and resolution of 22 October 1920 (Minutes of the Tenth Session of the Council, Brussels, 20-26 October 1920, Public Meeting, 27 October 1920), at 13 and Annex 115, at 142-45 (File R1407/27/7747/2764, available at https://archives.ungeneva.org/tenth-council-of-the-league-of-nations-minutes-of-the-meeting-held-in-brussels-20-26-october-1920-public-meeting-27-october-1920, accessed 7/7/23).

[88] PCIJ, *Advisory Opinion on Certain Questions Relating to Settlers of German Origin in the Territory Ceded by Germany to Poland*, 10 September 1923, PCIJ Series B No. 6; PCIJ, *Advisory Opinion on Acquisition of Polish Nationality*, 15 September 1923, PCIJ Series B, No. 7; PCIJ, *Treatment of Polish Nationals and Other Persons of Polish Origin or Speech in the Danzig Region*, 4 February 1932, PCIJ Series A/B, No. 44; PCIJ, *Minority Schools in Albania*, 6 April 1935, PCIJ Series A/B, No. 64.

[89] Report of Work of the League of Nations in Relation to Protection of Minorities Prepared by a Committee Constituted by the Council of the League in its Resolution of 7 March 1929 in Azcárate, *League of Nations* 1945 (n. 85), 201 and 204.

[90] For the procedure involving the Secretariat, the Council, the 'Committee of Three', and the minorities section, see Simpson, *Human Rights* (n. 24), 130-32.

[91] Tittoni report 1920 (n. 87), 185. See also Simpson, *Human Rights* (n. 24), 130.

[92] Report of Work of the League of Nations 1929 (n. 89), at 201, 204, and 208.

1937.[93] Part III of the treaty was on 'Protection of Minorities'.[94] That part contained detailed rules on fundamental rights, education, language, and so on, and it notably granted members of minority groups the right to individual and collective petitions regarding violations of the minority protection provisions of the agreement.[95] The institutions were two minority offices in Polish and in German Upper Silesia respectively, a mixed commission under a Swiss president, and an arbitral tribunal under a Belgian president.

Besides an inter-State procedure, individual complaints were possible. 'Persons belonging to a minority' could address a petition to the 'Office of Minorities of the State to which they belong' (defined by the agreement) which was then forwarded to the 'President of the Mixed Commission for his opinion'. If the petitioner was not satisfied, he or she could 'appeal to the Council of the League of Nations'.[96] In the life of the Convention, 2,283 complaints, involving many more individuals, were submitted, but the mixed commission (under the presidency of the Swiss Felix Calonder) issued only 127 opinions.[97] The numbers show that most issues were settled by negotiation. The arbitral tribunal could be seized in a reference procedure ('evocation') by national courts on questions of the interpretation of the 1922 Convention.[98] It decided some 4,000 cases on, for example, rights to citizenship and free movement.

Most of the findings of the mentioned bodies were against Poland. After the rise of Nazism in Germany, members of the Jewish community availed themselves of the procedure and obtained redress against anti-semitic policies in German Upper Silesia.[99] But overall, the minority protection system of the League did virtually nothing for Jews. The special Upper Silesian system was—in comparison to the general League system—much more effective. It was legalised in appearance, but the 'legal forms clothed a system of diplomatic negotiation'.[100]

[93] Upper Silesia Convention 1922 (n. 55). On the following, see Simpson, *Human Rights* 2004 (n. 24), 134-45.

[94] Part III replicated provisions of a prior multilateral treaty (*Traité concernant la reconnaissance de l'indépendance de la Pologne et la protection des minorités of 28 June 1919* (n. 84), signed at the same date and place as the peace treaty of Versailles), between the USA, the British Empire, France, Italy, Japan, and Poland) and made them applicable to Upper Silesia (see chapeau of Part III of the 1922 Convention).

[95] Part III, Division III 'Rights of Petition and Means of Redress' in the Upper Silesia Convention 1922 (n. 55), Arts. 147-158.

[96] Upper Silesia Convention 1922 (n. 55), Art. 149.

[97] Simpson, *Human Rights* 2004 (n. 24), 137.

[98] Upper Silesia Convention 1922 (n. 55), Art. 588.

[99] Text of a petition by M. Franz Bernheim, dated 12 May 1933, concerning the situation of the Jewish minority in German Upper Silesia (LoN OJ, July 1933 (Issue 7), 929-33, Annex 1451); and Proceedings of the Council, Agenda Items 3281, 3288, 3290, 3291, 3294, and 3297 (LoN OJ, July 1933 (Issue 7); and Opinion of the Committee of Jurists (LoN OJ, July 1933 (Issue 7), 934-35, Annex 1451a).

[100] Simpson, *Human Rights* 2004 (n. 24), 142.

2.5.3 The Relevance of the Regime for Individuals

The 'new method of guarantee'[101] was intended to de-escalate, sanitise, and collectivise the political implications of the minorities question. Previous meddling by the kin States which sought to protect 'their' kin fuelled disloyalty of the minorities towards their State of residency. That had been a constant source of dispute, especially among neighbouring States. Therefore the Great Powers supervision was to be replaced by the action of League bodies seen as 'collective and impersonal'.[102]

The overall purpose of the minority protection regime was twofold. Its primary objective was to prevent quarrels among States. The former director of the minorities questions section of the League of Nations, Pablo de Azcárate, insisted that 'the system was neither humanitarian nor juridical', that its aim was 'purely political'.[103] This was however a one-sided view. The PCIJ in contrast had in 1923 said that '[t]he *main object* of the Minorities Treaty is to assure respect for the rights of Minorities and to prevent discrimination against them by any act whatsoever of the Polish State'.[104]

Neither objective was in the end reached, not least because Germany abused the situation of the German minorities abroad (the biggest and the best organised group) as a pretext for invading its neighbours. The affected States implemented the treaty provisions in a minimalist fashion.[105] With rising nationalism, they (and also the kin States) did their best to undermine the system. However, the main reason for the system's collapse were probably not its intrinsic flaws (such as its selective geographical coverage and vague provisions), but the dismantlement of the League and of the international order as a whole: 'The rights of national minorities can command no more respect in a lawless world than any other rights.'[106]

The entire minorities protection machinery had, according to contemporaries, 'by no means a brilliant record of achievement'.[107] Still, four points of relevance for the humanisation of international law stand out. First, the minority schemes' operation was an 'important phase of the essential process of breaking down the concept of the sovereign, irresponsible state'.[108] This is in itself key for the enhanced and 'immediate' international legal status of the individual.

Secondly, the then novel international procedures available to minorities offered the first access for individuals to international bodies with complaints against their own State of nationality. Typically, the specific guarantees especially relevant for

101 Robinson et al., *Minorities Treaties* 1943 (n. 78), 84.

102 *ibid.*

103 Azcárate, *League of Nations* 1945 (n. 85), 14.

104 PCIJ, *German Settlers* 1923 (n. 88), 25 (emphasis added).

105 On the translation into domestic law and application by courts, see Robinson et al., *Minorities Treaties* 1943 (n. 78), 193, and 238-39.

106 Janowsky, *Nationalities* 1945 (n. 82), 165.

107 William Rappard, 'Minorities and the League' International Conciliation Document No. 222 (1926), 330-43, at 340.

108 Claude, *National Minorities* 1955 (n. 78), 29.

minorities such as admission to public service, free use of their language, and the establishment of schools were reserved for the nationals of the State of residence.[109] This was a difference to the 'law of aliens' and to the international options for foreigners to institute arbitration against their host State.

Thirdly and relatedly, the then novel international procedures available to minorities were the fulcrum around which the scholarly debate on the international legal personality of the individual (and to a much lesser extent their rights) pivoted:[110] the probably prevailing opinion was that the international instruments did not confer any rights on minorities, and that these remained 'objects of international legislation'; they enjoyed the guarantee in fact but not in law.[111] Only isolated voices perceived direct international rights of minorities and concluded that they were therefore international legal persons.[112] However, commentators did not clearly distinguish between possible procedural rights on the one side and substantive rights on the other side, nor did they properly distinguish collective (group) rights from individual rights.

Fourthly, the calls for 'generalisation' of the minorities regime stimulated and merged with the ideas about international human rights. We have seen that equal rights or representation for members of minority groups were most likely only a side effect of the League minority protection scheme. Importantly, the guarantees for members of minorities did nothing to protect majorities (or individuals as such) from ill-treatment by their State. Moreover, the regime was selectively imposed only on the States of central and eastern Europe. Exactly this lacuna was targeted by those States and authors who time and again demanded a '*generalisation*' of the regime.[113]

[109] See, e.g., Arts. 7-9 of both the Polish Treaty of 28 June 1919 (n. 84) and the Treaty of Peace between the Principal Allied and Associated Powers and the Serb-Croat-Slovene State, 10 September 1920 (*American Journal of International Law* 14 (1920), Supplement: Official Documents (October 1920), 333-43). In contrast, life and liberty and non-discrimination was guaranteed to all inhabitants (see, e.g., Art. 2 of both treaties). Both in scholarship and State practice, the denomination as a 'minority' was often reserved for the group of persons possessing the nationality (citizenship) of their State of residence. *cf.* Rosting, 'Protection of Minorities' (n. 83), 641. The citizenship requirement as a precondition for the applicability of international rules on minority protection was overcome only in the 1990s and early millennium. See Venice Commission, Report on Non-citizens and Minority Rights, Study No. 294/2004 (CDL-AD(2007)001) of 18 January 2007.

[110] See in more detail section 5, below.

[111] Otto Junghann, *Das Minderheitenschutzverfahren vor dem Völkerbund* (Tübingen: Mohr 1934), 33-34 and 7.

[112] Segal, *L'individu* 1932 (n. 70), 133-62, 174. Carl Schaeffer and Heinrich Brode, *Völkerrecht* (19th-21st edn, Leipzig: Hirschfeld 1932), 29, saw a trend in the direction of an international legal personality of minorities.

[113] In the meetings of the League Assembly's sixth committee ('Political questions'), several delegates supported such 'generalisation', spearheaded by M. Frangulis as the delegate of Haiti (LoN OJ, Special Supplement No 120 (Geneva 1933), 32. *cf. ibid*, at 34 (Japan); at 46 (Netherlands); and at 47 (Romania). In scholarship, see André Mandelstam, 'Der internationale Schutz der Menschenrechte und die New-Yorker Erklärung des Instituts für Völkerrecht' *Zeitschrift für ausländisches öffentliches Recht und Völkerrecht* 2 (1931), 335-77, at 367. See critically Howard Calderwood, 'The Proposed Generalisation of the Minorites Regime' *American Political Science Review* 28 (1934), 1088-98.

'Generalisation' ingeniously implied two things: first and primarily, the request was that all other States should offer such guarantees. This was, for example, the official explanation for Poland's withdrawal from the system: 'While waiting for the establishment of a *general and uniform system for the protection of minorities*, my government sees itself obliged to refuse, from today on, all collaboration with the international organs concerning the control of the application by Poland of the system for the protection of minorities.'[114] But because the Great Powers adamantly refused to commit themselves to minority protection, their refusal could be—so the academic proponents of the call for generalisation hoped—sidelined by the introduction of an overall ('universal') scheme of individual human rights protection. Along that line, 'generalisation' also meant that all inhabitants (generally) should be protected: 'there should be no denial of civil rights because of race, religion or nationality; that is the general principle of the minority treaties ought to be universally recognized'.[115]

Such a scheme would benefit all individuals in all States, and at the same time realise equality among States. In fact, the inter-war advocates of a 'universal' human rights instrument mainly (whether for tactical reasons or by conviction) wrote about rectifying the situation of inequality among States.[116] It looks as if the quest for an equal playing field, namely for State equality, stood (as in the fields of labour, refugees, and mandates) in the foreground, with the improvements for individuals as a welcome side-effect.

Overall, the post-Versailles minority protection schemes were, despite their ultimate collapse, the most relevant historic experience for the subsequent evolution of an international human rights law.[117] This concerns both the material non-discrimination clauses and—more importantly—the international institutional and procedural arrangements to handle individual and group complaints *against their State of nationality*.

Especially the complaint mechanisms in the Upper Silesian 'experiment'—to use the arbitral tribunal's president's word—has rightly been praised as a 'vital lesson',[118] as a model for subsequent international minority management schemes,[119] and even for the institutional arrangements made in 1950 for the European Convention of Human Rights.[120]

[114] LoN, Actes de la Quinzième Session Ordinaire de l'Assemblée (1934), Séances Plénières, at 43 (emphasis added).

[115] Quincy Wright, in World Citizens' Association, *The World's Destiny and the United States: A Conference of Experts in International Relations* (Chicago, IL: Donnelly 1941), 107.

[116] Mandelstam, 'Schutz der Menschenrechte' 1931 (n. 113), 367; see also Hans Wehberg, 'Probleme der rechtlichen Organisation der Welt – Die New Yorker Tagung des Institut de Droit International' *Die Friedenswarte* 29 (1929), 353-63, at 355; Antoine-F. Frangulis, 'Droits de l' Homme (garantis internationalement par voie juridictionelle)', in Antoine-F. Frangulis (ed.), *Dictionnaire Diplomatique III, supplément* (Paris: Académie Diplomatique Internationale 1937).

[117] Simpson, *Human Rights* 2004 (n. 24), 107.

[118] Kaeckenbeeck, *Upper Silesia* 1942 (n. 55), 482.

[119] Azcárate, *League of Nations* 1945 (n. 85), 159-60.

[120] Simpson, *Human Rights* 2004 (n. 24), 134.

3. Individual Access to International Courts and Tribunals

Another phenomenon that manifested the ambiguous international legal status of individuals and potentially reinforced it was the wide gamut of tribunals and commissions that dealt with individual claims against foreign governments.

The legal nature of the claims and the legal position of the individual claimants in these—what could be called 'diagonal'—proceedings was controversial at the time and remains ambiguous today.[121] In the paradigm of diplomatic protection of the time, the harm done to the private actor by a foreign State was qualified as being, from the perspective of international law, a harm inflicted on the individual's home State that was injured 'in the person of its subjects'.[122] The home State could pick up the case, by which the dispute 'entered the domain of international law and became a dispute between two States' in which the home State then asserted *its* state-owned rights on the international plane.[123] A new and rather massive practice of diagonal arbitration cast doubts on this statist construction and gave rise to the question whether the individuals themselves were the owners of international law-based rights, both procedural rights and substantive ones.

3.1 The aborted International Prize Court of 1907

According to the projected *Hague Convention (XII) relative to the Creation of an International Prize Court*, an individual ('neutral individual' or 'an individual subject or citizen of an enemy Power') would have been able to appeal to the International Prize Court as an appellate court against decisions of the national prize courts. The draft convention was an outcome of the second Hague peace conference, but failed to secure ratifications and never entered into force. Individuals would have been able to contest the lawfulness of a 'prize', that is, the capture of a merchant ship or its cargo in a naval war where such capture encroached on the individual's property.[124] The project was novel in two respects, in foreseeing a genuine institutionalised court (as opposed to a mere arbitral tribunal) and in giving individuals access to that court. Already at the Hague conference of 1907,

[121] On the legal position of the individual in the diagonal proceedings against States in the interbellum, see Kate Parlett, *The Individual in the International Legal System* (Cambridge: CUP 2011), 65-84; Astrid Kjeldgaard-Pedersen, *The International Legal Personality of the Individual* (Oxford: OUP 2018), 85-94.

[122] PCIJ, *Mavrommatis Palestine Concessions Case*, Judgment, 30 August 1924, PCIJ Series B, No. 3, 12.

[123] *ibid.*

[124] Convention (XII) relative to the Creation of an International Prize Court, 18 October 1907, available at: https://ihl-databases.icrc.org/en/ihl-treaties/hague-conv-xii-1907, accessed 7/12/23, Arts. 4 and 5.

proponents stated that the 'individual appeal is in line with the progress of international law'.[125]

In opposition, statists such as Erich Kaufmann downplayed the significance of that plan as an indication of a legal personhood of the individual. Kaufmann notably highlighted the exceptional state of war in which the belligerent States should not be confronted with each other as parties. Moreover, the home State could prohibit its nationals to accede to the court.[126]

Despite its defeat, the projected court was almost invariably mentioned by the 'individualist' writers. This is warranted because the reason for the court's failure was not any hostility against the novel individual complaint mechanism but controversy over the substantive prize law to be applied.[127] In result, the pre-war plans on the Prize Court justifiably were one of the most important reference points for the post-war legal debate on the international status of the individual.

3.2 The Central American Court of Justice (1907-18)

Between 1907 and 1918, a Central American Court of Justice was in operation, and this was the first ever international court to which individuals had access.[128] It had from the outset been established for a limited period of ten years after the last ratification of its founding convention.[129] The court could hear (after exhaustion of domestic remedies), 'questions which individuals of one Central American country *may raise* against any of the *other* Contracting Governments, because of the violation of treaties or conventions, and other cases of an international character; no matter whether their own government supports said claim or not'.[130] The court dealt with a total of ten cases, seven of which were brought by individuals. Only one of the individual complaints, by the Nicaraguan national Alejandro Bermúdez Núñez against alleged arbitrary and illegal expulsion from Costa Rica, resulted in court proceedings, but was unsuccessful on the merits.[131]

[125] Statements of Francis Hagerup (Norway) and Colonel Eugène Borel, as summarised in William Isaack Hull, *The Two Hague Conferences and their Contributions to International Law, published for the International School of Peace Ginn & Company, Boston 1908* (New York, NY: Kraus Reprint Co. 1970), 431 (also cited in Kjeldgaard-Pedersen, *Personality* (n. 121), 82).

[126] Erich Kaufmann, 'Règles générales du droit de la paix' *Recueil des Cours* 54 (1935), 420-21.

[127] Dietrich Schindler and Jiří Toman, 'Introductory Note', in Dietrich Schindler and Jiří Toman (eds.), *The Laws of Armed Conflicts* (Dordrecht: Martinus Nijhoff 1988), 825.

[128] Jean Eyma, *La Cour de Justice Centre-Américaine* (Paris: E Sagot 1928).

[129] Convention for the Establishment of a Central American Court of Justice (Costa Rica, El Salvador, Guatemala, Honduras, Nicaragua), 20 December 1907 (*American Journal of International Law* 2 (1908), Supplement 231-43). On the limitation of time, see Art. XXVII.

[130] *ibid*, Art. II (emphases added).

[131] Demanda Intentada por el Sr. D. Alejandro Bermúdez Núñez, contra el Gobierno de Costa Rica, 13 April 1914, in *Anales de la Corte de Justicia Centroamericana* Sumario de Los Núms 9 Á 11, Tomo IV. Enero a Mayo 1914, 1-119, available at https://portal.ccj.org.ni/wp-content/uploads/010-T-4-N-9-11-1.pdf, accessed 12/12/23.

The individual's standing before this short-lived court attracted disproportionate attention; almost all 'individualist' writers of the inter-war period referred to it. They did not mention that the Central American Court was in political terms 'less international' than the courts and tribunals that were discussed at the same time in Europe. The five central American States had formed a political union both in the colonial period (the *Captaincy General of Guatemala* within the Spanish Empire) and in various phases after their independence in 1821.[132]

The convention established a direct international procedural individual right. It was not mediated by their governments, because the plaintiffs did not need the support of their own government. In substance, Bermúdez Núñez had invoked various provisions of an amity treaty, notably its national treatment clause.[133]

The possibility of central American citizens to bring proceedings against States has been assessed as a 'revolutionary measure' in international law.[134] But this appraisal must be qualified. First, the situation was in geo-political terms almost 'domestic', so that Manley Hudson found it '*proper*, in view of the *widespread conception of Central America as a unit*, to allow individuals to bring suits against governments'.[135] Second, the treaty and the court pursued also, or even primarily, a public interest purpose, as the Court in *Bermúdez Núñez* highlighted: it interpreted the relevant provision as *not* intending to serve the interests of individuals in obtaining diplomatic asylum, but rather the public interest of preserving inter-State peace.[136] Finally and most importantly, the individual complaints were explicitly foreclosed against the plaintiff's own State of nationality.[137] This feature distinguished the Central American scheme from the minority complaints and shielded the relationship between a State and its nationals from international scrutiny.

3.3 Post-War 'Mixed Arbitration'

More than fifty provisions of the peace treaties after World War I foresaw 'mixed arbitral tribunals'/'tribunaux arbitraux mixtes' (TAMs) that, *inter alia*, decided

132 Notably as the Federal Republic of Central American States from 1823 to 1841, with various later attempts at a reunification of all or several States.

133 General Treaty on Peace and Amity signed at Washington on 20 December 1907, Oxford Historical Treaties: Parry's Consolidated Treaty Series, 206 CTS 63, Art. VI.

134 Rosa Riquelme Cortado, 'Central American Court of Justice (1907-18)', in Anne Peters and Rüdiger Wolfrum (eds.), *The Max Planck Encyclopedia of Public International Law* (Oxford: OUP 2012), para. 21.

135 Manley O. Hudson, 'The Central American Court of Justice' *American Journal of International Law* 26 (1932), 759-86, at 785 (emphasis added).

136 *Anales CJC* 1914 (n. 131), 96-97. *cf.* also Parlett, *Individual* 2011 (n. 121), 61-62 and 65; Kjeldgaard-Pedersen, *Personality* 2018 (n. 121), 83.

137 See the wording of Convention for the Establishment of a Central American Court of Justice 1907 (n. 129), Art. II.

individual-State ('diagonal') disputes on claims such as outstanding debts, damage to property, confiscations, and expropriations, resulting from war or revolution.[138] The United States, which had not ratified the Treaty of Versailles, concluded agreements on separate commissions.[139] Based on the peace treaties, a total of thirty-nine mixed arbitral tribunals decided about 90,000 to 100.000 cases until they were gradually phased out by 1939.[140] The vast majority were contractual disputes between individuals that are not of interest for this chapter. Kate Parlett lists only nineteen diagonal cases against States.[141]

One frequently analysed provision was Article 297(e) of the Treaty of Versailles under which 'nationals of Allied and Associated powers *shall be entitled to compensation*' for war-related damage or injury to their property, rights, or interests in German territory, to be borne by Germany.[142]

At their time, the TAMs sparked an intense debate on the international legal position of the private claimants. Several arbitral awards explicitly qualified the framework as constituting individual rights of nationals of the victor States to compensation, to be exercised independently or against the policy of their home State.[143] However, the mixed arbitral tribunals declined jurisdiction for proceedings brought against Germany or France by those States' own nationals[144]—a move which might be interpreted as suggesting State ownership of the claims.

A similar bulk of practice stems from the Mexican claims commissions' work from 1923 to 1934. These commissions had been established by various agreements between Mexico and seven States in order to deal with the consequences

[138] For a contemporary treatment of TAMS, see Walter Schätzel, 'Die Gemischten Schiedsgerichte der Friedensverträge' *Jahrbuch des Öffentlichen Rechts der Gegenwart* 18 (1930), 378-455. For current literature, see Michel Erpelding and Hélène Ruiz Fabri (eds), *The Mixed Arbitral Tribunals, 1919-1939* (Baden-Baden: Nomos 2023); Marta Requejo Isidro and Burkhard Hess, 'International Adjudication of Private Rights: The Mixed Arbitral Tribunals in the Peace Treaties of 1919-1922', in Michel Erpelding, Burkhard Hess, and Hélène Ruiz Fabri (eds.), *Peace through Law: The Versailles Peace Treaty and Dispute Settlement after World War I* (Baden-Baden: Nomos 2019), 239-76.

[139] These proceedings were conducted in the form of diplomatic protection by the US: Parlett, *Individual* 2011 (n. 121), 73-74; Kjeldgaard-Pedersen, *Personality* 2018 (n. 121), 88-89.

[140] For these figures, see Michel Erpelding and Hélène Ruiz Fabri, 'Introduction: International Adjudication and the Legacy of the Mixed Arbitral Tribunals', in Erpelding and Ruiz Fabri (eds), Mixed Arbitral Tribunals 2023 (n. 138), 9-23, at 12. For older statistics from 1930, see Schätzel, 'Schiedsgerichte' 1930 (n. 138), 378-455, at 449-52.

[141] Parlett, *Individual* 2011 (n. 121), Appendix III.

[142] Treaty of Versailles, 28 June 1919, 225 CTS 188 (emphasis added). The claims were to be decided by mixed tribunals (Art. 304).

[143] German-British arbitral tribunal, *Executors of F. Lederer (deceased) v. German Government*, Award of 13 December 1923, Recueil des décisions des tribunaux arbitraux mixtes, institués par les traités de paix (TAM) 3 (1924), 762-70, at 768; German-French arbitral tribunal, *Sigwald v. État allemand*, Award of 27 August 1926, TAM 6 (1927), 888-91, at 890.

[144] See, e.g., German-Belgian arbitral tribunal, *Hubert et Gesnot v. Princesse d'Arenberg et État allemand*, Decision of 24 January 1922, TAM 1 (1922), 739-40, at 740; German-French arbitral tribunal, *Office français de vérification et de compensation v. la Société Orosdi-Back*, Decision of 20 March 1922, TAM 1 (1922), 914-16, at 916; German-Yugoslav arbitral tribunal, *Wilhelm Schumacher v. État allemand et État serbe-croate-slovène*, Decision of 27 April 1922, TAM 2 (1923), 596-602, at 600.

of the Mexican revolution. Abraham H. Feller in 1935 analysed the claimants in the proceedings before these commissions, notably the relationship between the harmed individual and their home State.[145] Under some conventions, the claims to be considered were explicitly qualified as claims '*of* citizens' or '*by* persons'.[146] In a 1926 award, the US-Mexican General Claims Commission held that 'the *private nature of the claim* inheres in it and is not lost or destroyed so as to make it the property of the nation, although it becomes a national claim in the sense that it is subject to the absolute *control of the nation espousing it*'.[147] But another commission held that '[t]here does not exist, in that system any relation of responsibility between the transgressing State and the injured individual for the reason that the latter is not subject to international law'.[148] In any case, even upon avowal that a claim was what we would today call a direct international right, the States often still controlled the entire proceedings, and made them resemble classic diplomatic protection.[149] Moreover, all TAMs were ultimately abolished by inter-State agreements without the consent of the concerned individuals, a fact that undermined the argument that the individuals held a legally entrenched position within the system.[150]

3.4 Individual Claims from Government Procurement, Contracts, and Bonds

Independently from the war, in an increasingly globalised commercial sphere, more and more private business actors had claims against foreign governments, for example due to foreign investment, public procurement contracts, or unpaid State bonds. In the context and against the background of the Hague peace conferences at which inter-State arbitration was debated and realised, the question of direct access of injured individuals to (new) international arbitral tribunals or courts was intensely debated. Notably the German merchants, seconded by scholars, pressured for diagonal arbitration, for example in the form of special chambers of the Permanent Court of Arbitration (PCA) that had been

145 Abraham H. Feller, *The Mexican Claims Commissions* (New York, NY: Macmillan 1935), 83-94.

146 See, e.g., General Claims Convention between the United States of America and the United Mexican States for the settlement of claims by the citizens of each country against the other, 8 September 1923, RIAA vol. IV (1951), 11-14, at 11, Art. I.

147 General Claims Commission, *USA (William A. Parker) v. United Mexican States*, Opinion of 31 March 1926, RIAA vol. IV (2006), 35-41, at 37 (emphases added).

148 US-Mexican Claims Commission, *Dickson Car Wheel company*, July 1931, RIAA vol. IV (2006), 669-91, at 678.

149 Parlett, *Individual* 2011 (n. 121), 84; Kjeldgaard-Pedersen, *Personality* 2018 (n. 121), 91-92.

150 Michel Erpelding and Jakob Zollmann, 'Epilogue: The Early and the Long End of the Mixed Arbitral Tribunals, 1920-1939, in Erpelding and Ruiz Fabri (eds), *Mixed Arbitral Tribunals* 2023 (n. 138), 529-45, at 536, with further references.

established in 1899. In a 1911 memorandum on behalf of a merchants' association (*Handelsvertragsverein*), Hans Wehberg argued that individual access to an international tribunal would be the 'capstone of the building' of arbitration as established by the Hague system.[151]

Serious contemplation was also given to the idea of standing of individuals in the planning for the PCIJ that began working in 1922. In the Advisory Committee of Jurists sitting in 1920, Albert de Lapradelle and B. C. J. Loder were in favour of such standing, but were defeated.[152]

The key consideration in favour of direct individual claims was that such proceedings would conveniently *depolitise the issues and avoid selectivity.*[153] This was neatly put by Edwin M. Borchard as early as 1913 and still resonates today: The problem of diplomatic protection was that a

> legal right of the individual may [...] be sacrificed to the political expediency of his government. With the constant growth of international contractual relations between individuals and foreign governments the fulfilment and enforcement of legal obligations towards individuals should be divorced from political considerations. The difference in the practice of governments in the support of contract claims gives an unequal advantage to the nationals of some States and correspondingly embarrasses the governments whose policy or practice it is to decline diplomatic pressure in such cases.[154]

Diagonal suits would avoid 'disagreeable diplomatic coercion' and 'what is always a potential germ of international difficulties'; and 'the peace of the world will be fostered by the removal of one great source of international conflict'.[155] Against these arguments, sceptics against any allowance for individuals to sue foreign States warned against 'countless and endless litigation',[156] and against 'derisory or vexatious requests'.[157]

[151] Hans Wehberg, *Ein internationaler Gerichtshof für Privatklagen*, Handelspolitische Flugschriften Heft 7 (Berlin: Liebheit & Thiesen 1911), 34.

[152] Permanent Court of International Justice and Advisory Committee of Jurists, *Procès-verbaux of the Proceedings of the Committee, June 16th–July 24th, 1920, with Annexes* (The Hague: Van Langenhuysen Brothers 1920), 205-06; 210-11. For more detail, see Kjeldgaard-Pedersen, *Personality* 2018 (n. 121), 49-51.

[153] Edvard Hambro, 'Individuals before International Tribunals' *Proceedings of the American Society of International Law at its Annual Meetings (1921-1969)*, vol. 35 (24-26 April 1941), 22-26, at 25.

[154] Edwin M. 'Borchard, 'Contractual Claims in International Law' *Columbia Law Review* 13 (1913), 457-99, at 498.

[155] *ibid*, 499.

[156] Jacques Dumas, 'La sauvegarde internationale des droits de l'homme' *Recueil des Cours* 59 (1937), 1-97, at 10.

[157] Kaufmann, 'Règles générales' 1935 (n. 126), 425.

3.5 Assessment

In practice, the admission of individual plaintiffs (to collect monetary compensation for either commercial or war-related injuries) co-existed with the ongoing exercise of States bringing such claims before international tribunals in the form of diplomatic protection.

In the academic debate, even those who favoured individual access to international dispute settlement did not necessarily accept that those individuals possessed direct international rights. For the commercial context (such as procurement) Wehberg qualified the legal relationships between the private creditors and the debtor States as public international law-like (‘*völkerrechtsähnliche Beziehungen*’).[158]

As for the TAMs, the individual right to sue a foreign State which was ‘in itself’ a ‘progress’ of the law, did not stand the test, wrote Schätzel.[159] It would have been quicker and easier to deal with these individual claims as part of the inter-State negotiations on reparations. Schätzel thus qualified the claims as held by the allied States (not by the citizens).[160] Indeed, various features of the procedure assured that the individuals were not masters of the proceedings. This led to the conclusion that the relevant entitlement to compensation was actually *owned* by the States, and individuals were merely allowed to reclaim them at the place of their State.[161] An alternative qualification was that ‘the claim right of the private person’ (‘*das Klagerecht der Privatperson*’) was no international right but ‘rooted solely in domestic law’.[162] Both competing views denied that there could be an international individual right: if the right was owned by the individual, it must be domestic, if it was an international right, it must be State-owned.

According to Erich Kaufmann, the role of individuals before the mixed tribunals ‘did *not* constitute a first step of a revolution of the traditional concepts of international law’.[163] Kaufmann explicitly denied the emergence of any general rule to open up international tribunals to individuals or any tendency to extend the role of individuals in ‘normal’ situations (unrelated to war and territorial reapportionments).[164] In contrast, Abraham H. Feller found the diverse practice of the Mexican claims commissions to be irreconcilable with the ‘orthodox theory’ that ‘[o]nly States are subjects of international law’.[165]

[158] Wehberg, ‘Gerichtshof’ 1911 (n. 151), 9.

[159] Schätzel, ‘Schiedsgerichte’ 1930 (n. 138), 454.

[160] Schätzel, *Mitteilungen der Deutschen Gesellschaft für Völkerrecht* 7 (1926) (discussion of talk by Ebers), at 44-45.

[161] Rudolf Blühdorn, ‘Le fonctionnement et la jurisprudence des Tribunaux Arbitraux Mixtes créés par les traités de Paris’ *Recueil des Cours* 41 (1932), 141-239, at 144-45.

[162] Georg Geier, *Das internationale Privatrecht der Gemischten Schiedsgerichte des Versailles Vertrages* (Murnau: Fürst 1930), 12.

[163] Kaufmann, ‘Règles générales’ 1935 (n. 126), 422 (emphasis added).

[164] *ibid*, 424.

[165] Feller, *Mexican Claims Commission* 1935 (n. 145), 84.

Overall, it cannot be concluded with certainty that the Washington treaty on the Central-American Court, the Versailles Treaty, similar provisions in other peace treaties, or the Mexican treaties conferred direct material and procedural rights on individuals. Neither the practice, nor the plans for individual access to the PCA or PCIJ that never materialised, manifested a paradigm-change.[166] Nevertheless, it cannot be denied that both the practice and the doctrine of diagonal arbitration moved individuals to the centre stage in specific transnational contexts.

4. International Rights in Domestic Courts: The PCIJ's *Danzig* Advisory Opinion of 1928

Individual access to domestic courts with a view to enforcing their rights flowing from international treaties fortifies the individuals' international legal status.[167] The reason is that domestic courts are at the same time international agents—what Scelle ingeniously called 'dédoublement fonctionelle'—and are in that role tasked with applying international law.[168] The *Danzig* advisory opinion of 1928 defined this mechanism.[169] Here the PCIJ recognised that international treaties may grant individual rights and that their violation is actionable before domestic courts. At issue was a 1921 agreement between Poland and what was then the Free City of Danzig (the final Agreement concerning Officials).[170] The question for the advisory opinion was whether the railway employees who had passed from the railway service of the Free City of Danzig (formerly Prussian railway) to Polish service were entitled to bring actions against the Polish railways administration in respect of pecuniary claims (such as rates of wages) before courts of the Free City of Danzig, based on this agreement.[171] The most relevant provision of the *Beamtenabkommen* was Article 6 which mentioned 'the principle of *respect for rights* which can be shown to have been *duly acquired*', and which committed the Polish railway to recognise and satisfy claims regarding promotions, appointments, rates of wages, etc.[172]

[166] Parlett, *Individual* 2011 (n. 121), 348; Kjeldgaard-Pedersen, *Personality* 2018 (n. 121), 91.

[167] This section partly reproduces passages from Anne Peters, *Beyond Human Rights* (Cambridge: CUP 2016), 29-31.

[168] Georges Scelle, 'Règles générales du droit de la paix' *Recueil des Cours* 46 (1933), 327-703, at 358.

[169] PCIJ, *Jurisdiction of the Courts of Danzig*, Advisory Opinion of 3 March 1928, PCIJ Series B, No. 15.

[170] *Endgültiges Beamtenabkommen* of 22 October 1921 between the Government of Poland and the Free City of Danzig, repr. in PCIJ Series C, No. 14-I, 1928, 152-57. After the defeat of Germany in World War I, Danzig was detached from the German Empire and established as a 'Free City' by the Allied victorious powers; it had treaty-making power.

[171] See PCIJ, *Courts of Danzig* 1928 (n. 169), 10. The Polish treasury raised objections and argued that the Danzig courts had no jurisdiction to entertain these actions, while the Danzig courts declared themselves competent.

[172] *Endgültiges Beamtenabkommen* 1921 (n. 170), Article 6. Neither contracting party adopted specific laws to transpose or otherwise integrate the agreement into municipal law (Kate Parlett, 'The PCIJ's

The advisory opinion is (probably intentionally) formulated in an ambiguous manner so that diametrically opposed conclusions can be drawn from it.[173] The crucial passage is: '[B]eing an international agreement, [it] *cannot, as such*, create direct rights and obligations for private individuals. But it cannot be disputed that the very object of an international agreement, according to the *intention* of the contracting parties, may be *the adoption by the Parties of some definite rules creating individual rights and obligations* and enforceable by national courts.'[174]

The first and second sentences of the key passage are in tension with each other. The first sentence claims that an international agreement normally does *not* create rights and duties for individuals. In the following second sentence, this legal presumption is rebutted (only) in the event that the treaty parties have specially intended to grant individual rights and have formulated them in a sufficiently precise ('definite') way.

In *Danzig*, the PCIJ then interpreted the *Beamtenabkommen*—taking the intention of the treaty parties into account—as a 'part' of the employment relationship between the railway officials and the Polish railways administration: 'That there is such an intention in the present case can be established by reference to the terms of the *Beamtenabkommen*.'[175] '[C]onsequently, the Danzig officials have [...] a right of action against the Polish Railways Administration for the recovery of pecuniary claims based on the *Beamtenabkommen*.'[176]

It is important now that the passage '[...] *the adoption by the Parties of some definite rules creating individual rights and obligations* and enforceable by national courts'[177] is unclear. What is meant by '*some definite rules*'? The dualist reading of this passage is that these must be rules of domestic law. According to this reading, which was advocated most prominently by the president of the PCIJ at the time, Dionisio Anzilotti, the court had indeed *not* determined that an international agreement could itself contain individual rights, but rather had only drawn attention to the fact that the treaty parties could create such individual rights *in their implementing legislation*. According to the dualist interpretation, it was crucial that a treaty party (in the case of the *Beamtenabkommen*, Poland) failing to implement

Opinion in *Jurisdiction of the Courts of Danzig*: Individual Rights under Treaties' *Journal of the History of International Law* 10 (2008), 119-45, at 128).

[173] On the intentional ambiguity, see Hersch Lauterpacht, *The Subjects of International Law*, reproduced in Hersch Lauterpacht, *International Law, Being the Collected Papers of Hersch Lauterpacht* (Cambridge: CUP 1970), chapter 5, 279-307, at 289: 'And yet the Court was so ingeniously restrained in the manner in which it gave the decision that some have regarded it not as a far-reaching modification, but as an affirmation, of the established doctrine.'

[174] PCIJ, *Court of Danzig* 1928 (n. 169), 17-18 (emphasis added).

[175] *ibid*, 18.

[176] *ibid*, 21.

[177] *ibid*, 17-18 (emphasis added).

the treaty into its domestic law could not in turn rely on its inaction to justify the treaty breach under international law vis-à-vis the other State party to the treaty.[178]

The opposite understanding of the advisory opinion was advocated by Hersch Lauterpacht. According to Lauterpacht, the first sentence of the cited key passage merely pays lip service to the established doctrine at the time. According to this view, '*some definite rules*' referred to the provisions of international treaties themselves. If the treaty parties so intended and if the treaty provisions are definite enough, those provisions can create individual rights that are also directly applicable (i.e. can be invoked before a domestic court). In this view, the advisory opinion is 'in effect a revolutionary pronouncement', and '[i]t is difficult to exaggerate the bearing of the Opinion on the subject'.[179] This reading of the key passage does in fact fit better with the conclusions of the advisory opinion.[180]

Lauterpacht's monist reading of the advisory opinion has prevailed. But even according to the *Danzig* opinion interpreted in this way, the direct application of a treaty provision was still the exception that has to be specially proven.

5. Individuals as 'International Legal Persons'

The novel legal bodies, instruments, procedures, and entirely new branches of international law sparked a doctrinal controversy on a possible international legal personality of the individual[181] — a debate which some at the time chastised as 'metaphysical' and 'quite academic'.[182] That said, several standard books of the time and some now forgotten textbooks did not mention individuals at all under the rubric of possible international legal persons[183] (or 'subjects').[184]

[178] See Dionisio Anzilotti, *Corso di Diritto Internazionale, Volume primo, Introduzione – Teorie Generali* (Padova: Cedam 1955), 339-40.

[179] Hersch Lauterpacht, *The Development of International Law by the International Court* (2nd edn, London: Stevens 1958), 174 and 175.

[180] See above, text with notes 175 and 176.

[181] Janne E. Nijman, *The Concept of International Legal Personality: An Inquiry into the History and Theory of International Law* (The Hague: TMC Asser Press 2004), chapter 3, 85-243; Nathasha Wheatley, 'Spectral Legal Personality in Interwar International Law: On New Ways of Not Being a State' *Law and History Review* 35 (2017), 753-88.

[182] Edwin M. Borchard, 'The Access of Individuals to International Courts' *American Journal of International Law* 24 (1930), 359-65, at 364.

[183] Julius Hatschek, *Völkerrecht als System rechtlich bedeutsamer Staatsakte* (Leipzig: Deichert 1923); William Edward Hall, *A Treatise on International Law* (8th edn, Oxford: Clarendon Press 1924); Eduard Otto von Waldkirch, *Das Völkerrecht: In seinen Grundzügen dargestellt* (Basel: Helbing & Lichtenhahn 1926); René Foignet, *Manuel élémentaire de droit international public* (13th edn, Paris: Rousseau 1926 and 14th edn, Paris: Rousseau 1929); Joseph Thomas Delos, *La Société Internationale et les principes du droit public* (Paris: Pedone 1929); Ernst Vanselow, *Völkerrecht* (Berlin: Mittler 1931); Friedrich Wilhelm von Rauchhaupt, *Völkerrecht* (München: Voglrieder 1936); Alessandri Mis, *Le droit international public* (Paris: Pedone 1941).

[184] These two terms were not always used interchangeably. I will use 'person' in the following.

The extreme position was that States only could be legal persons of international law.[185] Implicitly drawing on a reimagined Roman law-based dichotomy between persons (*personae*) and things (*res*), individuals were relegated to the realm of things; they were 'objects' not 'subjects' of international law.[186]

The 'States-only' position was typically held by German and Italian authors who were, at the end of the nineteenth century, preoccupied with their nations' State-building exercise, but also by most other scholars.[187] Josef Kunz in 1925 called it the *communis opinio*.[188] The view was indeed so common that even young Hersch Lauterpacht—who would after 1942, under the impression of the Holocaust and the extinction of almost his entire family, spearhead international criminal law and the international protection of human rights—in 1927 still based his legal analysis on that premise: 'Of course, International Law being a law between States only and exclusively.'[189] This was likely written under the influence of his teacher Lassa Oppenheim. From there it then followed (tautologically) that individuals could never have international legal rights or obligations: 'For how could International Law, which is a law between States, give rights to individuals concerning their relations to a State?', Oppenheim asked rhetorically.[190] And he gave the answer: 'International Law *cannot* grant international rights to individuals, for international rights and duties can exist only between States, or between the League of Nations and States.'[191]

But that States-only position became dubious upon a careful analysis of the new legal instruments, accompanied by the first sharp doctrinal conceptualisation of 'international legal person'—a term that had previously not received much of a 'definition' for the purpose of international law. A radical small group of authors (spearheaded by Nicolas Politis[192]) argued that only human beings from flesh and blood could be, 'in the last analysis',[193] the true and only addressee of international—and in fact of all law. In the 1930s the main proponents of this view were Georges

[185] Henry Wheaton and Coleman Phillipson, *Wheaton's Elements of International Law* (5th edn, London: Stevens and Sons 1916), 34; von Liszt, *Völkerrecht* 1918 (n. 35), 42-43; Oppenheim, *International Law* 1920 (n. 36), 457-58; Heinrich Triepel, 'Les rapports entre le droit interne et le droit international' *Recueil des Cours* 1 (1923), 77-121, at 81; Dionisio Anzilotti, *Corso di diritto internazionale* (3rd edn, Roma: Athenaeum 1928), 113; Kaufmann, 'Règles générales' 1935 (n. 126), 309-620, at 407.

[186] Oppenheim, *International Law* 1920 (n. 36), 460 (§ 290); Knubben, *Subjekte des Völkerrechts* 1928 (n. 34), 487-527, at 516; Anzilotti, *Corso* 1928 (n. 185), 124; Alfred von Verdross, 'Règles générales du droit international de la paix' *Recueil des Cours* 30 (1929), 271-518, at 348; Cezary Berezowski, 'Les sujets non souverains du droit international' *Recueil des Cours* 65 (1938), 5-87, at 19.

[187] Roland Portman, *Legal Personality in International Law* (Cambridge: CUP 2010), chapter 5, 42-79.

[188] Kunz, *Völkerrechtliche Option* 1925 (n. 46), 1.

[189] Hersch Lauterpacht, 'Revolutionary Propaganda by Governments' *Transactions of the Grotius Society* 13 (1927), 143-64, at 143.

[190] Oppenheim, *International Law* 1920 (n. 36), 457 (§ 289).

[191] *ibid*, 459 (§ 289) (emphasis in original).

[192] Politis, *Nouvelles tendances* 1927 (n. 43), 45 and 66.

[193] James Leslie Brierly, 'Règles générales du droit de la paix' *Recueil des Cours* 58 (1936), 5-237, at 47.

Scelle,[194] Hans Kelsen,[195] James Brierly,[196] and Hersch Lauterpacht.[197] More moderate writers recognised a 'partial',[198] 'limited',[199] 'conditioned',[200] 'indirect',[201] or 'passive'[202] international legal personality of humans, flowing at best from specific treaty law and thus apt to deploy only an *inter partes* (not *erga omnes*) effect.

Awarding the epithet of 'international legal person' of course depended on the doctrinal circumscription of that concept which was problematised only after World War I. A smaller group of authors favoured a broad definition that looked at the substantive law only, while the prevailing doctrine endorsed a narrower conception and additionally asked for procedures. The first group of authors found *material rights* of individuals to be determinative of their legal status.[203] Some also pointed to the individuals' substantive *obligations* (notably the treaty-based criminalisation of piracy, slave trade, human trafficking, and war-related obligations).[204] A yet smaller group of scholars found the social or formal law-*making* capacity to be the crucial criterion, and notably Georges Scelle considered individuals to be vested with such a power.[205]

In contrast, the majority of the writers of the time were willing to concede the high pedigree label of international legal person only to those actors who not only possessed substantive rights but also enjoyed procedural standing before international bodies. So human beings could be international legal persons only to the extent they were able to avail themselves autonomously (without relying on

[194] Georges Scelle, 'Introduction, le milieu intersocial' *Précis de droit des gens: Principes et systématique*, vol. I (Paris: Sirey 1932), 42: 'Les individus seuls sont sujets de droit en droit international public.'

[195] Hans Kelsen, 'Théorie Générale du Droit International Public – Problèmes Choisis' *Recueil des Cours* 42 (1932), 121-351 and 142.

[196] Brierly, 'Règles générales' 1936 (n. 193), 47: 'only individuals are susceptible of being subjects of this law, as of all other [law]' ('seuls les individus sont susceptibles d'être sujets de ce droit-là, comme de tout autre').

[197] Hersch Lauterpacht, 'Règles générales du droit de la paix' *Recueil des Cours* 62 (1937), 95-422, at 215.

[198] Giorgio Balladore Pallieri, *Diritto internazionale pubblico* (Milano: Giuffrè 1937), 277-79.

[199] Romano, *Corso* (n. 9), 76-77; Jean Pierre Adrien François, 'Règles générales du droit de la paix' *Recueil des Cours* 66 (1938), 1-294 at 117.

[200] Berezowski, 'Sujets' 1938 (n. 186), 18.

[201] Louis Le Fur, 'La théorie du droit naturel depuis le XVIIe siècle et la doctrine moderne' *Recueil des Cours* 19 (1927), 259-442, at 350, footnote 1.

[202] Verdross, 'Règles générales' 1929 (n. 186), 349; Karl Strupp, 'Les règles générales du droit de la paix' *Recueil des Cours* 47 (1934), 466.

[203] Godehard Josef Ebers, 'Sind im Völkerrecht allein die Staaten parteifähig' *Mitteilungen der Deutschen Gesellschaft für Völkerrecht* 7 (1926), 5-46, at 17; Hans Herz, 'Le sujet en droit international public' *Revue internationale de la théorie du droit* 10 (1936), 100-11, at 110; Lauterpacht, 'Règles générales' 1937 (n. 197), 95-422, at 100 and 213. For a clear distinction between substance and procedure, the capacity to *have* rights, and the capacity *to act* in law, see Strupp, 'Règles générales' 1934 (n. 202), 257-596, at 421.

[204] Nicolas S. Politis, 'Le problème des limitations de la souveraineté et la théorie de l'abus des droits dans les rapports internationaux' *Recueil des Cours* 6 (1925), 5-116, at 9.

[205] Scelle, 'Règles générales' 1933 (n. 168), 327-703, at 367: 'pouvoir social de créer des situations juridiques'. For a focus on law-making power, see also Verdross, 'Règles générales' 1929 (n. 186), 271-518, at 321, 347, and 349.

diplomatic protection by their home State) of proceedings before international courts and similar forums in order to enforce their *rights* against States that had allegedly violated such rights.[206] Equally, individuals were international persons not already by virtue of being saddled with international legal *obligations* but only when an international rule itself provided for a direct sanction against them.[207] Where no such international procedures existed, humans remained—even if endowed with material rights and obligations—international persons in an 'imperfect sense',[208] or 'sujets simples', with 'droits internationaux imparfaits'.[209] They were not '*Rechtsgenossen*'.[210]

This linkage of status to procedure was inspired by the novel international mechanisms to which individuals had access and which marked a tangible—and in juridical terms clear and obvious—difference to prior international legal instruments, which in a fuzzy way had sought to benefit individuals. Conceptually, this narrow definition of legal personality reminds of the Anglo-Saxon priority of procedures ('no right without a remedy'). Thus, the proponents of an international legal personality of the individual pointed to the new individual complaint procedures (notably the projected Prize Court, the Central-American Court, and the TAMs)[211] as prime indicators or evidence of the individual's new and enhanced status under international law.[212]

The anti-individualist authors drew different conclusions from the very same institutions. These writers insisted on the 'extraordinary' situation, qualified the tribunals as 'very rare exceptions' which confirmed the rule, and recalled that the institutions were always revocable by the States.[213] Therefore, individuals were only incidentally benefitted, by legal 'reflex'.[214] In conclusion, it would be 'false' to

[206] Franz von Liszt and Max Fleischmann (revised by), *Das Völkerrecht: systematisch dargestellt* (12th edn, Berlin: Springer 1925), 86 (this statement was not yet contained in the 11th edn of 1918); André Mandelstam, 'La protection internationale des droits de l'homme' *Recueil des Cours* 38 (1931), 125-232, at 199-200; Verdross, 'Règles générales' 1929 (n. 186), 323-412, 328; J. W. Garner, 'Le développement et les tendances récentes du droit international' *Recueil des Cours* 35 (1931), 605-720, at 694; Segal, *L'individu* 1932 (n. 70), 166-69; Kaufmann, 'Règles générales' 1935 (n. 126), 309-620, at 416.

[207] Kelsen, 'Théorie Générale' 1932 (n. 195), 117-352, at 152-53.

[208] Hans Kelsen, *Principles of International Law* (2nd edn, New York, NY: Holt, Rinehart & Winston 1966), 234.

[209] Georges Ténékidès, *L'individu dans l'ordre juridique international* (Paris: A. Pedone 1933), 214.

[210] Ernst Wolgast, *Völkerrecht: mit einem systematischen Verzeichnis der völkerrechtlichen Kollektivverträge* (Berlin: Stilke 1934), 794.

[211] See section 3, above.

[212] von Liszt and Fleischmann, *Völkerrecht* 1925 (n. 206), 86; Politis, 'Abus de droit' 1925 (n. 204), 1-122, at 8-9; Alfred Verdross, *Die Verfassung der Völkerrechtsgemeinschaft* (Wien/Berlin: Julius Springer 1926), 159; Ebers, 'Staaten' 1926 (n. 203), 14-15; Maurice Bourquin, 'Règles générales du droit de la paix' *Recueil des Cours* 35 (1931), 1-232, at 43; Segal, *L'individu* 1932 (n. 70), 167; Romano, *Corso* (n. 9), 76-77; Brierly, 'Règles générales' 1936 (n. 193), 5-237, at 92; Hambro, 'Individuals' 1941 (n. 153), 22-26, at 24; Vladimir R. Idelson, 'The Law of Nations and the Individual' *Transactions of the Grotius Society* 30 (1944), 50-66, at 60.

[213] Heilborn, *Stellung des Menschen* 1927 (n. 32), 8; Kaufmann, 'Règles générales' 1935 (n. 126), 420-21; see also Kunz, *Völkerrechtliche Option* 1925 (n. 46), 4.

[214] Strupp, 'Règles générales' 1934 (n. 202), 467.

conceive these three procedures as 'a witness of a new conception of international law'.[215]

Doctrinally, the classification of the individual as an international legal person sat easily with a 'monist' conceptualisation of the relationship between international law and domestic law. Hans Kelsen,[216] Georges Scelle,[217] Hersch Lauterpacht,[218] and others,[219] all explained or associated the individual's international legal standing with monism.

In contrast, the great dualists tended to deny the international legal personality of the individual. In the dualist paradigm, individuals could (almost by definition) never be the direct addressees of international rights or obligations. Rather, such obligations were addressed to States only, and had to be transposed by the States into their domestic law (conceived as a completely distinct legal order); these *domestic* laws then could obligate or entitle individuals, only against their home State.[220] Dionisio Anzilotti spoke of an 'evident confusion of the international legal order with a non-existent legal order of humanity'.[221] According to the dualist scheme, international customary law or treaties which seemingly spelled out individual rights or obligations in reality obliged or authorised the States to enact the requisite norms. The resulting rights or obligations were *not* international rights, but rights derived from municipal laws.[222]

For Heinrich Triepel, it was 'most important' that 'the individuals' obligations toward their State or their fellow citizens *can never conflict* with their international obligations, since they do not have any such obligations'.[223] In this logic, it was fully consistent that the individual could therefore never contest the non-fulfilment or violation of an international treaty before an international body. Only domestic remedies would be at the individual's disposal.[224] Crucially, from that perspective, individuals could not use international law against their own State of nationality to which they owed unqualified loyalty.[225]

215 Kaufmann, 'Règles générales' 1935 (n. 126), 421.

216 Hans Kelsen, 'Les rapports de système entre le droit interne et le droit international public' *Recueil des Cours* 14 (1926), 231-329, at 286.

217 Georges Scelle describes himself as '[t]rès nettement partisan d'un monisme *absolu*', 'Règles générales' 1933 (n. 168), 33 (emphasis in the original).

218 Lauterpacht, 'Règles générales' 1937 (n. 197), 126 and 232.

219 François, 'Apatrides' 1935 (n. 30), 283-376, at 318.

220 Paul Heilborn, 'Die Subjekte des Völkerrechts', in Karl Strupp (ed.), Julius Hatschek (founder), *Wörterbuch des Völkerrechts und der Diplomatie*, Vol. II (Berlin: de Gruyter 1925), 684-86, at 685; Leo Strisower, 'Einige Bemerkungen über Staatsverträge, welche die Rechtslage der Individuen betreffen' *Zeitschrift für öffentliches Recht* 4 (1925), 272-98, at 284; Strupp, 'Règles générales' 1934 (n. 202), 257-596, at 407-08.

221 Anzilotti, *Corso* 1928 (n. 185), 122 ('la confusione evidente che qui si fa tra l'ordinamento giuridico internazionale e un preteso diritto dell'umanità').

222 Heinrich Triepel, *Völkerrecht und Landesrecht* (Leipzig: Verlag von C. L. Hirschfeld 1899), 254; Oppenheim, *International Law* 1920 (n. 36), § 289 (p. 342-43); Anzilotti, *Corso* 1928 (n. 185), 123.

223 Triepel, *Völkerrecht* 1899 (n. 222), 254 (emphasis added).

224 On diplomatic protection, see the text accompanying note 122.

225 Triepel, *Völkerrecht* 1899 (n. 222), 261; for wording, see the text accompanying note 240.

As these debates show, the international legal personality of the individual was (and is) not merely a terminological squabble, but concerns the overall structure of international law, the scholarly method, and it is a normative issue. What is at stake is not only the penetration of the shield of State sovereignty but more fundamentally even the 'normality' of international law: if international law—with its direct outreach to the individual—is seen as a social phenomenon, not a product of State 'will', then it is a law as strong and as legitimate as any other body of law.

6. Rationales, Paradigms, and Principles

The overarching policy objective of those who sought to carve out and strengthen the international legal status of the individual was surely an enhanced legal protection. New and massive harms were committed against individuals who were discriminated, expelled, stripped of their nationality, etc. The gap in legal protection arose because the home State (which was often itself the perpetrator) was not willing or able to care for the individuals, or because the problem could not be remedied by one State alone. Additionally, the Great War itself, which had led to several of the new issues (notably refugees and minorities), came to be seen as an outgrowth of exaggerated statism and nationalism, undergirded in international law by a strong principle of sovereignty. And notably for the population of the mandate territories, maybe also for the proletariat, an international legal status of the individual also implied their 'improvement'. Finally, and more forward-looking, some of the individualist authors in the 1920s and 1930s additionally sensed the rise of totalitarianism and fascism, the complete subjection of the individual to the State, and sought to erect a bulwark against these politics.[226]

6.1 From *ius naturalism* to realism

The conceptual moves and theoretical underpinnings to reach those objectives spanned the entire gamut of paradigms available at the time. Some authors displayed an affinity to *ius naturalism*[227] or a fuzzy naturalism.[228] Politis relied on 'equity', the 'juridical conscience of peoples', and civilisation.[229] Lauterpacht invoked 'compelling reasons of progress of international law and morality'.[230]

[226] Nijman, *Concept* 2004 (n. 181), 87, 126-27, 130, 147-48, 171, 187, and 225.
[227] Bourquin, 'Règles générales' 1931 (n. 212), 1-232, at 41-42.
[228] Le Fur claimed that 'the legal personality must be the simple transfer of the *real* personality into law, and must be accorded to every individual'. ('La personnalité juridique doit être la simple traduction juridique de la personnalité *réelle*, qu'elle doit être reconnue à tout individu.') He thus implied that the law simply depicts or follows reality. Le Fur, 'Théorie du Droit' 1927 (n. 201), 259-442, at 404 (emphasis added).
[229] Politis, *Nouvelles tendances* 1927 (n. 43), 62-63 (my translation).
[230] Lauterpacht, 'Règles générales' 1937 (n. 197), 215.

In contrast, both Scelle and Kelsen claimed to be 'realists'.[231] For Kelsen, the legal term 'person' was merely the 'personified expression of the unity of a given legal system regulating human action'.[232] The legal person was a purely juridical 'auxiliary' construct in order to identify at whom rights or obligations, and sanctions, in a given legal order, were addressed at. The person (also the individual as a legal person) was 'a complex of rights and obligations'.[233] For the purposes of the law, individuals were not natural, but juridical persons.[234]

Georges Scelle, who analysed law as a social phenomenon,[235] taught that all law ultimately consisted of social relationships or 'social formations', whose agents were always individuals, acting in different roles.[236] Because individuals could interact among each other across the entire globe, they were all members of the 'vast ecumenic society which calls itself humanity'.[237] Therefore, '[a]n international society, like any national society, is a society of individuals, and only of individuals'.[238] Scelle moreover followed Léon Duguit and espoused a peculiar concept of the legal person that denied individual 'rights' and spoke only of 'competences'.[239] The methodological shift was accompanied by an invocation of new legal principles. The ideas invoked to bolster the enhanced international legal status of the individual were *democracy* and *solidarity* (section 6.3). These acquired the function of counter-principles to *sovereignty* which will be discussed first (section 6.2).

6.2 Against Unfettered State Sovereignty

The conceptualisation of the individual as the ultimate international legal person was the flipside of a transformation of the State. In the second half of the nineteenth century, in the heydays of statism, the State was considered a real entity, a living organism, an end in itself, even sacred. The defenders of the international legal role of the individual reacted against this exaggeration. They attacked both the concept and role of States and argued against the States' ostensible differentia specifica, sovereignty.

For Triepel still (writing in 1899), 'the *duty of those subject to the State* [Unterthanen] *to obey the laws of the State* – irrespective of the relationship thereof to international law – is entirely unconditional'.[240] Triepel had denied the possibility

231 Kelsen, 'Théorie générale' 1932 (n. 195), 121-351, at 144; Scelle, 'Règles générales' 1933 (n. 168), 332.
232 Kelsen, 'Théorie générale' 1932 (n. 195), 142-43.
233 *ibid*, 143.
234 *ibid*, 143-44.
235 Scelle, 'Règles générales' 1933 (n. 168), 339.
236 *ibid*, 342-43.
237 *ibid*, 342.
238 *ibid*, 343.
239 Scelle, *Précis de droit* vol. I 1932 (n. 194), 26; vol. II. (Paris: Sirey 1934), at 292.
240 Triepel, *Völkerrecht* 1899 (n. 222), 261 (emphasis added).

of direct international rights or obligations of individuals because this would risk relaxing the individuals' absolute subjection to their State. But the dangers of such statism had already materialised through World War I (and of course even more shockingly in World War II). Against such experience, the individualists, firstly, descriptively and conceptually thought to dismantle the hypostasis of the State as a 'superman' (Kelsen)[241] and its 'anthropomorphic abstraction' (Scelle).[242] Nicolas Politis exposed the State to be a 'pure abstraction'. States as 'fictions' were only 'relational devices' for humans which composed them, and only 'their personality counts'.[243] That said, notably Scelle did not necessarily assign a minor role to the State but favoured strong social and welfarist policies.

The reconceptualisation of the State had a systemic significance for international law: according to Politis, international law as a whole since the Great War had been undergoing a phase of transformation from the international law of States into a genuinely universal law of human beings.[244] This also affected the scholarly method. Mirkine-Guetzévich saw 'la protection internationale de l'individu comme un "postulat" de la science juridique moderne'.[245] The idea that international society is composed of States was, wrote Scelle, a 'false view' that was responsible for the worthlessness and paralysis of the 'traditional science of the law of nations'.[246]

In addition to the proper description and analysis of international law, there was the normative concern with responsibilising power holders. Unfettered State sovereignty was abused to the detriment of humans, and therefore needed to be checked. For Antoine Hobza, individual rights (such as freedom of religion) could (and should) be stipulated in an international treaty so as to interrupt the 'general irresponsibility of the state in function of its sovereignty'.[247] André Mandelstam put it categorically: the fate of the 'new international law of tomorrow' (consisting—as he saw it—notably in the international protection of human rights), would depend on the 'definitive solution of the great problem of the sovereignty of the state'.[248]

One solution to fix that great problem was to deconstruct the billiard-ball State and to displace the 'real centre of legal and moral responsibility' from the 'metaphysical personality of the State' to the 'individual'.[249] This then meant that State sovereignty was neither accepted as absolute (or impenetrable), nor as the foundational principle of international law. International law needed to obtain a new,

[241] Kelsen, 'Rapports' 1926 (n. 216), 281 ('surhomme').

[242] Scelle, 'Règles générales' 1932 (n. 168), 343.

[243] Politis, *Nouvelles tendances* 1927 (n. 43), 76.

[244] *ibid*, 75-76.

[245] Boris Mirkine-Guetzévich, 'Préface', in Egidio Reale, *Le régime des passeports et la Société des Nations* (Paris: A Rousseau 1930), XIII.

[246] Scelle, 'Règles générales' 1932 (n. 168), 343.

[247] Antoine Hobza, 'Questions de droit international concernant les religions' *Recueil des Cours* 5 (1924), 367-424, at 380.

[248] Mandelstam, 'Protection' 1931 (n. 206), 125-232, at 172.

[249] Lauterpacht, 'Règles générales' 1937 (n. 197), 215.

'objective' basis, independent from the will of States.[250] International law had 'exactly the same foundation as domestic law: it is a social product'.[251]

The critique of the dominant conception of sovereignty also led to a recasting of the overall purpose of international law and to the claim that 'man is the objective of [all] law. This is the modern tendency of the science of international law'.[252] In 1941 such reasoning was presented as

> the very strongest argument in favour of enlarging the scope of the individual in international law. The dogma of sovereignty is in reality the very negation of international law invoked whenever a state wishes to pursue a line of policy against the interest of the community of States. The strongest reason for working in favour of a better position of the individual in international law is exactly that it can counteract extreme nationalism and the omnipotence of the State which has caused so many catastrophes in the past.[253]

Concomitantly, the relative scope of the *domaine réservé*, relative to the development of international rules, as the PCIJ acknowledged specifically in an opinion concerning the nationality of individuals in 1923, was key.[254] The possibility of the 'shrinking' of exclusive domestic jurisdiction then later led the way to a more full-fledged international protection of the individual. As Norman Bentwich predicted in 1945: 'Another large sphere of State activity which, it is fairly certain, will be taken out of the sphere of exclusive domestic jurisdiction, and become of international concern, is the treatment of the individual by the State.'[255]

Overall, although not a zero-sum game, the ascendancy of the individual in international law to some extent ousted the State from its place as the pivot of the international legal system, and also pierced the shield of sovereignty.

6.3 Democracy and Solidarity

Two principles, democracy and solidarity, were built up to perform the dual legal function as counterprinciples against sovereignty and as the attendant legal bases of the legal status of the individual. For Scelle, the various new international regimes and procedures (as mentioned in this chapter) responded to the problem of the 'autonomy of the will of the legal person' and manifested that the principle of

250 Ebers, 'Staaten' 1926 (n. 203), 18-19.
251 Politis, *Nouvelles tendances* 1927 (n. 192), 77.
252 Mirkine-Guetzévich, 'Préface' 1930 (n. 245), VII-XIV, at XII.
253 Hambro, *Individuals* 1941 (n. 153), 26 (footnote omitted).
254 PCIJ, *Nationality Decrees Issued in Tunis and Morocco*, 1923, Advisory Opinion of 7 February 2023, PCIJ Series B No. 4, at 24.
255 Norman Bentwich, 'The Limits of the Domestic Jurisdiction of the State' *Transactions of the Grotius Society* 31 (1945), 59-89, at 62.

democracy had been transferred to international law and that the governed held governing powers.[256] Politis requested, 'in order to grant international law the democratic character reclaimed by our epoch, to place at its foundation, instead of the aristocratic idea which subordinates men to the State, the principles furnished by the study of the individual with his likes'.[257] For Otfried Nippold, the idea of equal rights for all and 'the idea that right, in the life of nations, shall prevail over might – beyond a doubt finds its adequate expression above all in democracy'.[258]

Second, the enhanced legal status of the individual was seen as a legal consequence of a postulated international principle of 'solidarity'.[259] Spiropoulos explained the 'legal condition of the individual' against the background of an ongoing 'battle' between sovereignty and solidarity among States as 'one of the characteristics of the international legal situation of our epoch'.[260] According to Politis, 'solidarity of human relations is the great modern social phenomenon. It has inspired a new doctrine of domestic public law which, from domestic public law, has extended its influence into international law.'[261] Scelle presented the most elaborate theory: The extant division of labour in any given group gives rise to an 'unvoluntary' solidarity. This 'social fact' was the 'origin' of all societies, including the international one, which therefore all consisted of individuals only.[262]

6.4 Rights

The language of rights was fairly marginal both in the legal instruments and in the immediate post-World War I debates on individuals in international law. Moreover, technical claim rights and fundamental human rights played a different role and had a different trajectory.

6.4.1 Claim Rights and Legal Personality

Those writers who affirmed the individual's international legal personality mainly derived that status from the complaint procedures offered to individuals. Those

[256] Scelle, *Précis* vol. II 1934 (n. 239), at 293-94.

[257] Politis, 'Abus de droit' 1925 (n. 204), at 8: 'pour donner au droit international *le caractère démocratique réclamé par notre époque*, de mettre à sa base, à la place de l'idée aristocratique qui subordonne l'homme à l'État, les principes fournis par l'étude de l'individu avec ses semblables.'

[258] Otfried Nippold, *The Development of International Law after the World War* (Oxford: Clarendon Press, 1923) (English translation of *Die Gestaltung des Völkerrechts nach dem Weltkriege* 1917), 104.

[259] *ibid*, 39: 'the whole procedure of international law is founded upon the idea of this solidarity'. For the French theory of 'solidarisme', see the promoter of the League of Nations, winner of the Nobel peace prize in 1920, Léon Bourgeois, *La solidarité* (first published in 1896, seven editions up to 1912, Paris: Librairie Armand Colin).

[260] Spiropoulos, 'L'individu' 1929 (n. 11), 195-269, at 197.

[261] Politis, *Nouvelles tendances* 1927 (n. 43), 75-76: 'La solidarité des relations humaines est le grand phénomène social moderne. Elle a inspiré une nouvelle doctrine du droit public interne qui, du droit public interne, a étendu son influence dans le droit international.'

[262] Scelle, 'Règles générales' 1932 (n. 168), 339-40 and 343.

who attached significance to the substantive individual entitlements in international instruments did not have fundamental human rights in mind.[263] Put differently, the post-World War I debate on the legal personality was disjunct from lingering *ius naturalist* remnants in international legal scholarship.

In none of the new interbellum legal regimes was the concept of an individual right elaborated, neither in the legal instruments themselves nor in accompanying doctrine. The word 'right' was used occasionally (and misleadingly such as in the title of the mentioned Declaration on the 'rights' of the Child[264]), but it apparently did not carry a strong meaning of entitlement and was not conceptualised in opposition to mere protection on the basis of 'objective' law or standards. Current observers conclude that the language of 'rights' for individuals in some treaties and decisions reflected no deliberate choice away from the idea of protection by rebound and in no way attempted to transform the structures of international law.[265]

Because the traditional doctrine had been fixated on States' 'rights', those who identified individual rights did not justify those with the holders' human-ness but rather performed a transfer of rights from States to individuals. Explicit pronouncements on international individual rights were rare and contrarious. For example, Georges Ténékidès on the one side identified a '"sui generis" character of the individual right that is relevant for international law'. 'The individual right that is created internationally forms an autonomous legal category.'[266] On the other side, Jean Pierre Adrien François saw no internationally based legal fundamental rights that could be reclaimed by individuals, and no rights were derivable from humanitarian considerations.[267]

6.4.2 Fundamental Rights and Human Dignity Post-World War I

Only isolated scholars brought the American and French revolution's ideas of unalienable, innate, and fundamental rights to bear also in twentieth century international law. Discussing the slave trade, human trafficking (of 'Whites' ['blanches']), emigration, nationality, the law of aliens, and extradition (i.e. the pre-World War I legal fields), Henry Bonfils and Paul Fauchille in 1914 claimed that 'man possesses certain rights which are inherent attributes of the human person. *These rights, innate, primordial, absolute* […] *are governed by international law.* — As a human, the physical individual is subjected to international law. […] The innate rights all have their base and their rationale in the double principle of individual liberty and inviolability of the human person.'[268]

[263] See accompanying text to note 203, above.

[264] Declaration of the Rights of the Child 1924 (n. 16).

[265] Parlett, *Individual* 2011 (n. 121), 348-49.

[266] Ténékidès, *L'individu* 1933 (n. 209), 204 ('droit individuel d'intérêt international').

[267] François, 'Apatrides' 1935 (n. 30), 317.

[268] Henry Bonfils and Paul Fauchille, *Manuel de droit international public* (7th edn, Paris: Rousseau 1914), at 251 (§ 397) (emphasis added).

Destruction and mutilation in World War I, famine, epidemic, and impoverishment could have added urgency to such reasoning. And in fact, activists, victims (e.g. disabled veterans), and humanitarian organisations in the 1920s formed 'a new, and transnationalised humanitarian movement' whose guiding principle was 'rights, not charity'.[269] Bruno Cabanes characterises the immediate post-World War I societal developments as a move 'from humanitarian rights [. . .] to human rights', as a 'revolution of rights in the 1920s'.[270] The 'transnational' rights were based on vague ideas, they were not universal, they were not necessarily technically anchored in international law, and they were 'applied to groups, not to individuals'.[271] Even if the invention of transnational rights was 'a decisive turning point'[272] already in the 1920s, it took longer to involve mainstream international scholarship and international politics.

That said, academic texts on international human rights began to be produced in the early 1920s. The most significant one was the Institut de Droit International's 'Déclaration des droits internationaux de l'homme', prepared by André Mandelstam as a rapporteur.[273] With its adoption on 12 October 1929, on 'Columbus day' (the 437th anniversary of the 'discovery' of the new world), the reference to the US American declaration of independence and bill of rights was quite obvious. Mandelstam boasted that the declaration would 'in the history of the law of nations without any doubt be appreciated as an event of highest significance, as the starting point of a new era'.[274] At the time, however, '[n]either the League nor any national government took the least notice'.[275]

6.4.3 Response to World War II

The political sphere was hit by the idea of human rights only decades later – 'suddenly and unexpectedly'.[276] According to Brian Simpson, (only) in 1944 public interest in human rights was so widespread that the theme could no longer be ignored by international politics.[277] The topos had emerged out of the work of

[269] Bruno Cabanes, *The Great War and the Origins of Humanitarianism, 1918–1924* (Cambridge: CUP 2014), at 300.
[270] *ibid*, at 307.
[271] *ibid*, at 16 and 301.
[272] *ibid*, at 301.
[273] Institut de Droit International, 'Déclaration des droits internationaux de l'homme' *Annuaire IDI* 35 (1929) part II, 298-300.
[274] Mandelstam, 'Schutz der Menschenrechte' 1931 (n. 113), 335-77 (370): 'In der Geschichte des Völkerrechts wird ohne Zweifel die New Yorker Deklaration als ein Ereignis von der höchsten Bedeutung, als der Ausgangspunkt einer neuen Ära gewürdigt werden.'
[275] Simpson, *Human Rights* 2004 (n. 24), 153.
[276] Mark Mazower, 'The Strange Triumph of Human Rights, 1933-1950' *Historical Journal* 47 (2004), 386.
[277] Simpson, *Human Rights* 2004 (n. 24), 219-20.

predominantly Anglo-American civil society groups, individual activists,[278] academics,[279] and learned societies.[280]

Initially only at the margins of the plans for a new peace order, reinforced by the spread of the knowledge about the Nazi crimes and horrors of the war that cost maybe 80 million human lives, human rights became the story what the war had actually been about.[281] Key political documents such as President Roosevelt's four freedom speech (6 January 1941) and the Atlantic Charter (14 August 1941) mentioned 'rights' but said nothing on international protection and enforcement mechanisms. In hindsight, these texts were reinterpreted and acquired a practical significance as milestones on the road to an international scheme of human rights protection.[282]

A tentative Chinese proposal for a clause on 'equality of all States and all races' in the founding document of the new world organisation (modelled on the Japanese proposal for the League Covenant) was rejected at the Dumbarton Oaks conference of the four key powers in summer 1944.[283] Only after France joined (on 7 May 1945) the group that later became the P5 did the protection of human rights emerge as one of the objectives of the new organisation as a whole.[284] Human rights now figure in the preamble,[285] as one of the purposes of the United Nations organisation (Art. 1(3)), and in Article 55 lit.(c) of the UN Charter. Wary to shield racialised laws, for example with regard to segregation, immigration, and the colonies, the leading States took care to keep references to human rights in the UN Charter as weak as possible. The wording was 'designed to have symbolic importance, but no

[278] On the 'rights of man campaign' by Herbert George Wells, see Jan H. Burgers, 'The Road to San Francisco: The Revival of the Human Rights Idea in the Twentieth Century' *Human Rights Quarterly* 14 (1992), 464-68.

[279] Hersch Lauterpacht, *An International Bill of Rights* (New York, NY 1945, reproduced Oxford: OUP 2013) was written before the text of the UN Charter was settled; the preface is dated October 1944. Unlike Lauterpacht's book, Jacques Maritain, *Les droits de l'homme et la loi naturelle* (New York, NY: Éditions de la maison française 1942) proposed a complete scheme for the international protection of human rights (*cf.* Simpson, *Human Rights* 2004 (n. 24), 205-06).

[280] See note 273, above, on the Institut de Droit International. The American Law Institute's (Committee of Advisers on Essential Human Rights), 'Statement of Essential Human Rights' *The Annals of the American Academy of Political and Social Science* 243 (1946), 18-26, was the principal source of inspiration for the first draft of the Universal Declaration of Human Rights (UDHR). This draft was authored by John Peters Humphrey, a UN staff member and Canadian national, in 1947 (Burgers, 'Road to San Francisco' 1992 (n. 278), 473; Simpson, *Human Rights* 2004 (n. 24), 196; Daniel J. Whelan, *Indivisible Human Rights: A History* (Philadelphia, PA: University of Pennsylvania Press 2010), 12.

[281] On the genesis of the human rights provisions in the UN Charter, see, seminally, Burgers, 'Road to San Francisco' 1992 (n. 278), 449-77; Simpson, *Human Rights* 2004 (n. 24), 157-220; Pamela Slotte and Miia Halme-Tuomisaari (eds.), *Revisiting the Origins of Human Rights* (Cambridge: CUP 2015).

[282] Simpson, *Human Rights* 2004 (n. 24), 175 and 182.

[283] Tentative Chinese Proposals for a General International Organization, 23 August 1944. Foreign Relations of the United Sates: Diplomatic Papers, 1944, Volume I, available at https://history.state.gov/historicaldocuments/frus1944v01/d422, accessed 7/12/2023. For the Japanese proposal of 1919, see note 12, above.

[284] Simpson, *Human Rights* 2004 (n. 24), 256.

[285] Ironically, the relevant passage of the preamble was drafted by the South African delegate Jan Smuts who was himself a proponent of racial segregation.

practical effect'.[286] The non-invocability of human rights was additionally secured with robust non-intervention clauses.[287] The symbolic kick-off of international human rights law then was the Universal Declaration of Human Rights (UDHR) of 1948.[288]

In these texts, *human dignity*, as developed both in Catholic social doctrine and in democrat and socialist theory and positivised in constitutional texts in the first three decades of the twentieth century, became a buzzword.[289] It was mentioned in Article II(a) of the Philadelphia Declaration of 1944 that put the ILO on a new footing, in the preambles of the UN Charter and of the UNESCO Constitution (both of 1945), and then in the UDHR of 1948.[290] Dignity has since then functioned as a cover-up for the so-far unattainable consensus on the theoretical foundations of international human rights.

Mark Mazower has argued that the initial UN human rights regime was 'in fact a step *backwards*' behind the League's minority protection scheme.[291] It was a convenient and weaker substitute for a regime that had been unpopular and had crashed, and which the leading powers certainly did not want to apply to themselves. The relevant States therefore collapsed minority protection into human rights. Thus, they engaged in window-dressing and managed to avoid the much-demanded generalisation of minority protection that was still on the table:[292] 'Behind the smokescreen of the rights of the individual, in other words, the corpse of the League's minorities policy could be safely buried.'[293]

7. Conclusion

The 'long' years after World War I, including World War II and its aftermath, up to the foundation of the United Nations, were a formative period for the humanisation of international law. It has been claimed that the interbellum suffered from an 'intellectual aridity'[294] in respect of human rights. Indeed, under the influence of legal positivism and dualism, international legal doctrine after World War I tended

[286] Simpson, *Human Rights* 2004 (n. 24), 243.

[287] *ibid*, 221-75; Mazower, 'Triumph' 2004 (n. 276), 387-88 and 393-94. Non-intervention is secured by Art. 2(1) and (7) of the UN Charter.

[288] The UDHR has been celebrated as a rupture by, e.g., Mary Ann Glendon, *A World Made New: Eleanor Roosevelt and the Universal Declaration of Human Rights* (New York, NY: Random House 2001).

[289] Christopher McCrudden, 'Human Dignity and Judicial Interpretation of Human Rights' *European Journal of International Law* 19 (2008), 655-724, at 664.

[290] *ibid*, 676-77.

[291] Mazower, 'Triumph' 2004 (n. 276), at 396 (emphasis added).

[292] See notes 113-116, above.

[293] Mazower, 'Triumph' 2004 (n. 276), at 389.

[294] Christian Tomuschat, *Human Rights between Idealism and Realism* (3rd edn, Oxford: OUP 2014), 26.

to push the idea of inherent fundamental rights of humans out of the realm of international law altogether. The potential legal personality of individuals was mainly tied to procedures.

The post-World War I international regimes that catered for individuals did not tread the moral high ground but responded to specific political and economic problems: refugees, the stateless, minorities, and mandate populations were the fall-out of war and revolution; and diagonal arbitration was a tool to resolve both war reparation matters and satisfy the needs of the transnationalised commerce. These novel international regimes on very concrete aspects of human vulnerability, coupled with a rich reflexion on international legal personhood, were the genuine contribution of the time.

That said, the interbellum legal practice (and maybe also the doctrine) that boosted and strengthened the international legal status of the individual mainly had macro-political objectives. The social conditions of workers needed to be improved in order to forestall the spill-over of communism to western Europe and for preventing a proletarian revolution. Access of individuals (ranging from minorities over mandate populations to State contractors) to international forums and bodies was good for preventing disputes between two governments that would otherwise be 'exaggerated' into an inter-State arbitration.[295]

The broader policy objective to 'privatise' transboundary disputes in order to avoid inter-State strife remains a key rationale of all current international litigation available for individuals against foreign States. In a parallel fashion, even fundamental human rights today are acknowledged to have additional purposes (outside personal interests of the rights holder), ranging from safeguarding a functioning democracy, fact-finding in criminal justice, or protecting public health or the environment with the help of freedom of opinion and speech. But that instrumental character of individual substantive and procedural rights does not make such rights less genuine and less valuable for those who invoke and use them. Rather, allowing victims to take justice into their own hands (for whatever further reasons) also renders their protection more effective. As Georges Kaeckenbeeck, president of the Upper Silesian Arbitral Tribunal, wrote on 'the peculiarity of the direct access of individuals to the Arbitral Tribunal: '[…] one thing remained absolutely beyond doubt: the protection of the population of territories subjected to changes of sovereignty is not and cannot be satisfactorily ensured by international organs which only the Governments themselves can set in motion.'[296]

[295] On the aborted prize court of 1907, see, e.g., Johannes Kriege, the German delegate, at the plenary conference of 1907 (in William Isaack Hull (ed.), *The Two Hague Conferences and their Contributions to International Law* (Boston: International School of Peace Ginn & Company 1908; reproduced in New York, NY: Kraus Reprint Co. 1970), 431 (also cited in Kjeldgaard-Pedersen, *Personality* (n. 121), 82).

[296] Kaeckenbeeck, *Upper Silesia* 1942 (n. 58), 482.

Ironically, the macro-political purpose of forestalling and alleviating inter-State conflict was not necessarily reached by the new regimes—quite the contrary. Several of the novel instruments and procedures burdened only some States selectively, and triggered hostility. The central and eastern European States 'deeply resented the system' of minority protection.[297] The asymmetry of the mixed tribunals fuelled the German aversion against the *diktat* of Versailles. Walter Schätzel decried the TAMs as an 'unprecedented abuse of the institution of arbitration' which one-sidedly implemented 'privileges' that the victors had imposed.[298] Fifty thousand private claimants were 'let loose' as adversaries against the German State, while German private claimants could not reclaim anything from the victor States.[299] So from an inter-State perspective, the empowerment of some individuals (leaving aside others) was a source of political tension.

The other irony is that the subordinate and ancillary objective of the new regimes and procedures, their humanitarian thrust, in the long run did carry the day. They mirrored the 'transnationalization of humanitarianism' that was 'one of the major trends of the post-war era'.[300] The new international legal regimes were the logical response to the transboundary quality of the humanitarian problems (refugees, statelessness, labour, minorities).

The 'legal conscience' of the 'epoch' may have been characterised—as one of the individualists wrote in 1930—by the '*international significance*' of the 'undeniable' rights of man.[301] Importantly however, it took both an internal methodological renovation away from legal positivism to a more sociological approach to international law and the external shock of the horrors of National Socialism and World War II to (re-)unite the new technicalities (including procedures) with more principled considerations on the inviolability of the human person. The combination of both technicality and principle then allowed the development of a practical scheme of international human rights protection.[302]

In all this, the 'legacy of benevolent paternalism within international law'[303] was very palpable, both in the statist and the individualist camp. The deniers of individual international personhood often professed that the ultimate telos of the

[297] Simpson, *Human Rights* 2004 (n. 24), 131.

[298] Schätzel, 'Schiedsgerichte' 1930 (n. 138), 452 and 380.

[299] *ibid*, 454-55.

[300] Cabanes, *Great War* 2014 (n. 269), 5.

[301] Mirkine-Guetzévich, 'Préface' 1930 (n. 245), VII-XIV (VII) (emphasis added).

[302] I do not take a stance on the question of whether this regime only became real in the 1960s and 1970s (with decolonisation and the fight against apartheid), as claimed by Samuel Moyn, *The Last Utopia* (Harvard, MA: Belknap Press 2010). The two universal covenants were adopted in 1966 and entered into force in 1977; human rights were brought into the east-west dialogue by the Helsinki Final Act of 1975.

[303] Miia Halme-Tuomisaari, 'Lobbying for Relevance: American Internationalists, French Civil Libertarians and the UDHR', in Slotte and Halme-Tuomisaari (eds.), *Origins of Human Rights* 2015 (n. 281), 330-80, at 331.

international legal order was to serve the interests of humans.[304] However, they sought to achieve this goal through the States as patrons, guarantors, or guardians. In the other camp, the supporters of an international legal personality of individuals desired man's 'international emancipation' from the States,[305] but such emancipation was implicitly or explicitly reserved for the white, able-bodied, straight, and male, while other individuals were seen in need of education, improvement, and civilisation. And never were the underdogs (members of the vulnerable groups such as children, minorities, members of indigenous populations) primary actors in the international arenas as opposed to mere targets of action.[306]

The interbellum practice, far from unequivocally raising the individuals' international status and detaching it from States, was mixed. When it came to confronting foreign States, the individual victims more often than not remained mediated by their home State which exercised classic diplomatic protection.[307] Also, minorities and mandate populations were officially dubbed as mere communicators of information that set in motion inter-State quasi-diplomatic procedures of settlement. This practice was punctuated by some contrary treaty language and decisions of (new) arbitral tribunals, that either explicitly acknowledged or (more often) only silently implied procedural standing and/or substantive rights for individuals against (foreign or own) governments, flowing directly from international instruments. Another strand of practice were individual complaints before *domestic* courts invoking the violation of treaty provisions that were seen to convey direct international rights, a procedural path opened up by the *Danzig* advisory opinion.[308] But all the judicial and arbitral decisions barely theorised or conceptualised their moves. Therefore, opposite doctrinal conclusions were drawn (and are still drawn) from those possibilities of individual action.

Finally, the addressees of presumptive post-World War I direct international rights of individuals were diverse: in the international labour conventions, the direct obligors were employers; for refugees and stateless persons, it was the State of residence. The TAMs and the Central American Court only allowed individuals' law suits against a foreign government. In contrast, under the minority treaties, the most specific and far-reaching guarantees were reserved for persons who possessed the nationality of the obliged State. Foreign citizens were sometimes not even included in the definition of 'minority'.[309] That means that both the material minority rights and procedural access to the complaints mechanisms were mainly directed against the *own* government.[310] For this reason (because it interceded

[304] Heilborn, *Stellung des Menschen* 1927 (n. 32), 4; Le Fur, 'Théorie du Droit' 1927 (n. 201), 259-442, at 350, footnote 1; Stélio Séfériadès, 'Principes généraux du droit international de la paix' *Recueil des Cours* 34 (1930), 177-492, at 310; Berezowski, 'Sujets' 1938 (n. 186), 78.

[305] Bourquin, 'Règles générales' 1931 (n. 212), 5-229, at 46.

[306] Halme-Tuomisaari, 'Lobbying for Relevance' 2015 (n. 303), at 331-32.

[307] See notes 122-123, above.

[308] See section 4, above.

[309] See note 109, above.

[310] Epitomised in the Upper Silesian Tribunal's decision in *Steiner and Gross* 1928 (n. 59).

with the bond of nationality and loyalty), the minority regime was a stronger incursion into State sovereignty than the mandate scheme or the mixed arbitration. It also bore more resemblance to the current human rights regime whose normal cases are infringements by the home State.

In some ways, the interbellum legal debate was less reductive than the present-day international legal landscape which is flooded by human rights. The then emerging international legal status of individuals was independent from the enjoyment of international human rights, simply because that paradigm did not exist. Retrieving that legacy brings into the picture the diversity of direct international rights and obligations of individuals beyond human rights, a diversity that refines and expands the place of the individual in international law.[311]

[311] Peters, *Beyond Human Rights* 2016 (n. 167).

PART 2

THE INDIVIDUAL IN THE THEORY OF INTERNATIONAL LAW

8
Legal Positivism and the Individual in International Law

Gleider Hernández

1. Introduction

To retrofit Julius Caesar's infamous cliché, positivism bestrides international law theory like a Colossus; it remains an unavoidable reference point upon which any contemporary analysis of international law rests. By this I mean that even if one is not methodologically positivist, and whatever claims might exist as to the changing zeitgeist, engagement with positivist legal thinking—in its most basic sense of studying *posited* or *willed* law[1]—continues to form the bedrock of academic and practical thinking about the international legal system. Positivism has proven central in establishing international law as a secular and autonomous discipline,[2] and in framing how international law has been practised, argued, and taught. Equally, it has been instrumental in establishing an account of international law as the legal order of inter-State relations and, throughout most of its history, has also led to the gradual, deliberate marginalisation of the individual as a legal subject; bearer of rights, obligations, or duties; or even as a potential source of international law.

In this chapter, I wish to engage with the intellectual history of international legal positivism and tease out the prior assumptions which it has internalised over time: the centrality of the State as international legal subject, and the concomitant sidelining of the individual. My aim is to excavate more fully how the methods of legal positivism came to dominate mainstream ways of thinking about international law, and the extent to which this dominance was achieved by embracing a State-centric or *voluntarist* account of international law. I contest that State-centrism is a *necessary element* of a positivist approach to international law. But I also challenge the idea that the airbrushing out of the individual engendered by State-centrism was simply an unintended outcome—an epiphenomenon—having

[1] A concise intellectual history of the notion of *droit positif* or *ius positivum* can be found in Stephan Kuttner, 'Sur les origins du terme "droit positif" ' *Revue historique de droit français et étranger* 15 (1936), 728-40.

[2] See David Kennedy, 'The Disciplines of International Law and Policy' *Leiden Journal of International Law* 12 (1999), 9-133; Martti Koskenniemi, *The Gentle Civilizer of Nations* (Cambridge: CUP 2001), laying out his core argument in the Introduction, 6-9.

Gleider Hernández, *Legal Positivism and the Individual in International Law* In: *The Individual in International Law*. Edited by: Tom Sparks and Anne Peters, Oxford University Press.
DOI: 10.1093/oso/9780198898917.003.0008

arisen over time and through the history of international legal thought. Rather, I take the view that if we understand 'positivism' as referring primarily to a question of method, in the sense of a scientific technique (in the broadest sense) through which we study and understand law, such a narrower definition can help to explain international law's development in this direction. Even though a positivist account of international law will normally avoid any normative explanation for the basis of law, I believe that even in its methodological approach, positivism carries with it certain presumptions as to law's structure. I will argue in this chapter that a positivist approach represents a choice, a choice that privileges order and coherence as necessary, desirable conditions for law and legal systems.

It may well be that the inner premises embodied by positivism, such as a promise of neutrality of law and legal institutions, the purported objectivity of its method, or the interaction of positivism with other methods across the range of human knowledge and knowability, hold emancipatory promise. But even if positivist methods can be deployed in the service of a fairly broad range of normative commitments, in the case of international law specifically, I contend that it has been used to justify and advance a State-centric account of international law—and this, to the detriment of the place of the individual.

In order to develop these arguments further, it is key to lay out some working definitions of positivism and other cognate concepts, notably the State-centred approach to international law which I will call *voluntarism* or *consensualism*. In Section 2, I introduce such definitions and try to illustrate them by application to some contemporary, self-described positivist accounts of the individual in international law. In Section 3, I retrace, briefly, the emergence of what is loosely understood as 'classical' international legal positivism, as it has proceeded from the early Modern period into its zenith of the pre-1914 period. Though State consent had long been part of the international vernacular, it was Lassa Oppenheim's early twentieth-century work which would consolidate the positivism-voluntarism dialectic, and which would entrench—as I will contend—the relegation of the individual within international law. In Section 4, I engage with the anxieties displayed by key mainstream thinkers and their engagement with this positivist-consensualist edifice throughout the mid-twentieth century; it was during this period that the dominance of this conceptual edifice began to unravel, and a degree of disciplinary self-reflection began to take place. In this section, I rely on four key western legal thinkers: Kelsen, Hart, Lauterpacht, and Scelle. This decidedly Eurocentric selection is not made blindly; I choose these thinkers precisely because of their dominance during the mid-twentieth century, both in the Global North and beyond, in defining the parameters for thinking about positivist international law.[3]

[3] The 'overwhelming Eurocentrism' of our discipline during the period, of course, has long been pointed out: see Koskenniemi, *Gentle Civilizer of Nations* 2001 (n. 2), 9.

On the basis of the preceding analysis, Section 5 concludes with the observation that the relationship between positivism and voluntarism (i.e. State-centrism) is one which remains contingent, and was neither logically nor conceptually necessary. In other words, the nature of international law as a system can likely accommodate a greater emphasis on the place of the individual, set in opposition to the State; or in fact, a range of other foci. In this concluding section, I have found it useful to rely on the recent work of Joseph Raz, a self-described positivist in the analytical jurisprudence tradition. I do so in keeping with my aim, in this chapter, to engage in an internal analysis of the place of the individual within positivist approaches to international law.

2. Contemporary International Legal Positivism

2.1 Some Working Definitions

Positivism remains a concept used by most international legal scholars and practitioners, but with little explanation. Too often it is presumed to embody some core claims, for example as Devika Hovell has identified them: that international law is connected to the will of States; that it is generated through formal sources which are the foundation of a self-contained and unified legal system; and that law can be dissociated from extra-legal factors and, through this, be considered both objective and determinate.[4] To a degree, this remains too general: my understanding of 'positivism' is narrower, as an approach or a *method* which regards law and legal systems as a deliberate or willed product of collective human endeavour, established through agency and decisions that consolidate over time.[5] I contend that this narrower understanding of positivism will substantiate my claim that the marginalisation of the individual has been achieved not through the core tenets of international legal positivism itself, but rather the way in which positivism, as a *method* of engaging with law, has been deployed in the service of other concepts.

To define positivism as a method helps to identify two further propositions which are relevant in relation to the place of the individual law. First, a positivist approach to the law nevertheless represents a view on law's structure: it is a choice to engage with law on the purported basis that one can do so purely through identification of valid legal rules and how they are to function, and by avoiding any engagement with its moral, ethical, or normative premises unless these are channelled into a legal system through another source. The approach purports to only

[4] See, e.g., the 'core claims' of classical international legal positivism can be found in Devika Hovell, 'The Elements of International Legal Positivism' *Current Legal Problems* 75 (2022), 71-109, at 74.

[5] See Hans Kelsen, *Pure Theory of Law* (Max Knight (tr.), 2nd edn, Clark, NJ: Law Book Exchange 2009), 31 and 32; Joseph Raz, 'Legal Positivism and the Sources of Law' in *The Authority of Law: Essays on Law and Morality* (Oxford: OUP 1979), 37. Both will be discussed in sections 4 and 5, below.

deal with the *lex lata*, or law as it is laid down, and not with any *lex ferenda*, or law as it might be desired to be.[6] From this first proposition, then, the second proposition follows: the validity of legal rules can be ascertained from recognised sources of the law within a self-contained, autonomous legal system, and the evaluation of valid law can be fully dissociated from any extra-legal criteria.[7] Understood thus, 'positivism' defines law as what has been posited validly, and a norm can only be described as *legal* on the basis that is derives its *validity* from being supported through the legal rules within that legal system.

Nothing in positivism (thus defined) excludes the legal personhood or importance of the individual within international law. It is in fact another core concept, related but distinct, which has served over time to consign the individual to the sidelines in respect of international law. I call this concept *voluntarism* or *consensualism*, and I use the terms interchangeably. They refer to the belief in the centrality of the State as both international legal subject and the source of international legal rules. Unlike a positivist *method* or approach, *voluntarism/consensualism* is an explicit *normative* position on the structure and basis of legitimacy of international law, according to which the proper basis of international law is rooted, exclusively or predominantly, in the will of its central legal subjects: States.

2.2 Redemptive Accounts of the Individual within International Law

To illustrate how they operate in relation to the place of the individual, and before turning to a genealogy of these concepts, I wish to engage briefly with two contemporary, self-described positivist accounts of the individual in international law. My claim is that both are rehabilitatory accounts which, even as they seek to map out the place of the individual in international law, do not question either the core tenets of a positivist method nor the limitations of a purely consensualist view on the nature of international law.

The first illustration can be found in Kate Parlett's 2011 monograph on the individual within the international legal system,[8] which aims to study the ebbs and flows in the place of the individual in international law across various international legal regimes. Parlett consciously adopts what she terms a 'rules-based approach',[9] privileging *lex lata* above all, which emerges as both resolutely positivist (in its

[6] See the defence of the relevance of this distinction in Jörg Kammerhofer, 'Legal Positivism', in Anne Peters (2021-) and Rüdiger Wolfrum (2004-20) (eds.), *Max-Planck Encyclopaedia of Public International Law* (Oxford: OUP 2023).

[7] For an emphatic view on this point, see Jörg Kammerhofer, *Uncertainty in International Law: A Kelsenian Perspective* (Abingdon: Routledge 2011), 250-51.

[8] Kate Parlett, *The Individual in the International Legal System: Continuity and Change in International Law* (Cambridge: CUP 2011).

[9] *ibid*, 7-9.

focus on validity) and also voluntarist, in its focus on States' conduct in its account of international law-making. It is a deliberate choice, seemingly to eschew broader normative claims or any further (re)theorising of the nature of international law.[10] Within this framework, classic 'Vattelian' State-centrism[11] remains intact, with a focus on how, during various periods, the recognition of individuals has recurred in international legal argument, and across various specialised regimes.[12]

Astrid Kjeldgaard-Pedersen's 2018 monograph on the international legal personality of the individual[13] takes a narrower, more cautious approach. Though Kjeldgaard-Pedersen also explores a broad range of specialised regimes within international law, she claims repeatedly that her work remains conceptually orthodox, again with a focus on *lex lata*—'it is not meant to be a *de lege ferenda* exercise[, nor] to promote a particular normative agenda'.[14] The rehabilitatory aspects of her approach are explicit, and avoid engaging critically with the voluntarist element which is presumed to be essential in international legal positivism. In her words, she aims to shed light on the 'epistemic bias against the international legal personality of the individual', 'to show that scholars, including those who pledge allegiance to positivism, have failed to provide a satisfactory account of the position of the individual *as a matter of positive international law*, and that this misconstruction influences the way in which international law is currently interpreted and applied in practice'.[15]

2.3 Positivism, Voluntarism, and the Relegation of the Individual

To my mind, Parlett and Kjeldgaard-Pedersen have engaged in thoughtful work, and have made important contributions to understanding the place of the individual through mainstream accounts. But it bears pointing out that they do not engage critically with the voluntarist element that, as discussed in Section 2.1, many international lawyers often presume to be a part of international legal positivism. Their strategy has been to internalise this voluntarist element in service of an argumentative method based in mainstream, accepted methods of international legal reasoning to explore whether the fabric of international law is sufficiently

[10] A point raised by Andreas Müller, 'Kate Parlett: *The Individual in the International Legal System*' *European Journal of International Law* 23 (2012) 294-99, at 297-98, where he suggests that its critique of the subject-object dichotomy is somewhat overstated.

[11] Parlett, *The Individual in the International Legal System* 2011 (n. 8), 11-13; Roland Portmann, *Legal Personality in International Law* (Cambridge: CUP 2010), chapter 2. Vattel's contribution to the doctrine of voluntarism is addressed in section 3.1, below.

[12] Parlett, *The Individual in the International Legal System* 2011 (n. 8), 26-29 (positivism in international law textbooks); and 38-40 (identifying alternative conceptions to State-centrism).

[13] Astrid Kjeldgaard-Pedersen, *The International Legal Personality of the Individual* (Oxford: OUP 2018).

[14] *ibid*, 5 and 14.

[15] *ibid*, 6.

elastic that the individual was, is, or can in fact receive recognition within it. In Kjeldgaard-Pedersen's own concluding words, 'contrary to common belief, the "States-only" conception of international legal personality has in fact never reflected the realities of practice—at least not for as long as there has been substantial practice to consider'.[16]

To my mind, we need to excavate further the conflation of positivism with consensualism within our field, which buttresses the myth of 'States-only' thinking and its pervasive effect on legal discourses and development. Parlett and Kjeldgaard-Pedersen rightly point out that the individual has never been wholly invisible. Nevertheless, over time, the individual has been portrayed as marginal—or dismissed outright—as the *outcome* of a positivist method combined with a voluntarist approach that defines international law as being exclusively concerned with, and made by, States. My argument is that to understand positivism as a *methodological fact*, we can better discern its historical contribution to the making of international law – and the marginalisation of the individual in favour of the State.

3. International Law in the Early Modern Period: The Retreat of the Individual

3.1 The Early Modern Period and the Embrace of Positivism

As international law developed within (primarily European) inter-State relations from the seventeenth century onwards, State consent came to be regarded as the ultimate source—or basis of obligation—of the law of nations. As States became central to the voluntarist conception of international law, this conception diminished the place of individuals over time. Even in the avowedly naturalist Salamanca School, one detects traces of voluntarism across the work of Francisco Suárez,[17] who—though with some degree of ambivalence—recognised how *ius gentium* arose in part through gradual trial and error and the practice of proto-State legal subjects, 'peoples', albeit as an auxiliary source of obligation.[18]

The consent of these emerging legal subjects would concretise as an important basis for international law obligations through Grotius' famed distinction between *ius naturale* and *ius gentium* (which he in fact called *ius volontarium*).[19] This was

[16] *ibid*, 230.

[17] As was described in Martti Koskenniemi, *To the Uttermost Parts of the Earth* (Cambridge: CUP 2021), esp. 135-43.

[18] See James Bernard Murphy, *The Philosophy of Customary Law* (Oxford: OUP 2014), 47, engaging with Francisco Suarez, *The Laws and God the Lawgiver* (Naples 1612) DL2, 20.1. See further Jean-François Courtine, 'Vitoria, Suarez et la naissance du droit de nature moderne', in Alain Renaut (ed.), *Naissances de modernité. 2 Histoire de la philsophie politique* (Paris: Calmann-Lévy 1999), 127-81.

[19] Hugo Grotius, *De jure belli ac pacis libri tres* (ed. Amstelaedami, 1720), *Prolegomena*, XII, 12-15, cited in Roberto Ago, 'Positive Law and International Law' *American Journal of International Law* 51

not yet the advent of positivism as we understand it: *ius naturale* persisted as a parallel, formal source of international legal obligation, and several of Grotius' near-contemporaries including Samuel von Pufendorf and Christian Wolff, even as they would focus increasingly on the tacit or explicit consent of States, would do so through a method and paradigm that we would generally associate with natural law. Mark Somos has described the period as an oscillation between the 're- and denaturalisation' of international law.[20]

At this juncture, *ius gentium* was not necessarily positivist, in the narrow methodological sense that it separated the study of law from 'extra-legal' considerations. Rather, it was a descriptive account that defined *ius gentium* simply as the 'law of peoples', a horizontal system located in the practice and belief of sovereign and equal States in their *inter se* relations.[21] Positivism would emerge as the preferred method through which to assess State conduct, as the Grotian framework would give way, in Emerich de Vattel's 1758 textbook *Le droit des gens*,[22] to a decisive move away from natural law. Vattel's key contribution was to move the focus nearly exclusively to *ius voluntarium*. By sidestepping existential questions of why the *ius voluntarium* was a valid source of law, he allowed for the identification of valid norms of positive law as separate from ethical or moral considerations.[23]

Vattel and his successors throughout the eighteenth and nineteenth centuries would not so much establish positivism per se. In fact, in some respects the move towards positivism was geared more as a reflex away from natural law. Positivism was deployed in service of rationality and rigour to the study of international law, mirroring a move in the study of domestic law, and arguably in a conscious attempt to professionalise the legal discipline and defend international law as a coherent system of legal norms.[24] During this period, recourse to consensualism as

(1957) 691-733, at 693, who suggests Grotius' use of the term derives from the earlier Suárez and even Aristotle, as an emphasis not only on posited law but on law that is *willed*.

[20] For a more nuanced account of these intellectual shifts in the German-speaking world, see Koskenniemi, *To the Uttermost Parts of the Earth* 2021 (n. 17), chapter 11, esp. 811-23, 832-37, and 861-65. See also Nicholas Onuf, 'Civitas Maxima: Wolff, Vattel and the Fate of Republicanism' *American Journal of International Law* 88 (1994) 280-303; Ago, 'Positive Law' 1957 (n. 19), 693; Martti Koskenniemi, *From Apology to Utopia* (reissued edn, Cambridge: CUP 2005), 80.

[21] Grotius, *De jure belli ac pacis libri tres* (n. 19); see also Hersch Lauterpacht, 'The Grotian Tradition in International Law' *British Yearbook of International Law* 23 (1946) 1-53, at 52-53.

[22] Koskenniemi, *To the Uttermost Parts of the Earth* 2021 (n. 17), 861-65. The authoritative work on Emerich de Vattel's legal theory remains Emmanuelle Jouannet, *Emer de Vattel et l'émergence doctrinale du droit international* (Paris: Pedone 1998).

[23] Of course, there were contemporaneous objections which invoked natural law to justify all manner of international legal rules. See especially, John Locke's fixation with a 'natural right of property' and Kant's idealistic concepts of law, freedom, and peace in Koskenniemi, *To the Uttermost Parts of the Earth* 2021 (n. 17), 634-36 (Locke), 901-04 (Kant).

[24] Richard Collins, 'Classical Legal Positivism in International Law Revisited', in Jörg Kammerhofer and Jean d'Aspremont (eds.), *International Legal Positivism in a Post-Modern World* (Cambridge: CUP 2014), 23-49, at 32-33; Koskenniemi, *Gentle Civilizer* 2001 (n. 2), 86-188.

the normative basis of international law was not axiological; even more than in the eighteenth century, it was in service of a move towards disciplinary autonomy.

The embrace of State-centrism was not purely ideological, but was about the adoption of truth-claims and a faith in objectivism and rationalism in the study of international law into an autonomous system. In this way, the legacy of the nineteenth century was not deference to sovereignty, but the emergence of sovereignty 'as the key *topos* of international law, leading the law into a formal and procedural direction, away from views about the substantive rightness or wrongness of particular types of behavior'.[25] In so doing, the emphasis on scientific rationality and the focus on the consent of the 'sovereign State' as the central international legal subject, however, wrought with it an unintentional, but very real dismissal of the individual as rights-bearer or legal subject within international law. As the State as legal actor took centre stage, the individual was ushered to the sidelines.

The embrace of positivist methods was not solely a means of harnessing the scientific rationality of the Enlightenment, but a strategic move to reinforce the centrality of the State as subject, actor, and source of international law.[26] During this period, various strands would draw on the vocabulary of *ius positivum* or positive law and would enmesh it, slowly but deliberately, with *ius voluntarium*, law laid down through the consent or will of States. The gradual elision of positivism with consensualism would narrow the scope of the concept of 'positive law' and thus facilitate its decoupling from theology or moral philosophy. Again, the focus on State consent within international law was partly tactical: in the absence of domestic legal institutions, the turn to a secular, rationalist method to engage with international law was seen as an appeal to the rationalist ideals of the period to ensure recognition of international law's character *as law*.[27] This process of secularisation fitted well with other intellectual developments flowing from Enlightment ideals: 'the idea which reduced legal positivism to a mere state voluntarism was widely accepted; and the *myth of the will of the state as the only origin of law was created*'.[28]

[25] Collins, 'Classical Legal Positivism' 2014 (n. 24). See further David Kennedy's remark that sovereignty in the nineteenth century was 'a doctrinal project of practicality [...] If nineteenth century international lawyers had a blind faith, it was in law, not sovereignty. Sovereignty was their construct, their response, a project of earnest doctrinal elaboration, opening a space for a new form of statecraft in an ancient legal fabric': David Kennedy, 'International Law and the Nineteenth Century: History of an Illusion' *Quinnipiac Law Review* 17 (1997) 99-138, at 121.

[26] See Janne Nijman, *The Concept of International Legal Personality: An Inquiry into the History and Theory of International Law* (The Hague: TMC Asser Press 2004), 110; and in relation to the preponderance of 'will' in the making of international law, see Koskenniemi, *Gentle Civilizer of Nations* 2001 (n. 2), 187-94.

[27] See, e.g., Samuel Pufendorf, *De jure naturae et gentium libri octo* (ed. Amstelodami, 1688), lib. I, cap. VI, 77 para 18, also cited in Ago, 'Positive Law' 1957 (n. 19), 695; but see generally Inge van Hulle, 'Nineteenth Century' (chapter 6), in this volume, who opens her chapter with the claim that the nineteenth century was 'the age in which state-centrism reigned supreme in international legal theory'.

[28] Ago, 'Positive Law' 1957 (n. 19), 699, and see further discussion from 695-702.

During the nineteenth century, this State-centric account would become deeply ingrained within international legal thinking, constituting, as David Kennedy has put it, the 'baseline against which to measure the discipline's progress and [contemporary] exceptionalism'.[29] It was during this period that international lawyers would confine the subjects of international law ever more restrictively to States, thus further excluding individual rights and subjectivity from mainstream thinking.[30]

The role of individuals would accordingly be conceived as that of indirect subject,[31] a move further entrenched by a relatively narrow, hegemonically European circle of scholars,[32] such as Germans Georg Jellinek[33] and Heinrich Triepel;[34] the Italian Dionisio Anzilotti;[35] and the naturalised Briton Lassa Oppenheim.[36] Certain groups or communities that did not achieve a certain standard of civilisation were not recognised as States and were thus deprived of subjecthood. The denial of individual, non-State rights thus was an effective legitimating element for imperial conquest and domination during the period.[37]

[29] Kennedy, 'International Law and the Nineteenth Century' 1997 (n. 25), 100. The State-centrism which dominated the epoch is also described further in Van Hulle, 'Nineteenth Century' (chapter 6), in this volume.

[30] See further the overarching argument in Koskenniemi, *Gentle Civilizer of Nations* 2001 (n. 2), 14, on how a portrayal of the pre-war era as unduly positivist ignores 'persistent strands of "naturalism" in the [19th] century's legal doctrine, constantly referring back to the moral and civilizing forces of European law and practices', again reaffirming the reconstruction point'.

[31] See, e.g., Louis Le Fur, 'La théorie du droit naturel depuis le XVIII siècle et la doctrine moderne' (Paris: Hachette 1928), 92. See also Henry Bonfils, *Manuel de droit international public* (4th edn, Paris: Libraire Arthur Rousseau 1905), 79; Jean Basdevant, 'L'affaire des pêcheries des cotes septentrionales de l'Atlantique entre les Etats-Unis d'Amérique et la Grande-Bretagne devant la Cour de la Haye' *Revue générale de droit international public* 19 (Paris: Pedone 1912), 421-582, at 519; Paul Fauchille, *Traité de droit international*, vol. I (Paris: Libraire Arthur Rousseau 1922), 761.

[32] For a concise narration, see Collins, 'Classical Legal Positivism' 2014 (n. 24).

[33] Georg Jellinek, *Die rechtliche Natur der Staatenverträge. Ein Beitrag zur juristischen Construktion des Völkerrechts* (Vienna: Hölder 1880), 19-28, articulating an early theory of the validity of international law as grounded in the will of a community of States, an 'objective' community of sorts that was distinct from its members but nevertheless reliant upon the free will of sovereign States as law-creating entities to limit themselves: the concept of *Selbstverpflichtung* or self-limitation through consent. See Jochen von Bernstorff, 'German Intellectual Historical Origins of International Legal Positivism', in Jörg Kammerhofer and Jean d'Aspremont (eds), *International Legal Positivism in a Post-Modern World* (Cambridge: CUP 2014), 50-80, at 66-73. This concept of *Selbstverpflichtung* has also been argued to be somewhat sociological, rather than rigidly voluntarist: see further Koskenniemi, *Gentle Civilizer* 2001 (n. 2), 199-206.

[34] Heinrich Triepel, *Völkerrecht und Landesrecht* (Leipzig: Hirschfield 1999); see further von Bernstorff, 'German Intellectual History' 2014 (n. 33), 75-77.

[35] Dionisio Anzilotti, *Corso di diritto internazionale* (3rd edn, Rome: Athenaeum 1928), 17; see further Giorgio Gaja, 'Positivism and Dualism in International Law: Dionisio Anzilotti' *European Journal of International Law* 3 (1992) 123-38; Angelo-Piero Sereni, *The Italian Conception of International Law* (New York, NY: Columbia University Press 1943), chapter 12 (on Anzilotti).

[36] Lassa Oppenheim, *International Law. A Treatise* (1st edn, London: Longman & Sons 1905); Lassa Oppenheim, 'The Science of International Law: Its Task and Method' *American Journal of International Law* 2 (1908), 313-56.

[37] See further Ntina Tzouvala, *Capitalism as Civilisation* (Cambridge: CUP 2020), esp. 58-62, on the 'logic of improvement' deployed to exclude such voices and facilitate their integration into the global imperial economy.

3.2 Coalescence: The Early Twentieth-Century Theory of Lassa Oppenheim

One can hardly overstate the influence of Lassa Oppenheim in consolidating the positivist-consensualist paradigm into what he called a coherent 'science of international law'.[38]

The first edition of Oppenheim's general textbook of international law would define the discipline through the language of consensualism: 'Law of Nations or International Law *(droit des gens, Völkerrecht)* is the name for the body of customary and conventional rules which are considered legally binding by civilised States in their intercourse with each other.'[39] Oppenheim's essentially relational account, which Devika Hovell calls a 'social thesis',[40] depicted the law as a material emanation; a 'reality' rooted in the common interests of States which had 'long since united the separate States into an indivisible community: the 'Family of Nations'.[41] Construed thus, the origin of international law is located through a positivist focus on law created by will, which in Oppenheim's theory required the individual consent of each State to any obligation binding upon it.[42] No State is wholly free, it was claimed: for example, no State could unilaterally subtract itself from existing, recognised international legal rules, which could only be changed by common consent.[43]

Oppenheim's theory equally depended on the identity of the cognitive subject: States:[44] 'international law is a law not above but between states; […] there is no central authority above the sovereign states which could compel them to comply […] or to submit their differences to a juridical decision'.[45] Instead, only a degree of self-help by the wronged State would be tolerated.[46] But another reading is that Oppenheim's positivism was instrumental; effectively to buttress his ontology of international law as a consensualist, State-based legal order. Oppenheim's pragmatism had its methodological limits, perhaps due to an early anxiety about evidence

[38] Oppenheim, *International Law* 1905 (n. 36), viii. The leading monograph on the contribution of Lassa Oppenheim (and Hans Kelsen) to international legal positivism is Mónica García-Salmones Rovira, *The Project of Positivism in International Law* (Oxford: OUP 2013), chapters 2 and 3 (Oppenheim) and chapter 4 (Kelsen); reviewed by the present author in Gleider Hernández, '*The Project of Positivism in International Law* (Mónica García-Salmones Rovira)' *Netherlands Yearbook of International Law* 62 (2015), 183-89.

[39] Oppenheim, *International Law* 1905 (n. 36), 2.

[40] See Hovell, 'Elements' 2022 (n. 4), 77-78.

[41] Oppenheim, *International Law* 1905 (n. 36), 19.

[42] Oppenheim, 'The Science of International Law' 1908 (n. 36), 332-33.

[43] Oppenheim, *International Law* 1905 (n. 36), 15-18. Oppenheim also tolerated a degree of 'tacit' consent, but with the caveat that the overwhelming majority of States in the 'Family of Nations' should agree to a given rule.

[44] *ibid*, 18-19: 'Since the Law of Nations is based on the common consent of individual States, not of individual human beings […] States solely and exclusively are the subjects of International Law'; and only they could be subjects of rights and duties thereunder.

[45] Oppenheim, 'The Science of International Law' 1908 (n. 36), 322.

[46] Oppenheim, *International Law* 1905 (n. 47), 13.

of State will: though international law might be based on customs and conventions, it would be informed somehow by deriving relevant principles from (at that time, purely domestic) judicial decisions, cases being 'law-shapers, law developers, law finders and law-excavators'.[47]

Oppenheim's adherence to a strict positivism was attenuated somewhat by his concept of the 'Family of Nations'. The so-called 'Family of Nations' was based on his theory of 'the interests which knit all the *individual civilised States* together and which create constant intercourse',[48] with more than a hint of *mission civilisatrice* thinking permeating his work.[49] As Benedict Kingsbury puts it, Oppenheim's theory 'embodied a normative or ethical view that a positivist understanding of international law was best able to advance the realization of international society of a higher set of values *to which Oppenheim adhered*'.[50] Oppenheim's 'Family of Nations' was no mere descriptive term, but a concept referring both to the members of the 'family' and its 'common interests', and thus a powerful analytical strategy. As Antony Anghie puts it:

> Despite the positivist claims that the sovereign was the exclusive basis for the international system, it was only if society was introduced into the system that positivists could approximate the idea of 'law' to which they urged adherence. Society, then, provides the matrix of ideas, *the analytical resources which allied with sovereignty*, could establish a positivist international legal order.[51]

There is a dizzying, Matryoshka-doll nesting of metaphors on which Oppenheim's concept 'Family of Nations' rests. Foremost, it served to consolidate the view of international society as composed exclusively of opaque, individualised States as legal subjects. This 'billiard ball'[52] approach, ironically, used domestic

[47] Oppenheim, 'The Science of International Law' 1908 (n. 36), 336-40, see García-Salmones Rovira, *The Project of Positivism* 2013 (n. 38), 55.

[48] Oppenheim, *International Law* 1905 (n. 36), 11.

[49] See Liliana Obregón, 'The Civilized and the Uncivilized', in Bardo Fassbender and Anne Peters (eds.), *The Oxford Handbook of the History of International Law* (Oxford: OUP 2012), 917-40; Tzouvala, *Capitalism as Civilization* (2020) (n. 37), chapter 2, 44-87;Jo-Anne Claire Pemberton, 'The So-Called Right of Civilisation in European Colonial Ideology, 16th to 20th Centuries' *Journal of the History of International Law* 15 (2013), 25-52. See further Koskenniemi, *Gentle Civilizer* 2001 (n. 2), 141 (on the exclusion-inclusion logic animating the 'Scramble for Africa'); Martti Koskenniemi, 'International law in Europe: Between Tradition and Renewal' *European Journal of International Law* 16 (2005) 113-24, at 117.

[50] Benedict Kingsbury, 'Legal Positivism as Normative Politics' *European Journal of International Law* 13 (2002) 401-37, at 431 (emphasis added); for similar conclusions, see García-Salmones Rovira, *The Project of Positivism* 2013 (n. 38), 118; Jean d'Aspremont, *Formalism and the Sources of International Law* (Oxford: OUP 2011), 142-46; Collins, 'Classical Legal Positivism' 2014 (n. 24), 33-34.

[51] Anthony Anghie, *Imperialism, Sovereignty, and the Making of International Law* (Cambridge: CUP 2005), 48 (emphasis added).

[52] I borrow the metaphor as popularised by Bruno Simma and Dirk Pulkowski, 'On Planets and the Universe: Self-Contained Regimes in International Law' *European Journal of International Law* 17 (2006), 483-529, and drawn from Arnold Wolfers, *Discord and Collaboration in International Society* (Baltimore: Johns Hopkins 1962), 19-24.

law analogies on legal personality to attribute those features in international law to States and States alone. The focus on States as the sole members of the 'Family' was thus instrumental in the airbrushing of any vestiges of the individual; the coherence of the 'Family' left no further space for individual participation or the assertion of individual rights.

4. Consolidation: The Twentieth Century

Oppenheim and his contemporaries opened the twentieth century by entrenching the doctrine we now understand as 'classical' international legal positivism, the specific alloy of positivist method and State-centrism which was achieved to the exclusion of all other legal subjects, including individuals. This theory has constituted the substrate of international law scholarship and practice since, and though not without its critics, retains a strong claim to represent the mainstream position of international lawyers even today.

The upheavals of the twentieth century generated existential hand-wringing about the basis for international law, with two influential strands which sought to redefine international law's relationship with the individual. First, I will turn to what I loosely term an internal critique, emerging during the interwar and immediate post-war period through the work of Hersch Lauterpacht and Georges Scelle in particular. Even if not strict positivists, both sought to redeem positivism as a methodology by—at least partially—decoupling it from pure voluntarism and emphasising the relevance of extra-legal foundations or considerations. To a degree, this reconfirms the relative ease with which positivist method can be deployed even by natural law theories, which are sometimes misrepresented as positivism's opposite. The second intellectual development is quite recent, and concerns the theoretical renewal of international legal positivism in the twenty-first century, which drew heavily from the mid-century positivist theories of Hans Kelsen and H. L. A Hart to emphasise once again, if only in a formal sense, the autonomy of international law as a self-contained system.

4.1 Post-1914: Lauterpacht's Redemptive, Neo-Grotian Account of Positivism

World War I inflicted untold suffering and horrors across the world. The capacity of States to commit mass atrocities became even more plain for all to see, and international lawyers struggled to make sense of their irrelevance, pointing in vain to valid legal rules that might have constrained the violence so recently unleashed. Perhaps it was in the wake of human tragedy, or being discouraged by the relative paucity of positive legal obligations; but some international lawyers began to rethink the foundations of international legal positivism being set in an exclusively State-centred voluntarism.[53] The most recognised advocate of such an approach is Sir Hersch Lauterpacht, whose concept of international law was self-styled as a return to the Grotian conception of international law as reinfusing the voluntarist 'law of nations' with a degree of humanistic normativism.[54] Lauterpacht would criticise orthodox positivism for being unduly rigid; but this was not a broadside against positivist *method*. Rather, Lauterpacht took issue primarily with consensualism—that is to say, the centrality of State sovereignty and consent to obligation, in particular in relation to their role in establishing the validity of international legal sources.[55]

Lauterpacht's concept of international law was a self-styled 'Grotian' approach, in the sense that for him, positive law willed by States could be unduly at variance with the reality, or 'facts' of the law.[56] Necessarily so, then, it was to be supplemented (though not superseded) by the 'law of nature', 'the universal law of humanity in which the individual human being, the ultimate unit of all law, rises sovereign over the limited province of the State'.[57] In some respects, of course, this displays an affinity towards *ius naturalism*, but to my mind, it was not so much an abandonment of the chief tenets of positivism as a means through which to approach the identification of valid legal rules.

This move is particularly prominent in his post-war writing, in which Lauterpacht maintained that international law, which 'is and must remain a law of independent, autonomous States',[58] could be perfectly well accommodated with a functionalist approach to international law that elevated collective security, peaceful dispute settlement, and above all, protection of the human person and of fundamental human rights as 'the ultimate purpose of *all law*'.[59] Nevertheless, Lauterpacht's defence of positivist method aimed at its redemption and continued

[53] See further, Peters, 'Before Human Rights' (chapter 7), in this volume.

[54] See further the argument in Hersch Lauterpacht, 'The Grotian Tradition' 1946 (n. 21); though Koskenniemi, *Gentle Civilizer of Nations* 2001 (n. 2), 357-59, would term it rather a 'Victorian' approach embodying a liberal narrative of progress.

[55] See, e.g., Hersch Lauterpacht, *Private Law Sources and Analogies in International Law* (London: Longman, Green & Stevens 1927), 43. From 51-54, he expounds on the point that many so-called 'positivist' scholars of international law had not consistently adhered to a voluntarist or consensualist paradigm.

[56] Koskenniemi, *Gentle Civilizer* 2001 (n. 2), 364, in particular examining the argument in Lauterpacht, *Private Law Sources and Analogies* 1927 (n. 55), 74-75.

[57] Lauterpacht, 'The Grotian Tradition' 1946 (n. 21), 29. As Koskenniemi, *Gentle Civilizer* 2001 (n. 2), 365 notes, Lauterpacht believed States remained an 'artificial personification' or proxy for human decisions.

[58] Hersch Lauterpacht, 'The Organization of Peace and the Revision of the Status Quo', in Elihu Lauterpacht (ed.), *International Law: Collected Papers*, vol. 1 (Cambridge: CUP 1970), 444; Hersch Lauterpacht, 'Règles générales du droit de la paix' *Recueil des Cours* 62 (1937), 97-422, at 416.

[59] See, e.g., Hersch Lauterpacht, *International Law and Human Rights* (London: Stevens & Sons 1950), 6, 46, and 77; Hersch Lauterpacht, 'The Reality of the Law of Nations', in Elihu Lauterpacht (ed.), *International Law: Collected Papers*, vol. 2 (Cambridge: CUP 1975), 47. See further Koskenniemi, *Gentle Civilizer* 2001 (n. 2), 364-66.

relevance as a method to understand international law practice and scholarship,[60] in particular through a theory of judicial interpretivism, similar to that of Ronald Dworkin in seeking some form of immanent purpose for the international legal system.[61] Two small doctrinal observations illustrate the point. The first is Lauterpacht's engagement with Kelsen's monism, too often contrasted with dualism in a simplistic attempt to distinguish between civil and common law traditions. However, Kelsen's monist theory concerned the unity of law; it was designed to subordinate politics and extra-legal considerations within a legal frame, and as Lauterpacht would have it, effectively to legalise a normative preference for peace.[62] The redemptory angle in Lauterpacht's approach towards positivism can also be seen in his well-known claims that international law, as a 'gapless' or complete international legal order, required international judges to ensure the impossibility of *lacunae* and to assert or apply legal rules even when State consent could not be established.[63] Crucially, this would be achieved by reference to the foundational, 'ultimate' purposes of international law, and not through a dogmatic reliance on a presumptive State freedom of action.[64] Lauterpacht's critique of classical positivism aimed squarely at its association with consensualism as international law's *basis for validity*; it was not a call to abandon positivism entirely. His main contribution to international legal thinking would be to reintroduce certain natural law elements to counterbalance a strict, normatively void interpretation of State consent. In his own words, 'State sovereignty, the incarnation of the supreme will of the State as the exclusive source of the law, must disdain the idea of persons owing their quality as subjects of the law to a source independent of the will of States. That source is the fact that, in relation to both rights and duties, the individual is the final subject of all law.'[65] This commitment to individual subjectivity was, to my mind, a rejection

[60] Iain Scobbie, 'The Theorist as Judge: Hersch Lauterpacht's Concept of the International Judicial Function' *European Journal of International Law* 8 (1997) 264-98 in fact concluded that 'Lauterpacht's theoretical construction of international law is rooted in Kelsenite legal epistemology'.

[61] I have written on the essentially interpretivist approach advocated by Lauterpacht: see, e.g., Gleider Hernández, 'Interpretation', in Jörg Kammerhofer and Jean d'Aspremont (eds.), *International Legal Positivism in a Post-Modern World* (Cambridge: CUP 2013), 317-48; Gleider Hernández, 'Interpretative Authority and the International Judiciary', in Andrea Bianchi, Matthew Windsor, and Daniel Peat (eds.), *Interpretation in International Law* (Oxford: OUP 2015), 166-85.

[62] Hersch Lauterpacht, 'Kelsen's Pure Science of Law', in Elihu Lauterpacht (ed.), *International Law: Collected Papers*, vol. 2 (Cambridge: CUP 1975), 72. See further Jochen von Bernstorff, *The Public International Law Theory of Hans Kelsen* (Cambridge: CUP 2011).

[63] Hersch Lauterpacht, *The Function of Law in the International Community* (Oxford: Clarendon Press, 1933), esp. 64-67. I have written extensively on the point: see further Gleider Hernández, *The International Court of Justice and the Judicial Function* (Oxford: OUP 2014), chapter VIII; see also Shabtai Rosenne, 'Sir Hersch Lauterpacht's Concept of the Task of the International Judge' *American Journal of International Law* 55 (1961), 825-62. But *cf.* Jörg Kammerhofer, 'Gaps, the *Nuclear Weapons* Advisory Opinion and the Structure of International Legal Argument between Theory and Practice' *British Year Book of International Law* 80 (2009), 333-60.

[64] Lauterpacht, *Function of Law* 1933 (n. 63), 94-96; Lauterpacht, *Private Law Sources and Analogies* 1927 (n. 55), 43-44.

[65] Hersch Lauterpacht, 'The Subjects of the Law of Nations (Part II)' *Law Quarterly Review* 64 (1948), 97-120, at 118. See further Roman Kwiecień, 'Sir Hersch Lauterpacht's Idea of State Sovereignty—Is it Still Alive?' *International Community Law Review* 13 (2011), 23-42, at 28-32.

of consensualism as the normative basis of international law, and not a rejection of positivism as his preferred approach to engaging with it.

4.2 The 'Scientific Sociology' of Georges Scelle

Georges Scelle's engagement with classical international legal positivism was predominant in French-speaking international law circles during the same period. As with Lauterpacht, Scelle's intellectual approach served more to dismantle voluntarism and its link to positivism, but was not an attack on the core tenets of positivist method. It is true that Scelle was a political activist, advocating for a *dépassement* (literally 'surpassing', or transcendence) of the State and State sovereignty through international law.[66] Nevertheless, his insistence on scientific 'truths' and his analysis of law as a phenomenon emanating from social relationships or 'formations', coupled with the articulation of his concept of *droit objectif* ('objective law'–which had nothing to do with natural law), led him to a crucial engagement with international legal positivism, with internationalism as a 'crucial fact'.[67] For him, objective law arose indeed from facts—the 'nature of things'—not from transcendent laws of nature as such.[68] Instead, 'objective law' would be *caused*, rather than willed, from phenomena rooted in social necessity (*'le résultant necessaire'*) for solidarity and inter-State relations, and could be ascertained from social facts and practices.[69] The distinction was both sociological and material, justifying his call for what he termed *la science juridique* or 'legal science'; but it was not formal. In this sense, Scelle was not voluntarist: within his concept of law, objective law could exist without tracing its validity to State consent, and found its validation in an international legal system with solidarity and the promotion of the individual at its heart.[70]

Scelle retained a heightened fidelity to positivism as an approach, what he called the *sovereignty of law*: in his view, positivism meant to constrain State sovereignty through legal means, and in particular by insisting on a relatively strict separation between law and politics or power relations.[71] Scelle's emphasis on solidarity as a legal value, not through some appeal to transcendent ethics or justice, was a factual observation that international law, *as an emanation of social necessity*, ought not to be constrained or instrumentalised for ideological or political purposes. This was

[66] Koskenniemi, *Gentle Civilizer* 2001 (n. 2), 329.

[67] Georges Scelle, *Précis de droit des gens*, vol. 1 (Paris: Sirey 1932), viii; see further Peters, 'Before Human Rights' (chapter 7), in this volume, section 6.1; pinpoint to be added at the proofs stage.

[68] Koskenniemi, *Gentle Civilizer* 2001 (n. 2), 328.

[69] Georges Scelle, 'Règles générales du droit de la paix' *Recueil des Cours* 46 (1933), 331-703, at 349. There is some similarity between the work of Scelle and that of Emile Durkheim: see further Sparks, 'Secular Natural Law' (chapter 10), in this volume, pinpoints to be added at the proofs stage.

[70] Scelle, *Précis de droit des gens* 1932 (n. 67), 13.

[71] *ibid*, ix-x; Scelle, 'Règles générales du droit de la paix' 1933 (n. 69), 348-49.

achieved by defining positive law as the 'translation' or the *outcome* of objective law being linked to social exigencies rooted in human conduct:

> La traduction normative de ces lois causales immanentes s'appelle le droit positif. Le droit positif n'est donc, par définition, que la transposition sur le plan normative des lois causales d'une société.[72]

Legal scholarship ought therefore to seek to identify the existence of law and legal norms through positivist means. However, the basis of international law's validity in the will of States would not be exclusive; it would, to a degree, be rooted in material, social realities. This is an important differentiator between Scelle and Lauterpacht, with the latter arguing from what can only be described as a sort of ethical rationalism.[73] Rather, Scelle's objective was to challenge the exclusivity of consensualism within international legal doctrine on which sovereignty was centred.[74] His theory, centred on individual protection and human rights, was not to favour the individual as the immediate subject of international law in a transcendent sense, but as an acknowledgment of 'social realities' which existed and had, over time, established how the interactions between States, as representatives of individuals and communities of individuals should proceed.[75] For Scelle, positivist methodology would need modernisation to conform with these social necessities and the observations of material facts, which were not normative commitments but *scientific* commitments.[76] Paradoxically, Scelle's insistence on the centrality of the individual as a matter of sociological necessity was not so much a departure from doctrinal voluntarism as a normative posture, but instead an attempt to adjust or refashion positivist methodology in the service of new material and scientific sensibilities.[77]

[72] Scelle, *Précis de droit des gens* 1932 (n. 67), 298 ('The normative translation of these immanent causal laws is called positive law. Positive law is therefore, by definition, nothing more than the normative transposition of a society's causal laws'). See also Scelle, 'Règles générales du droit de la paix' 1933 (n. 69), 349.

[73] One inspiration for this has been the argument for 'ethical rationalism' as laid out by Patrick Capps and Shaun Pattinson (eds.), *Ethical Rationalism and the* Law (Oxford: Hart 2017), chapter 1, 1-16.

[74] Scelle, *Précis de droit des gens* 1932 (n. 67), 13-14. Importantly, Scelle rejects the 'recognition of a special, privileged legal essence to the personified state collectivity', observing that only the individual would be capable of willing something, and that therefore, the State was a social milieu existing to guarantee individual protection.

[75] *ibid*, 15-16.

[76] Florian Couveinhes-Matsumoto, 'Georges Scelle: Les ambiguïtés d'une pensée prémonitoire' *Revue d'histoire des facultés de droit et de la culture juridique, du monde des jurists et du livre juridique* (2006) 339-406, at 351-54. See also Hubert Thierry, 'The Thought of Georges Scelle' *European Journal of International Law* 1 (1990) 193-209, at 194 and 197.

[77] Scelle, *Précis de droit des gens* 1932 (n. 67), 56. He is even more explicit in Georges Scelle, *Théories du gouvernement international* (Paris: Presses universitaires de France 1934), 55: '[l]e critère formel est antiscientifique. La nature intrinsèque d'un acte ne se détermine que par le critère matériel: celui du contenu de l'acte' ('[t]he formal criterion is antiscientific. The intrinsic nature of an act can only be determined by the material criterion: that of the content of the act'). But see Couveinhes-Matsumoto. 'Georges Scelle' 2006 (n. 76), 357-58, who notes that Scelle does not justify why material social facts are, scientifically at least, more relevant.

Of course, one might just have easily chosen to focus on a range of scholars writing during the period who also challenged classical international legal positivism; but through their influence, both Lauterpacht and Scelle remain exemplars of a much broader international legal debate taking place at the time. Though each had their distinct approach, both departed from voluntarism, focusing on an engagement with the individual as international legal subject. They sought a reconciliation of the individual-State relationship *through* positivism as a method or technique. Drawing from natural law accounts, sociology, and other inspirations, their approaches evinced two alternative paths through which a focus on the individual might have rebalanced the relationship between positivism and voluntarism. My key conclusion: through this integration of the individual, they sought to reform positivism, and not to reject it entirely in favour of another methodological approach.

4.3 International Law as a System: The Prominence of Kelsen and Hart

Both Hans Kelsen[78] and H. L. A Hart[79] have been deployed often in contemporary accounts for those seeking to rehabilitate legal positivism on the international plane. For international lawyers, their legacy is of a *formal* character, and was not about finding a new normative basis for international law, whether in the legal subjectivity of the individual or elsewhere. That is precisely the point: their theories have allowed international law to claim to retain a degree of coherence and a commitment to universality, achieved through methodological systematicity and an emphasis on coherence. Positivist methodology, and not a challenge to consensualism, has been at the heart of this rehabilitatory effort, and it is perhaps fitting that both Kelsen and Hart were both primarily legal theorists in the domestic legal mould, dealing with systems of law in which individuals were both the primary legal subject and actor (or official). However, most of their theorising could be applied by analogy to any formal legal system, based on whatever normative posture, be it consensualism (Oppenheim and others), human dignity (Lauterpacht), or social necessity (Scelle). To sketch out a highly compressed account, Kelsen's theory of law as a pure social system elucidated a theory of systemic

[78] See, e.g., Jörg Kammerhofer, 'Kelsen – Which Kelsen? A Re-Application of the Pure Theory to International Law' *Leiden Journal of International Law* 22 (2009), 225-50; von Bernstorff, *The Public International Law Theory of Hans Kelsen* 2011 (n. 62); García-Salmones Rovira, *The Project of Positivism* 2013 (n. 38), chapters 2-3.

[79] See, e.g., Jean d'Aspremont, 'Herbert Hart in Today's International Legal Scholarship', in Jörg Kammerhofer and Jean d'Aspremont (eds.), *International Legal Positivism in a Post-Modern World* (Cambridge: CUP 2014), 114-50, esp. at 144-50; *cf.* Mehrdad Payandeh, 'The Concept of International Law in the Jurisprudence of H.L.A. Hart' *European Journal of International Law* 21 (2010), 967-96.

autonomy that admits of, and needs no, extra-legal justification.[80] But the basis of law for Kelsen, his *Grundnorm* or 'basic norm', is beyond law and legal scholarship: it is as an 'original law-making fact' beyond the positive law.[81] Kelsen's exclusion of normativity from positivist thinking opens a potential gap international lawyers have exploited: a systematic conception of international law requires no necessary connection to State-centrism or the rejection of the individual. Importantly, if Kelsen's theory of legal systems is applied to international law, nothing precludes international law—a fully operative structure—from shifting or adjusting its basic norm over time, provided that the legal structure could still derive its validity from any new norm.[82]

Similarly, H. L. A. Hart's 'social thesis' avoids the question of the basis of law's validity entirely: in its focus on the distinctive features of law *qua* law, the study of the foundations of law is reduced, infamously, to the province of 'descriptive sociology'.[83] But Hart's famous account of legal systems as composed of primary (or duty-imposing) rules[84] as well as secondary rules of a more 'law-empowering' nature,[85] focuses on an autonomous systemic character and not any normative foundation for law. In particular, Hart's concept rests upon a rule of recognition which rests upon *acceptance* by 'some powerful subset of the members of the community […] "officials" […] accept the secondary rules': Hart's famous internal point of view adhering to the rule on the basis of that it is law.[86] Importantly, when applied to international law, there is no necessary element of State-centrism; if anything, Hart's social thesis of recognition renders international law as an autonomous formal system, the rules of which are 'derived from the practice of law-applying authorities'.[87] Hart's concept of law does not require the dismissal of the individual; it can be premised on any substantive norm that social facts would help to build up, be it a greater emphasis on the subjectivity of the individual or another foundational concept.

A few key observations emerge from Kelsen and Hart's accounts. Foremost, international law can operate as a self-contained system, on the basis of its own internal rules and without recourse to external sources. Unlike Oppenheim's account, international law does not need to rely on voluntarism to the point where the individual is reduced to a mere object. Yet, paradoxically, the positivist approaches

[80] What Kelsen himself calls, in German, '*Eigengesetzlichkeit*': see Hans Kelsen, *Reine Rechtslehre* (2nd edn, Vienna: Deuticke 1960), iii; Hans Kelsen, *Das problem der Souveränität und die Theorie des Völkerrechts* (2nd edn, Tübingen: JCB Mohr 1928), 276-78, cited and interpreted in English by von Bernstorff, *The Public International Law Theory of Hans Kelsen* 2011 (n. 78), 127; Hans Kelsen, *General Theory of Law and State* (Cambridge, MA: Harvard University Press 1945), xiv.

[81] Kelsen, *Pure Theory of Law* 2009 (n. 5), 199.

[82] See further, section 5, below.

[83] See H. L. A Hart, *The Concept of Law* (3rd edn, Oxford: Clarendon Press 2012), vi.

[84] *ibid*, 81.

[85] *ibid*, 91-99.

[86] d'Aspremont, 'Herbert Hart in Today's International Legal Scholarship' 2014 (n. 79), 122-124.

[87] d'Aspremont, *Formalism and the Sources of International Law* 2011 (n. 50), 15.

of Kelsen and Hart cannot help to identify the *foundations* of the international legal order except as lying beyond the reach of the tools offered by law. If positive international law does not require any specific normative or moral basis, neither Hart's nor Kelsen's respective theories shed much light on the place of the individual, beyond the fact that they do not exclude the individual. Individual rights, or concepts of human dignity, *could* be a normative or moral consideration, or a preferred social commitment embedded into the law itself. In this respect, Hart's and Kelsen's theories exemplify the extent to which positivism can be reduced almost—though perhaps not quite—exclusively to a method. In the final section, I will try to explore some of the consequences which flow from this observation in relation to international law's engagement with the individual.

5. Conclusion: A Potential for Foundational Change?

We circle back now to the individual in positivist legal theory of international law, according to which in a legal system, norms must be *valid* (in the sense that they are legally recognised as norms and thus produce legal effects) in order to be considered as properly legal.[88] But if that is so, conceptually at least it is possible to detach the validity of a norm or rule from its content. The normative basis of international law as being rooted in the consent of States as its normative basis remains a product of historical events and developments, a result of decisions over time. As I hope I have shown, a positivist account of international law does not make it necessary to deny the relevance or role of the individual: this is a product of historical circumstance.

It is this last point on which I wish to dwell. Certainly, the positivism-voluntarism amalgam is deeply embedded in the orthodox account of international law, both as a matter of international law's (post-nineteenth-century) history and as a prominent teaching of (nearly) every major textbook. But law is not a static form: if anything, it is relatively malleable, as it allows for the accommodation of small changes in legal and social practices over time. In this respect, I wish to explore a concept developed by Joseph Raz, the 'paradox of change', as a useful heuristic device to understand how a legal system built on one normative basis might become 'self-justifying', in that its reasons for validity might shift over time, or even be replaced through the ordinary processes of legal change: '[t]he same law can be valid for a variety of reasons, and these may change without the law changing'.[89]

Raz's 'paradox of change' concept rests on the idea that at one stage the structure or legal system can acquire a degree of self-legitimation quite apart from its

[88] Joseph Raz, *Practical Reasons and Norms* (Oxford: OUP 1975), 84.

[89] Joseph Raz, *Between Authority and Interpretation* (Oxford: Clarendon Press, 2009), 350-51, at 344 (in relation to domestic constitutions).

original foundations. As Raz puts it in relation to constitutions, 'at least old ones, do not derive their authority from the authority of their authors. […] They are self-validating. They are valid just because they are there, enshrined in the practices of their countries.'[90] The same can be said of international law; that over time, interpretive practices of legal officials (in domestic law, judges; in international law, perhaps a broader category including legal advisers to States, those advising international organisations, and others) and such internal referents come over time to supplant the extra-legal forces that might have superseded this or that foundational rule; and we do not need to resort to formalist techniques like the *Grundnorm* to exclude these from the scope of legal scholarship.[91]

By way of conclusion, is any of Raz's thinking useful in a chapter on positivism and the individual in international law? I take some inspiration from Alexander Somek, who has suggested that the 'true spirit' of legal positivism resides not in the insistence on the form of a legal system or its reliance on this or that dogma (e.g. Hart's dogma of social facts), but on a degree of malleability, in the sense that a legal system carries the seeds with it to outgrow the normative basis for which it was intended, and to become rooted in another foundation.[92] Put more simply, legal positivism is a method that deconstructs the idealised constructions of legal materials but without, somehow, eliminating their normative meaning.[93] And if that is the case, the distinction between positivism (a question of method) and consensualism (a normative claim on the proper basis of the international legal system) could perfectly accommodate the gradual accretion of a new foundation which could supplant the State-centrism which has long formed a part of international law's founding myth.

In any event, an undue fixation on consensualism has its own costs, elevating State priorities above other considerations that might be held by non-State actors, whether characterised as human dignity; a tentative definition of 'global public goods';[94] or any other interests of ethical, political, or social concern. In theory, international law could be wholly positivist but ground the ultimate justification for law-making and—in keeping with the question posed in this book—allow for a wider account of individuals as law-creative subjects of international law. It is hardly anti-positivist to contend that such a development may have occurred, or

[90] *ibid*, 348; see also Ago, 'Positive Law and International Law' 1957 (n. 19), 704-05, who regarded Kelsen's theory of the *Grundnorm* as self-contradictory, in that his positivism could not explain the origin, or validity, of 'the most important of all the norms'.

[91] Hovell, 'Elements' 2022 (n. 4), 76 characterises, as an 'uncomfortable paradox', the inability for positivist theory to cognise the ultimate norm of a legal system through positivist methodology. For her, this embodies a disciplinary *renvoi* to so-called 'black boxes of political and constitutional theory' on which international law's normativity rests.

[92] I draw loosely here from Alexander Somek, 'The Spirit of Legal Positivism' *German Law Journal* 12 (2011), 729-56, at 753.

[93] ibid, 754.

[94] See, e.g., Nico Krisch, 'The Decay of Consent: International Law in an Age of Global Public Goods' *American Journal of International Law* 108 (2014), 1-40.

is in the process of quickening, which might give some comfort to critics of international law's State-centrism. It would be equally arguable, and it is worth contemplating that a shift in gaze away from State-centrism as the basis for international law might not lead ineluctably towards the emancipation of individuals through international law, but instead reveal an international law founded on the accumulation of capital by bourgeois elites, the upholding of racist or imperial structures of domination, or the continued, exploitative resource extraction which threatens the sustainability of this planet. Though positivism might not itself provide the tools for resistance or for reform, its value lies, I think, in its explanatory potential, to understand how the law came to be, and the limits built into it.

9

The Individual in International Law from the Contemporary Sacred Natural Law Perspective

*Rafael Domingo**

1. Introduction

In recent years, there has been a renaissance of natural law studies, including the study of so-called sacred natural law.[1] Unlike rational natural law theories addressed by other chapters in this volume, sacred natural law theories are rooted in theological and scriptural accounts of created reality, and they combine reason and revelation in their elaboration and justification of legal arguments.[2]

For sacred natural law theories, God, creation, nature, reason, and morality are inseparably connected. The created universe offers testimony to God's laws and communicates moral knowledge. For some sacred natural theories, natural law is known both naturally (through inclination, intuition, and reason)[3] and supernaturally (through spiritual knowledge and religious sources that illuminate and complete natural knowledge). According to these theories, the natural and the supernatural are not two merely juxtaposed dimensions, but two interconnected dimensions of a unique multidimensional reality that includes legal, political, moral, and spiritual dimensions. Each dimension of reality is both autonomous in

* I want to thank the editors, Anne Peters and Tom Sparks, as well as Felix Maria Arocena, Gary S. Hauk, Francesca Iurlaro, Alexandra Kemmerer, John Witte Jr., and the reviewers for their interesting suggestions and thoughtful comments.

[1] For an overview, see Stephen J. Grabill, *Rediscovering the Natural Law in Reformed Theological Ethics* (Grand Rapids, MI: William B. Eerdmans 2006); David VanDrunen, *Divine Covenants and Moral Order: A Biblical Theology of Natural Law* (Grand Rapids, MI: William B. Eerdmans 2014), 1-36; Anver M. Emon, Matthew Levering, and David Novak (eds.), *Natural Law: A Jewish, Christian, and Islamic Trialogue* (Oxford: OUP 2014); Norman Doe (ed.), *Christianity and Natural Law: An Introduction* (Cambridge: CUP 2017).

[2] See Sparks, 'Secular Natural Law' (chapter 10), in this volume. For an overview on the distinction, see Richard Tuck, 'The "Modern" Theory of Natural Law', in Anthony Pagden (ed.), *The Languages of Political Theory in Early-Modern Europe* (New York, NY: CUP 1987), 99-119; VanDrunen, *Divine Covenants and Moral Order* 2014 (n. 1), 1-36; Doe, *Christianity and Natural Law* 2017 (n. 1), esp. xiii-xvii and 1-16.

[3] See Jacques Maritain, *Man and the State* (Washington DC: The Catholic University of America Press 1998), 91.

Rafael Domingo, *The Individual in International Law from the Contemporary Sacred Natural Law Perspective* In: *The Individual in International Law*. Edited by: Tom Sparks and Anne Peters, Oxford University Press.
 DOI: 10.1093/oso/9780198898917.003.0009

its own sphere of application and integrated into a deeper dimension—the legal in the political, the political in the moral, and the moral in the spiritual dimensions.[4]

In order to achieve the greatest degree of harmony in reality, and to understand and protect the human person as a multidimensional individual being, each dimension needs to recognise the existence, influence, and function of the other dimensions, which in some sense act as a filter or check on the excesses of the others. For instance, an unjust law (such as a Nazi law or a slave code) might be valid in the legal and the political dimensions of reality but immoral under the higher moral dimension. Some natural law scholars, following Saint Augustine and Saint Thomas Aquinas,[5] would say that an unjust law is not a true law (*lex iusta non est lex*), but a corruption of law; others would affirm that it is true positive law but contrary to morality or justice. Regardless of the specific categorisation, what is crucial is the substantial difference between a law promulgated in accordance with the standards of the moral dimension and one promulgated in contradiction to those moral standards.

This multidimensionality of reality clarifies why no legal theory can fully account for law from the legal dimension alone, just as no moral theory makes perfect sense of morality from the moral dimension—and for that matter, nothing in physics can fully interpret the physical dimension of reality. In this sense, the so-called Böckenförde dictum is illustrative and certainly true: 'The liberal, secularized state is sustained by conditions it cannot itself guarantee.'[6] The premises of a secular liberal State cannot be fully explained by the political dimension alone, because the fundamental conditions and qualities of justice, freedom, and dignity touch all the dimensions of reality in which the human person acts (the political, the moral, the spiritual), not just the political one.

While natural law theories of various sorts have long been a central teaching of Christian theology, ethics, anthropology, and jurisprudence, natural law has been more marginal in Judaism and Islam.[7] Recently, however, as a result of a fertile inter-religious dialogue, some theories of natural law increasingly are being developed in Jewish and Muslim traditions.[8] However, it would be problematic to talk

[4] See Rafael Domingo, 'Why Spirituality Matters for Law: An Explanation' *Oxford Journal of Law and Religion* 8 (2019), 326-34.

[5] See Saint Augustine, *De libero arbitrio* 1.5.11 (Francs E. Touscher (ed. and tr.), Philadelphia: Peter Reilly Co. 1937), and Thomas Aquinas, *Summa Theologiae* I-II, q. 96, a. 4, c (online edition, Enrique Alarcon (ed.), Corpus Thomisticum, *S. Thomae de Aquino Opera Omnia*, Pamplona: University of Navarra 2000).

[6] Ernst-Wolfgang Böckenförde, 'The Rise of the State as a Process of Secularization' [1967], in Mirjam Künkler and Tine Stein (eds.), *Ernst-Wolfgang Böckenförde: Religion, Law, and Democracy: Selected Writings*, vol. 2 (Thomas Dunlap (tr.), Oxford: OUP 2020), 152-67, at 167. For a commentary on this dictum, see Tine Stein, 'The Böckenförde Dictum — On the Topicality of a Liberal Formula' *Oxford Journal of Law and Religion* 7 (2018), 97-108.

[7] Norman Doe, 'Natural Law in the Interfaith Context: The Abrahamic Religions', in Doe, *Christianity and Natural Law* 2017 (n. 1), 184.

[8] See David Novak, *Covenantal Rights: A Study in Jewish Political Theory* (Princeton, NJ: Princeton University Press 2000); David Novak, *Natural Law in Judaism* (Cambridge: CUP 2008); Anver M.

about a Jewish natural law tradition or an Islamic natural law tradition in the same way that we talk about the Christian natural law tradition. Many Jewish scholars think that the idea of natural law is alien to the sources and character of Judaism.[9] Something similar can be said more strongly about Islamic legal scholars, who consider the law of revelation to be sufficient.[10]

Among Christian traditions, sacred natural law theories have been more developed and discussed in Protestantism and Roman Catholicism than in Orthodox Christianity, which makes no distinction between sacred and rational natural law.[11] Contemporary natural law approaches have been provided by, among others, such Christian thinkers as (alphabetically) Ernst-Wolfgang Böckenförde, Norman Doe, John Finnis, Robert P. George, Mary Ann Glendon, Javier Hervada, Russell Hittinger, Matthew Levering, C. S. Lewis, Jacques Maritain, Martin Rhonheimer, Robert Spaemann, David VanDrunen, and Michel Villey.[12] The role that each author gives to sacred natural law is different, and many times they use arguments that are opposite from one another (e.g. Hittinger vs Finnis[13]), but all the authors agree on the relevance of the transcendent dimension for the development of legal order.

2. Sacred Natural Law as a Metalegal Concept

Sacred natural law theories are more comprehensive and integrated than rational natural law theories. They offer a bigger picture of the foundations of normativity based on the creative purpose, providence, and wisdom of God, maker of the universe and universal law-giver. They investigate and integrate abundant sources to discern the content and meaning of sacred natural law—nature and creation, experience and intuition, practical reason and divine revelation—in order to protect the person as a whole.

Sixteenth-century Italian jurist Alberici Gentili was among the first western jurists to recognise and argue clearly for the role of sacred natural law in the

Emon, *Islamic Natural Law Theories* (Oxford: OUP 2010); Emon, Levering, and Novak, *Natural Law: A Jewish, Christian, and Islamic Trialogue* 2014 (n. 1).

[9] On this topic, see Abraham Joshua Heschel, *Heavenly Torah as Refracted through the Generations* (New York, NY: Continuum 2006).

[10] For an overview, see Anver M. Emon, *Islamic Natural Law Theories* (Oxford: OUP 2010).

[11] Stanley S. Harakas, 'Eastern Orthodox Perspectives on Natural Law' *American Journal of Jurisprudence* 24 (1979), 86-113.

[12] See Rafael Domingo, 'El Derecho y la Moral. Cien años de soledad' *Scripta Theologica* 52 (2020), 763-92 and John Witte Jr., 'Natural Law in Europe and America (1600-)', in Hans-Josef Klauck et al. (eds.), *The Encyclopaedia of the Bible and Its Reception*, vol. 20 (Berlin: DeGruyter 2022), [add page range in proofs].

[13] Russell Hittinger, *A Critique of the New Natural Law Theory* (Notre Dame, IN: University of Notre Dame Press 1988).

development of a secular law of nations and rational law of nature. While some medieval scholars anticipated some of his insights, Gentili was distinct in arguing for a concept of a secular law of nations that did not question either the supremacy of the laws of God over human law, or the understanding of natural law as divine law, or, as a result, the supremacy of natural law over civil law.[14] Gentili's theory of legal secularisation was a theistic theory of secularisation, one firmly based on Christian principles and ideals and their role in the legal sphere, including the sphere of the law of nations, the *ius gentium*.

Nonetheless, Gentili insisted that the legal and spiritual dimensions remain separate, even if they are connected. His influential dictum *Silete theologi in munere alieno* (Be silent, theologians, about things that are foreign to you!)[15] underscored the necessary autonomy of the disciplines of law and theology as well as his belief that questions related to the law of nations and, therefore, to natural law should be dealt with and resolved by legal scholars. Jurists, not theologians, are the true and final interpreters of the law, he insisted, even if they draw widely on sacred sources. Gentili's dictum has been claimed centuries later by scholars of European public law to argue for the complete secularisation of the law and the absolute divorce of law and theology. This later modern view, however, goes far beyond the limits Gentili himself intended.[16]

A generation later, the Dutch jurist Hugo Grotius argued similarly for the place of biblical and other expressions of sacred natural law within the secular legal sphere. His famous legal works on the law of nations, war and peace, maritime law, and international law thus drew heavily on the Bible and Christian teachings, and he wrote commentaries on the Bible as well as a famous tract on *The Truth of the Christian Religion*, which bled into his legal work.[17] Nonetheless, he insisted that the legal sphere must be autonomous and that the law of nature and nations could and should exist and operate fully 'even if there were no God'.[18] But, as Janne E. Nijman has pointed out, Grotius' famous *etiamsi daremus* experiment, however, never meant to disconnect humanity and human nature from the work of God in

[14] See Rafael Domingo and Giovanni Minucci, 'Alberico Gentili and the Secularization of the Law of Nations', in Rafael Domingo and John Witte Jr. (eds.), *Christianity and Global Law* (London: Routledge 2020), 98-111.

[15] Alberici Gentili, *De iure belli libri tres* (John C. Rolfe (tr.), New York: Oceana Publications 1964), 1.12.92, 57. On this topic, see Giovanni Minnucci, *Silete theologi in munere alieno. Alberico Gentili tra diritto, teologia e religione* (Milan: Monduzzi Edizione 2016).

[16] See Carl Schmitt, *The Nomos of the Earth in the International Law of the Ius Publicum Europaeum* (Gary L. Ulmen (tr.), New York, NY: Tellos Press 2006), 126.

[17] Hugo Grotius, *The Truth of the Christian Religion* (first published 1640, this edn: Maria Rosa Antognazza (ed.), Indianapolis: Liberty Fund 2012).

[18] Hugo Grotius, *De Iure Belli ac Pacis Libri Tres*, Prolegomena, para 11 (first published 1625, this edn: James Scott (ed.), Francis Kelsey (tr.), Oxford: Clarendon Press, 1925), 13: 'etiamsi daremus [. . .] non esse Deum'.

this world. Rather, Grotius depends on the relationship between God and human beings for his theory of the *Ius naturae et gentium*.[19]

Like these two early modern legal giants, I hold to the value of maintaining a sacred natural law alongside a rational natural law. I do not see any opposition between a theistic approach to law that includes appreciation for sacred sources of law and a positive, secular international legal order that is based on treaties, conventions, and declarations. So long as the theistic framework is optional and noncoercive, the starting point of any legal framework for both believers and nonbelievers today should be theistically oriented.[20] A theistic orientation of the law prevents the legal system from being reduced into a mere legal set of conventional rules. If that were to happen, law would not protect human persons in their multidimensional integrity, would not have built-in safeguards against tyrannical abuse, and would not foster a solidary collaboration between believers and nonbelievers in the search for justice and peace in our globalised world.

Beyond providing a theistic orientation and a necessary check on law and rational legal discourse, sacred natural law theories emphasise the strong connectivity between theology (including natural theology) and jurisprudence. Historically in the west, jurisprudence was firmly rooted in and shaped by theology.[21] As Gottfried Leibniz emphasised, 'the similarity between the two disciplines is surprising'.[22] In my opinion, theology should continue to buttress the pillars of secular law, including international law, from the outside by supporting the dignity and freedom of individuals, developing a culture of human rights, and blocking the assumption of a divine role by international legal authorities and institutions: if God exists, no human power has the right to become a god.[23]

How is it possible to protect the necessary autonomy of international law and other legal systems when nonlegal sources are legitimated and when law is understood as interconnected with other different dimensions of reality, not least the spiritual? In my view, sacred natural law can and should operate in the legal system as a *metalegal concept*, not a legal one. Metalegal concepts illuminate the legal concepts and arguments from outer, higher dimensions. They do not use the essential method of legal systems—coercion. Nor do they generate specific legal doctrines of contract, agreement, or treaty, but instead involve higher principles like honour,

[19] Janne E Nijman, 'Grotius' Imago Dei Anthropology: Grounding Ius Naturae et Gentium', in Martii Koskenniemi, Mónica García-Salmones Rovira, and Paolo Amorosa (eds.), *International Law and Religion: Historical and Contemporary Perspectives* (Oxford: OUP 2017), 87-110, at 106.

[20] See Rafael Domingo, *God and the Secular Legal System* (Cambridge: CUP 2016), 167 and Rafael Domingo, 'The Metalegal God' *Ecclesiastical Law Journal* 16 (2014), 147-67.

[21] See Carl Schmitt's famous dictum that 'all significant concepts of the modern theory of the state are secularized theological concepts', in *Political Theology: Four Chapters on the Concept of Sovereignty* (George Schwab (tr.) Chicago, IL: The Chicago University Press 2005), 36.

[22] See Gottfried Wilhelm Leibniz, *The New Method of Learning and Teaching Jurisprudence* (Carmelo Massimo de Iuliis (tr.), Clark, NJ: Talbot Publishers 2017), pt. 2, para. 4, 33.

[23] See Rafael Domingo, 'Theology and Jurisprudence: A Good Partnership?' *Journal of Law and Religion* 32 (2017), 79-85.

promise, or covenant. Nor do they require full acceptance by all citizens, because technically the metalegal is not 'in force'. Metalegal concepts are not part of the legal system in the strictest sense, but they are part of the legal order in the broadest sense, just as the type of soil and the landscape around a house are not strictly part of the house but are critical for its construction and its views.

Metalegal concepts are categories, values, and ideas beyond the legal dimension that yet have legal significance in legal systems – in our case international law.[24] To have legal significance does not mean that a metalegal concept has a direct legal effect in the strictest sense,[25] but instead can be seen more through illumination, support, guidance, or understanding. Indeed, a metalegal concept can enter into practice as a light that shines and guides, as a framework that attracts, or as an aid or support to advancement.[26] Sometimes, metalegal concepts are also recognised as rights or values (e.g. religious freedom). In these cases, metalegal concepts operate in the legal realm as both legal and metalegal concepts. But this is not the case for the concept of sacred natural law in the international law order, where sacred natural law is a mere metalegal concept.

Although not strictly legal, metalegal concepts do not obscure the essence of international law; on the contrary, they illuminate international law at its heart. Metalegal concepts support international law by linking it with other dimensions of human knowledge and understanding. Metalegal concepts are also sources of value in the realm of international law and international relations. An example: whether norms are classified as peremptory (*ius cogens*) depends on Article 53 of the Vienna Convention more than on a direct decree of God,[27] but the reality of a divine providence adds value to the idea of *ius cogens*. Peremptory norms are connected to immutability, permanence, and perpetuation granted by divine providence.

The birth of the European Union is a good example of this kind of illumination provided by metalegal concepts. The first and crucial steps of the long European integration process after the World War II were possible, at least in some notable degree, because of the spiritual stature of the so-called European founding fathers: Konrad Adenauer, Robert Schuman, Jean Monnet, Alcide De Gasperi, and Joseph Bech, among others. They were able to build a new Europe from the blood and ashes of the battlefields through reconciliation, forgiveness, and communion (three metalegal concepts), and by overcoming any kind of domination, revenge, and retaliation.[28]

[24] On these metalegal concepts, see Domingo, *God and the Secular Legal System* 2016 (n. 20), 29-32; Domingo, 'The Metalegal God' 2014 (n. 20), 147-67.

[25] On legal causation, see Herbert L. A. Hart and Tony Honoré, *Causation in the Law* (2nd edn, Oxford: Clarendon Press 1985).

[26] In the same vein but applied to divine law, see Remi Bragué, *The Law of God: The Philosophical History of an Idea* (Lydia G. Cochrane (tr.), Chicago, IL: University of Chicago Press 2007), 264.

[27] Jeremy Waldron, 'What is Natural Law Like?', in John Keown and Robert P. George (eds.), *Reason, Morality, and Law: The Philosophy of John Finnis* (Oxford: OUP 2013), 72-89, at 88.

[28] See Desmond Dinan, *Origins and Evolution of the European Union* (2nd edn, Oxford: OUP 2014).

3. The Image of God as the Ultimate Ground for the Protection of the Person in International Law

The image-of-God doctrine—the idea that God created humanity in the divine image—provides some spiritual, moral, and anthropological standards that have important implications for international law and legal science in general, especially for illuminating the ideas of human dignity and equality. In fact, centuries ago, Grotius founded his anthropological approach to the law of nations in this Imago Dei doctrine.[29]

As is well known, the book of Genesis stresses the relevant position of human beings in the world by saying that humankind was created in the *image and likeness of God.*[30] Biblical scholars of every tradition have discussed the meaning of this expression for centuries, developing many different and even controversial approaches.[31] In recent Protestant and Catholic theology,[32] following, among others, Saint Augustine[33] and Saint Thomas Aquinas,[34] one finds the strongest affirmation that the notion of humanity made in the image of God validates the relevant place of each person in the universal order and inside the political community. Each person is substantially a mirror of God, reflecting their personal relationship with God. In other words, the relationship or representation and resemblance to God are constitutive of—that is, inseparable from—the human being.

This image of God is fundamentally personal, not only in the sense that each human being, male or female (Gen. 1:27), is made in the image of God, but also in the sense that the image is of an incarnated divine person, Jesus Christ, and ultimately the image of a personal triune and loving God. The plural pronoun used in the Genesis narrative ('Let us make humankind in our image after our likeness') emphasises this Trinitarian context.[35]

In the next sections, we will analyse how the Imago Dei doctrine sheds light on, among other concepts, the legal notions of human dignity, individual freedom and responsibility, solidarity, pluralism, diversity, and even the emerging idea of global law.

[29] Nijman, 'Grotius' Imago Dei Anthropology' 2017 (n. 19), 87-110.

[30] Genesis 1:26-28; 5:1-3; and 9:6.

[31] The impact of original sin in the image-of-God bearers, for instance, is interpreted in many different ways in many Christian denominations. See VanDrunen, *Divine Covenants and Moral Order* 2014 (n. 1); Doe, *Christianity and Natural Law* 2017 (n. 1); Gabrielle Thomas, *The Image of God in the Theology of Gregory of Nazianzus* (Cambridge: CUP 2019).

[32] Edith Stein, *Finite and Eternal Being* (Kurt F. Reinhardt (tr.), Washington DC: ICS Publications 2002).

[33] Augustine of Hippo, *The Trinity* (2nd edn, John E. Rotelle (ed.), Edmund Hill (tr.), Hyde Park, NY: New City Press 2012), 9-10.

[34] Thomas Aquinas, *Corpus Thomisticum. S. Thomae de Aquino Opera Omnia* (Enrique Alarcón (ed.), Pamplona: Universitatis Studiorum Navarrensis 2000), I q. 93.

[35] Thomas A. Smail, 'In the Image of the Triune God' *International Journal of Systematic Theology* 5 (2003), 22-32 and James Hanvey, 'Dignity, Person, and Imago Trinitatis', in Christopher McCrudden (ed.), *Understanding Human Dignity* (Oxford: OUP 2013), 209-28.

4. Human Dignity: The Status of the Image-of-God Bearers

Dignity is a polyhedric concept with many nuances and implications.[36] It is the human being's most radical and inherent quality, and one of the constitutive ideas of the entire body of international human rights. It is more than a right, basic good, value, or principle.[37] It is the transcendental ground, the fundamental premise for human equality, human freedom, and human rights and duties. As the preamble to the Universal Declaration of Human Rights states, the 'recognition of the inherent dignity and of the equal and inalienable rights of all members of the human family is the foundation of freedom, justice and peace in the world'.[38]

Sacred natural law provides a metalegal and objective validity to the general idea of dignity as the status of every human being made in the image of God.[39] Without a theistic approach, dignity easily can be reduced to a subjective substantial self, a pure capacity for rational autonomy, a mere self-respect as a necessary condition for living well and taking seriously moral responsibilities,[40] or a simple right to be recognised as a legal person. In the worst case, it can be transformed into a formal, vacuous concept without a specific function in the international realm because of its calculated ambiguity. And when the idea of human dignity weakens, the international human rights system falters.

According to sacred natural law theories, the status conferred by dignity to human beings is neither temporary nor territorial, but personal and constitutive of any human being. In this sense, human beings are unique. The status provided by dignity implies—among other goods—respect, human freedom and responsibility, human equality, and human rights.

The image-of-God doctrine strengthens the respect of human beings because they are in a special relationship with God. Human beings are not an accident in cosmic history; they are a whole and an end. They are creatures made with some features of their Creator: they are active creatures who freely collaborate with their Creator in the development of the universe and the fulfilment of the Creator's plans.

[36] On dignity, see Robert Spaemann, *Love and the Dignity of Human Life: On Nature and Natural Law* (Grand Rapids, MI: William B. Eerdmans 2011); McCrudden, *Understanding Human Dignity* 2013 (n. 35); Jeremy Waldron, *Dignity, Rank, and Rights* (Oxford: OUP 2015); Michael Rosen, *Dignity: Its History and Meaning* (Cambridge, MA: Harvard University Press 2018); Martin Schlag, 'Christianity and the Principle of Dignity', in Domingo and Witte, *Christianity and Global Law* 2020 (n. 14), 214-30.

[37] On human dignity and international law, see Paolo Carozza, 'Human Dignity', in Dina Shelton (ed.), *International Human Rights Law* (Oxford: OUP 2013), 345-60.

[38] See UNGA, Universal Declaration of Human Rights, A/RES/217(III)A.

[39] On the connection between human dignity and image of God, see Bernd Oberdorfer, 'Human Dignity and Image of God' *Scriptura* 204 (2010), 231-39; Hanvey, 'Dignity, Person, and Imago Trinitatis' 2013 (n. 35); Janet Soskice, 'Human Dignity and the Image of God', in McCrudden, *Understanding Human Dignity* 2013 (n. 35), 229-43.

[40] See, e.g., Ronald Dworkin, *Justice for Hedgehogs* (Cambridge, MA: The Belknap Press of Harvard University Press 2011), 13-14.

Human freedom is a marvellous expression of the divine image, because creation was essentially an act of loving divine freedom, not a necessary emanation from the divine. If human creatures are free, it is because God the Creator is free and created humans in the divine image – that is, with capacity for freedom, responsibility, and love.

Dignity is shared by all human beings, without exception, and it is a unique and equalising status. Thus, human equality is also an expression of the fact that all human beings have been made in the same unique image of God, which is the image of one God living eternally in three equal persons: Father, Son, and Holy Spirit. Each divine person, although distinct from the others in view of their relationships, does not divide unity, because there is no diversity of being among them. On the other hand, each divine person of the Trinity is equal to the Trinity itself. As Saint Augustine pointed out: 'so total is the equality in this triad that not only is the Father not greater than the Son as far as divinity is concerned, but also Father and Son together are not greater than the Holy Spirit, nor is any single person of the three less than the Trinity itself.'[41]

This profound understanding of the value of each human being as a bearer of the divine image produces a natural deference for human rights, which are the basic manifestations in the legal dimension of this spiritual image.[42] Reflecting the image of God, human rights have an individual but also a communitarian scope. Self-giving enables human beings to experience their individual lives as completely united with the lives of others. When one exercises rights in a self-giving (communitarian) attitude, rights become transformed from enforceable protected interests into 'enforceable protected services',[43] and society strengthen its ties of union.

5. Universal Moral Principles Shared by the Image-of-God Bearers

The image of God represented in the human being is a living image of a living God. This image has the potential to inspire sound principles for judging when human affairs and actions might either preserve or harm the quality of the divine image in every human person. For this reason, according to most sacred natural law

[41] Saint Augustine, *The Trinity (De Trinitate)* (first published c. 417, this edn: John E. Rotelle (ed.), Hyde Park, NY: New City Press 2012), 8.1, 241.

[42] On the relation between Christianity and human rights, see John Witte Jr. and Frank Alexander (eds.), *Christianity and Human Rights* (Cambridge: CUP 2010). For a different approach, see Samuel Moyn, *Christian Human Rights* (Philadelphia, PA: University of Pennsylvania Press 2005) and Samuel Moyn, 'Christianity and Human Rights', in Domingo and Witte, *Christianity and Global Law* 2020 (n. 14), 323-36.

[43] On the idea of right as service, see Álvaro d'Ors, *Nueva introducción al estudio del derecho* (Madrid: Civitas 1999), § 62 and Rafael Domingo, 'Álvaro d'Ors', in Rafael Domingo and Javier Martínez-Torrón (eds.), *Great Christian Jurists in Spanish History* (Cambridge: CUP 2018), 343-59, at 356.

theories, human beings are able to know naturally some aspects of God's basic law, which is written on the human heart.

In his letter to the Romans, Saint Paul confirms this important doctrine when he affirms that the natural law written on human hearts allows human beings to know moral obligations naturally, even without knowing the Mosaic law: 'Indeed, when Gentiles, who do not have the law, do by nature things required by the law, they are a law for themselves, even though they do not have the law.'[44] Paul explains how Jews, under Mosaic law, and Gentiles, under a law manifested by nature, can share some basic universal moral standards. Many of these moral standards and conventional practices are, of course, contextual and depend on cultural traditions. However, some natural law principles as such remain as a source of binding common principles among all human beings beyond the inevitable cultural differences.

This doctrine of a universal natural law written in human hearts has an extraordinary impact in international law because it recognises the individual as a true original source of legal validity: *ex persona ius oritur* (the law comes from the individual). The doctrine also supports the idea that no legal system, including the international legal system, is self-contained, because some aspects of legal systems are ordered beyond the systems.

The moral natural law written in human hearts should lead the international law-making process to limit any potential arbitrariness of nation-State sovereignty. According to natural law, there is in the deepest dimensions of human existence a law that remains unchangeable, whose derogation by political authorities is not allowed by nature. It is a sort of natural *ius cogens*, which enlightens positive *ius cogens* and human governance. The rule of *pacta sunt servanda* (agreements must be kept), which is basic to both natural and positive law, is a good example of how natural law impinges on international law at the fundamental level. Along with this respect for promises and contracts, sacred natural law demands, among other things, respect for the integrity of creation and its resources, as well as reparation of injustice.

6. Pluralism, Diversity, and the Image of God

To be bearers of the image of God serves to identify human beings as persons but not to make them uniform. The image of God is a source of pluralism and diversity since it is the image of a triune personal living God. The idea of person is essentially rooted in relationship and diversity. Each person is different from every other. Precisely this difference allows affirming that, despite being God the Absolute One, a distinction of three divine persons is possible based on their

[44] Romans 2:14-15.

relations of origin: the Father generates, the Son is begotten, and the Holy Spirit proceeds. Made in the triune image of God, each member of humanity is different and should be protected in that difference. This diversity enriches human society and supports pluralism as a political value. Pluralism is based on unity, because the former comes from the latter, not vice versa. Pluralism is the way of living out unity in diversity in democratic political societies.

Sacred natural law theories support a unifying foundational pluralism instead of the individualistic pluralism of well-ordered societies.[45] Individuals do not determine their personal fulfilment and flourishing by stipulating a minimum hypothetical contract to live in society. Unity is neither contractual nor based on a conception of the self as independent from any conception of the good, but rather is deeper than that: unity is the oneness of the image of God reflected in each human being within the political community. The image-of-God unity is precontractual, prepolitical, and prelegal. It transcends, precedes, and shapes any kind of organisation of democratic societies.

7. Solidarity and the Image-of-God Doctrine

The word 'solidarity', derived from the Latin *solidus* (solid), is as fresh as it is revolutionary, as rich as it is classical, and as strong as it is necessary. Although the word was first pronounced in French (*solidarité*) and in the context of the French Revolution,[46] the idea of solidarity is as old as the Bible, Greek philosophy, and Roman law, the three great pillars of western civilisation.

The word 'solidarity' is used technically in the most varied areas of private and public law. Yet beyond all technicalities and differences lies the central intuition that gave rise to solidarity in Roman law. Roman law uses 'solidary' (*in solidum*) to describe joint and several liability – for example, when several debtors, several creditors, or several wrongdoers share entirely and at the same time in certain obligations stemming from a stipulation, a contract, or a private wrong (*delictum*).[47]

The Roman jurist Gaius, in his well-known *Institutes*, resorts eight times to the expression *in solidum*. For example, in *Institutes* 3.121, Gaius tells us that, before the emperor Hadrian changed the law by means of an official letter (*epistula*), sureties were bound jointly and severally for the entire amount of the debts of the principal debtor, and the creditor was at liberty to collect the whole debt either from

[45] John Rawls, *A Theory of Justice* (first published 1971, rev. edn: Cambridge, MA: Belknap Press of Harvard University Press 1999), 397-405.

[46] See Marie-Claude Blais, *La solidarité. Histoire d'une idée* (Paris: Éditions Gallimard 2007); Serge Audier, *La pensé solidariste* (Paris: Presses Universitaires de France 2010). See also Kurt Bayertz (ed.), *Solidarity* (Dordrecht: Kluwer 1999) and Hauke Brunkhorst, *Solidarity: From Civic Friendship to a Global Legal Community* (Cambridge, MA: MIT Press 2005).

[47] Lucio Parenti, *In solidum obligari. Contributo allo studio della solidarietà da atto lecito* (Naples: Edizioni Scientifiche Italiane 2012).

the debtor or from each of the sureties.[48] In another example, in *Institutes* 4.71, Gaius explains that when a father places his son or his slave in charge of a ship or other business, the liability is *in solidum*—that is, shared by the father and the son or slave.

Based on the same central idea of Roman law solidarity, the sacred natural law principle of solidarity states that each person, as a full image-of-God bearer, is *liable* for the protection of the whole image of God, not only in the person's individual self but also in every other human being, as well as in any community of human beings, including the global human community. Since God is a spirit, the image of God is not divisible, and therefore the liability to protect this image always extends to the whole (*in solidum*). Thus, just as there is no distinction between the individual divine image and the divine image of every member of the political community of human beings, so there is no substantial distinction between the individual ethos and the ethos of any political community – that is, between the individual good and the common good of local, intermediate, and global communities.

As the image of God is only one, so the good is also one. In God, there are three persons but not three goods. The Father is the whole good, the Son is the whole good, and the Holy Spirit is the whole good. The good, like God, and therefore like the image of God, cannot be divided but only shared. Thus, the common good is part of the individual good and vice versa. Any wall of separation between the common and the particular good is artificial. In contrast, individual interests can conflict with each other and with the local, the national, or the international interest. The reason for this difference is that interest is always individualistic and therefore fragmentary. Common interest is the sum of individual interests; it is the totality of particularities, but not the universality of the diversity. Common interest promotes cooperation, the process of working together for the same purpose, but not solidarity in the fullest sense. International law is based on international cooperation among sovereign states; global law, however, goes to the next step: the solidary unity of the global community.[49]

The image-of-God doctrine reveals the need to transform cooperation into solidarity: one cannot possess the image of God just for oneself. If human beings are united and there is an indivisible common good, anything that happens to another matters, especially if it affects dignity. Common good thus becomes a moral requirement. The image of God universalises the idea of neighbour, without reducing it to a simple abstraction, and asks for practical commitment.[50]

[48] Gaius, *The Institutes of Gaius* (first written c. 161, this edn: Francis De Zulueta (ed.), Oxford: Clarendon Press 1953), 3.121.

[49] See Rafael Domingo, 'Christianity, Solidarity, and Law', in John Witte Jr. and Rafael Domingo (eds.), *The Oxford Handbook on Christianity and Law* (Oxford: OUP, 2023), chapter 60.

[50] See Joseph Ratzinger (Benedict XVI), Encyclical Letter *Deus Caritas Est*, 25 December 2005 (Vatican City: Libreria Editrice Vaticana 2005), § 15.

8. Subsidiarity and the Image-of-God Doctrine

Intimately united to responsibility and freedom is the principle of subsidiarity, which tries to protect the priority of the person, and specifically the individual's inalienable freedom, against strong intervention by higher and more powerful social structures and groups.[51] Developed specifically by Catholic social teaching,[52] the foundational idea of the principle of subsidiarity lies in the ontological priority of each human person (and each person's freedom), as an image-of-God bearer, to any kind of social grouping or community. Thus, the starting point of any well-structured legal system, including international law, should be the individual and not the political community.

Subsidiarity protects the necessary freedom to fulfil personal responsibilities. Subsidiarity allows individuals the fulfilment of solidary obligations that cannot be delegated to higher structures. Cooperation, support, and help from more powerful groups are legitimised only when individual or lower groups are not able to accomplish their purpose on their own. In this sense, subsidiarity is a complementary principle of solidarity.[53] Subsidiarity constitutes the limit of a potentially fake solidarity transformed into paternalism or domination or social privatism.

Although always governing with the aim of protecting the individual, the European Union has used the principle of subsidiarity with a more technical and narrow meaning. It represents only a principle of administrative decentralisation to regulate the exercise of the Union's nonexclusive powers. Article 5(3) of the Treaty on European Union states that in areas which do not fall within the exclusive power of the European Union—that is, in areas shared by the European Union and the member States—'the Union shall act only if and in so far as the objectives of the proposed action cannot be sufficiently achieved by the Member States, either at the central or at regional and local level, but can rather, by reason of the scale or effects of the proposed action, be better achieved at Union level'.[54]

[51] On subsidiarity, see Paolo Carozza, 'Subsidiarity as a Structural Principle of International Human Rights Law' *American Journal of International Law* 97 (2003), 38-79; Gerald L. Neuman, 'Subsidiarity', in Dina Shelton (ed.), *International Human Rights Law* (Oxford: OUP 2013), 360-78; James E. Fleming and Jacob T. Levy (eds.), *Federalism and Subsidiarity* (New York, NY: New York University Press 2014); Maria Catherine Cahill, 'Subsidiarity', in Gerard V. Bradley and E. Christian Brugger (eds.), *Catholic Social Teaching: A Volume of Scholarly Essays* (Cambridge: CUP 2019), 414-32; Thomas C. Kohler, 'Christianity and the Principle of Subsidiarity', in Domingo and Witte *Christianity and Global Law* 2020 (n. 14), 303-20.

[52] See Pius XI, Encyclical Letter *Quadragesimo Anno*, 15 May 1931, § 80; John Paul II, Encyclical Letter *Centesimus Annus*, 1 May 1991 (Vatican City: Libreria Editrice Vaticana 1991), § 48; Benedict XVI (Joseph Ratzinger), Encyclical Letter *Caritas in Veritate*, 29 June 2009 (Vatican City: Libreria Editrice Vaticana 2009), §§ 57-58; For an overview, see Kohler, 'Christianity and the Principle of Subsidiarity' 2020 (n. 51).

[53] See Francis, Encyclical Letter *Fratelli Tutti*, 3 October 2020 (Vatican City: Libreria Vaticana 2020), § 187.

[54] See Consolidated version (2016) of the Treaty on European Union (TEU), 13 December 2007, EU OJ C 326, 26/10/2012 P.0007-0390.

9. The Global Law Community of the Image-of-God Bearers

At the heart of sacred natural law lies the idea that all human beings form a united natural community of image-of-God bearers, which grants metalegal legitimacy to the global human community and its specific law—the global law.

The global human community is first and foremost a community of human persons, not a society or federation of sovereign states.[55] Of course, the only way for persons to work together in a global context would be through different global institutions, supranational entities, nation-States, transnational corporations, NGOs, and other nonstate actors that integrate the global human community.[56] But working through these global actors does not remove the person as a global citizen from the spotlight. The centrality of the person, and as a result humanity as such, is the key that opens the door to a new constitutionalism beyond the State, and the sacred natural law supports this movement from a spiritual dimension.

The global human community is universal because it includes each and every human being without exception. And it is unique. This is why the global human community cannot be structured as a unique sovereign world State or a mere federation of sovereign States. To exist, a sovereign State requires the existence of at least one other state susceptible to being excluded from its territorial jurisdiction. There is no sovereign State without other sovereign States.[57] The concept of the State, like that of sibling or friend, requires otherness: for any of these to exist, there must be at least two of its kind. One is not enough.

The most important consequence of universality is that the global human community is a nonvoluntary community, but a necessary one.[58] As such, the global human community requires no consent for membership, and indeed consent is not possible: no human being could ever leave this community and join another one, as no human being can give up the condition of being an image-of-God bearer. This compulsory membership has to be balanced by a high degree of citizen participation in the decision-making process, and by reducing the goal of global law to a minimum: the protection of those specific human goods that necessarily have to be satisfied and protected globally (global public goods), such as global peace and security, global health, and conservation of the planet.

[55] The argument is developed in Rafael Domingo, 'The New Global Human Community' *Chicago Journal of International Law* 12 (2012), 567-87; Rafael Domingo, 'Global Law and the New Global Human Community' *Revista Brasileira di Direito* 13 (2017), 27-39; Rafael Domingo, 'Derecho global y comunidad humana global', in Jorge Fabra Zamora (ed.), *Las transformaciones del derecho en la globalización* (México, DF: Universidad Autónoma de México 2020), 45-58.

[56] For more on these new actors, see Anne Peters et al., 'Non-State Actors as Standard Setters: Framing the Issue in an Interdisciplinary Fashion', in Anne Peters et al. (eds.), *Non-State Actors as Standard Setters* (Cambridge: CUP 2009), 1-32 in the editors' introduction.

[57] This argument was firmly defended by Hermann Heller, *Die Souveranität. Ein Beitrag zur Theorie des Staats- und Völkerrechts* (Berlin: Walter DeGruyter 1927), 20-23.

[58] For the legal consequences of compulsory membership in communities, see Tony Honoré, 'Nécessité Oblige', in Tony Honoré, *Making Law Bind* (Oxford: Clarendon Press 1987), 120-21.

10. The Inherent Connection between International Law and Love

If God is love[59] and, again, the human being is made in God's image, then human beings were created to love and be loved. As a transformative power that leads human beings to communion with God and others, love is the fulfilment of any law,[60] including international law. Love of God and love of neighbour are interwoven, even inseparable, because ultimately love is divine. It comes from God, unites us to God, and makes us one, overcoming all divisions. Because love is divine, it is free.[61]

As an expression of love that is compatible with justice, international law accepts the idea of forgiveness (e.g. condonation or remission of sovereign debt). Forgiveness re-establishes the order as a whole by acquitting offenders and thereby placing them in a spiritually higher dimension of justice. Hannah Arendt refers to forgiveness as 'the necessary corrective for the inevitable damages resulting from action'.[62] Forgiveness establishes 'redemption from the predicament of irreversibility'[63] and 'serves to undo the deeds of the past, whose "sins" hang like Damocles' sword over every new generation'.[64] For this reason, as Martha Minow points out, 'there is value in considering how and when law can usefully make space for forgiveness'.[65]

The true development of international law should be understood in the light of love and forgiveness. Justice is not the opposite of love. There is no real tension or conflict between true justice and true love. Moreover, love presupposes justice. There is no love without justice, nor is it possible to achieve the plenitude of justice without love. 'Love that perpetrates injustice is malformed love', affirms Nicholas Wolterstorff.[66] Law provides the necessary platform for justice to flourish, and justice provides the unique platform for love to flourish. On the other hand, love ennobles justice and strengthens legal systems.

Justice is indeed 'the first virtue of social institutions, as truth is of systems of thought',[67] but only if it is referred to as a loving justice. Love will always be necessary in order not to reduce the human person into a 'legal person' or even a 'legal object'. Whoever tries to eliminate love and forgiveness is trying to eliminate the image of God in humanity. The rule of law demands a rule of love. For this reason,

[59] First Letter of John 4:16.

[60] Romans 13:9-10.

[61] On love, see the still interesting and fresh work byClive S. Lewis, *The Four Loves* (Fort Washington, PA: Harvest Book Company 1971).

[62] Hannah Arendt, *The Human Condition* (2nd edn, Chicago, IL: University of Chicago Press 1971), 238.

[63] *ibid*, 236.

[64] *ibid*, 237.

[65] Martha Minow, 'Forgiveness, Law, and Justice' *California Law Review* 103 (2015), 1615-45, at 1645.

[66] Nicholas Wolterstorff, *Justice in Love* (Grand Rapids, MI: William B. Eerdmans 2015), xvii.

[67] Rawls, *A Theory of Justice* 1999 (n. 45), 3. On page 586, he refers to 'the primacy of justice'.

any international legal system that ignores love is preparing to remove the true law and to diminish the protection of the dignity of persons in their integrity.

11. Conclusion

Sacred natural law theories are strongly oriented to the individual because every person has been created in the image of God. Consequently, sacred natural law theories support the priority of the person in the international legal realm. Insofar as sacred natural law theories are not mandatory but optional, respect individual moral conscience, and acknowledge the obligatory force of positive law, they are valid for developing a universal (not compulsory) international metalegal framework that illuminates positive law.

More than a century ago, the German jurist Otto Gierke (1841-1921) rejected as mistaken all the attempts to reduce natural law to a bodily existence – that is, to a sort of 'simulacrum'. But he insisted that the 'undying spirit' of natural law will never be extinguished: 'If it is denied entry into the body of positive law', he concluded, 'it flutters about the room like a ghost, and threatens to turn into a vampire which sucks the blood from the body of Law'.[68]

The development of a *transcendent global law* should use the best contributions and arguments of the sacred natural law traditions and overcome some futile discussions about the *nature* of natural law. Transcendent global law might lead the transformation of a very often self-interest-oriented international community of nation-States into a value-oriented global human community of image-of-God bearers. In this process, not only the jurists but also the philosophers and, especially, the theologians condemned to silence have something to say. Using Gentili's language, Latin, this paper comes to an end by inviting the theologians to stop their long silence and open their mouths wide again to illuminate the secular law from outside: *Adaperite, theologi, ora vestra, et scientia vestra afferte iuri lucem!*

[68] Otto Gierke, *Natural Law and the Theory of Society*, vol. 1 (first published 1883, this edn: Ernest Barker (tr.), 2nd edn, Cambridge: CUP 1934), 226.

10
The Individual in Secular Natural Law Theories of International Law

*Tom Sparks**

1. Introduction: Humanisation and Natural Law

I take as my starting point for this discussion the proposition that international law is reorienting to centre the individual. That contention—described as the 'humanisation' of international law[1]—has in my view been convincingly demonstrated and must be accepted.[2] In myriad ways, international law and its different subfields make provision for individuals.

As theorists of law, our task is to consider humanisation from a legal philosophical standpoint. If we treat humanisation as a legal fact, the onus of showing that those developments can be reconciled with any given theoretical paradigm falls on its adherents. To the extent that we accept the premise of humanisation, if it is argued that humanisation is not consistent with a positivist (or economic, critical, or realist) account of the law, it is the paradigm, and not the development, which should be thrown into doubt. To do otherwise essentialises intellectual constructs and commits what Pierre Bourdieu calls 'the most serious epistemological mistake in the social sciences, namely, that which consists of putting "a scholar inside the machine"'.[3] In Andrea Bianchi's terms, becoming 'unduly constrained by the

* The author thanks Anne Peters, Mark Somos, Gleider Hernández, Josh Jowitt, Angelo Jr Golia, Richard Sparks, Felix Herbert, and the participants in the project workshop for their feedback and many discussions which have been vital in shaping this chapter. The remaining errors, infelicities, and failures of logic—doubtless, numerous—are my responsibility alone.

[1] See Peters and Sparks, 'Introduction' (chapter 1), in this volume; Golia, 'Global Law and the Individual' (chapter 14), in this volume.

[2] This task has been achieved by Anne Peters, *Beyond Human Rights: The Legal Status of the Individual in International Law* (Jonathan Huston (tr.), Cambridge: CUP 2016). *Beyond Human Rights* is an updated and translated version of *Jenseits der Menschenrechte: die Rechtsstellung des Individuums im Völkerrecht* (Tübingen: Mohr Siebeck 2014). See further Ruti Teitel, *Humanity's Law* (Oxford: OUP 2011); Kate Parlett, *The Individual in the International Legal System: Continuity and Change in International Law* (Cambridge: CUP 2011) ; Astrid Kjeldgaard-Pedersen, *The International Legal Personality of the Individual* (Oxford: OUP 2018).

[3] Pierre Bourdieu, 'The Scholastic Point of View' *Cultural Anthropology* 5 (1990), 380-91, at 384. (first published 1989, this edn: Loïc Wacquant (tr.)).

Tom Sparks, *The Individual in Secular Natural Law Theories of International Law* In: *The Individual in International Law*. Edited by: Tom Sparks and Anne Peters, Oxford University Press. © Tom Sparks 2024.
DOI: 10.1093/oso/9780198898917.003.0010

pressure of having always to conform with self-imposed, rigid intellectual paradigms'. Doing so commits 'the fallacy of taking the things of logic for the logic of things'.[4]

With Bourdieu's warning in mind, I undertake two tasks here in relation to secular natural law; that is, those natural law theories which build on premises other than divine truth.[5] I consider first whether humanisation is consistent with a secular natural law framework; and secondly what the fact of humanisation implies for the credibility of secular natural law as the paradigm by which to explain the international legal system. In section 2, I address the key question posed in this volume: to assess the degree of coherence between my theoretical paradigm and humanisation. In the case of natural law, however, some adjustment is needed: few would question whether humanisation and natural law are compatible. Rather, section 2.1 digs a little deeper, and asks the twin questions of whether the phenomenon of humanisation *needs* to rely on a natural law framework, and whether accepting a natural law framework would *necessarily* result in a humanised natural law. To the former, I provisionally answer in the affirmative. To the latter, I answer that the connection is well established under all or most existing secular natural law theories, but it cannot be said that all natural law theories, whatever their basis, would *necessarily* lead to the same human-centrism. The discussion raises a connected issue, however, which is addressed in section 3: if detached from divine truth, how can secular natural law respond to the sceptical challenge that any principle selected as the basis of a natural legal system must inevitably be arbitrary? Section 4 offers one possible answer, from within the sceptical paradigm itself: it discusses the socially constructed morality of Émile Durkheim to argue that his framework would describe the humanised legal order of modernity. Section 5 concludes.

2. Humanisation and (Natural) International Law

Natural law is the dirty little secret of humanisation scholarship. Though a few scholars in the tradition—including myself—happily accept a role for natural law, by many others it is accepted only reluctantly,[6] or the question of theoretical basis is quietly avoided.[7] In the theory-agnosticism of many humanisation scholars, a desire to avoid engaging with the connection between humanisation and natural

[4] Andrea Bianchi, 'The Unbearable Lightness of International Law' *London Review of International Law* 6 (2018), 335-59, at 358.

[5] Rafael Domingo refers to such theories as 'rational' natural law approaches: see Domingo, 'Sacred Natural Law' (chapter 9), in this volume.

[6] Peters, *Beyond Human Rights* 2016 (n. 2), 25.

[7] See, e.g., Kjeldgaard-Pedersen, *International Legal Personality* (n. 2), and discussion in the text accompanying notes 14-19, below.

law is visible. As Anne Peters comments, although a 'neo-natural law paradigm is best suited for justifying an "original" international personality of the individual [...] such a paradigm hardly satisfies today's scientific standards of intersubjective comprehensibility'.[8] She later concludes that nevertheless, 'the independence of the individual's legal personality from the State requires recourse to a basic principle that precedes the State',[9] conceivable as 'a kind of positivized natural law'.[10]

Other scholars—with greater or lesser enthusiasm—also refer to natural law as the basis of a humanised international law. Antônio Augusto Cançado Trindade refers to the 'historical process of humanization of International Law' as one in which international law is 'always attentive to fundamental values, comes to occupy itself more directly with the realization of superior common goals'. He comments that '[f]urthermore, the international (active) subjectivity of the individuals fulfils a true necessity of their *legitimatio ad causam*, to vindicate their rights, emanated directly from International Law'.[11] Similarly, Antonio Cassese, commenting on the second Additional Protocol to the Geneva Conventions of 1949, noted a tendency to have recourse to natural law where positive law runs out: the drafters, he says, 'turned to natural law, or to a new form of natural law, as is the case every time positive law is inadequate'.[12] Ruti Teitel, while acknowledging that 'the effects of post-Enlightenment thinking made abundantly clear the limits of natural law', argues nevertheless that what she terms 'the law of humanity rises to this moment of legal and political transformation, as it presents a value system that mediates natural and positive law'.[13]

At the other end of the spectrum are those scholars of humanisation who avoid engaging with natural law. Kate Parlett typifies such an approach when she defines her focus as one of the actualities of the international order, and not on its foundations. She calls hers a '"rules-based" approach', which 'finds resonance in positivism because it is focussed on discerning the existence of legal rules on the basis of the sources of international law. In this sense, a rules-based approach also distinguishes between the law as it is (*lege lata*) and normative arguments as to what the law should be (*lege ferenda*)'.[14] She continues that '[a]s such, it is not necessary to take a position on theoretical approaches to international law', but concedes that the rules-based approach 'remain[s] open to the possibility that there may be rules which emanate from sources other than the traditional source of state-based

[8] Peters, *Beyond Human Rights* 2016 (n. 2), 25.

[9] *ibid*, 428.

[10] *ibid*, 430.

[11] Antônio Augusto Cançado Trindade, 'International Law for Humankind: Towards a New Jus Genitum' *Recueil des Cours* 316 (2005), 9-439, at 282 (emphasis omitted). See further 57-58, 147-48, 177-202, and 265-73.

[12] Antonio Cassese, *The Human Dimension of International Law: Selected Papers* (Oxford: OUP 2008), 124.

[13] Teitel, *Humanity's Law* 2011 (n. 2), 33.

[14] Parlett, *Individual in the International Legal System* 2011 (n. 2), 8. (References omitted).

consent'.[15] Astrid Kjeldgaard-Pedersen is more careful still in steering her study away from the theoretical underpinnings of international law, noting that according to her Kelsenian 'a posteriori' approach, '[w]hether individuals have rights and obligations under international law is […] entirely an empirical question'. As such, her 'purpose is not to promote a particular normative agenda'.[16] Though Kjeldgaard-Pedersen notes the criticism of Kelsen by—for example—Lauterpacht that the lacuna of the *Grundnorm* could be filled by natural law,[17] she prefers to follow Kelsen in leaving the *Grundnorm* unfilled.[18] As I have argued elsewhere, in so doing Kjeldgaard-Pedersen reduces the range of her account: though she can assess whether individuals *can* be(come) legal persons under international law (in contrast to her primary target: the 'states only' conception of international personality, which denies this possibility), the determined reliance only on empirical factors leaves unaddressed the question of whether or not individuals *inherently are* its (original) persons, relegating States to the rank of secondary, constructed persons.[19]

So far, so cautious. Few of the names most associated with the humanisation thesis—with the exception primarily of Cançado Trindade—openly embrace natural law. Critics of humanisation have been quick to detect the whiff of naturalistic thinking, however. Tara Melish, in a critique of *Beyond Human Rights*, comments that Peters' framing 'presupposes a view of law as independent from and superior to politics and power, a view not easily squared with everyday realities'.[20] Emma Dunlop, too, is quick to condemn Peters' project as activist, declaring that '[d]espite her assertion Peters is not […] engaged in a neutral exercise of "diagnosis". She is invested in this process of "humanization", if the process is indeed occurring.'[21] Klaus Gärditz, commenting on the *Bridge of Varvarin* judgment of the German *Bundesverfassungsgericht*, commended the Court for 'wisely withst[anding] the temptation to adopt modern *theoretical* concepts of individualization of international law to reinterpret the existing *positive* body of international humanitarian law'.[22] In my view, the critics are—partially—correct. I do not concur with the negative connotation they ascribe to natural law but, certainly, I see humanisation and natural law as natural bedfellows.

[15] *ibid*, 8.

[16] Kjeldgaard-Pedersen, *International Legal Personality* 2018 (n. 2), 6.

[17] *ibid*, see, e.g., 31.

[18] *ibid*, 43-46.

[19] Tom Sparks, 'Astrid Kjeldgaard-Pedersen: The International Legal Personality of the Individual' *German Yearbook of International Law* 61 (2018), 594-97.

[20] Tara J. Melish, 'Review of Anne Peters, Beyond Human Rights' *American Journal of International Law* 113 (2019), 654-64, at 657.

[21] Emma Dunlop, 'Reply to Anne Peters' *European Journal of International Law* 20 (2009), 556-60, at 556.

[22] Klaus Ferdinand Gärditz, 'Bridge of Varvarin' *American Journal of International Law* 108 (2014), 86-95, at 91 (emphasis in original).

2.1 Natural Law and Humanisation

Before proceeding, it is necessary to define secular natural law.[23] Natural law theories share the primary characteristic that they regard the positive law as only part of the universe of legal norms. In addition to law made through processes such as legislation, there exist norms which are hierarchically superior to positive law and the process of its creation, and which thus cannot be altered by means analogous to (for example) amending a statute. Most theories conceive of this superior level of norms as *morality*. All positive norms must comply with the natural law, although that does not mean that the natural law determines every aspect of the legal system. All variants of the tradition of which I am aware accept that there are certain matters which may and should be regulated solely by the positive law – it is necessary for the functioning of society that there be regulations concerning on which side of the road to drive, for example, but unlikely that natural law dictates the choice between the left and the right. Nevertheless, every rule of positive law must conform with the demands of the natural law. Thus, even within traffic law natural law may prescribe certain outcomes—natural law would likely demand that the use of vehicles to cause deliberate harm is regulated, for example—but in other cases the legislature will be able to choose between multiple natural law-compliant outcomes.

Different theories of natural law conceive of the natural morality to which the natural law refers as thicker or thinner, and as standing in different relation to the subjects of the positive law (legal persons). For some natural lawyers, natural law is directly applicable to the subjects of law, and can directly create rights and obligations. This, broadly, can be understood as the position adopted in the establishment of the Nuremberg trials: it is generally agreed that when these proceedings were established, no recognised offence of genocide (for example) existed in international law, in German criminal law, or in the criminal law of the allied powers.[24] The acts tried at Nuremberg, however, were of such a morally repugnant character that morality reaches through the positive law and gives rise to a directly applicable *legal* offence, which can be treated by *legal* means; that is, in this instance, a criminal trial resulting in sentence or acquittal.[25]

[23] Compare the parallel but separate sacred tradition of natural law, discussed in Domingo, 'Secular Natural Law' (chapter 9), in this volume.

[24] Though for an important nuance, see Ziv Bohrer, 'International Criminal Law's Millennium of Forgotten History' *Law and History Review* 34 (2016), 393-485.

[25] Note, however, that there have been arguments to the effect that the Nuremberg offences can be treated as a matter of positive law. For a discussion, though ultimately concluding that arguments in favour of a positivist heritage fail fully to convince (because, in his view, the trials were a near-direct application of principles of justice), see Quincy Wright, 'Legal Positivism and the Nuremberg Judgment' *American Journal of International Law* 42 (1948), 405-14, at 407-08; and further Neal Koch, 'Classical Legal Positivism at Nuremberg Considered' *Case Western Journal of International Law* 9 (1977), 161-66. For an alternative view, see Ziv Bohrer, 'Nuremberg and Grotius's Scholarship as Non-Grotian Moments: On Novelty-Bolstering in International Law' *Grotiana* 44 (2023), 30-64.

Other natural law theories, by contrast, do not emphasise natural law as directly applicable to law's subjects, focusing instead on accordance with the natural law as a criterion of validity for positive rules of law. A classic statement of this position is Gustav Radbruch's:

> Der Konflikt zwischen der Gerechtigkeit und der Rechtssicherheit dürfte dahin zu lösen sein, daß das positive, durch Satzung und Macht gesicherte Recht auch dann den Vorrang hat, wenn es inhaltlich ungerecht und unzweckmäßig ist, es sei denn, daß der Widerspruch des positiven Gesetzes zur Gerechtigkeit ein so unerträgliches Maß erreicht, daß das Gesetz als »unrichtiges Recht« der Gerechtigkeit zu weichen hat. […] Denn man kann Recht, auch positives Recht, gar nicht anders definieren denn als eine Ordnung und Satzung, die ihrem Sinn nach bestimmt ist, der Gerechtigkeit zu dienen.[26]

Here Radbruch sets a high threshold: a positive law may survive if it is unjust to a degree, but once the conflict between any given rule of the positive law and natural law reaches a tipping point, the positive law will give way to the natural. Other theorists have a lower tolerance for conflict between the natural and positive laws, but these are differences of degree rather than kind.[27]

A third variant of natural law theory may be mentioned, which differs in the nature of its 'morality'. Lon Fuller influentially and controversially argued in favour of a minimal and procedural 'morality' with which, in his account, law-making must comply in order to produce law properly-so-called. Law, said Fuller, is the activity of 'subjecting human conduct to the governance of rules',[28] and it must, he therefore argued, be connected with the human—and human conduct—sufficiently to enable that enterprise to be successful.[29] From these foundations he derived eight 'routes to failure' in law-making, for example by failure to make generalisable rules, legislating retroactively, or creating contradictory demands.[30] Failure to comply

[26] Gustav Radbruch, 'Gesetzliches Unrecht und übergesetzliches Recht' *Süddeutsche Juristen-Zeitung* 1 (1946), 105-108, at 107. 'The conflict between justice and legal certainty may well be resolved in this way: the positive law, secured by legislation and power, takes precedence even when its content is unjust and fails to benefit the people, unless the conflict between statute and justice reaches such an intolerable degree that the statute, as 'flawed law', must yield to justice. […] For law, including positive law, cannot be otherwise defined than as a system and an institution whose very meaning is to serve justice.' Translation by Bonnie Litschewiski Paulson and Stanley Paulson, from Gustav Radbruch, 'Statutory Lawlessness and Supra-Statutory Law (1946)' *Oxford Journal of Legal Studies* 26 (2006), 1-11, at 7.

[27] See, e.g., Joshua Jowitt's comment that a rule of law which fails to comply with the Principle of Generic Consistency (which Jowitt adopts from Alan Gewirth) would 'definitionally fail to be law': Joshua Jowitt, 'Legal Rights for Animals: Aspiration or Logical Necessity' *Journal of Human Rights and the Environment* 11 (2020), 173-98, at 187-88. For the Principle of Generic Consistency, see Alan Gewirth, 'The Basis and Content of Human Rights' *Georgia Law Review* 13 (1978-79), 1143-70.

[28] Lon Fuller, *The Morality of Law* (New Haven, CT: Yale University Press 1969), see, e.g., 106 and *passim*.

[29] *ibid*.

[30] *ibid*, 39-41.

with these standards, Fuller said, would result in rules which cannot be called law, while the inverse—meeting the 'eight kinds of legal excellence' (generality, clarity, non-contradiction, and so on)—means compliance with the 'inner morality of law'.[31] His 'Morality of Law' thus derived has been criticised by, for example, H. L. A. Hart and Joseph Raz on the grounds that his account is too thin to be called 'moral': we might as well, quips Hart, speak of a 'morality' of poisoners or, to take Raz's example, of a 'moral' sharpness of knives.[32] Nevertheless, both (if reluctantly) seemed to accept the applicability of Fuller's criteria, although rebranding them as an aspect not of law's 'morality' but of the rule of law.[33]

Fuller's account is valuable, and I return to it later in this discussion.[34] For present purposes, however, I agree with Raz and Hart that whatever the virtues of Fuller's 'morality' of law (and there are many), it is primarily to a more substantive set of standards that the term 'natural law' should be taken to apply.

Before turning to the question of what those 'substantive' standards should be taken to comprise, it is useful to pose two further abstract questions to further explore the connection between natural law and humanisation. I noted my belief in the introduction to section 2 that natural law and humanisation are complementary, but how deeply are the two connected? Would acceptance that international law is humanising mean that we *must* accept a natural law understanding of the system – in other words, does humanisation *need* natural law? On the other side, if one accepts that international law *is* a natural law-based system, would that *necessarily* imply that it is also humanised (or humanising)? The next sections take those questions in turn.

2.1.1 Does Humanisation Need Natural Law?

A conclusion that humanisation *needs* natural law would imply that no other framework can explain the changes in the international legal system which can together be called its humanisation. It would imply that all lawyers who ascribe to the humanisation thesis *necessarily must accept* that the international legal system is based on natural law. As such, it is the task of this book, and not only this chapter, to consider to what extent a range of frameworks are consistent with or could explain those developments. Nevertheless, some preliminary observations may be offered. For that purpose, this chapter focuses on the age-old discussion between *ius naturalism* and *ius positivism*.

[31] *ibid.*

[32] H. L. A Hart, 'The Morality of Law. By Lon L. Fuller' *Harvard Law Review* 78 (1965), 1281-96, at 1286; Joseph Raz, 'The Rule of Law and Its Virtue', in Joseph Raz, *The Authority of Law: Essays on Law and Morality* (Oxford: Clarendon Press 1979), 210-29, at 225.

[33] See, e.g., Raz, 'Rule of Law' 1979 (n. 32), 223-26; H. L. A. Hart, 'Positivism and the Separation of Law and Morals' *Harvard Law Review* 71 (1958), 593-629, at 623-24. See also the discussion in Jeremy Waldron, 'Positivism and Legality: Hart's Equivocal Response to Fuller' *New York University Law Review* 83 (2008), 1135-69.

[34] See section 4.1, below.

As discussed in section 2.1, different humanisation scholars have different reasons for embracing or rejecting natural law. For Parlett and Kjeldgaard-Pedersen, the normative foundations of humanisation can be left aside, with the phenomenon being assessed purely on an empirical level. For Teitel, natural and positive law in combination give rise to humanisation, though she offers little discussion of that relationship. The same lack of detailed discussion applies to the work of Cançado Trindade and Cassese, although here reaching a different conclusion: both authors seem to regard it as straightforward that humanisation relies on a natural law framework.

The most extensive and sophisticated discussion of this point is to be found in Anne Peters' *Beyond Human Rights*. Peters turns—apparently with trepidation—to natural law, largely as a result of her focus on individual legal personality.[35] It is here that Peters finds the distinction between 'mere' rights of individuals as objects within a State-centred international legal system, and individuals as co- (or even prior?) legal *subjects* alongside States. She is faced, though, with the ever-present positivist critique of humanisation: that the developments associated with humanisation are mere rules of the moment within a legal order the rule-makers of which are States. As such, the critique runs, such developments are revocable and ephemeral. As Peters comments, it 'would be a serious deficit of the international personality of the individual if the individual's legal status necessarily had to be granted by the State'.[36] Humanisation can only indicate a lasting change in the international legal system—as opposed to a temporary development which could be withdrawn at any time—if the international legal personality of the individual is in some sense insulated against deliberate change by States.[37] Having first examined treaty law, customary law, and general principles as potential sources for such a protected norm of individual personality—and finding each wanting[38]—Peters concludes that '[u]ltimately, the independence of the individual's international legal personality from the State requires recourse to a basic principle that precedes the State'.[39] She continues: as 'long as positive international law is not generated by "direct" democratic procedures without mediation by the States, and as long as natural law is not an option, then international law is subject to ultimate control by the States'.[40]

Peters' analysis here is, in my view, correct. It is, perhaps, possible to conceive of a humanised international legal system based solely on positive law. Such a system could display all the markers identified by humanisation scholars, save one: in such a system, the individual's status is in no way entrenched, and it could be revoked by States as easily as it was granted. Such a system is humanised only superficially: in

[35] Peters, *Beyond Human Rights* 2016 (n. 2), 408-35.
[36] *ibid*, 408-09.
[37] *ibid*, 409-11.
[38] *ibid*, 413-27.
[39] *ibid*, 428.
[40] *ibid*, 434.

its fundaments, it remains State-centric. To the extent, then, that the label of humanisation is intended to convey a development at a deeper level, something more is needed.

Based on the foregoing, it is possible to return to the question of whether humanisation needs natural law. It is possible to construct a humanisation argument based purely on the positive law, but such a humanisation is inevitably superficial and revocable: it amounts to little more than a claim that States have *chosen* to place more emphasis on the welfare of individuals and communities, and may make a different choice in the future. If humanisation scholars wish to advance a deeper argument, one with normative force, they must appeal to a principle beyond the positive law. In my view, humanisation scholars with the ambition to describe a deep change to the international legal system must accept and defend a natural law basis for the international legal system.

2.1.2 Does Natural Law Need Humanisation?

The inverse question can also be posed: is humanisation the inevitable consequence of understanding international law as a natural law-based system? Or: are all natural law scholars inevitably also humanisation scholars?

The sheer variety of natural law approaches makes such a question difficult to answer, and ideal and empirical approaches yield different results. If taken in historical perspective, however, we must conclude that there is no necessary connection between a natural law framework and values which align with the contemporary humanisation discourse. Sacred natural law, especially, has a deeply chequered history of exclusionary discourses, in which the conformity (or otherwise) of communities with religious values and the demands of scripture law condition their status and value under international legal norms.[41]

In the abstract, secular natural law approaches should perform better by this metric: after all, the focus on rationality rather than scripture should firmly embed individuals within communities as the centre of the (international) legal system. Different thinkers have selected different starting points, all of which are understood (by their proponents) to be universal: Patrick Capps, for example, follows a long tradition both sacred and secular in adopting human dignity;[42] while Joshua Jowitt (building a neo-natural law on a Gewirthian foundation) selects agency as his starting point.[43] Such frameworks have, however, come under attack from two sides. First, it has been widely noted that the 'universal' individual which features

[41] See, influentially, Antony Anghie, *Imperialism, Sovereignty and the Making of International Law* (Cambridge: CUP 2004), 17-28, 52-65, and *passim*.

[42] Patrick Capps, *Human Dignity and the Foundation of International Law* (Oxford: Hart 2010).

[43] Jowitt, 'Legal Rights for Animals' 2020 (n. 27); and further Joshua Jowitt, *Agency, Morality and Law* (Oxford: Hart 2023). Jowitt uses a framework based on the work of Alan Gewirth who, however, himself demurred from adopting a natural law conclusion. See, e.g., Alan Gewirth, 'The Ontological Basis of Natural Law: A Critique and an Alternative' *American Journal of Jurisprudence* 29 (1984), 95-121.

in the thought experiments underpinning secular natural law theories tends to align with the characteristics of a white, male, and heterosexual ideal liberal subject.[44] Secondly, by focusing on capacities such as agency or qualities like dignity, it is possible to *reduce* the centrality of humanity to law: as some have pointed out, these are qualities which in some measure are possessed by a wider class of potential 'persons' than human individuals only.[45] Indeed, some scholars in this school explicitly embrace such a broader community of legal persons: Joshua Jowitt uses a natural law framework compellingly to argue that the 'individuals' which the law encompasses must include nonhuman animals.[46]

Agency, dignity, and cognate concepts—such as Amartya Sen's and Martha Nussbaum's well-being,[47] or the idea of 'nested practical identities' on which Christine Korsgaard constructs a neo-Kantian framework,[48] for example—are common starting points for a secular natural law enquiry. Certainly, such concepts are well placed to anchor 'the individual' at the centre point of the legal system. By basing (secular natural) law on features of the internal mental life of individuals (as with agency), their interests (as with well-being), or their ability to live what they consider to be a good life (as with dignity), the law must necessarily accord individuals personality and condition its demands according to those starting points. While we can accept that many—though I would argue, not all—of these secular natural law theories as they have been developed and deployed in historical perspective have had the effect of centring law on a hegemonic and unrealistic view of

[44] This argument has been made most influentially, perhaps, by Catherine MacKinnon, 'Are Women Human?', in Catherine MacKinnon (ed.), *Are Women Human?: And Other International Dialogues* (Cambridge, MA: Belknap Press of Harvard University Press 2006), 41-43; and in international law by Hilary Charlesworth, Christine Chinkin, and Shelley Wright, 'Feminist Approaches to International Law' *American Journal of International Law* 85 (1991), 613-45, at 617, 632, and 637-38. See also, for different perspectives, Raimon Panikkar, 'Is the Notion of Human Rights a Western Concept?' *Diogenes* 30 (1982), 75-102, at 86; Ratna Kapur, 'Human Rights in the 21st Century: Take a Walk on the Dark Side' *Sydney Law Review* 28 (2006), 665-87, at 673-75; Abdallāh Aḥmad an-Naʿīm, 'The Cultural Mediation of Human Rights: The Al-Arqam Case in Malaysia', in Joanne R Bauer and Daniel A Bell (eds), *The East Asian Challenge for Human Rights* (Cambridge: CUP 1999), 147-68; and discussion in Janne Mende, 'Are Human Rights Western—And Why Does It Matter? A Perspective from International Political Theory' *Journal of International Political Theory* 17 (2021), 38-57, at 44-51. For analysis from a feminist perspective, see Houghton, 'Feminist Approaches' (chapter 12), in this volume.

[45] See, e.g., the discussion of debates around the concept on dignity by Kant, Schopenhauer and contemporaries in Paul Cliteur and René van Wissen, 'Human Dignity as the Foundation for Human Rights: A Discussion of Kant's and Schopenhauer's Work with Respect to the Philosophical Reflections on Human Rights' *Rechtstheorie* 35 (2004), 157-74, at 164-66, and *passim*.

[46] Jowitt, 'Legal Rights for Animals' 2020 (n. 27); Joshua Jowitt, 'Monkey See, Monkey Sue? Gewirth's Principle of Generic Consistency and Rights for Non-Human Agents' *Trinity College Law Review* 19 (2016), 71-96. For a fuller treatment, see Jowitt, *Agency, Morality, and Law* 2023 (n. 43).

[47] Amartya Sen, 'Elements of a Theory of Human Rights' *Philosophy & Public Affairs* 32 (2004), 315-56; Amartya Sen, 'Human Rights and Capabilities' *Journal of Human Development* 6 (2005), 151-66; Martha C. Nussbaum and Amartya Sen (eds), *The Quality of Life* (Oxford: Clarendon Press 2009).

[48] Christine M Korsgaard, *The Sources of Normativity* (Onora O'Neill (ed.), Cambridge: CUP 1996); Christine M. Korsgaard, *The Constitution of Agency: Essays on Practical Reason and Moral Psychology* (Oxford: OUP 2008).

what it means to be an 'individual',[49] and thus have left much to be desired in their application, they remain in ideal terms individual-centric theories of law.

These—and similar—individual-centric theories of natural law have dominated secular natural law frameworks throughout history. More recently, though, a form of secular natural law has been developed that centres not on humans, but rather on the earth system. As Judith Koons explains, 'at the heart of [Earth Jurisprudence] lies the premise of a necessary shift in thinking from a purely human-centred to an Earth-centred system of law and governance'.[50] As Peter Burdon develops the framework, Earth Jurisprudence can be understood as a series of three concentric rings. At the outer level sits what Burdon calls 'the Great Law', a scientifically informed supreme layer of normativity, based on the needs, cycles, and patterns of the earth system.[51] Importantly, the requirement to align human behaviour with the 'Great Law' is not equivalent to the doctrine of sustainable development, or cognate concepts: preserving the health of the earth system is not for the good of humans, but rather for the good of the earth system in itself.[52] Nested within the 'Great Law' sits human law comprising, in turn, natural law (the second of the three rings), and the innermost, smallest ring: the positive law.

Earth Jurisprudence neither renders human interests irrelevant, nor denies human agency in translating the demands of the 'Great Law' into specific provisions within legal systems. It does, however, decentre humanity and individuality, embracing instead the networks of interactions which make up eco and earth systems. Although such law remains human law, in the sense that it is humans who access and interpret it, it would be conceivable (if things were to reach such a pass) that the demands of the 'Great Law' may conflict with the needs or interests of particular human groups, or even with those of the species as a whole. Humans make up only a small part of the earth system, and their interests must thus be weighted accordingly.[53]

I return, with this in mind, to the question posed at the beginning of this section: does a natural law framework (necessarily) imply a humanised legal system? In empirical terms, the vast majority of (secular) natural law frameworks developed

[49] I would argue, in particular, that the Gewirthian framework, as developed by Jowitt, is sufficiently all-encompassing to escape this critique, as is (in my view) Korsgaard's 'nested practical identities' concept, while Sen and Nussbaum's capabilities framework was expressly developed as a corrective to inadequate mainstream conceptions of human rights.

[50] Judith E Koons, 'What Is Earth Jurisprudence: Key Principles to Transform Law for the Health of the Planet' *Penn State Environmental Law Review* 18 (2009), 47-70, at 48 (references omitted).

[51] Peter D Burdon, 'A Theory of Earth Jurisprudence' *Australian Journal of Legal Philosophy* 37 (2012), 28-60, at 38-46.

[52] *ibid*, at 44.

[53] This point is not made in explicit terms in the Earth Jurisprudence scholarship (to my knowledge), but seems to me to be an inevitable conclusion of the argument. It may, perhaps, be implied by Koons' discussion of Thomas Berry's concept of 'communion', in which '[l]ife on Earth may be seen as a circle [...] [e]ven the predator and prey relationship bespeaks of a circle of intimacy. Beings on earth serve as food for others': Koons, 'What Is Earth Jurisprudence' 2009 (n. 50), 61-62 (references omitted).

and discussed throughout history *would* demand a human-centred international legal system, in which the rights, needs, and interests of individuals would be prioritised. It is clear, too, however, that the term 'individual' would require further clarification in this regard, and that 'individual'-centred and 'human'-centred systems may not enjoy the easy equivalence which is often assumed (including in Anne Peter's and my introduction to this volume).[54] Is such an alignment, though, *necessary*? Beyond the empirical approach, I can only conclude that in ideal terms there is no *necessary* reason that secular natural law approaches must centre humanity. Earth Jurisprudence, while a minority approach, is nevertheless a clear indication that a secular natural law theory need not begin from any characteristic (such as dignity, agency, or well-being) that is inherent to humanity, but may instead emphasise the *natural*.

The question may be more easily answered, however, if we restrict the scope to the specific problem of *international* law; that is to say, the choice between the State and another entity (modally: the human individual) as the 'authentic' person of the international legal system.[55] Put another way, is international law a dualist system in which legal communities (States) *in and between themselves* create a legal order in which they thus are the system's 'persons'; or does the international legal system—like the legal orders within it—ultimately depend on and refer to the authentic personhood of an 'original' person (such as the human individual)? Two answers are possible, but both lead to the same conclusion: that a secular natural international legal system is not a State-centric order. First, there is no (secular) natural law theory of which I am aware that would privilege the State-form in and of itself: even in extreme accounts of the formation of the State, such as Hobbes', the State is an aggregation of the rights of individuals—who are the 'authentic' holders of natural rights—and exists for their protection.[56] In my view, it is only through a view of the State as exercising a divine right (sacred natural law) or as being an expression of pure compulsion (as, for example, in Austinian positivism) can the State be considered as a thing in itself,[57] independent from the individuals which comprise it. Secondly, even if such a theory were proposed, it is hard to envisage a theory which would privilege the good of States in themselves rather than the values the State exists to serve, be they human, or encompassing a wider (ecological) concept of individuality.

The key is contingency. Natural law seeks something constant in which to anchor its supra-legal normative claims. The form of the State, however, is anything

[54] Peters and Sparks, 'Introduction' (chapter 1), in this volume.

[55] This term is adapted from Rafael Domingo, *The New Global Law* (Cambridge: CUP 2010), 124-26; and the discussion in Peters, *Beyond Human Rights* 2016 (n. 2), 24-25.

[56] Thomas Hobbes, *Leviathan: Or the Matter, Forme and Power of a Common Wealth Ecclesiasticall and Civil* (Andrew Crooke 1651), §§ XV, XVI-XVII.

[57] Note that I seek, here, a normative account of the State *as such*, and so exclude accounts which describe the dominance of the State-form without endorsing it, such as that provided by historical materialism.

but constant. It is now beyond question that the myth of the modern State as having emerged following the peace of Westphalia owes much more to the desire of nineteenth- and twentieth-century positivists to be able to claim a deep genealogy for their anti-naturalist legal theory than to true similarities between the entities which emerged from the Thirty Years War and the contemporary State.[58] Indeed, and given rapid developments in human rights law, environmental law, international institutional law, regional economic integration, global communications technologies, and the balance of power between States and multinational corporations, it would be quite possible to argue that the contemporary State is only partly comparable to those entities which emerged from another brutal conflict in 1945. Even leaving aside these more recent variations, however, and presuming for a moment that we accept that the State has not materially changed since 1648, we would need to confront the fact that the post-Westphalian State represents only a fragment of a vastly longer history of the social and political organisation of human societies. As such, it has generally been to steadier values—predominantly the human or the natural—which scholars seeking constancy have referred.

3. 'Nonsense Upon Stilts'

And yet it has been observed that even these steadier values cannot be regarded as immutable. Jeremy Bentham's highly rhetorical denunciation of the temerity of the 1789 French revolutionaries in proclaiming their 'droits naturels, inaliénables et sacrés de l'homme'[59] that '[n]atural rights is simple nonsense: natural and imprescriptible rights, rhetorical nonsense—nonsense upon stilts'[60] has at its heart this scepticism. This 'terrorist language',[61] as Bentham has it, cannot be accepted as an imprinter of immutable truth, rather:

> What is the real source of these imprescriptible rights—these unrepealable laws? Power turned blind by looking from its own height: self-conceit and tyranny

[58] See Stéphane Beaulac, 'The Westphalian Legal Orthodoxy - Myth or Reality' *Journal of the History of International Law/Revue d'histoire du droit international* 2 (2000), 148-77; Andreas Osiander, 'Sovereignty, International Relations, and the Westphalian Myth' *International Organization* 55 (2001), 251-87; Quentin Skinner, 'A Genealogy of the Modern State' *Proceedings of the British Academy* 162 (2009), 325-70; Partel Piirimäe, 'The Westphalian Myth and the Idea of External Sovereignty', in Hent Kalmo and Quentin Skinner (eds.), *Sovereignty in Fragments: The Past, Present and Future of a Contested Concept* (Cambridge: CUP 2010), 64-80.

[59] *Déclearacion des Droits de l'Homme et du Citoyen de 1789*, Conseil Constitutionnel, available at <https://www.conseil-constitutionnel.fr/le-bloc-de-constitutionnalite/declaration-des-droits-de-l-homme-et-du-citoyen-de-1789>, accessed 24/11/2023. '... natural, unalienable and sacred rights of man' (official translation).

[60] Jeremy Bentham, 'Anarchical Fallacies; Being an Examination of the Declarations of Rights Issued during the French Revolution', in John Bowring (ed.), *The Works of Jeremy Bentham, Published under the Superintendence of his Executor*, vol. II (Edinburgh: William Tait 1843), 489-534, at 501.

[61] *ibid.*

> exalted into insanity. No man was to have any other man for a servant, yet all men were forever to be their slaves. Making laws with imposture in their mouths, under pretence of declaring them—giving for laws anything that came uppermost, and these unrepealable ones, on pretence of finding them ready made. Made by what? Not by a God—they allow of none; but of their goddess, Nature.[62]

Bentham taps into then-active philosophical discussions around academic scepticism and the impossibility—as that school teaches—of knowing *anything* with certainty,[63] and condemns the revolutionaries for setting their judgement above that of others: 'In us is the perfection of virtue and wisdom: in all mankind besides the extremity of wickedness and folly. Our will shall consequently reign without controul [*sic.*], and for ever: reign now we are living—reign after we are dead.'[64]

In contemporary theory, a similar point has been advanced by Kyle Murray, building on foundations laid by the linguistic relativist, Richard Rorty. Rorty (in) famously denies the possibility of objective truth on the basis that our only tool for the investigation of what is true is language. But while, he says, we can verify the truth of propositions within the parameters of a particular linguistic frame of reference—their *coherence*—we can reveal nothing deeper about them: 'There is no ground-floor level of truth where we have direct confrontation between reality and thought or language unmediated by justifying assertions. Rather, truth is by coherence. There once was played a coherent language-game in which it was legal to say there are devils, and in that language-game we now play in English it is true to say there are brown desks. But science may some day replace this language-game by another.'[65] In other words, the statement 'there are brown desks' can be either true or false within the meaning of those words in the English language as it is presently used, but it can tell us nothing more fundamental about the nature of 'desks' or the qualities of 'brown'. 'And with that', says Murray, applying the observation to law, 'the realist project is doomed'.[66] For if we cannot even verify the existence of 'brown desks', still less can we discern or uncover any 'moral truths':

> One cannot be sure that what one is 'detecting' or 'seeing' is anything more than the meaning we give to 'the world' or the so-called 'moral aspects' within it. The process of paying careful attention to the world, the moral facts, reality etc, cannot be shown to amount to anything more than paying attention to our own preferred

[62] *ibid.*

[63] Mark Somos, 'Reason and Scepticism', in Richard Whatmore and Brian Young (eds.), *A Companion to Intellectual History* (Chichester: John Wiley & Sons 2016), 417-37, and *passim*, esp. 431-34.

[64] Bentham, 'Anarchical Fallacies' 1843 (n. 60), 501.

[65] Richard Rorty, 'Science and Metaphysics: Variations on Kantian Themes, by Wilfred Sellars' *Philosophy* 45 (1970), 66-70, at 68.

[66] Kyle L. Murray, 'Philosophy and Constitutional Theory: The Cautionary Tale of Jeremy Waldron and the Philosopher's Stone' *Canadian Journal of Law & Jurisprudence* 32 (2019), 127-58, at 134.

descriptions. With ultimately nothing beyond the preferred descriptions of individuals and groups to be appealed to, all that remains are the competing claims and beliefs themselves, and those who make them.[67]

To the sceptic, those who claim that there are moral principles are either acting in bad faith or are deceiving themselves – clinging to 'metaphysical blankets', as Murray puts it with Benthamite sarcasm. 'Whatever', he says, 'helps you sleep at night'.[68]

This is an extreme example of a broader category of arguments from indeterminacy – arguments which challenge the possibility of natural principles (legal or moral) on the basis that it is impossible with certainty to define their content. These include the idea of moral relativism *simpliciter*, including in the tradition deriving from Hume,[69] as well as that of cultural relativism.[70] A common form of argument from indeterminacy is reported by Andrei Marmor: 'we may have, as we do, very different conceptions about what the moral-political conditions of legitimacy should be, and what would make various laws better or worse than others'.[71] A similar premise underlies Neil MacCormick's appeal to 'the sovereignty and freedom of the individual conscience' as justification for his 'moralistic case for an a-moralistic law'.[72] How can natural lawyers respond to arguments from indeterminacy of these and other kinds?

One approach is to seek to ground the values of objective morality more firmly. It is worth noting, in this regard, that arguments relating to law have a lower barrier to surpass than do arguments relating to pure philosophy: law is relational, and the solipsist's position is thus not sustainable. It is impossible meaningfully to posit the existence of law without presuming the existence of other minds.[73] An important natural law argument capable of building from this point is Joshua Jowitt's reinterpretation of Alan Gewirth's theory of agential rights.[74] Gewirth sought to construct

[67] *ibid.*

[68] *ibid*, 135.

[69] David Hume, *A Treatise of Human Nature* (first published 1739, this edn: L. A. Selby-Bigge (ed.), Oxford: Clarendon Press, 1896), Book III, pt. I, § I, at 456-58.

[70] The term 'cultural relativism' was first used by Mieville Herskovits, building on work by Franz Boas: see Melville J Herskovits, *Man and His Works: The Science of Cultural Anthropology* (New York, NY: Alfred A Knopf 1948), 61-78, esp. 63-64 and Franz Boas, *Race, Language and Culture* (New York, NY: MacMillan 1940), 636. Within international law, a particularly important aspect of this idea is captured by the concept of human rights colonialism, described influentially by Makau Mutua, 'Savages, Victims, and Saviors: The Metaphor of Human Rights' *Harvard International Law Journal* 42 (2001), 201-46 and *passim*, esp. at 204-07 and 236-37.

[71] Andrei Marmor, 'Legal Positivism: Still Descriptive and Morally Neutral' *Oxford Journal of Legal Studies* 26 (2006), 683-704, at 704.

[72] Neil MacCormick, 'A Moralistic Case for A-Moralistic Law' *Valpariso University Law Review* 20 (1985), 1-42, at 17.

[73] I am grateful to Mark Somos for this point.

[74] Jowitt, *Agency, Morality, and Law* 2023 (n. 43); and further Alan Gewirth, *Reason and Morality* (Chicago, IL: University of Chicago Press 1978); Gewirth, 'The Basis and Content of Human Rights'

a generalisable argument in favour of individual rights from two premises: first, that we accept the existence of other agents; and secondly, that we regard our own agency as a necessary and sufficient criterion for our own *claim* to bear rights associated with our agency (note: no stronger than a *claim*). If we *claim* rights for ourselves based on our agency, we must *grant* the same rights to any other being which shows signs of being an agent, in order to avoid self-contradiction.[75] Jowitt comments that 'by grounding his test for the moral permissibility of action in the unavoidable fact of our individual agency', Gewirth 'identifies a critical morality; one that is [. . .] not the contingent collective morality that a given society may extrapolate from its own subjective cultural requirements'.[76] As such, for a Gewirthian, one of the primary arguments in favour of his framework is that it obviates the objection from cultural relativism.[77]

I find the Gewirthian framework compelling. Nevertheless, it could be objected that by founding all morality on agency, the quintessential concept of western liberalism, Gewirthian frameworks escape cultural relativism only by elevating western values to the status of premises.[78] What if we want to take cultural relativist arguments more seriously? The next section explores a middle path, grounded in the sociological theory of Émile Durkheim, which while rejecting relativism, nevertheless does not need to claim the discovery of a timeless, universal truth. It may be that such an approach can offer a firm foundation for a natural international legal personality of the individual.

4. A Law for Human Society – Constructing a New Natural Law

Presuming that we grant the relativist conclusion—that there are no absolutes; or that, if there are, they are inaccessible because of the contingency inherent in the means by which we reason conceptually—are there nevertheless grounds to believe that legal systems can coherently and legitimately base themselves on natural law? I will answer that question affirmatively; and will further argue that even if we begin our enquiry from a moral relativist starting point there are good reasons to believe that legal systems *necessarily must* incorporate natural law.

1978-79 (n. 27); Gewirth, 'The Ontological Basis of Natural Law: A Critique and an Alternative' 1984 (n. 43).

[75] Jowitt, *Agency, Morality, and Law* 2023 (n. 43), 16-19.

[76] *ibid*, 15 (references omitted).

[77] See, e.g., Jowitt's response to cultural relativism arguments: *ibid*, 21-22.

[78] For the avoidance of doubt, my own view is that Jowitt successfully defends Gewirthian theory against such charges: *ibid*, 21-22. I nevertheless see the counterfactual as valuable.

4.1 Society and Morality

I referred in section 2.1 to Lon Fuller's process-based 'morality' of law, in which Fuller contends that key virtues in law-making (certainty, non-contradiction, non-retroactivity, and so on) must be implied into the criteria of legality because law, to be law properly-so-called, must be capable of governing human conduct.[79] Despite vehement objections to other parts of his thesis, legal positivists and natural lawyers alike have seemingly, albeit in some cases grudgingly,[80] accepted Fuller's basic proposition: that law is a social activity and serves a specific function.[81] Jowitt refers to this shared, functional understanding of law as the 'agreed referent', the basic, common proposition which allows positivists and natural lawyers to enter into dialogue.[82] That there is agreement thus far means, in turn, that the present enquiry can treat the following minimal, but vital, statement as uncontroversial: when we speak of law, it is always to the law *of a society* that we refer. Its purpose is, ultimately, always to guide conduct within that society; that is to say, the conduct of *persons*.

The connection between law and society was a preoccupation of Émile Durkheim. Durkheimian theory may appear, at first sight, an odd place to start a search for universal moral principles for use by natural law. As Gabriel Abend notes, 'Durkheim is a genuine normative relativist'.[83] Durkheim accepted the concept of moral truth—and in particular, accepted that morality could in important ways be understood as *objective*—but tied moral truth to the society to which it applies. Moral principles, he argued, 'develop in history and in the realm of historic causes […] it changes as conditions change'.[84] He takes the example of ancient Rome and its practices, such as the ubiquitous acceptance of slavery, which to the modern eye are morally unacceptable: 'If the ancient Romans had not the broad conception of humanity we possess today, it is not because of any defect attributable to their limited intelligence, but because such ideas were incompatible with the nature of the Roman state. […] It is because changes have occurred in the social structure that have necessitated this change in morals.'[85] He summed up the

[79] Fuller, *Morality of Law* 1969 (n. 28), see, e.g., 106 and *passim*.

[80] For a brief discussion of H. L. A. Hart's and Joseph Raz's responses, see the text accompanying notes 27-34, above.

[81] Note that even those who object, as Brian Tamanaha does, generally do so on the basis that such an observation is not specific enough to serve as a *sole* definition of law, and not on the basis that they dispute the accuracy of the proposition itself: see Brian Z Tamanaha, *A Realistic Theory of Law* (Cambridge: CUP 2017), 43-54.

[82] Jowitt, *Agency, Morality, and Law* 2023 (n. 43), 77-78; drawing on Deryck Beyleveld and Roger Brownsword, *Law as Moral Judgment* (Agincourt, Ontario: Carswell Legal Publications 1986), 120.

[83] Gabriel Abend, 'Two Main Problems in the Sociology of Morality' *Theory and Society* 37 (2008), 87-125, at 102.

[84] Émile Durkheim, *The Division of Labor in Society* (George Simpson (tr.), New York, NY: The Free Press 1964), 53.

[85] *ibid.*

position pithily: 'We know well that morality has varied. [... I]t is in the nature of things that morality should vary. The moral system of the Romans and Hebrews was not our own, nor could it have been so.'[86]

If Durkheim subscribed so strongly to moral relativism, what help can he offer to the current investigation? For all that he was a relativist, Abend notes that he was simultaneously an objectivist. For Durkheim, that morality is relative does not imply that it can be defined by the individuals living within a social structure. 'It is not', as Abend argues, 'that whatever each society decides or agrees to call virtue thereby becomes virtuous for them'.[87] Rather, Durkheim 'holds the very strong thesis that [social] science can determine the truth of moral judgments'.[88] These judgements of the truth or otherwise of moral propositions do not derive from the opinions of the people within a society, whether understood as a general mass of opinion or the views of society as a whole formalised as law. Rather, they are to do with the structure of the society itself.

By 'structure' Durkheim does not refer to hierarchy, nor to those things which lawyers might readily understand by that term—courts, parliaments, basic norms, constitutions, and so on. To those, he would have given the label 'institutions' and, certainly, institutions can be a part of a social structure. But 'structure' is also much deeper and more pervasive, encompassing culture, religion, shared practices, customs, class divisions, education, organisation of work, the stories we tell our children, and even language.[89] Structure is any social fact that may condition individual action or decision, that is external to the individual themselves; that is, is distinct from agency. When Durkheim says, therefore, that morality is determined by structure, he is not referring to something immutable and constant, but nor is it something which can be amended on terms remotely comparable to processes of legislative change. Rather, changes to structure are changes to society itself. It may be affected by individual and social decisions, movements, and developments, but only if they are sufficiently significant to affect deeply the way society organises itself. It is only these fundamental, structural changes that will change its morality.[90]

The morality of a given society encompasses a great number of principles, some of which will be more and some less deeply entrenched; some attached to more ephemeral, changeable aspects of the social structure, some to aspects that are deeper, and more embedded. Durkheim identifies one particularly deeply rooted

[86] Émile Durkheim, 'A Discussion on the Effectiveness of Moral Doctrines', in William S. F. Pickering (ed.), H. L. Sutcliffe (tr.), *Durkheim: Essays on morals and education* (London: Routledge 1979), 129-39, at 130-31.

[87] Abend, 'Two Main Problems' 2008 (n. 83), 102.

[88] *ibid.*

[89] Steven Lukes, *Émile Durkheim, His Life and Work: A Historical and Critical Study* (2nd edn, Stanford, CA: Stanford University Press 1985), 150-55.

[90] Roger Cotterrell, 'Justice, Dignity, Torture, Headscarves: Can Durkheim's Sociology Clarify Legal Values?' *Social & Legal Studies* 20 (2011), 3-20, at 5.

principle, which he sees as the basis of morality in all complex societies:[91] the individual.

4.2 Multiculturalism and the Individual

Durkheim was fascinated by the forces that hold societies together, and enable individuals and groups to co-exist within social settings despite their differences. Durkheim posited that in early human societies—and perhaps still in some isolated or indigenous cultures—what makes the leap from kinship to social group possible are shared beliefs and practices; shared rituals and prohibitions.[92] To these, he gives the label of 'religion', while noting that the 'religious' nature of a belief or practice need have nothing to do with gods. Rather, 'a religion is a unified system of belief and practices relative to sacred things, that is to say, things set apart and surrounded by prohibitions—beliefs and practices that unite its adherents in a single moral community'.[93] Moreover, he intimately connects that discussion with his concept of law: 'This religious formalism' he argues, is 'probably the first form of legal formalism.'[94]

In early human societies, according to Durkheim, a religion shared by all members of the community suffices to provide a basis for its shared social life. That observation holds good whether the 'religion' in question is understood according to the conventional usage of that term—that is to say, refers to the shared worship of a god or equivalent entity or entities—or according to Durkheim's wider conception of a shared belief or practice, potentially including a shared sense of morality or an agreed legal code.[95] The situation is more complex, though, in contemporary societies, which tend to be multicultural, multi-ethnic, and (in the conventional sense) multi-religious. What serves as the basis of togetherness—the civic religion—in cosmopolitan societies? Durkheim argues that in such societies:

[91] Cotterrell says: 'contemporary western societies', but I am not aware that Durkheim made such a stipulation, nor am I convinced that one is required. Durkheim emphasises that the more pluralistic or multicultural a society becomes, the more important the value of the individual becomes, and it may be that on this basis he would exclude tribal or other monocultural societies. However, certainly in the modern world, the description of plural societies (whether in terms of race, religion, culture, class, language, or other factors) would apply to all—or virtually all—States: compare Steven Lukes, 'Durkheim's "Individualism and the Intellectuals"' *Political Studies* 17 (1969), 14-30, at 26-28 and Roger Cotterrell, 'The Sociological Concept of Law' *Journal of Law and Society* 10 (1983), 241-56, at 250.

[92] Émile Durkheim, 'Religion and Ritual', in Anthony Giddens (ed.), *Émile Durkheim: Selected Writings* (Cambridge: CUP 1972), 219-38, at 224-28.

[93] Émile Durkheim, *The Elementary Forms of Religious Life* (Carol Cosman (tr.), Oxford: OUP 2001), 46.

[94] *ibid*, 35. For a discussion in the context of international law, see Immi Tallgren, 'The Durkheimian Spell of International Criminal Law?' *Revue interdisciplinaire d'études juridiques* 71 (2013), 137-69, at 165-66.

[95] For a discussion of ritual in the internal aspect of norms, see Reza Banakar, *Normativity in Legal Sociology: Methodological Reflections on Law and Regulation in Late Modernity* (Cham: Springer International Publishing 2015), 216.

> [T]he members of a single social group will no longer have anything in common other than their humanity, that is, the characteristics which constitute the human person in general. This idea of the human person, given different emphases in accordance with the diversity of national temperaments, is therefore the sole idea that survives, immutable and impersonal, above the changing tides of particular opinions[.][96]

This focus on individuality must be distinguished from the individualistic: it is not 'liberalism', 'the inevitable consequence' of which would be '[i]ntellectual and moral anarchy'.[97] Rather, 'individualism thus understood is the glorification not of the self, but of the individual in general. Its motive force is not egoism but sympathy for all that is human, a wider pity for sufferings, for all human miseries, a more ardent desire to combat and alleviate them, a greater thirst for justice.'[98] As Roger Cotterrell expands, '[i]t does not give the individual a kind of primacy over society, as liberal thought typically does. It is society (its need for solidarity in circumstances of modern complexity and diversity) that invests each individual (irrespective of personal conditions or character) with absolute moral value. Society does not exist only to fulfil the needs of the individual; rather, individualism is valuable because it corresponds with [. . .] society's requirements for solidarity and unity.'[99]

Durkheim regards this conclusion as true, but relative. It applies to 'a particular kind of' society,[100] and should the basic conditions of society vary from place to place or time to time, then so too will the principles of morality which underpin it. As Cotterrell puts it,

> To be true to Durkheim's kind of normative relativism, I think it is necessary also to recognise that aspects of moral individualism (and interpretations of the meaning of dignity and autonomy) are likely to change as societies change, and that this value system, essential though it is in Durkheim's picture of how modern society can and should exist, certainly does not exhaust the complex and sometimes conflicting moral requirements of diverse types of social relations of community.[101]

And yet, 'Durkheimian morality is *not* just what people think in a given time and place. [. . .] Durkheim claims that sociology can study social life objectively as

[96] Lukes, 'Durkheim's "Individualism"' 1969 (n. 91), 26.
[97] *ibid*, 24. See further Banakar, *Normativity in Legal Sociology* 2015 (n. 95), 225-26.
[98] Lukes, 'Durkheim's "Individualism"' 1969 (n. 91), at 24.
[99] Cotterrell, 'Justice, Dignity, Torture' 2011 (n. 90), 6-7.
[100] *ibid*, 7.
[101] Roger Cotterrell, 'Durkheim on Justice, Morals and Politics', in Roger Cotterrell (ed), *Émile Durkheim: Justice, Morality and Politics* (London: Routledge 2016), xi-xxiv, at xxi.

a matter of "social fact". In doing so, it can identify moral principles and practices compatible with (or even necessary to) stable social relations in particular kinds of societies.'[102] That nuance is particularly important in the present context, because it is *pluralism and diversity* that Durkheim identifies as requiring the entrenchment of the shared respect for humanity as the moral basis for social relations. The more diverse societies become, he argues, the greater the need for the unifying factor of common humanity. As such, and if we accept Durkheim's premises, his observation should only have gathered force since Durkheim's time, both for the societies which comprise the international community, and for that community itself.

4.3 The Individual and the International

Durkheim, writing in the late nineteenth century, did not expressly apply his sociology to international society. I argue that there are, however, good reasons to consider his work relevant to this context. For assistance in drawing the links, I turn to Anthony Giddens.

Modern, complex societies are, Giddens argues, characterised by disembedding mechanisms. These mechanisms 'remove social relations from the immediacies of context. [They] presume, yet also foster, the separation of time from space as the condition of the time-space distanciation which they promote'.[103] He gives the examples of money, as well as systems of recognition of expertise (such as professional qualifications or trade-body memberships). Both have the effect of removing the need for individual knowledge of—and trust in—particular individuals with whom we have dealings in social settings, but allowing us instead to rely on social structures. This expands the range over which social relations can be established beyond the circle of people with whom we have direct, personal relationships: 'Trust here is vested, not in individuals, but in abstract capacities.'[104]

Simultaneously, globalisation, facilitated by disembedding, gives rise to different levels of social interaction. Where all social interaction used to take place within defined and relatively stable communities of relatively static individuals, globalisation enables local and national levels of interaction, as well as 'the intensification of worldwide social relations which link distant localities in such a way that local happenings are shaped by events happening many miles away, and vice versa'.[105] Without needing to imply a nascent 'world state', '[t]hese processes mark an overall movement towards "one world"', albeit that it may remain a somewhat 'fractured' world.[106] The consequence of these shifts is that 'the nation-state has

[102] Cotterrell, 'Justice, Dignity, Torture' 2011 (n. 90), 5.
[103] Anthony Giddens, *The Consequences of Modernity* (Cambridge: Polity Press 1995), 42.
[104] *ibid*, 39.
[105] *ibid*, 77. See also Banakar, *Normativity in Legal Sociology* 2015 (n. 95), 27-29.
[106] Giddens, *Consequences of Modernity* 1995 (n. 103), 66.

become "too small for the big problems of life, and too big for the small problems of life." At the same time as social relations become laterally stretched and as part of the same process, we see the strengthening of pressures for local autonomy and regional cultural identity.'[107]

Although Giddens does not explicitly make the connection, the conditions he describes within world society (i.e. the international community and the natural and legal persons which comprise it) seem highly attuned to those which, Durkheim would have argued, require that society be premised on a shared morality of respect for humanity. The outward (disembedding, globalising) pressure of globalisation brings individuals, communities, and States into ever-closer contact with other communities which have different values, beliefs, and forms of social organisation; in parallel, that outward pressure creates a countermovement: an inward (localising) pressure towards the safe and familiar, which emphasises local cultural similarity even within existing social structures. Both pressures demand a common basis for inter- and intra-community communication, while making such a common basis difficult to find. Durkheimian thought holds that it is only humanity, the individual, which can provide that common factor: 'moral individualism becomes more important the more complex and differentiated societies become'.[108]

What though, concretely, are the demands of Durkheim's individual-centred morality in international society? What prohibitions and shared convictions, to return to Durkheim's conception of the shared basis of social life, are to be applied, and how should those be reflected in international law? To answer these questions would require a more extensive discussion than the current chapter allows, but a preliminary answer can be attempted.

Cotterrell has discussed how Durkheim's sociological morality informs the domestic legal systems of plural societies. The law would need to protect, he argues, '[i]deas of common humanity, in the form of human rights and human dignity'.[109] What is more, the interpretation of those broad headings can be further informed by Durkheim's theory. Cotterrell discusses the morality of punishing offenders, torture, and the morality (or otherwise) either of wearing or banning headscarves, and several broad principles emerge: physical integrity, personal autonomy, the equal worth of individuals, and the freedom of communication between all individuals within society.[110] These values map closely onto another concept with clear relevance for the international system: self-determination. I have elsewhere

[107] *ibid*, 79; citing Daniel Bell, 'The World and the United States in 2013' *Daedelus* 116 (1987), 1-31, at 13-14.

[108] Cotterrell, 'Justice, Dignity, Torture' 2011 (n. 90), 10; and further Martin Ramstedt, 'On the Relationship between Normative Pluralism and Justice after Multiculturalism', in Håkan Hydén et al. (eds.), *Combining the Legal and the Social in Sociology of Law: An Homage to Reza Banakar* (Oxford: Hart 2023), 83-92, at 86-88.

[109] Cotterrell, 'Justice, Dignity, Torture' 2011 (n. 90), 10.

[110] *ibid*, 11-17.

discussed the significance of the concept of self-determination for the international legal order,[111] and have argued that in particular what I name 'polity-based self-determination' is a keystone of the contemporary international legal system.[112] It is this principle, I argue, which underpins State sovereignty, in both its internal and external aspects: States are comprised of self-determining peoples which, by virtue of their self-constitution as a political community claim a right to make decisions concerning their shared socio-political life without external interference.[113] Gleider Hernández and I have argued that the principle is a norm of *ius cogens* status.[114]

A common moral commitment (in Durkheimian terms) to the value of the individual maps on to human rights, respect for human dignity, and self-determination within the international legal system. Those principles establish the legitimacy of the system of independent, sovereign States, and concurrently set the limits of that sovereignty. Something more, though, can also be derived from those principles: they cast serious doubt on the original, or sole, personality of the State in the international legal sphere. As self-determination makes clear, it is from their populations—their continuing polity-based self-determination—that States come into being, are maintained, and receive their legitimacy. Far from being the sole relevant persons, States receive a delegated personhood from the individuals and communities which comprise them.

It was remarked at the beginning of this section that modernity is characterised by a lateral stretching of networks of communication: individuals within one State are brought into immediate contact with individuals and social groups elsewhere. '[I]nterpersonal communication', the social fabric Durkheim seeks to protect is no longer only 'society-wide',[115] but occurs across 'one world'.[116] Under these, the conditions of modernity, the model of 'black box' statehood cannot be maintained, if ever it held water. While there are numerous cases in which it is convenient to treat State structures *as* persons,[117] we should dispense with the fiction that they *are*. State personhood is relegated to a subsidiary, contingent form, and we return to the 'natural person' as the natural person of law.

[111] Tom Sparks, 'Grotian Moments in the Law of Self-Determination: Law, Rhetoric, and Reality' *Grotiana* 43 (2022), 159-86, at 159-61 and 167-70; Tom Sparks, *Self-Determination in the International Legal System: Whose Claim, to What Right?* (Oxford: Hart 2023), chapter 1.

[112] Sparks, *Self-Determination* 2023 (n. 111), chapter 1.

[113] *ibid*, chapter 1, and further chapter 4.

[114] Gleider Hernández and Tom Sparks, 'Categorising Self-Determination: Four Forms' *German Yearbook of International Law* 63 (2020), 223-54, at 239-40.

[115] Cotterrell, 'Justice, Dignity, Torture' 2011 (n. 90), 10.

[116] Giddens, *Consequences of Modernity* 1995 (n. 103), 66.

[117] Stilz argues that '[s]ignificant moral values [...] are served by organizing our political world as a structure of self-governing units': Anna Stilz, *Territorial Sovereignty: A Philosophical Exploration* (Oxford: OUP 2019), 9-10.

5. Conclusion: A Human Law

Natural law insists that the law takes account of the human individual. According to natural lawyers, a law which fails to uphold basic needs, interests, and values not only fails to be 'good' law, but ceases to be 'law' at all. This chapter has sought to answer three connected questions. First, it investigated the connection between natural law and the thesis that international law is humanising. Section 2 posed interconnected questions of whether the humanisation thesis demands a natural framework, and whether a natural law framework would inevitably produce a humanised international law. I concluded that the most appropriate basis for a humanised international legal system would be a natural law foundation and, albeit with caveats, that it is likely that an international legal system premised on natural law would be a human-centred system: while it is not the case that all natural law theories centre the human individual, none was identified which would centre the State.

In turn, however, those discussions prompted a further question: if we seek to found the international legal system on something more certain—less contingent—than the will of States, how can it respond to the positivist challenge that by reaching beyond the positive law it invites contingency? Numerous answers could be posed to such a question, and it is by no means necessary to accept the sceptical premise. I referred, for instance, to Jowitt's re-examination of the Gewirthian framework as a potential, compelling basis for a non-contingent theory of natural law.[118]

I wanted to explore, however, whether it would be possible to accept the idea of contingency—for example, in the form of the cultural relativism thesis—and nevertheless to construct a meaningful argument for a natural law basis for the international legal system. I concluded that it is possible, provided that one begins from a starting point that is sceptical, rather than solipsistic. To do so, I focused on the sociological morality of Émile Durkheim, and argued that a Durkheimian basis for international law would demand respect for humanity, manifested as key limits on State power and action such as human dignity, human rights, and the principle of self-determination. Indeed, Durkheim would likely argue that such a shared moral concern for humanity is the only possible basis for a social order (the international system) that is characterised by such diversity, and would make that claim as an analytical—not normative—proposition. The trends of globalisation, pluralisation, and cross-cultural communication on which Durkheim premised that conclusion at the turn of the twentieth century have only accelerated in the years since his death.

I have sought to show in this chapter that there are powerful arguments for believing that (complex) legal systems must centre individuals, as a necessary aspect

[118] See the accompanying text to notes 74-77, above.

of morality. That conclusion is demanded by conventional natural law reasoning, where rational analysis leads us to the moral worth of the individual as a matter of logical principle. As I have sought to show, however, so too are we led to that end-point via another route, even if we accept the sceptical position that no recourse can be made to a timeless, immutable moral system. All roads lead to Rome? Perhaps so. Even a sceptic's international legal system must, it seems, acknowledge the central figure of the individual: the true telos of law and society.

11
The Status of the Individual in International Law
A TWAIL Perspective

Bhupinder S. Chimni

1. Introduction

The determination of the subjects of a legal system is a matter of critical import as it is internally related to its telos. Unsurprisingly, their identification raises important epistemological and ontological questions. The debate on the question of subjecthood in the international legal system involves, among other things, an assessment of the nature and character of the global order; the history, role, and condition of international law; pathways to the future; and relevant empirical and technical questions. In view of the complex nature of the issues involved, and the deep ideological and political divides in global society, it is not surprising that there is a diversity of views on whether the individual is a subject of international law. In the Cold War period, for instance, many western scholars contended that the individual is a subject of international law while Soviet scholars strongly contested this view. The two standpoints reflected opposing assessments of the nature and outcomes of the international capitalist system, one based on liberal theory and the other on Marxism Leninism, and flowing from them the role of international law in realising what were distinct visions of the future. The end of the Cold War in favour of western liberal democracies meant that the view that the individual is a subject of international law gained ground. Of course, this understanding also signalled the resolve to prevent events that preceded the Cold War that is, genocide and a world war that caused immense human suffering. Today, the liberal vision of the future, encapsulated in the hope of protecting the dignity of all individuals, is sought to be taken forward through humanising international law and transforming it into a human-centred law.

Earlier, the debate on subjecthood was between exponents of positivism and natural law with the latter inclined to treat individuals as subjects of international law. But in view of developments in different areas of international law over the last few decades, in particular international human rights law, even positivists, who rely on formal legal criteria to determine subjecthood, have come to conclude

Bhupinder S. Chimni, *The Status of the Individual in International Law* In: *The Individual in International Law*. Edited by: Tom Sparks and Anne Peters, Oxford University Press.
DOI: 10.1093/oso/9780198898917.003.0011

that the individual is at least a partial subject of international law. In the view of positivist scholars, the determination is supported by the existence of the rights and duties of individuals, and the ability to make claims, in a wide range of international legal instruments.[1] But a strand of mainstream international law scholarship (MILS), inclusive of variants of positivist, natural law, and liberal standpoints, goes further and embraces methodological individualism to argue that individuals are the real subjects of international law. This thesis is also supported by reference to diverse developments in the international order that include the erosion of sovereignty principle, rapid technological developments that call for urgent focus on individual rights, and a perceived relationship between human rights and peace.

Insofar as critical international law scholarship (CILS) is concerned it encompasses different responses to the issue of subjectivity. But, generally speaking, CILS contests the view that the individual is a subject of international law. Of these, third world approaches to international law (TWAIL), feminist approaches to international law (FtAIL), and Marxist approaches to international law (MAIL) combine legal-formal and particular historical sociological perspectives to arrive at distinct understandings of the status of the individual in international law. These approaches look beyond the individual to explore and bring to the fore the social categories of class, gender, race, and caste, and their past and present relationship to international law, to differentiate between formal and authentic subjects of international law.

The present chapter turns to TWAIL to review the status of the individual in contemporary international law and the possibility of the emergence of a human-centred law.[2] There is of course no singular or unique TWAIL approach to the question. This chapter relies on insights from postcolonial theory, Marxism, and socialist feminism to contend that the emergence of a human-centred international law, and the arrival of the individual as an authentic subject of international law, is constrained by deep structures of global capitalism, patriarchy, and racism. It argues that the debate on the question of subjecthood must move beyond positivism and natural law, or the imperatives of the Cold War, to the sociology of international order and make a distinction between formal and authentic subjects of international law. It suggests that in order to evaluate the status of the individual in international law, account must be taken of the operation of three logics at the international level, namely the 'logic of capital', the 'logic of territory', and the 'logic

[1] 'Individuals are now recognised as subjects of international law, though only with respect to certain areas of that discipline.' Mahmoud Cherif Bassiouni, *Introduction to International Criminal Law* (2nd rev. edn, Leiden: Martinus Nijhoff Publishers 2013), 60.

[2] The TWAIL view on the status of the individual in international law in the ancient and medieval periods in different civilisations has yet to be fully articulated. But there is literature on international humanitarian law and human rights law that bears on the status of the individual in pre-modern international law. In this regard, see the separate opinions of Judge Christopher Weeramantry in the *Gabčíkovo-Nagymaros* case and the *Nuclear Weapons* advisory opinion; Nagendra Singh, *India and International Law: Ancient and Medieval* (New Delhi: S. Chand and Co 1973).

of culture'. The 'logic of capital' shapes global social relations, the 'logic of territory' determines the ways in which global social relations come to impact internal social relations, and the 'logic of culture' determines in their matrix the extent to which structures of class oppression, patriarchy, and racism are embedded in internal and international society. It is the three logics in combination, assessed at national and global scales, that help answer the question whether an individual is an authentic (as against a formal) subject of international law. To put it differently, TWAIL offers *a social relations understanding* of the status of the individual in contemporary international law and, based on it, advances an *intersectional and integrated* view on the question of subjectivity.[3] In the final analysis, TWAIL is sceptical of the liberal claim of deep humanisation of international law.[4] TWAIL does not attribute fundamental significance to the distinction made between rights and humanisation scholarship, with the former focused on international human rights and humanitarian laws and the latter committed to the transformation of the very discipline of international law to advance the goal of human dignity.[5] In the TWAIL view, the humanisation of international law needs to be assessed *primarily* in relation to the role of imperialism in the international order.[6] This problem cannot be addressed without engaging with the 'logic of capital', as the universalising thrust of capitalism necessarily translates into imperialism. In short, the humanisation of the international legal system must mean the diminishing role of imperialism in international affairs. It must also mean the absence of use of coercion and force in the pursuit of that goal, other than to prevent genocide or gross violations of human rights. Finally, the humanisation of international law must involve reducing the

[3] The idea of an 'authentic subject' of international law is not to be conceived of in essentialist terms, that is, assigned a unique and universalist meaning. It is for each individual to reach an understanding of what 'authenticity' means for them. The social relations perspective calls for the removal of structural institutional barriers, whether in the form of capitalism, patriarchy, racism, or casteism, and accompanying cultures and ideologies, to create conditions that allow an individual to realise their potential in life while participating in community life. On the larger debate in philosophy, see the *Stanford Encyclopedia of Philosophy*, 'Authenticity', available at https://plato.stanford.edu/entries/authenticity/#RecAccAut, accessed 7/7/23. A social relations approach has been used by others to shed light in different domains of international law. See, e.g., Sara L. Seck, 'A Relational Analysis of Enterprise Obligations and Carbon Majors for Climate Justice' *Oñati Socio-Legal Series* 11 (2021), 254-84.

[4] For one sceptical view examining theoretical debates on the question of the inflation of human rights, see Tara J. Melish, 'Book Review: Anne Peters, *Beyond Human Rights: The Legal Status of the Individual in International Law* (Jonathan Huston (tr.), Cambridge: CUP 2016)' *American Journal of International Law* 113 (2019), 654-64.

[5] Humanisation scholars include Myres S. McDougal, Harold D. Lasswell, and Lung-chu Chen, 'Human Rights and World Public Order: A Framework for Policy-Oriented Inquiry' *The American Journal of International Law* 63 (1969), 237-69; Antônio Augusto Cançado Trinidade, *The Access of Individuals to International Justice* (Oxford: OUP 2011); Ruti Teitel, *Humanity's Law* (Oxford: OUP, 2011); Peters, *Beyond Human Rights* 2016 (n. 5).

[6] Generally speaking, the term 'imperialism' is used to describe a set of structures, processes, ideologies, and practices in the economic, legal, social, and political domains that produce and reproduce over time dependent and dominated groups, peoples, and nations. Imperialism is also the outcome of an asymmetrical power relationship between advanced capitalist nations and less developed nations.

exploitation and alienation of marginalised groups in international society. But these issues are at best inadequately addressed by humanisation scholarship.[7]

Be that as it may, the chapter does not seek to argue that the developments in different areas of international law that extend the growing rights and duties of individuals do not reflect progressive development of international law. Indeed, it would be churlish to deny that codifying the rights of individuals under international law matters; it is a move towards promoting global democracy in the same way as at the domestic level the institution of rights supports the sustenance of democratic States. But the matter of subjectivity cannot be reduced to a question of merely ascertaining the existence of a *legal* subject (as against a social or political subject and without distinguishing between the abstract and the concrete) or the existence of formal rights. One may however hasten to add that the posited distinction between formal and authentic subjects is not meant to deny the autonomy or significance of the legal sphere (i.e. its internal rules, logic, and dynamics) but to point to its limits in transforming the individual into a subject who can be assured human dignity. There is a parallel in the sphere of politics. Hannah Arendt, for instance, observed that the political sphere is 'the only realm where men can be truly free'.[8] But while the freedom to act and struggle in the political domain is of enormous value, it cannot translate into true freedom unless accompanied by enabling developments in other spheres of life. In other words, the division of the human subject into legal, social, or political subjects is a useful heuristic device but cannot be the basis on which final determinations can be made with respect to any of them. In the legal sphere there is a need to transcend the limits of a law-centred view of subjectivity to take cognisance of and integrate developments in non-legal spheres. However, which non-legal developments are seen as critical to produce an authentic subject of international law depends on a scholar's individual theoretical standpoint. Thus, in the debates on the subject, MILS, including humanisation scholarship, has neglected the relationship of the question of subjecthood to capitalism or colonialism or neocolonialism. It could therefore even be argued that the debate on the status of the individual is a move to sustain and legitimise an oppressive imperialist global order. To be sure, that is not the whole truth. Such a claim would neglect the utopian strain in international law. It would also disregard developments in international law or the efforts of some of the finest legal minds to address problems of our times, especially the role of international law in promoting human rights. But it is equally true that MILS has not addressed the question of the exploitation and oppression for centuries of large social groups and

[7] In the rest of the chapter the acronym MILS is used to cover both mainstream and humanisation scholarship.

[8] Hannah Arendt, *On Revolution* (New York, NY: Penguin Books 1963), 104.

nations. TWAIL seeks to capture its absence and/or ambivalence on the matter in the debates on the 'subjects' of international law.[9]

2. TWAIL View: A Social Relations Perspective

In arriving at an understanding of the emergence of the individual as an authentic subject of international law, at least two questions need to be asked. First, is the status of the individual to be determined by reference to rights listed in international legal instruments or should these be accompanied by the capacity to claim them? To put it differently, should *locus standi* be viewed as a pre-condition rather than as an outcome of subjectivity?[10] This question does not receive attention in this chapter, for whatever the response the relevant practices are too thin to sustain the conclusion that the individual is a genuine subject of international law. A second question that needs to be explored is whether the expansion of individual rights, both under general international law (GIL) and international human rights law (IHRL), has reformed national and global social orders to an extent that it can be concluded that the individual is an authentic subject of international law.[11] More specifically, have structures and processes of production, distribution, and consumption at national and global levels that have a direct bearing upon the life chances of individuals been sufficiently transformed through the intervention and operation of international law to allow an individual to live a life of dignity? In making an assessment, TWAIL does not disregard the significance of the expansion of the universe of individual rights under IHRL or GIL. It merely argues that substantial changes in the material structures of global governance are a precondition for the individual to emerge as a genuine subject of international law. A human-centred international law cannot emerge in an unequal and unjust global order. Such an order can only give rise to a dehumanised international law.

2.1 The Distance from MILS

In order to elaborate the distinctive standpoint of TWAIL it is necessary at first to touch on some strands of MILS which argue that the individual is the real subject of international law. According to Georges Scelle, as Hubert Thierry has observed, 'the individual is not only the immediate subject of the "law of people", but is the

[9] Likewise, while TWAIL greatly values the principle of sovereign equality of States, it recognises that the formal equality between States coexists with deep inequalities in power and resources.

[10] Gerasimos Fourlanos, 'Subjectivity in International Law and the Position of the Individual' *Nordisk Tidsskrift for International Ret* 53 (1984), 9-25, at 21.

[11] Peters, *Beyond Human Rights* 2016 (n. 5), 1 and 7.

only subject, because he alone is capable of willing and of being responsible."[12] Likewise, Hersch Lauterpacht views the individual as the final subject of international law. In his review of Lauterpacht's landmark book *International Law and Human Rights*, Myres McDougal noted the sociological reasons offered for treating the individual as the real subject of international law: 'the realization of the dangers besetting international peace as the result of the denial of fundamental human rights', 'a period of history in which the destructive potentialities of science and the power of the machinery of the State threaten the very existence of civilized life', and 'the interdependence of States which requires regulation is the interdependence of the individuals who compose them'.[13] But Lauterpacht did not want his normative preference to rest only on a natural law standpoint as it would come to be viewed as simply the expression of a hope.[14] He therefore 'tempered' his approach by conceding the importance of the practice of States.[15] He observed that whether an individual is a subject of international law 'is largely [a question] of ascertaining what is the intention of States—and, generally, the practice of States—in each particular case. The conferment of such rights may cover either particular rights or the so-called fundamental rights of the individual in general.'[16] The combination of elements drawn from sociology, natural law, positivism, and methodological individualism in Lauterpacht's work has informed much later mainstream scholarship.

In contemporary times, Judge Antônio Augusto Cançado Trinidade, a passionate defender of the idea of the individual being a subject of international law, also relies on these eclectic sources to contend that from the sixteenth century the goal was the humanisation of inter-State relations and treating individuals as the real subject of international law.[17] It received a setback with Hegelian legal philosophy in the nineteenth century with its emphasis on absolute State sovereignty that resulted in a 'harmful influence' on the project of promoting a human centred law.[18] But the twentieth century saw the individual as a subject of international law rescued with innumerable scholars arguing the case.[19] Judge Cançado Trinidade believes that 'the direct access of the human rights person to international justice [...] represents the essence of the international protection of human rights' and

[12] Hubert Thierry, 'The European Tradition in International Law: Georges Scelle' *European Journal of International Law* 1 (1990), 193-209, at 204.

[13] Myres S. McDougal, 'International Law and Human Rights' *Yale Law Journal* 60 (1951), 1051-56, at 1052. See also Charles G. Fenwick, 'Review of Lauterpacht, International Law and Human Rights' *American Political Science Review* 45 (1951), 229-30.

[14] Natasha Wheatley, 'Spectral Legal Personality in Interwar International Law: On New Ways of Not Being a State' *Law and History Review* 35 (2017), 753-88, at 756.

[15] Roland Portman, *Legal Personality in International Law* (Cambridge: CUP 2011), chapter 7, 126-72.

[16] Hersch Lauterpacht, 'The Subjects of the Law of Nations' *Law Quarterly Review* 64 (1948), 97-119, at 112; Puliyakot K. Menon, 'The Legal Personality of Individuals' *Sri Lanka Journal of International Law* 6 (1994), 127-56.

[17] Trinidade, *The Access of Individuals to International Justice* 2011 (n. 6), chapter 1, 1-17.

[18] *ibid*, 2.

[19] *ibid*, 6-13.

is becoming a reality today.[20] In his view, this development contributes to upholding 'the international rule of law, and also to the realization of justice at the international level'.[21] However, he recognises that there are serious problems to be overcome at the level of practice in making individual complaints mechanisms effective.[22]

Scholars who have been critical of both natural law and positivist views have taken a slightly different route in affirming that the individual is a subject of international law. Thus, for example, while McDougal agreed with Lauterpacht that the 'primary political goal of humanity' should be the 'further transformation of the law of nations from a law of States to a law of international society with the individual human being at the very center of its constitutional structure', he achieved this outcome through advancing a distinct concept of international law, defining it as a process of authoritative decision-making.[23] The resulting focus on participants in that process sidestepped the need for an empirical survey of positive law to determine whether the individual is a subject of international law. The individual as a participant became, alongside the State and other non-State actors such as corporations and international organisations, a subject of international law.[24] In the Cold War period, this view helped contrast the position of liberal democracies with that of the socialist bloc nations that rejected the role of individual in the international legal process.

In the TWAIL view none of these takes on the status of the individual speaks to the constraints imposed by deep structures (of universalising capitalism, patriarchy, and racism) on making the individual an authentic subject in international law. Above all, they fail to account for the phenomenon of imperialism, a principal feature of international relations since the seventeenth century, which has caused terrible and endurable harm to individuals living in weak nations in both colonial and postcolonial eras.[25] These views also neglect the fact that it was inter-imperialist competition that was at the root of the two world wars which saw horrific violation of international humanitarian laws. This explains why it was only in the inter-war period of the last century that the claim of the individual being

[20] *ibid*, xxvii.

[21] *ibid*, 16.

[22] See generally, Strengthening and Enhancing the Effective Functioning of the UN Human Rights Treaty Body System Individual Complaint Mechanisms, Recommendations from Members of Academia and Civil Society in View of the 2020 UN Human Rights Treaty Body Review, available at: https://hertieschool-f4e6.kxcdn.com/fileadmin/2_Research/1_About_our_research/2_Research_centres/Centre_for_Fundamental_Rights/Documents/Recommendation_report_February_2020.pdf, accessed 7/7/2023.

[23] *ibid*, 1056.

[24] Rosalyn Higgins, 'Conceptual Thinking about the Individual in International Law' *British Journal of International Studies* 4 (1978), 1-19.

[25] In this chapter the word 'imperialism' is used to denote a set of structures, processes, ideologies, and practices in the economic, legal, social, and political domains that produce and reproduce over time dependent and dominated groups, peoples, and nations. Imperialism is essentially the outcome of an asymmetrical power relationship between advanced capitalist nations and other nations.

a subject of international law first came to be strongly advanced by scholars (e.g. Georges Scelle, Nicholas Politis, Hans Kelsen, and Frederick Dunn) and tribunals (the *Danzig Railway Officials* case).[26] As Natasha Wheatley puts it, 'it was only the cataclysmic ruptures wrought by the First World War that turned personality into a pressing preoccupation for international law and order'.[27] The complex new situations (e.g. the mandate system and minority treaties) that emerged from the war, many without precedence, also encouraged the belief that 'international law could fashion its own persons'.[28] It only needs to be added that many of the subjects of the new imaginary were not happy with how personality was being made; the colonies protested and European nations such as Poland and Czechoslovakia did not want their sovereignty compromised in the name of minorities.[29]

It is unsurprising that a second iteration on individuals being subjects of international law came in the aftermath of World War II, which made the horrors of World War I pale in comparison. It led to the adoption of the Universal Declaration of Human Rights (UDHR) and the pronouncement by the Nuremberg Tribunal on the responsibility of individuals for committing war crimes and crimes against humanity. It famously observed that 'crimes against international law are committed by men, not by abstract entities, and only by punishing individuals who commit such crimes can the provisions of international law be enforced'.[30] In mentioning these developments MILS rarely refers to the fact that when the UDHR was adopted and Nuremberg Tribunal made its pronouncement, entire peoples and nations were being exploited, oppressed, and denied the status of subjects of international law. Meanwhile, in the *Reparations* case the International Court of Justice (ICJ) further opened up the discourse on subjects. While it noted that a subject must be 'capable of possessing international rights and duties' and should have the 'capacity to maintain its rights by bringing international claims',[31] it created space for subjects other than international organisations by observing that 'the subjects of law in any legal system are not necessarily identical in their nature or in the extent of their rights, and their nature depends upon the needs of the community'.[32] As a result of these developments, and the onset of the Cold War, the support for the individual as a subject of international law grew, now accompanied by

[26] PCIJ, *Pecuniary Claims of Danzig Railway Officials Who Have Passed into the Polish Service, Against the Polish Railways Administration (Advisory Opinion)*, 1928, PCIJ Series B No. 15. See Kate Parlett, 'The PCIJ's Opinion in Jurisdiction of the Courts of Danzig. Individual Rights under Treaties' *Journal of the History of International Law* 10 (2008), 119-46; Catherine Brölmann and Janne Nijman, *Legal Personality as a Fundamental Concept of International Law* (Amsterdam: Law School Legal Studies Research Paper No. 2016-43).

[27] Wheatley, 'Spectral Legal Personality' 2017 (n. 15), 759.

[28] *ibid*, 763.

[29] *ibid*, 776.

[30] The Nuremberg Trial, 6 FRD 69, 110 (Int'l Military Tribunal 1946).

[31] ICJ, *Reparation for Injuries Suffered in the Service of the United Nations*, Advisory Opinion, (1949) ICJ Reports 174, at 179.

[32] *ibid*, 178.

the phenomenon of neocolonialism. The global scenario has not changed since. In sum, the production of subjectivity in international law is the work of developments that are intimately associated with the phenomenon of imperialism. It would be difficult to understand the evolution of the status of the individual as a subject in international law outside the constellation of factors that spawned inter-imperialist competition and the competition between capitalism and socialism. The focus on individuals became an ideological device in MILS to displace a critique of deep structures of capitalism and imperialism.

The relevant ideological and material factors continue to be differently evaluated along with the weight of legal developments. Therefore, even today, 'opinions are strongly divided over both the status and the legal position of the individual in international law, as well as what constitutes the background and frontiers of this legal position'.[33] It may be useful to recapitulate the reasons for the divided house in current debates. First, as Anne Peters points out, 'international law has no general codified norm governing the definition and attribution of international legal personality', neither in 'relevant treaties nor generally accepted principles of customary international law'.[34] In the event, the notion of international legal personality is, 'merely a "void," fillable *and emptyable* at will by states [...] it can be "entirely empty or without function if no specific rights are granted" '.[35] Second, the atomistic understanding of individuals that underlies MILS's discourse on subjects of international law has been persuasively contested by communitarian and critical thinkers who point to the significance of social relations in giving substance to rights. Third, there is the continuing neglect of the history of imperialism, of which colonialism was one phase, and the accompanying exploitation and oppression of nations of the Global South in the postcolonial era making it difficult to take seriously the view that a human centred law had emerged. In order to flesh out the TWAIL perspective the latter two grounds of contestation deserve further comment.

2.2 The Social Relations Perspective: Abstract and Concrete

In addressing the question of whether an individual is a subject of international law MILS overlooks the fact that the individual is inevitably embedded in a web of social relations. This reality is recognised even by IHRL, as many rights can only be exercised in association and community with others.[36] But in its cogitation on the

[33] Alexander Orakhelashveli, 'The Position of the Individual in International Law' *California Western International Law Journal* 31 (2000), 241-76, at 241.

[34] Peters, *Beyond Human Rights* 2016 (n. 5), 35.

[35] Melish, Review of Peters, *Beyond Human Rights* 2019 (n. 5), 658 (emphasis in original); quoting Peters, *Beyond Human Rights* 2016 (n. 5), 59.

[36] Robert McCorquodale, 'Self-Determination: A Human Rights Approach' *International and Comparative Law Quarterly* 43 (1994), 857-85.

question of subjecthood MILS abstracts from real world contexts in which individuals live and die and relies instead on an asocial individual.[37]

Karl Marx was among the first to advance a communitarian critique of the liberal understanding of society as constituting an aggregate of individuals.[38] In his well-known *Theses on Feuerbach* he pointed out that 'the human essence is no abstraction inherent in each single individual' but in reality 'is the ensemble of the social relations'.[39] Or, as the communitarian scholar Michael Walzer has, in our times, put it, 'the deep structure even of liberal society is communitarian […] that we are in fact persons and that we are in fact bound together'.[40] Clearly the choices individuals exercise using a spectrum of rights is framed within an existing 'pattern of social relations'.[41] There is thus no pre-social or unencumbered self that can be declared a subject of law.[42] Of course, amidst prevailing social relations it is recognised that 'the best life is still the one where the individual chooses what is worth doing, achieving, or being, though it may be that this choice has to be made within a certain framework which is itself unchosen'.[43] Marx went much further and pointed out that 'genuine community and full individual development will become possible only when we regain control of our economic and social relations and organize society in such a way as to allow for our all-round activity as universal beings'.[44] In doing so he was emphasising, among other things, the significance of productive activities in determining an individual's status in society.

The fact is that the relationship of the individual with society is inescapable in any effort to understand the real (or non-formal) status of the individual in international law. The social relations in any society, both material and cultural relations, can be captured and assessed in many ways by deploying, among other things, the categories of class, gender, and race. A first attempt at using such a category in inter-State relations came during the October Revolution. The former Soviet Union used the vocabulary of class to approach the question of subjects of international law. In view of the fact that all existing societies were divided along class lines, 'Soviet legal scholars […] rejected, unanimously, the notion of the individual as subject

[37] On a social relations perspective to rights and law, see generally Jennifer Nedelsky, *Law's Relations: A Relational Theory of Self, Autonomy, and Law* (Oxford: OUP 2011). As Nedelsky notes, social relationships are not seen as constitutive of the individual self (at 3).

[38] Michael Walzer, 'The Communitarian Critique of Liberalism' *Political Theory* 18 (1990), 6-23, at 8.

[39] Karl Marx, 'Theses on Feuerbach' (1845), appended to Friedrich Engels, 'Ludwig Feuerbach and the End of Classical German Philosophy' (1888), reproduced in Institute of Marxism-Leninism (ed.), *Karl Marx and Fredrick Engels: Selected Works*, vol. 1 (Moscow: Progress Publishers, 1973), 13-15, at 14.

[40] Walzer, 'The Communitarian Critique' 1990 (n. 39), 10.

[41] *ibid*, 10 and 21.

[42] And, as Walzer points out, 'that insofar as liberalism tends toward instability and dissociation, it requires periodic communitarian correction', *ibid*, 21.

[43] Daniel A. Bell, 'A Communitarian Critique of Liberalism' *Analyse & Kritik* 27 (2005), 215-38, 225.

[44] Sean Sayers, 'Individual and Society in Marx and Hegel: Beyond the Communitarian Critique of Liberalism' *Science & Society* 71 (2007), 84-102, at 95.

of international law'.[45] This position was critiqued after the end of the Cold War by insider Rein Müllerson, who observed that the Soviet Union had 'over-emphasized the role [...] *of the classes*'.[46] It tended in his view to overlook, at least in practice, that all individuals, irrespective of their class, must possess fundamental rights.

TWAIL contends that what is required is not the abandonment of the category 'class' (or gender or race) but a dialectical approach that does not either underplay the significance of formal individual rights or the deep social fractures in society. It goes further and recommends an intersectional approach that retains the centrality of class without *a priori* privileging it over gender, race, or caste.[47] This dual approach may be illustrated with reference to women's rights. TWAIL, like FtAIL, values the advances in individual rights of women but evaluates their impact by locating them in prevailing gender relations in global society. This procedure leads to the inexorable conclusion that women have not become authentic subjects of international law as the institution of patriarchy continues to have a strong presence. To be sure, there are a variety of assessments of the impact of the codification of women's rights on the ground. Thus, for example, the radical feminist scholar Catherine McKinnon has a more sanguine assessment of the effect of women's rights than the liberal Hilary Charlesworth.[48] However, few adherents of FtAIL would suggest that the adoption of women's rights has seriously weakened the institution of patriarchy. In short, the status of the individual is not simply determined by the bundle of rights an individual has, or the procedural standing in enforcing them, but by social relations that are freedom enhancing.[49] It is therefore a leap of faith to move from accepting the importance of women's rights to claiming that these rights bring real freedom. Thus, unless gender relations are transformed through the radical reframing, *inter alia*, of family, property, and workplace laws, the realisation of individual rights will not bring about a new social order. In other words, if the individual is to become a genuine or authentic subject of international law it has to be preceded by a transformation of internal social orders; in the final analysis, the emancipation of an individual is not a legal but an historical act. In bringing about social transformation, which of the categories of class, gender, race, or caste will be privileged will depend on the nature and goals of particular social movements.

[45] Rein Müllerson, 'Human Rights and the Individual as Subject of International Law: A Soviet View' *European Journal of International Law* 1 (1990), 33-43, at 33-34 and 35.

[46] *ibid* (emphasis added).

[47] Bhupinder S. Chimni, *International Law and World Order Approaches* (2nd edn, Cambridge: CUP 2017).

[48] *ibid*, 378-80 and 419-21.

[49] For in Marx's words, 'Rights can never be higher than the economic structure of society and its cultural development conditioned thereby': Karl Marx, 'Critique of Gotha Programme' in *Karl Marx and Friedrich Engels: Selected Works*, vol. 3 (Moscow: Progress Publishers, 1970), 19.

2.3 Transnational Social Relations

The categories of class, gender, and race also have an international dimension that, crucially, bears upon the realisation of individual rights, especially in the Global South. TWAIL argues that, like all other aspects of modern international law, the status of individuals cannot be grasped outside the relational matrix established by the political economy of imperialism. For instance, in the colonial era aliens had special rights facilitated by capitulation agreements and the law of state responsibility *vide* the doctrine of minimum standards of civilisation.[50] It is of relevance here that Scelle, the foremost proponent of the view that the individual is the subject of international law, suggested that individuals of colonised nations could become subjects only if the latter formed a federal unity with the Metropolitan nation.[51] Likewise, neither Lauterpacht nor McDougal seriously addressed the violation of human rights of colonial peoples or called for decolonisation.

Even today, MILS continues to ignore the political economy of imperialism which shapes in crucial ways the nature and character of social relations in nations of the Global South.[52] Even strands of critical approaches such as FtAIL do not assign significance to the 'logic of capital'. Thus, for instance, neither radical nor liberal feminisms pay sufficient attention to the consequences of the universalisation of capitalism. In the event, the TWAIL perspective is more aligned to socialist feminist thinking that simultaneously questions the institutions of capitalism, imperialism, and patriarchy. To put it differently, in order to assess whether an individual is a subject of international law there is a need to move the discourse from the question of rights to that of justice.[53]

The TWAIL social relations perspective may be further clarified by reviewing the relationship between individual rights and the rights to self-determination and development, as these directly link subjectivity to societal development. Common

[50] Frederick Dunn wrote in 1941: 'Only a relatively small proportion of the treaties entered into since the middle of the last century have dealt with the relations of States as political atoms. The great majority of them have been concerned with the rights and interests of private individuals with their ability to travel about freely from country to country, to carry on trade across national boundaries with some degree of predictability ... to be protected in matters of public health and morals and a host of other things which are not at all concerned with the advancement of the political interests of States.' Frederick Dunn, 'The International Rights of Individuals' *Proceedings of the American Society of International Law* (1941), 14-15.

[51] Thierry, *European Tradition* 1990 (n. 13), 206.

[52] This is often done by terming the latter approach 'economic determinism'.

[53] 'If the global problem today is [...] the relatively unchecked globalization of capital, postcolonial political deformations, and superpower imperialism combining to dis-enfranchise peoples in many parts of the first, second, and third worlds from the prospects of self-governance to a degree historically unparalleled in modernity, other kinds of political projects, including other international justice projects, may offer a more appropriate and far-reaching remedy for injustice defined as suffering and as systematic disenfranchisement from collaborative self-governance.' Wendy Brown, 'The Most We Can Hope For ...: Human Rights and the Politics of Fatalism' *South Atlantic Quarterly* 103 (2004), 451-63, at 461-62. See also Samuel Moyn, *Human Rights are Not Enough: Human Rights in an Unequal World* (Boston, MA: Harvard University Press, 2019).

Article 1 of the International Covenant on Civil and Political Rights (ICCPR) and the International Covenant on Economic, Social and Cultural Rights (ICESCR) states 'that all peoples have the right of self-determination'. In its General Comment on the article, the Human Rights Committee (HRC) observed that 'its realization is *an essential condition for the effective guarantee and observance of individual human rights* and for the promotion and strengthening of those rights'.[54] This view echoes the common preambular paragraph of ICCPR and ICESCR, which states that 'the ideal of free human beings enjoying civil and political freedom and freedom from fear and want can only be achieved *if conditions are created* whereby everyone may enjoy his civil and political rights, as well as his economic, social and cultural rights' (emphasis added). The Declaration on the Right to Development, 1986 takes the relational view further by explicitly treating the right as both an individual and a collective right. In a recent comment, Nico Schrijver makes the important observation that the right of development is '*a bridging right* because *it connects the rights of individuals (citizens) with those of groups and peoples, including indigenous* peoples'.[55] He goes on to explain that 'it is a fact of life that many human rights are mainly experienced in community, as part of a group or population, while they also have meaning for each individual. The right to development therefore aptly connects individual and collective human rights'.[56] In other words, it is difficult to see how individuals can enjoy social, economic, and cultural rights without there being progress at the societal level. In sum, both the rights of self-determination and development exemplify the social relations perspective, as these relate the status of the individual to the conditions and state of development of peoples and nations. It is the intimate interface between individual rights and social development that determines whether an individual can be an authentic subject of international law. In the absence of this dialectic, developments in international law giving individual rights tend to acquire significance far beyond their impact on the ground.

The TWAIL perspective however goes beyond examining social relations inside nations to, *inter alia*, highlight the emergence of transnational class relations. The material status of the individual not only depends on whether they live in the Global North or the Global South but also whether they belong to the dominant social and political groups and classes. The growing inequalities inside nations have meant the emergence of a transnational capitalist class (TCC) on the one hand and a transnational oppressed class (TOC) on the other.[57] A social relations perspective

[54] United Nations, Office of the High Commissioner for Human Rights, General Comment No. 12: Article 1 – The Right to Self Determination of Peoples (13 March 1984), available at: https://www.refworld.org/docid/453883f822.html, accessed 7/7/2023, at 1 (emphasis added).

[55] Nico Schrijver, 'A New Convention on the Human Right to Development: Putting the Cart before the Horse?' *Netherlands Quarterly of Human Rights* 38 (2020), 84-93, at 92 (emphasis added).

[56] *ibid.*

[57] Chimni, *International Law and World Order* 2017 (n. 48), 506-09.

notes the growing global divide between the poor and rich to contend that, in the final analysis, the material status of an individual depends on the evolving transnational class relations. It bears on the ability of an individual to know of and access rights made available by different international instruments.

2.4 Participation, Resistance, and Subjectivity

If the rights to self-determination and development are to be actualised, or inequalities across nations to be addressed, it is critical that the individual has the right to participate in relevant decision-making processes at the internal and international levels. Indeed, in the TWAIL view, the actualisation of the right to participate is fundamental to determining whether an individual is a subject of international law. On the formal plane, these rights are part of the corpus of rights available under IHRL. For instance, Article 25(a) of the ICCPR grants every citizen 'the right and the opportunity [...] to take part in the conduct of public affairs, directly or through freely chosen representatives'. The provision recognises that unless the agency of the individual in the social and political spheres is actively recognised by international law, they cannot assume the status of a subject. In its General Comment No. 25 (1996), the HRC observed that citizens can 'take part in the conduct of public affairs by exerting influence through public debate and dialogue with their representatives or through their capacity to organize themselves'.[58] In fact, as Jeremy Waldron argues, the right to participate is 'fundamental' for the realisation of other rights of the individual since 'we are hardly in a position to say that [someone's rights are taken] seriously if at the same time we ignore or slight anything *he* has to say about the matter'.[59]

On the international plane, this right to participate is the essence of the all-affected principle and may manifest itself through the participation of NGOs.[60] While some mainstream scholars deny the right of participation to civil society or NGOs in international law-making others recognise a 'legitimate expectation of participation'.[61] Those against the right of participation ignore the fact that 'the voices of certain powerful minorities – corporations, interest groups and so on – are already taken into account as a matter of fact in the process of international

[58] United Nations, Human Rights Committee, International Covenant on Civil and Political Rights, General Comment No. 25, 27 August 1996, CCPR/C/21/Rev. 1/Add. 7, at para. 8.

[59] Cited by Nahuel Maisley, 'The International Right of Rights? Article 25(a) of the ICCPR as a Human Right to Take Part in International Law-Making' *European Journal of International Law* 28 (2017), 89-113, at 107. Jeremy Waldron, *Law and Disagreement* (New York, NY: OUP 1999), 251.

[60] Bhupinder S. Chimni, 'The Limits of the All Affected Principle: Attending to Deep Structures' *Third World Thematics* 2 (2018), 807-12; Jochen von Bernstorff, 'New Responses to the Legitimacy Crisis of International Institutions: The Role of "Civil Society" and the Rise of the Principle of Participation of "The Most Affected" in International Institutional Law' *European Journal of International Law* 32 (2021), 125-57.

[61] Maisley, 'Right of Rights' 2017 (n. 60), 92-95.

law-making, simply because they have the resources and the connections necessary for this purpose'.[62] Therefore, 'guaranteeing a right to participation [to NGOs] would imply levelling the playing field for other voices, which have greater difficulties in being heard'.[63] In recent decades there has been a growing degree of acceptance of the right to participate at the international level.[64] Where the right to development is concerned Amartya Sen's notion of 'development as freedom' captures this significant dimension of the relationship between individual rights and development.[65] Sen persuasively argues that the right to development can be realised only if there is democratic participation in the framing of policies and laws. The reality, however, is that the all-affected principle is respected more in breach. Individuals or their civil society representatives are either unable to find an opportunity or effectively participate in international decision-making. Once again the material realities are opposed to the recognition of an individual as a subject of international law.

The individual is then left with no option but to join other individuals to protest or resist policy decisions that have been taken at national or global levels. TWAIL therefore argues that the individual becomes a subject of international law not only through recognition of their status in international law from above but also through recognition of international law from below, which ensures that the voices of social movements representing the TOC are heard.[66] In fact, global civil society movements have helped inscribe in positive law the rights of workers, women, children, refugees, disabled persons, internally displaced persons, indigenous peoples, and stateless persons. They have also drawn attention to the concerns of the TOC through protests against extant international law regimes. The process of protesting gained momentum with the Rio Conference on Environment and Development in 1992 and has continued since. Global civil society organisations have organised protests at meetings of the International Monetary Fund (IMF), the World Bank, and the World Trade Organization (WTO). The 1999 Seattle protests at the site of the WTO ministerial meeting captured the imagination of the world. The meetings of the World Social Forum (WSF) have given the forum the means to coordinate the direct actions of civil society organisations coming from different nations.

In other words, international organisations must respect individual rights if they are to be considered real subjects of international law. As the ICJ in the *WHO* case observed: 'international organizations are subjects of international law and, as such, are bound by any obligations incumbent upon them under general rules of

[62] *ibid*, 106.
[63] *ibid*.
[64] *ibid*, 98-99.
[65] Amartya Sen, *Development as Freedom* (New Delhi: OUP 2000).
[66] Balakrishnan Rajagopal, *International Law from Below: Development, Social Movements and Resistance from Below* (Cambridge: CUP 2003).

international law'.[67] Andrew Clapham has likewise noted that international organisations are bound by 'appropriate customary international law of human rights'.[68] This view is also supported by general comments and resolutions of international human rights bodies. Thus, for instance, the Committee on Economic Social and Cultural Rights (CESCR) has called upon the international financial institutions (IFIs) 'to pay enhanced attention in their activities to respect for economic, social and cultural rights'.[69] The principles of emerging Global Administrative Law (GAL)—transparency, participation, and accountability—also come into play.[70] The application of IHRL has led to some positive developments, such as the creation of the World Bank Inspection Panel (WBIP) to hear the concerns of project affected persons (PAPs).[71] WBIP is a fact-finding body which allows private individuals access to express their grievances. It is seen as 'an extraordinary development' that has enhanced the transparency and accountability of IFIs.[72] However, while global civil society has been active in demanding rights and accountability, and international organisations are beginning to respond, there is clearly much more to be done.[73] In fact, the reality is that many of the developments in this regard have been unable to reform the global order in ways that mean the individual can be deemed an authentic subject of international law.

2.5 The Ultimate Test: Condition of Stateless Persons and Refugees

In assessing whether an individual is a subject of international law it is worth looking at an area of international law that addresses the concerns of perhaps the

[67] ICJ, *Legality of Threat or Use of Nuclear Weapons*, Judgment, (1996) ICJ Reports 66, at 89-90.

[68] Andrew Clapham, *Human Rights Obligations of Non-State Actors* (Oxford: OUP 2006), 151.

[69] Smita Narula, 'The Right to Food: Holding Global Actors Accountable Under International Law' *Columbia Journal of Transnational Law* 44 (2006), 691-800, at 745.

[70] However, on the limits of GAL, see Bhupinder S. Chimni, 'Cooption and Resistance: Two faces of Global Administrative Law' *New York University Journal of Law and Politics* 37 (2005), 799-827.

[71] Its objective is 'to address the concerns of the people who may be affected by Bank projects and to ensure that the Bank adheres to its operational policies and procedures during design, preparation and implementation phases of projects': World Bank, 'The Inspection Panel', available at: https://www.worldbank.org/en/programs/accountability/brief/the-inspection-panel, accessed 7/7/23. At a minimum, requesters must show in writing that they live in the project area (or represent people who do) and are likely to be affected adversely by project activities; they believe that actual or likely harm results from failure by the Bank to follow its policies and procedures; their concerns have been discussed with Bank management and they are not satisfied with the outcome. See generally Bhupinder S. Chimni, 'International Financial Institutions and International Law: A Third World Perspective', in Daniel D. Bradlow and David Hunter (eds.), *International Financial Institutions and International Law* (The Netherlands: Wolters Kluwer 2010), 31-63.

[72] Eisuke Suzuki and Suresh Nanwani, 'Responsibility of International Organizations: The Accountability Mechanism of Multilateral Development Banks' *Michigan Journal of International Law* 27 (2005), 177-225, at 187-88.

[73] Robert O'Brien et al., *Contesting Global Governance: Multilateral Economic Institutions and Global Social Movements* (Cambridge: CUP 2000), 3.

most vulnerable individuals in the world, namely, the stateless or/and refugees. The right of stateless persons to nationality and the right of an asylum seeker not to be refouled are the most fundamental of individual rights. It is the unfortunate condition of stateless persons that made Hannah Arendt speak of the 'right to have rights', an expression that equally applies to refugees.

In order to address the problem of statelessness two international conventions on stateless persons were adopted in the post-World War II era, namely, the 1954 Convention on the Status of Stateless Persons and the 1961 Convention on the Reduction of Stateless Persons. Yet today the number of stateless persons is on the rise. It has been estimated that the number of stateless persons at present is close to 15 million and likely to grow in the future.[74] Insofar as refugees are concerned, the UN Convention on the Status of Refugees was adopted in 1951 (later amended by the 1967 Protocol) and it promised safe haven to asylum seekers. In signalling that asylum seekers/refugees had rights, especially that of non-refoulement, the convention appeared to give substance to the claim that an individual was a subject of international law. But the reality in recent decades has been troubling. While the convention continues to provide a degree of protection, it is becoming increasingly clear that the fate of refugees is precarious. After the end of the Cold War, during which the convention served as an instrument, western liberal democracies have been unwilling to provide asylum to refugees, nearly all of whom were coming from the Global South. In the last three decades, three generations of non-entrée measures have been put in place to keep asylum seekers and refugees out.[75] In other words, the undermining of the refugee regime gathered strength once the flow of refugees assumed a South-North dimension.[76] This is particularly troubling not only because 86 per cent of refugees are located in the Global South, but also because most of those refugees have fled nations where the western world has actively intervened in one way or another (these include Afghanistan, Iraq, Libya, Sudan, Syria, and Venezuela).[77] The tragedy of asylum seekers was symbolically captured by the image of a three-year-old Syrian boy, Aylan Kurdi, lying dead on a Turkish beach. The total number of migrant deaths in the Mediterranean alone from 2014 to 2022 has been 21,470.[78] While the recently adopted Global Compact

[74] Institute on Statelessness and Inclusion, 'The World's Stateless: Deprivation of Nationality' (2020), available at: https://files.institutesi.org/WORLD%27s_STATELESS_2020.pdf, accessed 7/7/23, at 14.

[75] Thomas Gammeltoft-Hansen and James Hathaway, 'Non-Refoulement in a World of Cooperative Deterrence' *Columbia Journal of Transnational Law* 53 (2015), 235-84.

[76] Bhupinder S. Chimni, 'The Geopolitics of Refugee Studies: A View from the South' *Journal of Refugee Studies* 11 (1998), 350-74.

[77] United Nations High Commissioner for Refugees, 'Global Trends: Forced Displacement in 2020', available at: https://www.unhcr.org/statistics/unhcrstats/60b638e37/global-trends-forced-displacement-2020.html, accessed 7/7/23, at 2.

[78] Statistica, 'Number of recorded deaths of migrants in the Mediterranean Sea from 2014 to 2022', available at: https://www.statista.com/statistics/1082077/deaths-of-migrants-in-the-mediterranean-sea, accessed 7/7/23. See also IOM, 'Missing Migrants Project', available at: https://missingmigrants.iom.int/, accessed 7/7/23.

for Refugees (2018) is a welcome development, it contains few concrete measures to address the non-entrée regime in place in the Global North.[79] It once again raises the question of whether, in advancing the claim that the individual is a subject of international law or of the humanisation of international law, formal criteria should suffice or whether ground realities should be taken into account.

3. Conclusion

In the past century there have been developments that lend support to the view that the individual is a subject of international law. These developments include the proliferation of human rights instruments conferring rights on individuals; the direct access of individuals in many instances to international bodies and tribunals to enforce rights; the recognition of the responsibility of individuals for the crime of genocide, war crimes, and crimes against humanity; the creation of a permanent international criminal court to try individuals responsible for such crimes; and the scholarly view that the individual is the real subject of international law.[80] However, this chapter argues that such a determination is the outcome of a flawed epistemology that embraces methodological individualism and legal determinism. The focus of any assessment of whether an individual is a subject of international law should not merely be on the atomistic individual or legal materials but on internal and global social relations as these impose structural constraints on realising the goal of human dignity. TWAIL thus distinguishes between formal and authentic subjects of international law. In its view, the central obstacles to realising the goal of individual human dignity and a human-centred law are, in the final analysis, the entrenched structures of exploitative capitalism, imperialism, patriarchy, racism, and casteism.

Be that as it may, another crisis, virus induced, is upon us. The spectre of growing poverty and inequality in the post-pandemic era threatens past gains in improving individual welfare.[81] Even those fleeing threats to their life and freedom are turned away. In a world in which an individual is unable to fulfil basic needs, and is the subject of alienation and violence in myriad forms, it would be cruel to declare them a subject of international law.[82] It is time to accept that while law

[79] Bhupinder S. Chimni, 'The Global Compact on Refugees: One Step Forward, Two Steps Back' *International Journal of Refugee Law* 30 (2018), 630-34.

[80] Higgins, *Conceptual Thinking* 1978 (n. 25), 1-19.

[81] Secretary-General's Nelson Mandela Lecture: 'Tackling the Inequality Pandemic: A New Social Contract for a New Era', available at: https://www.un.org/sg/en/content/sg/statement/2020-07-18/secretary-generals-nelson-mandela-lecture-%E2%80%9Ctackling-the-inequality-pandemic-new-social-contract-for-new-era%E2%80%9D-delivered, accessed 7/07/23; United Nations, Human Rights Council, Report of the Special Rapporteur on Extreme Poverty and Human Rights, The parlous state of poverty eradication, A/HRC/44/40, at para. 35. See also United Nations, 'The Sustainable Development Goals Report 2020' (Cambridge: CUP 2020).

[82] Bhupinder S Chimni, 'The Past, Present and Future of International Law: A Critical Third World Approach' *Melbourne Journal of International Law* 8 (2007), 499-515.

has constitutive effects, it remains, in the final analysis, a secondary force in internal and international social orders. In short, legal determinism is as flawed as economic determinism. Any discussion on the individual being a subject of international law must extend to the examination of critical non-legal spheres that are the major determinants of the life chances of individuals, whether in the Global North or in the Global South.

12

The Individual in Feminist Approaches to International Law

*Ruth Houghton**

1. Introduction

Individuals, and in particular women, have always been at the core of feminist international legal scholarship. The primacy of the legal subjecthood of States in international law is something that feminists have long sought to disrupt.[1] Through a focus on the concerns of women, the impact of international law on women, and the role of women and women's networks in law-making,[2] feminists have challenged the State-centric frame of international law. When examining what a feminist approach tells us about the relationship between the individual, State, and international law, it becomes clear that for current feminist scholars the concern is less whether individuals have legal personality, as they have sought to demonstrate this already, but rather how the individual is conceptualised, and specifically the gendered and racialised construction of women as subjects of international law.

Feminist international lawyers challenge the masculine bias of international law, which had given rise to an assumed heterosexual male body underpinning international law's conceptualisation of the individual.[3] Scholars such as Dianne Otto and Gina Heathcote, have criticised liberal (and neo-liberal) international law, which is predicated on a male subjectivity.[4] This chapter focuses on critiques of the

* With thanks to Sophie Doherty, Nikki Godden-Rasul, and Matthew Nicholson for their discussions and comments on earlier drafts of this work, and thanks to Emily Jones, Aoife O'Donoghue, Jane Rooney, Se-shauna Wheatle, Esra Demir Gürsel, and Marina Veličković for their comments and suggestions on this chapter.

[1] For a history that questions this primacy of the state, see Kate Parlett, *The Individual in the International Legal System: Continuity and Change in International Law* (Cambridge: CUP 2011); Astrid Kjeldgaard-Pedersen, *The International Legal Personality of the Individual* (Oxford: OUP 2018).

[2] See, e.g., Deborah Stienstra, *Women's Movements and International Organizations* (Hampshire: Macmillan 1994), 47-48; Hilary Charlesworth and Christine Chinkin, *The Boundaries of International Law: A Feminist Analysis* (Manchester: Manchester University Press 2000), 14; Dianne Otto, 'The Exile of Inclusion: Reflections on Gender Issues in International Law over the Last Decade' *Melbourne Journal of International Law* 10 (2009), 11-26.

[3] Charlesworth and Chinkin, *Boundaries of international law* 2000 (n. 2), 129.

[4] See, e.g., Dianne Otto, 'Feminist Approaches to International Law', in Anne Orford and Florian Hoffmann with Martin Clark (eds.), *The Oxford Handbook of the Theory of International Law* (Oxford: OUP 2016), 488-504, at 498; Gina Heathcote, 'On Feminist Legal Methodologies: Spilt, Plural and Speaking Subjects' *feminists@law* 8 (2018), 1-20, at 7.

Ruth Houghton, *The Individual in Feminist Approaches to International Law* In: *The Individual in International Law*. Edited by: Tom Sparks and Anne Peters, Oxford University Press. © Ruth Houghton 2024.
DOI: 10.1093/oso/9780198898917.003.0012

liberal subject in international law. Whilst liberal feminists embrace the universality of the liberal subject,[5] there are concerns that the level of abstraction overlooks women's lives. Responding to the abstract individual gives rise to a 'bind' for feminists;[6] if international law adopts the 'abstract', universal subject, then it risks overlooking the specific conditions of women around the world. However, if it focuses on these specific conditions, international law risks further marginalisation of women.[7] This chapter seeks to map how different feminist perspectives have responded to this concern.

This chapter will utilise both feminist international law scholarship and feminist legal theory, to highlight the tensions between different feminist approaches, including liberal feminists, radical feminist approaches, and intersectional and post-colonial feminisms.[8] There is no singular feminist approach to the individual in international law; rather this chapter suggests four principles for a feminist approach to a human-centric international law. First, a responsiveness to the risks of essentialism. Second, and relatedly, resisting the proliferation of feminine 'characters' in international law. Such generalisations and universalising of women have the potential to silence and oppress. Feminist international law scholars should be alert to these silences and oppressions that can arise in certain characterisations of the individual, to ensure that they are not replicated. Third, the need for contextualised plural subjectivities. Fourth, encouraging and facilitating reflexive dialogues across feminisms.[9]

This chapter starts by unpacking 'women' or 'woman' as the subject of feminist approaches to international law, to expose the risks of essentialism (section 2). One approach is to focus on 'women' as a strategic category,[10] which offers an alternative to the universal male individual of liberalism. For liberal feminists, focusing on 'women' has had successes,[11] as seen with gender mainstreaming in specific areas

[5] Siobhán Mullally, *Gender, Culture and Human Rights: Reclaiming Universalism* (Oxford: Hart 2006), 1; Vanessa Munro, *Law and Politics at the Perimeter: Re-evaluating Key Debates in Feminist Theory* (Oxford: Hart 2007), 59.

[6] See Faye Bird, '"Is this a Time of Beautiful Chaos?": Reflecting on International Feminist Legal Methods' *Feminist Legal Studies* 28 (2020), 179-203, at 180.

[7] Dianne Otto, 'Disconcerting "Masculinities": Reinventing the Subject of International Human Rights', in Doris Buss and Ambreena Manji (eds.), *International Law: Modern Feminist Approaches* (Oxford: Hart 2005), 105-29, at 123-24.

[8] For an introduction to these different feminisms, see Berta E. Hernández-Truyol, 'Crossing Borderlands of Inequality with International Legal Methodologies – the Promise of Multiple Feminisms' *German Yearbook of International Law* 44 (2001), 113-69.

[9] Gina Heathcote, *Feminist Dialogues on International Law: Successes, Tensions, Futures* (Oxford: OUP 2019), 72. See also Vasuki Nesiah, 'Priorities of Feminist Legal Research: A sketch, a draft agenda, a hint of an outline . . .' *feminists@law* 1 (2011), 1-4.

[10] For a discussion, see Ratna Kapur, 'The Tragedy of Victimization Rhetoric: Resurrecting the "Native" Subject in International/Post-Colonial Feminist Legal Politics' *Harvard Human Rights Journal* 15 (2002), 1-13; Jaya Ramji-Nogales, 'Revisiting the Category "Women"', in Susan Harris Rimmer and Kate Ogg (eds.), *Research Handbook on Feminist Engagement with International Law* (Cheltenham: Edward Elgar 2019), 240-53, at 240.

[11] See Doris Buss and Ambreena Manji, 'Introduction', in Doris Buss and Ambreena Manji (eds.), *International Law: Modern Feminist Approaches* (Oxford: Hart 2005), 1-16, at 3-4; Karen Engle, 'International Human Rights and Feminisms: When Discourses Keep Meeting', in Doris Buss and

of international law.[12] Other feminist scholars question whether 'woman' is an appropriate category at all,[13] as it risks essentialism through reproducing the idea of a homogenous concept of 'woman' and reproduces gendered-binaries where women are compared against men when included within subjecthood.[14] Section 3 outlines the 'feminine characters' that are constructed by international law and section 4 considers the different feminist approaches that are proffered within feminist theory to move beyond these essentialised, dehumanised characters. Intersectional approaches and post-colonial feminisms, move beyond 'woman' as the organising category and call for a 'contextualised legal subject' and 'plural subjectivities', which reframes the foundations of international law.[15] A consideration of those different approaches highlights the need for discussions across feminist, queer, critical race, and post-colonial perspectives on the individual in international law (section 5).

2. Responsive to the Risks of Essentialism

Feminist international law scholarship asks the 'women' question in part to document the 'absence and exclusion of women from law-making fora',[16] but also to disrupt the primacy of the State in international law. For Zoe Pearson, the international feminist project is concerned with the 'Who of international law; who is involved in creating international law, whose concerns are heard and addressed'.[17] As such, feminist scholarship in international law provides a wealth of examples of women as participants in international law-making. In particular, there are accounts of women in peace processes and constitutional processes, and the instrumental work of women operating across the local, national, and international scales of governance lobbying for international organisational and legal change.[18] Examples

Ambreena Manji (eds.), *International Law: Modern Feminist Approaches* (Oxford: Hart 2005), 47-66, at 51-52.

[12] *cf.* Sari Kouvo who argues that gender mainstreaming can 'distort equality and social justice politics': Sari Kouvo, 'The United Nations and Gender Mainstreaming: Limits and Possibilities', in Doris Buss and Ambreena Manji (eds.), *International Law: Modern Feminist Approaches* (Oxford: Hart 2005), 237-52, at 239.

[13] See, e.g., Otto, 'Disconcerting "Masculinities"' 2005 (n. 7), 107.

[14] *ibid*, 123-24.

[15] Ulrika Andersson, 'Trafficking in Human Beings: Vulnerability, Criminal Law and Human Rights', in Sari Kouvo and Zoe Pearson (eds.), *Feminist Perspectives on Contemporary International Law: Between Resistance and Compliance* (Oxford: Hart 2011), 177-92, at 179; Heathcote, *Feminist Dialogues* 2019 (n. 9), 72.

[16] See Hilary Charlesworth, 'The Women Question in International Law' *Asian Journal of International Law* 1 (2011), 33-38, at 33.

[17] Zoe Pearson, 'Feminist Project(s): The Spaces of International Law', in Sari Kouvo and Zoe Pearson (eds.), *Feminist Perspectives on Contemporary International Law: Between Resistance and Compliance* (Oxford: Hart 2011), 47-68, at 48.

[18] See, e.g., Ignacio de la Rasilla, 'Concepción Arenal and the Place of Women in Modern International Law' *Legal History Review* 88 (2020), 211-53; Immi Tallgren (ed.), *Portraits of Women in International Law: New Names and Forgotten Faces?* (Oxford: OUP 2021); Rebecca Adami

include Catherine O'Rourke's work in transitional justice on women's roles in peace processes and constitutional transitions,[19] as well as Aoife O'Donoghue's piece demonstrating the role of women in the League of Nations.[20] Earlier feminist scholarship, such as Hilary Charlesworth and Christine Chinkin's work, highlighted examples of women's movements lobbying for change in international law, such as the organisation of women outside the World Anti-Slavery Convention in London in 1840, and the International Congress of Women held in the Hague in 1915, to discuss the prevention of war.[21] Otto, in particular, emphasises the role of local and international women's networks in influencing the policies and practices of the UN.[22] Such examples are useful for challenging narratives of the State as the singular subject of international law and men as the only participants.

Asking the 'Women Question'[23] disrupts the liberal narrative of the individual as male; 'woman' provides 'a subject that repudiates the atomized, decontextualized, and ahistorical subject of liberal rights discourse'.[24] However, 'woman' also suggests a single homogenous category or group. Whilst some feminist scholars argue that 'a unitary subject' is useful for strategic activism because 'that enables women to continue to make claims based on a commonality of experience',[25] others have highlighted the problems of essentialism. Some feminist scholars, including from Black feminist, post-colonial feminist, and queer feminist perspectives, would question whether 'woman' as a subject in feminist approaches to international law is desirable.[26] Focusing on 'woman' risks replacing the universal male individual, with a universal 'woman'.

This essentialism of 'woman' is especially prevalent when combined with cultural essentialism and racism.[27] Josephine Jarpa Dawuni discusses the use of 'the singular "African woman"' in international law and its scholarship, which constructs an 'often-faceless and nation-less "African" woman'.[28] Similarly, Chandra

and Dan Plesch (eds.), *Women and the UN: A New History of Women's International Human Rights* (Abingdon: Routledge 2021).

[19] Catherine O'Rourke, 'Feminist Strategy in International Law: Understanding Its Legal, Normative and Political Dimensions' *European Journal of International Law* 28 (2017), 1019-45.

[20] Aoife O'Donoghue, 'Article 7 of the Covenant of the League of Nations', in Rosemary Auchmuty and Erika Rackley (eds.), *Women's Legal Landmarks* (Oxford: Hart 2018), 125-33; Charlesworth and Chinkin, *Boundaries of international law* 2000 (n. 2), 15.

[21] Stienstra, *Women's Movements* 1994 (n. 2), 47-48; Charlesworth and Chinkin, *Boundaries of international law* 2000 (n. 2), 14.

[22] Otto, 'The Exile of Inclusion' 2009 (n. 2), 11.

[23] See Charlesworth, 'The Women Question' 2011 (n. 16), 33.

[24] Kapur, 'The Tragedy of Victimization Rhetoric' 2002 (n. 10), 5.

[25] *ibid.* On page 11, Kapur argues that in limited circumstances, essentialism has strategic purpose. See also Ramji-Nogales, 'Revisiting the Category "Women"' 2019 (n. 10), 240.

[26] Otto, 'Disconcerting "Masculinities"' 2005 (n. 7), 123-24.

[27] Kapur, 'The Tragedy of Victimization Rhetoric' 2002 (n. 10), 2.

[28] Josephine Jarpa Dawuni, 'Marti-Legal Feminism: An African Feminist Response to International Law', in Susan Harris Rimmer and Kate Ogg (eds.), *Research Handbook on Feminist Engagement with International Law* (Cheltenham: Edward Elgar 2019), 445-62, at 446.

Talpade Mohanty criticised the categorisation and therefore construction of a homogenous 'Third World women'.[29] Such essentialising ignores the harms and oppressions faced by women as a result of the intersections of race, gender, class, ableism, and sexuality. For Dawuni, to disrupt the categorisation of the 'African woman', there needs to be a shift to the 'contributions of *individual* women' as a way of moving beyond the essentialisation of a constructed collective of women.[30] A focus on the agency, personal contributions, and the many 'forms of diversity' of African women moves towards a more 'nuanced' approach to the individual.[31] The need to centre individual women's lives and achievements demonstrates the utility of an individual-centric approach to international law, but it has to be one that focuses on diversity and not essentialist characterisations.

Some feminists note the utility of the category of 'women' for strategic purposes.[32] Otto notes the work done by 'woman' as a category to highlight gendered harms.[33] However, this sort of 'strategic essentialism' should be limited to specific purposes and to challenge dominant ideologies.[34] Understanding how strategic essentialism is used and when requires a contextualised and intersectional approach. Jaya Ramji-Nogales argues that 'woman' can provide a starting point for political mobilisation, but that discord and disagreement should be expected and encouraged.[35]

The two approaches suggested by Dawuni and Ramji-Nogales—on the one hand focusing on *individual* women's lives and on the other, strategic use of 'woman' that encourages disagreement, discord, and discussions—can help elaborate the four principles for a feminist approach to the individual suggested in this chapter. A responsiveness to essentialism requires a critique of the harm caused by essentialism, but also the acknowledgement of its specific strategic uses by women throughout histories of legal and political reform (principle 1). Relatedly, Dawuni's work highlights the need to disrupt the imposed categorisations on women that arise from essentialism (principle 2). Ramji-Nogales' call for discord and disagreement amongst feminists highlights the need for reflexivity across feminisms so that approaches to the individual are not 'closed' but remain open, which can be facilitated by plural subjectivities (principles 3 and 4). To further understand the need for a shift to plural subjectivities, the next section examines the problematic effects of one-dimensional characterisations of women in international law.

[29] Chandra Talpade Mohanty, 'Under Western Eyes: Feminist scholarship and colonial discourses' *Boundary* 12 (1984), 333-58, at 351, also cited in Dawuni, 'Marti-Legal Feminism' 2019 (n. 28), 452.

[30] Dawuni, 'Marti-Legal Feminism' 2019 (n. 28), 446.

[31] *ibid.*

[32] Kapur, 'The Tragedy of Victimization Rhetoric' 2002 (n. 10), 5.

[33] Otto, 'Disconcerting "Masculinities"' 2005 (n. 7), 123-24.

[34] Kapur, 'The Tragedy of Victimization Rhetoric' 2002 (n. 10), 11.

[35] Ramji-Nogales, 'Revisiting the category "women"' 2019 (n. 10), 240.

3. Resist the Proliferation of Feminine Characters in International Law

Whilst women are present within international law, scholars note it is often as victims and 'mothers, or potential mothers, in need of protection'.[36] Feminists have highlighted these characters discussed within international law and how these caricatures prevent discussions of 'women' in all their diversity.[37] As Andrea Bianchi summarises the critique: 'Women are not subjects in their own right, and their voice is hardly ever heard.'[38]

While the strategic essentialist uses of 'woman' as a category can articulate the agency, political mobilisation, and therefore subjecthood of women, the imagery of the 'African woman'; 'Third World woman'; as well as the wives,[39] mothers, and other characters constructed in international law and international legal scholarship, can objectify women.[40] The tension between subject and objectification is a tension that reverberates throughout feminist debates on the 'subject' of international law. This section unpacks that tension by focusing on examples of the 'feminine characters' constructed in international law and its scholarship to explore the processes of objectification and subject-formation.

Tracing the stereotypical gendered tropes of women as mother and victim, Otto criticises the way in which women have been encapsulated into the idea of the 'individual'.[41] These stereotypes found in international human rights law and international criminal law[42] serve to reassert 'the masculinity of the universal subject of human rights law'.[43] Women are compared with the masculine 'autonomous individual',[44] and what we are left with is a binary of female victim and male protector. As Otto argues:

> Each of these female personas produces and is dependent upon a binary male representation: the protected subject constitutes her 'protector' in the form of the

[36] Hilary Charlesworth, 'Feminist Methods in International Law' *American Journal of International Law* 93 (1999), 379-94, at 381.

[37] See, e.g., Karen Engle, 'Female Subjects of Public International Law: Human Rights and the Exotic Other Female' *New England Law Review* 26 (1992), 1509-26; Anne Orford, 'Muscular Humanitarianism: Reading the Narratives of the New Interventionism' *European Journal of International Law* 10 (1999), 679-711, at 685-89.

[38] Andrea Bianchi, *International Law Theories: An Inquiry into Different Ways of Thinking* (Oxford: OUP 2016), 186.

[39] See Otto, 'Disconcerting "Masculinities"' 2005 (n. 7), 106.

[40] Dawuni, 'Marti-Legal Feminism' 2019 (n. 28), 450.

[41] Otto, 'Disconcerting "Masculinities"' 2005 (n. 7), 128, also cited in Buss and Manji, 'Introduction' 2005 (n. 11), 10-11.

[42] See Daniela Nadj, 'The Culturalisation of Identity in an Age of "Ethnic Conflict" – Depoliticised Gender in ICTY Wartime Sexual Violence Jurisprudence' *International Journal of Human Rights* 15 (2011), 647-63.

[43] Otto, 'Disconcerting "Masculinities"' 2005 (n. 7), 128 also cited in Buss and Manji, 'Introduction' 2005 (n. 11), 10-11.

[44] Otto, 'Disconcerting "Masculinities"' 2005 (n. 7), 114-15.

head of the household and [...] the 'victim' subject affirms the need for the masculine bearer of 'civilisation' and saviour of 'good' women from 'bad', and often 'native', men.[45]

Much of the early discussion on the 'shift' to the individual within international law is found in international human rights law and international criminal law,[46] and it is in these discourses that we find a discussion on 'victims'. Much feminist thought, therefore, has been directed towards the construction of 'victims' in international human rights law and international criminal law.[47] However, the broader concern about objectification and risks of essentialism are applicable across international law and its scholarship. The next two subsections use these discussions from international human rights law and international criminal law to help draw conclusions on the construction of the individual woman within international law.

3.1 Women as Victims in International Law

There is a long line of feminist scholarship that has demonstrated the problems with the 'victim-subject' as a feminine and racialised character in international law.[48] Ratna Kapur highlights how international human rights discourse promoted 'this image of the authentic victim subject while advocating for women's human rights'.[49] Ulrika Andersson critiques the focus on vulnerability in human-trafficking law and discourse.[50] Other scholars have demonstrated similar trends in international criminal law with respect to sexual violence.[51] Feminist scholars also critique the UN Security Council (UNSC) approach to gender, for example Otto critiques UNSC Resolution 1820 because 'women are again defined primarily by their violability, and protective responses return with a vengeance'.[52] Simplistic

[45] *ibid*, 106.

[46] Ruti Teitel, *Humanity's Law* (Oxford: OUP 2011), 4; Parlett, *Individual in the International Legal System* 2011 (n. 1); Kjeldgaard-Pedersen, *The International Legal Personality of the Individual* 2018 (n. 1), 13.

[47] See Buss and Manji (eds.), *Modern Feminist Approaches* 2005 (n. 11); Susan Harris Rimmer and Kate Ogg (eds.), *Research Handbook on Feminist Engagement with International Law* (Cheltenham: Edward Elgar 2019).

[48] See Kapur, 'The Tragedy of Victimization Rhetoric' 2002 (n. 10); Maria Grahn-Farley, 'The Politics of Inevitability: An Examination of Janet Halley's Critique of the Criminalisation of Rape as Torture', in Sari Kouvo and Zoe Pearson (eds.), *Feminist Perspectives on Contemporary International Law: Between Resistance and Compliance* (Oxford: Hart 2011), 109-29, at 126;Jayne Huckerby, 'Feminism and International Law in the Post 9/11 Era' *Fordham International Law Journal* 39 (2016), 533-90.

[49] Kapur, 'The Tragedy of Victimization Rhetoric' 2002 (n. 10), 2.

[50] Andersson, 'Trafficking in Human Beings' 2011 (n. 15), 177.

[51] See Nadj, 'The Culturalisation of Identity in an Age of 'Ethic Conflict' 2011 (n. 42).

[52] UNSC, Resolution 1820 (2008), 19 June 2008, UN Doc. No. S/RES/1820; Otto, 'The Exile of Inclusion' 2009 (n. 2). See also Dianne Otto and Gina Heathcote, 'Rethinking Peacekeeping, Gender Equality and Collective Security: An Introduction' in Dianne Otto and Gina Heathcote (eds.), *Rethinking Peacekeeping, Gender Equality and Collective Security* (London: Palgrave Macmillan, 2014), 1-20, at 2; Vanja Hamzić, 'International law as violence: competing absences of the other', in Dianne

characterisations of women are present in soft law, such as the World Bank Environmental and Social Framework (ESF) and the Sustainable Development Goals (SDGs).[53] The construction of women as vulnerable is present in the 2017 World Bank ESF as women are grouped with other vulnerable groups in the Environmental and Social Standard on Labour and Working Conditions.[54] Within the SDGs, emphasis is placed on the role of member States in empowering women and girls,[55] thus constructing women as 'passive recipients of development' rather than as 'agents of change'.[56] The repeated discursive grouping of 'women and girls' throughout the SDGs compounds the idea of women as vulnerable.[57] Christine Struckmann demonstrates how the SDGs reliance on liberal feminism and the emphasis placed on participation in the labour market overlooks the 'the structural drivers of women's subordination and oppression', including the interconnected role of political, economic, and social dimensions of inequalities.[58]

Otto points out that 'the "victim" subject [...] is produced by colonial narratives of gender, as well as by notions of women's sexual vulnerability'.[59] As such, 'the victim subject has reinforced gender essentialism and cultural essentialism',[60] which then means that 'the victim subject reinforces the depiction of women in the Third World as perpetually marginalized and underprivileged'.[61] Otto has demonstrated how the victim-subject is presented as in need of protection 'from her own collective communal culture'.[62]

The victim-subject is represented as needing to be saved by the male protector, as well as by the White western feminist, who is 'seen as ideally placed' to join the

Otto (ed.), *Queering International Law: Possibilities, Alliances, Complicities, Risks* (Abingdon: Routledge 2017), 76-90, at 77 and 85.

[53] See Marcel M. T. A Brus, 'Soft Law in Public International Law: A Pragmatic or a Principled Choice? Comparing the Sustainable Development Goals and the Paris Agreement', in Pauline Westerman et al. (eds.), *Legal Validity and Soft Law* (New York, NY: Springer International Publishing 2018), 243-66 (SDGs); Giedre Jokubauskaite, 'The Legal Nature of the World Bank Safeguards' *Verfassung in Recht und Übersee* 51 (2018), 78-102 (discussion on ESF as soft law).

[54] See World Bank, 'The World Bank Environmental and Social Framework', 2017, 31. During the consultation process, participants had raised concerns about the definition of vulnerability that was being used: see World Bank, 'Meeting of Labour Experts on the Second Draft of the World Bank's Environmental and Social Standard 2: Labour and Working Conditions (ESS 2)' (18 September 2015, Washington DC).

[55] UNGA, 'Transforming Our World: The 2030 Agenda for Sustainable Development', 21 October 2015, UN Doc. No. A/RES/70/1, at Goal 5.c and at paras. 3 and 20.

[56] Christine Struckmann, 'A Postcolonial Feminist Critique of the 2030 Agenda for Sustainable Development: A South African Application' *Agenda* 32 (2018), 12-24, at 17.

[57] For a discussion, see Ann-Kathrin Rothermel, 'Gender in the United Nations' Agenda on Preventing and Countering Violent Extremism' *International Feminist Journal of Politics* 22 (2020), 720-41, at 729.

[58] Struckmann, 'A Postcolonial Feminist Critique' 2018 (n. 56), 13.

[59] Otto, 'Disconcerting "Masculinities"' 2005 (n. 7), 106.

[60] Kapur, 'The Tragedy of Victimization Rhetoric' 2002 (n. 10), 2.

[61] *ibid*, 6.

[62] Otto, 'Disconcerting "Masculinities"' 2005 (n. 7), 114-15.

rescue mission.[63] Anne Orford warns about the temptation for White western feminists to 'save' the 'Third World'.[64] Such ideas can underpin problematic calls for 'sisterhood' that are constructed through 'a colonialist Western feminism that presumed "sisterhood is global"', which worked to 'down[play] thorny issues of differences between women'.[65] These claims to 'sisterhood' act, as Inderpal Grewal and Caren Kaplan note, as 'a kind of Western cultural imperialism'.[66] Feminist international law must disrupt these problematic constructions of 'victim' and 'sisterhood', by centring women's particularised history and their multiple experiences of intersecting power dynamics.[67]

There have been acknowledgements of the need to move away from the victim-subject to women's agency in international law, for example UNSC Resolution 1325 'cast[s] women in active leadership roles by emphasising the need to increase their representation at all levels of decision-making related to conflict prevention, management and resolution'.[68] The shift from victim to contributor disrupts 'the traditional narrative of women's weakness and vulnerability' and negates the 'need for (male/state/military) protection'.[69] However, there are concerns that such gains could be lost, especially since UNSC Resolution 1820 saw a return to the imagery of victimhood and vulnerability.[70] Ann-Kathrin Rothermel demonstrates the role of 'problematic imaginaries' of women as victims on the one hand, and as '"natural" peacemakers' on the other which has filtered into the UN Agenda on Preventing and Countering Violent Extremism.[71] Although more recent UNSC resolutions have encapsulated the agency of UNSC Resolution 1325,[72] examples such as UNSC Resolution 1820 and the agenda on Preventing and Countering Violent Extremism

[63] Anne Orford, 'Feminism, Imperialism and the Mission of International Law' *Nordic Journal of International Law* 71 (2002), 275-96, at 276.

[64] *ibid.*

[65] Inderpal Grewal and Caren Kaplan (eds.), *Scattered Hegemonies: Postmodernity and Transitional Feminist Practices* (Minnesota: University of Minnesota Press 1994), 17; also cited in Susan M. Roberts, 'Gendered Globalization', in Lynn A. Staeheli, Eleonore Kofman, and Linda J. Peake (eds.), *Mapping Women, Making Politics: Feminist Perspectives on Political Geography* (Abingdon: Routledge 2004), 127-40, at 131.

[66] Grewal and Kaplan (eds), *Scattered hegemonies* 1994 (n. 65), 17.

[67] *ibid.* See also Elisabeth Prügl, *The Global Construction of Gender: Home-Based Work in the Political Economy of the 20th Century* (New York, NY: Columbia University Press 1999). For a discussion on the problems of 'sisterhood', see Kapur, 'The Tragedy of Victimization Rhetoric' 2002 (n. 10), 37.

[68] UNSC, Resolution 1325 (2000), 31 October 2000, UN Doc No. S/RES/1325; Otto, 'The Exile of Inclusion' 2009 (n. 2). See also Sari Kouvo and Zoe Pearson, 'Introduction', in Sari Kouvo and Zoe Pearson (eds.), *Feminist Perspectives on Contemporary International Law: Between Resistance and Compliance* (Oxford: Hart 2011), 2-9.

[69] Otto, 'The Exile of Inclusion' 2009 (n. 2), 17.

[70] *ibid.*

[71] Rothermel, 'Gender in the United Nations' 2020 (n. 57), 720-21.

[72] UNSC, Resolution 1888 (2009), 30 September 2009, UN Doc. No. S/RES/1888; UNSC, Resolution 1889 (2009), 5 October 2009, UN Doc No. S/RES/1889; Dianne Otto, 'Power and Danger: Feminist Engagement with International Law through the UN Security Council' *Australian Feminist Law Journal* 32 (2010), 97-121, at 102-03.

show the pervasiveness of these stereotypical images of women.[73] Indeed, as Patricia Hill Collins argues the power of stereotypical images lies in their ability to 'make racism, sexism, poverty, and other forms of social injustice appear to be natural'.[74]

3.2 Women as Mothers in International Law

Another recurring female character in international law is the 'mother'. International law constructs the image of 'mother' as tied to images of the heterosexual married couple, and 'a nuclear family',[75] and often the 'mother' is constructed as a woman in need of protection and is therefore 'more an object than a subject of international law'.[76]

Scholars have noted how a conceptualisation of motherhood in conflict and in peace-processes, relies on the idea that mothers are best-placed to bring about peace.[77] This is informed by the problematic idea that mothers are naturally peaceful, and the ethics of care argument that women reason differently to men.[78] Drawing on the example of the Mothers of Srebrenica, scholars note how this conceptualisation of motherhood potentially sidelines the concerns and experiences of these women, as well as potentially marginalising other women.[79]

Charlesworth criticises the Beijing Platform for Action for its 'limited vision of women's roles' as mothers.[80] The Platform for Action focused on 'women's experiences as including "balancing work and family responsibilities, as mothers, as professionals, as managers, as entrepreneurs"'.[81] This highlights that 'the traditional role of mother remains crucial for women, and all that is added is the need

[73] Otto, 'Power and Danger' 2010 (n. 72), 118; Rothermel, 'Gender in the United Nations' 2020 (n. 57).

[74] Patricia Hill Collins, *Black Feminist Thought: Knowledge, Consciousness, and the Politics of Empowerment* (10th anniversary edn, Abingdon: Routledge 2000), 69.

[75] *ibid*, 182.

[76] Otto, 'Disconcerting "Masculinities"' 2005 (n. 7), 106.

[77] Orford, 'Feminism, Imperialism' 2002 (n. 63), 282; Olivera Simic, 'What Remains of Srebrenica? Motherhood, Transitional Justice and Yearning for Truth' *Journal of International Women's Studies* 10 (2009), 220-36, at 222; Sanne Weber, 'From Victims and Mothers to Citizens: Gender-Just Transformative Reparations and the Need for Public and Private Transitions' *International Journal of Transitional Justice* 12 (2018), 88-107, at 102.

[78] Carol Gilligan, *In a Different Voice: Psychological Theory and Women's Development* (Cambridge MA: Harvard University Press 1982), 25-31; MacKinnon in response argues that any difference in reasoning is a result of subordination; she criticises the attachment of 'feminine' reasoning to women; see Isabel Marcus and Paul Spiegelman (moderators), Ellen C DuBois et al. (conversants), 'Feminist Discourse, Moral Values and the Law – A Conversation' *Buffalo Law Review* 34 (1985), 11-87, at 74-75.

[79] Simic, 'What Remains of Srebrenica?' 2009 (n. 77), 229.

[80] Hilary Charlesworth, 'Martha Nussbaum's Feminist Internationalism' *Ethics* 111 (2000), 64-78, at 73.

[81] Fourth World Conference on Women, *Beijing Platform for Action* (New York, NY: United Nations Division for the Advancement of Women, 1995) para. 245(b); Charlesworth, 'Martha Nussbaum's Feminist Internationalism' 2000 (n. 80), 73.

to participate in the free market economy'.[82] Such a position has not changed dramatically since the 1990s. Although the Beijing Platform for Action stressed shared and equal responsibilities between men and women at home,[83] it was in 2005 that the Committee on Economic, Social and Cultural Rights recognised paternity leave as part of the right to social security,[84] but a 2019 report reviewing the implementation of the Beijing Declaration and Platform for Action found that 'only slightly more than half of all countries provided fathers with paid statutory leave entitlements, usually of relatively short duration',[85] and '[t]he provision of unpaid care and domestic work disproportionately remains women's responsibility the world over'.[86]

These ideas of 'equal sharing of responsibilities for the family by men and women' in the Beijing Declaration and Platform for Action, which is said to lead to a 'harmonious partnership [which is] critical to their well-being and that of their families'[87] constructs the image of 'mother' as tied to an image of the heterosexual married couple and the notion of a nuclear family. Discussing the right to found a family in the Yogyakarta Principles on the Application of International Human Rights Law in Relation to Sexual Orientation and Gender Identity, Otto has shown how the principles

> merely reconfigure, rather than contest the heteronormative family model. They assume, for example, that the primary purpose of the family is to procreate, that the foundational family relationship is a monogamous couple and that the interests of children will be a primary concern.[88]

Upholding the heterosexual family ignores alternative approaches to family.[89] It also fails to reflect the diversity of women's experiences;[90] as Collins

[82] Dianne Otto, 'Holding up Half the Sky, but for Whose Benefit? A Critical Analysis of the Fourth World Conference on Women' *Australian Feminist Law Journal* 6 (1996), 7-28, at 27; Charlesworth, 'Martha Nussbaum's Feminist Internationalism' 2009 (n. 80), 73.

[83] United Nations, Beijing Declaration and Platform of Action, adopted at the Fourth World Conference on Women, 27 October 1995, A/CONF.177/20 (1995), at para. 15.

[84] United Nations Committee on Economic, Social and Cultural Rights, General Comment No. 16: The Equal Right of Men and Women to the Enjoyment of All Economic, Social and Cultural Rights (Art. 3 of the Covenant), 11 August 2005, E/C.12/2005/4, at para. 2; Dianne Otto, 'Queering Gender [Identity] in International Law' *Nordic Journal of Human Rights* 33 (2015), 299-318, at 305.

[85] United Nations Economic and Social Council, Review and appraisal of the implementation of the Beijing Declaration and Platform for Action and the Outcomes of the Twenty-Third Special Session of the General Assembly, 13 December 2019, E/CN.6/2020/3, at 21.

[86] *ibid*, 20.

[87] UN, *Beijing Declaration* 1995 (n. 83), para 15.

[88] Otto, 'Queering Gender' 2015 (n. 84), 314-15, citing the 'Yogyakarta Principles on the Application of International Human Rights Law in Relation to Sexual Orientation and Gender Identity' (International Commission of Jurists, 2007) A-G.

[89] For a discussion, see Otto, 'Queering Gender' 2015 (n. 84), 314-15.

[90] For a discussion on the 'contradictory experiences' of family for Black women, see Kapur, 'The Tragedy of Victimization Rhetoric' 2002 (n. 10), 8, fn 22.

demonstrates, ideas of motherhood and family were used to oppress Black women in America.[91] Furthermore, Afrocentric feminist notions of family include Black women's experiences as othermothers that exposes the myth of the nuclear family.[92] Othermothering is where women take on caring roles for children outside blood relations, in either formal or informal arrangements, and which emerged from West African communal and interdependent living and was important as part of Black women's survival tactics and educational practices during slavery.[93] Othermothering reminds us that motherhood is not just a biological relationship, but a social relationship too. It is these examples that show motherhood as a relational experience.[94] Heathcote reminds us that 'imagining of motherhood as uniform and as experienced in the same way by women within and across communities is not only dismissive of cultural variations in meaning and understanding of maternal subjectivity but also silences the different experiences of disabled, migrant, lesbian, and trans people as mothers'.[95] A homogenous, heterosexual idea of motherhood informs international law, and excludes other experiences.

3.3 Critiquing the Caricatures

These constructed images of women rely on stereotypes that work to objectify and to oppress women.[96] These gendered characterisations arise when women are compared to the masculine universal subject, and they risk dehumanising and silencing people.[97] In highlighting the objectification of African women by international law and international legal scholarship, Dawuni argues that objectification is the 'skewed representation of women from African countries', where the focus is on 'what happens to these women, rather than what these women make happen', and as a result 'the woman becomes the object of fascination'.[98] Processes of objectification are built on the intersection of race, gender, sexuality, and class.[99]

To disrupt the objectification of African women, Dawuni calls for a process of 'subjectification', where the focus shifts to 'addressing the personal agency,

[91] Collins, *Black Feminist Thought* 2000 (n. 74).

[92] *ibid*, 178. See also Dawuni, 'Matri-Legal Feminism' 2019 (n. 28), 445.

[93] Stanlie M James, 'Mothering: A Possible Black Feminist Link to Social Transformation?', in Stanlie M James and Abena P. A. Busia (eds.), *Theorizing Black Feminisms: The Visionary Pragmatism of Black Women* (Abingdon: Routledge 2005), 45-56, at 46.

[94] Thank you to Esra Demir-Gürsel for guidance on this point. For a discussion, see Kristin Savell, 'The Mother of the Legal Person', in Susan James and Stephanie Palmer (eds.), *Visible Women: Essays on Feminist Legal Theory and Political Philosophy* (London: Hart 2013), 29-68, at 66-67.

[95] Heathcote, *Feminist Dialogues* 2019 (n. 9), 162.

[96] See discussion on stereotypes in Collins, *Black Feminist Thought* 2000 (n. 74), 69.

[97] Dawuni, 'Marti-Legal Feminism' 2019 (n. 28), 453.

[98] *ibid*, 450.

[99] See Collins, *Black Feminist Thought* 2000 (n. 74), 72.

contributions, and cultural and other forms of diversity the African woman brings to international feminist scholarship and advocacy'.[100] Dawuni's process of subjectification echoes Orford's subject-constitution.[101] Orford's discussion on the constitution of the subject shows that the processes of subjectification (or subject-constitution) and objectification are overlapping and informed by gender stereotypes and racial bias.[102] As an example of these overlapping processes, Orford, building on Gayatri Spivak's work, highlights how the construction of the White western feminist in the nineteenth century was predicated on the objectification of the 'Other'.[103]

The constructed feminine characters found in international law and imposed on women are not liberating or empowering for women.[104] The characters or stereotypes work to negate the voice of women; the use of such images can lead to paternalistic, imperialistic, and conservative responses to women's issues.[105] Images of mothers and victims 'entrench' gender dichotomies,[106] reproducing 'gendered bodies and sexed subjects'.[107] Rothermel shows how the UN Agenda for Protecting and Countering Violent Extremism combines the materialistic logic of the 'good mother' with a paternalistic logic of protecting victims, which works to construct 'women [as] the objects of policies rather than agents in their own right' and to cement the role of the State and international institutions as having 'the "power to empower"', rather than recognise the work women do to empower themselves.[108]

Feminist international legal scholarship must work to disrupt these characterisations. To do so, international feminist scholarship should ensure that discussions are intersectional and aware of the potential silencing effects of objectification, generalisations, and essentialism. Feminist approaches to the individual in international law will warrant reflexivity to account for the contextualisation. International law must consider 'multiple historically, culturally, and socially determined subjectivities instead of falling back on universalized assumptions about women's realities and their subject position'.[109] The question then becomes how to do this.

[100] Dawuni, 'Marti-Legal Feminism' 2019 (n. 28), 450.

[101] Orford, 'Feminism, Imperialism' 2002 (n. 63), 284. See also Gayatri C. Spivak, 'Can the Subaltern Speak? Speculations on Widow-Sacrifice' *WEDGE* 7/8 (1985), 120-30, at 128.

[102] Orford, 'Feminism, Imperialism' 2002 (n. 63), 283-84.

[103] *ibid.*

[104] Kapur, 'The Tragedy of Victimization Rhetoric' 2002 (n. 10), 18.

[105] *ibid*, 27.

[106] See Nadj, 'The Culturalisation of Identity in an Age of 'Ethic Conflict' 2011 (n. 42), 657; Nicola Henry, 'The Fixation on Wartime Rape: Feminist Critique and International Criminal Law' *Social & Legal Studies* 23 (2014), 93-111.

[107] Heathcote, *Feminist Dialogues* 2019 (n. 9), 100.

[108] Rothermel, 'Gender in the United Nations' 2020 (n. 57), 734.

[109] Kapur, 'The Tragedy of Victimization Rhetoric' 2002 (n. 10), 29.

4. Beyond Feminine Characters, Towards Plural Subjectivities

If, as Pearson suggests, feminist approaches to international law are about the 'who' in international law, sections 2 and 3 demonstrate the need to consider how the 'who' is constituted in international law and international legal scholarship.[110] Whilst there have been calls to reclaim 'woman' as a useful category of analysis, other scholars call for a new approach to legal subjects. In seeking to expose the failings of the male, bounded liberal subject, feminism provides a plethora of approaches, and this section will map several of them: the reclaiming of liberalism's universal subject; the 'Two Sexes Model'; the 'Gender-Hybrid Model'; the 'Resistive Subjects' model; and plural subjectivities. These different approaches demonstrate the tensions in feminist theories, but as Heathcote notes, 'shifting [to] plural legal subjects found within gender and feminist theories',[111] provides an opportunity for dialogue amongst feminisms and other critical scholarship, to think through these tensions.[112]

One feminist approach to the 'crisis of subjectivity' in feminist legal thought[113] is to re-embrace liberalism. In liberalism the individual is the basic unit of society, it 'exists prior to social organization' and is 'rational and self-interested'.[114] Feminist scholars criticise the liberal construction of the individual as anti-social; the liberal legal subject is 'self-contained'[115] and 'socially decontextualized'.[116] The liberal individual is 'stripped of embodied particularities in order to appear neutral'.[117] Feminists have highlighted how the supposed neutrality of the liberal subject is constructed on 'male attributes'.[118] For Christine Battersby, '[t]he philosophical self is male *precisely because* he is devoid of all traces of femininity [...] the very invocation of the idea of gender difference renders the legal person problematic'.[119]

[110] Pearson, 'Feminist Project(s)' 2011 (n. 17), 48.

[111] Heathcote, *Feminist Dialogues* 2019 (n. 9), 81.

[112] *ibid*, 20 and 81.

[113] Maria Drakopoulou, 'The Ethic of Care, Female Subjectivity and Feminist Legal Scholarship' *Feminist Legal Studies* 8 (2000), 199-26.

[114] Ann Scales, *Legal Feminism: Activism, Lawyering and Legal Theory* (New York, NY: New York University Press 2006), 64; also cited in Rosemary Hunter, 'Contesting the Dominant Paradigm: Feminist Critiques of Liberal Legalism', in Margaret Davies and Vanessa Munro (eds.), *Ashgate Research Companion to Feminist Legal Theory* (Dartmouth: Ashgate 2013), 13-30, at 13.

[115] Ngaire Naffine, 'Can Women be Legal Persons?', in Susan James and Stephanie Palmer (eds.), *Visible Women: Essays on Feminist Legal Theory and Political Philosophy* (Oxford: Hart 2013), 69-90, at 82.

[116] Anna Grear, 'Sexing the Matrix: Embodiment, Disembodiment and the Law – Towards the Re-gendering of Legal Rationality', in Jackie Jones et al. (eds.), *Gender, Sexualities and Law* (Abingdon: Routledge 2011), 39-52, at 44; also cited in Hunter, 'Contesting the Dominant Paradigm' 2013 (n. 114), 13.

[117] Grear, 'Sexing the Matrix' 2011 (n. 116), 39-52, at 44.

[118] Stephanie Palmer, 'Critical Perspectives on Women's Rights: The European Convention on Human Rights and Fundamental Freedoms', in Anne Bottomley (ed.), *Feminist Perspectives on the Foundational Subjects of Law* (London: Cavendish 1996), 223-42, at 225-26.

[119] Christine Battersby, *The Phenomenal Woman* (Cambridge: Polity Press 1998), 2-8; also cited in Joanne Conaghan, *Law and Gender* (Oxford: OUP 2013), 187.

However, Siobhán Mullally argues that liberalism's 'appeal to universal norms and principle' needs to be 'reclaimed' by feminists 'if feminism is to retain its critical, emancipatory edge'.[120]

Feminist scholars embracing liberalism have sought to defend the universality and abstract nature of the individual 'because it offers the possibility of articulating universal principles which are not dependent upon essentialist invocations of sex/gender'.[121] Indeed, '[g]iven the complexity and problematicity of sex and gender as categories, [some feminists have argued that] the very *sexlessness* of liberalism, once for feminists its principal weakness, in this context becomes a key strength'.[122] Elizabeth Kiss argues that the universal subject encompasses everyone and facilitates the 'inclusion of everyone in moral and social life', and it also provides 'justice for all regardless of their particular experiences or identities'.[123] Yet, it is this claim to universality and the dismissal of the particular that post-colonial, critical race, and queer feminists have criticised because it becomes based on homogenous ideas.

As noted in section 2, adopting an 'abstract' universal subject risks overlooking the specific conditions of women around the world, but focusing on these specific conditions risks further marginalisation because 'it is against those very specificities that the privileged figure of the masculine universal is defined'.[124] The tension arises through an approach that seeks to 'include' women within the individual in international law. As shown throughout this chapter, the process of including women as rights-holders, duty bearers, or as participants in international law decision-making, creates women as subjects of international law, but at the same time *how* these women are included, which can be through the use of depersonalised caricatures, objectifies women whether it is as victims, mothers, or ideal peacemakers. Otto argues that '[t]his dynamic suggests that, paradoxically, the cost of women's inclusion may be their continuing marginalisation'.[125] She doubts 'whether a focus on women's specificities will ever achieve women's full inclusion in universal representations of humanity'.[126] This demonstrates the limitations of the mere inclusion of 'woman' within the liberal individual; instead there is a need to reconceptualise what is meant by the individual as a subject of international law. A shift to a human-centric international law must also move beyond mere

[120] Mullally, *Gender, Culture and Human Rights* 2006 (n. 5), 1; also cited in Munro, *Law and Politics at the Perimeter* 2007 (n. 5), 59.

[121] Munro, *Law and Politics at the Perimeter* 2007 (n. 5); also cited in Conaghan, *Law and Gender* 2013 (n. 119), 85.

[122] Conaghan, *Law and Gender* 2013 (n. 119), 85.

[123] Elizabeth Kiss, 'Justice', in Alison M Jaggar and Iris Marion Young (eds.), *A Companion to Feminist Philosophy* (Wiley-Blackwell 1999), 487-99, at 496; also cited in Munro, *Law and Politics at the Perimeter* 2007 (n. 5), 59.

[124] Otto, 'Disconcerting "Masculinities"' 2005 (n. 7), 123-24.

[125] *ibid*, 123-24.

[126] *ibid*.

'inclusion' towards the rescripting of gender and the reframing of foundations in international law.

In the 2006 article 'Lost in translation', Otto reflects on methods for responding to the paradox of women's inclusion. For ease, I have labelled the approaches she outlines as the 'Two Sexes Model', the 'Gender-Hybrid Model' and the 'Resistive Subjects' model. She first considers the 'women's-rights-are-human-rights-strategy' (or the 'Two Sexes Model') which would reflect two sexes in human rights law instead of 'trying to force [the] masculine universal to be more gender inclusive'.[127] But she rejects this approach as further entrenching essentialism and strengthening gendered-dichotomies,[128] and she instead outlines a project of dismantling the gender-binary. She argues that 'gender must be re-scripted as something other than a dichotomy'; it should be 'multiplicitious'.[129] As humans are 'understood as constituted by a multiplicity of ideas and practices', they are 'gender hybrids'.[130] This Gender-Hybrid Model acts to dismantle the current gender hierarchies. In 2006, Otto expressed how dismantling gender hierarchies felt unachievable,[131] but Otto's work and the work of queer theorists in international law show the ever-pressing need to revisit this rescripting of gender.[132] A failure to see gender as multiple and fluid risks excluding marginalised gender-variant communities, including non-western gender identities.[133]

One prevailing concern with the 'Gender-Hybrid' model, specifically, rather than re-scripting gender more broadly, is the concern that the masculine norm of the individual would still be reasserted as the 'universal image of the hybrid'.[134] What is needed to ensure that the masculine norm does not prevail is an approach that exposes how subjects are constructed, the role of gender norms (i.e. ideas of how men and women should act) in these processes, and how these norms are resisted through everyday activities. To respond to this concern, Otto turns to Kapur's work on 'peripheral and resistive subjects' to foreground 'those subjects who disrupt the presently sexed and imperial order' of human rights law, but also international law.[135]

'Resistive subjects' are perceived as 'chaotic, disorderly and demonised "others"', who are on the fringes of society.[136] Focusing on 'resistive subjects' located outside

[127] Dianne Otto, 'Lost in Translation: Re-scripting the Sexed Subjects of International Human Rights Law', in Anne Orford (ed.), *International Law and its Others* (Cambridge: CUP 2006), 318-56, at 352-53.

[128] *ibid*, 352-53.

[129] *ibid*, 354.

[130] *ibid*, 355.

[131] Otto, 'Lost in Translation' 2006 (n. 127), 355.

[132] Dianne Otto (ed.), *Queering International Law: Possibilities, Alliances, Complicities, Risks* (Abingdon: Routledge 2019).

[133] Sandra Duffy, 'Contested Subjects of Human Rights: Trans and Gender-variant Subjects of International Human Rights Law' *Modern Law Review* 84 (2021), 1041-65.

[134] Otto, 'Lost in Translation' 2006 (n. 127), 355.

[135] Kapur, 'The Tragedy of Victimization Rhetoric' 2002 (n. 10), 29-34: also cited in Otto, 'Lost in translation' 2006 (n. 127), 355.

[136] Otto, 'Lost in Translation' 2006 (n. 127), 355.

of the Global North acts as 'a reminder to articulate gender as embedded in racialised, heteronormative, and colonial histories'.[137] But crucially, the resistive subject also shows how women challenge gendered and racial 'dichotomies and hierarchies'.[138] Kapur documents Indian women's struggles in courts and political protests to challenge the image of the Indian woman as a 'victim'.[139] Throughout their protests[140] and the court cases,[141] the Mothers of Srebrenica disrupted stereotypes of mothers as being located within the private sphere; their campaign was 'resistant to entrenched cultural expectations that women would be passive victims and that their physical bodies would largely remain in the private realm'.[142] Other examples include Sylvia Tamle's account of women's naked protests in Uganda that subvert the 'scripts of subordination' that are engraved on women's bodies.[143] Dawuni's focus on African women's individual agency works to resist the image of the 'African Woman' as a victim.[144] It is important to note that the 'resistive' subject does not seek to link agency and resistance,[145] but rather works to disrupt the 'victim' category which can work to deny women's agency. As such, this approach exposes the role of gender, race, religion, and sexuality in the construction of the 'victim' subject. Beyond accounts of the 'victim', Kapur's work shows us that rather than fixed accounts of 'woman' as the subject of feminist approaches to international law, a more 'fluid and dynamic account of subjectivity' is needed.[146]

Building on Otto's and Kapur's work, Heathcote proposes to consider 'difference as the organising methodology for feminist legal theories'.[147] To avoid replacing one universal male norm with another universal category, Heathcote moves beyond the singular example of the resistive subject to plural subjectivities, adding into conversation Rosi Braidotti's work on the 'nomadic subject' ('a cross boundary,

[137] Heathcote, *Feminist Dialogues* 2019 (n. 9), 98.

[138] Otto, 'Lost in Translation' 2006 (n. 127), 356.

[139] Kapur, 'The Tragedy of Victimization Rhetoric' 2002 (n. 10), 30-31.

[140] See Marie E Berry, *War, Women, and Power: from Violence to Mobilization in Rwanda and Bosnia-Herzegovina* (Cambridge: CUP 2018), 168.

[141] European Court of Human Rights, *Stichting Mothers of Srebrenica v. Netherlands*, Third Section, Decision of 11 June 2013, Application No. 65542/12, at paras 115-16; Jacob Katz Cogan, 'Stichting Mothers of Srebrenica v Netherlands' *American Journal of International Law* 107 (2013), 884-90, at 884; Supreme Court of The Netherlands, *Mothers of Srebrenica Association et al. v. The Netherlands*, Judgment of 19 July 2019, ECLI:NL:HR:2019:1223 (English translation: ECLI:NL:HR:2019:1284), at para 4.8.2; Cedric Ryngaert and Otto Spijkers, 'The End of the Road: State Liability for Acts of UN Peacekeeping Contingents After the Dutch Supreme Court's Judgment in Mothers of Srebrenica' *Netherlands International Law Review* 66 (2019), 537-53, at 551.

[142] Berry, *War, Women, and Power* 2018 (n. 140), 168.

[143] Sylvia Tamale, 'Nudity, Protest and the Law in Uganda' *Feminist Africa* 22 (2017), 52-86, at 79.

[144] Dawuni, 'Marti-Legal Feminism' 2019 (n. 28), 446.

[145] Kapur, 'The Tragedy of Victimization Rhetoric' 2002 (n. 10), 37; For a discussion on the concern of linking agency with resistance, see Esra Demir-Gürsel, 'The Distinction Between the Freedom of Religion and the Right to Manifest Religion: A Legal Medium to Regulate Subjectivities' *Social & Legal Studies* 22 (2013), 377-93, at 385.

[146] Heathcote, *Feminist Dialogues* 2019 (n. 9), 100.

[147] Heathcote, 'On Feminist Legal Methodologies' 2018 (n. 4), 11.

stateless post-human' and 'multicultural individual'),[148] and Avtar Brah's work on 'diasporic subjects' (which disrupts the identity politics based on nation-States as the 'migrant's multi-located sense of belonging').[149] Plural subjectivities are situated in 'specific geo-political and historical locations',[150] showcasing the diversity of lived experiences[151] and disrupting the fixed categorisations of women. Their metaphorical focus on movement across borders reflects the continually changing nature of the subject,[152] as well as challenging the nation-centric position of the individual in international law.[153] Combining the peripheral, nomadic, and diasporic subjects, Heathcote demonstrates how there can be no 'fixed account' of the individual in international law.[154] Rather, feminist approaches should look to a 'fluid and dynamic account of subjectivity'.[155]

Plural subjectivities, predicated on difference as the organising principle,[156] necessitates the reframing of the individual and international law. If the individual of liberalism is disrupted by gendered difference,[157] the plurality of difference in Heathcote's approach fractures the idealised subject of the individual in international law. Feminists challenge binaries such as, male/female, woman/man, and public/private. These binaries should be understood as being more fluid.[158] As such, the subject-object binary in positivist approaches to international law is drawn into question.[159] The discussions in feminist scholarship on the 'characters' in international law demonstrate how the binary between subject-object continues to work to uphold gender inequalities: as women are constructed as subjects in international law, there are pervasive stereotypes that objectify and dehumanise women. Arguably, this means that a shift in the international legal literature to 'participants'[160] or a human-centric approach might not move us away from the pervasive subject-object distinction. What is needed is a focus on the ongoing

[148] Rosi Braidotti, *Nomadic Subjects: Embodiment and Sexual Difference in Contemporary Feminist Theory* (2nd edn, New York, NY: Columbia University Press 2011).

[149] See Heathcote, 'On Feminist Legal Methodologies' 2018 (n. 4), 13 referencing Avtar Brah, *Cartographies of Diaspora: Contesting Identities* (Abingdon: Routledge 1996).

[150] Rosi Braidotti, 'Writing as a Nomadic Subject' *Comparative Critical Studies* 11 (2014), 163-84, at 180.

[151] Heathcote, 'On Feminist Legal Methodologies' 2018 (n. 4), 12.

[152] Braidotti, 'Writing as a Nomadic Subject' 2014 (n. 150), 171-73.

[153] *ibid*, 179; Heathcote, 'On Feminist Legal Methodologies' 2018 (n. 4), 11.

[154] Heathcote, 'On Feminist Legal Methodologies' 2018 (n. 4), 13.

[155] *ibid*, 13-14.

[156] *ibid*, 11.

[157] Battersby, *The Phenomenal Woman* 1998 (n. 119), 2-8; Conaghan, *Law and Gender* 2013 (n. 119), 187.

[158] Otto, 'Queering Gender' 2015 (n. 84), 309.

[159] See the discussions in Robert McCorquodale, 'The Individual and the International Legal System', in Malcolm Evans (ed.), *International Law* (5th edn, Oxford: OUP 2018), 259-86, at 260-61.

[160] Rosalyn Higgins, *Problems and Process: International Law and How We Use It* (Oxford: OUP 1994), 49-50. McCorquodale argues that 'participant', rather than the subject vs object conceptual framework is more useful. See McCorquodale, 'The Individual' 2018 (n. 159), 301.

processes of objectification to resist an essentialised subject and move beyond reductive caricatures.

5. A Call for Ongoing Dialogues on the Individual in International Law

Heathcote's 'plural subjects' emerge from the 'shifting plural legal subjects found within gender and feminist theories',[161] and in that respect Heathcote offers a way to think through the debates between different feminisms. Otto and Heathcote call for dialogues between feminist, queer, intersectional, and post-colonial feminisms and theories.[162] As such, the shift to plural subjectivities can be brought into conversation with Andersson's 'contextualised legal subject',[163] which reiterates the structural and discursive factors that work to construct a subject. Contextualising a legal subject requires reflection on gender, class, sexuality, race, ethnicity, as well as history, to understand all 'other factors relevant to their life experience'.[164] Bringing the 'contextualised legal subject' into conversation with a 'resistive subject', shows the importance of understanding both the dynamics of structural norms on the construction of the subject and how people navigate, conform with, or resist these norms. If, as Otto notes, focusing on women's specificities can risk further marginalisation,[165] the complex specificities of contextualised plural subjects demonstrate the need to reframe international law away from the liberal individual, and away from an approach that seeks only to 'include' women in the universal individual subject.

The contextualised 'plural subjectivities' is useful for conversations across feminist perspectives of international law because it asks feminists to consider 'the effect of additional power differentials'.[166] It is a mechanism that opens up the 'assumptions of feminist approaches rather than being limited to participation or quotas for inclusion'.[167] Whilst liberal feminists call for equal gender participation (and even quotas) in international institutions and decision-making, other feminists call for broader discussions on who is included and excluded in these processes.[168] The World Bank ESF is a useful example for unpacking this broader question of 'inclusion'. The World Bank consultation process for the ESF was

161 Heathcote, *Feminist Dialogues* 2019 (n. 9), 81.
162 Otto, 'Queering Gender' 2015 (n. 84), 300; Heathcote, *Feminist Dialogues* 2019 (n. 9).
163 Andersson, 'Trafficking in Human Beings' 2011 (n. 15), 177 and 179.
164 Alice Edwards, 'From the Margins to the Mainstream and Back Again', in Sari Kouvo and Zoe Pearson (eds.), *Feminist Perspectives on Contemporary International Law: Between Resistance and Compliance* (Oxford: Hart 2011), 133-36, at 135.
165 Otto, 'Disconcerting "Masculinities"' 2005 (n. 7), 123-24.
166 Heathcote, *Feminist Dialogues* 2019 (n. 9), 3.
167 *ibid*, 14.
168 For a discussion, see *ibid*, 153.

heralded as a 'global' endeavour, reaching 8,000 stakeholders across sixty-three countries. It provides an example of individuals, civil society, investors, states, and international organisations as participants in the creation of soft law. Yet, a study of the consultation process reveals the limitations. For example, access was limited both because of the short-notice periods and the geographical location of meetings. This worked to further marginalise marginalised communities and meant they were less likely to be heard in the consultation process. At times, there was a failure to consider the 'contextualised subjectivities' of individuals wishing to participate, including the geographical remoteness of communities, a failure to consider access to translators for local languages, and disabled access and Braille documentation not always being available.[169] This consultation exercise shows that mere 'inclusion' of individuals as participants within decision-making processes is not sufficient. A feminist, plural subjectivities critique of this World Bank consultation would highlight the power differentials between the different stakeholders participating that shaped who was listened to, the need for more attention to the contextualised plural subjectivities of persons to ensure voices are heard, and a reflection on who was included and who was excluded in the process.[170]

Use of plural subjectivities is important for feminist international legal academics as well. As Rosemary Hunter notes, the representations of women by feminist scholars can be 'as rigid, limiting, constraining, totalizing and oppressive as legal representations'.[171] Heathcote cautions that the 'failure to attend to' plural subjectivities 'perpetuates the reassertion of the status quo that pivots on a version of humanity and subjectivity drawn from the Western enlightenment man that haunts legal liberalism'.[172] To mitigate that risk, feminists writing on international law 'need to remain aware of our own historical location, avoid one-dimensional representations, present subjects as complex and multi-dimensional'.[173] The plural subjectivities approach helps to avoid the risks of essentialism and moves away from the reductive feminine caricatures that are found in international law through ongoing reflexive conversations across feminist, queer, post-colonial, and intersectional theories. A plural subjectivities approach is not limited to feminist approaches to the individual; it should be used to inform mainstream international law.[174]

[169] Ruth Houghton, 'Looking at the World Bank's Safeguard Reform through the Lens of Deliberative Democracy' *Leiden Journal of International Law* 32 (2019), 465-82, at 475-76; for a discussion on consultation processes for the SDGs, see Struckmann, 'A postcolonial feminist critique' 2018 (n. 56), 21.

[170] See Heathcote, *Feminist Dialogues* 2019 (n. 9), 153.

[171] Hunter, 'Contesting the Dominant Paradigm' 2013 (n. 114), 18.

[172] Heathcote, *Feminist Dialogues* 2019 (n. 9), 80.

[173] Ratna Kapur, *Erotic Justice: Law and the New Politics of Postcolonialism* (London: Glass House Press 2005), 128-31; Hunter, 'Contesting the Dominant Paradigm' 2013 (n. 114), 18.

[174] See Hilary Charlesworth, 'Talking to Ourselves? Feminist Scholarship in International Law', in Sari Kouvo and Zoe Pearson (eds.), *Feminist Perspectives on Contemporary International Law: Between Resistance and Compliance* (Oxford: Hart 2011), 17-32, at 17.

The models and approaches outlined in the previous section indicate the tensions across feminist theories, which oscillate between the universal and the particular. However, the plural subjectivities approach, built on subjectivities across feminist, post-colonial, and queer theories, facilitates a reflexive dialogue on these tensions. It negates a singular response to the nature of the individual in international law. A feminist human-centric approach to international law should be alert to the risks of essentialism as well as the complex processes of objectification that can also give rise to dehumanised essentialised images of people. By shifting to focus on plural subjectivities and by ensuring reflexivity on the nature of the individual in international law, a feminist human-centric international law can mitigate these risks.

6. Conclusion

Asking the 'woman' question can disrupt the state as the primary subject in international law by highlighting the work done by women and women's networks. Asking the 'woman' question also gives rise to a debate on whether women can be included within the universal subject of liberalism. The problems that arise from that process of inclusion lead to discussions that challenge the very foundations of international law. The first sections of this chapter, picking up on Otto's critiques, demonstrated the pitfalls of 'including' women within international human rights law and international law, as both are predicated on the universal liberal subject. The gender-mainstreaming that has occurred in specific areas of international law has constructed a series of feminine characters, such as mothers and victims, as well as entrenching an essentialised idea of 'woman'. Part of this process of inclusion, then, is the process of objectification, where racialised and gendered imagery is used. To avoid replicating gendered and racialised hierarchies in a feminist human-centric approach to international law, this chapter suggests four principles: first, a responsiveness to the risks of essentialism; second, resisting the proliferation of feminine 'characters' in international law; third, the need for contextualised plural subjectivities,[175] and fourth, ongoing reflexive dialogues across feminisms.

Rather than seeking merely to include women within a universal subject of the individual, Otto and Heathcote argue for a rethinking of the foundations of international law. Combining peripheral, nomadic, and diasporic subjects, Heathcote centres 'plural subjectivities'. Starting from 'plural subjectivities' requires different foundations of international law as plural subjects challenge the binaries of male-female and object-subject, as well as gendered and racialised hierarchies. As this

[175] Heathcote, *Feminist Dialogues* 2019 (n. 9), 72.

chapter demonstrates, there is no singular approach to the question of the subject in feminist approaches to law, and therefore dialogues across feminist theories, as well as including queer, post-colonial, and other theories are needed. A feminist human-centric approach to international law, built on 'plural subjectivities', will require further and ongoing dialogues that centre the need to contextualise plural subjects, considering gender, race, sexuality, ableism, and class.

13
A Marxist Account of the Individual in International Law

*Marina Veličković**

1. Introduction

Karl Marx was far fonder of individuals than he was of law.[1] I base this conclusion not on what he has written about the individual, but rather on what he has written about the law. While his position on law is relatively straightforward (he had such distaste for it that he imagined it becoming obsolete), his account of the individual is both more convoluted and quite contradictory. These are the four things that we do know. For Marx individuals are determined by the historical epoch in which they live; specifically: their relationship to nature, to their own labour, and to their fellow humans is defined by the dominant mode of production.[2] Further, an individual is not unique because they are imbued with intrinsic properties other animals do not have, instead, productivity through which they create both their material world and their sense of self is what ultimately makes them different.[3] In capitalism an individual is defined by the fact that landlessness forces them to sell their labour for a wage, thus constantly commodifying a part of themselves. Finally, an individual can only be free in communism, because it is only then that they will be able to achieve their full individuality.[4] Individuality stands for freedom to explore any branch or vocation, and engage in and become accomplished in as many

* This chapter has benefited greatly from feedback by Kirsten Campbell, Robert Knox, Ntina Tzouvala, Ruth Houghton, Justina Uriburu, and Haris Husarić. I am also indebted to the meticulous work of the commentator (Kanad Bagchi), reviewers (Bhupinder S. Chimni and Gleider Hernández), and editors (Tom Sparks and Anne Peters). Finally, I owe immense thanks to Alma Midžić, who selflessly shared her knowledge and resources with me, helping me get a better understanding of environmental activism in the Balkans.

[1] Marx was critical of abstract individuals, but apparently quite fond of 'living human individuals': Ian Forbes, *Marx and the New Individual* (London: Unwin Hyman 1990), 30-33.

[2] This means that a person is not an abstract thing, and their characteristics are not universal characteristics of all people; Karl Marx, 'Private Property and Communism', in *Economic and Philosophic Manuscripts* (1844), available at: https://www.marxists.org/archive/marx/works/1844/manuscripts/comm.htm, accessed 7/7/23; Forbes, *New Individual* 1990 (n. 1), 45.

[3] Karl Marx, 'Part I: Feuerbach. Opposition of the Materialist and Idealist Outlook', in *The German Ideology* (1845), available at: https://www.marxists.org/archive/marx/works/1845/german-ideology/ch01a.htm, accessed 7/7/23.

[4] Marx, *German Ideology* 1845 (n. 3).

Marina Veličković, *A Marxist Account of the Individual in International Law* In: *The Individual in International Law*. Edited by: Tom Sparks and Anne Peters, Oxford University Press. © Marina Veličković 2024.
DOI: 10.1093/oso/9780198898917.003.0013

activities as one may wish,[5] or to put it differently, it stands for 'real, substantive freedom, participation, equality, and self development'.[6]

I take this as my starting point and ask: can international law have a meaningful role in transition from capitalism to communism, thus contributing to the establishment of material conditions which would enable human individuality? I argue that it cannot because the logic of capitalism is embedded in its very form, making it impossible for international law to overcome its history of complicity in violence and dispossession (section 2). I then ask a second question: are there still ways in which individuals can use international law (specifically international human rights law) in struggles which are anti-capitalist and emancipatory?[7] To answer this question, I first outline Marxist critiques of human rights (section 3), and I then explore the ways in which the limitations that Marxist scholars point out have been negotiated by activists in practice (section 4). Drawing on the work of environmental activists in Bosnia and Herzegovina I argue that there may be some utility in using human rights to articulate radical demands in institutional settings, but I ultimately conclude that law cannot and should not be at the centre of emancipatory movements.

2. Marxist Conceptions of International Law

To explore whether and in what ways international law might help bring about the end of capitalism I resort to history and theory. I turn to Marxist accounts of history of international law because they problematise the liberal narratives of international law as a mark of human progress. Instead, in a Marxist retelling international law emerges as central to dispossession of land and resources and to the violence inherent in that. First, I draw on Bhupinder S. Chimni to tease out the ways in which international law has historically played the role of a handmaiden to capitalism,[8] and then I refer to Ntina Tzouvala's work to argue that this alliance is not a thing of the past. I finally turn to theory to propose that international law is unlikely to abandon its role in the reproduction and expansion of global capitalism in the future, because the logic of capitalism is embedded in its very form.

[5] *ibid.*

[6] Bartholomew terms this 'rich individuality': Amy Bartholomew, 'Should a Marxist Believe in Human Rights' *The Socialist Register* 26 (1990), 244-64, at 254-55.

[7] I conceptualise emancipation as a process of subversive action which could eventually lead to individuality.

[8] In particular, I draw here on Chimni's periodisation of historical epochs. He charts five periods in the history of international law: old colonialism (1500-1760), new colonialism (1760-1875), imperialism (1875-1945), neocolonialism (1945-85), and global imperialism (1985-); Bhupinder S. Chimni, *International Law and World Order: A Critique of Contemporary Approaches* (Cambridge: CUP 2017), 442 and 480.

2.1 A Marxist History of International Law

A Marxist reading of history is a materialist reading, which means that ideas cannot be studied separately from the mode of production in the epoch of their genesis; or more simply, for Marxists ideas are always tied to material conditions in the society from which they emerge.[9] I offer a brief sketch of what different junctures in international law might look like if viewed through a Marxist lens.

We begin with 'Old colonialism': an era of primitive accumulation of land and resources which enabled European transition from feudalism to capitalism.[10] While this process cannot be viewed separately from domestic processes of land enclosures, its distinctiveness in creating a regime of racialised exploitation needs to be underscored.[11] Central to this project was the legal constitution of indigenous populations as less human than the White European colonisers. Brown and black bodies were stripped of their humanity and turned into commodities.[12] Viewed from this perspective international humanity was formed through a process of dehumanisation. White humanity could appear universal, because those who were racialised were dehumanised; European humanity could appear global, because those from the periphery were not perceived as subjects of humanity; mercantile humanity could appear humane because those who were exploited for it were considered inhuman. Power to define humanity was then also power to dehumanise, and historically international law was not external to this process, but essential to it. Antony Anghie's work is also hugely important here.[13] Further, a materialist reading of history of international law would also reflect on the ways in which the natural law doctrines of the hugely influential Salamanca School historically developed in response to colonial expansion; as a way of legalising and legitimating colonial violence.[14] This way of reframing history shows how ideas evolved in response to the material conditions at the time of their genesis.

The second stage—new colonialism—was a departure from 'the backwardness of the manufacturing sector in Europe' which had marked the age of the old colonialism.[15] 'New colonialism' saw a shift in policy so that colonies were used

[9] Susan Marks, 'Introduction', in Susan Marks (ed.), *International Law on the Left: Re-Examining Marxist Legacies* (Cambridge: CUP 2008), 1-29, at 2; China Miéville, 'The Commodity-Form Theory Of International Law', in Susan Marks (ed.), *International Law on the Left: Re-Examining Marxist Legacies* (Cambridge: CUP 2008), 92-132, at 96-97; Robert Knox, 'Marxist Approaches to International Law', in Anne Orford and Florian Hoffmann (eds.), *The Oxford Handbook of the Theory of International Law* (Oxford: OUP 2016), 306-29, at 307.

[10] Chimni, *International Law and World Order* 2017 (n. 8), 481.

[11] *ibid*, 481-85; Robert Knox, 'Valuing race? Stretched Marxism and the logic of imperialism' *London Review of International Law* 4 (2016), 81-126.

[12] Knox, 'Valuing Race' 2016 (n. 11), 108-112.

[13] Anthony Anghie, *Imperialism, Sovereignty and the Making of International Law* (Cambridge: CUP 2005).

[14] For more on this, see Martti Koskenniemi, 'Empire and International Law: The Real Spanish Contribution' *University of Toronto Law Journal* 61 (2011), 1-36.

[15] Chimni, *International Law and World Order* 2017 (n. 8), 486.

more for market expansion and less for resource extraction.[16] The third stage was nineteenth-century imperialism, which was marked by an increase in inter-imperialist competition for space and resources.[17] The contemporaneous turn to positivism in international law provided a theoretical framework in which State will could be centred and *simultaneously* limited to 'civilised societies' thus excluding the periphery.[18] Similarly to how divinity was necessary to legitimate claims to land, rationality was necessary to legitimate the logic of the capitalist market. The intellectual shift from natural international law to positive international law is then in this materialist account reframed as a consequence of the shift from the primitive accumulation stage of capitalism in which international law was used to accumulate land and resources, to the imperialist stage of capitalism in which international law was used to expand the reach of the domestic market.

This was followed by the two final stages: neocolonialism which Chimni describes as subjugation of newly independent States through 'transnational corporations and banks, unequal exchange, a system of conditionalities […] and manipulative aid',[19] and 'global imperialism'.[20] For Chimni the end goal of 'global imperialism' is the creation of a global economic space, in which goods, capital, and services could move freely.[21]

Ntina Tzouvala's book looks at the past to offer insight in how this (dystopian) future might come about. Tzouvala argues that the ideas of non-western inferiority and of the possibility that this could be remedied through the influx of western capital has been constitutive of modern international law.[22] In the book, Tzouvala links the nineteenth-century concept of the 'standard of civilisation' with the expansion of the capitalist mode of production.[23] She argues that 'the "standard of civilisation" oscillated between two logics': the 'logic of improvement', which premised equality of States on 'comprehensive internal reform in accordance with the imperatives of capitalist modernity', and the 'logic of biology', which made such equality impossible by designating non-western communities as inferior.[24] Tzouvala then explores how this pattern of argument was used in different historical epochs to legitimate the global expansion of capitalism. Of particular interest here is her chapter on the occupation of Iraq and the war in Syria, in which she explores how the language of 'civilisation' has survived in the age of neoliberalism, enabling western administrations of non-western States to implement neoliberal

[16] *ibid*, 487.
[17] *ibid*, 489-96.
[18] China Miéville, *Between Equal Rights: A Marxist Theory of International Law* (Leiden: Brill 2005), 240-43; see also Ntina Tzouvala, *Capitalism as Civilisation: A History of International Law* (Cambridge: CUP 2020), chapter 2, at 44-87.
[19] Chimni, *International Law and World Order* 2017 (n. 8), 497.
[20] *ibid*, 506-07.
[21] *ibid*, 507.
[22] Tzouvala, *Capitalism as Civilisation* 2020 (n. 18), 1.
[23] *ibid*, 44-46.
[24] *ibid*.

reforms under the banner of the international rule of law.[25] Tzouvala's work then demonstrates that the world need not be borderless so that movement of goods, capital, and services across borders could be free, it merely needs to become entirely civilised. It also demonstrates that the future, with the exception of small pockets of resistance, is already here.

2.2 History vs Theory

And yet, despite this bloody history, Marxist international legal scholars disagree about the potential for international law to be meaningfully reformed. In this section I provide an overview of their different positions about the 'potentialities of law to achieve change and redistribution'.[26] Or, to put it more succinctly, I consider: according to these different readings, can international law be a part of a socialist international? And what, if any, significance does this have for the individual?

The most enthusiastic believer in the potential for reform is Bhupinder S. Chimni. His integrated approach to Marxist international law (IMAIL) integrates Marxism, feminism, and third world approaches to law (TWAIL) to develop a multifocal lens through which to critique international law's complicity in injustice.[27] What sets IMAIL apart from Marxist theory that preceded it is its belief in the possibility of reform of international law. As Akbar Rasulov argues in his review of Chimni's book, this work is particularly refreshing because it attempts to integrate profound critique and a deep commitment to international law.[28] However, Chimni's agenda for reform falls short.[29] His vision of reformed international law is determined by what the system is not: neither in the service of global capitalism, nor built on international socialism. Instead, this new international law tries to thread a middle path between two political systems which Chimni sees as having blood on their hands.[30] But beyond this contour there is little to pin one's hopes on, and the absence of detail in Chimni's account of possibilities stands in sharp contrast with his exceptionally detailed critique.[31]

In contrast, Susan Marks warns against basing one's progressive critique on international law, but she stops short of concluding that law has no emancipatory

[25] *ibid*, 167-211. See also Ntina Tzouvala, 'Food for the Global Market: The Neoliberal Reconstruction of Agriculture in Occupied Iraq (2003-4) and the Role of International Law' *Global Jurist* 1 (2017), 117-24.

[26] I owe my gratitude for this phrasing to Justina Uriburu.

[27] Chimni, *International Law and World Order* 2017 (n. 8), 499-550.

[28] Akbar Rasulov, 'A Marxism for International Law: A New Agenda' *European Journal of International Law* 29 (2018), 631-55.

[29] *ibid*, 651-53.

[30] Chimni, *International Law and World Order* 2017 (n. 8), 543-50.

[31] The 'Alternative Futures' section of the book is merely seven pages long, in comparison to over 100 pages outlining IMAIL, and the total book length of over 600 pages.

potential.[32] However, it is important to note that for Marks this emancipatory potential lies in the critique of the system rather than in the system itself. For Marks then, individuals have a bigger role to play: their emancipation might not be achieved through law (passive), but through critique (active). Robert Knox, unlike Chimni and Marks, is more committed to Marxism than to international law, and so he sees international law as potentially useful only to the extent to which it can be used to erode the capitalist legal order.[33] In his pivotal piece on strategy and tactics in international law, Knox argues that international law can be used tactically to achieve strategic aims of the Marxist political project.[34] However, he also cautions that there is a danger that each attempt to engage with liberal international law on its own terms may strengthen it instead of weakening it, and that this possibility of co-optation should factor into strategic decision-making.[35] Knox's account, in particular, opens up space for individuals to engage with international law *on their own terms*. The key difference between Chimni and Marks on the one hand, and Knox on the other, is that Knox does not conceptualise individuals through their relationship to international law (they are not merely rights-holders, law-makers, or even critics), but rather as political subjects for whom international law is no more than a tool at their disposal. Whether and how they use this tool is to be determined by them, in the context of their local political struggles.

Finally, in contrast to Knox, China Miéville rejects any possibility that international law may serve emancipatory aims; for him, international law can never be extricated from imperialism, and it could never serve any master other than global capital.[36] This outright dismissal does not leave any space for individuals to try and subvert international law; there is no choice to be had about its potential utility in broader political struggles. Where Knox leaves some space for agency of his individual subject, Miéville lets structure entirely subsume the space for resistance.

Miéville's scepticism is not merely historical. Drawing on Evgeny Pashukanis's commodity-form theory of law Miéville argues that in capitalism the logic of commodity exchange is embedded in the very form of international law. This means that even if international law can overcome its history, it is trapped by its internal logic. Commodity-form theory is woven together from three inter-related claims: that 'the logic of the legal form is the logic of the commodity form';[37] that form determines the content of law, rather than that form can be derived from an analysis of content;[38] and finally that violence is inherent in law.[39]

[32] Susan Marks, 'International Judicial Activism and the Commodity-Form Theory of International Law' *European Journal of International Law* 18 (2007), 199-211, at 202.

[33] Robert Knox, 'Marxism, International law and Political Strategy' *Leiden Journal of International Law* 22 (2009), 413-36; Robert Knox, 'Strategy and Tactics' *Finnish Yearbook of International Law* 21 (2010), 194-229.

[34] Knox, 'Strategy and Tactics' 2010 (n. 33).

[35] Knox, 'Political Strategy' 2009 (n. 33), 435.

[36] Miéville, *Between Equal Rights* 2005 (n. 18), 8.

[37] Miéville, 'The Commodity-Form' 2008 (n. 9), 106.

[38] *ibid*, 107 and 180-20.

[39] *ibid*, 116.

The first claim is based on a materialist reading of legal history. In capitalism, classes were constituted through the process of primitive accumulation in which the working class lost its access to its means of subsistence and in which the capitalist class emerged as owners of previously commonly owned natural resources.[40] Capitalism is then marked by the violent separation of the working class from their means of (re)production, which forces the working class to sell its labour for wages in order to ensure its own survival.[41] Further, as Umut Özsu demonstrates in his work on primitive accumulation, this process is not merely historical, it is ongoing.[42] Law plays a central role in masking this fundamental inequality and presenting this exchange of labour for wages as an exchange among equal parties.[43] Law enables the conceptualisation of individuals as abstract, legal subjects. Pashukanis argues that the constitution of all subjects of law as formally equal is a form of fetishisation because this formal equality conceals material inequality.[44] For him, fetishism is implicit in the commodity-form, and so this process is not an unfortunate side effect of law's operation, rather it is central to the very form of law in global capitalism. Akin to domestic law's role in masking inequality between individuals, international law conceals inequality between States. International law presumes that all States are equally sovereign and thus engage in commodity exchange on equal terms.[45]

The second and third claims are closely related. For Pashukanis, the function of the legal form is to regulate social relations, and so the form can only be rooted in particular relationships (material reality) and cannot be derived from the content of law (legal provisions). Instead, rules 'are secondary, and [. . .] their specific content is contingent'.[46] Further, since the function of the legal form is to facilitate commodity exchange, and commodity exchange implies the possibility of ownership (and thus of power to exclude others from use), violence is implicit in the legal form.[47] In domestic settings the State has a monopoly on violence and so violence implicit in the legal form is violence of the State;[48] in international law, however, the absence of a sovereign means that what determines disputes is the violence

[40] For an explanation of primitive accumulation, see Knox, 'Marxist Approaches' 2016 (n. 9), 311. For more on the role of international law in primitive accumulation, see Mark Neocleous, 'International Law as Primitive Accumulation; Or, the Secret of Systemic Colonization' *European Journal of International Law* 23 (2012), 941-62; Umut Özsu, 'Grabbing Land Legally: A Marxist Analysis' *Leiden Journal of International Law* 32 (2019), 215-33.

[41] Knox, 'Marxist Approaches' 2016 (n. 9), 310-12.

[42] Özsu, 'Grabbing Land Legally' 2019 (n. 40).

[43] Knox, 'Marxist Approaches' 2016 (n. 9), 310-12.

[44] Evgeny Pashukanis, 'International Law', in Piers Beirne and Robert Sharlet (eds.), *Pashukanis: Selected Writings on Marxism and Law* (first published 1925, this edn: London: Academic Press 1980), 180-81.

[45] *ibid*; Miéville, 'The Commodity-Form' 2008 (n. 9), 75-116.

[46] Miéville, 'The Commodity-Form' 2008 (n. 9), 107.

[47] *ibid*, 116.

[48] Walter Benjamin, 'Critique of Violence', in Marcus Bullock and Michael W. Jennings (eds.), *Walter Benjamin: Selected Writings* (Cambridge, MA: Belknap Press of Harvard University Press 1996).

of the participants.[49] According to Miéville, what makes international law specific is that 'violence retains its particularistic, rather than abstract impersonal (State) character'.[50] However, since States are materially unequal, their capacity for coercion is also unequal; and since content of law is determined through coercion, it follows that different States can influence the development of legal content to different extents.[51] The fetishised equality of States then does not only conceal their material inequality, it also helps obscure how this inequality shapes legal content.

While Miéville's (and Pashukanis's) argument that the link between international law and capitalism is not merely historical, and that instead the logic of capitalism is imbedded in the logic of law is persuasive, it could also be critiqued as overly State-centric, in that it does not account for any other international legal actors whose economic power could challenge the primacy of States. The account assumes a permanence of States as units of socio-economic organisation; and their continued relevance in global affairs. Moreover, the account also reifies international law, and it fails to account for its very real contradictions and gaps, for the chinks in the seemingly impenetrable armour. Despite his profound critique, Miéville's book still tells a story of law, with the world within which it exists only appearing at the margins.

And this is the point: the question whether international law can be reformed is a question about international law, asked on international law's terms. It assumes the centrality of international law to Marxism; it assumes that to arrive at a political future of our choosing we must do something *about* international law: reform it, critique it, scrap it. In the remainder of the chapter I am interested in a different question: what, if anything, can individuals do *with* international law? It is true that the world of rich individuality that Marx envisioned is not the world of international law, but that does not mean that international law cannot provide tools which can help individuals participate in the slow process of social change. Or to translate this into Robert Knox's famous terminology—perhaps international law can still have *tactical* utility, even if engagement with it cannot serve the strategic goals of Marxism.

3. Is There Marx in International Law?

In this section, I first consider whether a materialist account of history is compatible with the idea that individuals can play a role in historical change. Then, I explore the potential for international human rights law to be used as means for individuals to engage with international law in ways that are emancipatory. I argue

[49] Miéville, 'The Commodity-Form' 2008 (n. 9), 117.
[50] *ibid*, 118.
[51] *ibid*, 120.

that indeterminacy and breadth, which have often been launched as critiques of human rights, can actually become tools for social movements. Finally, I explore *how* environmental activists from Bosnia and Herzegovina used human rights in their struggle for the preservation of a local river: I consider what kinds of victories they gained through law and what battles they have chosen to conduct on different terrain.

3.1 Moving Beyond the Agency vs Structure Debate

If we accept that individuality is the end point of social transition to communism, the question that remains is: what role can individuals play in this historical process? Answers to this range from a total rejection of human capacity to effect historical change,[52] to arguments that Marxism can be a useful tool for elucidating the complex relationship between human agency and structure,[53] and they often depend on the authors' disciplinary quest.[54] Most useful for my current enquiry is the strand of scholarship which explores the ways in which Marxism can illuminate our understanding of the role of individual in actual processes of social change.[55] For example, Ian Forbes proposes that materialism is not a rejection of social transmission and evolution of ideas, instead it is a call to ground the cognitive in the historical.[56] This means that concrete human individuals can play a role in 'intergenerational cognitive progress' or more simply, in social change.[57]

However, it is important to emphasise the role of community in Marx's writing. According to Marx individuality can only be achieved in a community, because it is 'only in community with others' that each individual has 'the means of cultivating his gifts in all directions'.[58] This is particularly relevant in the context of resisting neoliberalism and its individualising tendencies. David Harvey describes the key features of neoliberalism as 'strong private property rights, free market

[52] Forbes highlights Althusser as the main advocate of this position: see Forbes, *New Individual* 1990 (n. 1), 1-13.

[53] Derek Layder, 'Problems in Accounting for the Individual in Marxist-Rationalist Theoretical Discourse' *British Journal of Sociology* 30 (1979), 149-63.

[54] For a sociology perspective, see Layder, 'Marxist-Rationalist Theoretical Discourse' 1979 (n. 53). For an anthropological reading, see Lawrence Krader, 'Marxist Anthropology: Principles and Contradictions, New Perspectives in the Science of Man, Part 1: Society Individual and Person' *International Review of Social History* 20 (1975), 236-72; Lawrence Krader, 'The Dialectical Critique of the Nature of Human Nature' *Critique of Anthropology* 2 (1976), 4-22. For a view from philosophy, see Adam Schaff, *Marxism and the Human Individual* (New York, NY: McGraw-Hill 1970); and see also Michael H. Mitias, 'Marx and the Human Individual' *Studies in Soviet Thought* 12 (1972), 245-54.

[55] Forbes, *New Individual* 1990 (n. 1), 60-62.

[56] *ibid.*

[57] *ibid.*

[58] Marx, *German Ideology* 1845 (n. 3). See also Marshall Berman, *All that is Solid Melts Into Air* (New York, NY: Penguin Books 1988), 97-98.

and free trade',[59] a shift from manufacture to financialisation,[60] and a turn towards 'deregulation, privatisation, and withdrawal of the State from many areas of social provision'.[61] Neoliberalism has led to the dispossession of the working classes and unprecedented enrichment of the elites under the banner of promotion and protection of individual freedom.[62] These material conditions have produced a neoliberal individual: existentially insecure, trapped in precarious employment, limited in their exercise of their political freedoms due to the rise of technological corporations which control the boundaries of free speech, privacy, and democratic decision-making.[63] Moreover, in recent years, with the rise of 'influencer culture' individuals themselves have become brands, ultimately collapsing the distinction between the self and the commodity. Neoliberal individuals are thus alienated and isolated, and so further quest for individual liberty is not likely to prove emancipatory.

Further, if we take the centrality of international law to global neoliberalism on the one hand, and the centrality of rhetoric of individualism to neoliberalism on the other, we might wonder whether the push for increased prominence of individuals in international law might in fact be a sign of law's neoliberalisation, and not of its humanisation. Therefore, in an act of resistance, I conceptualise the individual who engages with human rights as a part of an organised struggle. They are not acting by themselves and for themselves, instead they are a symbol of a larger movement.[64] International human rights then must provide means for individual, as well as for community emancipation. This emancipation entails the end of capitalism, so international human rights would have to provide the tools which could help this process of economic transition. Emancipation is a dialectic process, and so the question is not whether international human rights can end capitalism (arguably no *single* thing can), instead the question is whether and in what ways they might be useful for emancipatory struggles along the way.

3.2 Top Marx for Human Rights?

I start this section with a brief outline of Marx's relationship with rights which was, contrary to common belief, not entirely antagonistic.[65] I then explore two Marxist

59 David Harvey, *Neoliberalism* (Oxford: OUP 2005), 2.
60 *ibid*, 32-33.
61 *ibid*, 3.
62 *ibid*, 16.
63 *ibid*, 69.
64 I return to this point in section 4 when I consider the tension between the individual-centric nature of rights and the collective nature of struggles for them.
65 I here focus on critiques which consider whether human rights are compatible with Marxism; to see more on how human rights and Marxism might be complementary, or how human rights might be enriched by insights from Marxist theory, see Brad R. Roth, 'Retrieving Marx for the Human Rights Project' *Leiden Journal of International Law* 17 (2004), 31-66.

critiques of human rights: Susan Marks' famous charge that human rights conceal the root causes of social inequality, and relatedly that human rights cannot remedy these (structural) disparities and can only offer partial relief. If one accepts this critique (as I do) the question of whether these partial remedies might still hold some utility remains. After this I consider a second, in a way more profound, critique of human rights: the critique that human rights are incompatible with Marxist emancipatory struggles because they conceal exploitation and instead focus on oppression.

3.3.1 Marx(ists) on Rights

As Paul O'Connell sets out in his article 'On the Human Rights Question' in which he launches a thoughtful defence of human rights as a (potentially) Marxist project, the issue of human rights was relatively unexplored in the decades after Marx's death.[66] Instead the focus of socialist movements and theorists was on 'economic theory, party building and social revolution'.[67] It was only in the 1980s that the interest in the topic was re-ignited[68] after Stephen Lukes published an article arguing that Marxism is fundamentally incompatible with human rights in *Praxis International*.[69] Drucilla Cornell and William McBride responded arguing that such a reading was too restrictive and that there was some space for Marxists to meaningfully engage with the human rights project.[70]

The controversy stems from Marx's own writings on rights, which as Amy Bartholomew points out are 'critical, differentiated, underdeveloped, and in more than a few instances, ambiguous'.[71] On the one hand Marx develops a searing critique of rights in *On the Jewish Question*, providing a limitless source of quotes for scholars to draw on, including:

> None of the supposed rights of man, therefore, go beyond the egoistic man, man as he is, as a member of civil society; that is, an individual separated from the community, withdrawn into himself, whole preoccupied with his private interest and acting in accordance with his private caprice.[72]

On the other hand, even in this text Marx still defends the Jewish people's right to equality within Germany. Moreover, both Marx and Engels 'wrote repeatedly in

[66] Paul O'Connell, 'On the Human Rights Question' *Human Rights Quarterly* 40 (2018), 962-88, at 970.

[67] *ibid.*

[68] Bartholomew, 'Should a Marxist Believe' (1990) (n. 6), 244-45; O'Connell 'Human Rights Question' (2018) (n. 66), 270.

[69] Steven Lukes, 'Can a Marxist Believe in Human Rights?' *Praxis International* 4 (1981), 334-45.

[70] Drucilla Cornell, 'Should a Marxist Believe in Rights?' *Praxis International* (1984), 4-45; William L. McBride, 'Rights and the Marxian Tradition' *Praxis International* 4 (1984), 57.

[71] Bartholomew, 'Should a Marxist Believe' (1990) (n. 6), 248.

[72] Karl Marx, *On the Jewish Question* (1844), available at: https://www.marxists.org/archive/marx/works/1844/jewish-question/, accessed 12/05/2021.

defence of the rights of free expression, protest and the right to vote'.[73] Thus, Marx saw some, if very limited utility, in rights, for they could be tools in broader political struggles, even if they could never lead to human emancipation. Engagement with rights is then a matter of pragmatism, or of 'uncompromising realism' to use Perry Anderson's term.[74]

However, what both O'Connell and Bartholomew fail to do is to historicise the 1980s renewed academic interest in this question. In an exercise of historical materialism, I want to propose that the concern (and scepticism) which was expressed on the left at the time can be seen as a response to the birth of neoliberalism and neoliberalism's claim to the rhetoric of individual freedom and rights. Neoliberal conceptions of human rights focus on individual freedom and choice, all the while making any meaningful freedom and choice an impossibility for billions who are impoverished through dispossession. Perhaps the critiques of human rights in the early 1980s were then not so much *against* human rights as they were against the sudden withdrawal of the State as the provider of welfare and basic socio-economic security. And to their credit, many of the critics were right: as David Harvey demonstrates, human rights have become a way for organisations to step into the role of the State in terms of provision of basic services, while their utility as a tool of resistance has been sidelined.[75] Critical legal scholars of the time were then perhaps not wrong in their assessment, but they may have missed an opportunity to (re)claim human rights. Perhaps they just capitulated before the battle had really started. In the following two subsections I explore two powerful critiques of human rights and tease out some of the ways in which human rights could potentially be reclaimed.

3.3.2 Structural Critique

Human rights have been criticised both for their inability to address structural causes of harm, and for the fact that in addressing more immediate (and one could argue more temporary) causes of harm they distract from these structural causes. Perhaps the most widely known critique in this strand was voiced by Susan Marks in her iconic piece on 'Human Rights and Root Causes'.[76] In the piece, Marks diagnoses a tendency of the human rights movement to proclaim their interest in addressing the 'root causes' of human rights abuses, but to then either misidentify effects as causes or to recognise actual root causes only to 'put them aside'.[77] In a similar vein Robin West argues that myopic focus on rights can distract from underlying structural inequalities and injustices.[78] Gordon, Swanson, and Buttigieg

[73] O'Connell, 'Human Rights Question' (2018) (n. 66), 969.
[74] Aptly quoted in *ibid*, 974.
[75] Harvey, *Neoliberalism* (2005) (n. 59), 178.
[76] Susan Marks, 'Human Rights and Root Causes' *Modern Law Review* 74 (2011), 57-78.
[77] *ibid.*
[78] Robin West, 'Tragic Rights: The Rights Critique in the Age of Obama' *William and Mary Law Review* 53 (2011), 713-46 and 719-27.

demonstrate this inability to simultaneously engage in rights advocacy and to accurately pinpoint structural causes of global inequalities in their Marxist analysis of Human Rights Watch.[79]

However, O'Connell argues that despite these shortcomings human rights can still be valuable in local struggles for resources such as housing, water, and land.[80] Unfortunately he does not provide examples of how exactly human rights are being used by these local organisations: whether as a way to articulate their claims, as a way to secure funding, or as a way to draw international attention to the issue at hand. The advantage of human rights is that they *could* be used in any of these ways, some of which have the potential to be emancipatory. The issue is that they are in fact often used in ways which deradicalise the demands and operation of local movements.[81] As Nela Porobić Isaković and Gorana Mlinarević demonstrate in their analysis of the work of women's rights NGOs in Bosnia and Herzegovina, rhetoric of rights and the projectisation of emancipatory struggles has led to depolitisation of feminist activism in Bosnia and Herzegovina, and has indeed obscured the movement's view of the underlying structural issues.[82] However, in the final section of the chapter, I explore how one grassroots movement successfully resisted this type of institutionalisation and depolitisation.

3.3.3 Exploitation vs Oppression

I, again, start with Susan Marks. In her paper 'Exploitation as an International Legal Concept' Marks explores the role of international law, including human rights law, in concealing the ways in which exploitation is embedded in global capitalism. Marks argues that international legal instruments, by only recognising forms of exploitation that stem from individual vulnerability, portray exploitation as an individual and not as a systemic ill.[83] Further, international law only recognises extreme forms of exploitation which entail direct, and not systemic, coercion. This has two inter-related aspects: on the one hand international legal discourse uproots exploitation from socio-economic inequalities that create conditions for it and obscures how these inequalities are reproduced through it, and on the other hand it identifies individual vulnerability as *the* primary cause of exploitation.[84]

On the surface this may appear to be the same strand of critique as the structural critique, but the significance of Marks' observation is not just in identifying

[79] Neve Gordon, Jacinda Swanson, and Joseph A. Buttigieg, 'Is the Struggle for Human Rights a Struggle for Emancipation?' *Rethinking Marxism* 12 (2000), 1-22.

[80] O'Connell, 'Human Rights Question' (2018) (n. 66), 963.

[81] *cf.* Conor Gearty, 'Do Human Rights Help or Hinder Environmental Protection' *Journal of Human Rights and the Environment* 1 (2010), 7-22.

[82] Gorana Mlinarević and Nela Porobić Isaković, 'Sustainable Transitions to Peace Need Women's Groups and Feminists: Questioning Donor Interventions in Bosnia and Herzegovina' *Journal of International Affairs* 72 (2019), 173.

[83] Susan Marks, 'Exploitation as an International Legal Concept', in Susan Marks (ed.), *International Law on the Left: Re-Examining Marxist Legacies* (Cambridge: CUP 2008), 281-307, at 283.

[84] *ibid*, 293-97.

the ways in which invisibility of exploitation conceals structural causes of injustice, but also in putting 'exploitation' on the international law agenda. As Barbara Foley argues, the concept of 'exploitation' is essential for class analysis because it foregrounds the process of gaining profit through 'extraction of what Marx called "surplus value" from the labour of those who produce the things that society needs'.[85] And class analysis enables us to consider how social identities and forms of oppression associated with them are a product of exploited labour.[86] Without this analysis social identities are presumed, and in the absence of questioning which would lead to their destabilisation, they are legitimated.[87] Human rights, by focusing on oppression on the basis of identity then obscure how these identities emerge and how these different forms of oppression are inter-related. This approach, to borrow phrasing from Raju Das, 'beaks down struggle into its smallest component parts',[88] and thus undermines cross-identity solidarity which is essential for success of emancipatory movements.[89] Further, focus on oppression instead of on exploitation means that questions of distributive justice are removed from the human rights agenda.

It is doubtful that human rights can adequately capture and address exploitation. As Marks points out, obligations of State, which are the focus of human rights, 'are largely exhausted by regulatory measures'.[90] This is because the oppression approach to human rights obscures the profit-making element of exploitation and forecloses questions of (re)distribution. Further, the focus on identity means that human rights struggle to accommodate movements that build solidarity across a range of identities, or on the basis of identities which are not legally recognised. However, in the following section I use the example of the food sovereignty movement to explore the ways in which it might be possible to reclaim the radical potential of identity politics,[91] and use human rights discourse and organisations for emancipatory purposes.

[85] Barbara Foley, 'Intersectionality: A Marxist Critique' *New Labor Forum* 28 (2019), 10-13, at 11. See also Meyerson's work on Black Marxsim on which Foley extensively draws: Gregory Meyerson, 'Rethinking Black Marxism: Reflections on Cedric Robinson and Others' *Cultural Logic* 3 (2000), 1-45, at 3.

[86] Foley, 'Intersectionality' 2019 (n. 85), 11.

[87] *ibid.*

[88] Raju Das, 'Identity Politics: A Marxist View' *Class, Race and Corporate Power* 8(1) (2020), 1-33 and 9.

[89] My argument here is not that identity differences should be dismissed, but rather that acknowledgment and accommodation of differences is merely a first step of building an emancipatory movement. For more on some of the ways in which women's activists, and especially African American women's activists, who formed such coalitions, see Tamar W. Carol, 'Intersectionality and Identity Politics: Cross-Identity Coalitions for Progressive Social Change' *Signs: Journal of Women in Culture and Society* 42 (2017), 600-607.

[90] Marks, 'Exploitation' (2008) (n. 83), 306.

[91] In this interview about his forthcoming book, *Race and Class in the Age of Trump*, Asad Haider discusses the genealogy of 'identity politics' and locates the genesis of the term *within the radical politics of the Combahee River Collective*: Rafael Khachaturian, 'The Emancipation of All: Marxism in the Age of Identity Politics' (*Verso Books Blog*, 29 July 2020), available at: https://www.versobooks.com/en-gb/blogs/news/4808-the-emancipation-of-all-marxism-in-the-age-of-identity-politics, accessed 5/6/23.

4. Rich Individuality

I started with an outline of a Marxist account of an individual, and more importantly for Marxist theory—of individuality. The goal of human emancipation, in Marxist terms, is being *free* to develop one's faculties as one wishes, whether that is through fishing, art and dance, or through medicine; rich individuality means that individuals would be able to choose their own path without any material restrains. The question I then asked, and tried to answer throughout the rest of the chapter, was: can international law be of aid to human emancipation. I considered the history and form of international law and concluded that international law, as a handmaiden of capitalism is unlikely to contribute to a transition to communism. I then turned to international human rights law in order to see if, as an individual-centred field of international law, it might still be used subversively, as a tool in emancipatory struggles. I concluded on a cautiously optimistic note of: *perhaps*. I now explore what *perhaps* might look like in practice. For this I first turn to Michael Fakhri's work on how two different movements reconceptualised and (subversively) employed the word 'sovereignty';[92] and then, drawing on Fakhri's argument about the tactical utility of legal language, I explore an example of my own: the struggle for the preservation of rivers in Bosnia and Herzegovina. I consider the role of human rights in the grassroots movement's activism; specifically the ways in which they ground their claims in rights language to give them an air of modesty, while struggling for ambitious political alternatives.[93] If rights are a tool, I ask, what kind of resistance can they help us build; can this resistance be anti-capitalist; can it be emancipatory?

In 'Third world sovereignty, indigenous sovereignty, and food sovereignty' Fakhri outlines how the Inuit community in the Arctic uses geographical reframing to give a new meaning to sovereignty, and how the food sovereignty movement has reconceptualised sovereignty to develop solidarity 'despite a diffuse definition and different interests'.[94]

The Innuit, in response to their exclusion from a summit that ended with a declaration pronouncing 'state authority over Arctic space, ecology and its indigenous communities',[95] produced a 'Circumpolar Inuit Declaration on Sovereignty in the Arctic'. In this declaration the Innuit first asserted themselves as 'a people […] as a collective of rights-holders and not stakeholders'.[96] Then

[92] Michael Fakhri, 'Third World Sovereignty, Indigenous Sovereignty, and Food Sovereignty: Living with Sovereignty Despite the Map' *Transnational Legal Theory* 9 (2018), 218-53.

[93] See also Gearty, 'Human Rights' (2010) (n. 81), 11, for an argument that the human rights' focus on the individual is only seemingly at odds with the environmental movement's preoccupation with environment; in practice, these movements share 'their commitment to change, their attitude to power and their mode of organising'. While this argument rings true in some instances, especially in relation to NGOs, my exploration of the grassroots activism reveals that there are some remaining tensions.

[94] Fakhri, 'Third World Sovereignty' (2018) (n. 92), 222.

[95] *ibid*, 235.

[96] *ibid*, 236.

by defining sovereignty in reference to multiple overlapping legal regimes and territories, they embedded their own sovereignty in a 'mesh of authority' in which no single legal regime (national, regional, international) dominates, thus rooting this *legal* term in the empirical reality of Inuit life and governance.[97] For present purposes: the emancipatory power of the declaration lies in the fact that it 'codifies experience of sovereignty'.[98] This can be contrasted with the history of colonial erasure of local boundaries and modes of governance in the name of expansion of capital and 'civilisation'.

In contrast, the ingenuity of the food sovereignty movement's approach lies not so much in their 'reclaiming' of sovereignty, as in their expansion of it. The movement uses the term sovereignty to attract a range of actors who are as diverse geographically as they are ideologically in order to mobilise around the 'right of peoples to healthy and culturally appropriate food produced through ecologically sound and sustainable methods, and their right to define their own food and agriculture system'.[99] The movement exploits the relative vagueness of the term sovereignty to expand its meaning: vagueness is here an advantage because it enables actors with different ideological and strategic goals to come and act together when their tactical goals align. Moreover, the movement uses legal language to articulate distributional and fairly radical demands in institutional settings.

Both of Fakhri's examples demonstrate different ways in which communities can come together and (re)claim international law in order to articulate demands which are fairly revolutionary. While neither of these interventions is, strictly speaking, Marxist (although there are Marxist organisations in the food sovereignty movement) their work offers a possible template for how Marxists can use international law 'tactically'.[100] Vagueness of law can actually be a useful tool for bringing together activists and organisations who share a common objective, while also being divided by slight ideological differences. Moreover, if the depoliticisation that legal language offers is employed tactically it can actually be used to frame radical ideas in status-quo terms. On the one hand, as Fakhri's work demonstrates, there seems to be obvious utility in this; on the other hand the Marxist in me wonders: can radical ideas be translated into law without losing that which makes them radical? Or to put it differently: if an emancipatory struggle is framed in status-quo terms, can the resulting victory be in any way subversive? To explore (but not answer) these questions I turn to an example close to home.

[97] *ibid*, 237-38.

[98] *ibid*.

[99] Declaration of Nyéléni, adopted at the Forum for Food Sovereignty (27 February 2007), available at: https://nyeleni.org/en/declaration-of-nyeleni/, accessed 5/6/23.

[100] I here again draw on Robert Knox's definition of the term: Knox, 'Strategy and Tactics' (2010) (n. 33).

4.1 Testing the Tool: Human Rights and the Struggle for Water as a Common Good

Before sunrise on 24 August 2017 around 100 regular policemen and 150 members of the special police arrived at the foot of a small wooden bridge over the river Kruščica in Central Bosnia, where some fifty women from the local village were sitting, arms interlinked, their bodies forming a human chain.[101] The women had been waiting. They had been guarding the river twenty-four hours a day, every day, since the first construction truck appeared on 2 August.[102] The truck was there to start the building works on a small hydropower plant which was to be built on the river.[103] In this sense Kruščica was utterly unexceptional: rivers across Bosnia and Herzegovina were being littered with small hydropower plants (around 300 were in some stage of development at the time).[104] Such was the proliferation of small hydropower plants at the time, that activists estimated that if all construction went ahead according to schedule there would be one hydropower plant per every 15 km of river flow throughout Bosnia.[105] Most of these small structures are privately owned, permits for them issued by the local authorities, often with no consultation of the local community whose lives are supported and shaped by these rivers.[106] The reason Kruščica became exceptional, was what happened next: visible violence.

[101] Association for Culture and Art - Crvena, Oštra Nula and Women's International League for Peace, 'Submission to the UN Universal Periodic Review of Bosnia and Herzegovina', 28 March 2019, available at: https://www.wilpf.org/wp-content/uploads/2019/08/UPR-Bosnia-Herzegovina_2019.pdf, accessed 5/6/23, at 13-14; Alma Midžić, 'Kruščica: Defending Balkan Rivers' *CommON(s)!*, 7 June 2018, available at: https://ourcommons.org/featured/kruscica-brave-women-balkan-rivers/, accessed 5/6/23.

[102] Midžić, 'Defending Balkan Rivers' (n. 101).

[103] Small hydropower plants are defined as plants with power of under 10mW. As such, they make a minimal contribution to the overall electricity production in Bosnia and Herzegovina, but have a disastrous impact on the local ecosystems and communities. See Alma Midžić, 'Quina és la prioritat: la comunitat, la protecció de l'aigua o la producció d'energia renovable? El cas de la construcció excessiva de centrals minihidràuliques a Bòsnia i Hercegovina' *Es Feres Estudis* 32 (2022), 52-69; Paul Hockenos, 'A Balkan Dam Boom Imperils Europe's Wildest Rivers' *Yale Environment* 360 (2018), available at: https://e360.yale.edu/features/a-balkan-dam-boom-imperils-europes-wildest-rivers, accessed 5/6/23.

[104] These power plants have the capacity of up to 10mW, which means that they do not significantly contribute to the general levels of electricity production, while having detrimental effects for the local ecosystems. Estimates as to the actual number vary between sources; an estimate of 300 is given in Crvena et al., 'Submission to the UPR' (n. 101), 13; 250 is given in Hockenos, 'A Balkan Dam Boom' (2018) (n. 103); and Alma Midžić sets the number at 341 small hydropower plants planned or under construction in 2021 in Midžić, 'Quina és la prioritat' (n. 103), 54.

[105] Alma Midžić, 'Kruščica i posljedice nasilja' *Perspectives: Political Analyses and Commentary* 8 (2021), 70-76, 70.

[106] As Larisa Kurtović argues, '[such] contracts are a crucial segment of the postwar political economy, which is controlled by a group of largely ethno-nationalist political parties, eager to find fresh means of filling their increasingly shrinking coffers, as well as keep their key business allies happy. And happy they are indeed, as these concession agreements also come with guarantees that the local electrical utilities will purchase that electricity at a favorable rate.' Larisa Kurtović, 'Riverine Struggles against Plunder and Dispossession: Water Defenders in Postwar Bosnia-Herzegovina' *EuropeNow* (18 May 2022), available at: https://www.europenowjournal.org/2022/05/17/riverine-struggles-against-plunder-and-dispossession-water-defenders-in-postwar-bosnia-herzegovina/, accessed 5/6/2023.

The police warned the women to move, and when they refused, the police attacked them with batons and boots, beating and dragging their bodies off the bridge.[107] The brutality was recorded and streamed online, giving the local struggle for the preservation of the river national visibility.[108] And while some of the public outrage was focused on the physical violence women had experienced, the activists were quite successful in getting *their* message across: this violence was just a visible manifestation of other forms of injustice the local community was being subjected to, including dispossession, and it was indicative of the State's complicity in this injustice.[109] The activists laid bare the ways in which the law itself was a part of the problem, a conduit for violence.

The framework within which hundreds of permits for construction of these hydropower plants were being issued was a *legal* framework. As such, law was being imposed as a terrain on which to conduct the struggle. Yet, a legal challenge is costly and time-consuming, both money and time being commodities that are in short supply in this poor rural community. Legal aid in Bosnia and Herzegovina does not cover these kinds of legal costs, another avenue presented and closed off through law.[110] The police had clearly broken the law when they violently attacked the protesters, but to bring a police brutality claim one needs a medical certificate proving injuries sustained: a certificate not a single victim was issued.[111] Keeping law enforcement accountable through law, it turned out, came with many in-built challenges. Finally, the women were not merely dragged off the bridge, they were dragged to the local police station and arrested, many of them subsequently charged with misdemeanours.[112] The total cost of their legal defence exceeded €10,000 (for reference, the average monthly income in this community is under €300).[113] And yet, despite the obvious ways in which the law was a part of the problem; the community also *tactically* referred to it throughout their struggle.

They disputed the legality of the permits: the women maintained that the public consultation process which included only forty local inhabitants out of the 2,500 who live in the village breached their rights to participate in democratic

[107] Midžić, 'Defending Balkan Rivers' (2018) (n. 101); Crvena et al., 'Submission to the UPR' (2019) (n. 101).

[108] Midžić, 'Kruščica i posljedice nasilja' (2021) (n. 105), 71.

[109] See especially Midžić, 'Defending Balkan Rivers' (2018) (n. 101) which draws on interviews with local activists.

[110] Midžić, 'Kruščica i posljedice nasilja' (2021) (n. 105), 71.

[111] Midžić, 'Defending Balkan Rivers' (2018) (n. 101).

[112] The charges were ultimately dismissed by the local judge who felt that it would be impossible to determine each of the women's individual responsibility: see Midžić, 'Defending Balkan Rivers' (2018) (n. 101); however the police found a way around this and instead kept issuing the women with fines of between 30 and 50 per cent of their monthly income for obstruction of the highway: see: Midžić, 'Kruščica i posljedice nasilja' (2021) (n. 105), 72. The total amount of these fines was around €3,000: Ena Bavčić, 'Monitoring the Right to Free Assembly: Bosnia and Herzegovina 2017-2018' (2019) available at: https://ecnl.org/sites/default/files/files/BosniaHerzegovina_Monitoring-assembly-report-2018.pdf, accessed 5/6/23.

[113] Midžić, 'Kruščica i posljedice nasilja' (2021) (n. 105), 72.

decision-making.[114] The police were accused of breaching a number of the women's human rights, including the right to freedom of expression, peaceful assembly, liberty, and security.[115] And, of central interest to me, the activists also framed their demands for the preservation of the river in terms of the right to water,[116] and right to life.[117] The river, which supplies around 150,000 people with drinking water (including the industrial city of Zenica and a small town of Vitez) and serves as a water source for the local village (in which some inhabitants are still not connected to the water supply network), was already at its biological minimum.[118] The building of the hydropower plants would have tipped the delicate balance that was struck over the edge, and the local village would have lost its access to drinking water.

Alma Midžić, a local activist and feminist, spent time with the community and interviewed them about their struggle and their objectives. What comes across in these interviews is the way in which the women make a rhetorical link between the river which provides them with water and their right to life, for which water is essential.[119] For them, the protection of their rights is inextricably linked to the protection of the river; the individual is embedded in their environment, not alienated from it. Their very conception of this right challenges the idea that there is a dichotomy between human rights and environmental protection. Through the use of seemingly neutral language, the women are actually articulating a fairly radical notion: that they are entitled to more than *bare life*; to a particular kind of life and a particular kind of relationship to their environment.

This relationship, for the women of Kruščica, was about having a say in how the river is being governed.[120] A struggle for the *commons*.[121] Commons can be understood as a system of community governance of goods and/or resources, which

[114] Midžić, 'Defending Balkan Rivers' (2018) (n. 101).

[115] See in particular the NGO report to the Human Rights Council: Crvena et al., 'Submission to the UPR' (2019) (n. 101), and Bavčić, 'Freedom of Assembly' (2019) (n. 112), which was published as a part of the European Center for Not-for-Profit Law (ECNL) monitoring programme.

[116] The right is further enshrined in domestic legislation which stipulates that in cases where a body of water could have multiple purposes (including recreational or commercial), supplying the population with drinking water takes priority: Zakon o Vodama FBiH, Art. 47(2).

[117] See, e.g., Midžić, 'Defending Balkan Rivers' (2018) (n. 101).

[118] Midžić, 'Quina és la prioritat' (2022) (n. 103), 64; Crvena et al., 'Submission to the UPR' (2019) (n. 101).

[119] Midžić, 'Defending Balkan Rivers' (2018) (n. 101). Midžić quotes Amela Zukan, one of the women, as saying: 'Why are they attacking us, we are not criminals, we just defended our right to water and life. That's everyone's right, isn't it?' See also the quote cited by Tahira Tibold: 'This is a struggle for life, for drinking water. Without electricity we can manage, but without water we cannot live.'

[120] Hata Hurem, as quoted in Midžić, 'Defending Balkan Rivers' (2018) (n. 101): 'The people slept and were blind until the struggle against the construction of a hydro power plant began. Then we opposed. Our fight is also a struggle for our vision of Kruščica. We used to have 3 hotels, this is a well-known picnic area, since we have a beautiful nature. We want to focus our work on conservation of nature and development of resources for resting and recreation, which we had before (in the time of Yugoslavia).'

[121] It is important to note here that I am interested in the commons from a perspective of local grassroots movements, not from the perspective of global governance. For a critique of the global commons in this context, see Surabhi Ranganathan, 'Global Commons' *European Journal of International Law* 27 (2016), 693-717.

consist of three elements in mutual relationship: 1) a resource to be governed, 2) community of users governing the resource, 3) institutions designed by users in order to govern the resource.[122] Defined in this way commons are not *inherently* anti-capitalist, just, or progressive; they are *made* radical through an ongoing commitment to 'social justice, democracy and ecological sustainability'.[123] The commons are then a rejection of the dichotomy between the public (State owned and managed) property and private property, and moreover (and more importantly), a rejection of the capitalist obsession with *ownership* as a form of exclusion. The primary lens through which resources are viewed is their use; commons are then not *things* but rather a set of relationships.[124] In the context of Marxist theory and materialist history, a claim to the commons can be seen as an attempt to resist the ongoing process of accumulation by dispossession. And while there are some disagreements as to whether these challenges are destined to remain small scale and local, or whether perhaps, States might have a role to play,[125] it is obvious that this form of resistance is always collective and never individual.

Women of Kruščica employed a different tactic for this aspect of their struggle: they ran for (and won) a number of seats on the local sub-municipal council, which plays a key role in local consultations regarding building permits. Their hope was that they would be able to use the existing institutional structures to govern the river the way the community sees fit. And they are not alone in this; regionally, a number of successful environmental groups have also built political platforms through which they have entered formal politics (including *Ne da(vi)mo Beograd* from Serbia and *Možemo!* from Croatia). The fact that these movements are using a variety of tools at their disposal, including direct action, human rights discourse, and formal politics is a good indicator that human rights can both have a role to play in social progress, and that their role is neither dominant nor crucial.

In the summer of 2022, almost five years after the 24 August attack on the women of Kruščica, the Parliament of the Federation of Bosnia and Herzegovina (FBiH) adopted an amendment to the law on electric energy prohibiting further construction of small hydropower plants in FBiH. This victory, while limited (private investors who were in the process of securing their permits are still given a three-year window to secure all the paperwork, but further permits will not be issued) is in no way pyrrhic. Tireless work of activists that had preceded the struggle for Kruščica, and which was made more visible by it, has resulted in a concrete legal

[122] Mary Dellenbaugh et al. (eds.), *Urban Commons: Moving Beyond State and Market* (Basel: Birkhäuser 2015), 13. For regional context, see also Tomislav Tomašević et al., *Commons in South East Europe: Case of Croatia, Bosnia & Herzegovina and Macedonia* (Sarajevo: Institute for Political Ecology 2018).

[123] Tomašević et al., *Commons in South East Europe* (2018) (n. 122), 49-50, drawing on Silke Helfrich.

[124] *ibid*, 46.

[125] David Harvey, in particular, argues that States might have an important role to play in governing some high-scale resources: David Harvey, *Rebel Cities: From the Right to the City to the Urban Revolution* (London: Verso 2012), chapter 3.

gain: the practice that had triggered the struggle has been abolished. However, the material conditions in which the practice was embedded did not change: natural resources are still treated as commodities, and these commodities are owned and managed by the State with no input from the local community. This case, then, confirms Robert Knox's assertion that legal tactics can only form a small part of the larger political strategy; but law is only as useful as our collective ability to decentre it and move beyond it.

5. Conclusion

I started by asking whether international law, taking into account multiple Marxist critiques of it, could be meaningfully reformed, so that it becomes compatible with the Marxist political project. Having concluded that such a shift was unlikely (and many would argue impossible), I asked a different question: can international law still be used by individuals in their emancipatory struggles? To explore this, I focused on human rights law and I analysed both the critiques and the praxis that shape the field. Ultimately, drawing inspiration and learning lessons from Bosnian environmental activists, I concluded that human rights can be a useful tool for articulating radical demands in neutral terms, but also that victories which can be achieved through these means are limited. Perhaps the most important lesson, for lawyers, is that the only way for law to be emancipatory is if it is only a small part of a broader political struggle; a tool to be used and then discarded when it outlives its usefulness.

Such understanding of the relationship between the individual, the State, and international law departs from both the State-centric and human-centred accounts in that it refuses to see this relationship as static and fixed: on this reading, it is the dynamic nature of the relationship that opens the possibility for its tactical use. It is precisely the ability to invoke *both* sovereignty (as in the example of the 'Circumpolar Inuit Declaration on Sovereignty in the Arctic') and legality (as in the example of the women of Kruščica) tactically that makes international law a potentially useful tool to begin with.

14

Global Law and the Individual

*Angelo Jr Golia**

1. Introduction

Since 28 January 2021, the Oversight Board (OB), the independent adjudication body established by Facebook/Meta to review its content moderation practices, has made decisions that are binding upon the social media company. Significantly, a review can be activated either by Meta itself via direct referral or by individual users who disagree with decisions to remove their posts or comments.[1] The first decisions not only overturned content removals but also issued nine policy recommendations.[2] Despite the lack of references to international human rights law (HRL) in Facebook's Community Standards and in the OB's own Bylaws, the OB referred to HRL in two ways. First, with an act of self-regulation,[3] the OB autonomously expanded the 'legal' basis of its review by referencing the UN Guiding Principles on Business and Human Rights (UNGP). Then, in its decisions, it developed a critique of Meta's decision-making process on content moderation, primarily based on Article 2 of the International Covenant on Civil and Political Rights (ICCPR).

A few months later, in May 2021, the District Court of The Hague rendered a landmark judgment, based in part on international law, in the case *Milieudefensie v Royal Dutch Shell*, which held a transnational corporation (TNC) responsible for the first time for its contribution to climate change.[4] The NGO *Milieudefensie* brought the case on its own behalf and on that of 17,379 individual claimants and six other NGOs. On the admissibility, the Court found that plaintiffs could bring a class action in the common interest of preventing dangerous climate change, since the interests of current and future generations of Dutch residents 'are suitable for

* For helpful comments on earlier drafts of this chapter, I am indebted to LI Zhenni, Ann Kathrin Lohse, Lisa Mardikian, Anne Peters, Theodor Shulman, Achilles Skordas, Tom Sparks, and Saskia Stucki. The usual disclaimers apply.

[1] 'Section 3 Oversight Board Bylaws', available at: https://oversightboard.com/governance/.

[2] 'Announcing the Oversight Board's first case decisions', available at: https://oversightboard.com/news/165523235084273-announcing-the-oversight-board-s-first-case-decisions/, accessed 11/10/21.

[3] 'The adoption of the Rulebook for Case Review and Policy Guidance', available at: https://oversightboard.com/sr/rulebook-for-case-review-and-policy-guidance, accessed 11/10/21.

[4] Rechtbank Den Haag, *Milieudefensie et al. v. Royal Dutch Shell PLC*, judgment of 26 May 2021, C/09/571932/HA ZA 19-379, available at: https://uitspraken.rechtspraak.nl/inziendocument?id=ECLI:NL:RBDHA:2021:5339, accessed 11/10/21.

Angelo Jr Golia, *Global Law and the Individual* In: *The Individual in International Law*. Edited by: Tom Sparks and Anne Peters, Oxford University Press. © Angelo Jr Golia 2024. DOI: 10.1093/oso/9780198898917.003.0014 bundling so as to safeguard an efficient and effective legal protection of the stakeholders'.[5] On the merits, Shell was found responsible based on domestic tort law[6] providing that a tortious or unlawful act includes 'an act or omission in violation of what is societally accepted according to unwritten law'. Under such an 'unwritten standard of care', the Court held, the company has an obligation to contribute to mitigating climate change by reducing its CO_2 emissions in line with the targets set in the 2015 Paris Agreement.[7] Significantly, the Court highlighted that HRL does not apply directly to corporations. In interpreting the domestic tort provision, however, it gave prominence to both binding and non-binding international law instruments, such as the European Convention on Human Rights (ECHR) and the International Covenant on Civil and Political Rights (ICCPR),[8] the Paris Agreement,[9] the UN Guiding Principles,[10] the Organisation for Economic Co-operation and Development (OECD) Guidelines for Multinational Enterprises, among others;[11] as well as climate science documents, most notably the Assessment Reports of the Intergovernmental Panel on Climate Change.[12] At the same time, the Court held that Shell has an 'individual responsibility' to reduce the emissions over which it has control and influence.[13] This means that it has an 'obligation of result' concerning Shell group's activities and a 'significant best-efforts obligation' regarding Shell group's business relations over which it has no immediate control, including end users.[14] In other words, the target of the Court's decision did not just focus on Shell as a legal person incorporated under Dutch law; it also, and fundamentally, considered Shell as a single, worldwide economic actor.

These are only two examples—taken from proceedings before a private adjudicator and a domestic court, respectively—that highlight more general patterns in the relationship between the individual and what is known as 'global law'.[15] In this chapter, I wish to explore three of these patterns, namely symbiosis, oscillation, and strategic subjectification.

Symbiosis. Global law and the individual are in a symbiotic relationship. This means that what we call the 'individual' supports the development and functions of global law and its specific features. This observation does not concern the fact

[5] *ibid*, para. 4.2.4. The Court applied the test under Dutch Civil Code, Book 3, Section 305a.
[6] Dutch Civil Code, Book 6, Section 162.
[7] Paris Agreement, 12 December 2015, FCCC/CP/2015/L.9/Rev/1.
[8] *Milieudefensie v. Shell* 2021 (n. 4), paras. 4.4.9-4.4.10.
[9] *ibid*, paras. 4.4.26-4.4.28, 4.4.42.
[10] *ibid*, paras. 4.4.2, 4.4.11-4.4.21.
[11] *ibid*, paras. 4.4.11, 4.4.14.
[12] *ibid*, paras. 2.3.5.4, 4.4.26-4.4.34
[13] *ibid*, paras. 4.4.13, 4.4.52.
[14] *ibid*, para. 4.1.4.
[15] Here provisionally understood as a regulatory mix of State-made and non-State-made rules that emerged, following globalisation processes, on the domestic, local, regional, and international levels and elaborated by public, private, and hybrid actors alike. For a more detailed account, see section 3, below.

that global law needs agents, like any other form of law, but rather that the *specific* construct of the 'individual', as it emerged during legal modernity, constitutes its necessary legal infrastructure. At the same time, in a global(ised) socio-legal context, global law, with its distinctive characteristics, creates new arenas for ongoing power struggles, disputes, and diverse expectations within decision- and law-making processes. In other words, global law provides the individual with access to (legal) possibilities that would otherwise be out of reach.

Oscillation. The symbiotic relationship between global law and the individual is characterised by a continuous and context-dependent oscillation—an expansion/restriction dynamic—of the individual's *legal* relevance, which depends on the varying need for conflict-based *iuris genesis*.[16] Such oscillation is contingent, not predetermined but rather open to contestation and reconfiguration. The legal spaces and possibilities created for the individual by global law may not inherently lead to progress or regress. Instead, like other forms that the law has taken over the centuries, these spaces and possibilities are influenced by power struggles and strategies that are *specific* to the current conditions. Such oscillation, in turn, has two effects. First, it pushes towards a heightened level of abstraction in the modern concept of the individual, further distancing it from anthropomorphic, 'realist' models. Second, it makes the interplay between three distinct yet interconnected dimensions of subjectification more visible: social individualisation, legal personification, and specific legal entitlements. I will refer to this interplay as 'global legal subjectification'.

Strategic subjectification. The symbiotic, oscillating relationship between global law and the individual facilitates the development of strategies of legal subjectification, some of which may potentially be used to counter problematic issues of globalisation. In other words, analysing the dynamics of the relationship between the individual and global law may offer strategic guidance to tackle some of the worst trends of (legal) globalisation, which contribute to the oppression, isolation, marginalisation, instrumentalisation, and alienation of people, as well as contributing to ecological and climate disasters.

The chapter proceeds as follows. Section 2 briefly explores the reasons for an analysis that focuses on the relationship between global law and the individual *beyond* the human rights paradigm. Section 3 offers a general overview of global law, emphasising the features most relevant to its relationship with the individual, notably the need for *iuris genesis* in the absence of strong centralised law-making. Section 4 explores the three patterns mentioned, namely symbiosis (section 4.1), oscillation (section 4.2), and strategic subjectification (section 4.3). This section is broken down further to emphasise potential strategies of subjectification that aim

[16] Broadly understood as the 'creation of legal meaning', following Robert Cover, 'Foreword: Nomos and Narrative' *Harvard Law Review* 97 (1983), 4-68, at 11.

to strengthen the role of the individual as a catalyst of global emancipation and politicisation. Section 5 concludes the chapter.

2. The Need for a 'Beyond Human Rights' Moment

Unlike the discourse of international law, scholarship explicitly focusing on global law has not had a fully fledged '*beyond human rights*' moment, that is, it has rarely theorised the role of the individual *beyond* the paradigm of human rights.

In the realm of international law scholarship, the relatively recent (re-)emergence of the individual paralleled the rise of twentieth-century HRL, which made its way into inter-State schemes and has led to significant structural changes: the proliferation of legal instruments conferring rights on individuals; direct access for individuals to international organisations and tribunals; and recognition of individual accountability for international crimes. However, the expansion of the scope of international law into new spheres—such as trade, investment, environment, climate, migration, health, criminal law, disaster relief—has raised the need to revisit the doctrine of legal subjects, to reconceptualise the legal position of the individual, and, in more recent times, to differentiate human rights in the narrow sense from other international individual rights.[17]

However, the scholarship *specifically* dedicated to (the notion of) global law has dealt predominantly with the individual as a rights holder,[18] with HRL perceived as a specific framework 'used' as a pool of legitimacy[19] to strengthen the either formal or informal authority of global governance institutions. This emphasis on human rights could partly be explained by the fact that, unlike Westphalian international law, 'global law' lacks a strong, relatively autonomous, overarching principle of legitimacy such as State sovereignty. Furthermore, in a literature characterised by interdisciplinarity and transdisciplinarity, most authors focus on the institutions, structures, and processes of emerging global legal dynamics, often overlooking the specific role of the individual. Indeed, if the individual is understood as equivalent to the legal person, that is, as a point of imputability of rights and obligations

[17] Among a rich literature, see Anne Peters, *Beyond Human Rights: The Legal Status of the Individual in International Law* (Cambridge: CUP 2016); see also Peters and Sparks, 'Introduction' (chapter 1), in this volume.

[18] See, among many others, Rafael Domingo, *The New Global Law* (Cambridge: CUP 2010), 142-44; Neil Walker, *Intimations of Global Law* (Cambridge: CUP 2014), 71-77; Samantha Besson, 'Human Rights as Transnational Constitutional Law', in Anthony F. Lang and Antje Wiener (eds.), *Handbook on Global Constitutionalism* (Cheltenham: Edward Elgar 2017), 234-63. To be sure, this simplifies a literature that has analysed the role of individuals in a variety of fields not always strictly related to human rights: see, among many, Jutta Brunnée and Stephen Toope, *Legitimacy and Legality in International Law: An Interactional Account* (Cambridge: CUP 2010); Tamar Megiddo, 'Methodological Individualism' *Harvard International Law Journal* 60 (2019), 219-65.

[19] *cf.* Chris Thornhill, 'A Sociology of Constituent Power: The Political Code of Transnational Societal Constitutions' *Indiana Journal of Global Legal Studies* 20 (2013), 551-603, esp. at 569-73.

deriving from the norms of a specific, self-contained legal system, then the very nature of global law—fragmented, fluid, permeable, and polycentric[20]—makes it difficult to frame its legal position, at least *beyond* the human rights regime.

But that is not all. Since its emergence in its current form, the very idea of global law has been faced with identity issues and criticism. They concern, for example, its nature as 'law' in any of the senses attached to the term according to modern, State-centred models,[21] and its difference, if any, with the transnational law discourse[22] or with (the philosophy of) cosmopolitan law. Importantly, these writings assert that the concept of global law enables a global neoliberal consensus largely shaped by the economic and military superpower that emerged in the immediate aftermath of the Cold War. This, in turn, results in market-based governmentality and the instrumentalisation and alienation of both living beings and the environment.[23]

While these issues cannot adequately be explored here, they justify the need for a more specific examination of the individual *within* global law that goes beyond the human rights framework. Such an examination, first, helps individuate the *proprium* of global law, compared to conceptual alternatives such as transnational law. Second, it contributes to a much-needed conceptual distinction between two different but often conflated trends: individualisation and humanisation. Third, analysing the relationship between individual and global law based on the global law's polycontexturality[24] may further substantiate claims, raised in international law scholarship, concerning the different legal status of investment, labour, and environmental rights.[25] Fourth, it helps imagine new forms of subjectification at the global level, that is, new forms of socio-legal interaction and collective struggle, potentially transcending the (neo-)liberal *acquis* of the rights form.

3. Global Law: An Overview

We can define 'global law' as the conceptual fallout of a situation where the increased inter-connectedness and autonomy of various social processes, triggered

[20] *cf.* Larry Catá Backer, 'The Structural Characteristics of Global Law for the 21st Century: Fracture, Fluidity, Permeability, and Polycentricity' *Tilburg Law Review* 17 (2012), 177-99.

[21] See, e.g., Martin Loughlin, 'The Misconceived Search for Global Law' *Transnational Legal Theory* 8 (2017), 353-59.

[22] Dating back at least to Philip Jessup, *Transnational Law* (New Haven, CT: Yale University Press 1956).

[23] *cf.* Bhupinder S. Chimni, 'Co-option and Resistance: Two Faces of Global Administrative Law' *NYU Journal of International Law and Politics* 37 (2005), 799-827; and more recently Aoife O'Donoghue, On Tyranny and the Global Legal Order (Cambridge: CUP 2021).

[24] That is, a situation characterised by a plurality of mutually irreducible social perspectives. They are not compatible with one another and can be overcome only by the rejection of values, which in turn leads to different binary distinctions. See Gotthard Günther, 'Life as Poly-Contexturality', in Gotthard Günther, *Beiträge zur Grundlegung einer operationsfähigen Dialektik*, vol. 1 (Hamburg: Meiner 1976), 283-306.

[25] Peters, *Beyond Human Rights* 2016 (n. 17), 318.

by globalisation and the ensuing need for global regulation, have not been accompanied by the establishment of centralised, unitary law-making authorities. Indeed, in its currently prevailing use,[26] 'global law' indicates forms of normativity accompanying—that is, simultaneously enabling and re-enforced by—the emergence of relatively autonomous and specialised global governance frameworks.[27] The institutions within various regimes and systems, such as global politics, global economy, global science, and global sport, generate a diverse range of both formal and informal[28] norms and normative practices that interact in different ways with sources of national and international law. These norms and practices include regulations and agreements emerging within international organisations (IOs), international non-binding declarations, memoranda of understanding, general comments, guidelines, public and private codes of conduct, transnational company agreements, standards, terms of service, rankings, and reports.

Indeed, to manage the growing complexity and maintain their autonomy, the specialised systems of global politics, economy, science, media, environment, sport, and other 'global' social spheres increasingly need to establish new normative frameworks. Traditional State-centred (both national and international) law alone no longer appears sufficient *precisely* because of the constraints caused by globalisation.[29] New law-making centres and normative practices have emerged which, on the one hand, interconnect (through interpretation, circulation of argumentative and legal models, implicit or explicit *renvoi*, etc.) with more traditional sources[30] and, on the other hand, may de facto replace them in specific regulatory fields.[31] This situation is also characterised by the rise of various interconnected public, private, and hybrid[32] actors: next to traditional, 'public law' IOs, the global governance system is now populated by domestic and international administrative agencies, transnational private actors, international and domestic courts and

[26] For a mapping of the different conceptions of global law, see Walker, *Intimations* 2014 (n. 18), 55-130. On imperial and colonial law as functional antecedents of global law, see Poul F. Kjaer, 'Global Law as Inter-Contextuality and as Inter-Legality', in Jan Klabbers and Gianluigi Palombella (eds.), *The Challenge of Inter-legality* (Cambridge: CUP 2019), 302-18.

[27] *cf.* Gunther Teubner, 'Global Bukowina: Legal Pluralism in the World Society', in Gunther Teubner (ed.), *Global Law without a State* (Aldershot: Dartmouth Gower 1997), 3-28, at 8. See also Pierrick Le Golf, 'Global Law: A Legal Phenomenon Emerging from the Process of Globalization' *Indiana Journal of Global Legal Studies* 14 (2007), 119-45.

[28] See only Joost Pauwelyn, Ramses Wessel, and Jan Wouters (eds.), *Informal International Lawmaking* (Oxford: OUP 2012).

[29] *cf.* Jean-Bernard Auby, *Globalisation, Law and the State* (Oxford: Hart 2017), 14-19.

[30] In the most recent literature, see Nico Krisch (ed.), *Entangled Legalities Beyond the State* (Cambridge: CUP 2021).

[31] A classic example is the Codex Alimentarius Commission, whose standards de facto regulate food security at the global level.

[32] See Gunther Teubner, 'Hybrid Laws: Constitutionalizing Private Governance Networks', in Robert A. Kagan, Martin Krygier, and Kenneth Winston (eds.), *Legality and Community: On the Intellectual Legacy of Philip Selznick* (Berkeley, CA: Berkeley Public Policy Press 2002), 311-33; Jean-Christophe Graz, 'Les hybrides de la mondialisation. Acteurs, objets et espaces de l'économie politique internationale' *Revue française de science politique* 56 (2005), 765-87; Oren Perez, 'Transnational Networked Authority' *Leiden Journal of International Law* 35 (2022), 265-93.

dispute-settlement bodies, and standard-setting bodies.[33] It is also noteworthy that the term 'global law' includes both[34] the substantive norms of these distinct processes[35] and the norms and techniques through which such processes interact, overlap, conflict, and exchange normative meaning among themselves as well as with national and international law.[36]

From a normative perspective, these processes have also set in motion at least two interconnected dynamics of depoliticisation. First, social processes once open to political struggle, characterised by non-predetermined outcomes and by the reversibility of decisional processes (e.g. maximisation of investment protection), are becoming increasingly juridified. Second, collective decision-making has shifted, in part, from State-centred structures and processes to global governance institutions and even private actors that overtly draw their legitimacy from technical expertise or output efficiency rather than from processes of political deliberation. At the same time, global law is characterised by different dynamics of repoliticisation,[37] from which new focal points and venues for political contention emerge—often from the collaboration of both hegemonic and non-hegemonic actors, movements, coordinated practices of participation and contestation, and transnational strategic litigation.

Conceptualised as the 'systematisation of anarchy',[38] global law does not imply an underdeveloped or *still* incomplete legal order. The incompleteness of global law is intrinsic to its nature. Instead, global law pertains to a multitude of interconnected and non-heterarchical normative processes[39] that, at least *potentially*, have a global reach. Global law is law that *could* be applied in a multiplicity of legal contexts that are not predetermined. The adjective 'global', then, does not refer to

[33] Among the most recent literature, see Rebecca Schmidt, *Regulatory Integration Across Borders: Public-Private Cooperation in Transnational Regulation* (Cambridge: CUP 2018).

[34] In the transnational law discourse, these two forms are indicated as 'transnational legal substance' and 'transnational legal process': see Harold H. Koh, 'Transnational Legal Process' *Nebraska Law Review* 75 (1996), 181-207.

[35] Among others, some regimes of international law such as the 2005 International Health Regulations of the World Health Organization (WHO); the sources of the *lex mercatoria*; the standards elaborated by the International Standard Organization; the Recommendations of the Financial Action Task Force; the Helsinki Declaration of the World Medical Association on the ethical principles for medical research involving human subjects; the Friendly Relations Declaration and the Stockholm Declaration on the Human Environment of the UN General Assembly; expert-based soft law such as the Global Pact for the Environment; the internal private regulation of TNCs such as Facebook's Standards of the Community; and some forms of religious and indigenous law.

[36] Among others, mechanisms of implicit or explicit *renvoi*; comparative and foreign law in judicial reasoning; international law-friendly interpretation; construction of open norms clauses such as due diligence, good faith, and duty of care through soft law instruments; systemic integration principles; 'constitutional tolerance'; comitology; and subsidiarity.

[37] See generally Anne Peters, 'Dual Democracy', in Jan Klabbers, Anne Peters, and Geir Ulfstein (eds.), *The Constitutionalization of International Law* (Oxford: OUP 2009), 263-341; Gunther Teubner, '*Quod omnes tangit*: Transnational Constitutions Without Democracy?' *Journal of Law and Society* 45 (2018), 5-29. For a criticism, see Ioannis Kampourakis, 'The Postmodern Legal Ordering of the Economy' *Indiana Journal of Global Legal Studies* 28 (2021), 101-52, esp. at 142-46.

[38] *cf.* Backer, 'The Structural Characteristics' 2012 (n. 20), 180.

[39] According to *ibid*, there are four: fracture, fluidity, permeability, and polycentricity.

actual territorial scope but to the absence of pre-determined territorial and normative boundaries.[40] This does not mean that global legal processes are without boundaries *tout court*. Instead, such boundaries are constantly redefined at the level of the single legal act.[41] Single acts of legislation, administration, adjudication, or contractual agreements incorporate or exclude various forms of normative content and address diverse subjects. As a result, they constantly redefine the distinction between what constitutes law and what does not, while reshaping the boundaries of the legal systems in which they operate.[42]

To be sure, in most cases, the single legal act must still conform to the conventional legal hierarchy. Adjudicators like The Hague District Court or the Facebook OB may still claim that they are applying domestic tort law or Facebook's Standards of the Community. However, they increasingly resort—often against the intention of their drafters—to a broader set of normative material. Courts and adjudicators, then, act not only as institutions embedded in one legal system or as branches of government, but increasingly as 'guardians' of global legal orders—relating to the governance frameworks of, for example, economy, climate, and freedom of expression. This situation also makes it more difficult for an external observer to identify in advance the normative material used to reach a decision and, therefore, to guess its concrete outcome.

A final point: the polycentricity of global law should be understood more precisely as polycontexturality.[43] This means that it is not just characterised by multiple centres but that these centres are placed in different territorial, functional, and institutional contexts and that their norm- and decision-making is guided by potentially conflicting rationalities. The right to property, for example, is interpreted in different ways by regional courts within the human rights regime (e.g. the European Court of Human Rights (ECtHR) and the Inter-American Court of Human Rights (IACtHR))[44] and in yet other ways by the dispute-settlement bodies of the global investment regime (e.g. investor-State dispute settlement (ISDS) bodies), despite frequent but still selective cross-references.[45] In each case, partially different normative materials serve as the basis for interpreting the relevant provisions. From the perspective of international law, it is precisely this polycontexturality that might offer further arguments to justify, for example, the different treatment of property rights depending on the context and the function

40 *cf.* Walker, *Intimations* 2014 (n. 18), 21.

41 *cf.* Hans Lindahl, 'A-Legality: Postnationalism and the Question of Legal Boundaries' *Modern Law Review* 73 (2010), 30-56; and more generally, Thomas Vesting, *Legal Theory* (Oxford: Beck-Hart 2018), 63-75.

42 Gunther Teubner, 'Breaking Frames: The Global Interplay of Legal and Social Systems' *American Journal of Comparative Law* 45 (1997), 149-69.

43 See Günther, 'Life' 1976 (n. 24).

44 *cf.* most recently Yuval Shany, 'International Courts as Inter-Legality Hubs', in Jan Klabbers and Gianluigi Palombella (eds.), *The Challenge of Inter-legality* (Cambridge: CUP 2019), 319-38.

45 *cf.* Silvia Steininger, 'What's Human Rights Got To Do With It? An Empirical Analysis of Human Rights References in Investment Arbitration' *Leiden Journal of International Law* 31 (2018), 33-58.

performed. In the context of the investment protection regime, they function to protect the system of global investments; in the context of the narrower framework of the HRL regime, their purpose is to protect the humanity of the individual –regardless of its meaning.

4. Patterns

An initial point to emphasise when discussing the patterns of the relationship between the individual and global law is the conceptual distinction with the issue of legal personality. Indeed, precisely because of the polycontexturality, incompleteness, and fluidity of global law, a unitary conception of *legal* personality would contradict its very nature. Instead, from the perspective of global law, the individual may have multiple legal personalities or none at all, depending on the specific system under consideration. One paradoxical feature of global law is that in order to function *as law*, it must presuppose the existence of socially constructed individuals who may not necessarily qualify as legal persons in all and each of the legal processes that comprise it. As the issue of legal personification loses centrality, the focus switches to the conditions under which an entity is *individualised* as a precondition for its legal relevance in a given system. In other words, from the perspective of global law, the central question is no longer: 'What are the legal conditions for the recognition of legal personality?' Instead, the central questions become: 'What kind of individual does global law presuppose?', and conversely: 'What kind of law does the individual need in the context of globalisation?'.

4.1 Symbiosis

To answer these questions, one may start by noting that global law is primarily based on the prototypical model of actorhood that emerged in western legal modernity:[46] anthropomorphic, abstract actors, formally equal to others, capable of expressing their will either immediately or mediately, and generally detached from specific societal belongings, with the notable exception of political membership (citizenship).[47] Freed from the constraints of a stratified society, like that of the Middle Ages, and from legal positions linked to status and role, the individual under modern law is a relatively abstract, decontextualised entity which can simultaneously *act* in different social spheres (as *homo politicus*, *economicus*, *scientificus*,

[46] cf. John W. Meyer and Ronald L. Jepperson, 'The "Actors" of Modern Society: The Cultural Construction of Social Agency' *Sociological Theory* 18 (2000), 100-20.

[47] *cf.* Gert Verschraegen, 'Hybrid Constitutionalism, Fundamental Rights and the State' *Netherlands Journal of Legal Philosophy* 40 (2011), 216-29.

etc.).[48] Similarly, modern law does not recognise the power of private individuals to unilaterally determine the legal status of other subjects. The functional differentiation typical of western modernity, distinguishing between state and society and between public and private, has led to the loss of *legally recognised* capacity for social power unilaterally to determine the legal status of other subjects.

These features are essential preconditions for the formation and development of global law. As seen in section 3, global law consists of a multiplicity of interconnected normative processes that cannot always rely on centralised legislation or administration, that is, hierarchical law-production based on the unilateral determination of the legal status of other subjects. For this reason, global law has to resort to modes of law-production that are based on at least potentially divergent claims of legally equal subjects, that is, adjudication and contract. For example, investor-State and commercial arbitration awards, panel reports of the World Trade Organization (WTO) Dispute Settlement Body,[49] contracts drafted or adjudicated following UNIDROIT principles and United Nations Commission on International Trade Law (UNCITRAL) Model Laws,[50] as well as formal or informal agreements among various administrative agencies constantly produce new rules that constitute the dynamic core of global economic law. In principle, these forms of legal interaction, based on the formal equality of participating entities, can potentially give rise to conflicts because of their adversarial modes of engagement. Such forms of legal interaction are crucial to advancing *iuris generative* processes. Therefore, global law 'needs' the individual to sustain its own *iuris genesis*, or at least it needs this more than its national/international counterparts do.

The second, closely related, reason why global law needs the individual concerns its polycontextural character. Given that normative frameworks based on divergent rationalities and contexts are fragmented and mutually irreducible, an actor able to raise claims in different legal systems, often characterised by limited communication, effectively connects them indirectly.[51] In other words, the socially constructed individual transmits legal meaning, especially through litigation, thus potentially linking different normative processes.[52] In their concrete development,

[48] *cf.* Niklas Luhmann, 'The Individuality of the Individual: Historical Meanings and Contemporary Problems', in Niklas Luhmann (ed.), *Essays on Self-Reference* (New York, NY: Columbia University Press 1990), 107-22, at 112.

[49] Which, as is known, is currently in crisis because of the US's obstruction of the appointment of members to its Appellate Body, resulting in a lack of a quorum under its rules. A number of WTO members agreed to participate in the Multi-Party Interim Appeal Arbitration Arrangement (MPIA) and other alternative appeal mechanisms pursuant to Art. 25 of the Dispute Settlement Understanding (DSU). An updated overview and a list of cases pending under such mechanisms are available at: https://wtoplurilaterals.info/plural_initiative/the-mpia/, accessed 11/10/21.

[50] See, e.g., Model Law on International Commercial Arbitration, 21 June 1985, GAOR 40th Session Supp. 17, Annex I.

[51] *cf.* Gert Verschraegen, 'Human Rights and Modern Society: A Sociological Analysis from the Perspective of Systems Theory' *Journal of Law and Society* 29 (2002), 258-81.

[52] This element has been highlighted especially in the 'transnational legal process' scholarship: see Koh, 'Transnational Legal Process' 1996 (n. 34); Maya Steinitz, 'Transnational Legal Process Theories',

global legal processes 'capture' individuals' claims not only to sustain their own *iuris genesis* but also to adapt to each other reflexively. In this sense, the capacity to 'cross' overlapping legal systems allows the abstract individual, typical of legal modernity, to push for normative developments in different global contexts, possibly leading to co-evolution, cross-fertilisation, and adaptation. By asserting their claims across different contexts, individuals facilitate the encounter between, and potentially the mutual adaptation or integration of, for example, global *political*, *economic*, and *scientific* justice, ultimately contributing to the sustainability of the inherent anarchy within global law.

The individual, for their part, also 'exploits' the specific features of global law. In the context of globalisation, the autonomous, modern individual increasingly needs normative realities that possess the specific characteristics of global law. The (de/re-)politicisation dynamics recalled in section 3 mean that claims can often be raised only in fora different from an individual's 'original' legal context and on the basis of diverse normative materials that do not always easily qualify as 'law'. In this sense, and although citizenship 'still plays a crucial role in mediating the balance between inclusion and exclusion in global society',[53] the rise of global law has partially directed practices traditionally linked to national citizenship—claims to rights and participation in law-making—away from centralised political institutions and relocated them, often through collective organisations or networks, in distinct global functional spheres.

Similarly, practices such as law-shopping, forum-shopping, or transnational litigation can be seen as a strategic selection of normative systems, based on the opportunities they offer—in terms of recognition of legal personality, procedural and substantive law, broader impact of the decision sought—to advance individual interests or policy agendas at the global level. In other words, global law offers the socially constructed actors typical of legal modernity the opportunity, for better or worse, to further emancipate themselves from the constraints inherent in forms of law-making primarily based on State and inter-State arrangements. In this sense, global law may well serve progressive and anti-colonial purposes and help reduce the gap between so-called developing and developed countries.[54]

in Cesare P. R. Romano, Karen J. Alter, and Yuval Shany (eds.), *Oxford Handbook of International Adjudication* (Oxford: OUP 2013), 339-56, at 350-56.

[53] Verschraegen, 'Hybrid Constitutionalism' 2011 (n. 47), 222.

[54] See, e.g., the Global Pact for the Environment, a process initiated in 2017 by a network of experts and supported by the General Assembly of the UN (UNGA, Towards a Global Pact for the Environment, 10 May 2018, A/RES/72/L.51) and the Draft Pan-African Investment Code (PAIC) adopted by the African Union Commission—Economic Affairs Department in December 2016 (available at: https://au.int/sites/default/files/documents/32844-doc-draft_pan-african_investment_code_december_2016_en.pdf, accessed 11/10/21), a model investment treaty elaborated with a view to promoting sustainable development.

The different stances of the ECtHR and the IACtHR regarding legal persons as right-holders may serve as an example here.[55] Similarly, especially in the context of global environmental law, it is apparent that single individuals and collective entities tend to push strategically for different types of soft law and scientific reports, to transform them into norms that are legally binding on other actors. Other contexts provide similar examples, for instance when it comes to investor rights.

To conclude this section, arguing that the relationship between global law and the individual is symbiotic means that they are co-dependent. Global law could emerge in this form only because legal modernity has shaped a *specific* model of actorhood. In the era of globalisation, it is predominantly global law that continues to construct the individual as a self-authorised agent. For better or worse, decisions like those rendered by the Hague District Court in *Milieudefensie* and Facebook's OB are only possible within the framework of global law.

4.2 Oscillation

Global legal processes give rise to patterns of oscillation by *selectively* expanding or restricting the possibility of conflict—and consequently the *legal* (ir)relevance of the socially constructed individual—depending on their need for *iuris genesis*.

On the one hand, global governance frameworks that rely, for one reason or another, on authoritative law-making or on epistemic or scientific authority tend to assign less importance to the individual in terms of legal personification and specific entitlements.[56] Alternatively, they rely on a more general human rights discourse, mainly ex post facto or as a source of output legitimacy rather than an operational necessity.[57] In both cases, there are no or only weak legal mechanisms available to individuals.

On the other hand, the individual has greater legal relevance in contexts where 'administrative' or 'legislative' modes of norm-production are relatively weak or absent. Even here, however, such relevance is influenced by the intrinsic dynamic of a given system: the global investments regime gravitating around investor-State arbitration, for example, assigns economic actors a central role and tends to marginalise other types of individuals. At the same time, human rights and

[55] See IACtHR, *Titularidad de Derechos de las Personas Juridicas en el Sistema Interamericano de Derechos Humanos*, Advisory Opinion of 26 February 2016, OC-22/16, at paras. 34-105, stating that, while legal persons do not hold the same rights as natural persons under the Inter-American Commission on Human Rights (IACHR), certain entities—specifically, trade unions, tribal and indigenous organisations, and individuals connected to legal entities—do have rights under the Convention and may petition the Inter-American System when those rights are allegedly violated.

[56] e.g., the absence of individual complaint mechanisms against the sanctions of the UN Security Council.

[57] e.g., the WHO, an IO that can rely on one of the strongest legal frameworks, international law-making (the International Health Regulations), and on epistemic/scientific expertise as a source of legitimacy.

environmental movements are striving to gain acknowledgement as relevant subjects in this same regime, for example in the form of *amici curiae* or stakeholders. In this regard, the oscillating subjectification within the investment regime can be seen as the arena where the conflict between two distinct governance frameworks and their conflicting rationality is played out: regulation and protection of global (neoliberal) economy versus regulation and protection of the global environment.

The oscillation pattern, in turn, has two other effects. First, it pushes the concept of the individual further away from anthropomorphic models and towards more abstract ones. Indeed, because global law must accommodate increasingly diverse and complex governance frameworks, the basic elements of the involved systems become more abstract. When individual entities and objects oscillate among distinct yet interconnected regimes, the need arises for the concept of the individual to become more abstract so that it can cover a broader range of situations. In this context, the perceived need for more effective global regulation of the environment, climate, and new technologies—along with the corresponding strategies pursued by relevant actors—broadens the either direct or indirect legal relevance of entities like non-human animals, ecosystems, rivers, algorithms, humanoid robots, and combinations thereof. Once these entities start to populate the realm of legal subjects in different systems, their conceptual genus needs to be more abstract (or rather: less anthropomorphic). It is one thing to include men, women, children, and collective entities predominantly conceived as groups of human beings (States, corporations) in the concept of the actor, but it is quite another thing to *also* include trees, rivers, non-human animals, etc. Such a concept departs more decisively from flesh-and-blood human beings and entities recognised as having specific ontological or psychological properties (e.g. will, interests, pain, reflexive capacities, empathy, action). In other words, global law tips the balance from realist towards phenomenological or constructivist imaginaries of the individual.[58] In this sense, the analysis of the oscillation/abstraction pattern adds a much-needed layer of complexity to an international legal discourse that often equates individualisation with humanisation.

But what does this allegedly more abstract concept look like? The individual presupposed by global law should be able to engage with multiple and overlapping normative processes that (may) have a global reach. In this regard, global processes seem to progressively tend towards a concept of the individual as a point of reference for socially constructed claims, either as a claimant or as an addressee. This individual 'needed' by global law is not necessarily the holder of a legal right or the bearer of a legal duty. The concept of rights seems to be too strictly related to *self-interest*, which already restricts the set of entities and events that may 'trigger' the

[58] *cf.* Meyer and Jepperson, 'The "Actors"' 2000 (n. 46), 101.

iuris genesis of global law. Rather, this individual would be any entity socially considered able to raise a claim, either immediately or mediately; or an entity socially considered to be the addressee of a claim. Although for now this is only a trend,[59] the social attribution to any entity of the capacity to raise a claim or to be the addressee of a claim progressively makes such an entity an individual, at least for the purposes of global law.[60] At least conceptually, other qualities such as the capacity to suffer; autonomous will; the capacity for social communication; and legal status such as legal personality, specific rights, and duties come later.

These observations lead us to the second effect related to the oscillation pattern: the increased visibility of the interplay between three distinct yet interconnected dimensions of legal subjectification at the global level, namely social individualisation, legal personification, and specific legal entitlements. These three dimensions often overlap or may even represent a *continuum*. For example, once society recognises the claim or expectation of non-human animals not to have unnecessary suffering inflicted upon them, they *are* individuals for the purposes of global law, regardless of who represents those claims or expectations by legal means, or how or where they do so. Once such claims translate into legal obligations upon others not to cause suffering, it is often only a short step to recognising correlative rights and eventually full-fledged legal personality.[61] The same would apply, for example, to the (socially constructed) claim of a river not to be polluted or of a specific ecosystem not to have its integrity compromised. However, social individualisation, legal personification, and the attribution of specific rights or obligations remain analytically distinct. The *interplay* between such dimensions in global law may be referred to as *global legal subjectification* and gives rise to different strategies by the actors involved – both hegemonic and non-hegemonic. In each of these cases, legal subjectification takes a different path and responds to different functional logics.

To be sure, the interplay between the three dimensions—social individualisation, legal personification, and the attribution of specific rights or obligations—also occurs in State-centred legal frameworks.[62] However, the specific features of global law make these dimensions even more apparent, and global law potentially

[59] See, e.g., IACtHR, *Medio Ambiente y Derechos Humanos*, Advisory Opinion of 15 November 2017, OC-23/17, at para. 59, stating that a violation of the right to a healthy environment could be found even without the identification of affected individuals.

[60] *cf.* Meyer and Jepperson, 'The "Actors"' 2000 (n. 46), 108.

[61] This is most apparent in the rulings of Ecuador's Constitutional Court which, based on Art. 10 of the 2008 Constitution, first granted rights to mangrove ecosystems and a cloud forest (Sentencia No. 22-18-IN/21 of 8 September 2021; *Los Cedros*, Sentencia No. 1149-19-JP/21 of 10 November 2021) and more recently explicitly recognised that individual animals are protected by the rights of nature which also includes the right to free development of animal behaviour (*Estrellita*, Sentencia No. 253-20-JH/22 of 27 January 2022). On these issues, see only Saskia Stucki, 'Towards a Theory of Legal Animal Rights: Simple and Fundamental Rights' *Oxford Journal of Legal Studies* 40 (2020), 533-60, at 437-549.

[62] One can consider the unique historical developments in the realm of law with regard to slaves, women, foetuses, and labour unions.

shapes them differently *for each of its centres*. Following their own logic and patterns, the various governance frameworks and regimes may frame the *legal* relevance of a socially constructed individual differently, ranging from their outright invisibility to indirect legal relevance, to the recognition of personality with only a few legal entitlements, to the full-fledged armoury of legal rights granted in that specific system.

4.3 Strategic Subjectification

The symbiotic, oscillating relationship between global law and the individual facilitates and helps imagine different strategies of legal subjectification at the global level. In this regard, the need strategically to diversify the criteria of the individual's relevance is triggered *both* by actors pursuing different agendas on different sides of the political spectrum (e.g. hegemonic States, military-economic elites, global law firms, NGOs, or environmental and animal activists) *and* by the intrinsic dynamics of globalisation.[63] Calls to treat animals as legal persons and for animal rights are not new in modern legal history.[64] But an animal rights movement and *global* animal law have fully emerged and gained momentum only recently, as biodiversity loss and climate-related emergencies have made questions such as the reduction of meat consumption more pressing.[65] Global law uses—indeed, has to use—strategies of subjectification to accompany its own dynamics. However, by using them, global law also becomes dependent on, and is potentially influenced by, their variations, thus remaining open to non-predetermined evolutionary trajectories.

Examples of strategic subjectification concern the distinction between TNCs (the unitary global *individuals*) and the single legal entities through which they operate and raise claims (the single companies, recognised legal personality in different legal systems).[66] *Mutatis mutandis*, the OSCE, although it is not a formally recognised international legal person, *acts* through domestic law entities and is increasingly considered a de facto IO.[67] Conversely, international legal

[63] *cf.* Elizabeth H. Boyle and John W. Meyer, 'Modern Law as a Secularized and Global Model: Implications for the Sociology of Law' *Soziale Welt* 49 (1998), 213-32, at 227.

[64] See, e.g., Henry S. Salt, *Animals' Rights: Considered in Relation to Social Progress* (London: Bell & Sons 1892).

[65] To be sure, this is a simplification of a more complex network of inter-relations, whereby the social and legal recognition of animal rights is based on both growing ethical/moral reasons as well as material conditions (i.e. environmental crises) that make it necessary to reconsider the exploitation of animals, which paves the way (in a materialist sense) for the ethics to be taken more seriously: *cf.* Saskia Stucki, *One Rights: Human and Animal Rights in the Anthropocene* (Cham: Springer 2023).

[66] Among the most recent literature, see Doreen Lustig, *Veiled Power. International Law and the Private Corporation 1886-1981* (Oxford: OUP 2020).

[67] See Niels Blokker and Ramses A. Wessel, 'Revisiting Questions of Organisationhood, Legal Personality and Membership in the OSCE: The Interplay Between Law, Politics and Practice', in

personality may strategically be granted to IOs in order for States to avoid legal accountability.[68] Although the issue goes beyond the scope of this chapter, a further example of this dynamic may even be found in processes in which political communities are subjectified as States.

In other cases, actors strategically avoid legal personification. A global movement such as Fridays for Future, which seeks to bring about environmental and climate regulation and relies on scientific evidence as a source of legitimation, is recognised as an increasingly significant individual actor within the global community. Its leaders deliberately do not pursue its legal personification – not even within the various national systems. Importantly, however, the global legal subjectification of 'Fridays for Future' does not exist in a legal void; it is supported by a legal infrastructure. It is sustained by a foundation established under Swedish law and several trademarks registered in 2020 at the European Union Intellectual Property Office (EUIPO). As such, it is protected by the full armour of intellectual property law, which is globally administered by organisations like the World Intellectual Property Organization (WIPO) and the WTO.

These few examples show that global law does not preclude that 'problems and functional needs are articulated by individuals and groups that choose the systems and organizations where to carry on their plans'.[69] A precise analysis of the strategies employed by various actors should consider the micro-level actions and communications attributed to socially constructed individuals with different interests, goals, and conceptions of justice. These differences among individuals play a significant role in shaping the mechanisms of sociolegal evolution.[70] In this sense, the processes of *global legal subjectification* remain open, non-predetermined, and subject to challenges and (re-)politicisation.

It is important to emphasise that the dynamics outlined in this section may increase the alienation and exploitation inherent in many global regimes. Indeed, by employing different strategies of subjectification, global legal processes can facilitate distinct forms of governmentality, which govern individuals based on their particular accumulation imperatives, especially those based on market-based rationality. This also means that even when emancipatory strategies are effective, the polycontexturality of global normative processes can facilitate tunnel vision, single-issue politics, and the domination of a particular knowledge or perspective (epistemic capture). For example, global environmental movements often struggle

Mateja Steinbrück Platise, Carolyn Moser, and Anne Peters (eds.), *The Legal Framework of the OSCE* (Cambridge: CUP 2019), 135-64.

[68] Jean D'Aspremont, 'Abuse of the Legal Personality of International Organizations and the Responsibility of Member States' *International Organizations Law Review* 4 (2007), 91-119.

[69] Guilherme Vilaca, 'Transnational Law, Functional Differentiation and Evolution' *E-Publica* 2 (2015), 41-83, at 67.

[70] *cf.* Gunther Teubner, *Law as an Autopoietic System* (Oxford: Blackwell 1993), at 44-45; Vesting, *Legal Theory* 2018 (n. 41), 150-57.

to converge with global labour rights movements, and the latter with refugee protection movements.[71] In another context, the relatively high level of protection afforded to indigenous peoples has created division and controversy concerning the concept of 'indigeneity', leading to intense debates about who should be included or excluded from this category of legal subjects. The strategies pursued in such cases often lead to unintended consequences for the identity and (self-) perception of the peoples they represent.[72] In other words, from this perspective, global legal subjectification can potentially lead to other forms of depoliticisation and co-optation.

Conversely, however, such a dynamic may also work as an emancipatory force. Indeed, in situations where legal systems and processes do not overlap and are self-contained—as in the ideal-typical legal modernity based on the internal/external divide and on strictly dualist theories of international law—recognition of legal personality within a particular system plays a dominant role in the process of subjectification. As long as national and international legal systems do not overlap (too much) and other kinds of normativity are not able to establish their own forms of legal subjectification, State-centred law plays a central role in the social construction of the individual by recognising legal personality, citizenship, and specific legal entitlements. Certainly, State institutions and laws retain a significant role. However, in a situation characterised by polycontextural, permeable, and fluid global normative processes, where each governance framework and/or system may have its own criteria of legal personification, the chances that a specific entity might *visibly* be a legal person *somewhere* increase dramatically. Therefore, an entity existing as a legal person or endowed with either direct or indirect legal entitlements in some territorial or functional context ('somewhere')—such as a citizen, investor, refugee, worker, or natural entity—potentially exists as an individual *elsewhere*. A river may not be a legal person outside New Zealand or Canada, but the fact that it is recognised as a legal person *there* increases its chances of being socially constructed as an individual *elsewhere*, thus becoming potentially relevant to legal processes *everywhere*. The abundance of relatively autonomous yet interconnected normative processes at the global level, then, makes State-centred law less relevant to determining social individualisation.

From a more normative standpoint, such observations emphasise the need to imagine emancipatory strategies of legal subjectification. Although the role of lawyers (and law in general) should not be overestimated, 'coding' the infrastructures of global law one way rather than another does have an impact on globalisation and

[71] *cf.* Thomas Kleinlein, 'Fragmentierungen im Öffentlichen Recht: Diskursvergleich im internationalen und im nationalen Recht' *Deutsches Verwaltungsblatt* 17 (2017), 1072-79, at 1078; Gunther Teubner, '*Quod Omnes Tangit*' 2018 (n. 37), 22-25.

[72] *cf.* Marie-Catherine Petersmann, 'Contested Indigeneity and Traditionality in Environmental Litigation: The Politics of Expertise in Regional Human Rights Courts' *Human Rights Law Review* 21 (2021), 132-56.

its evolution.[73] In this sense, global law can potentially retain and even strengthen its emancipatory and repoliticising potential by establishing forms of legal subjectification that allow for the expression of non-self-interested claims. Here, I would like to highlight three potential macro-strategies.

4.3.1 New Legal Concepts and Regimes

A first and relatively conventional strategy involves shifting the equilibrium of the oscillation pattern through the introduction of new legal 'coding'. By shaping new concepts and regimes concerning socially constructed individuals, this strategy aims to make otherwise invisible actors emerge and to increase repoliticisation dynamics. 'Seeing' an entity as an individual using new concepts and legal frameworks is a way to assert normative demands against them or, conversely, to deny them the benefit of a corporate veil. Consequently, the concept of the individual as the socially constructed locus of a claim may work as a starting point that is then respecified and regulated differently in each context. Indeed, new legal concepts and frameworks should be 'imagined' by carefully calibrating both responsibilities and rights according to the specific risks and opportunities that they present to global society.

As seen in section 4.3, it is the relative legal invisibility of TNCs and transnational networks as unitary global actors—*as individuals*—that plays a significant role in driving some of the most concerning trends associated with global law. In this field, in order to attach legal obligations to de facto international institutions and other actors, scholars are increasingly trying to broaden or introduce legal concepts of TNC,[74] IO,[75] and transnational networks[76] to include entities which, even without international legal personality, exercise de facto authority over other individuals.

Similarly, other scholarly proposals aim to develop overarching principles of accountability for these entities, as well as their members or nodes. In this vein, a potential model is the proposal, 'Guiding Principles on Shared Responsibility in International Law', a project that aims to codify and advance the rules of shared

[73] See generally Katharina Pistor, *The Code of Capital: How the Law Creates Wealth and Inequality* (Princeton, NJ: Princeton University Press 2019) and, from within international legal scholarship, see Martti Koskenniemi, 'International Law as "Global Governance"', in Justin Desautels-Stein and Christopher Tomlins (eds.), *Searching for Contemporary Legal Thought* (Cambridge: CUP 2017), 199-218, at 215-16.

[74] See Kevin B. Sobel-Read, 'Reimagining the Unimaginable: Law and the Ongoing Transformation of Global Value Chains into Integrated Legal Entities', *European Review of Contract Law* 16 (2020), 160-85.

[75] See Rosalyn Higgins, *Problems and Process: International Law and How We Use It* (Oxford: Clarendon Press, 1994), 47-48; Dapo Akande, 'International Organizations', in Malcolm Evans (ed.), *International Law* (5th edn, Oxford: OUP 2018), 227-58, at 233; Angelo Jr Golia and Anne Peters, 'The Concept of International Organization', in Jan Klabbers (ed.), *Cambridge Companion to International Organizations Law* (Cambridge: CUP 2022), 25-49, at 33-34 and 48-49.

[76] See Angelo Jr Golia and Gunther Teubner, 'Networked Statehood: An Institutionalised Self-contradiction in the Process of Globalisation?' *Transnational Legal Theory* 12 (2021), 7-43.

responsibility of 'international persons'.[77] The project's purpose is to harmonise the rules of shared responsibility, which were previously established by the International Law Commission for States and IOs in cases involving an indivisible injury to which contribution may be individual, concurrent, or cumulative. In this project, the phrase 'international person' as potential duty-bearer refers only to States and IOs, but the authors specify that this focus is 'without prejudice to the possibility that other actors, such as individuals or other non-state actors, bear international obligations and share responsibility in certain circumstances'.[78]

In terms of international law-making, an interesting example is the legally binding instrument to regulate the activities of TNCs and other business enterprises, currently under negotiation at the intergovernmental working group established in 2014 by the UN Human Rights Council.[79] For our purposes, it is noteworthy that the drafts circulated to date obligate States to regulate 'business activities of transnational character'.[80] In this way, although the draft treaty would not directly impose any obligation on TNCs under international law, it would switch the focus of international regulation from the single entities incorporated at the domestic level to the unitary economic actor—the global *individual*—responsible for the human rights violations. Importantly, it would do so without having to recognise the autonomous international legal personality of TNCs.

At the domestic level, some legislators are moving in the same direction. Following the relative success of the General Data Protection Regulation (GDPR)[81] as a global standard, the EU and several European countries are increasingly resorting to different techniques of 'territorial extension'[82] in an attempt to exploit the so-called 'Brussels effect'.[83] This is particularly evident when it comes to various forms of 'global supply chain' regulations, which impose obligations of vigilance, due diligence, or non-financial reporting on businesses incorporated or based in

[77] André Nollkaemper et al., 'Guiding Principles on Shared Responsibility in International Law' *European Journal of International Law* 31 (2020), 15-72. For networks, see Golia and Teubner, 'Networked Statehood' 2021 (n. 76), 33-40.

[78] Nollkaemper et al., 'Guiding Principles' 2020 (n. 77), 22 (Commentary to Principle 1, para. 1).

[79] UN, Human Rights Council, Elaboration of an international legally binding instrument on transnational corporations and other business enterprises with respect to human rights, 14 July 2014, A/HRC/RES/26/9.

[80] See Open-ended Intergovernmental Working Group on Transnational Corporations and Other Business Enterprises with Respect to Human Rights, Third revised draft of the legally binding instrument to regulate, in international human rights law, the activities of transnational corporations and other business enterprises, 17 August 2021, available at: https://www.ohchr.org/sites/default/files/LBI3rdDRAFT.pdf, accessed 11/10/21, Art. 1(4).

[81] EU: Regulation 2016/679 of the European Parliament and of the Council on the protection of natural persons with regard to the processing of personal data and on the free movement of such data of 27 April 2016.

[82] *cf.* Joanne Scott, 'Extraterritoriality and Territorial Extension in EU Law' *American Journal of Comparative Law* 62 (2014), 87-126.

[83] That is, the power to shape the global business environment due to the sheer weight of its market, especially through standards in areas such as competition regulation, consumer health and safety, and environmental protection. See Anu Bradford, *The Brussels Effect: How the European Union Rules the World* (Oxford: OUP 2020).

their jurisdictions. These regulations may impose sanctions on these businesses for human rights violations occurring within their supply chains.[84]

At the level of international adjudication, one emancipatory strategy of subjectification might be to expand the use of counter-claims[85] and denial-of-benefits clauses[86] in international investment arbitration. *Mutatis mutandis*, this strategy may also involve selectively granting legal entitlements to, and imposing liability on, 'new' individuals such as non-human animals,[87] natural entities, or artificial intelligence programmes.[88]

4.3.2 Speaking with the Voiceless

A second strategy is closely related to the first. It consists of strengthening, both substantively and procedurally, the role of civil society actors as catalysts for renewed political engagement at the global level. This might mean establishing appropriate legal frameworks to support the transnational bargaining power of social actors, for example by strengthening the legal protection afforded to the right to strike or by means of so-called transnational company agreements in the realm of social and labour law.[89] In the European context, an interesting model is the proposal developed by the European Trade Union Confederation (ETUC) in 2014 for an Optional Legal Framework for transnational agreements.[90] Similar

[84] See, among other jurisdictions, the UK: The Modern Slavery Act 2015 (Transparency in Supply Chain) Regulations 2015, SI 2015/1833, Regulation 2; France: Loi 2017-750 relative au devoir de vigilance des societies meres et des enterprises donneuses d'ordre of 23 March 2017 (Law on the Law of the duty of oversight of parent companies and commissioning enterprises); The Netherlands: Wet zorgplicht kinderarbeid of 24 October 2019 (Law on the introduction of a duty of care to prevent the supply of goods and services produced using child labour); Germany: Lieferkettensorgfaltspflichtengesetz of 11 June 2021 (Supply Chain Due Diligence Law); EU: Directive 2014/95/EU of the European Parliament and of the Council on non-financial reporting of 22 October 2014; and Regulation 2017/821 of the European Parliament and of the Council on conflict minerals imports of 17 May 2017. At the moment, the European Commission and the European Parliament are elaborating a legislative proposal for a 'European Due Diligence Act' which will most probably take the form of a directive.

[85] See ICSID, *Urbaser S.A. et al. v. The Argentine Republic*, Award of 8 December 2016, ICSID Case No. ARB/07/26, at paras. 1182-221; ICSID, *David R. Aven et al. v. Republic of Costa Rica*, Award of 18 September 2018, ICSID Case No. UNCT/15/3, at paras. 737-42.

[86] Meant to avoid the misuse of investment agreements as a 'free ride' by third-country interests or undesirable forms of 'treaty-shopping' by private actors. See, e.g., UNCITRAL, *Philip Morris Asia Limited v. The Commonwealth of Australia*, Award on Jurisdiction and Admissibility of 17 December 2015, PCA Case No. 2012-12, at para. 585; ICSID, *Pacific Rim Cayman LLC v. Republic of El Salvador*, Decision on the Respondent's Jurisdictional Objections of 1 June 2012, ICSID Case No. ARB/09/12, at paras. 4.60-4.92.

[87] For an overview of the case law of the ECtHR on animal welfare, see Tom Sparks, 'Protection of Animals Through Human Rights: The Case-Law of the European Court of Human Rights', in Anne Peters (ed.), *Studies in Global Animal Law* (Berlin: Springer 2020), 153-71.

[88] See Anna Beckers and Gunther Teubner, *Three Liability Regimes for Artificial Intelligence: Algorithmic Actants, Hybrids, Crowds* (Oxford: Hart 2022).

[89] Isabelle Schömann et al. (eds.), *Transnational Collective Bargaining at Company Level. A New Component of European Industrial Relations?* (Brussels: European Trade Union Institute 2012).

[90] European Trade Union Confederation (ETUC) Resolution: Proposal for an Optional Legal Framework for transnational negotiations in multinational companies, March 2014, available at: https://www.etuc.org/en/document/etuc-resolution-proposal-optional-legal-framework-transnational-negotiations-multinational, accessed 11/10/21. According to this proposal, the decision would bestow legal significance upon transnational collective agreements, which currently have an ambiguous legal status.

partnerships may well emerge at the global level, for example in the context of climate regulation under the umbrella of the UN Framework Convention on Climate Change (UNFCCC) and the Paris Agreement.[91]

Another example of this strategy would be using both existing and new litigation strategies to transform claims based on individual rights into political issues at the global level.[92] If it is not possible to directly bring global capitalism and global injustice, which are depersonified social processes, to trial, then (global) law must find new ways to hold the entities that enable their most destructive dynamics accountable. Borrowing an argument formulated in the field of climate litigation,[93] one could assert that such strategies have the potential to foster renewed political engagement. They accomplish this by uniting movements, fostering the exchange of ideas among various stakeholders around the world, and shedding light on global injustices. In this regard, the *Milieudefensie* decision has already become a classic illustration of how domestic and international norms may be thematised as global law to put entire business models rather than just a corporate person on trial.

Similarly, at the procedural level, the IACtHR's 2017 advisory opinion concerning the eligibility of individuals to petition the Inter-American System is a relevant point of reference because it allows only certain collective actors, based on the type of claims and interests they represent.[94] However, it would truly advance this field if collective, organised actors had more opportunities to raise claims on behalf of individuals they do not directly represent. In this context, a point of reference could be the collective complaint procedure introduced by the Additional Protocol to the European Social Charter (ESC).[95] This procedure allows social partners and NGOs to raise questions concerning the non-compliance of a State's law or practice with one of the provisions of the ESC directly—that is, without domestic remedies having been exhausted—before the European Committee of Social Rights (ECSR). Notably, the claimant organisation need not be a direct victim of the alleged violation to lodge a complaint, nor does the claimant need to be based in the

The legal basis of the decision would be Art. 6 of the Treaty on European Union (TEU) and Arts. 152, 154, and 156 of the Treaty on the Functioning of the European Union (TFEU), and would have the form of either a Decision of the Council and of the Parliament (Art. 288 TFEU) or a Decision of the social partners (Art. 155 TFEU).

[91] See Charlotte Streck, 'Strengthening the Paris Agreement by Holding Non-State Actors Accountable: Establishing Normative Links between Transnational Partnerships and Treaty Implementation' *Transnational Environmental Law* 10 (2021), 1-23.

[92] *cf.* Gunther Teubner, 'Horizontal Effect Revisited. A Reply to Four Comments' *Netherlands Journal of Legal Philosophy* 10 (2011), 275-85, at 279.

[93] See Matthias Petel, 'Analyse de l'usage stratégique des droits humains au sein du contentieux climatique contre les États' *Max Planck Institute for Comparative Public Law & International Law Research Paper No. 2020-33*, available at: https://papers.ssrn.com/sol3/papers.cfm?abstract_id=3692955, accessed 11/10/21.

[94] See *Titularidad* 2016 (n. 55).

[95] Council of Europe, Additional Protocol to the European Social Charter Providing for a System of Collective Complaints, 9 November 1995, ETS No.158.

jurisdiction in which the violation occurred. It is telling that the ECSR decisions adopted within this procedure were the only international instances to find explicitly that the several measures implementing EU austerity policies violated (social) human rights.[96]

4.3.3 The Individual Beyond the Right

A third and more radical strategy, recently outlined by Christoph Menke[97] and endorsed by Katharina Pistor,[98] consists of assigning significance to a 'new' form of the individual that transcends or exists independently of the conventional rights framework of modernity. This conventional framework is considered too entangled by the capitalist and bourgeois societal norms that emerged from legal modernity, along with the colonialist/imperialist legacy of modern international law.[99] According to this proposal, no civil rights should be sacrosanct forever. Instead, all rights and claims to rights should be systematically evaluated in relation to those of others. In a global order where no rights are intangible, where all may—but nobody has to—participate, the conventional rights framework is replaced by the *pure claim*, and the legal person by the *pure individual*. This profoundly transforms the concept of right, turning it into a counter-right, that is, into a temporal empowerment for change. It is therefore no longer a legal tool invoked to defend a pre-existing, crystallised status quo or the subject's self-will. By disempowering or at least shifting the focus away from the rights discourse, this transition aims to reinvigorate politics. Contrary to the individuals of legal modernity who assert sovereignty, the *activity* of their own will, the individuals envisaged in the context of these counter-rights *reclaim* their own exclusion, *affirm* their vulnerability, their *passivity*. As Menke contends, the revolution of the counter-right involves the uprising of the 'insurrectionary slave'.

This strategy might seem abstract[100]—even utopian—but a potential model could be identified in the Fridays for Future movement mentioned in section 4.3. Fridays for Future is a global movement, mainly composed of school-aged activists who participate in globally coordinated protests and acts of civil disobedience

[96] See, e.g., European Committee of Social Rights, *Federation of employed pensioners of Greece (IKA-ETAM) v. Greece*, Decision of 7 December 2012, Complaint No. 76/2012; *European Roma and Travellers Forum v. France*, Decision on the merits of 24 January 2012, Complaint No. 64/2011; see Karin Lukas, 'The Collective Complaint Procedure of the European Social Charter: Some Lessons for the EU?' *Legal Issues of Economic Integration* 41 (2014), 275-88.

[97] See Christoph Menke, *Critique of Rights* (Cambridge: Polity Press 2020), 267-91.

[98] Pistor, *The Code* 2019 (n. 73), 231-34.

[99] See, among many others, Antony Anghie, *Imperialism, Sovereignty and the Making of International Law* (Cambridge: CUP 2005); Sundhya Pahuja, 'The Postcoloniality of International Law' *Harvard International Law Journal* 46 (2005), 459-70; José-Manuel Barreto (ed.), *Human Rights from a Third World Perspective: Critique, History and International Law* (Newcastle upon Tyne: Cambridge Scholars 2013).

[100] Pistor, *The Code* 2019 (n. 73), 232-33 points to the significant problems involved in the massive political-legal changes required by Menke's proposal.

to demand that political leaders take action to tackle the climate emergency. The movement consists predominantly of people who, because of their age, are excluded from most electoral and political procedures of institutional politics. Rather than rejecting their status as 'children', however, they reclaim it. The basis of their (counter-)rights lies *precisely* in their reclaimed passive status, in their exclusion. They invoke global social change *precisely* based on this status.

The example of Fridays for Future also brings us full circle concerning global law. Indeed, one may argue that the perspective of global law, with its distinct characteristics, suggest two ways in which Menke's proposal could be further developed: first, by extending these counter-rights to collectives, organisations, social movements, and networks, without replacing individual rights to resistance; second, by developing a wide range of counter-rights designed to address various forms of motivational constraints and accumulation imperatives in distinct societal contexts, such as the consolidation of power in politics, the accumulation of profit in the economy, and the accumulation of knowledge in science, and so on.[101]

5. Conclusion

An examination of the relationship between the individual and global law reveals a multifaceted reality that does not lend itself to a single interpretation. However, analysing such a relationship through the frameworks of the three patterns of symbiosis, oscillation, and strategic subjectification helps unveil the individual's *specific* role in an ongoing transformation that is relevant to international law *itself*. At its core, this transformation involves the transition from models of legal production that revolve almost exclusively around the State to models of legal production in which private and hybrid actors, legal pluralism, and various forms of epistemic communities assume a more prominent role.[102]

Indeed, this analysis offers insights to differentiate between global law and its conceptual alternatives. Global law is neither a cosmopolitan law, based on universal political, economic, or other principles of rationality, nor is it simply a transnational law that regulates cross-boundary processes and involves private and hybrid actors. Although the importance of semantic disputes should not be overestimated, one possible reason why global legal processes are indeed 'global' and not just 'transnational' may be that they depend on the individual, who is conceived as a socially constructed entity and as such is potentially relevant *everywhere*, that

[101] *cf.* Gunther Teubner, 'Counter-Rights: On the Trans-Subjective Potential of Subjective Rights', in Paul F. Kjaer (ed.), *The Law of the Political Economy: Transformations in the Functions of Law* (Cambridge: CUP 2020), 372-93.

[102] See, most recently, Martti Koskenniemi and Sarah Nouwen, 'The Politics of Global Lawmaking: A Conversation' *European Journal of International Law* 32 (2021), 1341-52.

is, *regardless* of the attribution of citizenship or the recognition of legal personality in a specific legal system.[103]

Similarly, this analysis may enrich parallel debates in international legal scholarship. First, and more generally, it challenges the common assumption that individualisation and humanisation are equivalent. Furthermore, it may offer evidence to support arguments that have already been developed in some strands of international law scholarship,[104] which suggest that subjective legal rights can differ depending on the specific functional context in which they are invoked or applied. For example, the distinction between international refugee rights and human rights, as well as between international labour rights and human rights, corresponds with the unique strategic requirements regarding legal recognition and entitlements within different global functional systems. This is so whether these systems are focused on governing refugee (and migration) flows, the dynamics of capital and labour that underpin the global economy, or the broader objective of protecting the inherent humanity of individuals. Importantly, this remains true regardless of whether these distinctions tend to emerge and align, as in the first scenario,[105] or diverge and create conflicts, as in the second scenario.[106]

However, within the realm of international legal scholarship, the analysis presented in this chapter may contribute to a shared postmodern 'anxiety',[107] related to the perception that 'global law' deviates from international law, which has traditionally been understood as a legal framework centred on sovereignty and State responsibility.[108] In other words, the study of the relationship between the individual and global law *today* contributes to relativising—at least from a historical perspective—the often too stark distinction between 'international' and 'global'. The conceptual structures and categories underlying international law crystallised in the State-centric nineteenth century in the hands of European powers with imperialist aspirations. These powers *selectively* and *strategically* facilitated and/or limited the cross-border movement of people and capital.[109] What lawyers are observing today and calling 'global law' seems to be influenced by similar trends and dynamics, but involve a significantly larger number of different actors, actors that 'need' the individual more than States do. Indeed, another question to consider is whether and how the *legal* concepts and vocabulary developed by international

[103] This mirrors, for example, the argument made by Çali, 'Global Constitutionalism' (chapter 15), in this volume, whereby the individual and their moral and legal significance play a central and wide-ranging role under the *global* constitutionalist approach to international law.

[104] Peters, *Beyond Human Rights* 2016 (n. 17).

[105] *ibid*, 450-57.

[106] *ibid*, 457-68.

[107] See Martti Koskenniemi and Päivi Leino, 'Fragmentation of International Law? Postmodern Anxieties' *Leiden Journal of International Law* 15 (2005), 553-79.

[108] See Koskenniemi and Neuwen, 'The Politics of Global Lawmaking' 2021 (n. 102).

[109] *cf.*, e.g., Inge Van Hulle, 'Nineteenth Century' (chapter 6), in this volume; and, more generally, Giovanni Arrighi, Terence Hopkins, and Immanuel Wallerstein, *Antisystemic Movements* (London: Verso 2012).

lawyers or even the framework of international law itself can or should adapt to such variety as well as to the strategic purposes of militants and activists across the political spectrum who aim to 'use' international law. Once more, a specific focus on the role of the individual may, at the very least, help 'map' the field enabling us to develop—to imagine--normative and strategic options.

This consideration suggests possibilities for further research. Although it was not possible to develop it here, any analysis of the relationship between global law and the individual should explore both the functional *and* the institutional contexts in which different forms of norm arise and interact. In other words, the analytical and normative challenge that global law poses for scholars is to consider such legal processes both as functional systems—the individual *and* the law of global politics, the law of global economy, the law of global science, the law of global environment, among others—*and* as systems of collective action/decision that exist alongside States (the individual *and* IOs, networks, TNCs). Legal theory, legal regulation, and even legal disputes must develop elaborate frameworks capable of comprehending the interaction between these dimensions. Only in this way will an authentically normative legal theory contribute to the emancipatory potential of (global) law and strengthen the transformative potential of its institutions.

15

Global Constitutionalism and the Individual

Başak Çalı

1. Introduction

This chapter explores how global constitutionalism provides insights into theorising and interpreting the relationship between individuals, States, and international law. However, four important caveats must be addressed before we begin. First, global constitutionalism is not a single, complete, and unified theory, but a research agenda with variants[1] and internal disagreements,[2] as is the case with other broad umbrella approaches or traditions. Second, global constitutionalism does not solely focus on the role of the individual in international law, it also proposes a wide range of constitutional principles to guide the interpretation of international law at domestic, regional, and international levels. These constitutional principles include *human rights*, *democracy*, *the rule of law*, *constituent power*, *separation of powers*, *proportionality*, and *subsidiarity*.[3] Global constitutionalism, however, does not presume *a priori* that the treatment of the individual at the international level mirrors the treatment of individuals in

[1] Compare, e.g., Jeffrey L. Dunoff and Joel P. Trachtman, 'A Functional Approach to International Constitutionalization', in Jeffrey L. Dunoff and Joel P. Trachtman (eds.), *Ruling the World: Constitutionalism, International Law, and Global Governance* (Cambridge: CUP 2009), 3-36 and Mattias Kumm, 'The Cosmopolitan Turn in Constitutionalism: An Integrated Conception of Public Law' *Indiana Journal of Global Legal Studies* 20 (2014), 605-28; see also Mattias Kumm, 'On the History and Theory of Global Constitutionalism', in Takao Suami et al. (eds.), *Global Constitutionalism from European and East Asian Perspectives* (Cambridge: CUP 2018), 168-200, at 170 where the author defines global constitutionalism as a 'jurisprudential approach' with 'competing theories of distinct issue-areas'.

[2] See, e.g., Neil Walker, 'The Return of Constituent Power: A Reply to Mattias Kumm' *International Journal of Constitutional Law* 14 (2016), 906-13; Mattias Kumm, 'Constituent Power, Boundaries and Identity: On the Justificatory Depth of Constitutionalism – A Rejoinder to Neil Walker' *International Journal of Constitutional Law* 14 (2016), 914-24; see also Christine E. J. Schwöbel, 'Situating the Debate on Global Constitutionalism' *International Journal of Constitutional Law* 8 (2010), 611-35.

[3] See, *inter alia*, Antje Wiener et al., 'Global Constitutionalism: Human Rights, Democracy and the Rule of Law' *Global Constitutionalism* 1 (2012), 1-15; Anne Peters, 'Proportionality as a global Constitutional Principle', in Anthony F. Lang and Antje Wiener (eds.), *Handbook on Global Constitutionalism* (Cheltenham: Edward Elgar 2017), 248-64; Anthony F. Lang Jr and Antje Wiener, 'A Constitutionalizing Global Order: An Introduction', in Anthony F. Lang Jr and Antje Wiener (eds.), *Handbook on Global Constitutionalism* (Cheltenham: Edward Elgar 2017), 1-20.

Başak Çalı, *Global Constitutionalism and the Individual* In: *The Individual in International Law*. Edited by: Tom Sparks and Anne Peters, Oxford University Press. © Başak Çalı 2024. DOI: 10.1093/oso/9780198898917.003.0015

domestic constitutional law. Instead, it invites a reflective adaptation of constitutionalism to the global sphere.[4] Whilst global constitutionalism approaches the point and purpose of international law in human-centred rather than in State-centred terms,[5] its main interest lies in developing a constitutionalist perspective on the humanisation of international law. Third, global constitutionalism is primarily characterised as a normative 'aspirational process':[6] that is, a process in which the constitutionalist significance of the individual may be present in certain existing features of international law, but may only be emerging or absent in others.[7] Therefore, interpreting international law from a global constitutionalist perspective is a constructive task, with the goal of guiding interpreters to emphasise constitutionalist elements in international law that already exist.[8] Fourth, and lastly, institutionalised expressions of the constitutional role of the individual in international law remain open-ended. As Anne Peters puts it, 'the idea is not to create a global, centralized government, but to constitutionalize global, polyarchic, and multilevel governance'.[9] This means that a normative commitment to a global constitutionalist focus on the individual does not necessarily require pre-defined institutional plans and outcomes.

Collectively, these four caveats mean that a broad range of concrete positions on the relationship between individuals, States, and international law can emerge within the framework of global constitutionalism. These can arise both when we explore the central role of the individual in the broader framework of constitutional principles in international law and when we interpret and appraise existing international law. Sharing a number of abstract theoretical commitments to constitutionalism, therefore, can still lead to pluralist understandings of how these commitments work in practice.[10] These differences may depend on the legal context in which the individual's role is being examined, such as sources of general international law, international human rights law, international criminal law, international trade law, or the international law of climate change.

[4] This is also called 'small c constitutionalism', notably coined by Kumm. See, Kumm, 'The Cosmopolitan Turn' 2014 (n. 1), at 608.

[5] See also Peters and Sparks, 'Introduction' (chapter 1), in this volume.

[6] Aoife O'Donoghue, *Constitutionalism in Global Constitutionalisation* (Cambridge: CUP 2014), at 154.

[7] See Anne Peters, 'Global Constitutionalism: The Social Dimension', in Takao Suami et al. (eds.), *Global Constitutionalism from European and East Asian Perspectives* (Cambridge: CUP 2018), 277-350.

[8] In this respect, global constitutionalism shares some common commitments with interpretivism as a method. On the methodological dimensions of interpretivism and international law, see Başak Çalı, 'On Interpretivism and International Law' *European Journal of International Law* 20 (2009), 805-22.

[9] Anne Peters, 'The Merits of Global Constitutionalism' *Indiana Journal of Global Legal Studies* 16 (2009), 397-411, at 404.

[10] See Cormac Mac Amhlaigh, 'Harmonising Global Constitutionalism' *Global Constitutionalism* 5 (2016), 173-206.

Given these preliminary caveats, this chapter focuses, first, on identifying the more abstract features of the global constitutionalist approach to the relationship between the individual, States, and international law and, second, on what implications may be drawn from these abstract features for the interpretation of international law. The chapter offers a twofold argument. First, it argues that the individual plays a central role for theorising the functions of States in international law, the structure of international law (most notably in contrast to positivist theories of international law), and the relationship between international law and domestic (constitutional) law. Secondly, the individual plays a significant heuristic role in the interpretation of existing international legal doctrines and proposals for international legal reform. The role of the individual in international law, however, is part of several interconnected constitutional values in a multilevel legal order, namely democracy, the rule of law, subsidiarity, and proportionality. Collectively, these two elements of the argument highlight the flexibility of global constitutionalism and its ability to remain in conversation with various theoretical approaches regarding the relationship between the individual, the State, and international law, most notably, natural law and critical approaches to international law. This flexibility, however, may constitute a strength as well as a weakness.

Section 2 begins with a discussion of the central role the individual has when theorising the relationship between individuals, States, and international law in global constitutionalism. The section then examines how the individual's significance aligns with the interconnecting constitutional principle of democracy and humanisation of international law. Section 3 turns to how global constitutionalism aims to shape the interpretation of existing international law and the future institutional development of international law. This section outlines the types of reforms that global constitutionalism could support or oppose in order to strengthen the individual's constitutionalised role in international law. Section 4 examines whether the individual's role in global constitutionalism is overdetermined. Section 5 concludes the chapter.

2. Global Constitutionalist Approaches to International Law and the Central Role of the Individual

The individual plays a central role in global constitutionalist approaches to international law in three distinct ways: (1) it helps global constitutionalism to reject the proposition that the structure of international law is based on sovereign consent only; (2) it aids global constitutionalism to focus attention on the accountability of international law towards individuals; and (3) it enables committing to the constitutionalist humanisation of international law.

2.1 The Central Role of the Individual in the Reconstruction of States and International Law

It is well known that positivist theories of international law define international law as primarily originating from the consent of sovereign States. Sovereign States make international laws together to ensure their mutual co-existence and cooperation. In positivist theories, State consent is not merely a social reality; it has also been defended as a means to safeguard an important normative value. This is the instrumental ability of consent to protect the diverse nature of the international system and to counterbalance any attempts by one group of States to dominate and impose their preferences over others.[11]

Global constitutionalism challenges this conventional positivist view of international law's consent-based structure, both in terms of its social reality and its normative value. In terms of its social reality, global constitutionalism relies on the strengthening of domestic constitutionalism and the expansion of international law from bilateralism to a consideration of broader community interests, especially since 1945. Global constitutionalism employs these developments to assert that both domestic and international law are experiencing a shared and discernible process of constitutionalisation.[12] Normatively, global constitutionalism promotes a functional understanding of sovereignty by emphasising that 'state sovereignty has its source and *telos* in humanity, understood as the principle that the state must protect human rights, interests, needs, and security'.[13] Thus, global constitutionalism views States as entities responsible for ensuring the well-being of individuals subject to constitutional constraints. It also links the legitimacy of States to how they treat their citizens. States are thus conceptualised as institutional vehicles to secure and respect individuals' rights.

The recognition of the dignity and equality of all individuals is central to global constitutionalists' understanding of State sovereignty. States, as institutional constructs, hold value not solely for their effective control of a territory and its population, but because they are or aim to be constitutionally organised in ways that demonstrate equal concern and respect to individuals. State sovereignty and the international legal order based on consent, therefore, should not be understood as an end in itself. Respecting State consent in international law is important, but only to the extent that such consent represents the collective will of individuals organised as a distinct group or nation. The concern for the individual and the value of

[11] See Prosper Weil, 'Towards Relative Normativity in International Law?' *American Journal of International Law* 77 (1983), 413-42.

[12] See Bruno Simma, 'From Bilateralism to Community Interests in International law' *Recueil des Cours* 250 (1994), 217-384; Anne Peters, 'Humanity as the A and Ω of Sovereignty' *European Journal of International Law* 20 (2009), 513-44.

[13] Peters, 'The Merits of Global Constitutionalism' 2009 (n. 9), at 543.

recognising individuals' political equality, therefore, are key to reconceptualising sovereignty.

Global constitutionalism relies on the intrinsic moral and equal worth of individuals to reject a sweeping formal defence of both internal and external State sovereignty.[14] In this respect, the global constitutionalist and natural-law approaches to sovereignty overlap. However, the global constitutionalist emphasis on the central role of individuals is not grounded exclusively in a theory of natural law, but also in a constructive interpretation of existing legal frameworks. Global constitutionalism, therefore, can be understood as engaging in a form of 'moralised description' of law.[15] This description relies on the actual constitutionalisation of individuals' rights in both domestic and international law as an observable and action-guiding social fact, rather than merely a moral aspiration.

Significantly, global constitutionalism does not limit its functional understanding of State sovereignty only to States that embrace constitutionalism in their domestic legal orders. Instead, it asserts that constitutionalism is pervasive enough to apply to all subjects of international law. Global constitutionalism, therefore, not only combines insights from traditions of political liberalism, republicanism, and democracy but also from those of cosmopolitanism.[16] This position represents a significant departure from those views—such as the influential one proposed by Rawls in the *Law of Peoples*[17]—which argue that non-liberal peoples cannot be assessed using liberal criteria in the context of international law.

Some variants of cosmopolitan global constitutionalism further maintain that individuals as constitutionally significant units matter not only for assessing the legal obligations of states in which they live, but also obligations of other states under international law.[18] As Mattias Kumm puts it, the concept of a group of free and equal individuals forming a community encompasses 'the idea of a community of free and equal persons governing itself within the framework of the state as part of an international community', an idea that 'is prior to and gives meaning to the idea of constituent power'.[19] This implies that individuals are not only normatively significant for the legitimacy of the States in which they live, but also play a

[14] See Mattias Kumm, 'The Legitimacy of International Law: A Constitutionalist Framework of Analysis' *European Journal of International Law* 15 (2004), 907-31.

[15] On constructive interpretation and moralised description, see Aaron James, 'Constructing Justice for Existing Practice: Rawls and the Status Quo' *Philosophy & Public Affairs* 33 (2005), 281-316, at 301.

[16] See Mattias Kumm, 'Constituent Power, Cosmopolitan Constitutionalism, and Post-Positivist Law' *International Journal of Constitutional Law* 14 (2016), 697-711.

[17] In Rawls' words: 'A main task in extending the Law of Peoples to non-liberal peoples is to specify how far liberal peoples are to tolerate non-liberal peoples.' See John Rawls, *Law of Peoples* (Cambridge, MA: Harvard University Press 1993), at 59.

[18] See Kumm, 'The Cosmopolitan Turn' 2014 (n. 1); Peters, 'Global Constitutionalism: The Social Dimension' 2018 (n. 7). See also Garrett Wallace Brown, 'Cosmopolitanism and Global Constitutionalism', in Anthony F. Lang and Antje Wiener (eds.), *Handbook on Global Constitutionalism* (Cheltenham: Edward Elgar 2017), 93-105.

[19] Kumm, 'Constituent Power' 2016 (n. 16), at 698.

role in understanding how we conceive the legitimacy of inter-State relations. For Kumm, in particular, all self-governing entities 'are under a prima facie duty *not to disable* [other self-governing entities], make them worse off than they would be if there was no other self-governing entity'.[20] States, therefore, are expected to have due regard to how their actions may effect distant others who are not immediate members of their national community, but are nevertheless members of the larger international community.[21]

As this discussion shows, the individual plays a significant role in reconstructing both the internal and external sovereignty of States. This reliance is not without its critics. One important criticism highlights that global constitutionalism overlooks the differences between domestic liberal constitutionalism and global constitutionalism and exaggerates the global cosmopolitan case for constitutionalism. They also highlight the absence of a strong constituent power to bring about cosmopolitan constitutionalisation in the international arena.[22] A second line of criticism points to the lack of attention global constitutionalism pays to pluralism, understood both as value pluralism and institutional pluralism in the international legal system.[23] In such a highly diverse context like the international society, the question is whether placing such a foundational emphasis on the abstract category of the individual is adequate.

In response to these criticisms, global constitutionalists defend the importance of individuals under what is termed 'small c' constitutionalism or 'micro-constitutionalism'.[24] Accordingly, even if concern for the individual is explicitly lacking in certain aspects of international law, it can still be advocated, as neither domestic nor international law is immune from constitutionalist analysis.[25] Global constitutionalism further acknowledges that there are indeed tensions between liberal democratic and cosmopolitan variants of constitutionalism. It, however, emphasises that legal theory is well suited to work with value pluralism as well as institutional pluralism through the law's ability to develop mediating principles. Constitutional principles of subsidiarity and proportionality, in particular, are the textbook constitutionalist responses to address competing values, interests, and rights in domestic, regional, or international law.[26] Subsidiarity allows constitutionalists to clarify the allocation of authority in a multilevel legal order, in

[20] Kumm, 'Constituent Power, Boundaries and Identity' 2016 (n. 2), at 919.

[21] *ibid.*

[22] Walker, 'The Return of Constituent Power' 2016 (n. 2), at 909.

[23] See Neil Walker, 'Constitutionalism and Pluralism', in Anthony F. Lang and Antje Wiener (eds.), *Handbook on Global Constitutionalism* (Cheltenham: Edward Elgar 2017), 433-44.

[24] Kumm, 'The Cosmopolitan Turn' 2014 (n. 1), at 608; Anne Peters, 'Compensatory Constitutionalism: The Function and Potential of Fundamental International Norms and Structures' *Leiden Journal of International Law* 19 (2006), 579-610, at 594.

[25] Peters, 'The Merits of Global Constitutionalism' 2009 (n. 9), at 398.

[26] See Andreas Føllesdal, 'The Principle of Subsidiarity as a Constitutional Principle in International Law' *Global Constitutionalism* 2 (2013), 37-62; Alec Stone Sweet and Jud Matthews, 'Proportionality Balancing in Global Constitutionalism' *Columbia Journal of Transnational Law* 47 (2008), 68-149.

particular between domestic and international institutions. Proportionality analysis, on the other hand, provides a framework in which conflicts between individual rights, as well as conflicts between rights and other public interests, are resolved by the most suitable entities or authorities.[27] In other words, global constitutionalism proposes to address the tensions between liberal democratic and cosmopolitan stances on constitutionalism in a piecemeal fashion, rather than in abstract terms by attending to the substantive issues at stake and identifying the entities or authorities best placed to address them. This perspective also provides fresh insight on the monism versus dualism debate in international law, which revolves around the domestic reception of international law, by suggesting that domestic and international law are in a synergistic relationship.

2.2 The Democratisation of International Law

Global constitutionalism supports the democratisation of multilevel governance regimes, thus aiming to ensure that individuals have a voice not only in domestic but also in international law-making. But this endorsement does not amount to the establishment of a global State where every individual directly participates. Instead, the global constitutionalist agenda focuses on ensuring that individuals are significantly involved in decisions that directly affect them and emphasises that national citizenship and domestic democratic voting rights in a single political community is one means of such participation.[28] This allows global constitutionalism to focus attention on the existing participatory gaps that arise in multilevel legal orders of the international system. The areas recognised as needing more democratisation encompass a variety of situations, including the way States exercise public authority over non-citizens in their territories; the extraterritorial exercise of State powers that have a significant impact on individuals outside their territories; how States fulfil their duties towards refugees; as well as the utilisation of public powers by international organisations. Global constitutionalists perspectives can critique participation models that exclude individuals based on citizenship[29] and question the lack of constitutionalist scrutiny regarding States' extraterritorial actions.[30]

[27] See Peters, 'Proportionality' 2017 (n. 3).

[28] See Anne Peters, 'Dual Democracy', in Jan Klabbers, Anne Peters, and Geir Ulfstein, *The Constitutionalization of International Law* (Oxford: OUP 2009), 263-341.

[29] See Robert E. Goodin, 'Enfranchising All Subjected, Worldwide' *International Theory* 8 (2016), 365-89.

[30] See Peters, 'Global Constitutionalism: The Social Dimension' 2018 (n. 7).

2.2.1 Constitutionalist Humanisation

The individual and the respect for their human rights are central to global constitutionalism. The central role of human rights in this approach overlaps in significant ways with what is called the 'humanisation of international law': that is, the aim of international law to protect individuals.[31] Advocates of the humanisation of international law within the global constitutionalist framework, however, rely on the importance of human rights in both domestic and international law. As such, this framework offers a constitutionalist perspective on humanisation.

Global constitutionalism promotes the idea that all State authorities have a constitutional obligation to advance the protection of human rights within their jurisdictions. This goes beyond simply granting human rights a place in the domestic constitution; it also involves promoting a human rights approach throughout all other domestic laws. However, the normative agenda of global constitutionalists concerning human rights protection extends beyond this focus on a single domestic jurisdiction. Specifically, global constitutionalism asserts that the protection of human rights is not limited to the domestic constitutionalist realm, but can effectively extend into the international constitutionalist sphere. It is widely recognised that there is no fundamental difference between constitutional fundamental rights and international human rights, and that domestic, regional, and international levels of human rights protection ultimately serve the common goal of guaranteeing decision-making procedures and outcomes that respect individuals' rights.[32] Global constitutionalism also maintains that this position is not idealistic, but is in fact supported by the development and institutionalisation of international human rights law and its discernible systemic effects on other areas of public international law. As a result, it is possible to expand the range of actors with human rights responsibilities. Therefore, human rights are capable of guiding and constraining the actions not only of States but also regional and international organisations, as well as powerful non-State actors. Global constitutionalism emphasises the paramount importance of ensuring the protection of human rights whenever any authority holds the potential to influence or limit the rights of individuals.[33]

The constitutionalist interpretation of human rights in international law goes beyond specifying which entities bear human rights obligations. It is also

[31] See Peters and Sparks, 'Introduction' (chapter 1), in this volume. See also Antônio Augusto Cançado Trindade, 'International Law for Humankind: Towards a New Jus Gentium' *Recueil des Cours* 316 (2005), 9-439; Peters, 'Humanity as the A and Ω' 2009 (n. 12).

[32] See Stephen Gardbaum, 'Human Rights as International Constitutional Rights' *European Journal of International Law* 19 (2008), 749-68. See also Samantha Besson, 'Human Rights as Transnational Constitutional Law', in Anthony F. Lang and Antje Wiener (eds.), *Handbook on Global Constitutionalism* (Cheltenham: Edward Elgar 2017), 234-47.

[33] For a doctrinal expression of this global constitutionalist vision, see German Constitutional Court, *BNDGesetz*, Judgment of 19 May 2020, 1 BvR 2835/17, paras. 1-332.

concerned with integrating a wide range of human rights considerations into decision-making procedures. For instance, Iain Ferguson argues that global constitutionalism supports a forward-looking 'collective politics of human rights'.[34] The collective politics of human rights highlights the dynamic role that human rights play in constitutionalisation of international law. This role is not only about expanding the range of accountability for human rights violations, but also about broadening the scope of human rights protections, for example by considering the constitutionalisation of third-generation or solidarity rights in the international legal order and endorsing the inclusion of human rights concerns into various branches of international law. This broadens the scope of application from traditional areas like consular protection to new fields such as climate change. Furthermore, this dynamic involvement in the collective politics of human rights may also enable global constitutionalism to actively engage with other theoretical approaches, such as feminist approaches to international law[35] and third world approaches.[36]

3. Interpretation and Reform of Current International Law

Given the importance placed on the concern and respect for individuals both as insiders and outsiders of self-governing communities, it is no surprise that the individual as a category fulfils several distinct heuristic orientation functions in guiding the interpretation of existing international law. This is also closely tied to the normative agenda of global constitutionalism, which aims to strengthen constitutional analysis in international, regional, and domestic contexts. This means that global constitutionalism supports a *pro persona* approach to framing the origins of international law; it advocates the systemic integration of international law across various branches, emphasising the rights of individuals. It also supports or endorses employing a perspective that promotes individual rights when interpreting existing arrangements of international law precisely because it views human rights as part of 'a core normative structure within an ever-fragmenting regime' of international law.[37] Therefore, the research agenda of global constitutionalism embraces the humanisation of the international-law agenda to enhance the broader constitutionalisation of international law.

[34] Iain Ferguson, 'Liberal Theory', in Anthony F. Lang and Antje Wiener (eds.), *Handbook on Global Constitutionalism* (Cheltenham: Edward Elgar 2017), 106-16, at 110.

[35] See Ruth Houghton and Aoife O'Donoghue, 'Ourworld: A Feminist Approach to Global Constitutionalism' *Global Constitutionalism* 9 (2020), 38-75.

[36] See Siddharth Mallavarapu, 'After fragmentation: Notes from the Global South' *Global Constitutionalism* 9 (2020), 424-36.

[37] O'Donoghue, *Global Constitutionalisation* 2014 (n. 6), at 96.

3.1 The Individual, Interpretation, and Global Constitutionalism

Global constitutionalism favours interpretations of international law that advance the constitutional standing of human rights across all branches of international law (similar to the role of fundamental rights in domestic constitutional settings). That is, human rights should not be treated merely as binding treaty law applicable between State parties; they should also be seen as constitutional principles with the capacity to influence the interpretation of international law more generally. This would involve supporting interpretations of existing international law that better align with a constitutionalist understanding of human rights in international law. For global constitutionalists, international law has rich doctrinal resources to facilitate this. However, these doctrinal resources are piecemeal and fragmented. The heuristic task at hand, therefore, is strategically to restore these doctrinal resources in a way that aligns with a constitutionalist perspective. In the following, I focus on three of these restorations offered by global constitutionalist approaches: the reconceptualisation of *ius cogens* norms, general principles of law, and the principle of systemic integration.

3.1.1 The Reconceptualisation of *Ius Cogens* Norms and Normative Hierarchy

To begin, global constitutionalism supports the category of peremptory norms of general international law and dismisses the legal positivist scepticism regarding the challenges of identifying such norms. A central feature of all constitutionalist thinking is that constitutional principles are of a higher order, and a hierarchy of norms exists between ordinary law and constitutional law. The peremptory norms fulfil this central hierarchical function in international law. Global constitutionalism would also not find it challenging to identify the norms that are apt for *ius cogens* status, because of the importance it assigns to individuals and the expression of their will as a political community.[38] In other words, from a global constitutionalist perspective, individuals' basic freedoms, as well as the right to self-determination, understood as a collective expression of these freedoms, can be justified as peremptory norms.[39]

3.1.2 General Principles of Law

Global constitutionalism would endorse a broader interpretation of the primary sources of international law in the context of human rights. In positivist international law, human rights law is often treated as part of treaty law. Establishing human rights as a matter of customary international law often involves debates

[38] See Andrea Bianchi, 'Human Rights and the Magic of Jus Cogens' *European Journal of International Law* 19 (2008), 491-508.

[39] See Kumm, 'History and Theory' 2018 (n. 1).

about whether there is settled practice recognised as law. Treatment of human rights as general principles of law is scarce.[40] From a global constitutionalist perspective, however, general principles of law can also act as a primary source of international human rights law.[41] It has been suggested, for example, that the overlapping recognition of fundamental rights in constitutions in almost all parts of the world could serve as the basis for these rights to be recognised as general principles of law.[42] Once fundamental rights are recognised as general principles of law, the development of soft human rights law can also be seen in a new light: soft law can then be understood not as the potential early beginnings of hard international law, but as interpretive specifications of existing general principles of law. These reinterpretations of existing international legal doctrines are possible because global constitutionalism considers domestic and international constitutionalism as mutually influential and interdependent. This understanding, in turn, gives comparative human rights law a prominent position in the identification of human rights norms in international law. Samantha Besson, for example, argues that the comparative method is not just a means to discover how others interpret human rights law, but is also a necessary tool to define what the constitutional framework of international law incorporates as human rights law.[43] She argues that this is because, in terms of ontology, human rights are part of a transnational legality; that is, legality shaped jointly by both domestic and international law.[44]

3.1.3 The Principle of Systemic Integration

The principle of systemic integration, as recognised by the Vienna Convention on the Law of Treaties, holds that relevant international law should be considered when interpreting an international treaty.[45] From a global constitutionalist perspective, this principle can have a significant role in extending the influence of human rights into other branches of international law, such as international trade or international investment law. It provides a means to consider human rights norms in the interpretation of these branches of international law.[46] This approach shares important commonalities with third-world approaches to international law,

[40] William A. Schabas, *Customary International Law of Human Rights* (Oxford: OUP 2021), 40-101.

[41] For earlier discussions of these, see also Bruno Simma and Philip Alston, 'The Sources of Human Rights Law: Custom, *Jus Cogens* and General Principles' *Australian Yearbook of International Law* 12 (1992), 82-108.

[42] See Thomas Kleinlein, 'Customary International Law and General Principles: Rethinking Their Relationship', in Brian D. Lepard (ed.), *Reexamining Customary International Law* (Cambridge: CUP 2016), 131-58.

[43] See Besson, 'Transnational Constitutional Law' 2017 (n. 32).

[44] *ibid*, 241.

[45] See Campbell McLachlan, 'The Principle of Systemic Integration and Article 31(3)(c) of the Vienna Convention' *International and Comparative Law Quarterly* 54 (2005), 279-320; Panos Merkouris, *Article 31(3)(c) VCLT and the Principle of Systemic Integration* (Leiden: Brill Nijhoff 2015).

[46] See Anne Peters, 'The Refinement of International Law: From Fragmentation to Regime Interaction and Politicization' *International Journal of Constitutional Law* 15 (2017), 671-704.

as the human rights that need to be considered are not limited to civil and political rights but also include economic, social, and cultural rights, as well as the rights of indigenous peoples.[47] In this respect, global constitutionalism aligns itself with the wide-ranging critiques of the neoliberal economic order.[48] However, what sets it apart is its insistence on constraining both the operation of power and the protection of human rights in the exercise of that power, thus aiming to bridge the divide between economic constitutionalism and social constitutionalism in the global sphere.

3.2 Reform Agendas: Participation of and Remedies for Affected Individuals

Global constitutionalism acknowledges that the protection of the individual and their rights in the international legal order is an ongoing process, and that there are institutional gaps in the system, particularly when individuals are not involved in decision-making processes that impact them or when they lack access to remedies. Global constitutionalism therefore supports the general idea that institutional arrangements should be reformed to ensure that the exercise of authority is accessible and accountable to individuals affected by it, and that individuals have access to effective remedies. The agenda for institutional reform encompasses more than just assigning supervisory functions to regional and international courts to compensate for deficiencies in the domestic constitutional protections of these rights, which the current institutional arrangements already provide.[49]

In terms of ensuring individuals' meaningful participation in the international system, global constitutionalists do not insist that the separation of powers or democratic participation, as found in domestic constitutional orders, must be replicated in the international legal order. Instead, they propose that meaningful participation of individuals can be facilitated through indirect means (such as individuals exercising checks and balances through delegated powers to national institutions) and through direct means by increasing civil-society and individual involvement in the decision-making processes of international organisations or treaty regimes.[50] Whether international institutions are geared towards

[47] See Bhupinder S. Chimni, 'The Past, Present and Future of International Law: A Critical World Approach' *Melbourne Journal of International Law* 8 (2007), 499-515; Larissa Ramina, 'TWAIL – "Third World Approaches to International Law" and Human Rights: Some Considerations' *Revista de Investigações Constitucionais* 5 (2018), 261-72.

[48] Mattias Kumm, 'An Empire of Capital? Transatlantic Investment Protection as the Institutionalization of Unjustified Privilege' *Verfassungsblog*, available at: https://verfassungsblog.de/an-empire-of-capital-transatlantic-investment-protection-as-the-institutionalization-of-unjustified-privilege/, accessed 7/7/23.

[49] Peters, 'Compensatory Constitutionalism' 2006 (n 24).

[50] O'Donogue, *Global Constitutionalisation* 2014 (n. 6), at 33. See also Andreas von Staden, 'No Institution is an Island: Checks and Balances in Global Governance', in Joana Mendes and Ingo Venzke

'compensating'[51] for the lack of individual participation in domestic institutions or whether they engage in public actions at the expense of domestic constitutional safeguards is also relevant to whether, and how, the international order is democratised. For example, international human rights courts that enable individuals to challenge deficiencies in domestic human rights protections would require a different approach to democratisation than the UN Security Council, which is capable of exercising direct authority over individuals without their meaningful participation in those decisions.

Concerns regarding the lack of effective international remedies for individuals who are subject to the exercise of powers by global governance institutions are a central part of the global constitutionalist reform agenda. These institutions range from the UN to other international organisations, such as international financial institutions and the World Health Organization. It is therefore likely that the global constitutionalist agenda would not only favour interpretations of the existing mandates of these institutions that prioritise human rights, but would also propose the establishment of new institutional arrangements that guarantee accountability to individuals significantly impacted by the exercise of power in the realm of global governance. In this respect, it is also important to emphasise that because of the division between ordinary politics and constitutional constraints, global constitutionalism is open to a greater judicialisation of the international legal order, if such judicialisation enhances individuals' access and their ability to seek remedies.[52]

The global constitutionalists' reform agenda would also support the expansion and strengthening of not only civil but also criminal remedies, that is, holding individuals accountable for breaches of international law. This is consistent with global constitutionalism's normative framework, which advocates for the accountability not only of States but also individuals who subvert the international constitutional order. In this respect, global constitutionalists would view the International Criminal Court as serving important functions within the framework of global constitutionalism for prosecuting individuals for crimes of aggression, crimes against humanity, or genocide,[53] as well as serving compensatory constitutionalist functions by providing the means to remove such individuals from office in their respective jurisdictions.[54] Apart from endorsing the current regimes, global

(eds.), *Allocating Authority: Who Should do what in European and International Law?* (Oxford: Hart 2018), 115-39.

[51] Peters, 'Compensatory Constitutionalism' 2006 (n. 24), at 580.

[52] Compare this with the scepticism associated with political constitutionalism. See Richard Bellamy, 'The Democratic Legitimacy of International Human Rights Conventions: Political Constitutionalism and the European Convention on Human Rights' *European Journal of International Law* 25 (2014), 1019-42.

[53] Alain Zysset, 'Global Constitutionalism and the International Criminal Court: A Relational View' *Glasgow Centre for International Law and Security Working Paper* (2020), available at https://gcils.org/wp-content/uploads/2020/10/GCILS-WP-1-Zysset.pdf, accessed 7/7/23.

[54] Rupert Elderkin, 'The Impact of International Criminal Law and the ICC on National Constitutional Arrangements' *Global Constitutionalism* 4 (2015), 227-53.

constitutionalism would also be in a position to support the expansion of criminal accountability to encompass a wider range of international crimes, and potentially even include corporate actors.

4. Global Constitutionalism, the Individual, and the Problems of Heterogeneity and Pluralism

A central challenge for global constitutionalism is whether its emphasis on individuals is overdetermining. That is, whether the various contexts in which the significance of the individual is asserted are too fragmented to offer an integrated understanding of the role of the individual in global constitutionalist thinking. This is particularly significant because global constitutionalism endorses a multilevel constitutional order in which various actors within domestic, regional, and international spheres are expected to give meaning to the moral value, agency, and rights of individuals across multiple levels and different contexts. The unity of value of the individual and their rights within such a complex institutional frameworks is bound to give rise to many conflicts.[55] These conflicts emerge not only within the boundaries of individual countries, where they involve clashes between the rights of individuals and collective interests (or the rights of others), but also between the rights of individuals in one country and collective interests (or the rights of others) in another country, or between the rights of individuals in one place and what can be described as global public collective interests. Consider, for example, the extensive surveillance measures undertaken by States extraterritorially to protect national security (or the collective rights of their own citizens to security). These measures may encroach upon the privacy rights of those subject to surveillance.[56] Similarly, measures mitigating the effects of the climate crisis may prevent individuals and communities in developing or least developed countries from enjoying economic rights.[57] Whilst global constitutionalism supports a 'collective politics' of human rights when addressing these conflicts in various contexts, there is also always a risk that the emphasis on the significance of the individual will lead to

[55] Neil Walker, 'Beyond Boundary Disputes and Basic Grids: Mapping the Global Disorder of Normative Orders' *International Journal of Constitutional Law* 6 (2008), 373-96, at 379-81; Armin von Bogdandy, 'Pluralism, Direct Effect, and the Ultimate Say: On the Relationship between International and Domestic Constitutional Law' *International Journal of Constitutional Law* 6 (2008), 397-413; Daniel Bethlehem, 'International Law, European Community Law, National Law: Three Systems in Search of a Framework', in Martti Koskenniemi (ed.), *International Law Aspects of the European Union* (Leiden: Martinus Nijhoff 1997).

[56] See Marko Milanovic, 'Human Rights Treaties and Modern Surveillance Policy in the Digital Age' *Harvard International Law Journal* 56 (2015), 81-146.

[57] See Simon Caney, 'Distributive Justice and Climate Change', in Serena Olsaretti (ed.), *Oxford Handbook of Distributive Justice* (Oxford: OUP 2018), 664-89.

questions about *which individual's* rights in *which locations* for *what normative reasons* will be prioritised by *which institutions*. In this respect, the diverse range of traditions that inform global constitutionalist thinking, including the liberal and social constitutional tradition, the cosmopolitan tradition, and critiques of human rights that highlight historical injustices within western liberal constitutionalist traditions,[58] may prove to be its Achilles heel. This is because these traditions offer different visions for assessing the nature and goals of human rights and their constitutionalist significance within international law. They do not form a seamless, coherent, or harmonious whole.[59]

In this respect, it is possible to identify two different but inter-related challenges related to overdetermination. The first challenge pertains to the reliance on a wide range of actors—domestic, regional, or global—to address international legal issues. The second challenge relates to dealing with the inevitable conflicts between individual rights and collective community interests, not only when they occur within a single State, but also between individuals or communities in one State and collective interests in another State or global public interests.

4.1 Commitment to a Multilevel Legal Order

When addressing the first challenge, global constitutionalism requires that all actors, regardless of their position, to acknowledge the basic presumption that we live in a multi-level legal order. Interpretation of the law at any level should thus proceed only after this foundational position of the interdependence of domestic and international law has been accepted.[60] This is because both domestic and international law are concerned with constitutional matters relating to establishing the suitable framework for the governance of collective action and determining how individuals and their rights can be protected. Samantha Besson, in particular, addresses this co-dependence by relying on what she terms the 'transnational legality' of human rights law.[61]

However, adhering to this initial presumption does not eliminate conflicts in the interpretation of various legal orders. Global constitutionalism opposes the idea of a cosmopolitan world State as the primary venue for resolving these conflicts. Instead, it defends the position that individuals can receive protection under

[58] See Karin Mickelson, 'Rhetoric and Rage: Third World Voices in International Legal Discourse' *Wisconsin International Law Journal* 16 (1998), 353-419; Obiora Chiendu Okafor, 'Newness, Imperialism and Legal Reform in Our Time: A TWAIL Perspective' *Osgoode Law Journal* 43 (2005), 171-91.

[59] Consider, e.g., that the role of the individual in a seemingly harmonious single political setting is subject to different interpretations. See, e.g., Philip Petit, 'Liberalism and Republicanism' *Australian Journal of Political Science* 28 (1993), 162-89.

[60] Kumm, 'The Cosmopolitan Turn' 2014 (n. 1), at 625.

[61] Besson, 'Transnational Constitutional Law' 2017 (n. 32), at 237.

domestic or international law, without a prima facie presumption as to which level is better. Because global constitutionalism views the international and domestic systems as co-constitutive, it necessities the acceptance of this principle of subsidiarity. In this regard, global constitutionalism differs from neo-natural approaches to international law, as exemplified by the writings of Antônio Augusto Cançado Trindade,[62] which assume that international law serves as the central source of individual rights.

Global constitutionalism, however, is criticised for optimistically assuming that all interpreters will treat human rights seriously and will adopt an appropriate understanding of subsidiarity, a concept which itself requires a substantial amount of interpretation when applied in specific contexts.[63] How the various orders can interact, especially when there is no solid legal and institutional relationship between multilevel interpreters, also structurally hinders multilevel dialogues among actors in different positions. In this respect, one concern that arises is whether the conception of global constitutionalism as a multilevel order can serve as a general theory of international law beyond Europe, where international, regional, and domestic law consistently interact in dense and iterative relationships.

In addition, there is significant variation in the development of the protection of individual rights in the context of liberal democratic constitutionalism and the protection of the extraterritorial dimensions of human rights in the context of the global economy, global migration, and the global climate crisis. This disparity is evident even in the ways in which liberal democratic States approach international law. This means that whilst a global constitutional perspective can indeed strengthen the protection of individual rights in domestic constitutional contexts,[64] it is not clear whether domestic or regional interpreters would be capable of advancing human rights protections or individual criminal responsibility in the context of global problems. Profound political disagreements across communities regarding how responsibilities and benefits should be distributed to advance the centrality of the individual in international law impose significant constraints on the reach of global constitutionalist analysis. In other words, the envisioned division of responsibilities between domestic, regional, and international courts in safeguarding human rights as proposed by global constitutionalism may only work in matters related to the promotion of individual human rights and accountability for individual crimes within a single jurisdiction. Attempts to emphasise the importance of individuals in the ways States interact with each other in the spirit of 'small c' constitutionalism may face charges of imposition, domination,

[62] See Antônio Augusto Cançado Trindade, *The Construction of a Humanized International Law* (Leiden: Brill 2017).

[63] Føllesdal, 'The Principle of Subsidiarity' 2013 (n. 26).

[64] See Yoon Jin Shin, 'Cosmopolitanising Rights Practice: The Case of South Korea', in Takao Suami et al. (eds.), *Global Constitutionalism from European and East Asian Perspectives* (Cambridge: CUP 2018), 245-74.

or naïve depoliticisation without the presence of 'big C' constitutionalism in the global sphere.

4.2 Global Conflicts of Human Rights and Public Interests

The second challenge of overdetermination that global constitutionalism faces is the complex task of incorporating an *a priori* commitment to the protection of individual rights within the comprehensive framework of international law while navigating conflicts between various human rights on one side and human rights and collective interests on the other. Anne Peters recognises this problem:

> Global constitutionalism can of course not provide a magic formula to glue together and to straighten out the internal contradictions and conflicts arising from the interplay of highly complex international legal regimes ranging from international trade law over foreign investment protection law to international tax law. But global constitutionalism does provide a specific lens through which to see the legal issues.[65]

A critical question in this respect is whether the perspective provided by global constitutionalism is precise enough to navigate the intricacies of conflicts between individual rights and collective interests worldwide, without adopting substantive positions on historic and current global inequalities within the international system. Peters suggests that a key advantage of global constitutionalism is its 'interdisciplinary connecting power'.[66] In other words, the global constitutional framework enables us to turn what might otherwise be non-issues into matters of international law. It also helps highlight the absence of integrated approaches that deal with the central role of the individual in different areas of international law. However, this orientation function still leaves ample space for interpretation if there is no clear policy agenda for how to integrate a constitutionalised legal focus on individuals in specific circumstances marked by profound political disagreements and historical economic inequalities.[67] The suggestion to adopt the principles of subsidiarity and proportionality as mediating doctrines of global constitutional law to manage conflicts[68] also faces a similar problem of overdetermination. A central, unresolved issue with employing the principle of proportionality as a global constitutionalist doctrine, for example, is the lack of an overarching framework that identifies whose individual interests in which jurisdictions should

[65] Peters, 'Global Constitutionalism: The Social Dimension' 2018 (n. 7), at 335.
[66] *ibid*, at 334.
[67] See Tarik Kochi, 'The End of Global Constitutionalism and Rise of Antidemocratic Politics' *Global Society* 34 (2020), 487-506.
[68] See Peters, 'Proportionality' 2017 (n. 3).

factor into a proportionality analysis in complex fields such as international investment, trade, and the climate crisis.[69] In other words, when the protection of individuals' rights in one country clashes with the individuals' rights in another country—which is often the case, for instance, with regard to individuals' intellectual property rights in one State versus individuals' right to health in another, as demonstrated by the COVID-19 pandemic—the rhetoric of global constitutionalism may not offer a sufficient basis for protecting all individual rights. Such instances require more substantive doctrines to justify trade-offs between the rights of disparate groups worldwide as a matter of global justice.[70]

5. Conclusion

This chapter has sought to demonstrate that the individual and their moral and legal significance play a central and wide-ranging role in global constitutionalist approaches to international law. In establishing the significance of the individual, global constitutionalism takes an eclectic approach. It draws from various traditions ranging from liberalism and republicanism to moral and legal cosmopolitanism and critical traditions. Relying on these diverse sources allows global constitutionalism to assign numerous normative and interpretive roles to the individual in international law. The individual plays a central role reconceptualising state sovereignty and state consent in international law. Furthermore, it also offers a 'lens' through which to interpret existing sources and doctrines of international law. By focusing on the individual, global constitutionalism can also endorse a wide range of initiatives aimed at reforming international law and further enhancing its continuous humanisation. These initiatives may involve the accountability of international organisations, the establishment of regulatory frameworks to protect individuals in the context of the globalised economy, or States' extraterritorial human rights obligations.

The individual's role in global constitutionalism shares common ground with the humanisation of international law thesis as well as other traditions, including the natural law tradition in modern international law and critical approaches to international law. Global constitutionalism advocates humanisation as a way of understanding the constitutionalist structure of international law, State sovereignty, and the interpretation of existing rules and principles in international law.

[69] See Thomas Cottier et al., 'The Principle of Proportionality in International Law: Foundations and Variations' *Journal of World Investment and Trade* 18 (2017), 628-72.

[70] On discussions in this domain, see Thomas Pogge and Darrel Moellendorf, *Global Justice: Seminal Essays* (St Paul, MN: Paragon House 2008).

The telos of humanisation strongly corresponds with global constitutionalism's support for empowering individuals to have greater participatory access to and remedies within international law. Global constitutionalism shares common ground with natural-law approaches to the extent that it supports a human-centred understanding of international law and rejects the legal positivist conception of international law. Like critical approaches to international law, global constitutionalism also highlights the transformative potential of international human rights law in the global and domestic legal orders. It accommodates considerations related to socio-economic and third-generation rights. Global constitutionalism's dynamic treatment of the role of the individual in international law thus enables it to accommodate a wide array of concerns from a broad range of constitutionalist traditions and critiques of international law. However, it remains unclear whether global constitutionalism provides sufficient normative clarity or specific mechanisms to address conflicts between individual rights or individual rights and collective interests beyond a single jurisdiction. Above all, global constitutionalism encourages us to give serious consideration to constitutionalism in international law and to actively engage with it.

16
The Individual in (International) Law and Economics

*Anne van Aaken**

1. Introduction

Contemporary economics, including Law and Economics, which applies economic theory and methodology to legal questions, adheres to an individualistic approach both in terms of methodology and normative principles. It is therefore not State-centred. From a normative perspective,[1] it traces its theories (welfare economics) back to utilitarianism, which is grounded in individualism (each human being's utility counts, rather than that of a monarch or a State). However, as economics aggregates each person's utilities into a social welfare function without accounting for factors like human rights that may not be reflected in individual utility, it can still be seen as having normative shortcomings. This led to New Welfare Economics, pioneered by economist and philosopher Amartya Sen, and founded not on the aggregated subjective utility of individuals, but rather on the objective measurement of human capabilities. This approach has become especially prominent in international policy. As a replacement for the simplistic measure of gross national product (GNP), the United Nation Human Development Index (HDI) is used to assess human development. It takes into account capabilities related to health, education, and income, and is rooted in Sen's approach. This has been further developed by the Sustainable Development Goals (SDGs), which can now be regarded as a central focus and reference point in international law and policy. The focus on individual, not State welfare, has a longstanding history in economics. It could be argued that economics adopted an individual-centric perspective before

* I would like to thank Başak Çalı, Anne Peters, Tom Sparks, and Gustavo Prieto as well as the participants of the workshop and gratefully acknowledge funding from the Alexander von Humboldt Foundation.

[1] In the context of social sciences and especially economics, the terms 'normative' and 'positive' are used as defined by Max Weber. They refer to the ability to distinguish a body of knowledge concerned with what *is* (analytical and empirical knowledge) from a set of judgements on what ought to be (value judgements): Max Weber, *The Methodology of the Social Sciences: The Meaning of 'Ethical Neutrality' in Sociology and Economics* (first published 1917, this edn: Edward A. Shils and Henry A. Finch (eds.; trs.), 1st edn, Glencoe, IL: The Free Press of Glencoe 1949), 1–49, at 11.

Anne van Aaken, *The Individual in (International) Law and Economics* In: *The Individual in International Law.* Edited by: Tom Sparks and Anne Peters, Oxford University Press.
DOI: 10.1093/oso/9780198898917.003.0016

international law did.[2] The normative individualism in Law and Economics aligns with the approaches in international law that prioritise the individual rather than the State.

Methodologically, it's worth noting that positive Law and Economics has consistently maintained an individualistic approach. In other words, it focuses on *individual* behaviour, not structures. This positive social science focuses on how individuals behave in relation to the law, or how they strategically interact, with game theory being a favoured tool among economists for studying such interactions. For a long time, Law and Economics confined its analysis to national law, focusing on individual behaviour. When international Law and Economics (ILE) emerged, it primarily employed the methodological tools of positive Law and Economics, rather than delving into the normative aspects of welfare economics and efficiency. In early international Law and Economics scholarship, much like international relations theory, there was a tendency to focus on the State as the primary unit of analysis. The individual, therefore, did not feature either normatively or methodologically in the analysis. This mirrors a Westphalian type of thinking in international legal scholarship. Nevertheless, the positive approach of Law and Economics has the capacity to analyse non-State actors and individuals in international law. In fact, the individual has often been considered the relevant unit of analysis, especially in the field of behavioural international Law and Economics. It is noteworthy that the United Nations is now calling for a shift towards behavioural economics in order to achieve its goals, including the SDGs.[3] Behavioural economics, in both its research focus and methodology, places a central emphasis on the individual. Thus, this chapter will outline the normative and positive potential of the Law and Economics approach, but will also suggest that there remains a research gap in ILE concerning the individual as a unit of positive analysis.

It could be argued that just as normative economics shifted towards New Welfare Economics, a Law and Economics approach emphasising individual well-being, which incorporates considerations of human rights, could parallel the broader trend towards humanisation in international law.[4] Given that economics, like international law and scholarship, is continually evolving as a field, it is remarkable how close they have become on a normative level. Convergence on the positive level is impossible, as legal science, at least if understood as doctrinal research, is not social science. However, what economics, particularly with its methodological advancements driven by the shift towards behavioural economics, can contribute

[2] Although, of course, there have always been strands within international legal scholarship that gave prominence to the individual. For instance, certain natural law traditions in international law like the Spanish Christian universalism of the fifteenth century did exhibit concern for individual rights and welfare; see Iurlaro, '1500-1648' (chapter 4), in this volume.

[3] UN Behavioral Science Report, 2021, available at: https://digitallibrary.un.org/record/3929741, accessed 27/11/23.

[4] *cf.* Peters and Sparks, 'Introduction' (chapter 1), in this volume.

is the methodological individualism inherent in economics. Thus, modern ILE is ideally positioned to provide a social-science perspective that supports the transition towards individualism in international law concerning human rights and development in normative thinking. In addition, methodological individualism equips ILE with the potential to align with the more diverse array of actors in international law, moving away from treating the State as a unitary actor. In harmony with the United Nations' shift towards behavioural sciences, this chapter utilises social-science insights into human behaviour—that is, behavioural sciences with a focus on behavioural Law and Economics—to demonstrate how New Welfare Economics and international law can align on a normative level.

The chapter proceeds as follows: section 2 explores the role of the individual in normative Law and Economics, addressing traditional welfare economics first and then New Welfare Economics. Section 3 discusses positive Law and Economics, that is, social-science analysis, and looks at the role of the individual in rational choice theory, which has also been used in ILE and other approaches to international law. It then turns to the use of behavioural Law and Economics and its focus on the individual. Section 4 describes the convergence between (international) Law and Economics and argues for an integrated view, for example as reflected in the SDGs, including normative and positive aspects of research. The last section concludes with an outlook for the future.

2. Normative Individualism in Welfare Economics and Its Potential for International Law

Moral philosophers, such as Jeremy Bentham, John Stuart Mill, and Adam Smith, the founding fathers of economics and utilitarianism, were among the earliest thinkers to emphasise the importance of the individual in their notions of what defines a 'good society'. Their primary concern was not the well-being of the monarch or a State as an entity. Instead, they emphasised the significance of every individual, including women[5] and slaves,[6] in determining whether a society was considered good. At that time, utilitarianism was progressive – its normative benchmark unit was the individual.[7] Before turning to New Welfare Economics, I will provide a brief overview of the fundamentals of traditional welfare economics as it has been used in Law and Economics and to a lesser extent in ILE, and the criticisms it has faced.

[5] Miriam Williford, 'Bentham on the Rights of Women' *Journal of the History of Ideas* 36 (1975), 167–76; Robert W. Dimand, Evelyn L. Forget and Chris Nyland, 'Gender in Classical Economics' *Journal of Economic Perspectives* 18 (2004), 229–40.

[6] Lea Campos Boralevi, *Bentham and the Oppressed* (Berlin: de Gruyter 1984), 142–64; John Salter, 'Adam Smith on Slavery' *History of Economic Ideas* 4 (1996), 225–51, at 233–36 and *passim*.

[7] David O. Brink, *Mill's Progressive Principles* (Oxford: OUP 2013).

2.1 Traditional Welfare Economics: Utilitarianism and Efficiency

Welfare economists typically endorse what Amartya Sen has labelled 'welfarism': the thesis that 'the relative goodness of alternative states of affairs must be based exclusively on, and taken as an increasing function of, the respective collections of individual utilities in these states'.[8] Thus, traditional welfare economics is based on utilitarianism and is entirely consequentialist in nature. The Chicago-school style of traditional Law and Economics, in turn, is based on traditional welfare economics. It therefore shares the pitfalls of utilitarianism[9] because it considers only individual subjective expected utility in the social welfare function.[10] While it may in theory include such factors as fairness, justice, equality, and rights—in short, all tangible and intangible goods—typically it does not incorporate these elements.[11] Given that there are *a priori* no constraints on what can be included in an individual's utility function, a challenge arises in distinguishing between preferences that could be considered meddlesome and objectionable from preferences that are allowed to carry weight in the welfare function.[12] A retreat to idealised preferences would require an explanation of what to idealise. Furthermore, adverse social conditions may systematically distort preferences, which are shaped by the individual's circumstances, such as poverty, discrimination, and law. Moreover, ever since Lionel Robbins' influential essay,[13] it has been clear that there is no scientifically rigorous method to make individual utilities interpersonally comparable, making it challenging to construct a readily computable social welfare function. Regardless of the selected method of aggregation, which means regardless of how individual preferences are combined or whose preferences are considered (whether nationally or internationally), there are serious difficulties in welfare economics that inevitably involve issues at the heart of moral and political philosophy. Irrespective of the efficiency criterion used (either Pareto or Kaldor-Hicks),[14] the 'view that rights cannot be intrinsically important is fairly engrained in economic tradition now established, and this is partly due to the influence of utilitarianism

[8] Amartya K. Sen, 'Utilitarianism and Welfarism' *Journal of Philosophy* 76 (1979), 463–88, at 468.

[9] For a thorough discussion on rule and act utilitarianism, see John J. C. Smart and Bernard Williams, *Utilitarianism: For and Against* (Cambridge: CUP 1973).

[10] On the development of the notion of utility in welfare economics, see Robert D. Cooter and Peter Rappoport, 'Were the Ordinalists Wrong About Welfare Economics?' *Journal of Economic Literature* 22 (1984), 507–30, at 515.

[11] Louis Kaplow and Steven Shavell, *Fairness versus Welfare* (Cambridge, MA: Harvard University Press 2002), 15–38.

[12] Amartya K. Sen, 'The Impossibility of a Paretian Liberal' *Journal of Political Economy* 78 (1970), 152–57, at 152.

[13] Lionel Robbins, *An Essay on the Nature and Significance of Economic Science* (London: Macmillan 1935). Measuring preference intensity, not just the ordering of preferences on an ordinal scale, is the crucial issue.

[14] For an extensive discussion, see Horst Eidenmüller, *Effizienz als Rechtsprinzip* (4th edn, Tübingen: Siebeck/Mohr 2015); Anne van Aaken, *'Rational Choice' in der Rechtswissenschaft: Zum Stellenwert der ökonomischen Theorie im Recht* (Baden-Baden: Nomos 2003).

(and specifically of welfarism, as part of the package)'.[15] The informational basis of welfare economics is too 'broad' on the one hand (including too many preferences) and too 'thin' on the other hand (ignoring non-utility based claims on social choice and welfare). This criticism is what led Amartya Sen to develop New Welfare Economics, to which I now turn.

2.2 New Welfare Economics: Individual Rights and Capabilities

Recognising the limitations of a purely subjectivist approach and the inappropriate informational basis of welfarism, Sen, a Nobel Prize winner for economics, developed so-called New Welfare Economics, which involves an objective valuation of human well-being while reflecting on the distinctiveness of each individual's needs. He engaged with possible alternatives to traditional welfare economics and to the Rawlsian approach,[16] namely John Rawls' idea of primary goods—essentially income, power, and legal rights—which Sen considered too crude to account for individual differences (e.g. disabilities).[17] Instead, Sen turned to capabilities (and functionings) as a philosophical organising concept. He based those on a neo-Aristotelian approach[18] where the basis of individual welfare is not a subjective notion of utility but the capability to lead 'the kind of lives they value—and have reason to value'.[19] This 'capabilities approach' (CA), developed with Martha Nussbaum,[20] has attracted the interest not only of welfare economists and philosophers but more recently of lawyers too.[21] On an even broader scale, Sen's approach has also captured the attention of international lawyers,[22] as demonstrated by his Grotius lecture in 2011.[23] His approach has

[15] Amartya K. Sen, *On Ethics and Economics* (8th edn, Oxford: Blackwell 1997), 49–50.

[16] John Rawls, *A Theory of Justice* (Cambridge, MA: Harvard University Press 1971).

[17] Amartya K. Sen, 'Equality of What?', in Amartya K. Sen (ed.), *Choice, Welfare and Measurement* (first published 1980, this edn: Cambridge, MA: Harvard University Press 1997), 353–69, at 368: 'Primary goods suffer from fetishist handicap in being concerned with goods, and even though the list of goods is specified in a broad and inclusive way, encompassing rights, liberties, opportunities, income, wealth, and the social basis of self-respect, it is still concerned with good things rather than with what these good things do to human beings'; see also Amartya K. Sen, *The Idea of Justice* (Cambridge, MA: Belknap Press of Harvard University Press 2009), 52–74.

[18] Sen, *On Ethics and Economics* 1997 (n. 15), at 3-11.

[19] Amartya K. Sen, *Development as Freedom* (New Delhi: OUP 2000), at 18.

[20] Martha C. Nussbaum and Amartya K. Sen, *The Quality of Life* (Oxford: OUP 1993); Martha C. Nussbaum, *Creating Capabilities: The Human Development Approach* (Cambridge, MA: Harvard University Press 2013); Martha C. Nussbaum, *Women and Human Development* (New York, NY: CUP 2000).

[21] Van Aaken, *'Rational Choice' in der Rechtswissenschaft* 2003 (n. 14); Brian Langille (ed.), *The Capability Approach to Labour Law* (Oxford: OUP 2019); Carrie Menkel-Meadow et al., *Amartya Sen and Law: Philosophers and Law* (London: Routledge 2020).

[22] Bhupinder S. Chimni, 'The Sen Conception of Development and Contemporary International Law Discourse: Some Parallels' *Law and Development Review* 1 (2008), 3–22.

[23] Amartya K. Sen, 'Thirteenth Annual Grotius Lecture Series: The Global Status of Human Rights' *American University International Law Review* 27 (2012), 1–15; Kim Lane Scheppele, 'Thirteenth

found widespread application, operationalisation, and measurement in various contexts.[24]

Sen's criticism of traditional welfare economics is based on the view that 'an adequate conception of development must go much beyond the accumulation of wealth and the growth of gross national product and other income-related variables'.[25] It leads to the powerful insight that poverty is 'a deprivation of basic capabilities' rather than simply a case of having low income.[26] Sen views 'development as freedom',[27] development being a process of expanding the real freedoms that people enjoy.[28] The idea of the capability approach is perhaps best expressed in Sen's own words:

> A functioning is an achievement, whereas a capability is the ability to achieve. Functionings are, in a sense, more directly related to living conditions, since they are different aspects of living conditions. Capabilities, in contrast, are notions of freedom, in the positive sense: what real opportunities you have regarding the life you may lead.[29]

Essentially, functionings are the various states and activities that make up a person's well-being, such as health, safety, and a good job, to more complex states, such as happiness, self-respect, and calm. Sen argues that the set of functionings an individual person can attain in a given period depends on the individual's current capability set. In his view, however, capabilities should be valued not only as a means to achieve functionings, but also for their intrinsic value.[30] That is, Sen attaches both instrumental and intrinsic value to capabilities. The capabilities approach emphasises that the things a person could do or be, as opposed to what they actually do or are, is an integral part of their welfare. This opportunity aspect of welfare assessment is reflected, for example, in equality and diversity theories and policies. The notions of agency and autonomy are central to the approach.

Sen constructs a 'goal-rights system' that assigns significance to negative and positive liberties, as he argues for 'a consequential system that incorporates the

Annual Grotius Lecture Response: Amartya Sen's Vision for Human Rights – and Why He Needs the Law' *American University International Law Review* 27 (2012), 17–35.

[24] Paul Anand et al., 'The Development of Capability Indicators' *Journal of Human Development and Capabilities* 10 (2009), 125–52. (Finding that indicators from various aspects of life are associated with life satisfaction, a finding that aligns with the multidimensional approaches to poverty and quality of life and the idea that people do not just solely value income (referred to as opulence in Sen's language). They also reference other measurement methods.)

[25] Sen, *Development as Freedom* 2000 (n. 19), 14.

[26] *ibid*, 20.

[27] *ibid*.

[28] Amartya Sen, 'Elements of a Theory of Human Rights' *Philosophy & Public Affairs* 32 (2004), 315–56, 328.

[29] Sen, *On Ethics and Economics* 1997 (n. 15), 36.

[30] Sen, *Development as Freedom* 2000 (n. 19), 13 and 18.

fulfilment of rights among other goals': 'It shares with utilitarianism a consequential approach (but differs from it in not confining attention to utility consequences only), and it shares with a libertarian system the attachment of intrinsic importance to rights (but differs from it in not giving it complete priority irrespective of other consequences).'[31] This shift in welfare economics towards a recognition of the significance of rights—not only first-generation but also second- and arguably third-generation rights—is noteworthy. It mirrors a holistic view of individual well-being, which also relies on individual rights. It might be argued that this approach 'stem(s) from the endeavour to ensure that all human beings can live full, healthy, and fulfilled lives'.[32] Sen also attaches importance to democracy for realising the goal of development as freedom.[33] He holds that the significance of democracy lies in 'three distinct virtues': '(1) its intrinsic importance, (2) its instrumental contributions, and (3) its constructive role in the creation of values and norms'.[34] As capabilities can be enhanced by public policy, the direction of public policy can likewise be affected by the effective use of participatory capabilities by the public. This two-way relationship is central to Sen's theory.[35] In his theory, democracy and participation are not only regarded as fundamental values in themselves but also as indispensable sources of information for policy-makers. His approach to individual well-being is not dependent on States as intermediaries. While this issue may not be prominently addressed in the theory, in practice, it may still be States that are responsible for ensuring and actualising those rights – or failing to do so.

While Sen refused to formulate a list of core capabilities, Nussbaum did. The elements she included may serve as illustrations:[36] *inter alia*, life; bodily health; bodily integrity; senses, imagination, and thought (informed and cultivated by an adequate education, including, but by no means limited to, literacy and basic mathematical and scientific training, protected by guarantees of freedom of expression with respect to both political and artistic speech, and freedom of religious exercise); affiliation (being able to live with and towards others, also protecting the freedom of assembly and political speech); social bases of self-respect and non-humiliation, human dignity (entails provisions of non-discrimination on the basis of race, sex, sexual orientation, ethnicity, caste, religion, national origin, and species); other species (being able to live with concern for and in relation to animals, plants, and the world of nature); control over one's environment (political, thus participating in political choices, and material, such as property).

31 *ibid*, 212.

32 Peters and Sparks, 'Introduction' (chapter 1), in this volume.

33 Sen, *Development as Freedom* 2000 (n. 19), 157.

34 *ibid.*

35 *ibid*, 18.

36 Nussbaum, *Women and Human Development* 2000 (n. 20). For her differences with Sen, see Nussbaum, *Creating Capabilities: The Human Development Approach* 2013 (n. 20).

Sen explicitly does not want to offer a transcendental institutional *theory* of justice, since 'we can proceed to address questions of enhancing justice and removing injustice, rather than to offer resolutions of questions about the nature of perfect justice'.[37] Remarkably, his idea of justice, rather than building just institutions abstractly, is closely connected to reality and behaviour, and thus to methodological individualism and social sciences.[38] His approach reflects a combination of deontology and consequentialism. I will take this up in section 3, when I turn to positive economics and how the combination of deontology and consequentialism is reflected in ILE and international law with a special view to the SDGs.

In summary, New Welfare Economics has embraced fundamental philosophical concepts rooted in a neo-Aristotelian approach. As a result, it eliminates the shortcomings of utilitarianism, maintaining its emphasis on the individual and establishing a connection to the normative issues raised by (international) lawyers. There is nothing in Sen's theory that would detract from a focus on the individual by introducing a mediation through States. Sen's contributions have been instrumental in promoting the capabilities approach as the dominant paradigm for policy discussions in the field of human development. Furthermore, he, along with others, inspired the creation of the HDI.[39] It is important to note that Sen's thinking is deeply entrenched in the real world and how it functions, thus never losing sight of positive economics and empirical research, to which I will turn in section 3. And indeed here, the State (as a unit of analysis) may also become an actor in advancing (or obstructing) humanity and humanisation.

2.3 Normatively Open Decision Theory Framework

International lawyers could also adopt an inclusive approach that considers various principles or criteria, such as fairness, human rights, equality, and allocative efficiency; the SDGs; or specific goals of international law, such as fighting corruption, which need to carefully assessed and balanced against each other within a transparent normative decision theory framework.[40] This approach would enable the adoption of a context-specific concept of efficiency or a selective welfare function, determined by established principles as codified, for example, in a constitution or

[37] Sen, *The Idea of Justice* 2009 (n. 17), x. And at xi, he compares his approach that of Rawls: 'there are some crucial inadequacies in this overpowering concentration on institutions (where behaviour is assumed to be appropriately compliant), rather than on the lives that people are able to lead. The focus on actual lives in the assessment of justice has many far-reaching implications for the nature and reach of the idea of justice.' (Footnote omitted).

[38] *ibid*, x.

[39] UN Development Programme, 'Human Development Reports', available at: http://hdr.undp.org/en/content/human-development-index-hdi, accessed 08/05/23.

[40] Normative decision theory models the optimal decision for a specific situation, assuming that decision-makers are rational.

international legal documents, such as the UN Charter or human rights treaties. In essence, it signifies morality as expressed through positive law.[41] It remains neutral in terms of normative values and instead relies on substantive normative criteria drawn from the specific legal domain under examination.[42] This approach can be used in national law but is even more pertinent for international law. This is especially noteworthy because the efficiency criterion in ILE has seldom been used. Indeed, ILE has traditionally lacked, from a normative perspective, any clearly defined welfare standard, including efficiency. In essence, ILE has predominantly been focused on positive analysis, with the notable exception being New Welfare Economics.

3. Positive Law and Economics: Methodological Individualism and Behavioural Assumptions

Methodologically, the Law and Economics approach explains any phenomena of interest on the macro level (e.g. the State level) by individual behaviour on the micro level (be it individuals, firms, or other non-State actors). This follows James Coleman's bathtub model[43] and opposes theories that either remain descriptive (e.g. system theory) or explain societal phenomena purely on the macro level via structural factors (e.g. Durkheim). While the fundamentally individualist approach is still upheld, psychologists and behavioural economists have challenged the *rationalist* actor assumption on cognitive and motivational grounds. They have done so by employing empirical methods, often through experiments or randomised controlled trials. The new strand of research has profoundly influenced modern Law and Economics scholarship.[44] It has also reached international law.

3.1 The Rational Choice Approach in Law and Economics

The Law and Economics approach is firmly committed to methodological individualism.[45] It has traditionally assumed rational actors, meaning that actors

[41] Anne Peters, *Beyond Human Rights: The Legal Status of the Individual in International Law* (Jonathan Huston (tr.), Cambridge: CUP 2016), 25.

[42] Van Aaken, *'Rational Choice' in der Rechtswissenschaft* 2003 (n. 14), 288-313.

[43] James Coleman, *Foundations of Social Theory*, vol. 1 (Cambridge, MA: Belknap Press of Harvard University Press 1998).

[44] Eyal Zamir and Doron Teichman (eds.), *The Oxford Handbook of Behavioral Economics and the Law* (Oxford: OUP 2014); Eyal Zamir and Doron Teichman, *Behavioral Law and Economics* (Oxford: OUP 2018).

[45] This doctrine demands that social phenomena must be explained by showing how they result from individual actions. It was first formulated in a more theoretical manner in Max Weber, Guenther Roth, and Claus Wittich, *Economy and Society* (first published 1922, this edn: Berkeley, CA: University of California Press 1978), 4–21.

pursue their (self-interested) goals purposefully under external constraints. In its thin form, individual behaviour is rational if it is goal-oriented, involves reflection and evaluation, and maintains consistency over time and across various decision scenarios. Thin models of rationality make few assumptions about human cognition, including the notions of completeness, transitivity, and independence of irrelevant alternatives.[46] The core principles of this paradigm include the pursuit of utility maximisation, the stability of preferences, rational expectations, and the optimal processing of information.[47] When addressing decisions involving uncertainty, the 'expected utility' concept[48] operates under the assumption that preferences remain consistent regardless of the circumstances in which they are revealed. This implies that the way decisions are described or presented does not influence the decision-making process, adhering to the 'descriptive invariance' axiom.[49] These assumptions do not reveal anything about the specific content or nature of preferences themselves. Instead, they form the basis for a formal concept of (thin) rationality. This already highlights the importance of the maximand, which has traditionally been presumed to be solely self-interest. Sen and many others have duly criticised this understanding of rationality, particularly on motivational[50] and cognitive[51] grounds.

In rationalist Law and Economics, it is crucial that any change in behaviour is attributed to a change in constraints or incentives (e.g. a budget constraint due to prices changes, legal constraints, or property rights), rather than a change in individual preferences. Preferences are presumed to be fixed for analytical purposes, as this assumption allows for changes in behaviour to be ascribed to alterations in circumstances, including a change in the law. Law is viewed as a 'giant price machine'[52] and acts as a purely external constraint or enabler.[53] The (behavioural)

[46] For a comprehensive exploration, see Shaun H. Heap et al., *The Theory of Choice: A Critical Guide* (3rd edn, Oxford: Blackwell 1997).

[47] Gary S. Becker, *The Economic Approach to Human Behavior* (Chicago, IL: University of Chicago Press 1976), 14.

[48] See Gary S. Becker, *Accounting for Tastes* (Cambridge, MA: Harvard University Press 1996), 5–7. The expected utility hypothesis is primarily a normative model that addresses how people should make decisions if they aim to be rational (normative decision theory). However, rationalists often use it as an assumption in descriptive models.

[49] Richard Cookson, 'Framing Effects in Public Goods Experiments' *Experimental Economics* 3 (2000), 55–79, at 55; Amos Tversky and Daniel Kahneman, 'The Framing of Decisions and the Psychology of Choice' *Science* 211 (1981), 453–58.

[50] Sen, *The Idea of Justice* 2009 (n. 17), chapters 1-2; and at 179: 'RCT does reflect an extremely limited understanding of reason and rationality.' See also Amartya K. Sen, 'Rational Fools: A Critique of the Behavioral Foundations of Economic Theory' *Philosophy and Public Affairs* 6 (1977), 317–44.

[51] Sen, *The Idea of Justice* 2009 (n. 17), part II; Russell B. Korobkin and Thomas S. Ulen, 'Law and Behavioral Science: Removing the Rationality Assumption from Law and Economics' *California Law Review* 88 (2000), 1051–144. For cognitive psychology insights, see section 3.3, below.

[52] Lawrence M. Friedman, 'Two Faces of Law' *Wisconsin Law Review* 1 (1984), 13–35, at 13.

[53] This is one of the main ways in which it differs from constructivist theories, which focus on the origins and changes of preferences, including through law. James Fearon and Alexander Wendt, 'Rationalism v. Constructivism: A Skeptical View', in Walter Carlsnaes, Thomas Risse, and Beth A. Simmons (eds.), *Handbook of International Relations* (London: Sage 2002), 52–72; Jutta Brunnée

economic approach looks directly at the influence of law on individual behaviour. Consequently, this approach can examine individuals both as decision-makers and as holders of rights, while also considering how they exercise those rights and the conditions they encounter, such as access to justice. It is thus well placed to cope with the humanisation of international law, given the phenomenon that 'international legal norms directly address and engage individuals'.[54]

3.2 The Rational Choice Approach in International Law and Economics

In ILE, the rational choice approach has also been used. Rationalist approaches in international law and international relations scholarship commonly stand on two pillars—the 'rational choice assumption' and the 'state as unitary actor' assumption.[55] Hence, everything depends on how State preferences are defined (if the State is the unit of analysis), and the various approaches of ILE (whether they lean more towards realism or institutionalism) may define these preferences differently. Scholarship typically focuses on the behaviour of States as single entities, though it is usually acknowledged that preferences may vary depending on the context or may not be internally consistent due to differences within the State's constituent actors. Nonetheless, a State's political leadership is considered of utmost significance.[56] Although authors are aware that this is a problem, they continue to rely on the State as the unit of analysis for the sake of simplicity, to reduce complexity, and to formulate hypotheses that can be empirically tested. This approach is often applied, even when examining subjects like human rights treaties.[57] This has also meant that individuals, whether viewed as decision-makers or as right bearers have not played a prominent role, if they have even been considered at all, in earlier ILE scholarship. This deficit is also evident in traditional international relations and legal scholarship. As Anne Peters and Tom Sparks put it: '[S]cholarship has treated the relationship between international law and the individual as one wholly mediated by States.'[58]

and Stephan J. Toope, *Legitimacy and Legality in International Law: An Interactional Account* (Cambridge: CUP 2010).

[54] Peters, *Beyond Human Rights* 2016 (n. 41), 1.

[55] Jack L. Goldsmith and Eric A. Posner, *The Limits of International Law* (Oxford: OUP 2005); Andrew Guzman, *How International Law Works: A Rational Choice Theory* (Oxford: OUP 2008); Joel P. Trachtman, *The Economic Structure of International Law* (Cambridge, MA: Harvard University Press 2008).

[56] Goldsmith and Posner, *The Limits of International Law* 2005 (n. 55), 6.

[57] Joel Trachtman, *The Future of International Law* (Cambridge: CUP 2013), chapter 6 (taking a contractarian view on human rights); Goldsmith and Posner, *The Limits of International Law* 2005 (n. 55), chapter 4.

[58] Peters and Sparks, 'Introduction' (chapter 1), in this volume, p. 2 (emphasis omitted). See also Tamar Megiddo, 'Methodological Individualism' *Harvard International Law Journal* 60 (2019), 219–65.

The assumption of the State as the unit of analysis is not inherently or fundamentally tied to rationalism itself. After all, liberal international relations scholarship frequently seeks to unpack the 'black box' that represents the State.[59] Indeed, a two-level or political economy explanation is often needed to understand the behaviour of States in the international arena. Dissecting the monolithic State and examining both internal (political) and transnational processes recognises the significance of emerging actors in this complex landscape, referred to as the 'Lego World' by Anne-Marie Slaughter.[60] In this context, the individual components within the State are the relevant units of analysis: non-State actors, such as international organisations, NGOs, and businesses, as well as various government agencies and even individuals. Individuals can be and are scrutinised as actors, rights holders, or as part of (international) organisations.

ILE has been slow to adopt this approach in the early 'big picture' literature,[61] but is moving in this direction.[62] In the realm of international trade law and international political economy, a political economy perspective, analysing different stakeholders[63] has traditionally been prevalent.[64] Moreover, when it comes to human rights and environmental treaties, compliance by States often necessitates consideration of a range of actors, including national courts and NGOs.[65] Ever more research looks at individual behaviour relevant to international law, including in the area of human rights.[66] It is therefore safe to say that ILE is taking methodological individualism more and more seriously. However, due to the

[59] Andrew Moravcsik, 'Taking Preferences Seriously: A Liberal Theory of International Politics' *International Organization* 51 (1997), 516–53, at 516.

[60] Anne-Marie Slaughter, 'Remarks, The Big Picture: Beyond Hot Spots & Crises in Our Interconnected World' *Penn State Journal of Law & International Affairs* 1 (2012), 286–302, at 295.

[61] See also note 55, above.

[62] For a template, see Anne van Aaken and Joel Trachtman, 'Political Economy of International Law: Towards a Holistic Model of State Behavior', in Alberta Fabricotti (ed.), *Political Economy of International Law: A European Perspective* (Cheltenham: Edward Elgar, 2016), 9–43.

[63] Helen Milner, 'Reflections on the Field of International Political Economy', in Michael Brecher and Frank P. Harvey (eds.), *Conflict, Security, Foreign Policy, and International Political Economy: Past, Paths and Future Directions in International Studies* (Ann Arbor, MI: University of Michigan Press 2002), 207–23; Duncan Snidal, 'International Political Economy Approaches to International Institutions', in Jagdeep S. Bhandari and Alan O. Sykes (eds.), *Economic Dimensions in International Law Comparative and Empirical Perspectives* (Cambridge: CUP 1998), 477–512.

[64] Gene M. Grossman and Elhanan Helpman, 'Trade Wars and Trade Talks' *Journal of Political Economy* 103 (1995), 675–708. This has recently put into question a purely rationalist paradigm: Gene M. Grossman and Elhanan Helpman., 'Identity Politics and Trade Policy' *Review of Economic Studies* 88 (2021), 1101–26; Anne van Aaken and Jürgen Kurtz, 'Beyond Rational Choice: International Trade Law and The Behavioral Political Economy of Protectionism' *Journal of International Economic Law* 22 (2019), 601–28.

[65] Beth Simmons, *Mobilizing for Human Rights: International Law in Domestic Politics* (Cambridge: CUP 2009).

[66] From a rationalist perspective, see Anne van Aaken, 'Making International Human Rights Protection More Effective: A Rational Choice Approach to the Effectiveness of Provisions of Ius Standi', in Stefan Voigt, Max Albert, and Dieter Schmidtchen (eds.), *International Conflict Resolution* (Tübingen: Mohr Siebeck 2006), 29–58; Veronika Fikfak, 'Against Settlement Before the European Court of Human Rights' *International Journal of Constitutional Law* 20 (2022), 942–75, who partially relies also on bounded rationality explanations.

pursuit of simplicity and the specific research question at hand, the State continues to hold a prominent position as the primary unit of analysis, with the individual often being seen as mediated by the State in such research.

3.3 New Developments: How Individuals Really Behave and the Implications for International Law

The rational choice paradigm as used in economics has been thoroughly challenged, since the 1970s, by experimental research that has revolutionised large areas of (law and) economics, including private, public, and criminal law,[67] as well as international relations scholarship.[68] Experiments are used to examine the social preferences and cognitive processes of individuals in controlled conditions.[69] Numerous experiments reveal deviations from narrow, cognitive rationality, as they illustrate that individuals frequently make decisions that do not adhere to the formal requirements of thin rationality. Furthermore, highlighting the role that factors such as fairness, envy, and altruism play in people's behaviour challenges the notion of deep-seated, motivational rationality, especially purely self-centred preferences. Therefore, the individual has shifted from being seen in isolated, atomistic terms to being understood within a social context.[70] Behavioural economics has played a transformative role, offering new insights into economic tools such as game theory or contract theory.[71] This enriched model of behaviour strives to understand how people really behave, further enhancing the individualistic perspective. Behavioural analysis can work on several levels of generality and with different units of analysis, ranging from the State to the individual, depending on the specific research question.

Those systematic deviations from rationalist assumptions—both cognitive and motivational—are increasingly integrated into international legal scholarship,[72]

[67] Zamir and Teichman, *Behavioral Law and Economics* 2018 (n. 44).

[68] Emilie M. Hafner-Burton et al., 'The Behavioral Revolution and International Relations' *International Organization* 71 (2017), Supplement S 1, S1–S31.

[69] They may be conducted in the field or in laboratory settings and can assess individual or group behaviour. For a discussion of their value in the realm of international law, see Jeffrey L. Dunoff and Mark A. Pollack, 'Experimenting with International Law: A Reader's Guide' *European Journal of International Law* 28 (2017), 1317–40.

[70] John B. Davis, *Individuals and Identity in Economics* (Cambridge: CUP 2010).

[71] For game theory, see Colin Camerer, *Behavioral Game Theory. Experiments in Strategic Interaction* (Princeton, NJ: Princeton University Press 2003); for contract theory, see Botond Koszegi, 'Behavioral Contract Theory' *Journal of Economic Literature* 52 (2014), 1075–118.

[72] Anne van Aaken, 'Behavioral International Law and Economics' *Harvard International Law Journal* 55 (2014), 421–81; Tomer Broude, 'Behavioral International Law' *University of Pennsylvania Law Review* 163 (2015), 1099–157; Anne van Aaken and Tomer Broude, 'Behavioral Economics and International Law', in Eugene Kontorovich and Francesco Parisi (eds.), *Economic Analysis of International Law* (Cheltenham: Edward Elgar 2016), 249–76; Doron Teichman et al., 'Nudge Goes International' *European Journal of International Law* 30 (2019), 1263–79; Daniel Peat, 'The Tyranny of Choice and the Interpretation of Standards: Why the ECtHR Uses Consensus' *NYU Journal of International Law and Politics* 53 (2021), 381–432; and many others.

influencing a growing body of scholarship that addresses issues of international legal theory,[73] treaty design, compliance,[74] international public goods and commons,[75] and special regimes,[76] as well as treaty negotiations.[77] In these contexts, the unit of analysis is often the individual, such as those who are imputed to the State, for example military commanders.[78] It can shed light on what international courts 'do in fact': experiments involving national judges[79] and international arbitrators[80] have revealed instances where these actors deviate from rationalist assumptions. Other research has used large n data sets to analyse international judicial decision-making.[81]

When individuals make decisions in the context of international law, either for a State, in an international organisation, or for themselves, their decision-making can be analysed from a behavioural perspective. Several biases and heuristics are especially relevant in the realm of international law. For example, while rational choice theory assumes that people perceive outcomes in absolute terms (expected utility), the well-established prospect theory posits that people ordinarily perceive outcomes as either gains or losses rather than final states. Gains and losses are defined in relation to a particular reference point – often, but not always, the status quo or a perceived entitlement established by law. A loss counts more than a gain (known as loss aversion), and actors tend to take more risks when dealing with potential losses. Loss aversion also increases the significance of default rules, which are prevalent in international law, including the analysis of sources. Default rules,

[73] Anne van Aaken and Moshe Hirsch (eds.), *International Legal Theory and the Cognitive Turn* (Oxford: OUP 2024).

[74] Anne van Aaken and Betül Simsek, 'Rewarding in International Law' *American Journal of International Law* 115 (2021), 195–241.

[75] Anne van Aaken, 'Behavioral Aspects of the International Law of Global Public Goods and Common Pool Resources' *American Journal of International Law* 112 (2018), 67–79.

[76] For trade law, see van Aaken and Kurtz, 'Beyond Rational Choice' 2019 (n. 64); for investment law, see Lauge Poulsen, *Bounded Rationality and Economic Diplomacy: The Politics of Investment Treaties in Developing Countries* (Cambridge: CUP 2015); for sources, see Tomer Broude, 'Explaining the Practical Purchase of Soft Law: Competing and Complementary Behavioral Hypotheses', in Harlan Grant Cohen and Timothy Meyer (eds.), *International Law as Behavior* (Cambridge: CUP 2019); for human rights law, see Fikfak, 'Friendly settlement' 2022 (n. 66) and the contributions in the Special Issue 'The Psychology of International Law' *European Journal of International Law* 30 (2019).

[77] Tomer Broude and Shai Moses, 'The Behavioral Dynamics of Positive and Negative Listing in Services Liberalization', in Martin Roy and Pierre Sauvé (eds.), *Research Handbook on Trade in Services* (Cheltenham: Edward Elgar 2016), 385–411.

[78] Ben Clarke, 'Contemporary Research on Proportionality in Armed Conflicts: A Select Review' *Journal of International Humanitarian Legal Studies* 3 (2012), 391–414; Shiri Krebs, 'Rethinking Targeted Killing Policy: Reducing Uncertainty, Protecting Civilians from the Ravages of Both Terrorism and Counterterrorism' *Florida State University Law Review* 44 (2017), 943–94.

[79] Chris Guthrie, Jeffrey J. Rachlinski, and Andrew J. Wistrich, 'Blinking on the Bench: How Judges Decide Cases' *Cornell Law Review* 93 (2007), 1–43.

[80] Susan Franck et al., 'Inside the Arbitrator's Mind' *Emory Law Journal* 66 (2017), 1115–73; Anne van Aaken and Tomer Broude, 'Behavioural Approaches to International Adjudication', in: Hélène Ruiz Fabri (ed.) *Max Planck Encyclopedia of Procedural International Law* (Oxford: OUP 2020).

[81] Peat, 'The Tyranny of Choice' 2021 (n. 72); Veronika Fikfak, 'Changing State Behaviour: Damages before the European Court of Human Rights' *European Journal of International Law* 29 (2019), 1091–125.

such as opt-in or opt-out rules, change the behaviour of actors, including States,[82] although according to rationalist assumptions they should not have any influence on decisions.

The endowment effect, namely the tendency to value objects and entitlements that people already have more highly than those they do not, may prevent efficient transactions and negotiations and therefore also hinder international co-operation.[83] Over-confidence—that is, actors having more confidence in their own judgements than the objective accuracy of those judgements warrants, is a common phenomenon. Together with the fundamental attribution error,[84] this may lead to more hawkish decisions in international conflict situations,[85] which has a profound impact, for example on international humanitarian law, as the United Nations has also acknowledged.[86] What those examples show is that States' behaviour must necessarily be linked back to individual decision-making. And, more importantly, many actors operating within the realm of international law play a relevant role in its practice, for example those engaged in frontline humanitarian negotiations.[87]

Framing effects similarly contradict the rationalist axiom of 'descriptive invariance'. A framing effect exists 'when different ways of describing the same choice problem change the choices that people make, even though the underlying information and choice options remain essentially the same'.[88] Numerous experiments explore those effects,[89] including in the context of public goods games. Framing has been shown to be relevant in international treaty negotiations and adjudication,[90] as well as in the perception of fact-finding missions.[91]

[82] Jean Galbraith, 'Treaty Options: Towards a Behavioral Understanding of Treaty Design' *Virginia Journal of International Law* 53 (2013), 309–64; Broude and Moses, 'The Behavioral Dynamics of Positive and Negative Listing in Services Liberalization' 2016 (n. 77).

[83] Daniel Kahneman, Jack L. Knetsch, and Richard. H. Thaler, 'Experimental Tests of the Endowment Effect and the Coase Theorem' *Journal of Political Economy* 98 (1990), 1325–48.

[84] The fundamental attribution error refers to the tendency to attribute other people's behaviour to their personal attitudes and motivations, rather than to environmental influences and constraints; for more detail, see Zamir and Teichman, *Behavioral Law and Economics* 2018 (n. 44), chapter 2.

[85] Daniel Kahneman and Jonathan Renshon, 'Hawkish biases', in Trevor Thrall and Jane K. Cramer (eds.), *American Foreign Policy and the Threat of Fear: Threat Inflation Since 9/11* (London: Routledge 2009).

[86] See note 3, above.

[87] See Anne van Aaken, Tomer Broude, Christoph Engel, and Katharina Luckner's research project with the Competence Center of Humanitarian Negotiations at the International Committee of the Red Cross, available at: https://frontline-negotiations.org/a-behavioral-analysis-of-humanitarian-negotiations-cchn-collaborates-with-international-research-team/, accessed 7/7/23.

[88] Cookson, 'Framing Effects in Public Goods Experiments' 2000 (n. 49), 55; for different theories about framing, see Tore Ellingsen et al., 'Social Framing Effects: Preferences or Beliefs?' *Games and Economic Behavior* 76 (2012), 117–30, at 118.

[89] Ellingsen et al., 'Social Framing Effects: Preferences or Beliefs?' 2021 (n. 88).

[90] Anne van Aaken and Jan Philip Elm, 'Framing in and through International Law', in Andrea Bianchi and Moshe Hirsch (eds.), *International Law's Invisible Frames—Social Cognition and Knowledge Production in International Legal Processes* (Oxford: OUP 2021), 35–54, with further references.

[91] Shiri Krebs, 'The Legalization of Truth in International Fact-finding' *Chicago Journal of International Law* 18 (2017), 83–163.

Behavioural game theory, that is, strategic interaction, has focused on the motivational aspect of behaviour and social preferences, especially in public goods games. When we consider the international order as a public good, these games become pertinent because they explain factors upholding the social order in a non-centralised setting. Repeated findings that individuals systematically engage in collective action to provide public goods without an external authority enforcer[92] have led some to label such outcomes as 'better than rational'.[93] These outcomes occur when reciprocity, reputation, and trust help to mitigate the strong temptations of immediate self-interest.[94] These experiments suggest that rationalist theories may be faulted for neglecting: (1) reciprocity *stricto sensu*; (2) the distinction between (perceived) fair and unfair sanctions; (3) altruism, spitefulness, and preferences for equality; (4) the role of trust and communication; (5) the intentions of other players; and (6) the 'type' of actor. Furthermore, scholars have claimed that these factors are 'probably relevant in all domains in which voluntary compliance matters'.[95] Clearly, international law is such a domain.[96] Especially in the context of international environmental law, where the effectiveness of the treaties is contingent on non-State actors, these insights hold significant value in achieving the objectives of such agreements.

When individual behaviour can be attributed to States or international organisations, behavioural economics can help to formulate a theory of cooperation in the realm of international affairs.[97] It is vital to meticulously examine the factors influencing cooperation in behavioural experiments to understand how States (or rather their respective representatives) structure their cooperation. For example, whether law uses an opt-in or opt-out system has considerable behavioural consequences.[98] Thus, the framework of treaty design that actors choose, such as decisions about default options, may be crucial to achieving cooperative benefits. Furthermore, behavioural research can shed light on the relevance of custom more

[92] Elinor Ostrom, 'A Behavioral Approach to the Rational Choice Theory of Collective Action' *American Political Science Review* 92 (1998), 1–22, at 2.

[93] Leda Cosmides and John Tooby, 'Better than Rational: Evolutionary Psychology and the Invisible Hand' *American Economic Review* 84 (1994), 327–32.

[94] Ostrom, 'A Behavioral Approach to the Rational Choice Theory of Collective Action' 1998 (n. 92), 3.

[95] Ernst Fehr and Bettina Rockenbach, 'Detrimental Effects of Sanctions on Human Altruism' *Nature* 422 (2003), 137–40, 137.

[96] See van Aaken, 'Behavioral Aspects of the International Law of Global Public Goods' 2018 (n. 75) and Anne van Aaken, 'Experimental Insights for International Legal Theory' *European Journal of International Law* 30 (2019), 1237–62.

[97] On the unit of analysis problem and further caveats of using behavioural economics and psychology in international law, see Anne van Aaken and Tomer Broude, 'Introduction to Special Issue 'The Psychology of International Law' *European Journal of International Law* 30 (2019), 1225–36. See also the contributions in *AJIL Unbound*, 115 (2021), 'The Limitations of the Behavioral Turn in International Law'.

[98] On organ donation, see Eric J. Johnson and Daniel Goldstein, 'Can Default Rules save Life?' *Science* 302 (2003), 1338–39. For international law, see Galbraith, 'Treaty Options: Towards a Behavioral Understanding of Treaty Design' 2013 (n. 82).

generally, given that custom creates mutual expectations of what the 'right thing to do' is. Behavioural research can also shed light on the enigma of compliance in collective action scenarios by focusing on the above-mentioned factors, which help maintain cooperation.[99] Furthermore, the behavioural approach has been crucial in development economics, where it focuses on the problem of poverty. In order to understand why and how individuals react (or not) to measures taken to improve their welfare and reduce poverty (e.g. in education and health, such as making use of micro-nutrition for children), randomised controlled trials have been conducted, often involving a comprehensive search for contributing psychological factors.[100] The goals of poverty reduction can only be achieved if behaviour is fully understood. And, as already mentioned, the United Nations has created a unit that deals with behavioural insights to achieve the UN's goals in several areas, either through the work of international organisations or by collaborating on projects with the affected individuals.[101] In essence, this means that the United Nations has started to link its actions back to individual behaviour, relying on behavioural insights, in its everyday work.

Both approaches—rationalism and behavioural economics—can be used to analyse State behaviour as well as individual behaviour relevant to international law. Given its close connection to psychology, the latter is often more focused on the individual than the State.

4. The Great Convergence: Sustainable Development Goals and How to Achieve Them

Certainly, the Westphalian system in international law used to be State-centred. However, this has changed, not only as a result of the legalisation and global recognition of human rights but also because there has been a fundamental shift in how we understand the international legal order.[102] This is also reflected in the SDGs,

[99] For an elaboration, see van Aaken, 'Experimental Insights' 2019 (n. 96). For the use of defaults in trade treaties, see Anne van Aaken, 'Making Trade Agreements Contribute to Sustainability: The Potential of Behavioural Science', in Geraldo Vidigal and Kathleen Claussen (eds.), *The Sustainability Revolution in International Trade Agreements* (Oxford: OUP 2024).

[100] Abhijit V. Banerjee and Esther Duflo, *Poor Economics: A Radical Rethinking of the Way to Fight Global Poverty* (New York, NY: Public Affairs 2011); for a more general discussion of behavioural economics in development economics, see Roberta Muramatsu and Flavia Avila, 'The Behavioral Turn in Development Economics: A Tentative Account through the Lens of Economic Methodology' *Brazilian Journal of Political Economy* 37 (2017), 363–80.

[101] See note 3, above.

[102] Christian Tomuschat, 'International Law: Ensuring the Survival of Mankind on the Eve of a New Century' *Recueil des Cours* 281 (1999), 13–438, at 162: 'States are no more than instruments whose inherent function it is to serve the interests of their citizens as legally expressed in human rights'; Tom Sparks, 'Towards a Human-Centred International Law: Self-Determination and the Structure of the International Legal System' *Durham theses, Durham University* (2017), available at Durham E-Theses Online: http://etheses.dur.ac.uk/12408/, accessed 7/7/23. This has also changed in jurisprudence; see,

which, although remaining soft law, can be considered the new guiding principles of the international legal order, serving as a focal and reference point for the actions of States, international organisations,[103] and non-State actors alike. They did not come out of a normative vacuum but reflect human-centred values and development. Most importantly, the SDGs are grounded in international law, making international law their normative framework.[104] Thus, they offer one example of how the normative convergence between international law and New Welfare Economics can materialise. The SDGs also illustrate the role that the insights of social science, particularly those from behavioural economics, play in making them a reality.

The HDI, based on Sen's approach of New welfare Economics, as explained in section 2, laid the philosophical groundwork. It guided the thinking that underlies the SDGs:

> There are many links between the human development approach and the 2030 Agenda. But it is worth noting up front that the two are fundamentally different things. The SDGs are a globally agreed tool for assessing development progress. Human development, meanwhile, is a philosophy—or lens—for considering almost any development issue one can think of. In other words, the SDGs provide a development destination. Human development allows one to design the route to get there.[105]

In addition to the philosophical basis and its normative integration into international law, realising the SDGs requires social-science expertise and appropriate behavioural assumptions.

At the level of international policy, the awareness that human well-being is a complex issue requiring a holistic approach led the United Nations General Assembly to create the SDGs of 2015, with the aim of achieving them by 2030. They are included in the 2030 Agenda for Sustainable Development.[106] The SDGs follow the Millennium Development Goals (MDG) of 2000, emphasising the interconnected environmental, social, and economic aspects of development by focusing

e.g., International Court of Justice (ICJ), *LaGrand (Germany v. United States of America)*, Judgment (2001) ICJ Reports 466, at para. 42.

[103] See, e.g., the programme of the WTO, 'The WTO and the Sustainable Development Goals', available at: https://www.wto.org/english/thewto_e/coher_e/sdgs_e/sdgs_e.htm, accessed 7/7/23; and the IMF, 'Sustainable Development Goals', available at: https://www.imf.org/en/Topics/SDG, accessed 7/7/23.

[104] Rakhyun E. Kim, 'The Nexus between International Law and the Sustainable Development Goals' *Review of European, Comparative and International Environmental Law (RECIEL)* 25 (2016), 15–26.

[105] Pedro Conceição, 'Human development and the SDGs', 24 June 2019, available at: http://hdr.undp.org/en/content/human-development-and-sdgs, accessed 7/7/23.

[106] UNGA, Transforming our World: The 2030 Agenda for Sustainable Development, 25 September 2015, A/RES/70/1.

on sustainability. Their holistic approach mirrors that of Amartya Sen. They include seventeen interconnected goals,[107] each of which typically includes eight to twelve specific targets. Each target has between one and four indicators used to measure progress towards reaching the objective in question. The targets are either 'outcome' targets (circumstances to be attained) or 'means of implementation' targets. Though the goals are broad and interdependent, two years after their initial introduction (6 July 2017), the General Assembly adopted a UN resolution to make them more 'actionable'.[108] A variety of tools are employed to track and visualise progress towards the goals and thus facilitate monitoring. All intend to make data more accessible and comprehensible.[109]

As the UN has acknowledged, achieving those goals—which include much of what is found in the New Welfare Economics approach and international treaties—requires the type of social-science expertise described in section 3, along with an understanding of what tools are effective in reaching these goals. The UN has therefore adopted the behavioural perspective, and has recently established a 'behavioral science unit'.[110] In summary, both the rationalist and, to an even greater extent, the behavioural approach provide the social-science methodology necessary to acquire knowledge on the (intended and unintended) consequences of the means chosen to achieve normatively desirable goals. These approaches contribute consequentialist insights to realise the aspirations of international law. In other words, social science helps to construct a more evidence-based international order that embraces human welfare and focuses on the individual, both normatively and as an actor. The United Nations therefore explicitly uses behavioural insights to advance the SDGs.

Although the SDGs are closely connected to (normative) New Welfare Economics in particular, ILE offer a positive social-science approach. It is essentially adaptable to various normative objectives and can be used for any normative goals and principles set by international law while also focusing on the individual as an actor. Therefore, ILE enables a normative approach that can be tailored to the specific issue or area in question, using the objectives relevant to the respective legal regime or treaty. This is so, for example when analysing the realisation of human rights from a behavioural perspective, for instance for examining access to justice.

[107] The seventeen SDGs are: (1) No Poverty, (2) Zero Hunger, (3) Good Health and Well-being, (4) Quality Education, (5) Gender Equality, (6) Clean Water and Sanitation, (7) Affordable and Clean Energy, (8) Decent Work and Economic Growth, (9) Industry, Innovation and Infrastructure, (10) Reducing Inequality, (11) Sustainable Cities and Communities, (12) Responsible Consumption and Production, (13) Climate Action, (14) Life Below Water, (15) Life On Land, (16) Peace, Justice, and Strong Institutions, and (17) Partnerships for the Goals.

[108] UNGA, Work of the Statistical Commission pertaining to the 2030 Agenda for Sustainable Development, 6 July 2017, A/RES/71/313.

[109] Our World in Data, 'Measuring progress towards the Sustainable Development Goals', available at: https://sdg-tracker.org, accessed 7/7/23.

[110] See note 3, above; and UN Behavioural Science Group, available at: https://www.uninnovation.network/un-group-pages/behavioural-science, accessed 1/12/23.

It can look not only at hard restraints and incentives for the various actors but also at the psychological mechanisms at play.[111] The Convention on International Trade in Endangered Species serves as another example,[112] emphasising the significance of consumer behaviour in efforts to reduce demand for products that threaten endangered species. A behavioural approach may better explain the frames needed to change consumer behaviour in order to achieve the purpose of the convention. The World Health Organization (WHO) employs behavioural sciences to nudge people towards healthier lifestyles, whether its related to communicable diseases, as seen in pandemics, or non-communicable diseases.[113] The UN Behavioural Science Unit employs the approach to foster peace, which is traditionally an issue of inter-State relations. The notion that peace, both within societies and on a larger scale, can be achieved solely through rational motives and logical reasoning is outdated; other elements such as social norms, narratives, and frames must be considered. Therefore, a view to the individual is indispensable.[114]

5. Conclusion

Many international lawyers see economics as being in conflict with the values of international law. This chapter has shown that this need not be so. First, economics is both a normative endeavour and a positive social-science approach. We must distinguish positive and normative economics, including their usefulness within the context of international law, for they can be applied independently. Furthermore, economics as well as Law and Economics are diverse and evolving fields, methodologically, normatively, and ideologically; they cannot be presented as a single approach. While there are good grounds to dismiss certain aspects of economics, such as traditional welfare economics, due to normative concerns, it makes sense to use those components that align with and are compatible with contemporary international law from a philosophical and normative perspective. Economics, in theory, has always focused on questions of agency and human actors but has done so in myriad ways. Normative economics has developed into an approach that puts humans and their rights at the centre of normative reflections and justice. Clearly, New Welfare Economics, combined with behavioural economics, which has also entered the complex field of development economics, closely aligns with the international agenda as embodied in the SDGs and ties in well with the

[111] See note 66, above.

[112] Convention on International Trade in Endangered Species of Wild Fauna and Flora (CITES), 3 March 1973, 993 UNTS 243.

[113] WHO, Behavioural sciences for better health initiative. Report by the Director-General, A75/25 (27 April 2022).

[114] Felix Kufus, 'What We Can Learn from Behavioural Science for Peace', *Futuring Peace*, July 15 2021, available at: https://medium.com/futuring-peace/what-we-can-learn-from-behavioural-science-for-peace-672842d82b74, accessed 7/7/23.

approach recently adopted by the United Nations. And although the SDGs as such may not be considered international law *stricto sensu*, they clearly guide the behaviour of States and international organisations. They are embedded not only in many international (human rights) instruments but also in other areas of international law, including anti-corruption and environmental law. This convergence is good news because it signifies a coming together of international law on the one hand and (law and) economics on the other, which will empirically enrich the policies needed to make the values of the international order, including humanisation, a reality. Economics, and especially behavioural economics, is well placed to bring the findings of social-science research focused on individual behaviour into the realm of international law. As succinctly expressed, normativity and reality need each other: '[I]f lawyer-economists do not make the mistake of claiming too much for what they are doing, and if they are willing to work at defining and analyzing pretty good instruments leading toward the just society, philosophers [and international lawyers] ought not be troubled.'[115]

[115] Guido Calabresi, 'An Exchange: About Law and Economics: A Letter to Ronald Dworkin' *Hofstra Law Review* 8 (1980), 553–62, at 561.

17
Individual Personhood in Anthropological Approaches to International Law

Marie-Claire Foblets

1. Introduction

Anne Peters and Tom Sparks have recognised that social and cultural anthropology is one of the relevant disciplinary angles for the study of international law, with its focus on the international personality of the individual and their protection. In this chapter, I highlight some criticisms arising from anthropology that touch on a central tenet of the 'humanisation thesis', namely that for their protection, 'individuals are, to a significant extent, the proper unit of concern for international law'.[1] The criticism draws on ethnographic research, and when it comes to defining the 'international personality of the individual' the findings show considerable diversity in how we define an 'individual'. Anthropologists and lawyers seem to begin from fundamentally different premises.[2] Anthropologists study the relationship between the individual and society (individual personhood) from the perspective of the realities on the ground, which are their primary objects of study. Traditionally, social and cultural anthropologists mainly concentrated on the study of the varied dynamics that reveal how social relations and networks operate *within* different human societies. More recently, anthropologists have started to explore the undeniable impact of globalisation on the lives of the societies they study. Their work increasingly focuses on the experiences of a growing number of people worldwide whose daily lives are marked by a profound rupture with the society around them. This includes unrecognised minorities, undocumented individuals, stateless persons, relocated communities, and indigenous communities left without protected status. Anthropology not only reveals that the promises of international law in relation to safeguarding the individual remain out of sync with

[1] See Peters and Sparks, 'Introduction' (chapter 1), in this volume.

[2] On these premises see, *inter alia*, Donovan James and H. Edwin Anderson, *Anthropology and Law* (New York, NY: Berghahn 2003); Annelise Riles, 'Representing in-between: Law, Anthropology, and the Rethoric of Interdisciplinarity', in Martha Mundy (ed.), *Law and Anthropology* (Aldershot: Ashgate 2002), 27-80; Michael Freeman and David Napier (eds.), *Law and Anthropology. Current Legal Issues* (Oxford: OUP 2009); John Comaroff, 'The End of Anthropology, Again: on the Future of an In/Discipline' *American Anthropologist* 112 (2010), 524-38.

Marie-Claire Foblets, *Individual Personhood in Anthropological Approaches to International Law* In: *The Individual in International Law*. Edited by: Tom Sparks and Anne Peters, Oxford University Press.
DOI: 10.1093/oso/9780198898917.003.0017

the actual lived experiences of an increasing number of people around the world today, but also highlights the need for a new, evidence-based approach to understanding and addressing their aspirations. What I develop here further builds on and confirms a thesis already amply developed in the literature, and not only in anthropology; namely, that efforts to promote respect for international standards of protection of the individual are often likely to fail until such a time that they relate directly to, and where possible are promoted through, local cultural, religious, and other communities.[3]

This chapter will proceed in two steps, each of which will be dealt with in a separate section.

In section 2, I provide a number of illustrations of the way anthropology analyses the concept of personhood. In many cultures the notion is understood quite differently from the way the western liberal tradition sees it, that is, as a self-determined, autonomous individual with various fundamental rights. I will draw from three distinct sources: first, kinship anthropology; second, anthropological criticisms of the concept of personal autonomy; and third, the notion of the 'dividual' in anthropology.

In section 3, I present three illustrations of attempts to introduce expressions of alternative conceptions of the person into international law. The first example draws on the concept of *kafala*, the shared commitment to care for a vulnerable child in Islam, which made its way into international law via the United Nations Convention on the Rights of the Child. The second example, by contrast, shows how a similar attempt to promote the values of inclusion of the person while also recognising and respecting differences in cultural perspectives failed. This is the case of the Bangkok Declaration, which was adopted at the World Conference Regional Preparatory Meeting in 1993 and was intended as a statement of the Asian region's stance on human rights. The third example draws on the Protocol on the Rights of Women in Africa, also called the Maputo Protocol, which entered into force on 25 November 2005.

I will be necessarily brief on each of the three illustrations; undoubtedly too brief to do justice to the complexity of the issues under scrutiny. Together, these examples help us to understand why anthropologists, starting from their field

[3] For an illustration of this thesis, see the work directed by Effie Fokas on the protection of religious freedom in the United States and Europe. For the protection to be effective, it requires mobilisation from the communities concerned, resorting to international courts if necessary. Fokas speaks of 'grassroots level awareness', and notably bases her observations on anthropologists who conduct fieldwork to collect data. See Effie Fokas, 'Directions in Religious Pluralism in Europe: Mobilizations in the Shadow of European Court of Human Rights Religious Freedom Jurisprudence' *Oxford Journal of Law and Religion* 4 (2015), 54-74; Effie Fokas, 'Grassroots Level Awareness about Religion at the European Court of Human Rights', in Jeroen Temperman et al. (eds.), *The European Court of Human Rights and the Freedom of Religion or Belief: The 25 Years since Kokkinakis* (Leiden: Brill 2019), 419-40; Pasquale Annicchino, 'The Geopolitics of Transnational Law and Religion', in Susanna Mancini and Michel Rosenfeld (eds.), *The Conscience Wars: Rethinking the Balance between Religion, Identity and Equality* (Cambridge: CUP 2018), 258-74.

observations and extending to the way they look at the role of international law with its (universal) standards for protecting the individual person as a legal subject, see the need to ensure greater openness and sensitivity to different cultural contexts.[4]

2. Personhood and Belonging: Insights Gained from Anthropological Approaches

Tom Sparks and Anne Peters define, for the purpose of international law, 'personhood as the capacity of an actor to bear rights or duties in a given legal order'.[5] They also consider indisputable the position that the humanisation of international law must be inclusive to non-western traditions that might be 'individualistic' in different ways or to lesser degrees.[6] This is where anthropology, with its knowledge gained from ethnographic observation, can make a contribution: what can be said about the many different ways in which meanings of personhood are configured in time and space through particular (social and cultural) contexts and empirical realities that shape their specificity and application? Do these multifarious configurations of personhood have status under international law, and if so, what insights and/or concerns guide the specific criteria for granting such recognition?

2.1 Kinship Underpinning Networks of Relationships

Social and cultural anthropology, being holistically oriented, seeks to understand the dynamic between specific societal conditions and the way(s) in which personhood is constructed in law as well as in other social domains. For the purposes of this chapter, I will begin with one specific illustration of the gap that continues to exist between the promises of an individual-focused international law and the lived reality of personality and personhood as studied by anthropologists, namely, the (legal) personality of the individual in the many societies worldwide where the logic of kinship continues to be the organising principle regulating relationships among individuals and between the individual and society.[7] Ethnographic

[4] For another illustration of anthropology's critical analysis of international law, see *inter alia*: Galit A. Sarfaty, 'An Anthropological Approach to International Economic Law', in Moshe Hirsch (ed.), *Research Handbook on the Sociology of International Law* (Cheltenham: Edward Elgar Publishing 2018), 296-318.

[5] See Peters and Sparks, 'Introduction' (chapter 1), in this volume.

[6] *ibid.*

[7] Kin-based relationships are traditionally defined as ties based on blood and marriage. They include lineal generational bonds (children, parents, grandparents, and great-grandparents), collateral bonds (siblings, cousins, nieces and nephews, and aunts and uncles), and affinal ties (i.e. through marriage). In *Kinship and Marriage*, Robin Fox defines the study of kinship in anthropology as 'the study of what man does with these basic facts of life—mating, gestation, parenthood, socialization, siblingship,

accounts demonstrate the primacy of kinship through detailed studies of the way alliances operate, the organisation of descent, sexuality, and sexual prohibitions, revealing the great diversity of rules that govern these relations. Therefore, more accurate knowledge of the rules and principles that regulate kin-based relationships, as well as of the terms assigned to them, could be valuable in accurately assessing how 'personhood' is constructed as legal subjectivity under situation-specific conditions.

One key observation in anthropology is that groups or communities often use the rules that govern kinship relations for their own purposes and to maintain the existing social order, both internally among the members of the group and in their relations with the outside world. This observation has yielded a kind of knowledge that remains highly valuable for understanding certain dynamics that govern individual behaviour until today. These dynamics often keep in place inherited structures of hierarchically conceived and predetermined patterns of behaviour among individuals and groups that at first glance may seem ill-suited to meet the standards of contemporary international human rights protection: early-age marriages[8] and endogamous marital relationships (that are at times also polygamous[9]) are but two illustrations of persistent practices characteristic of kin-based relationships and that would be interesting to study through the prism of the humanisation thesis, which refers primarily to the legal personality of individuals and their protection within, as well as beyond, State legal orders. An anthropological approach primarily investigates why a given group or community would want to retain such kin-based practices and institutions. Investigations often show that any attempt to eradicate these practices without sufficiently taking into account what they mean for the people concerned, risks removing the protection that such practices can at times still offer without providing an equivalent alternative.

Today, particularly in societies with well-established social security systems, it is widely believed that the influence and significance of kinship ties have considerably diminished, while other conventions, with individual self-determination paramount, have taken over, replacing traditional, kin-based logics.[10] Through

etc.'. According to Fox, human societies are 'working with the same raw material as exists in the animal world, but [we] can conceptualize and categorize it to serve social ends': Robin Fox, *Kinship and Marriage: An Anthropological Perspective* (Harmondsworth: Penguin Books 1967), 30.

[8] On early-age marriages, see Nadjma Yassari and Ralf Michaels (eds.), *Die Frühehe im Recht: Praxis, Rechtsvergleich, Kollisionsrecht, höherrangiges Recht* (Tübingen: Mohr Siebeck 2021); on polygamous marital relationships, see Béatrice Bourdelois, *Mariage polygamique et droit positif français* (Paris: G.L.N. Joly 1993).

[9] See, *inter alia*, Anika Liversage, 'Polygamy, Wellbeing, and Ill-being amongst Ethnic Muslim Minorities', in Marja Tillikainen (ed.), *Wellbeing of Transnational Muslim Families* (London: Routledge 2020), 78-93.

[10] See, e.g., Andrew Azzopardi and Shaun Grech (eds.), *Inclusive Communities: A Critical Reader* (Rotterdam: SensePublishers 2012); Anne Griffiths, Sanna Mustasaari, and Anna Mäki-Petajä-Leinonen (eds.), *Subjectivity, Citizenship and Belonging in Law: Identities and Intersections* (Abingdon: Routledge 2017); Thomas Hoffmann and Göran Larsson (eds.), *Muslims and the New Information and Communication Technologies: Notes from an Emerging and Infinite Field* (Dordrecht: Springer 2013).

detailed ethnographic accounts, anthropologists demonstrate, however, that still today individuals have more to gain in various situations from the protection they receive from a kinship system—whether it is based on individual consent or not—than from any other (international) legal regime or mechanism of support.[11] Kinship serves as a collective defence against the risks posed by factors such as rampant globalisation and the lack of alternative means for assisting those who are rendered particularly vulnerable by such social and economic transformations. The bonds of kinship, whether by consanguinity, affinity, or group affiliations, continue to play an important and even necessary role because of the obligations they carry; to share, to care, and to provide hospitality and mutual assistance.[12] In one case it might be the payment of a relatively large dowry that makes it possible to fulfil these obligations;[13] in another, it might be the expectation that financially successful members of a kin group will look after their relatives—near or far—and allow them to stay with them either temporarily or for extended periods.[14]

The logic of kinship can also help preserve a collective identity over a long period, notably in diaspora situations where endogamous marriages are particularly valued.[15] Research shows that these practices often occur in situations of socio-economic deprivation and should not necessarily be automatically attributed to 'culture'.

How then, as Peters and Sparks suggest, are we to ensure that the humanisation of international law and its reliance on human rights protection 'opens itself to non-western traditions' that are less individual-centred? Today, individual human rights are enshrined in law in most countries. The mainstream legal literature on human rights argues that (individual) human rights should benefit everyone.[16] In

[11] Ethnographic accounts offer a very nuanced picture, showing by means of empirical observation the continued importance of kinship ties as social *conventions*, and demonstrating how they make up the normative framework to which many individuals still belong and, more generally, their profound impact on the everyday reality of those involved. See, e.g., Miriam Benteler (ed.), *Perspektiven auf Verwandtschaft: Soziale Beziehungen in Europa und Asien. Perspectives on Kinship: Social Relations in Europe and Asia* (Berlin: Weißensee Verlag 2015); Tatjana Thelen and Erdmute Alber (eds.), *Reconnecting State and Kinship* (Philadelphia, PA: University of Pennsylvania Press 2018).

[12] See, e.g., Erdmute Alber and Heike Drotbohm (eds.), *Anthropological Perspectives on Care: Work, Kinship, and the Life-Course* (New York, NY: Palgrave Macmillan 2015); Rob Geen (ed.), *Kinship Care: Making the Most of a Valuable Resource* (Washington DC: Urban Institute Press 2013); Loraine Gelsthorpe, Perveez Mody, and Brian Sloan (eds.), *Spaces of Care* (Oxford: Hart 2020); Haldis Haukanes and Frances Pine (eds.), *Generations, Kinship and Care: Gendered Provisions of Social Security in Central Eastern Europe* (Bergen: University of Bergen 2005); Rosie Harding, Ruth Fletcher, and Chris Beasly (eds.), *ReValuing Care in Theory, Law and Policy: Cycles and Connections* (London: Routledge 2017).

[13] Jørgen S. Nielsen and Rubya Mehdi (eds.), *Embedding Mahr in the European Legal System* (Copenhagen: Djøf Forlag 2011).

[14] Kieran McLean Eadie, 'The Application of Kafala in the West', in Nadirsyah Hosen (ed.), *Research Handbook on Islamic Law and Society* (Cheltenham: Edward Elgar Publishing 2018), 48-76.

[15] Banu Çitlak et al. (eds.), *The New Diversity of Family Life in Europe: Mobile Ethnic Groups and Flexible Boundaries* (Wiesbaden: Springer 2017); Ralph Grillo, *Muslim Families, Politics and the Law: A Legal Industry in Multicultural Britain* (London: Routledge 2015); Alison Shaw and Aviad Raz (eds.), *Cousin Marriages: Between Tradition, Genetic Risk and Cultural Change* (New York, NY: Berghahn Books 2015).

[16] Thomas Risse, Stephen C. Ropp, and Kathryn Sikkink (eds.), *The Power of Human Rights: International Norms and Domestic Change* (Cambridge: CUP 1999).

reality, however, such a normative expectation is misleading. Ethnographic studies show in detail the many obstacles that hinder the realisation of this expectation. One of these obstacles is the fact that the concept of an international legal order that 'is oriented towards the interest and the needs of human beings with the help of legal institutions and mechanisms'[17] and is protected by an increasing number of existing international human rights treaties, is derived from specific historical circumstances that have not exerted influence on all human societies to the same extent or in the same way. As a result, the supposed universal acceptance of human rights that give precedence to the needs and interests of the persons concerned is highly questionable.[18] Kinship studies in anthropology show that the lived experience of individuals and the groups they form is complex and cannot be properly examined solely on the basis of the protection criteria as defined by international human rights law.[19] Taking inspiration from the work of, among others, Amartya Sen (see section 3) some anthropologists have therefore started exploring the degree to which the acceptance of pluralism within international human rights law could possibly serve as a way of dealing with diversity, both within and across societies.[20]

When human rights standards are applied to specific kin-based practices, such as early-age marriages or endogamy, they often lead to the conclusion that these practices cannot be granted protection under international law. This is because they do not meet the criteria for respecting individual autonomy as a norm, which obliges one to respect the decisions of an adult with decision-making capacity. In Europe, there are numerous examples in case law where officials such as family judges, juvenile courts, prosecutors, or other administrators responsible for granting permission to enter a country (e.g. in the context of family reunification) invoke the principles of the best interests of the child and their right to free consent as an adult to determine that the relationship in question cannot (yet) be granted effect under domestic law. This leads to what is commonly referred to as 'limping' situations in the literature: situations that lack recognition in at least one of the domestic jurisdictions to which the situation is connected, either through habitual residence or citizenship. Limping situations put the individuals involved

[17] See Peters and Sparks, 'Introduction' (chapter 1), in this volume.

[18] See, *inter alia*, Eva Brems et al. (eds.), *Human, Rights Encounter Legal Pluralism: Normative and Empirical Approaches* (Oxford: Hart 2017); Jack Donnelly, *Universal Human Rights in Theory and Practice* (Ithaca: Cornell 1989); Louisa Riches, 'Legal and Normative Pluralism, Hybridity and Human Rights: The Universal Periodic Review', in Nicola Lemay-Hébert and Rosa Freedman (eds.), *Hybridity: Exploring Power, Social Structure and Institutions Beyond the Liberal West* (Abingdon: Routledge 2017), 161-81; Yvonne Donders, 'Cultural Pluralism in International Human Rights', in Ana Filipa Vrdoljak (ed.), *The Cultural Dimension of Human Rights* (Oxford: OUP 2013), 205-39.

[19] See, *inter alia*, Sally Engle Merry, *Human Rights and Gender Violence: Translating International Law into Local Justice* (Chicago, IL: University of Chicago Press 2006).

[20] Amartya Sen, 'How to Judge Globalism', in Frank Lechner (ed.), *The Globalisation Reader* (Malden, MA: Wiley-Blackwell 2012), 16-21.

in a difficult legal position: their situation may be perfectly legal in the country of origin,[21] but is denied effect in the country of residence.

In practice, these principled notions of human rights, stemming from the fear that some parties involved may not have freely consented to a certain situation, do not prevent these situations from happening or from continuing to play, in their own way and in the particular context within which they apply, their protective role.[22] On the contrary, in the past three or four decades, new roles for kinship ties have been emerging that allow relatives to continue supporting each other, at times across national borders and jurisdictions.[23] In their own way, these practices are the confirmation of their profoundly social nature.[24] In a globalised world, therefore, kinship still has a significant role, enabling groups to use the logic of kinship to address their own needs and protection independently, primarily as a result of the dramatic inability of public authorities to offer any equivalent support or protection to appropriately respond to the situation.[25]

[21] Daphna Hacker, *Legalized Families in the Era of Bordered Globalization* (Cambridge: CUP 2017); Susanne Rutten, Benedicta Deogratias, and Pauline Kruiniger-van Maanen (eds.), *Marital Captivity: Divorce, Religion and Human Rights* (The Hague: Eleven International Publishing 2019).

[22] Jennifer Cole and Christian Groes-Green (eds.), *Affective Circuits: African Migrations to Europe and the Pursuit of Social Regeneration* (Chicago, IL: The University of Chicago Press 2016); Megan Gaucher, *A Family Matter: Citizenship, Conjugal Relationships, and Canadian Immigration Policy* (Vancouver: University of British Columbia Press 2018); Christian Groes-Green and Nadine T. Fernandez (eds.), *Intimate Mobilities: Sexual Economies, Marriage and Migration in a Disparate World* (New York, NY: Berghahn Books 2018).

[23] Remittances, to take just one example, are a widespread form of solidarity between members of extended families on a global scale. For millions of people around the world who have not migrated and have stayed in their country of origin, they represent an indispensable form of income for maintaining a certain level of well-being. The amount of money transferred every year from rich to considerably poorer countries is considerable; such remittances thereby constitute a major global economic activity. See, *inter alia*, Serge Feld, *International Migration, Remittances and Brain Drain: Impacts on Development* (Cham: Springer International 2021); Jorgen Carling, 'Remittances: Eight Analytical Perspectives', in Tanja Bastia and Ronald Skeldon (eds.), *Routledge Handbook of Migration and Development* (London: Routledge 2020), 114-24; Emmanuel K. K. Lartey, *The Effect of Remittances on the Current Account in Developing and Emerging Economies* (Washington DC: The World Bank [Policy Research Working Papers] 2018).

[24] Venetia Evergeti and Elisabetta Zontini, 'Introduction: Some Critical Reflections on Social Capital, Migration and Transnational Families' *Ethnic and Racial Studies* 29 (2006), 1025-39; Dominik Kohlhagen, *Diasporas africaines et mondes du droit: une anthropologie juridique d'une migration entre Douala et Berlin* (Villeneuve d'Ascq: Atelier National de Reproduction des Thèses 2013); Pashaura Singh and Louis E. Fenech (eds.), *The Oxford Handbook of Sikh Studies* (Oxford: OUP 2014).

[25] Loretta Baldassar and Laura Merla (eds.), *Transnational Families, Migration and the Circulation of Care: Understanding Mobility and Absence in Family Life* (New York, NY: Routledge 2014); Julia Carter and Simon Duncan, *Reinventing Couples: Tradition, Agency and Bricolage* (London: Palgrave Macmillan 2018); Francesca Decimo and Alessandra Gribaldo (eds.), *Boundaries within: Nation, Kinship and Identity among Migrants and Minorities* (Cham: Springer 2017); Azra Hromadžić and Monika Palmberger (eds.), *Care across Distance: Ethnographic Explorations of Aging and Migration* (New York, NY: Berghahn Books 2018); Majella Kilkey and Ewa Palenga-Möllenbeck (eds.), *Family Life in an Age of Migration and Mobility: Global Perspectives through the Life Course* (London: Palgrave Macmillan 2016).

2.2 The Principle of Individual Autonomy

Fundamentally, what stands in the way of the recognition in international law of certain kin-based practices is the presumed lack of *individual autonomy* left to the persons bound by the rules imposed on them by the kinship system. From a liberal perspective, implementing the principle of autonomy appears straightforward. In this view a legal subject is able to assert their subjective rights by exercising their free will. This allows individuals to form social relationships with other subjects (individual or collective) as they see fit. In the context of domestic law, these relationships are given their normative authority through contracts, which are legally binding agreements between the parties involved.

In their efforts to comprehend the vast range of perspectives on what it means to be an individual human being, anthropologists have, ever since the inception of the discipline, been striving to acquire a type of knowledge about human societies that enables them to scrutinise the specific differences and similarities among societies in terms of the constitution of the person. They have noticed significant differences in how a human being attains personhood in the deepest social and cultural sense; being born does not in itself automatically confer personhood. Anthropology convincingly demonstrates that the model of individual autonomy, in which the criterion for judging the validity of an individual's (legal) act is based on their free and informed consent is far from being prevalent worldwide: 'Not all cultures value personal autonomy.'[26] This observation may in turn help explain why individuals do not automatically embrace international legal standards when tensions arise between these standards and their cultural practices and traditions.

A critical analysis of empirical reality and its increasing complexity from the perspective of individuals' lived experiences does indeed suggest that the concept of an autonomous, individuated, self-regarding, and self-determined person is often merely illusory, a *legal fiction*. 'This is a conception of subjectivity grounded in secular modernity', the American legal anthropologist Sally Engel Merry stated.[27] Indeed, anthropological scholarship shows that personal autonomy ought, at the very least, to be reconsidered in light of the diverse underlying assumptions regarding the attributes that constitute 'the person'.[28] The complex dimensions of

[26] David Copp, 'Rationality, Autonomy and Basic Needs', in Neil Roughley (ed.), *Being Humans: Anthropological Universality and Particularity in Transdisciplinary Perspectives* (Berlin: De Gruyter 2000), 334-55, at 348.

[27] Sally Engle Merry, 'Relating to the Subjects of Human Rights: The Culture of Agency in Human Rights Discourse', in Michael Freeman and David Napier (eds.), *Law and Anthropology: Current Legal Issue Volume 12* (Oxford: OUP 2008), 385-407, at 386; see also Copp, 'Rationality, Autonomy and Basic Needs' 2000 (n. 26), 334-55.

[28] For examples of work that are based on anthropological research, see, *inter alia*, Ernestine McHugh, *Love and Honor in the Himalayas: Coming to Know Another Culture* (Philadelphia, PA: Pennsylvania University Press 2001); Annelies Moors, 'Adopting a Face Veil, Concluding an Islamic Marriage: Autonomy, Agency and Liberal-Secular Rule', in Marie-Claire Foblets et al. (eds.), *Personal Autonomy in Plural Societies. A Principle and its Paradoxes* (London: Routledge 2018), 127-39; Sarah Lund Skar, 'Marry the Land, Divorce the Man: Quecha Mariage and the Problem of Individual

autonomy, agency, and consent in the contemporary era are not only discussed by anthropologists. In recent years, authors of various disciplines have worked on the issue of individual agency and consent, targeting, among other notions, abstract interpretations of the concept of personal autonomy in political theory.[29] Emphasis is placed on the elusive nature of this notion, what it means in liberal theory, and how it is flawed both from a theoretical and an empirical point of view.

It should not be underestimated how many ethnic groups, cultures, faith-based communities, etc. maintain a normative system which deprives (some of) its members of certain protections or liberties that human rights law seeks to guarantee. Examples range from body-marking practices and restrictive dress codes to discriminatory inheritance rights.[30] The critical question is: can the principle of personal autonomy also serve as the basis for a person's decision freely to renounce the rights and freedoms guaranteed to them by international human rights law?

Anthropological scholarship cautions those who, perhaps driven by a strong commitment to human rights, refuse to believe that any person would willingly consent to certain controversial (from a human rights point of view) traditions or practices, if only because these traditions do not promote emancipation. As Monique Deveaux put it:

> Both the idealized conception of autonomy as free will and the more moderate conceptions of autonomy as requiring self-determination or the capacity for self-definition and authenticity in the context of a socialized existence obscure the context of important decisions that people may make. [...] in overlooking the complexity of individuals' own relationship to tradition, it would appear that the liberal autonomy framework would dispose the liberal State towards regulating

Autonomy', in Vigdis Broch-Due (ed.), *Carved Flesh/Cast Selves: Gendered Symbols and Social Practices* (Oxford: Berg 1993), 129-46; Marielle Risse, *Community and Autonomy in Southern Oman* (Cham: Palgrave Macmillan 2019).

[29] See, e.g., Jennifer Nedelsky, 'Reconceiving Autonomy: Sources, Thoughts and Possibilities' *Yale Journal of Law and Feminism* 1 (1989), 7-36; Sarah Conly, *Against Autonomy: Justifying Coercive Paternalism* (Cambridge: CUP 2012); Geoffrey Brahm Levey (ed.), *Authenticity, Autonomy and Multiculturalism* (New York, NY: Routledge 2015); Sawitri Saharso, 'Is Freedom of the Will but a Western Illusion?', in Barbara Arneil et al. (eds.), *Sexual Justice/Cultural Justice. Critical Perspectives in Political Theory and Practice* (Abingdon: Routledge 2007), 122-38.

[30] See, *inter alia*, Asivati Lorraine Chiweza, 'The Challenges of Promoting Legal Empowerment in Developing Countries: Women's Land Ownership and Inheritance Rights in Malawi', in Dan Banik (ed.), *Rights and Legal Empowerment in Eradicating Poverty* (Farnham: Routledge 2008), 2001-16; Jennifer Heath (ed.), *The Veil: Women Writers on Its History, Lore and Politics* (Berkeley, CA: University of California Press 2008); Stefan Eisenhofer, *Painted People: die Faszination des Zweiten Gesichts* (Munich: Kunth 2005); Sulistyowati Irianto, 'Inheritance Rights and Gender Justice in Contemporary Indonesia', in Adriaan Bedner and Barbara Oomen (eds.), *Real Legal Certainty and Its Relevance: Essays in Honour of Jan Michiel Otto* (Leiden: Leiden Publications 2018), 193-212.

or even censuring too wide a range of social customs that arguably should be accommodated.[31]

The warning applies to situations that in recent years have been on the rise. In Europe, professionals in plural societies, including legal practitioners, surgeons, midwives, and school principals, encounter situations in their daily work where people have chosen to renounce certain 'protective' (human) rights in favour of following the customs or beliefs of their culture or religion.[32] These professionals are faced with the dilemma of how to reconcile their professional ethics with the person's presumably autonomous decision to renounce their 'rights'. One could speak of situations of 'internormativity',[33] which often give rise to a veritable 'power struggle' between diverging systems of rules: will the practitioner 'force' the person to align themselves with human rights requirements, or is there space for accommodation?[34]

One way to facilitate the task of those responsible for making these often-difficult choices is to provide them with a mechanism for coordinating the different sets of norms at play.[35] One of these mechanisms is recourse to 'ordre public' or public policy exception:[36] in practice, in contemporary liberal thinking, recourse

[31] Monique Deveaux, 'Personal Autonomy and Cultural Tradition: The Arranged Marriage Debate in Britain', in Barbara Arneil et al. (eds.), *Sexual Justice/Cultural Justice. Critical Perspectives in Political Theory and Practice* (Abingdon: Routledge 2007), 139-66, at 145.

[32] Paulo Pinto de Albuquerque and Andrea Scoseria Katz, 'Is Religion a Threat to Human Rights or Is It the Other Way Around?: Defending Individual Autonomy in the ECtHR's Jurisprudence on Freedom of Religion', in Robert Uerpmann-Wittzack et al. (eds), *Religion and International Law: Living Together* (Leiden: Brill Nijhoff 2018), 277-93.

[33] It is clear that these dilemmas are not exclusive to conflicts between cultures and/or communities but can also occur within communities: Emmanuelle Bernheim, 'Le "pluralisme normative": un nouveau paradigme pour appréhender les mutations sociales et juridiques?' *Revue Interdisciplinaire d'Études Juridiques* 67 (2011), 1-41.

[34] On the complexities of a person's feelings of attachment, and how to address them, see, *inter alia*, Heidi Keller, 'Introduction: Understanding Relationships - What we Would Need to Know to Conceptualize Attachment as the Cultural Solution of a Universal Development Task', in Hiltrud Otto and Heidi Keller (eds), *Different Faces of Attachment. Cultural Variations on a Universal Human Need* (Cambridge: CUP 2014), 1-26.

[35] At least three types of these mechanisms can be distinguished. The first is that of subordination: in their relations with the State (as well as with international law), alternative or parallel systems remain subordinate. Second, and at the other end of the spectrum, is the mechanism of self-regulation, whereby groups, communities, or social organisations successfully continue to apply their own regulations within their given sphere of activity or competence. These groups to some extent rival the State, which in turn must tolerate this competition from parallel normative systems that are often better adapted to the social relations they govern. In the literature, this is described as 'strong pluralism' (see especially Jean-Guy Belley, 'Le Droit comme "terra incognita": Conquérir et construire le pluralisme juridique' *La Revue Canadienne Droit et Société/Canadian Journal of Law & Society* 12 (1997), 1-15, at 5). A third coordination mechanism is one that allows individuals to *choose (optio iuris)* between the competing normative systems and to decide for themselves which set of norms they will adhere to.

[36] See, *inter alia*, Nathalie Bernard-Maugiron and Baudouin Dupret (eds.), *Ordre public et droit musulman de la famille en Europe et en Afrique du Nord* (Brussels: Bruylant 2012); Jean-Michel Ducomte, 'Entre respect des libertés publiques et garantie de l'ordre public: l'évolution de la normativité en matière de laïcité', in Jean Baubérot, Micheline Milot and Philippe Portier (eds.), *Laicité, laicités: Reconfigurations et nouveaux défis (Afrique, Amérique, Europe, Japon, Pays arabes)* (Paris, Éditions de la Maison des sciences de l'homme 2014), 319-43.

to this exception means that the freedom of the individual to exercise their autonomy is subject to severe restrictions. In such cases, the will of the individual person remains without practical effect wherever exercising it would encourage the continuation of a practice or tradition that is considered incompatible with the standards of protection as defined under binding law as it applies in the domestic legal order. The underlying assumption is that a person holding fundamental rights cannot possibly be expected voluntarily to renounce those rights. A widespread practice, which is being categorically refused formal recognition in the vast majority of European countries, is, for example, religious marriages that are not registered with the competent civil authorities in the spouses' country of residence. Consequently, these marriages do not receive the legal protections associated with formal marriages.[37] This could be viewed as a form of 'imposed protection'. Such 'protection' however, risks having the opposite effect: it institutes a 'filter' system in people's lives. Recourse to human rights to justify public policy arguments can lead to practices being labelled as deviant or 'contentious', and consequently they may not be granted recognition under State law, and at times might even be criminalised. In such cases, the State often fails to offer a suitable alternative that would provide the parties involved with an appropriate remedy or protection.[38]

Imposed protection or a rigid and uncompromising human rights approach, therefore, comes down to denying individual actors the capacity to seek, *from within*, renewal and adaptation of certain traditions or practices specific to the group or community in question. It makes the exercise of autonomy dependent upon so many conditions that are external to the situation at hand so that, *in effect*, it results in a denial of that autonomy. Setting the bar high by strongly insisting on alignment with international human rights criteria of protection of an individual person's rights—even if that may be the preferred long-term option—can, therefore, from a short-term perspective, render the goal unattainable, with the risk that a person could lose the protection they have with existing social arrangements and consequently this could lead to their marginalisation. As a result, individuals facing a situation that (from the point of view of State legal order) clearly infringe upon their personal rights may choose not to take action against it even when they have the option to do so. They make this choice because other priorities are more important to them than asserting their 'human rights'. In Europe, for example, it is challenging to explain the abovementioned astonishingly high occurrence of unregistered religious marriages that persist and that, given their prevalence, meet

[37] See, *inter alia*, Russell Sandberg, *Religion and Marriage Law. The Need for Reform* (Bristol: Bristol University Press 2021).

[38] In practice, much depends on the extent to which institutional actors are prepared to take an active role in giving a person true support. To give just one example: offering shelters for women fleeing intolerable family situations is only a first step. It must be followed by a more sustainable and comprehensive system of support to help the women overcome the crises that they were trying to escaping from. This is often a complex and highly delicate task for support staff.

with little resistance within their respective communities.[39] The literature has developed innovative concepts and approaches to study situations like these, such as 'strategic essentialism', 'asymmetric anti-essentialism', 'cultural voluntarism', 'multicultural jurisprudence', and 'multiculturalism without culture', to cite but a few.[40] These concepts were primarily developed to address the challenge of balancing women's rights with cultural values and norms.[41] Women may have their own reasons for not seeking protection under international law standards.

By scrutinising human behaviour ethnographically, that is, by using an in-depth, long-term, field-based approach,[42] anthropologists have observed that certain practices, even if they seem to conflict with international standards of protection of the (human rights of) individuals, have deep historical roots and play a role in the complex process of shaping and reshaping personal and social identities. They regulate people's sense of belonging and, in so doing, have a role to play in maintaining the structures that hold groups and societies together. In examining motivations and behaviour in human societies, anthropologists encounter a wide range of practices that regulate 'personhood'. However, they make sure to understand these practices *within the subjects' own context*. 'Autonomy consists in

[39] See, *inter alia*, Akhtar, Rajnaara, Rebecca Probert and Annelies Moors, 'Informal Muslim Marriages: Regulations and Contestations' *Oxford Journal of Law and Religion* 7 (2018), 367-75.

[40] See especially Avigail Eisenberg, 'Identity, Multiculturalism and Religious Arbitration: The Debate over Shari'a Law in Canada', in Barbara Arneil et al. (eds.), *Sexual Justice/Cultural Justice. Critical Perspectives in Political Theory and Practice* (Abingdon: Routledge 2007), 211-30; Catriona Mackenzie, 'Relational Autonomy, Sexual Justice and Cultural Pluralism', in Barbara Arneil et al. (eds.), *Sexual Justice/Cultural Justice. Critical Perspectives in Political Theory and Practice* (Abingdon: Routledge 2007), 103-21; Chandran Kukathas, 'Is Feminism Bad for Multiculturalism?' *Public Affairs Quarterly* 15 (2001), 83-98; Saba Mahmood, 'Agency, Performativity, and the Feminist Subject', in Lene Sjørup and Hilda Rømer Christensen (eds.), *Pieties and Gender* (Leiden: Brill 2009), 13-45; Saba Mahmood, *Politics of Piety: The Islamic Revival and the Feminist Subject* (Princeton, NJ: Princeton University Press 2005); Uma Narayan, 'Essence of Culture and a Sense of History: A Feminist Critique of Cultural Essentialism' *Hypatia* 13 (1998), 86-106; Uma Narayan, 'Minds of Their Own: Choices, Autonomy, Cultural Practices, and Other Women', in Louise M. Antony and Charlotte E. Witt (eds.), *A Mind of One's Own: Feminist Essays on Reason and Objectivity* (New York, NY: Routledge 2002), 418-32; Anne Phillips, 'It's My Body and I'll Do What I Like With It: Bodies as Objects and Property' *Political Theory* 39 (2011), 724-48; Anne Phillips, *Multiculturalism without Culture* (Princeton, NJ: Princeton University Press 2007).

[41] See especially Conly, *Against Autonomy* 2012 (n. 29); Sarah Conly, 'Seduction, Rape and Coercion' *Ethics* 115 (2004), 96-121; Marilyn Friedman, 'Women's Rights, Oppressed Minorities and the Liberal State', in Barbara Arneil et al. (eds.), *Sexual Justice/Cultural Justice: Critical Perspectives in Political Theory and Practice* (London: Routledge 2007), 89-102; Marilyn Friedman, *Autonomy, Gender, Politics* (Oxford: OUP 2003); Maleiha Malik, 'Progressive Multiculturalism: Minority Women and Cultural Diversity' *International Journal on Minority and Group Rights* 17 (2010), 447-67; Jill Marshall, 'Freedom of Religious Expression and Gender Equality: *Sahin v Turkey*' *Modern Law Review* 69 (2006), 452-61; Sawitri Saharso, 'Feminist Ethics, Autonomy and the Politics of Multiculturalism' *Feminist Theory* 4 (2003), 199-215; Sawitri Saharso, 'Female Autonomy and Cultural Imperative: Two Hearts Beating Together', in Will Kymlicka and Wayne Norman (eds.), *Citizenship in Diverse Societies* (Oxford: OUP 2000), 224-42; Ayelet Shachar, 'Demystifying Culture' *International Journal of Constitutional Law* 10 (2012), 429-48; Ayelet Shachar, 'Feminism and Multiculturalism: Mapping the Terrain', in David Owen and Anthony Laden (eds.), *Multiculturalism and Political Theory* (Cambridge: CUP 2007), 115-48.

[42] In the conventional sense given to fieldwork in anthropology, it demands 'the full-time involvement of a researcher over a lengthy period of time [. . .] and consists mostly of ongoing interaction with the human targets of study on their home ground': John van Maanen, *Tales of the Field: On Writing Ethnography* (Chicago, IL: University of Chicago Press 1988), 2.

governing our actions by our values and plans to the best of our ability given our epistemic situation, at least in so far as the internal requirements are concerned', writes David Copp.[43] For the anthropologist, there is no other *scientifically* valid, empirically based way to understand these practices.

One might feel some discomfort with regards to ethnographic writings, as in some cases they seem to offer 'mere' descriptions. However, an anthropologist's primary focus is to examine the underlying normative logic that determines why one practice is considered acceptable by the observing group while others are not.[44] Why, in the perception of the outside world, are some practices considered ordinary and unproblematic, while others are deemed *un*acceptable, even though the pressure to conform to these practices or expectations is quite similar in both cases? These questions are addressed by anthropologists.

2.3 Webs of Interdependency

Like practitioners of any discipline, anthropologists have recourse to conceptual frameworks that enable them to study their subjects as comprehensively as possible, and if an appropriate framework does not exist, they develop it.[45] What constitutes 'a person' in a given societal context? Around the world, societies that embrace modern liberalism, with its concept of a functional and conscious person (whether adult or those in development), by emphasising personal autonomy and freedom, provide only a single model for how to conceive of identity and social cohesion.[46]

A finding that emerges from numerous ethnographic studies, and which has become commonplace in anthropology, is the deeply *relational* nature of the human subject. Personhood is embedded in a web of relations and occurrences that have powerful effects on what it takes to become 'complete' persons in a given societal context. The American anthropologist and South Asianist McKim Marriott adopted the notion of the 'dividual' to describe a mode of being that is fundamentally constituted of distinguishable components, with modes of personhood that are characterised by multiscale interdependencies.[47] Some years later the British

[43] Copp, 'Rationality, Autonomy and Basic Needs' 2000 (n. 26), 347.

[44] An anthropologist's appraisal and interpretation of what constitutes child care, for example, are relative in the sense that they relate to the culture in which they apply. This holds true for any standard or value.

[45] The concept of 'webs of interdependency', this subsection's heading, is borrowed from Jean Comaroff and John Comaroff, 'In/ter/dependence: An Afterword' *Focaal* 90 (2021), 70-73, at 71; Jean Comaroff and John Comaroff, *Theory from the South: Or, How Euro-America is Evolving Toward Africa* (Boulder, CO: Paradigm Publishers 2012), 21, 184.

[46] Merry, 'Relating to the Subjects' 2008 (n. 27).

[47] McKim Marriot, 'Hindu Transactions: Diversity without Dualism', in Bruce Kapferer (ed.), *Transaction and Meaning: Directions in the Anthropology of Exchange and Symbolic Behavior* (Philadelphia, PA: Institute for the Study of Human Issues 1976), 109-42.

anthropologist Marylin Strathern reinstated the concept of the dividual in her book *The Gender of the Gift*.[48] It is undoubtedly thanks to her work that the term was subsequently adopted by several other anthropologists. However, at the same time it became the subject of fierce debate among scholars. Based on the work of Marriott, but also drawing from Marcel Mauss' idea of gift exchange, Strathern understands Melanesians as 'dividual': partibility and permeability are markers of Melanesian persons, the collective as unity of many is achieved by eliminating what differentiates them. For Strathern, agency in the Melanesian context stands in stark contrast to the western concept that envisages individuals as constantly existing in a 'permanently subjective state', where they are the sole cause and source of activity.[49] Two main points of criticism against the concept have been raised. First, that 'dividual' personhood is, like the western 'individual', constructed from an idealist perspective and invites an ahistorical and relativistic reading. The second point is that aspects of 'dividual personhood' are equally present in the modern western person, so the primary relational sociality of the human being is not limited solely to small-scale or non-modern societies that were historically studied by anthropologists.[50] It is undoubtedly true that both 'dividual' and 'individual' encompass, each in its own way, the concept of relatedness. They are also present, to varying degrees, in every single interpersonal relationship.

Be that as it may, the concept of the 'dividual personhood' preserves its merit by shedding light on why, in particular socio-historical contexts, it might not be possible for a person to develop their own individuality without taking into account the social expectations that defines a 'genuine', 'real', or 'complete' person. The semantic field of 'dividuum' and 'dividuality', as developed and discussed in anthropological scholarship, thereby offers an interpretation that may help explain why certain groups and communities in contemporary times persist in *resisting* the liberal stand with its strong emphasis on individual choice.

That said, it is also true that the efforts of anthropologists to elaborate an analytical apparatus that allows them to describe, as faithfully as possible, the 'webs of interdependence'[51] they see unfolding are not limited to the concept of 'dividual personhood'. Feminist writers have introduced the term 'relational autonomy' to characterise the situation of women who make choices that are at odds with the goal of achieving gender equality.[52] According to this view, when women

[48] Marilyn Strathern, *The Gender of the Gift: Problems with Women and Problems with Society in Melanesia* (Berkeley, CA: University of California Press 1988).

[49] *ibid*, 338.

[50] On this discussion, see Sabine Hess, 'Strathern's Melanesian "Dividual" and the Christian "Individual": A Perspective from Vanua Lava, Vanuatu' *Oceania* 76 (2006), 286-96; Antje Linkenbach and Martin Mulsow, 'Introduction: The Dividual Self', in Martin Fuchs et al. (eds.), *Religious Individualisation: Historical Dimensions and Comparative Perspectives* (Berlin: De Gruyter 2019), 322-43.

[51] See notes 26 and 27.

[52] For instance, Jennifer Nedelsky 1989 (n. 29) first proposed the concept of 'relational autonomy'. Others also use it as; see, e.g., Susan B. Boyd, 'Autonomy for Mothers? Relational Theory and Parenting

make 'illiberal' choices primarily due to their social connections and networks, it would be wrong to assume that they have not made their own conscious decisions. Consequently, their decisions should still be respected because they reflect a reasoning, whether expressed explicitly or implicitly, that has its own grounds.[53]

The concepts of 'dividual personhood' and 'relational autonomy' are just two examples of the conceptual framework developed by anthropologists. Both concepts exemplify how anthropologists engage in a more complex examination of 'personhood' when studying people's decision-making processes. Personhood is shaped by many different interdependent relationships, each with its own combination of normative demands and possibilities. These relationships are based on a blend of diverse and at times contradictory normative expectations, of which international law is only one.[54] To be sure, the conceptual framework will continue to be further refined and adapted to suit the specific circumstances of each situation being studied.

Whether it concerns kinship logics, the principle of individual autonomy, or alternative concepts suggested by authors who have examined the functioning of societies that do not prioritise the individual as the humanisation thesis in international law suggests, all three illustrations prompt us to embrace a more nuanced understanding of particular societal contexts. They encourage us to find a middle ground between local and international standards of personhood in the realm of international law.

3. Cross-Cultural Understandings of the Needs and Interests of Human Beings in International Law

Is there space for alternative conceptions of the person in international law? In this section, I explore three attempts to introduce a more contextual understanding of

Apart' *Feminist Legal Studies* 18 (2010), 137-58; Susan B. Boyd, 'Motherhood and Autonomy in a Shared Parenting Climate', in Jackie Jones et al. (eds.), *Gender, Sexualities and Law* (London: Routledge 2011), 255-68; Maneesha Deckha, 'Non-Human Animals and Human Health: A Relational Approach to the Use of Animals in Medical Research', in Jennifer L. Llewellyn and Jocelyn Downie (eds.), *Being Relational: Reflections on Relational Theory and Health Law* (Vancouver: University of British Columbia Press 2012).

[53] For an example, see Samia Bao, *Gender and Justice in Family Law Disputes* (Waltham, MA:, Brandeis University Press 2017).

[54] The question of when individuals actually make choices of their own free will is one that dates back to antiquity. For centuries philosophers have debated how to determine whether decisions are authentic in the sense that they reflect autonomous reasoning processes. While authors usually use the concept of autonomy, on occasion they conflate this idea with agency. What is the difference between autonomy and agency? For some theorists, autonomy concerns the framework of the mind or the ability to make decisions without undue influence. Agency is usually a term used to refer to acting on decisions. While it is recognised that these concepts are closely linked, the distinction between them is not always very clear.

the notion of personhood into international law. The first can be perceived as successful as it led to the formal incorporation of a clause in the text of the United Nations Convention on the Rights of the Child. The second and third illustrations, while not as successful on the face of it, nevertheless serve to show the types of issues that are likely to arise in a context-specific engagement with international law that emphasises particular local realities.

3.1 Recognition of Islamic *Kafala* in International Law

The first example draws on the concept of the shared commitment to care for a vulnerable child in Islam, a practice known as *kafala*, which made its way into international law via the United Nations Convention on the Rights of the Child (hereafter CRC).[55] The inclusion of *kafala* in that convention is 'the first time an exclusively Islamic concept is recognized in a binding international instrument'.[56] Unlike adoption, which is a type of 'transfer', taking children permanently out of the original family and entrusting them to adoptive parents who assume exclusive parental authority, *kafala* offers a solution that allows a child to be cared for by various adults without severing the connection between the child and their original family. *Kafala* is seen as a system that allows for continuity in a child's well-being by entrusting the child to relatives who are more capable than the biological parents in providing for their needs. It is similar to fostering, but draws its inspiration from Islam,[57] which gives it a particular legitimacy in the eyes of the parties involved. *Kafala* is thus a practice whereby the responsibility for a child's education and upbringing can be shared between closely related adults who moreover share

[55] More specifically, Article 20 of the UN Convention on the Rights of the Child (UNCRC), 2 September 1990, A/Res/44/25 states:

1. A child temporarily or permanently deprived of his or her family environment, or in whose own best interests cannot be allowed to remain in that environment, shall be entitled to special protection and assistance provided by the State.
2. States Parties shall in accordance with their national laws ensure alternative care for such a child.
3. Such care could include, inter alia, foster placement, *kafalah* of Islamic law, adoption or if necessary placement in suitable institutions for the care of children. When considering solutions, due regard shall be paid to the desirability of continuity in a child's upbringing and to the child's ethnic, religious, cultural and linguistic background. [Emphasis added].

[56] Usang Maria Assim and Julia Sloth-Nielsen, 'Islamic *Kafalah* as an Alternative Care Option for Children Deprived of a Family Environment' *African Human Rights Law Journal* 14 (2014), 322-45, at 322; David Johnson, 'Cultural and Regional Pluralism in the Drafting of the UN Convention on the Rights of the Child', in Michael Freeman and Philip E. Veerman (eds.), *The Ideologies of Children's Rights* (Dordrecht: Martinus Nijhoff 1992), 95-114, at 95.

[57] The care of orphans and vulnerable children is of utmost importance in Islam, and to provide them with a filial environment and a sense of harmony and continuity, the practice of *kafala* is usually negotiated within the extended family, often involving close relatives of the child's biological family. Nadjma Yassari, 'Adding by Choice: Adoption and Functional Equivalents in Islamic Law and Middle Eastern Law' *American Journal of Comparative Law* 63 (2015), 927-62.

the same religious beliefs. Children under *kafala* arrangements are called *makfuls*, and their guardians *kafils*.[58] The recognition of *kafala* in international law has been welcomed by many authors as a compromise that reflects 'the role of cultural and religious factors in the drafting of international instruments and the place of compromise in resolving differences among state parties'.[59]

The extent to which *kafala* is, in practice, internationally recognised and therefore granted its appropriate legal effect varies from one place to another. In Europe, for instance, public authorities are wary of allowing recourse to *kafala*, especially when it involves children born in a country where Islamic law applies and who later will join adults residing in a European Union member State. This stems from concerns that *kafala* might be misused as a legal pretext to facilitate the transfer of a child from one country to another, thereby circumventing restrictive regulations regarding family reunification.[60]

The Court of Justice of the European Union (CJEU), however, believes that if an assessment confirms a genuine family relationship, including dependency, between the *makful* and the *kafil*, EU member States are obliged, under the right to respect for family life and the best interests of the child,[61] to permit the entry and residence of the *makful* under Art. 3(2) of Directive 2004/38.[62]

Following the CJEU's reasoning, it may be inferred that where there is a genuine and interdependent relationship between a *makful* and a *kafil*, States (i.e. the host country), after having undertaken an extensive assessment of the specific personal circumstances involved, may be obliged to allow family reunification. Whether this is indeed the case in practice, however, would need further investigation.[63]

[58] Given that the ties between biological parents and the child are not severed, due to strong beliefs in Islam about the importance of maintaining filial relations, the child will not be entitled to the *kafil*'s family name or inheritance. In practice, however, it is possible for a child to be given an inheritance through testamentary succession; see Nadia Sonneveld, 'Afstamming in tijden van medisch begeleide voortplanting en adoptie', in Pauline Kruininger (ed.), *Op gespannen voet. Islamitische verwantschappen, huwelijken en echtscheidingen in Nederland* (Den Haag: Boom Juridische Uitgevers 2015), 39-52.

[59] The drafting of the CRC was set against the background of a compromise, as is frequently the case when negotiating the terms of international conventions. As Assim and Sloth-Nielsen put it, 'Islamic *kafalah* represents one of such compromises in an attempt to accommodate the differences of the various State parties to CRC': Assim and Sloth-Nielsen, 'Islamic *Kafalah*' 2014 (n. 57), 325.

[60] See, *inter alia*, Alessandra Lang, '*Kafala* and Family Reunification of Third-Country Nationals', in Elisabetta Bergamini and Chiara Ragni (eds.), *Fundamental Rights and Best Interests of the Child in Transnational Families* (Cambridge: Intersentia 2019), 97-114.

[61] Charter of Fundamental Rights of the European Union, 7 December 2000, 2012/C 326/02, Art. 24.2.

[62] Case C-129/18 *SM v. Entry Clearance Officer*, Judgment of the Court (Grand Chamber) of 26 March 2019, para. 71.

[63] Jinske Verhellen, 'Erkenning van een kafala uit Marokko zonder adoptie in België' *Tijdschrift voor Familierecht* (2021), 257-61; see also Ray Jureidini and Said Fares Hassan, 'The Islamic Principle of Kafala as Applied to Migrant Workers: Traditional Continuity and Reform', in Ray Jureidini and Said Fares Hassan (eds.), *Migration and Islamic Ethics* (Leiden: Brill 2019), 92-109.

While it may be difficult to completely eliminate the risk of using *kafala* as a way to bypass restrictive immigration laws in Europe, the risks it entails are not nearly as severe as another form of abuse of *kafala*. This is when a *kafala* arrangement's primary purpose is not the protection and welfare of a child, but is instead a means to serve the interests of employers and companies who, through commercial and business transactions, exploit extremely vulnerable migrant employees. This practice is well illustrated by a revealing study conducted by Mohammed Dito that focuses on the situation in the Gulf States.[64] Occasional field studies by anthropologists reveal examples of extreme exploitation of migrants whose work permits are obtained through recourse to *kafala*, creating a highly imbalanced power dynamic between employer and employee.[65]

Things are not always as clear-cut as one would like them to be. On the one hand, the CRC's openness to an alternative form of conceiving of and providing for the care and protection of a human being, in this case a child, is to be welcomed; on the other hand, abuse is always a risk, and studies such as that of Mohammed Dito's reveal some serious legal and institutional flaws within *kafala*. The potential for abuse should not, however, be used to justify foreclosing an approach in international law that advocates 'the formation of cross-cultural understandings of individualism'.[66] Nevertheless, it goes without saying that this cannot be used as a free pass for trafficking of children or vulnerable persons, exploiting cheap labour, or any other form of abuse.

3.2 International Law with an Emphasis on Local Realities

The second and third illustrations demonstrate that international law can benefit greatly from adopting a nuanced understanding of the characteristics of the social context to which they are presumed to apply and what type of questions arise when greater importance is given to local realities. Doing so, particularly on issues of human rights protection, has the potential to enhance its relevance and legitimacy worldwide and be truly transformative.

[64] Mohammed Dito, 'Kafala: Foundations of Migrant Exclusion in GCC Labour Markets', in Abdulhadi Khalaf, Omar AlShehabi, and Adam Hanieh (eds.), *Transit States: Labour, Migration and Citizenship in the Gulf* (London: Pluto Press 2015); Anh Nga Longva, *Walls Built on Sand: Migration, Exclusion and Society in Kuwait* (Boulder, CO: Westview Press 1997).

[65] Longva, *Walls Built on Sand: Migration, Exclusion and Society in Kuwait* 1997 (n. 65). When Iraq invaded Kuwait in 1990, the sight of tens of thousands of non-Kuwaiti Arabs, Indians, East Asians, and westerners fleeing or trapped in occupied territory made the outside world aware that Kuwaitis were an absolute minority in their own country. Basing her analysis on extensive fieldwork and archival research Longva examines the system of *kafala*, under which foreign workers enter and reside in the country, illustrating how the practice has become the most critical source of power for native Kuwaitis with regards to immigrants.

[66] See Peters and Sparks, 'Introduction' (chapter 1), in this volume.

3.2.1 The Bangkok Declaration: Reversing the Order of Civil and Political Rights and Social and Economic Rights?

The Bangkok Declaration was adopted at the World Conference Regional Preparatory Meeting in 1993. In the lead-up to the Second World Human Rights Conference held in Vienna in June 1993, the Bangkok Declaration was intended as a statement of the Asian region's stance on human rights, in which a group of primarily East and Southeast Asian States recognised 'that while human rights are universal in nature, they must be considered in the context of a dynamic and evolving process of international norm-setting, bearing in mind the significance of national and regional particularities and various historical, cultural and religious backgrounds'.[67]

However, the attempt failed, and at the World Conference in Vienna, a strikingly unequivocal statement was instead adopted to the effect that 'the universal nature of [all human rights and fundamental freedoms] is beyond question'.[68] One main reason for this was the strong emphasis that the Bangkok Declaration's signatory States placed on respect for the right to development and the autonomy of individual States' to decide how they will ensure that these rights are respected without external interference or imposition. While not explicitly stated, the Bangkok Declaration as a whole can be interpreted as giving social and economic rights priority, which is a reversal of the traditional emphasis given to civil and political rights. Joanne Bauer goes so far as to say that the Bangkok Declaration contains an opposition to universal human rights 'made on the ground that human rights as such do not accord with "Asian values" '.[69] Whether this is an overstatement or not, the Bangkok Declaration was indeed rejected at the conference. Several authors saw this rejection as a panic reaction by western countries. On the part of the signatory States of the Bangkok Declaration, their insistence on the use of such strong language was no doubt 'shaped almost entirely by the rise in economic power in Asia'.[70]

Yet, the Bangkok Declaration's signatory States' initiative was not completely ignored. In fact, Michael Dowdle, who calls himself a liberal jurist, said: '[W]e can see why the claims of the Bangkok Declaration deserve much more serious intellectual attention than they have heretofore enjoyed.'[71] To put it in the wording of the initiative in the final version of the Vienna Declaration: 'While the significance of national and regional particularities and various historical, cultural and

[67] UNGA, Vienna Declaration and Programme of Action, 12 July 1993, A/CONF.157/23, para. 5 (Part I).

[68] *ibid*, para. 1 (Part I).

[69] Joanne Bauer, 'The Bangkok Declaration Three Years After: Reflection on the State of the Asia–West Dialogue on Human Rights' *Human Rights Dialogue* 1 (1996), 1.

[70] *ibid*.

[71] Michael W. Dowdle, 'How a Liberal Jurist Defends the Bangkok Declaration', in Lynda S. Bell, Andrew J. Nathan, and Ilan Peleg (eds.), *Negotiating Culture and Human Rights* (New York, NY: Columbia University Press 2001), 125-52, at 135.

religious backgrounds must be borne in mind, it is the duty of States, regardless of their political, economic and cultural systems, to protect all human rights and fundamental freedoms.'[72]

Three decades have passed since then, and the Bangkok Declaration remains a milestone document. The demand for recognition from countries that are taking a renewed interest in their own traditions and intellectual heritage, not rejecting human rights as such, but requesting a more balanced approach to it, remains just as relevant today.

3.2.2 The Maputo Protocol on the Rights of Women in Africa: Accommodating Domestic Realities

Another initiative that perhaps even better illustrates the need to accommodate social and cultural diversity in the way human rights protection is conceived and put into practice is the Protocol on the Rights of Women in Africa, also called the Maputo Protocol.[73] On 11 July 2003 in Maputo, Mozambique, the Assembly of the African Union adopted a protocol to the African Charter on Human and People's Rights that specifically addresses gender equality and is intended to supplement the general protections guaranteed under the Charter. It reads as an invitation, in particular to African States, to 'engage in a more constructive and productive dialogue that reflects an in-depth understanding of each country's context and milestones on the way forward towards transformed gender relations'.[74] Of the fifty-five States that are members of the African Union, forty-nine of them have signed the Maputo protocol, and forty have ratified it.[75] With unmistakable enthusiasm Jing Geng states that:

> With respect to the intersection between global standards and local values, one strength of the Protocol is its ability to reconcile culture and broader aspirations of gender equality. [. . .] In contrast to the idea that human rights are culturally intrusive and foreign to Africa, the Maputo Protocol is an instrument that was created by African women for African women. Therefore, it is a product of African origin with African ownership.[76]

[72] UNGA, Vienna Declaration 1993 (n. 68), para. 5 (Part I).

[73] Protocol to the African Charter on Human and People's Rights on the Rights of Women in Africa, 11 July 2003; see, *inter alia*, Celestine Nyamu Musembi, 'Pulling Apart?: Treatment of Pluralism in CEDAW and the Maputo Protocol', in Anne Hellum and Henriette Sinding Aasen (eds.), *Women's Human Rights: CEDAW in International, Regional and National Law* (Cambridge: CUP 2013), 183-213.

[74] Protocol to the African Charter on Human and People's Rights (n. 73), 632.

[75] See, *inter alia*, Jing Geng, 'The Maputo Protocol and the Reconciliation of Gender and Culture in Africa', in Susan Harris and Kate Ogg (eds.), *Research Handbook on Feminist Engagement with International Law* (Cheltenham: Edward Elgar 2019), 411-29.

[76] *ibid*, 412-13.

She takes a closer look at three contentious practices: female genital mutilation (FGM), polygamy, and the right to live in a positive cultural context. She does this with a view to demonstrating 'the extent to which the Protocol has located women's rights in the African context and moved beyond the obstacles in the gender and culture debate'.[77] The Protocol takes a firm stance of complete intolerance to all forms of FGM, including scarification, medicalisation and/or para-medicalisation. It also obliges States to put in place policies which, in the long term, would make any recourse to these practices impossible. In the case of polygamy, the Protocol is more nuanced, urging interested parties to remain realistic. Many customary practices related to marriage are still common (and are supported by customary law) including, where Islamic personal laws apply, polygamous marriages, whereby a man is simultaneously married to several wives. In their own way, particularly in rural communities, polygamous marriages provide a protective framework to which there is no alternative, and to abolish this framework would render existing family structures even more fragile. This observation is found in many anthropological studies that seek to understand as closely as possible the internal dynamics of kinship logics in Africa, both in the past and today.[78] The Protocol negotiators agreed on a compromise position which consists of referring to monogamous marriage as the preferred form of marital relationship, but without going so far as to impose it as the exclusive form of commitment among spouses.

The same realistic approach can be seen in the Protocol with regards to customs and ancestral traditions. Article 17 states that: 'Women shall have the right to live in a positive cultural context [...].' Those familiar with the law as it applies in Africa are aware of the huge diversity of systems concerned, involving complicated interactions of customs and traditions that vary based on regions, communities, and histories. This diversity is not only still very topical, but it is also highly dynamic, as groups and communities continue to adapt the rules that apply to them according to the circumstances and needs that arise. The Protocol takes this reality into account, and also introduces an innovative element, although it is not significant. This element reflects the will of the negotiators to strike a balance between, on the one hand, the acceptance of the African diverse social and cultural context as it is, which encompasses a wide range of norms, and, on the other hand, the promotion of broader human rights norms in pursuit of greater equality. In Article 17 it is specified that henceforth women will also have the right 'to participate at all levels in the determination of cultural policies'. This will obviously not happen overnight. What is interesting about Article 17 is that, in terms of the respect due to customs and traditions, it combines two approaches; one realistic in its recognition of present-day realities, and the other forward-looking in a spirit of gradual evolution.

[77] *ibid*, 422.

[78] See notes 7 and 22-25.

In the conclusion of her article on the Maputo Protocol, Geng observes that: 'From a theoretical perspective, the immediate effect is that the Maputo Protocol complicates the simple narrative of a passive, racialised woman oppressed by her culture or the idea of an inevitable clash between culture and women's rights.'[79]

Three illustrations do not, of course, exhaust the subject, but serve to show both the complexity and the importance of the position of Peters and Sparks when they state that international law must be open to supporting non-western traditions that might be 'individualistic' in different ways or to different degrees.[80] It is this openness, combined with a self-reflective and analytical position and with due regard to local contexts, that will ensure that international law has the desired impact on the lives of individuals. This openness also allows the vast knowledge acquired by anthropologists, in the field and through detailed studies of the most diverse human societies, to assert itself as valuable and valued disciplinary expertise that can help international law in its efforts to reconcile cultural diversity and human rights standards, in a more sustainable way.[81]

One author who has worked extensively on the intersection between global standards and local values, and is therefore frequently cited in the anthropological literature, is Amartya Sen.[82] His work demonstrates an approach used in anthropology to study how we can transcend the 'clash of cultures' and achieve the broader aspirations of human rights protection. Sen is one of the global authoritative voices strongly committed to addressing how justice can be realised for each and every person, not merely in an abstract sense of respect for human rights, but by considering the social, political, and economic realities on the ground around the world. Of course, many realities are not comparable to situations in western liberal democracies, and the approaches used to apply the principles of justice should not be compared.[83] For example, which standards should serve as the reference point in circumstances where conditions of tolerance are not met? Sen does not

[79] Geng, 'The Maputo Protocol' (n. 75), 427.

[80] See Peters and Sparks, 'Introduction' (chapter 1), in this volume.

[81] The challenge of how to adequately transpose ethnographic knowledge into legal reasoning is a topic of discussion within the field of anthropology today: can anthropologists be present at the moment when a decision maker (a court, a legislature, or any other corporate or non-governmental organisation) could benefit from ethnographic expertise, and how would it impact the decisions to be taken? See, among others, Pamela J. Stewart and Andrew Strathern (eds.), *Anthropology and Consultancy: Issues and Debates* (New York, NY: Berghahn 2005); Barry Morris and Rohan Bastin (eds.), *Expert Knowledge: First World Peoples, Consultancy, and Anthropology* (New York, NY: Berghahn 2004); Robert J. Currie, 'The Bounds of the Permissible: Using "Cultural Evidence" in Civil Jury Cases' *Canadian Journal of Law and Society* 20 (2005), 75-86; Elliott Oring, 'Folklore and Advocacy' *Journal of Folklore Research* 41 (2004), 259-67; Victoria Sanford and Asale Angel-Ajani (eds.), *Engaged Observer: Anthropology, Advocacy and Activism* (New Brunswick: Rutgers University Press 2006).

[82] On Amartya Sen, see also van Aaken, '(International) Law and Economics' (chapter 16), in this volume.

[83] See Brian Z. Tamanaha, 'A Reconstruction of Transnational Legal Pluralism and Law's Foundations', in Nico Krisch (ed.), *Entangled Legalities Beyond the State* (Cambridge: CUP 2022), 449-77.

approach this question with reference to an abstract ideal, but rather by beginning from considering the specific situation a person is in and examining their freedom of action (or, as Sen puts it, 'the liberty to achieve') within their concrete circumstances. 'I would argue that any theory of justice (1) identifies a space in which inter-personal comparisons are made for judging individual advantages, and (2) specifies a "combining" procedure that translates the demands for justice to operations on the chosen space.'[84] It is not surprising that Sen's work is widely cited by anthropologists, as they recognise the value of his approach for their own research.

4. Conclusion

To what extent can international law help in finding the right balance between an approach that demonises certain practices and 'rushes to dark judgments about [...] others', as Richard Shweder expresses it provocatively,[85] and a policy that would allow groups and communities to continue to live according to their traditions and practices even where these may be incompatible with the values of contemporary international law? As things stand, the answer must be a nuanced one.

As I have attempted to demonstrate using specific examples, anthropologists take as their starting point their observations in the field, and emphasise the importance of greater openness and sensitivity to diverse cultural contexts within the framework of international law, with its (universal) standards for the protection of the individual person as a legal subject. From their observations *in situ*, they also know that for a dialogue about effective international human rights protection to take place and produce sustainable effects, that dialogue must reflect an in-depth understanding of the context under study and of the lives of those the protection is intended to benefit. Whether anthropology focuses on kinship logics, the principle of individual autonomy of the person, or alternative concepts of personhood, such as 'dividuum' or 'dividuality', it invites us to embrace a more nuanced understanding of particular societal contexts and to mediate between local and international standards of personhood in international law.

Is there space in international law for alternative conceptions of the person? As they emphasised in their introduction, Peters and Sparks not only position themselves as advocates of a humanisation of international law that accommodates diversity, but they see this openness as a condition for enabling a debate to take place: 'If the humanisation debate integrates such traditions, the debate itself might contribute to the formation of cross-cultural understandings of individualisms.'[86]

[84] Amartya Sen, 'Gender Inequality and Theories of Justice', in Martha C. Nussbaum and Jonathan Glover, *Women, Culture, and Development: A Study of Human Capabilities* (Oxford: Clarendon Press 1995).

[85] Richard A. Shweder, 'The Goose and the Gander: The Genital Wars' *Global Discourse* 3 (2013), 348-66, at 364.

[86] See Peters and Sparks, 'Introduction' (chapter 1), in this volume.

In their view, as I see it, international law has much to gain from adopting a nuanced understanding of the particularities of local realities.

Anthropological studies, in their own way, support this advocacy: they provide evidence of the crucial role that concrete societal contexts continue to play in the organisation of social relationships worldwide. A better understanding of that reality is likely to enable a less critical and more assured approach in international law, and especially in the realm of human rights law. This approach seeks to ensure the recognition and necessary protection of certain forms of social organisation enabling them to fully function in harmony with international law, rather than in violation of it.

Anthropologists, who are familiar with the complexities of the empirical realities of societies around the world, suggest that a human-centred view of international law should embrace a combination of two approaches: one that is realistic in its recognition of present-day realities, and another that is forward-looking in a spirit of gradual adaptation processes.

The debate regarding the relationship between international or 'universal' human rights standards on the one hand, and different cultural perspectives and contexts on the other, needs to be continued. It is too important to be dismissed or hastily concluded. This is the way I see the 'raison d'être' of the space that Peters and Sparks have generously given, in this collective volume, to an application of interdisciplinary methodologies to the study of international law. And there is every reason to continue this effort.

18
Conclusions
Reconsidering the Individual in International Law

Anne Peters and Tom Sparks

1. Historical and Theoretical Findings

This volume, taken as a whole, seeks to add historical depth and theoretical sophistication to the debate on the role of the individual in international law. The contributions have, firstly, undermined the contention that the international legal system has always been an order created by, between, and for the benefit of sovereign State entities. Secondly, they provided nuanced answers to many of the critiques of the humanisation thesis.[1] The chapters also call attention to a number of questions which remain unanswered.

In demonstrating that individuals held a place in international law prior to the humanised 'moment' of the 1990s and early 2000s,[2] or even prior to the longer post-1945 human rights era,[3] the book also refines initial claims made by humanisation scholars themselves who have characterised the humanisation of international law as a 'paradigm shift',[4] a shift of the normative foundations of the legal order,[5] 'a true juridical revolution',[6] or 'a fundamental mutation'.[7] Thereby, scholars had highlighted the novelty of the international legal status of the individual. In so doing, protagonists of the humanisation claim had taken upon themselves the

[1] For these critiques, see Peters and Sparks, 'Introduction' (chapter 1), in this volume, section 4, pp. 18–26.

[2] Ukri Soirila, *The Law of Humanity Project: A Story of International Law Reform and State-Making* (Oxford: Hart 2021), 2-3.

[3] It has been announced that this era has now entered its 'twilight' or has ended: Eric Posner, *The Twilight of Human Rights Law* (Oxford: OUP 2014); Costas Douzinas, *The End of Human Rights: Critical Legal Thought at the Turn of the Century* (Oxford: Hart 2000); Stephen Hopgood, *The Endtimes of Human Rights* (Ithaca, NY: Cornell University Press 2013).

[4] Anne Peters, *Beyond Human Rights: The Legal Status of the Individual in International Law* (Jonathan Huston (tr.), Cambridge: CUP 2016), 408.

[5] Ruti Teitel, *Humanity's Law* (Oxford: OUP 2011), 4. See also Tom Sparks, who referred to a 'shift in the foundations of the system' in 'Towards a Human-Centred International Law: Self-Determination and the Structure of the International Legal System' (unpublished thesis, Durham University 2017), available at: http://etheses.dur.ac.uk/12408/, accessed 28/11/23.

[6] Antônio Augusto Cançado Trindade, 'International Law for Humankind: Towards a New Jus Gentium (I)' *Recueil des Cours* 316 (2005), 9–439, at 274.

[7] Alain Pellet, 'Le droit international à la lumière de la pratique: L'introuvable théorie de la réalité' *Recueil des Cours* 414 (2021), 25-547, at 380 (our translation).

Anne Peters and Tom Sparks, *Conclusions* In: *The Individual in International Law.* Edited by: Tom Sparks and Anne Peters, Oxford University Press. DOI: 10.1093/oso/9780198898917.003.0018

burden of historical proof: in seeking to establish a 'change' to the established structure of the international legal system, they were required to explain and justify how the new, individual-focused legal order is capable of displacing the system of States by which and for which the system was (or so it is said) created. The preceding chapters tell a somewhat different—and more nuanced—story.

1.1 The Individual in International Law's History

The first part of the book deals with the history of international law. The chapters investigate the changing legal relationship between the individual and the State, at different stages of the development of international law.

Eleanor Cowan (chapter 2) begins by considering the concept of international law in antiquity. Although she notes a continuing controversy concerning the applicability of that term to antiquity, there is, she argues, 'a growing willingness to view ancient international relations as relevantly concerned with international law'.[8] In parallel, there is a 'difficulty inherent in conceptualising the ancient individual',[9] because '[a]ncient Greco-Roman communities are commonly represented as associations of families rather than associations of individual citizens'.[10] Contrary to this common view, Cowan concludes that the 'Roman *ius gentium* was fundamentally and from the outset concerned with adjudicating disputes between individuals'.[11] Nevertheless, antiquity's interest in the individual is not modernity's: the 'individual is not the primary concern of [the *ius gentium*'s] thinking, but the operation of recognisable international law instruments and ideas in a world in which the State itself defied simple definition suggests that the ancient world is a good case-study of the extent to which legal relationships were social relationships.'[12]

This theme carries forward into Dante Fedele and Alain Wijffels' discussion of law in the Middle Ages (chapter 3). As in antiquity, it is clear that neither the concept of the State nor that of the individual is directly comparable to the contemporary use of those terms. '[T]here was no clear link between sovereignty and territory', Fedele and Wijffels comment, 'instead we find a complex interweaving and overlapping of jurisdictions'.[13] As a consequence: '"international law" cannot be understood as it has been by mainstream historiography since the nineteenth century […]; rather, it should be considered a multi-normative framework that governed inter-polity and cross-jurisdictional relations between a great variety

[8] Cowan, 'Antiquity' (chapter 2), in this volume, p. 32 (references omitted).
[9] *ibid*, p. 35.
[10] *Ibid*, p. 35 (references omitted).
[11] *ibid*, p. 36.
[12] *ibid*, p. 45.
[13] Fedele and Wijffels, 'Medieval International Law' (chapter 3), in this volume, p. 49.

of actors'.[14] Fedele and Wijffels discuss two exemplary case studies: prisoners of war and individual reprisals, each 'of particular relevance for tracing the notion of "individuality" in medieval (international) law'.[15] They conclude that although medieval law would not have recognised a distinct category of international law, 'it dealt with a wide variety of issues of governance and relations', several of which 'would qualify today as issues of international law'.[16] Nevertheless, and albeit with certain notable exceptions, collective and group identity was dominant over individuality. Moreover, the extent to which an individual could *qua* individual come to the attention of the law on international matters was correlated strongly with social class—notably, as they conclude, it is only 'at the upper levels of the social and political hierarchy' that 'individualisation [is] visible'.[17]

Francesca Iurlaro (chapter 4) discusses the period from 1500 to 1647. She identifies two ways—Iurlaro terms them two 'tendencies'—in which individuals acquired importance for international legal reasoning. First, exemplarity was widely used in teaching, understanding, and communicating law. Here, analogies to exemplary individuals were drawn to indicate the proper behaviour also of non-individuals, including States: 'In early modern *ius gentium*, *exempla* were not merely imbued with vaguely moralising undertones; they were also used so extensively as representations for moral arguments that they attained a canonical status.'[18] The second tendency was porosity: 'exempla offer a semantic strategy of negotiation between individuals and the collectivity', Iurlaro argues.[19] Iurlaro notes that the 'power of examples rests on a specific political argument, namely, that individuals and collectivities can define each other by imitating, projecting, or analogising patterns of behaviour'. Together, these tendencies are, she cautions, reflections of 'the reality of individuals engaging in international actions rather than evidence that individuals' legal status was fully recognised' in the modern sense.[20]

Mark Somos takes up the investigation in 1648 (chapter 5). The 1648 Peace of Westphalia is defined by conventional histories of international law as the break point between pre-modernity and the modern law of nations. In this 'Grotian moment',[21] it is said, the modern doctrine of State sovereignty sprung into being, reshaping the inchoate practices of the *ius gentium* into a *ius inter gentes*—a 'law of nations' which recognised the world as divided into sovereign, opaque units. As such, according to this traditional account, individuals became solely the concern

14 *ibid*, p. 49.
15 *ibid*, p. 51.
16 *ibid*, p. 63.
17 *ibid*, p. 64.
18 Iurlaro, '1500-1648' (chapter 4), in this volume, p. 71.
19 *ibid*, p. 67.
20 *ibid*, p. 66.
21 See Tom Sparks and Mark Somos, 'Grotian Moments: An Introduction' *Grotiana* 42 (2021), 179–91; and further Matthew Cleary et al., 'Grotian Moments and Appeals to Authority in Law and History' *Grotiana* 44 (2023), 65-93.

of intra-State law. Somos tells a more complex story, charting how 'individuals gained international legal standing at the State's expense in the applicable theories of Hobbes, Cumberland and Thomasius; how the sovereign reclaimed powers and rights from the individual in the system of Heineccius; and how the legal standing of the individual and the State rose in tandem in Pufendorf and Vattel as the scope of law expanded and incorporated new formal inventions.'[22] This was not the unmitigated triumph of sovereignty, but rather an era of rich and highly theorised debate over the proper relationships between individuals, States, and other actors.

Inge Van Hulle (chapter 6) discusses international law in the nineteenth century. The period is, at first sight, a strange place to seek the individual: as Van Hulle notes, '[t]he nineteenth century is the age in which State-centrism reigned supreme in international legal theory'.[23] Nevertheless, Van Hulle notes that a 'broad and contextual perspective on individuals' different roles in nineteenth-century international law destabilises the conceptual distinction between the international and the domestic and the global and the local as the actions of individuals blurred the boundaries between nation-States'.[24] She discusses the numerous roles that individuals played which destabilise the States-only conception of international law—'[t]he nationalist, the freedom fighter, the abolitionist, the humanitarian, the investor, the merchant, etc.'.[25] She also highlights that deep-rooted doctrines of today's international law began life as 'attempts to curtail or promote the calls of individuals', including 'diplomatic protection, extraterritoriality […] and international humanitarian law'.[26] Van Hulle concludes that a re-examination of the time-period shows 'that the nineteenth century was as much a century of State centrism as it was one in which individuals took a leading role in crafting international law.'[27]

In the final chapter of the historical part (chapter 7), Anne Peters brings the investigation to what is often understood to be the birth of modern-day international law: the signing of the UN Charter in 1945. She begins by recalling the cataclysm of the World War I,[28] and argues that out of international law's 'crisis',[29] grew an 'extraordinarily active period of legal innovation',[30] in the course of which the 'States only' international law of the nineteenth century 'evolved to accommodate those human groups and their members which could for various reasons not be protected by

[22] Somos, '1648-1789' (chapter 5), in this volume, p. 100.
[23] Van Hulle, 'Nineteenth Century' (chapter 6), in this volume, p. 101.
[24] *ibid*, p. 101.
[25] *ibid*, p. 117.
[26] *ibid*, p. 117.
[27] *ibid*, p. 117.
[28] Peters, 'Before Human Rights' (chapter 7), in this volume.
[29] *ibid*, p. 119; citing Jan de Louter, 'La crise de droit international' *Revue Générale de Droit International Public* 26 (1919), 76-110.
[30] Peters, 'Before Human Rights' (chapter 7), in this volume, p. 119; citing Martti Koskenniemi, 'History of International Law, World War I to World War II', in Anne Peters and Rüdiger Wolfrum (eds.), *The Max Planck Encyclopedia of Public International Law* (Oxford: OUP 2011), para. 4.

one State alone'.[31] She concludes that the interbellum did not 'unequivocally rais[e] the individual's international status and detach […] it from States'.[32] Individuals gained some international recognition in various guises (as refugees, stateless persons, minorities, mandate populations, merchants, and others). New international procedures allowed them to enforce their international claims against foreign States or even their home State.[33] The rationale of these new legal regimes was not to protect human dignity or vulnerability but to serve macro-political objectives, notably to prevent inter-State conflict. But the 'irony is that the subordinate and ancillary objective of the new regimes and procedures, their humanitarian thrust, in the long run did carry the day'.[34] Following the 'shock of the horrors of National Socialism and World War II', and coupled with a methodological shift 'away from legal positivism to a more sociological approach to international law', the post-1945 era saw 'the development of a practical scheme of international human rights protection'.[35]

1.2 The Individual in the Theory of International Law

The theoretical part of the book builds on the history: given that international law cannot be understood as having always and irredeemably been a States-only order, how could and should we understand the relationship between States and individuals? In ten chapters applying different theoretical approaches to international law, the authors each explore how their paradigm understands the relationship between States and individuals in the contemporary international legal order, and whether a legal system built in accordance with the precepts of each framework could be 'human-centred'.

The second part begins with chapters that re-examine the traditional positivism/naturalism debate, in the context of international law and the humanisation debate. Gleider Hernández (chapter 8) considers international legal positivism in the context of humanisation; while Rafael Domingo and Tom Sparks, respectively, reappraise the sacred and secular traditions of natural law (chapters 9 and 10).

In chapter 8, Hernández assesses whether a positivist framework is compatible with an individual-centred international legal system, and so (indirectly) tests the contention that only a natural law framework can provide a basis for humanisation.[36] Hernández distinguishes between two concepts which, he argues, have become unduly conflated in definitions of modern international legal

[31] Peters, 'Before Human Rights' (chapter 7), p. 119.
[32] *ibid*, p. 162.
[33] *ibid*, pp. 137–146.
[34] *ibid*, p. 161.
[35] *ibid*, p. 161.
[36] Hernández, 'Legal Positivism' (chapter 8), in this volume.

positivism: methodological legal positivism and voluntarism.[37] The former is, in Hernández's view, a technique or methodology for law-identification which, drawing on Herbert Hart and Hans Kelsen, he defines as requiring that norms of the legal system be established in accordance with the methods dictated by—respectively—the 'rules of recognition' or more basic norms. The latter is an ideological commitment to a *particular* rule of recognition (to use Hart's vocabulary), that is State consent.[38] Drawing on Joseph Raz and Alexander Somek, Hernández argues that legal systems are not immutable and that their foundations may migrate over time. He concludes that an international legal system which replaced or combined State consent with other values—including respect for the human individual—as aspects of the rule of recognition could remain fully consistent with methodological positivism.[39]

Rafael Domingo begins chapter 9 by defining sacred natural law as 'rooted in theological and scriptural accounts of created reality'. These accounts 'combine reason and revelation in their elaboration and justification of legal arguments'.[40] Focusing on Christian natural law thinking, Domingo proceeds to elucidate the value of a sacred natural law framework for a human-centred legal order. He highlights the 'image-of-God doctrine—the idea [in Judeo-Christian theology] that God created humanity in the divine image'—which underpins 'ideas of human dignity and equality'.[41] In turn, the inherent dignity of humans as bearers of the image of God gives rise to universal moral principles ('among other things, respect for the integrity of creation and its resources, as well as reparation of injustice');[42] respect for diversity ('[m]ade in the triune image of God, each member of humanity is different and should be protected in that difference');[43] and principles of solidarity[44] and subsidiarity.[45] In the final analysis, the centring, through the primacy of the image of God, of individual image-of-God-bearers highlights that the 'global human community is first and foremost a community of human persons, not a society or federation of sovereign states'.[46]

The final chapter in the *ius naturalism/ius positivism* section is Tom Sparks' exploration of the relationship between the humanisation thesis and secular frameworks of natural law (chapter 10). Sparks asks, first, whether the humanisation thesis needs to rely on natural law; and secondly, whether natural law necessarily implies a humanisation of law. He answers the first question positively; in

37 *ibid*, p. 167.
38 *ibid*, pp. 169–170.
39 *ibid*, pp. 186–187.
40 Domingo, 'Sacred Natural Law' (chapter 9), in this volume, p. 189 (references omitted).
41 *ibid*, p. 195.
42 *ibid*, p. 198.
43 *ibid*, p. 198.
44 *ibid*, p. 199.
45 *ibid*, p. 201.
46 *ibid*, p. 202 (references omitted).

his opinion, a stable basis for a humanisation of international law can be founded only in secular natural law.[47] The second question he answers negatively: *a priori*, secular natural law need not centre on values relating to humanity or the individual. Empirically, however, the vast majority of natural law theories do indeed find their basis in dignity, agency, well-being, or other similar individualist values.[48] Sparks then asks whether natural law theory is defeated by objections of contingency,[49] and concludes that 'there are powerful arguments for believing that (complex) legal systems must centre individuals, [. . .] even if we accept the sceptical position that no recourse can be made to a timeless, immutable moral system'.[50]

Bhupinder S. Chimni (chapter 11) offers a view of the humanisation of international law from a TWAIL perspective.[51] A TWAIL approach 'suggests that in order to evaluate the status of the individual in international law account must be taken of the operation of three logics at the international level, namely, the "logic of capital", the "logic of territory", and the "logic of culture"'.[52] However, mainstream humanisation scholarship has, Chimni argues, 'at best inadequately addressed' in particular the 'logic of capital' and its role in recreating imperial structures of domination through 'the universalising thrust of capitalism'.[53] Indeed, given that humanisation scholarship does not pay attention to (the consequences of) capitalism and (neo)colonialism, it could 'even be argued that the debate on the status of the individual is a move to sustain and legitimise an oppressive imperialist global order'.[54] Moreover, according to Chimni, even well-meaning humanisation scholarship tends to focus overly on formal legal markers of personhood, and is blind to 'the entrenched structures of exploitative capitalism, imperialism, patriarchy, racism, and casteism' that prevent individuals from actualising their personhood in reality.[55]

Ruth Houghton (chapter 12) applies feminist approaches. At one level, it is clear that humanisation and feminist frameworks are aligned: feminist scholars, Houghton comments, 'have long sought to disrupt' the 'State-centric frame of international law'.[56] They have thereby also contributed to lifting individuals from the status as an object of international law. In addition, they highlight a 'masculine bias' in which 'an assumed heterosexual male body underpin[s] international law's conception of the individual'.[57] While replacing male subjects with female subjects 'disrupts the liberal narrative of the individual as male[, . . .] "woman" also suggests

47 Sparks, 'Secular Natural Law' (chapter 10), in this volume, pp. 211–213.
48 *ibid*, p. 216.
49 *ibid*, p. 216.
50 *ibid*, p. 228.
51 Chimni, 'TWAIL' (chapter 11), in this volume.
52 *ibid*, p. 232.
53 *ibid*, p. 232.
54 *ibid*, p. 234.
55 *ibid*, p. 248.
56 Houghton, 'Feminist Approaches' (chapter 12), in this volume, p. 251 (references omitted).
57 *ibid*, p. 251 (references omitted).

a single homogenous category or group'.[58] The liberal narrative can thus itself objectify female subject(s) of law, when the default male subject is supplemented by female characters which are little more than caricatures—such as the 'mother', or the 'African woman'.[59] Instead, Houghton argues, the 'idealised' account of the individual needs to be 'fracture[d]', while the 'subject-object binary in positivist approaches to international law is drawn into question'.[60] She concludes that in place of the 'pervasive subject-object distinction', '[w]hat is needed is a focus on the ongoing processes of objectification'.[61] In other words, feminist international legal theory would argue that both methodologically and substantively there is a need to *individualise* international law, to move away from crude stereotypes of international law's persons, to a more diverse, richer, and more rounded account of the human in international law.

Completing the trio of critical approaches, Marina Veličković (chapter 13) offers a Marxist view on the individual in international law. Veličković is not convinced that international law has an emancipatory potential or can meaningfully contribute to bettering the living conditions of individuals. In the absence of international law's demise, however, she asks 'what, if anything, can individuals do *with* international law?'[62] As an answer, Veličković offers a case study of the struggle for water rights by the community of Kruščica in central Bosnia, in which a movement led by the women of the community achieved meaningful victories through political and legal forms of resistance.[63] That victory, Veličković says, 'is in no way pyrrhic'.[64] It is, however, limited: 'the material conditions in which the practice was embedded did not change: natural resources are still treated as commodities, and these commodities are owned and managed by the State with no input from the local community'.[65] She concludes that (international) law can serve emancipatory ends, but 'only [if it is] a small part of a broader political struggle; a tool to be used and then discarded when it outlives its usefulness'.[66] In that struggle, a Marxist assessment of the (instrumental) value of law 'departs from both the State-centric and human-centred accounts in that it refuses to see this relationship as static and fixed: on this reading, it is the dynamic nature of the relationship that opens the possibility for its tactical use'.[67]

Moving beyond critical approaches, Angelo Jr Golia (chapter 14) considers the place of the individual in a global law framework. In global law, 'the individual may

[58] *ibid*, p. 254.
[59] *ibid*, p. 254.
[60] *ibid*, p. 267.
[61] *ibid*, p. 267.
[62] Veličković, 'Marxist Account' (chapter 13), in this volume, p. 280.
[63] *ibid*, pp. 289–292.
[64] *ibid*, p. 292.
[65] *ibid*, p. 292.
[66] *ibid*, p. 293.
[67] *ibid*, p. 293.

have multiple or no legal personalities, depending on the specific system under consideration'. Therefore, the key question is not '[w]hat are the legal conditions for the recognition of legal personality?', but rather, '[w]hat kind of individual does global law presuppose?'[68] Golia highlights that a specific *kind* of individual is an 'essential precondition […] for the emergence and development of global law'.[69] Global law's individual 'is primarily based on the prototypical model of actorhood that emerged in western legal modernity'.[70] Global law *needs* the individual as a generator of legal meaning.[71] Moreover, individuals provide the transport medium by which (formally) non-connected legal systems are brought into communication, and it is in these interactions that global law grows. '[T]he socially constructed individual transmits legal meaning', Golia comments. Individuals thus 'facilitate the encounter between and potentially the mutual adaptation or integration of global political, economic, and scientific justice'. They thereby contribute to the sustainability of the 'anarchy within global law'.[72]

Başak Çalı's approach in chapter 15, is—like global law—a product of an increasingly interconnected (legal) world. Global constitutionalism, Çalı says, is an umbrella approach that 'proposes a wide range of constitutional principles to guide the interpretation of international law at domestic, regional, and international levels. These constitutional principles include human rights, democracy, the rule of law, constituent power, separation of powers, proportionality, and subsidiarity'.[73] All of these principles relate to the individual. This means that global constitutionalism 'approaches the point and purpose of international law in human-centred rather than in State-centred terms': it 'presume[s] *a priori* that the treatment of the individual at the international level mirrors the treatment of individuals in domestic constitutional law'.[74] Çalı notes that 'the focus is on the constitutionalisation of individuals' rights in both domestic and international law as a discernable tangible social reality, rather than merely a moral aspiration'.[75] It is thus beyond doubt that global constitutionalism is aligned with the idea of an individual-centred international law. As Çalı writes: 'Global constitutionalism advocates humanisation as a way of understanding the constitutionalist structure of international law, State sovereignty, and the interpretation of existing rules and principles in international law'.[76]

The same observation applies to the law and economics framework, discussed by Anne van Aaken in chapter 16. The contemporary law and economics approach,

[68] Golia, 'Global Law' (chapter 14), in this volume, p. 303.
[69] *ibid*, p. 304.
[70] *ibid*, p. 303 (references omitted).
[71] *ibid*, p. 304.
[72] *ibid*, p. 304 (emphasis omitted).
[73] Çalı, 'Global Constitutionalism' (chapter 15), in this volume, p. 321 (emphasis omitted).
[74] *ibid*, p. 321.
[75] *ibid*, p. 324.
[76] *ibid*, p. 338.

van Aaken says, is 'an individualistic approach both in terms of methodology and normative principles', and 'is therefore not State-centred.'[77] From a normative point of view, van Aaken highlights the development of new welfare economics by Amartya Sen, which centres individuals and 'the things a person could do or be'—the individuals' *capacities*.[78] While 'in practice, it may still be States that guarantee and realise [individual] rights', van Aaken notes that Sen's theory, normatively, 'is not dependent on States as intermediaries'.[79] Van Aaken highlights that in methodological terms, too, the law and economics approach to international law necessarily centres the individual, given that 'the individual [is] the relevant unit of analysis' in economic approaches, and has been so since its 'behavioural turn'.[80] Van Aaken concludes with a discussion of the sustainable development goals, an area of international life in which New Welfare Economics, behavioural approaches, and international law are brought into direct conversation. This 'convergence', she argues, 'will empirically enrich the policies needed to make the values of the international order, including humanisation, a reality.'[81]

In chapter 17, Marie-Claire Foblets discusses anthropological approaches to law. In contrast to the methodological individualism of law and economics, the anthropological approach might almost be characterised as methodologically anti-individualist. Foblets argues that in reality, individuals need to be understood in the contexts of their communities and societies—she highlights in particular kin relations—and not as decontextualised, a-social entities. Rather, '[p]ersonhood is shaped by many different interdependent relationships, each with its own combination of normative demands and possibilities. These relationships are based on a blend of diverse and at times contradictory normative expectations, of which international law is only one.'[82] Therefore, anthropological approaches are not straightforwardly aligned with an individual-centred international legal order. Foblets, however, sees promise in the future closer collaboration of humanisation scholars and anthropologists which, she argues, can 'provide evidence of the crucial role that concrete societal contexts continue to play in the organisation of social relationships worldwide'.[83] She concludes that 'a human-centred vision of international law should embrace a combination of two approaches: one that is realistic in its recognition of present-day realities, and another that is forward-looking in a spirit of gradual adaptation processes'.[84]

[77] van Aaken, '(International) Law and Economics' (chapter 16), in this volume, p. 341.
[78] *ibid*, p. 346.
[79] *ibid*, p. 346.
[80] *ibid*, p. 342.
[81] *ibid*, p. 360.
[82] Foblets, 'Anthropological Approaches' (chapter 17), in this volume, p. 377.
[83] *ibid*, p. 386.
[84] *ibid*, p. 386.

2. New Histories of the Individual in International Law

Taken together, the chapters of the first, historical part respond to critique that the humanisation thesis is blind to history. The critique runs that international law's 'humanisation' played out only in a 'specific moment in the history of international law',[85] and was preceded by a deep history of State centrism which, following the closing of the humanist window, reasserted itself. Humanisation applied only to conditions pertaining in the international legal system for a brief period from the preparation of the Universal Declaration of Human Rights in 1945, when the international human rights system was born, to around 2010, when the 'liberal trend' in international affairs went into retreat.[86] As such, according to the critics, humanisation's proponents need to show that a shift away from this deeply historically embedded statism is possible, against the burden of history.

Against this objection, the investigations in this book cast doubt on those critiques of humanisation which assess it as a momentary development, occurring within narrow temporal horizons. The historical chapters debunk the idea that international law has paid full regard to individuals only in the present day (i.e. since 1945, or even only since the 1990s). They show that at every point in the history of international law individuals, along with the communities which comprise them, have been central to the daily practice and development of that law. More than that: individuals have in all eras been active participants in international affairs, and in ways that go beyond the banal fact that States are represented by individuals. They are international law's rebels and its pirates; its slaves and slave traders; its hostages, war criminals, and investors. This reassessment of international law's history focusing on the role of the individual thus corrects a number of omissions or elisions in the standard account of international law's history.

Making visible the variety of roles which individuals have in international law, the analysis demonstrates that at no point, not even in the positivist fervour of the nineteenth century, was a 'States only' conception of international law sufficient to capture the complexities of the international legal system. Although for most of the history under consideration there was no understanding of international individual 'rights' which would be directly comparable to the contemporary understanding of that term, certainly for much of that time individuals were the direct beneficiaries of international protections, were subject to international regulation, or were taken into account in international legal reasoning. Thus, for example, international rights to and regulation of ransom in the medieval period,

[85] Soirila, *The Law of Humanity Project* 2021 (n. 2), at 2; Gerhard Hafner, 'The Emancipation of the Individual from the State under International Law' *Recueil des Cours* 358 (2013), 263-441, at 437-44.

[86] Ukri Soirila qualifies humanisation scholarship as a 'project' that began in the 1990s and dates the anti-humanisation 'backlash' to around 2010: see Soirila, *The Law of Humanity Project* 2021 (n. 2), at 1-2, 164, and 125. Turning points might be the unlawful 2003 Iraq war led by the USA and its allies, or the 2008 global financial crisis.

the exemplary individuals of the sixteenth century, the noblemen and revolutionaries of the seventeenth and eighteenth centuries, and the philanthropist of the nineteenth century all indicate concern for and interest in the fate of individuals. Mitigated heavily by understandings of the relevant times, they perhaps even bespeak a status for individuals similar to legal personhood.

All of this indicates that, on the one hand, international law was not a '*natural*' inter-State structure that was 'humanised'. On the other hand, it would be too simplistic to cast the States-only 'phase' of international law as itself a historical aberration from a 'naturally' individual-centred individual legal system which preceded and followed it. To do so would be anachronistic, projecting today's concepts of individuality, sovereignty, and subjectivity onto the past.[87] This form of historiography, which involves reading history backwards in order to present contemporary structures as naturally flowing from the developments of the past is often, as Sabine Marschall identifies, part of the process of 'forging [...] a compelling foundation myth, which traces the roots and defines the beginning of [a political] order'.[88] 'Every new political order forms a group identity through a process of selective remembering and invention of usable pasts', she comments.[89]

Creation myths may serve an important function in the formation of a political order (as a fact and as a concept) or, in our case, in shaping our understanding of the international political order. In most cases, though, creation myths tell us more about what present-day users of that history *want* the political order to be than they do about the historical forces which have shaped the order itself. Telling an alternative, individual-focused history of international law is a useful corrective, or re-contextualisation, of standard historical accounts. That said, we should not repeat the mistake of believing that, *because* individuals played roles of various kinds relevant to the international legal system at different stages of its development, *therefore* individuals are its subjects today.

The chapters to this volume, too, are (inevitably) selective. All history is incomplete. It would thus be important, as part of a forward research agenda for humanisation scholarship, to supplement this history with further accounts. Numerous possibilities exist; we highlight two in particular.

First, the historical chapters to this volume have told a longue durée history of international law. New projects to focus more deeply on specific, *shorter time-periods* are needed, to complement these historiographical insights. Doing so would enable historians both to supplement the large scope histories told here with an account of international law in day-to-day practice, and to investigate practice

[87] David Kennedy, 'The Disciplines of International Law and Policy' *Leiden Journal of International Law* 12 (1999), 9-134, at 90.

[88] Sabine Marschall, 'Forging National Identity: Institutionalizing Foundation Myths through Monuments' *South African Journal of Cultural History* 19 (2005), 18-35, at 20-22.

[89] ibid, 19-20.

relating to the individual in international law beyond Europe, and so to contribute to a global history.

Secondly, it would be valuable to use an *alternative periodisation*. In this volume, we consciously chose to adopt the conventional periodisation of international law, in order directly to reassess standard histories, albeit recognising that this periodisation is both limiting and Eurocentric. Departing from that periodisation would very likely invite new connections, cast discrepancies in new light, and offer a fresh set of insights on the legal position of the individual throughout the history of international law. Further historical research is needed to continue the task of 'temporalis[ing]' the status of the individual in international law. Humanisation does not fall out of time, but has a past, present, and future. Situating the legal idea in time allows the diagnosis of its operation to be sharpened.[90]

3. New Theoretical Perspectives on the Individual in International Law

The second part's theoretical chapters offer a rich treatment both of humanisation as a legal-theoretical idea and of the relative legal positions of States and individuals within the international system more broadly. Taken together, the findings allow us to respond to the critiques of the humanisation thesis that we identified in the introductory chapter.[91]

The doctrinal and 'realist' objection is that the claims of a humanisation of international law are superficial and fail to account for the *underlying structure* of a system which remains, ultimately, *State consent-based*.[92] As we discussed above, objections of this kind tend to rely on a history of international law that is now discredited. To cast humanisation as historically anomalous is therefore flawed.[93] Looking beyond history, the objection can be answered in three ways. First, it may be recalled that while all the theoretical paradigms discussed in this book would accept a role for State consent in making international law, none insist that consent *exclusively* is the means by which international law is made. Most strikingly, Gleider Hernández distinguishes between positivism and voluntarism, arguing that a methodological commitment to positivism need not imply that State consent is the only route to international law-making, nor that consent by itself is sufficient to make law.[94] Secondly, even if we accept a role for State consent in law-making,

[90] *cf. mutatis mutandis* for human rights: David M. Scott, 'Human Rights', in Jean d'Aspremont and John Haskell (eds.), *Tipping Points in International Law: Commitment and Critique* (Cambridge: CUP 2021), 172-95, at 187-88.

[91] See Peters and Sparks, 'Introduction' (chapter 1), in this volume, section 4.

[92] For this critique, see *ibid*, pp. 19–20.

[93] See section 2, above.

[94] Hernández, 'Legal Positivism' (chapter 8), in this volume, p. 185.

none of the theoretical approaches discussed support the contention that international law is *structurally* consent-based. Some authors (and frameworks) leave the source of normativity international law in abeyance (positivism, law and economics, anthropology); while others explicitly deny that it originates in consent (sacred and secular natural law, global constitutionalism, global law), and for still others the question of its structure is inseparable from the systems of exploitative power relations which sustain a division between privileged and unprivileged subjects (TWAIL, Marxism).

Thirdly, we note that the majority of writers who embrace methodological positivism and have deeply engaged with the Jellinekian idea of *Selbstverpflictung* (self-commitment) have found self-commitment wanting as a basis for normativity.[95] Rather, they acknowledge that positivist reasoning must ultimately be grounded in a source of obligation which is not itself explicable on positivist terms.[96] Whereas a domestic legal theorist can at this point refer to domestic socio-political process to fill the normative gap, international legal theorists are left with (broadly) three choices: to argue that the system degenerates into an exercise of pure power and coercion (as do many scholars in critical traditions);[97] to find the basis of obligation in natural law;[98] or to align the foundational legal principles of international law and domestic law, as global constitutionalism does.[99]

The last idea—that international law may find its normative basis in constitutionalist principles—is of particular interest for humanisation scholars, because it recalls States' telos. In chapter 1, we conceptualised States as projections of their populations onto the international legal sphere. As such, they are at least to some extent limited in their legitimate actions by the needs and interests of flesh-and-blood human individuals and communities which comprise them.[100] On this basis, the 'realist' insistence on State consent poses more questions than it answers, and should itself be seen as an invitation to consider consent's limits.

The authors in this volume also address the objection that the humanisation thesis is premised on an outdated and even flawed *natural law paradigm*.[101] Certainly, as the critics identify, natural law and humanisation have an intuitive

[95] See, e.g., Wolfgang Friedmann, *The Changing Structure of International Law* (London: Stevens and Sons 1964), 85; Alf Ross, *A Textbook of International Law: General Part* (London: Longmans, Green and Co. 1947), 37-40.

[96] Hans Kelsen's and Herbert Hart's theories are perhaps the best known: see the discussion in Hernández, 'Legal Positivism' (chapter 8), in this volume, pp. 184–185.

[97] This is implied, for example, in Veličković, 'Marxist Account' (chapter 13), in this volume, pp. 277–278.

[98] Domingo, 'Sacred Natural Law' (chapter 9), in this volume; Sparks, 'Secular Natural Law' (chapter 10), in this volume.

[99] Çalı, 'Global Constitutionalism' (chapter 15), in this volume. See also Takao Suami, 'Dead or Alive? Global Constitutionalism and International Law after the Start of the War in Ukraine', *Global Constitutionalism* (forthcoming 2023), 1-30. To a lesser extent, global law could also be said to fit within this category: Golia, 'Global Law' (chapter 14), in this volume.

[100] Peters and Sparks, 'Introduction' (chapter 1), in this volume, pp. 16–17.

[101] *ibid*, p. 20.

connection: both Rafael Domingo and Tom Sparks, writing respectively from the perspectives of the (Christian) sacred and secular approaches to natural law, conclude that the application of a natural law framework to international law would entrench within that legal system certain values associated with the needs and interests of the human person. The chapters reveal a greater level of complexity, however. Humanisation is not only conceivable on natural law terms: other frameworks, too, demand a human-centred international law. Başak Çalı notes that a global constitutionalism framework 'relies on the intrinsic moral and equal worth of individuals to reject a sweeping formal defence of internal and external State sovereignty'.[102] While she acknowledges an alignment with the values espoused by natural law theories, she rejects the idea that a constitutionalist framework depends on natural law-style reasoning: 'the global constitutionalist emphasis on the central role of individuals is not grounded in a theory of natural law, but rather in constructivist interpretation'.[103] Global law, too, on Angelo Jr Golia's account, employs 'phenomenological or constructivist imaginaries of the individual',[104] rather than relying on natural law-styles of reasoning. Nevertheless, global law also recognises, and even ' "needs" the individual', Golia says, 'to sustain its own *iuris genesis*'.[105]

To conclude, the equation of humanisation and natural law is at best incomplete: a far wider range of theoretical approaches can provide the underpinnings for a legal system centred on human beings, from constitutionalism, to global law, and economic approaches to law. That finding supports the substantial body of high-quality positive law analysis that has been done in this area, including by scholars with no ideological commitment to natural law.[106] By contrast, the adherence to discredited forms of categorical positivism by the 'States-only' conception of international law begins to appear tainted with ideology.

The chapters also respond to the reproach that the upgrading of the status and role of the individual human being in international law is a *western paradigm*, both because its historical development has been dominated by western States and because human individual-centred doctrines, far from expressing universal values, are premised on parochial, western conceptions of human dignity, autonomy, and agency.[107] The historical contention cannot be doubted, but the claim of philosophical parochialism requires some additional consideration. A first nuance is that autonomy is not uniquely a western concept, and other traditions exist that

[102] Çalı, 'Global Constitutionalism' (chapter 15), in this volume, p. 324.
[103] *ibid*, p. 324.
[104] Golia, 'Global Law' (chapter 14), in this volume, p. 307.
[105] *ibid*, p. 330.
[106] Kate Parlett, *The Individual in the International Legal System: Continuity and Change in International Law* (Cambridge: CUP 2011), e.g. at 8; Astrid Kjeldgaard-Pedersen, *The International Legal Personality of the Individual* (Oxford: OUP 2018), e.g. at 6.
[107] Peters and Sparks, 'Introduction' (chapter 1), in this volume, p. 20. A form of this argument is made by Foblets in 'Anthropological Approaches' (chapter 17), in this volume, pp. 375–377.

could have provided alternative foundations for those developments. In parallel, one should note that the 'western' quality of humanism and of human rights is routinely invoked by authoritarian power-holders outside the 'west' to shield their privileges. That in itself, however, is not sufficient to ground the universalist claim that underlies the idea of an international legal order centred on the individual. For (humanised) international law to have legitimacy in all regions of the world, humanisation needs to open itself to non-western traditions which might be less or in different ways 'individualist'.[108] In this book, for example, Marie-Claire Foblets refers to the anthropological concept of 'dividual personhood', intended to contrast *in*dividualism with 'forms of personhood that are characterised by multiscale interdependencies'.[109] Similarly, Chinese heritage comprises practices of self-mastery and self-culturing that might be usefully fed into the international human rights discourse, against the stereotypical invocation of ostensible 'Asian values'.[110] Māori philosophy and the Ubuntu tradition of southern Africa are approaches which emphasise the importance of community rather than 'self-postulating' individuality. Māori philosophy holds, for example that 'we come into being not as autonomous entities, but as always and already in, or *as* relations'.[111] Humanisation scholarship should seek to integrate such traditions in order to develop a more truly universal claim. If it can do so successfully, the humanisation debate itself might contribute to the formation of a cross-cultural, nuanced, and inclusive individualism.

The idea of individual-as-subject has been the subject of critique, too, by post-structuralism, critical legal studies, critical post-humanism, and the new materialism, which have all *deconstructed the category of the 'subject'* that forms an important building block of the humanisation thesis.[112] At this point we need to distinguish the philosophical from the legal analysis. In law, the 'subject' remains an indispensable category for attributing legal responsibility. It has, though, always been 'a bit of a legal fiction'[113]—both for States and for individual human

[108] *cf.* Soirila, *The Law of Humanity Project* 2021 (n. 2), 13 who deems a 'more heterogeneous, situated and localised' approach desirable and feasible.

[109] Foblets, 'Anthropological Approaches' (chapter 17), in this volume, p. 375; citing McKim Marriot, 'Hindu Transactions: Diversity without Dualism', in Bruce Kapferer (ed.), *Transaction and Meaning: Directions in the Anthropology of Exchange and Symbolic Behavior* (Philadelphia, PA: Institute for the Study of Human Issues 1976), 109-42.

[110] Erica Fox Brindley, *Individualism in Early China: Human Agency and the Self in Thought and Politics* (Honolulu, HI: University of Hawaii Press 2010), 131-35, esp. 132. The term 'Asian values' was coined by Lee Kuan Yew, Singapore's leading politician (Prime Minister from 1959 to 1990, member of cabinet from 1990 to 2004). For the entire debate, among many others, see Stephen C. Angle, *Human Rights and Chinese Thought: A Cross-Cultural Inquiry* (Cambridge: CUP 2002); Ying Ren, 'The Theoretical System of Human Rights with Chinese Characteristics' *Chinese Studies* 7 (2018), 210-19.

[111] Te Kawehau Hoskins, 'A Fine Risk: Ethics in Kaupapa Māori Politics' *New Zealand Journal of Educational Studies* 47 (2012), 85-99, at 90 (references omitted). See further Mvuseleleo Ngcoya, '*Ubuntu*: Toward an Emancipatory Cosmopolitanism?' *International Political Sociology* 9 (2015), 248-62.

[112] Peters and Sparks, 'Introduction' (chapter 1), in this volume, p. 21.

[113] Tarik Kochi, *Global Justice and Social Conflict: The Foundations of Liberal Order and International Law* (Abingdon: Routledge 2020), 214 (on the related idea of a constitutionalisation of international law).

beings. For example, the individual as constructed by the global law framework (chapter 14) distinguishes the individual-as-legal-subject 'decisively from flesh-and-blood human beings and entities recognised as having specific ontological or psychological properties'. Instead, global law relies on 'phenomenological or constructivist imaginaries of the individual'.[114] Similarly, Ruth Houghton—writing from a feminist perspective—calls for pluralistic forms of subjecthood to replace the totemic, singular subject, in order to escape the de-humanising effects of trying to capture a diversity of persons under a narrow ideal of subjecthood built around the white, male individual.[115] Being a legal and artificial device, 'subjecthood' can be freshly conceived in departure from the traditional, essentialised subject. It should draw insights from current debates on novel (posited) legal subjects (persons) such as networks and artificial intelligence,[116] and on developments regarding non-human subjects including animals,[117] and elements of nature.[118] The quality of a 'subject' (and of an 'individual') could be ascribed not due to certain inherent features such as self-reflexivity, but based on relationships of accountability and responsibility.[119] Such a reconceptualisation would in the end not lead to the 'death' of the subject, but rather to a proliferation of subjects with different rights and responsibilities.

A different critique is that the orientation of international law towards human individuals has lopsidedly privileged rights over the *duties and responsibilities* of the community-bound individual.[120] Along this line, Chimni comments that the concept of an individual-centred legal order 'is the outcome of a flawed epistemology that embraces methodological individualism and legal determinism'.[121] Foblets convergently notes that anthropologists have tended to regard the strong notion of personal autonomy which is prevalent in western politico-legal theory as an 'elusive' notion, which 'is flawed both from a theoretical and an empirical point of view'.[122] The argument resonates with discussions in the historical part of this volume: in chapter 2 (on antiquity) and chapter 3 (on the medieval period), the authors explore whether, in those periods, 'individual' would have been

114 Golia, 'Global Law' (chapter 14), in this volume, p. 307.

115 Houghton, 'Feminist Approaches' (chapter 12), in this volume, pp. 266–267.

116 See, e.g., the discussion in Anna Beckers and Gunther Teubner, *Three Liability Regimes for Artificial Intelligence: Algorithmic Actants, Hybrids, Crowds* (Oxford: Hart 2021), 23-31, and *passim*.

117 For an approach which mobilises the idea of subjecthood in favour of legal rights for animals, see Joshua Jowitt, 'Legal Rights for Animals: Aspiration or Logical Necessity' *Journal of Human Rights and the Environment* 11 (2020), 173-98.

118 See section 4.3.3, below, on 'greening humanisation'.

119 Marie-Catherine Petersmann, 'Life Beyond the Law – From the "Living Constitution" to the "Constitution of the Living"' *Zeitschrift für ausländisches öffentliches Recht und Völkerrecht* 82 (2022), 769-99, at 780. See influentially Dieter Suhr, *Entfaltung der Menschen durch die Menschen* (Berlin: Duncker & Humblot 1976); Jennifer Nedelsky, *Law's Relations: A Relational Theory of Self: Autonomy, and Law* (Oxford: OUP 2011).

120 Peters and Sparks, 'Introduction' (chapter 1), in this volume, p. 22.

121 Chimni, 'A TWAIL Perspective' (chapter 11), in this volume, p. 248.

122 Foblets, 'Anthropological Approaches' (chapter 17), in this volume, p. 370.

understood as a relevant legal category at all.[123] Likewise, global law (chapter 14), rather than treating as sustainable western legal theory's construction of the 'true', atomised individual, places its emphasis on social systems as inventors of legal individuality: 'this individual would be any entity socially considered able to raise a claim, either immediately or mediately; or an entity socially considered to be the addressee of a claim'.[124] These authors identify an important blind spot in the dominant understanding of individualism.

We therefore suggest bringing duties and responsibilities back into the picture. Neither a humanisation nor an individualisation of international law is logically or structurally limited to the establishment of rights as opposed to obligations. Quite to the contrary, the continuation of humanisation would seem to demand a better conceptualisation of international law-based duties of individual actors (including but not limited to corporate actors) towards other individuals.[125] Indeed, this move would reconnect to the historical milestones of the humanisation of international law, such as the Nuremberg trial and the Tadić proceedings which were concerned with the individual's obligation not to commit crimes under international law.[126] Further interesting research questions relate to the concept of fundamental duties of individuals such as posited in Article 29(1) of the Universal Declaration on Human Rights and elaborated in detail in the African Charter on Human and Peoples' Rights.[127] Another question is the normative priority of duties over rights, as preferred in many religious traditions[128] and in more recent ecological approaches.[129]

A quite different observation is that the humanisation of international law is associated with a (by its critics, unwelcome) *'proliferation' of human rights*.[130] The response of some scholars has been to recommend a 'radical moderation' of human rights claims and a 'human rights triage' to separate the 'central' from the 'marginal' rights (usually a euphemism for privileging civil and political rights over economic and social rights).[131] In contrast, Jens Theilen has argued that 'excess' does

[123] Cowan, 'Antiquity' (chapter 2), in this volume; Fedele and Wijffels, 'Mediaeval International Law' (chapter 3), in this volume.

[124] Golia, 'Global Law' (chapter 14), in this volume, p. 307.

[125] For a good discussion of the individual's obligations under international law, see Eva Brems, *Human Rights: Universality and Diversity* (The Hague: Martinus Nijhoff), 424-41; for a highly relevant discussion on moral rights and obligations in a globalised world, see Onora O'Neill, *Justice Across Boundaries: Whose Obligations?* (Cambridge: CUP 2016).

[126] See Peters and Sparks, 'Introduction' (chapter 1), in this volume, pp. 3–4.

[127] Part I of the African Charter is on 'Rights and Duties' with chapter II (Arts. 27-29) on duties towards 'family and society, the State and other legally recognized communities and the international community'.

[128] On Jewish law, see Robert M. Cover, 'Obligation: A Jewish Jurisprudence of the Social Order' *Journal of Law and Religion* 5 (1987), 65-74.

[129] Daniel Matthews, 'Law and Aesthetics in the Anthropocene: from the Rights of Nature to the Aesthesis of Obligations' *Law, Culture, and the Humanities* 19 (2023), 227-47.

[130] Peters and Sparks, 'Introduction' (chapter 1), in this volume, p. 22.

[131] Hurst Hannum, *Rescuing Human Rights: A Radically Moderate Approach* (Cambridge: CUP 2019) (quotes at 157, 161, and 163). Not all observers condemn the emergence of more human rights: Wellman

not damage human rights. Human rights need excess, because those threatened by human rights claims routinely push back and seek to deny those rights' transformative power.[132] To the extent that the proliferation argument is to be understood as an argument in favour of 'first generation' over other rights, a partial response can be drawn from the contributions to this book. Certainly, such a privileging of 'first generation' rights would be contradicted by a law and economics analysis, as told by Anne van Aaken. The New Welfare Economics approach incorporated into the UN Sustainable Development Goals, for example, on van Aaken's account is built on the 'capabilities' framework, an approach which does not permit a division between 'generations' of rights.[133]

Beyond this, we can legitimately ask why, in circumstances that critics call 'proliferation', specifically the human rights framework needs to carry the burden of the 'new' human rights. We tend to reject the idea that greater 'human rights realism'[134] is warranted, or that there is a need to 'rescue' human rights.[135] While certain 'new' rights very clearly merit the status of fundamental human rights, there are others which do not need to be given the same label. The rights in this latter category often protect significant human interests and values. In a non- or weakly humanised legal system, all such values must be gathered under the heading of human rights, simply for lack of an alternative legal category. However, in a more sophisticated humanised legal order and other better fitting structures and institutions, for example 'ordinary' rights, may be mobilised in order to secure those values. In this way, a more robust humanisation of international law can provide space for progressive, individual-centred principles which avoid overburdening the specific concept of human rights.[136]

concludes that the 'proliferation' has done 'much more good than harm': Carl Wellman, *The Proliferation of Rights: Moral Progress or Empty Rhetoric?* (Boulder, CO: Westview Press 1999), at 182.

[132] Jens Theilen, 'Inflation of Human Rights: A Deconstruction' *Leiden Journal of International Law* 34 (2021), 831-54, at 852. Theilen brilliantly lays out how the reproach that human rights have unduly proliferated 'reinforces the current dominant neoliberal understanding of human rights' and is 'a form of gatekeeping with deeply conservative political effects' (at 850).

[133] See van Aaken, '(International) Law and Economics' (chapter 16), in this volume, pp. 345–348; citing, *inter alia*, Martha C Nussbaum and Amartya K Sen, *The Quality of Life* (Oxford: OUP 1993).

[134] Nathalie R Davidson, 'Human Rights Realism' *Vanderbilt Journal of Transnational Law* 54 (2021), 31-81, proposing limits to legal accountability for gross human rights violations in order to avoid negative political consequences especially for peace processes.

[135] Hannum, *Rescuing Human Rights* 2019 (n. 131), 157.

[136] For renewed defences of rights (from different theoretical angles), see Kathryn McNeilly, *Human Rights and Radical Social Transformation: Futurity, Alterity, Power* (Abingdon: Routledge 2017); Karima Bennoune, 'In Defense of Human Rights' *Vanderbilt Journal of Transnational Law* 52 (2019), 1209-35; Alison Brysk and Michael Stohl (eds.), *Contracting Human Rights: Crisis, Accountability, and Opportunity* (Cheltenham: Edward Elgar 2019), Anne Peters, 'The Importance of Having Rights' *Zeitschrift für ausländisches öffentliches Recht und Völkerrecht* 81 (2021), 7-22; Sanja Dragić, *Post-Backlash Human Rights Law* (Leiden: Brill 2022).

Another reproach against the humanisation thesis is that it is *unscholarly*.[137] Our response is that neither academic honesty nor methodological rigour requires the scholar's 'neutrality' towards the object of study. After all—a truism nowadays—all knowledge is 'situated'.[138] Knowledge (especially about the law) is generated in concrete historical and social contexts. This context inevitably has an influence on the research question, methods, and interpretation of the (legal) data. Relatedly, scholars cannot escape their normative predispositions, which inevitably influence any legal analysis to some degree—an observation which is as valid for statist-positivist scholarship as it is for humanisation scholars. But it is one thing to acknowledge that legal work examining the individual and the law cannot be done from a 'neutral' standpoint and another thing explicitly to perform such work with a predetermined legal outcome. While the latter would count as advocacy, the former assuredly may qualify as scholarship if the writers at least implicitly indicate their normative orientation, aspire to maintain some critical distance to the object of study, and seek to understand the legal issues at hand from as many angles as possible. If these precepts are followed, 'engaged scholarship' can be successful, that is, it can generate legal knowledge.[139] In fact, excellent, methodologically rigorous scholarship has been published on humanisation.[140] To dismiss that work out of hand is itself unscholarly.

4. New Impulses from History and Theory for the Humanisation of International Law

In this concluding section, we flag impulses for further research on the humanisation of international law. We first discuss possible new doctrines (section 4.1) for the continued conceptual development of humanisation, in which we focus on participation. Section 4.2 then considers the substantive development of humanisation, and highlights newly humanising legal fields. Finally, in section 4.3 we further engage with three critiques highlighted in the introduction but not yet discussed in detail: the critique of neoliberalism, the critique of imperialism, and the environmental critique. All three are productive challenges whose insights must and can be integrated by humanisation scholarship. Section 4.4 concludes by looking to the future.

[137] Peters and Sparks, 'Introduction' (chapter 1), in this volume, p. 23.

[138] Donna Haraway, 'Situated Knowledges: The Science Question in Feminism and the Privilege of Partial Perspective' *Feminist Studies* 14 (1988), 575-99.

[139] *cf.* Catharine A. MacKinnon, 'Engaged Scholarship as Method and Vocation' *Yale Journal of Feminism* 22 (2010), 193-205.

[140] Among many, we would highlight in particular Parlett, *The Individual* 2011 (n. 106); Kjeldgaard-Pedersen, *International Legal Personality* 2018 (n. 106).

4.1 New Doctrines

Both the historical and theoretical parts of the book have frequently relied on the notion of participation. Francesca Iurlaro and Inge Van Hulle both highlighted the ways in which, irrespective of whether individuals were conceived as 'subjects', international law in the respective periods could not avoid taking account of individuals as *participants* in the international legal system.[141] Ruth Houghton, in her account of feminist perspectives, calls for international law to (re-)focus on participation, as a means to 'move us away from the pervasive subject-object distinction'.[142] In a different vein, Bhupinder S. Chimni finds it 'critical that the individual has the right to participate in relevant decision-making processes' if 'the rights to self-determination and development are to be actualised'.[143] These findings could lead to a reappraisal of the New Haven approach that has, since the 1950s, sought to erode the dichotomy of 'subjects' and 'objects', claiming that there are only 'participants in the world power process', with individuals being participants alongside States and others.[144] In a similar vein, Emmanuel Roucounas recently argued that '[t]he "individual" meets the characteristics of a user of international law. Thus, as a user, of international law, the individual should be considered a "posited person" beyond the controversial concept of the subject.'[145] It seems worth examining the extent to which the humanisation framework can be realigned to incorporate a focus on participation as an addition, or even alternative, to traditional notions of subjecthood. This might resonate with legal scholars' insistence on '(post)subjectivity' in international law.[146]

4.2 New Legal Fields

The critical objection that humanisation has been historically contingent on a short period in the history of international law is belied by the fact that two salient issue areas of international law—international climate law and *ius contra bellum*—are

[141] Iurlaro, '1500-1648' (chapter 4), in this volume; Van Hulle, 'Nineteenth Century' (chapter 6), in this volume.

[142] Houghton, 'Feminist Approaches' (chapter 12), in this volume, p. 267.

[143] Chimni, 'A TWAIL Perspective' (chapter 11), in this volume, p. 244.

[144] Myres McDougal, 'International Law, Power, and Policy: A Contemporary Conception' *Recueil des Cours* 82 (1953), 133-260, at 173-74; Rosalyn Higgins, *Problems and Process: International Law and How We Use It* (Oxford: Clarendon 1995), 50; W. Michael Reisman, 'Foreword: Veritas vos liberabit', in Jean d'Aspremont (ed.), *Participants in the International Legal System: Multiple Perspectives on Non-State Actors in International Law* (London: Routledge 2011), xxxv–xxxvi.

[145] Emmanuel Roucounas, *A Landscape of Contemporary Theories of International Law* (Leiden: Brill Nijhoff 2019), 519.

[146] Catherine Brölmann and Janne Nijman, 'Personality', in Jean d'Aspremont and Sahib Singh (eds.), *Concepts for International Law: Contributions to Disciplinary Thought* (Cheltenham: Edward Elgar 2019), 678-90, at 689.

currently being imbued with claims founded in human rights and other human interests.[147] Scholars, domestic and international courts, and others are creatively feeding human rights-based arguments into the special legal institutions and instruments of the two legal fields, mostly to make the relevant regimes more effective. These developments are fairly recent and thus disprove the assertion that humanisation has come to an end.

In international *climate law*, the 'traditional' human rights to private life and bodily integrity have been activated by courts to force States to set and comply with their carbon emission reduction targets, and to step up adaptation and mitigation.[148] Also the pending request for an International Court of Justice (ICJ) advisory opinion on State obligations with regard to climate change asks the Court, *inter alia*, to analyse obligations flowing from the UN Declaration on Human Rights.[149] The Brazilian Supreme Court declared the Paris Agreement to be a 'type of human rights treaty' and thereby awarded it a 'supranational' status.[150] With these legal developments, a mutual feedback loop has been set in motion: climate change has been 'humanised' while human rights have been 'climatised', to quote Christel Cournil and Camila Perruso.[151]

In the *ius contra bellum*, the recent Russian aggression against Ukraine has given additional momentum to its humanisation.[152] This is all the more striking, as this field of law had in 1945 been firmly conceptualised as operating exclusively in the relations between States. The prohibitions of the use of force and of aggression were seen to protect only the sovereignty and territorial integrity of States.[153] With this

[147] For the objection of the historical contingency of the humanisation of international law, see Peters and Sparks, 'Introduction' (chapter 1), in this volume, p. 19.

[148] See only the most prominent cases: Supreme Court of The Netherlands, *The State of The Netherlands (Ministry of Economic Affairs and Climate Policy) v. Stichting Urgenda*, Ruling No. 19/00135 of 20 December 2019; Federal Constitutional Court of Germany, Order of the First Senate of 24 March 2021, 1 BvR 2656/18; Republic of Chile and Republic of Colombia, Request for an Advisory Opinion on Climate Emergency and Human Rights to the IACtHR of 9 January 2023 (pending). In scholarship, see Julia Dehm, 'Post Paris Reflections: Fossil Fuels, Human Rights and the Need to Excavate New Ideas for Climate Justice' *Journal of Human Rights and the Environment* 8 (2017), 280-300; John Knox, 'Bringing Human Rights to Bear on Climate Change' *Climate Law* 9 (2019), 165-79; César Rodriguez-Garavito (ed.), *Litigating the Climate Emergency: How Human Rights, Courts, and Legal Mobilization can Bolster Climate Action* (Cambridge: CUP 2021). See further Council of Europe, *Manual on Human Rights and the Environment* (3rd edn, COE 2022), available at: https://rm.coe.int/manual-environment-3rd-edition/1680a56197, accessed 22/12/23.

[149] UNGA, Resolution adopted by the General Assembly on 29 March 2023, Request for an advisory opinion of the International Court of Justice on the obligations of States in respect of climate change, 4 April 2023, A/Res/77/276.

[150] *PSB et al. v. Brazil*, ADPF 708, Judgment of 30 June 2022, para. 17.

[151] Christel Cournil and Camila Perruso, 'Réflexions sur "l'humanisation" des changements climatiques et la "climatisation" des droits de l'homme: Emergence et pertinence' *La Revue des droits de l'homme* 14 (2018), 1-37.

[152] Though see discussion in Suami, 'Dead or Alive?' 2023 (n. 99), *passim*, esp. 28-29.

[153] For a discussion, see Erin Pobjie, 'Victims of the Crime of Aggression', in Stefan Barriga and Claus Kreß (eds.), *The Crime of Aggression: A Commentary* (Cambridge: CUP 2017), 816-60. Another inroad into the pure inter-State view of the *ius contra bellum* has been the acceptance of self-defence against attacks by non-State (collective) actors – only marginally related to the humanisation of this area of law.

argument, the English House of Lords had, in 2008, rejected a human rights claim brought by mothers of British soldiers killed in the Iraq war of 2003. Even though this war violated the United Nations Charter, its illegality did not lead to a breach of the right to life of the employed soldiers: the UK had not—according to the House of Lords—violated its duties of protection and care under Article 2 of the European Convention on Human Rights (ECHR).[154] By contrast, the UN Human Rights Committee in its General Comment No. 36 of 2019 opined that 'States parties engaged in acts of aggression as defined in international law, resulting in deprivation of life, violate ipso facto article 6 of the Covenant'.[155] By logical extrapolation, human rights violations of this kind would not only be committed against the individuals (both civilians and combatants) in the victim State but—even more against the grain of the traditional logic of war—would also violate the rights of the aggressor State's own combatants, independent of the subjection of these soldiers to the command of their home State under domestic law, and independent of the legality or illegality of the activity under international humanitarian law.[156] This legal argument—if accepted—would have far-reaching repercussions, *inter alia* for the obligation to prosecute the crime of aggression and for the obligation to provide remedies to the individual victims.[157] This then even leads to a quest for remedies for harm and damage caused to combatants, notably those of the defending State.[158]

In a similar fashion, the current controversy on the lawfulness of so-called wars of recovery, that is, armed operations that seek to regain territory that had been unlawfully occupied, brings to the fore the relevance of individual rights in such territorial conflicts. The dilemma 'reveals, in its starkest terms, the normative tension within the contemporary international law on the use of force: mainly, between its traditional focus on a statist perception of self-defence, which is centred on state rights such as territory and sovereignty, and a creeping individualist sensibility, which seeks to place individual rights at the core of the international legal regime in its entirety'.[159] The novel focus on the individual in the *ius contra bellum* has been criticised as conveying a 'reductive individualism'.[160] Its merits and problems

[154] UKHL, *R v. The Prime Minister and others*, Judgment of 9 April 2008, UKHL 20.

[155] United Nations, International Covenant on Civil and Political Rights, Human Rights Committee, Comment No 36, 3 September 2019, para. 70.

[156] Frédéric Mégret and Chiara Redaelli, 'The Crime of Aggression as a Violation of the Rights of One's Own Population' *Journal on the Use of Force and International Law* 9 (2022), 99-137.

[157] Eliav Lieblich, 'The Humanization of Jus ad Bellum: Prospects and Perils' *European Journal of International Law* 32 (2021), 579-612.

[158] Hannes Jöbstl and Dean Rosenberg, 'The Humanization of War Reparations: Combatant Deaths and Compensation in Unlawful Wars' *Michigan Journal of International Law* 45 (forthcoming 2024), available at: https://ssrn.com/abstract=4526714, accessed 29/11/23.

[159] Eliav Lieblich, 'Wars of Recovery' *European Journal of International Law* 34 (2023), 349-81, at 351. See further Claus Kreß, 'Die Europäische Menschenrechtskonvention und das völkerrechtliche Gewaltverbot', in Angelika Nußberger (ed.), *Menschenrechte als Alpha und Omega des Rechts? Zur Auseinandersetzung der Fachdiziplinen mit der aktuellen Rechtsprechnung zu den Menschenrechten in Europa* (Tübingen: Mohn Siebeck 2023), 149-68.

[160] *cf.* Lieblich, 'Humanization' 2021 (n. 157), at 584, fn 17.

will play a crucial part for all future moves to hold Russia and it leading figures to account for the ongoing aggression. To conclude, the most striking international legal response to two major urgent challenges of our times—warming and war—has been the activation of international human rights and the concomitant shift of focus of the relevant legal regimes towards individuals.

4.3 Three Productive Challenges

Standing out in the various points of critique that we addressed above (in section 3), three challenges persist and require further and deeper study.

4.3.1 Overcoming Neoliberalism

One of the reproaches has been that the mindset of international legal humanism is a veneer on the surface of neoliberal structures of domination in international law, and that it has been highjacked by neoliberalism.[161] Two of the book's authors forcefully develop this critique; Bhupinder S. Chimni and Marina Veličković. Veličković notes that there is an alignment between capitalism and the structures of international law, such that international law itself is central to creating and maintaining the capitalist world order. She contrasts the communitarianism of Marxist thought with the 'alienated and isolated' neoliberal individuals who, as a result of their isolation, are incapable of meaningful resistance. In these circumstances, Veličković comments, 'we might wonder whether the push for increased prominence of individuals in international law might in fact be a sign of law's neoliberalisation, and not of its humanisation'.[162] Chimni, in a similar vein, charges individualisation scholars with callousness in their failure to engage with underlying structures of oppression: '[i]n a world in which an individual is unable to fulfil basic needs, and is the subject of alienation and violence in myriad forms, it would be cruel to declare them a subject of international law'.[163] That is not to say, as Veličković demonstrates with her case study of women's resistance against water rights violations in Bosnia, that a humanised international legal system has no potential to contribute to individual emancipation.[164] But, both authors agree that the system's capacity to do so will always be limited by its failure to 'speak to the constraints imposed by deep structures (of universalising capitalism, patriarchy, and racism) on making the individual an authentic subject in international law'.[165]

[161] Peters and Sparks, 'Introduction' (chapter 1), in this chapter, p. 25.
[162] Veličković, 'Marxist Account' (chapter 13), in this volume, p. 282.
[163] Chimni, 'TWAIL Perspective' (chapter 11), in this volume, p. 248.
[164] Veličković, 'Marxist Account' (chapter 13), in this volume, pp. 292–289.
[165] Chimni, 'TWAIL Perspective' (chapter 11), in this volume, p. 237; see also Veličković, 'Marxist Account' (chapter 13), in this volume, pp. 280–280.

The concern that humanisation scholars—wittingly or unwittingly—become apologists for neoliberal, neocolonial structures of domination in international law must be treated seriously. That said, the concepts of human rights, human security, human dignity, and humanity are not neoliberal per se. Even if conceived as a counterpoint to State sovereignty, these concepts share the desire to discipline the State. However, such disciplining need not necessarily amount to cutting back the social services that the State delivers. A proper reorienting of international law towards human needs and interests must take note of the Janus-faced nature of the State: while States have historically proven to be the worst violators of human rights, they are also the guarantors for security (including social security), protectors against (new) power holders ranging from big tech to big crime, and loci for cultural and community life. Before the establishment of a novel system that protects human interests of these kinds otherwise than through the several States, States must be understood in terms of this ambiguity.[166] Humanisation sees a need to protect individuals from States, but without discarding States, which themselves continue to serve important human values.

Moreover, we can and should distinguish between the atomised individual as an artefact of neoliberalism and the individual as a self-determining entity. Scholars can further substantiate this distinction: the humanisation of international law must be better attuned to economic inequalities. It should be harnessed against persistent and rising material inequality of wealth and income of humans within and between States.[167] Components of such a post-liberal humanisation are, *inter alia*, the operationalisation of international socio-economic rights, especially across borders, combined with the conceptualisation of States as 'trustees of humanity',[168] the international principle of transnational solidarity for humans across borders,[169] and the accountability of transnational business actors for human rights abuses.[170] To conclude, a *post*-liberal theory of humanisation is perfectly conceivable and feasible.[171]

[166] Humanisation is, in general, neither committed to the idea of the State, nor committed to its replacement. For a defence of the State-form as the most appropriate means to meet human values, see Anna Stilz, *Territorial Sovereignty: A Philosophical Exploration* (Oxford: OUP 2019); for a perspective which foresees the replacement of States with a cosmopolitan legal order, see, influentially, David Held, *Democracy and the Global Order: From the Modern State to Cosmopolitan Governance* (Cambridge: Polity Press 1995).

[167] Anne Peters, 'Global Constitutionalism: The Social Dimension', in Takao Suami et al. (eds.), *Global Constitutionalism from European and East Asian Perspectives* (Cambridge: CUP 2018), 277-350.

[168] Eyal Benvenisti, 'Sovereigns as Trustees of Humanity: On the Accountability of States to Foreign Stakeholders' *American Journal of International Law* 107 (2013), 295-333. See Elena Pribytkova, 'Are there Global Obligations to Assist in the Realization of Socio-Economic Rights?' *New York University Journal of International Law and Politics* 54 (2022), 379-484, at 431 and 473.

[169] Rüdiger Wolfrum, 'Solidarity and Community Interests: Driving Forces for the Interpretation and Development of International Law' *Recueil des Cours* 416 (2021), 9-479, esp. chapter 5 (298-339).

[170] Anne Peters et al., 'Business and Human Rights: Towards a "Smart Mix" of Regulation and Enforcement' *Zeitschrift für ausländisches öffentliches Recht und Völkerrecht* 83 (2023), 415-60.

[171] Sim describes a range of political positions captured under the heading of 'post-liberalism', from 'liberal democracy 2' to far-right inspired post-truthism: Stuart Sim, *Post-Truth, Scepticism & Power* (Cham: Springer International Publishing 2019), 145-52, esp. 151; discussing John Gray,

4.3.2 Decolonising Humanisation

The second lasting challenge is to overcome the legacy of colonialism in humanisation. In part this refers to the need, already discussed above, to reduce the western bias in humanisation's conceptual underpinnings by integrating other voices and philosophical traditions. We have highlighted that, in our view, new research on the humanisation of international law should pay a far greater attention than hitherto to non-western philosophical traditions, in particular those that do not share western philosophy's focus on the Kantian individual,[172] as well as traditions which combine communalism and individualism.[173] Doing so will help to build a theory of humanisation that is not only more inclusive and legitimate, but also more conceptually robust and better able to meet the needs of tomorrow's individuals and communities.

Perhaps of yet greater concern is that Chimni sees humanisation as itself being a tool of imperialism (formal and informal):

> [T]he production of subjectivity in international law is the work of developments that are intimately associated with the phenomenon of imperialism. It would be difficult to understand the evolution of the status of the individual as a subject in international law outside the constellation of factors that spawned inter-imperialist competition and the competition between capitalism and socialism. The focus on individuals became an ideological device in [mainstream international legal scholarship] to displace a critique of deep structures of capitalism and imperialism.[174]

Chimni's observation could and should motivate work that aligns humanisation scholarship and TWAIL, so that they can mutually support each other's aims. While the paradigm of humanisation may so far lack a robust response to (neo)colonialism, TWAIL has been identified as lacking a 'vision of what a just, moral international order would look like',[175] and as having 'failed to produce a coherent set of new ideas about what international law should be, how it should

Post-Liberalism: Studies in Political Thought (London: Routledge 2013). We use the term post-liberalism here not to refer to any particular political alignment, but instead to refer to a human-centred theory of international law without a necessary commitment to any particular economic model.

[172] See notes 109-113 and accompanying text, above.

[173] Kuba Krys et al., 'Outside the "Cultural Binary": Understanding Why Latin American Collectivist Societies Foster Independent Selves' *Perspectives of Psychological Science* 17 (2022), 1166-87.

[174] Chimni, 'TWAIL Perspective' (chapter 11), in this volume, p. 238.

[175] Naz Khatoon Modirzadeh, '"[L]et Us All Agree to Die a Little": TWAIL's Unfulfilled Promise' *Harvard Journal of International Law* 65 (forthcoming), available at: http://dx.doi.org/10.2139/ssrn.4406477, accessed 29/11/23. Modirzadeh, in an internal critique of the approach, argues that TWAIL lacks a sufficiently developed concept of justice (at page 17 of the SSRN version).

function, what it should seek to do in the world, and how to get there'.[176] The above-mentioned post-liberal[177] humanism which takes the individuals seriously both in themselves and in their social and cultural context might be helpful in articulating TWAIL's missing concept of justice. While there are points on which there is no prima facie agreement between TWAIL and international legal humanism—for example on the need for a reassertion of sovereignty by States of the Global South[178]—at a minimum TWAIL and humanism are surely aligned in their answer to the question *for whom* these two frameworks (both TWAIL and a renewed humanism) should work. The humanisation of international law has the potential to contribute to postcolonial justice.

4.3.3 Greening Humanisation

The third lasting challenge for the humanisation of international law is that of responding to the ongoing ecological crisis. In the anthropocene, with the climate catastrophe unfolding, and the sixth mass extinction underway, the call to recognise the human being, the 'anthropos', as the normative reference point of international law is (rightly) suspect.

At this juncture, one strand of scholarship suggests that personhood and (international) rights also be extended to animals,[179] landforms, ecosystems, and other elements of nature.[180] Others, to the contrary, oppose such extensions which, to their mind, 'actually reinforce—rather than curtail—the modernist cuts between humans and non-humans'.[181] These scholars propose that the category of personhood and rights should be eliminated altogether in order to remove the primary cause of the law's neglect for nature.

[176] *ibid*, 4 and 16-17; see also Michael Fakhri, who asks: 'What is TWAIL's political agenda? What does TWAIL stand for and against?': Michael Fakhri, 'Introduction – Questioning TWAIL's Agenda' *Oregon Review of International Law* 14 (2012), 1-16, at 7-8.

[177] See note 172 and accompanying text, above.

[178] Modirzadeh, '"[L]et Us All Agree"' (n. 175), at 53-62. By contrast, humanisation scholarship is sceptical of State sovereignty, whether in the Global North or Global South. Further work will be needed to seek common ground on such points. On the State, see Peters and Sparks, 'Introduction' (chapter 1), in this volume, section 3.4.

[179] See, e.g., Visa A. J. Kurki, *A Theory of Legal Personhood* (Oxford: OUP 2019); Saskia Stucki, *One Rights: Human and Animal Rights in the Anthropocene* (Cham: Springer International Publishing 2023); Joshua Jowitt, *Agency, Morality and Law* (Oxford: Hart 2023).

[180] Influentially, Christopher D. Stone, 'Should Trees Have Standing? Toward Legal Rights for Natural Objects' *Southern California Law Review* 45 (1972), 450-501. Out of the vast literature, see only Craig Kauffman and Pamela Martin (eds.), *The Politics of Rights of Nature* (Cambridge, MA: MIT Press 2021); Daniel Corrigan and Markku Oksanen (eds.), *Rights of Nature* (Abingdon: Routledge 2021); Frank Adloff and Tanja Busse (eds.), *Welche Rechte braucht die Natur?* (Frankfurt: Campus 2021); Jana Norman, *Posthuman Legal Subjectivity: Reimagining the Human in the Anthropocene* (Abingdon: Routledge 2021); Mihnea Tănăsescu, *Understanding the Rights of Nature: A Critical Introduction* (Bielefeld: Transcript 2022); César Rodríguez-Garavito, 'The More Than Human Rights (MOTH)' Project at NYU, available at: https://mothrights.org, accessed 30/11/23.

[181] Marie-Catherine Petersmann, 'In the Break (of Rights and Representation): Sociality beyond the Non/human subject' *International Journal of Human Rights* (forthcoming 2023), 1-25, at 2.

At this point, humanisation scholars can and should engage in a productive conversation with critical posthumanism. Thinkers in that tradition seek 'to dismantle the idea that the human sits in hierarchical supremacy over other subjects – including the environment and non-humans'.[182] Posthumanist scholars recognise humankind's embeddedness within natural systems, and accept that other forms of life are morally significant,[183] coupled with a conviction that the human rights-focused 'liberal response' to the ecological challenges falls short.[184] They see a need to 'de-anthropocentre'—to borrow from Marie-Catherine Petersmann—the response to environmental crises in a 'corrective to the narrow anthropocentric focus on human life'.[185]

A human-centred approach to international law can, in our view, properly address the ecological challenge if it navigates between two extreme trends that lead—we think—to dead ends. It needs to avoid both a simply backward-looking, repetitive, rehumanisation on the one side, and throwing the human under the bus, on the other side.[186] Between these extremes lies a middle course of 'more-than-human legalities'.[187] Such approach would be to critically work through the foundations of humanism and question some of the traditional premises, notably the hierarchy of humans over the rest of the world and the isolation of the single human person. Based on such an approach, a humanisation of international law could contribute to constructing an international legal order that responds to the overlapping ecological crises which international society now faces. In the end, a green, 'entangled humanism'[188] that is equivalent to a 'human-inclusive eco-centrism'[189] seems a promising paradigm for the international law of the future.

[182] Emily Jones, 'Posthuman International Law and the Rights of Nature' *Journal of Human Rights and the Environment* 12 (2021), 76-101, at 83.

[183] Marie-Catherine Petersmann adopts Judith Butler's vocabulary of 'grieveable' life: Petersmann, 'Life Beyond the Law' 2022 (n. 119), 722; citing Judith Butler, *Frames of War: When is Life Grieveable* (Brooklyn, NY: Verso 2016).

[184] Petersmann, 'Life Beyond the Law' 2022 (n. 119), at 780.

[185] *ibid.* See also Iyan Offor, 'Second Wave Animal Ethics and (Global) Animal Law: A View from the Margins' *Journal of Human Rights and the Environment* 11 (2020), 268-96; Brian Favre, 'Is There a Need for a New, an Ecological, Understanding of Legal Animal Rights?' *Journal of Human Rights and the Environment* 11 (2020), 297-319.

[186] Stefan Herbrechter et al., 'Critical Posthumanism: An Overview', in Stefan Herbrechter et al. (eds.), *Palgrave Handbook of Critical Posthumanism* (Cham: Springer Nature 2022), 3-26, at 16.

[187] Irus Braverman, 'Law's Underdog: A Call for More-than-Human Legalities' *Annual Review of Law and Social Science* 14 (2018), 127-44, 137.

[188] William Eugene Connolly, *Facing the Planetary: Entangled Humanism and the Politics of Swarming* (Durham, NC: Duke University Press 2017).

[189] Geoffrey Garver, 'Are Rights of Nature Radical enough for Ecological Law?', in Kirsten Anker et al. (eds.), *From Environmental Law to Ecological Law* (Abingdon: Routledge 2021), 90-103, at 96 and *passim*.

4.4 The Way Forward

The chapters in this book have revealed a longstanding push-and-pull between the individual and the State which has been formative for international law from its earliest days, and have shown that a wide range of theoretical approaches to international law demand that the international legal system pay greater attention to individuals. Building from these insights, in this concluding chapter we have responded to the critiques typically levelled at the humanisation idea, many of which are shown, when viewed from historical and various theoretical perspectives, to miss their mark. The paradigm of humanisation of international law is robust.

That is not to say, though, that humanisation is without its flaws and blind spots. We have highlighted three critiques in particular which demand serious and open-minded consideration: that humanisation inadvertently becomes a stalking horse of neoliberalism; that it fails to address the gross injustice of (neo)colonialism and international inequality; and that it retains and reinforces a spent anthropocentrism oblivious of environmental breakdown.[190] Humanisation cannot allow itself to be satisfied with formal markers of personhood—the 'cruelty' of which Chimni has denounced[191]—and other ephemera; rather, humanisation scholarship must be subversive, progressive, and rebellious. Its adherents must be 'braver in presenting their view of a better world and taking concrete steps' to bring it about.[192]

A focus on inequality, deprivation, and inter-community justice can help to recover humanisation's radicalism and purpose in the contemporary world. But the humanisation of the future must also be able to respond to a multifaceted ecological crisis, in which anthropocentrism, the dark face of humanism, has played a major and negative role. In order not to repeat the same old faulty thinking, we must reconsider the habitual equation between an 'individualised' and a 'humanised' legal order; between the processes of individualisation and humanisation.[193] Several chapters of this book have already doubted whether these terms may be taken as synonymous: Especially a global law paradigm—which we find explains well the legal landscape as it is currently evolving—must treat as a (legal) individual any entity or artefact considered to possess the markers of (legal) individuality, up to and including 'trees, rivers, non-human animals, etc.'.[194] In parallel, an atomised, individual personhood is not truly representative of *human* personhood, which

[190] In a similar vein, Soirila has argued that an 'updated' humanisation is needed, which would 'be more aware of the networks of power it is embedded in, oppose itself more directly against neoliberalism, seek to make itself more useful and visible for persons and groups engaged in grassroot struggles, and find enhanced techniques for addressing issues of material inequality': Soirila, *The Law of Humanity Project* 2021 (n. 2), 149.

[191] Chimni, 'TWAIL' (chapter 11), in this volume, p. 248; and further discussion in note 164 and accompanying text, above.

[192] Soirila, *The Law of Humanity Project* 2021 (n. 2), 159.

[193] Peters and Sparks, 'Introduction' (chapter 1), in this volume, pp. 4–5.

[194] Golia, 'Global Law' (chapter 14), in this volume, p. 307.

exists—and can only exist—within social settings.[195] The combination of both approaches leads to the insight, that Individuals can be non-human, and humans are not fully individual.

A more mature theory of humanisation would focus on the *situated individual* in international law. *Situated individualism* would reintegrate the individual into collective communities and into natural systems without dissolving the one into the other. Basing humanisation on a more nuanced, situated, and communitarian individual responds better to the shortcomings—the 'insanity', to use Mvuselelo Ngcoya's term—of the 'rugged, sovereign individual' derived from the western philosophical canon.[196] In so doing, we argue, humanisation might be brought into alignment with anthropological and TWAIL approaches to law, which demand a more sophisticated treatment of individuals within communities.

Moreover, situating the individual will provide opportunities, too, for the integration of human personhood into a wider—human and non-human—community. Individuals need to be resituated within social structures, which themselves must be situated within the eco- and earth systems upon which they depend, and on which their activities impact. Giving the individual a proper place in international law is necessary in order to shape international legal responses to the excesses of capitalism, abuses of (neo)colonialism, and the environmental devastation.

Simply giving up on the human (be it in favour of a new statism or towards the legal subject's dissolution into networks, ligatures, matter, or whatever) would mean to leave behind all those members of the human population for whom the era of 'humanisation' has barely begun.[197] It would overlook that a secure legal space is—to paraphrase Rosa Luxemburg[198]—needed exactly by the others, the ones who are deprived, and not by those who have the say and who already have everything.

For this reason, far from abandoning the individual as a focal point of international law, we need to stay critically connected with humanist traditions, while productively engaging with the critiques articulated not least in this book. This will spur the reorientation of humanism, 'properly pluralized, reformulated' (to speak with Donna Haraway), as a lens for understanding and developing international law.[199]

[195] Foblets, 'Anthropological Approaches' (chapter 17), in this volume, pp. 375–377.

[196] Ngcoya, '*Ubuntu*' 2015 (n. 111), at 253. Soares offers a conceptual history of individualism: Conceição Soares, 'The Philosophy of Individualism: A Critical Perspective' *International Journal of Philosophy & Social Values* 1 (2018), 11-34, at 12-18.

[197] See, *mutatis mutandis* (on human rights) Theilen, 'Inflation of Human Rights' 2021 (n. 132), 853; Scott, 'Human Rights' 2021 (n. 90), 191.

[198] Rosa Luxemburg, 'Freiheit ist immer Freiheit des anders Denkenden', in Paul Levi (ed.) *Die Russische Revolution: Eine kritische Würdigung. Aus dem Nachlass von Rosa Luxemburg* (Berlin: Verlag Gesellschaft und Erziehung 1922), 109.

[199] Donna Haraway, *When Species Meet* (Minneapolis, MI: University of Minnesota Press 2008), 17. This is in line with a posthumanism that does not see itself as coming 'after' or superseding humanism but rather as a posthumanism that thinks with (and against) humanism: Zahi Zalloua, *Being Posthuman: Ontologies of the Future* (London: Bloomsbury 2021), 22-23.

Such an approach can preserve and build on the humanist tradition's legacy of transformative change,[200] while opening it to new critical impulses. In so doing, the situated and embedded individual has the potential to fire a 'second wave', a renewed individual-centred approach to international law. Further scholarship is needed to realise that potential.

[200] See *mutatis mutandis* Herbrechter et al., 'Critical Posthumanism' 2022 (n. 186), 16.

Index

For the benefit of digital users, indexed terms that span two pages (e.g., 52–53) may, on occasion, appear on only one of those pages.

www.ingramcontent.com/pod-product-compliance
Lightning Source LLC
LaVergne TN
LVHW020056220926
848484LV00002BB/509
* 9 7 8 0 1 9 8 8 9 8 9 1 7 *